Stoneman's Raid
1865

ALSO BY CHRIS J. HARTLEY

Stuart's Tarheels: James B. Gordon and His North Carolina Cavalry

Stoneman's Raid
1865

Chris J. Hartley

JOHN F. BLAIR
PUBLISHER
Winston-Salem, North Carolina

JOHN F. BLAIR
PUBLISHER
1406 Plaza Drive
Winston-Salem, North Carolina 27103
www.blairpub.com

Manufactured in the United States of America

JACKET IMAGE

Painting by Don Troiani, www.historicalimagebank.com

Library of Congress Cataloging-in-Publication Data

Hartley, Chris J.
  Stoneman's Raid, 1865 / by Chris J. Hartley.
    p. cm.
  Includes bibliographical references and index.
  ISBN 978-0-89587-377-4 (alk. paper)—ISBN 978-0-89587-392-7 (e-book) 1. Stoneman's Raid, 1865. 2. United States—History—Civil War, 1861-1865--Cavalry operations. 3. North Carolina—History—Civil War, 1861-1865—Cavalry operations. 4. Virginia—History—Civil War, 1861-1865—Cavalry operations. 5. United States. Army. Cavalry—History—Civil War, 1861-1865. 6. Raids (Military science)—History—19th century. 7. Stoneman, George, 1822-1894. I. Title.
  E477.9.H37 2010
  973.7'38--dc22
                              2010017954

DESIGN BY DEBRA LONG HAMPTON

To
Laurie, Caroline, and Taylor Ann with all my love

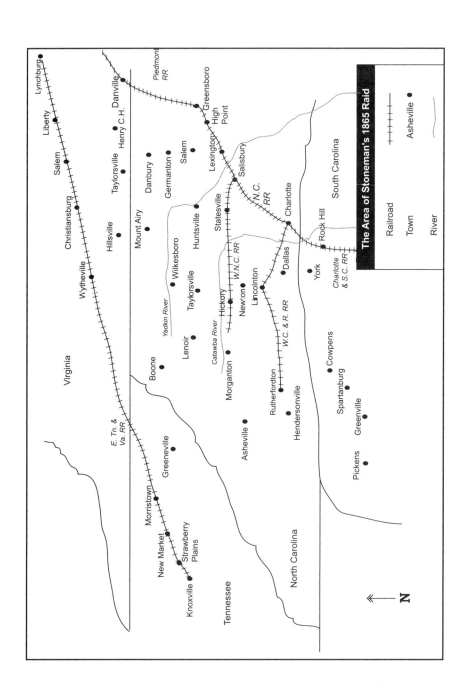

The Area of Stoneman's 1865 Raid

Railroad
Town • Asheville
River

Contents

Maps and Illustrations

x

Virgil Caine is the name, and I served on the Danville train,
'Til Stoneman's cavalry came and tore up the tracks again.
In the winter of '65, we were hungry, just barely alive.
By May the tenth, Richmond had fell,
It's a time I remember, oh so well.

The night they drove old Dixie down,
And the bells were ringing.
The night they drove old Dixie down,
And the people were singin'.
They went, "La, la, la, la, la, la, la, la, la, la, la, la, la, la, la."

Preface

Inspiring a Song and a Movie

It was a time of turmoil and war. Brother confronted brother. Long-cherished beliefs were trampled underfoot. Generations were at loggerheads. And young men died by the thousands on hotly contested battlefields.

America was coming apart at the seams.

The year was 1969.

In the midst of this upheaval, one of the most popular musical groups of the day recorded "The Night They Drove Old Dixie Down."[1] The Band's ground-breaking rhythm-and-blues-tinged rock-and-roll song told a story about the 1960s using events that had occurred in the 1860s. During the Civil War, America experienced death and disorder on a far greater scale than during the Vietnam War. The year 1865 saw the Confederacy's defeat and massive social change with the end of slavery and the beginning of Reconstruction. The Band's song told how an old Rebel named Virgil Caine survived those momentous changes, but in a way that was more about the tumultuous time in which the song was released. Subtle echoes of Vietnam and contemporary social struggles hid in its mournful tune and lyrics.

The obscure 1865 cavalry raid of Major General George Stoneman served as the unlikely backdrop for "The Night They Drove Old Dixie Down." It is surprising that The Band did not choose a more famous Civil War battle, such as Gettysburg or Vicksburg. Even more surprising is the fact that the song did not even come from the pen of an American. Its composer, J. Robbie Robertson, and four other members of the group were natives of Canada. Only The Band's drummer, Levon Helm, was an American—a Southerner from Arkansas, to be exact. When asked about the song's creation, lead singer Robertson explained that the tune came first, followed by lyrics that seemed to fit. "At some point, [the concept] blurted out of me," he recalled. "Then I went and I did some research and I wrote the lyrics to the song." It was, he said, "the only thing I could think of at the time."[2] Whatever the inspiration, "The Night They Drove Old Dixie Down" went on to great popularity and was later covered by artists such as Joan Baez and Bob Dylan, as well as more recent performers including Bruce Hornsby and the Black Crowes. Some of those versions omit the Stoneman reference, possibly because the phrase "Stoneman's cavalry" has been interpreted as "so much cavalry."[3]

In 1970, Stoneman's Raid resurfaced in another popular medium, a made-for-TV movie entitled *Menace on the Mountain*. Starring Mitch Vogel and Jodie Foster, the Walt Disney film tells the story of a teenage boy who struggles to protect his family from Yankee deserters who have seized its home while the father is off at war. The movie was based on the true story of an outlaw gang that ravaged western North Carolina in the spring of 1865 from a stronghold called Fort Hamby. The real outlaws were led by a deserter from Stoneman's cavalry.

Thanks to The Band and Walt Disney, George Stoneman's last campaign enjoys the rare distinction of being the only minor Civil War campaign to inspire a classic rock song and a TV movie. Yet few Americans, even those familiar with the song or the movie, know anything about the raid, much less whether or not it actually "drove old Dixie down" or spawned a "menace on the mountain." The raid is forgotten today because it was overshadowed by other dramatic events, including Lincoln's assassination, the surrender at Appomattox, and the collapse of the Confederacy. It is hardly surprising that the raid remains little more than a historical footnote.

Only a handful of published histories mention it at all. The first such account appeared in Cornelia P. Spencer's 1866 book, *The Last Ninety Days of the War in North Carolina*. Spencer devoted three chapters to "an authentic narrative of all leading incidents connected with Stoneman's Raid." Upon its publication, the book was generally hailed as accurate, but it was heavily influenced by the Lost Cause movement.[4] Since then, a number of local histories from areas the raid visited have appeared, but they are often long on hearsay and short on documentation.

Scholarly studies of the raid are few. John G. Barrett's *The Civil War in North Carolina* contains an insightful and well-researched chapter on the raid, and William R. Trotter's *Bushwhackers* provides a solid four-chapter overview. Appalachian State University professor Ina W. Van Noppen's 1961 book, *Stoneman's Last Raid*, offers the most complete account of the raid to date. A fine work in its own right, *Stoneman's Last Raid* nonetheless omits numerous important primary sources and fails to assess the impact of the raid on the South's postwar recovery. It is also long out of print.

Otherwise, most historians have said little about the raid, and virtually none has answered the perplexing string of questions it raises—above all, was Stoneman's 1865 raid successful? In his seminal book *Never Call Retreat*, Bruce Catton is pithy in his evaluation of the raid but does suggest that it was well executed. "Operating under a better general, he was a better cavalryman," Catton writes, contrasting Stoneman's performance under the leadership of General George Thomas with his earlier and controversial performance under General Joseph Hooker. Professor Van Noppen describes the raid as a "splendidly conceived, ably executed attack upon the war potential and the civilian population of the South as well as upon its military resources." Others are less charitable. Shelby Foote offers a few paragraphs about the raid in his three-volume Civil War narrative but leaves readers with the singular impression that it mostly vexed Union leadership.[5]

Union leaders and participants held a broad range of opinions about the raid. Ulysses S. Grant was no admirer. "They were all eminently successful," Grant wrote collectively of Stoneman's Raid and two others launched that spring, "but without any good result." Major General William T. Sherman, Grant's most trusted subordinate, thought better of it. He thought that Stoneman's last raid, together with the contemporaneous cavalry raids, dealt a fatal blow to the Confederacy. Veterans of the raid could not have agreed more. "It may be safely said," wrote one former cavalryman, "that no similar enterprise in the history of the war accomplished so much of importance with so little public attention." Ohio trooper Frank Mason went farther. "We were cutting the last avenues of escape that lay open to Lee, and we were a part of the machine by which the last great army of the Confederacy was to be hopelessly ensnared," he wrote. "The collapse was approaching, and we, every man of us [in Stoneman's cavalry], would be in at the death."[6]

Other reasons also compel a study of this raid. Over a span of two months, Stoneman's horse soldiers traveled more than one thousand miles across parts of six Confederate states, destroying railroads, bridges, telegraph wires, and other military resources. In the process, the raid probably directly involved more non-combatants in a military action than any other single event of its scale during the war. Lacking a supply line, Stoneman's men had to take whatever they needed (or in some cases wanted) wherever they found it. This meant that the civilians in the raiders' path had to endure considerable hardship and suffering. The Southern Claims Commission files in the National Archives bulge with claims for compensation for provisions, horses, and various valuables confiscated by the raiders. Numerous oral and written folk tales and legends about the raid survive to attest to the mayhem the Federals wrought. A handful of stories even praise the soldiers for their kindness and generosity.[7]

Although many of these tales are suspect, they eloquently convey the anger of the raid's victims. One eyewitness compared the raid to an avalanche. That feeling has lingered in the places it touched. The state of North Carolina has erected nineteen historical markers to commemorate the raid—among the most for any historical event. If these markers signify the local scope and the significance of the raid, they have also stirred painful memories. When the first markers were erected on the eve of World War II, disgusted citizens tore them out of the ground and threw them into a river.[8]

The raid offers numerous surprises. Although it lacked huge armies and took place in small towns and backwoods locales, it still saw desperate fighting at such unfamiliar places as Wytheville, Henry Court House, Salisbury, Morganton, and Asheville. It also featured a cast of prominent men, including not only George Stoneman but other Union soldiers including Ulysses S. Grant, William T. Sherman, George Thomas, Alvan Gillem, and Myles Keogh, as well as Confederate soldiers P. G. T. Beauregard, Joseph E. Johnston, John Pemberton, and Robert E. Lee. In the end, the raiders even figured in two other momentous events: the Appomattox campaign and the pursuit of Confederate president Jefferson Davis.

So observers are left asking if Virgil Caine was right when he claimed that Stoneman's Raid "drove old Dixie down." In answering that question, this study will assess the contribution of Stoneman's Raid to Union victory and its impact on the South's postwar recovery.

The story begins in a bustling log cabin in central Virginia.

Part One

Stoneman's Raid

Major General George Stoneman, commander of the District of East Tennessee, was eager to restore his reputation.

Chapter 1

Has Stoneman Started Yet?

Preparations: Winter 1864–65

The noise of the vast Union supply base at City Point, Virginia, filled the air but made no impression on Lieutenant General Ulysses S. Grant. Ignoring the din of laboring animals, men, and machinery, Grant, inside his log-cabin headquarters, instead mulled over a strategic problem. It was March 1865, dawn of the fifth spring of the war. The forty-two-year-old commander in chief of all Federal armies had a plan that should finally defeat the Confederacy. Unfortunately, one of his commanders balked. That man was Major General George Stoneman.[1]

Nearly two months earlier, Grant had ordered Stoneman to launch a raid into the Confederate heartland. The raid was to strike key parts of the enemy's infrastructure—railroads, bridges, supplies, and communications—while larger forces attacked the Confederacy's armies. Despite the raid's importance, a single horseman had yet to march. Frustrated, Grant knew that each passing day made it less likely the raid would help end the war.

This quandary also gave Grant a new reason to doubt George Stoneman, who already had two strikes against him. In 1863, Stoneman had commanded a much-maligned raid during the Chancellorsville campaign. And he was notorious for having been captured during an ill-fated raid in Georgia a year later. Was

*Lieutenant General Ulysses S. Grant grew frustrated
when Stoneman's Raid started later than he wanted.
The tardy start forced him to change the strategy of the
raid.*
Library of Congress

the New York–born general about to add to his legacy of failures?

His patience exhausted, Grant sent a peremptory order to Stoneman's immediate superior, Major General George H. Thomas. The commanding general
wrote simply and clearly: "If Stoneman has not got off on his expedition, start
him at once with whatever force you can give him."[2]

George Stoneman was born on August 8, 1822, the oldest of ten children.
His early life was centered in Busti, a wilderness town in western New York. In

this environment, young George quickly grew into a "tall, stalwart, and athletic farmers boy." His educational opportunities were limited to the district school and the village academy in neighboring Jamestown, but he made the best of it. At Jamestown Academy, Stoneman earned solid marks and the praise of his headmaster. By the time he turned seventeen, he had prepared himself for a career as a surveyor. Plans to move to Missouri to work on public lands did not bear fruit, however, so a year later Stoneman took a teaching job near Busti. The short-lived stint lined his pockets with a mere $12.50 a month, but Stoneman would later fondly recall his time as a country schoolmaster. He thought it "the most profitable, and best sp[e]nt four months" of his whole life.[3]

But it was an article in a national publication that changed Stoneman's life. In 1841, a magazine published a piece about the United States Military Academy that captured the young schoolmaster's imagination. With visions of military glory in his mind, he decided to seek admission. A year later, despite his family's lack of connections, Stoneman won a congressional appointment to West Point. The military school on the Hudson River became his true foundation. He met a number of men there who would play future roles as wartime adversaries and comrades. His roommate was an eccentric young Virginian named Thomas J. Jackson; other classmates included Darius Couch, A. P. Hill, George B. McClellan, and George Pickett. Stoneman proved to be an average student who was not always well behaved. On one occasion, he was given demerits for allowing women into a tent during a field exercise. Nonetheless, Stoneman made his way through the coursework and in 1846 graduated thirty-third in a class of fifty-nine.[4]

That summer, Stoneman left the classroom behind and began the work of a soldier. He expected to receive orders to fight in the Mexican War but was instead commissioned brevet second lieutenant in the First Dragoons, a unit bound for duty in the West. Ordered to meet his unit at Fort Leavenworth, Kansas, he arrived after the dragoons left for the frontier. Instead of being sent after the regiment, he drew an unexpected assignment. The United States Army of the mid-nineteenth century was mainly a frontier constabulary, and its duties included promoting loyalty among the Mormons. During the fall and winter of 1846–47, to show support to the Mormons and help establish federal control in the West, a "Mormon Battalion" marched from Fort Leavenworth to Santa Fe, New Mexico Territory, and then to San Diego, California Territory. Stoneman served as the battalion's assistant quartermaster. Assignments like this one convinced Stoneman that he had chosen his profession well. "I glory in it," he told a friend.[5]

After joining the First Dragoons, Stoneman served at various posts on the West Coast for the next five years. In the process, he fell in love with California. "To say that it is perfect would hardly be extravagant," he wrote of the state's beauty and climate. He even flirted with the idea of quitting the army and making California his permanent home. One day, he would return to the state and even serve as its governor, but for now the idea of leaving the military was implausible. With the dragoons, Stoneman instead discovered the hardships of a Western assignment, including his first combat as he battled Indians from tribes including the Coquille and Yuman. In 1853, when Secretary of War Jefferson Davis approved exploration of railroad routes to the West, Stoneman was assigned to help escort survey parties studying the terrain. This task took him deep into the hostile, beautiful wilds of the Sierra Nevadas and the Coast Range. At the close of this assignment, Stoneman was rewarded with a promotion to first lieutenant.[6]

During 1854 and 1855, Stoneman served briefly as aide-de-camp to General John E. Wool, commander of the Department of the Pacific. He also returned to the First Dragoons as regimental adjutant. Another and better opportunity presented itself in due course. On March 3, 1855, Jefferson Davis promoted Stoneman to captain and assigned him to the new Second United States Cavalry, one of the first two cavalry units ever created by the United States Army. The unit's leadership was studded with future Civil War luminaries. Albert Sidney Johnston and Robert E. Lee were the ranking officers, and men such as William J. Hardee, John Bell Hood, Joseph E. Johnston, David S. Stanley, and George Thomas also served. Even Stoneman's fellow captains Earl Van Dorn and Edmund Kirby Smith would find themselves in key roles in the country's next war. The regiment was assigned to frontier duty in Texas.[7]

About this time, Stoneman first encountered a problem that would plague him for the rest of his life—a severe case of hemorrhoids, also called piles. Characterized by inflammation, itching, and bleeding, hemorrhoids can become quite painful if they protrude outside the body. That is exactly what happened to Stoneman. A difficult challenge for anyone who rode a horse for a living, the malady probably developed from long hours on horseback and a low-fiber diet. While serving in Texas, Stoneman even underwent an operation, but it failed to correct the problem. He would have to find relief by other means. As he once confided to a friend, neither a cold nor a fever "affects me as my disease affects me, and if I don't get better soon I shall take a trip down into a more congenial clime and see if the south will not *agree* with me better than the north." Unfortunately, a change of climate did not help either. After the war, surgeons examining his problem speculated that death itself might have been a better fate.[8]

Gritting his teeth against the piles, Stoneman did not waver from his duty. A new foe awaited the United States Army in Texas in the form of Mexican marauders. To deter the bandits, Stoneman's company settled at Camp Cooper, a distant cantonment in the Comanche Reserve. Raids from Mexico drew the attention of the regiment and soon pulled Stoneman into an international incident that marked the first setback of his career. On March 15, 1860, with two companies of the Second Cavalry and seventy-five Texas Rangers in tow, he crossed the Rio Grande to chase the Mexican bandit Juan Cortina. Discovering Cortina's camp, Stoneman ordered his detachment to charge. The troopers did so successfully, killing, wounding, and capturing more than three hundred men. Or so they thought. The next morning, the troopers discovered that they had charged a Mexican army camp by mistake. Stoneman apologized but stubbornly refused to withdraw when faced down by a fresh contingent of Mexican soldiers. In fact, he remained in Mexico for several days before he gave up his search for Cortina.[9]

Problems with renegades were soon forgotten as internal strife divided the nation. Stoneman's Civil War career began with promise. When the secession crisis culminated in Texas, he commanded Fort Brown, an outpost on the left bank of the Rio Grande opposite Matamoras, Mexico. General David E. Twiggs, commanding the Department of Texas, was a Southern loyalist who decided to hand over the Federal facilities in Texas to the state. He ordered Stoneman to turn over Fort Brown to the secessionists. In a celebrated moment of obstinacy, the New Yorker refused and instead dodged a formal surrender by leading his company to a port on the Gulf Coast and escaping on a steamer. Thereafter, in the uncertainty of the war's early days, Stoneman cycled through two posts in quick succession, first at the Cavalry School in Carlisle, Pennsylvania, and then as commander of cavalry in the defenses of Washington. A new rank went along with the second assignment; he was appointed major of the First United States Cavalry, to date from May 9, 1861.[10]

In the war's early days, Stoneman carried a reputation as a solid administrator, organizer, and disciplinarian who cared for the welfare of his men and animals.

"Stoneman we believe in," wrote one Massachusetts soldier. "We believe in his judgment, his courage, and determination. We know he is ready to shoulder responsibility, that he will take good care of us and won't get us into places from which he can't get us out." That was the type of man that George B. McClellan, Stoneman's West Point classmate and the commander of the Department of the Ohio, wanted at his disposal. "Give me such men as . . . Stoneman," he requested, "& I will answer for it with my life that I meet with no disaster." Accordingly, in July 1861, Stoneman joined the staff of the department, which was conducting operations in western Virginia. Stoneman went to work as assistant inspector general and quickly confirmed his commander's high opinion of him, prompting McClellan to block a move to send Stoneman west to serve as Major General John C. Fremont's chief of staff. When McClellan was promoted to command the Army of the Potomac the following month, he created the post of chief of cavalry and took Stoneman with him to fill it. Stoneman, promoted to brigadier general of volunteers, quickly learned that the title was all name and no sub-stance. At the time, cavalrymen were doled out to infantry corps, and each corps also had a chief of cavalry. Employment of the dispersed horse soldiers remained at the discretion of the corps commanders, so the chiefs of cavalry amounted to no more than staff officers. With no authority to command cavalry in the field, these "chiefs of cavalry" could only inspect regiments, handle paperwork, and transmit orders. Stoneman complained about this misuse of horsemen, arguing that they should be employed as a whole rather than in parts. The army would suffer grievously from this arrangement before rectifying the problem.[11]

If he could not command men in the field, Stoneman could at least prepare the Army of the Potomac's cavalry. From the start, he visited camps and picket lines frequently, and he did not like what he saw. To improve the mounted arm, he emphasized discipline and drill in the ranks and encouraged his men to re-frain from looting and plundering. He worked to improve rations, medical facili-ties, and equipment. He asked McClellan to bring in an experienced instructor to teach the men the way of the horse soldier. The New Yorker also railed against poor leadership and requested that the War Department set up review boards to get rid of weak officers, especially those who led because of politics, not abil-ity. Improvements came slowly on his watch, but they formed the basis for what would one day be a cavalry force without equal.[12]

In November 1861, Stoneman excused himself from duty to marry Mary Oliver Hardesty, a young lady from a prominent Baltimore family who was fourteen years younger than her beau. Rumors suggested that secessionist beliefs marred his new family, but such charges did not deter Stoneman. Returning to the business of war, he found his next challenge in the spring of 1862, when McClellan attacked Richmond via the Peninsula. As the Army of the Potomac sailed to and advanced along the long finger of land formed by the York and James rivers, Stoneman directed a successful but sluggish pursuit of withdrawing Confederates. In June, Brigadier General J. E. B. Stuart's Confederate cavalry changed the tone of the campaign with a bold circuit of the Army of the Potomac. Responsibility for the fiasco did not fall at Stoneman's feet, but the ride did nothing for the reputation of Federal horse soldiers. As the Seven Days' Battles began, Robert E. Lee's Army of Northern Virginia pushed McClellan's forces back from the Confederate capital. Stoneman's difficulties were not limited to the enemy, however, as his hemorrhoids worsened. He remained in the saddle as long as he could, but his condition was severe. One cavalryman described him as suffering from "infirmities that would have kept a man of less fortitude in hospital." The pain finally forced Stoneman to apply for sick leave. McClellan reacted by ordering him replaced, which prompted the cavalryman to cancel his leave and meet with McClellan to retain his position. Yet despite the army commander's apparent dissatisfaction, Stoneman was one of few Federal horse leaders to finish the campaign with his reputation intact. He had performed with some skill on the Peninsula, but as one historian has suggested, Stoneman fell far short of greatness.[13]

That summer, he left the cavalry for an infantry command. The New Yorker experienced mixed success while serving as a commander of foot soldiers. That fall, while directing the First Division of the Third Corps, he failed to stop J. E. B. Stuart's Confederate cavalry during its second raid around the Army of the Potomac. He had a legitimate chance to do so, but his soldiers were so scattered that they could not respond effectively. However, Stuart did not retard Stoneman's ascent of the Union army's ladder. Rising to command the Third Corps of the Army of the Potomac, Stoneman was promoted to major general in November. In December 1862, he distinguished himself during the Battle of Fredericksburg when his corps conducted a stout defense of the army's left flank.[14]

In February 1863, Major General Joseph Hooker, the new commander of the Army of the Potomac, made perhaps the best move of his career when he reorganized the army's cavalry. By freeing the cavalry from infantry control and placing it in a single unit, Hooker breathed new life into his mounted arm. The army commander also appointed Stoneman to lead the new Cavalry Corps. The first major test of the corps came during Hooker's spring 1863 drive to Richmond, which ended in a fierce battle around Chancellorsville, deep in Virginia's Wilderness. Hooker's plan was to grapple with Lee while Stoneman severed Lee's communications, forcing a Confederate withdrawal. Stoneman would then serve as a blocking force as Lee retreated, while Hooker pounced on the fleeing Confederates.[15]

Stoneman's first raid should have begun on April 14, 1863, but nature intervened when the horse soldiers tried to cross the Rappahannock River. Rain began falling with a vengeance soon after the cavalry's first troopers reached the opposite bank. Within a few hours, the river rose seven feet and the roads turned into molasses. Stoneman had to cancel the crossing, much to the chagrin of President Abraham Lincoln. While waiting for the weather to clear, Hooker defended his cavalry commander and also rethought his plan. Not once but twice, Hooker discarded his ideas about what Stoneman should accomplish. One set of orders directed Stoneman to "subdivide your command, and let them take different routes, and have some point of meeting on your line of general operations. These detachments can dash off to the right and left, and inflict a vast deal of mischief, and at the same time bewilder the enemy as to the course and intentions of the main body." A second set of orders, issued on April 28, instructed Stoneman to divide his command and send one column toward the Orange and Alexandria Railroad and the other toward Louisa Court House. On April 29, in the light of these confusing directives, Stoneman's cavalry— about seventy-four hundred men in six brigades—finally crossed the river. But they plodded along like turtles, owing to an apparent lack of preparation by the cavalry's leadership.[16]

Stoneman's first column, commanded by Brigadier General William Woods Averell, started off well enough but ran into trouble at Rapidan Station. Displeased with the column's performance, Hooker recalled Averell. Meanwhile, Stoneman's main column enjoyed more success. The blue-clad troopers started slowly but captured Louisa Court House on May 2. Detachments scoured the countryside to tear up tracks, destroy bridges, and visit destruction upon Confederate depots. The next stop was Thompson's Crossroads, where Stoneman adopted a policy that would become his modus operandi. In a meeting with his commanders, Stoneman announced that "we had dropped in that region of the country like a shell, and that I intended to burst it in every direction, expecting each piece or fragment would do as much harm and create nearly as much terror as would result from sending the whole shell, and thus magnify our small force into overwhelming numbers." Accordingly, the column's ten regiments split into seven separate detachments and exploded across the Virginia countryside. Troopers struck railroad facilities and bridges and even ventured into the outskirts of Richmond, creating excitement and consternation wherever they went.[17]

On May 5, Stoneman decided his troopers had "accomplished all that we were sent to perform." Moreover, he had heard nothing from Hooker and had seen no evidence of a Confederate retreat. Worse yet, the men had picked up rumors that Hooker had been defeated. As a result, the cavalry commander pointed his horsemen toward a reunion with the Army of the Potomac. After a tiring and hard march, Stoneman's weary column, minus a handful of detachments that had returned to Union lines via other routes, recrossed the Rappahannock on May 8.[18]

As the raiders rejoined the army, most believed they had been successful. For once, Union cavalrymen had done the raiding behind the enemy's lines. A swath of destruction and demoralization lay in their wake, and the human cost had been modest, all of which boosted the morale of the Federal horsemen. One fellow general called it "the most successful cavalry raid we have had in this war." Secretary of War Edwin M. Stanton even sent a circular to generals and state governors celebrating the expedition. The mood was tempered, however, by some negative reactions. Considering Hooker's simultaneous defeat at Chancellorsville, several critics charged that Stoneman's raid had robbed the Army of the Potomac of much-needed cavalry on the battlefield, while the raid itself had accomplished little. Indeed, the damage inflicted was repaired in less than two weeks, and the raid took a substantial toll on horseflesh. The army commander agreed that the New Yorker had failed and told him so. In fact, Hooker thought Stoneman deserved much of the blame for the campaign's failure. The reasons were many, Hooker thought—Stoneman was slow, he left important bridges untouched, he failed to take Richmond when he had the chance, and he did not follow orders. "Stoneman . . . had married just before a Rebel wife and at the same time was terribly afflicted with the piles, and between the two he had become completely emasculated," Hooker bitterly wrote. "I might as well have had a wet shirt in command of my cavalry." He began to make noises about replacing his cavalry chief.[19]

Stoneman got the message. After the raid, he gracefully bowed out and applied for leave. The general order announcing the leave blamed his health, and that was not inaccurate because the raid had worsened the bleeding from his hemorrhoids. In fact, Stoneman immediately sought treatment from a West Point surgeon, who recommended a three-month break. Still, everyone knew the real reason for his departure. Hooker needed a scapegoat, and George Stoneman was the man. Within two weeks, Hooker elevated Major General Alfred Pleasonton to command the cavalry, ending the New Yorker's tenure with the Army of the Potomac.[20]

But rest did not end Stoneman's discomfort. Illness continued to plague him, and so did the consequences of the ill-fated raid. The combination collided one day in the office of Secretary of War Stanton. Now angered by the raid, Stanton called Stoneman to the War Department on several occasions to give him "a severe talk." According to Stanton's clerk, the last visit proved too much for Stoneman. "His face was thin and he looked as if he needed rest, sleep, and medicine. While waiting in the big room adjoining to see the Secretary, he fainted and fell to the floor," the clerk wrote. A surgeon managed to revive Stoneman, and Stanton came out of his office to see what the fuss was about. Taken aback by the crumpled general, Stanton took pity and postponed their next meeting until Stoneman's health improved. However, his clerk wondered if the piles had anything to do with the incident. "I always thought that he fainted in contemplation of the purpose of the stern Secretary," he wrote.[21]

Stoneman needed a long sick leave, but despite the doctor's wishes he took only a month off. A desk assignment awaited. On July 28, 1863, the War Department created the Cavalry Bureau, and Stoneman became its first chief, over Stanton's objections. Designed to coordinate cavalry training and the purchase and care of cavalry equipment and horses, the bureau was the army's answer to the mounting toll on men and horses. Although hampered by competition and resentment from the Quartermaster and Ordnance departments, Stoneman managed to produce some positive results. Under his direction, the Cavalry Bureau provided thirty-five thousand horses and established important depots where recruits and horses could be received, organized, and trained and where veterans could be remounted. He also helped restore the horseflesh crippled by his own raid. By October 1863, he had gathered more than sixteen thousand horses in various depots for rest, recuperation, and treatment. Stoneman did not overlook the cavalry's arms either. In a creative moment, he devised and circulated a questionnaire to help evaluate the various carbines in service.[22]

Well done or not, paperwork and bureaucracy held little appeal for the New Yorker. Stoneman wanted to return to the field. In January 1864, he got his wish with the help of John Schofield. Initially, Schofield tapped his old friend to command the Twenty-third Corps, but a subsequent reorganization sent Stoneman back to his first love—the cavalry. His new command was the Cavalry Corps of the Department of the Ohio, and that was cause for celebration. "I am on my way to the army in Tennessee, having thank God got out of the cavalry bureau and into the field again," he wrote a friend. As if to mark Stoneman's return, a new and daunting assignment surfaced. In March 1864, General William T. Sherman gathered several armies, including the Army of the Ohio, with the goal of subduing General Joseph E. Johnston's Army of Tennessee around Atlanta.

Despite numerous problems with his new command, Stoneman ably readied his horsemen for the field. Many of his troopers were inexperienced and poorly equipped. Others lacked discipline. Nonetheless, Stoneman had his force ready for action by May 12. But this success did not mark a fresh start; instead, Stoneman's star continued its slow descent to its nadir. Ordered to cross the Chattahoochee River and attack the Atlanta and West Point Railroad, Stoneman ran into Confederate resistance at Moore's Bridge. Citing high risks, the corps commander burned the bridge and turned away. Sherman came away unimpressed, attributing the failure to laziness. In the ranks, some troopers wondered if Stoneman had lost his nerve.[23]

By July, after weeks of inching southward, Sherman was ready to launch what he hoped would be the final assault on Atlanta. Despite Stoneman's poor showing at Moore's Bridge, Sherman still considered the New Yorker a "cavalry-officer of high repute." He gave Stoneman an important role in strangling Atlanta's defenses. While his infantry swung right toward the vital railroad junction of East Point, Sherman divided his cavalry into two columns and sent them off to raid the Macon railroad. Stoneman commanded one column of about sixty-five hundred men from his own corps and Brigadier General Kenner Garrard's cavalry division. Brigadier General Edward M. McCook commanded the other, which boasted about four thousand troopers. "These two well appointed bodies," Sherman reported, "were to move in concert . . . and on . . . July 28, they were to meet on the Macon road near Lovejoy's [Station] and destroy it in the most effectual manner. I estimated this joint cavalry could whip all of [Joseph] Wheeler's [Confederate] cavalry, and could otherwise accomplish its task."[24]

*Major General William T. Sherman first broached
the idea of a cavalry raid to support the Union's 1865
offensive.*
LIBRARY OF CONGRESS

For George Stoneman, past failures fueled the present, and this moment was no different. Hearing of "Cump" Sherman's plans, he proposed an addendum. Once he reached the railroad, why not continue to Macon and Andersonville? In Macon sat Camp Oglethorpe, a modest outpost that housed a few hundred prisoners and several factories that churned out revolvers, rifle stocks, ordnance, medicine, and other goods of war. Farther on lay Andersonville, home of more Confederate resources and an infamous prisoner-of-war camp. "There was something most captivating in the idea," Sherman wrote, "and the execution was within the bounds of probability of success." The general agreed to

Stoneman's proposal, as long as he first defeated any Confederate cavalrymen, broke the Macon railroad, and sent Garrard back to the army.[25]

Recalling the slow start of the Chancellorsville raid, Stoneman made sure there was no delay this time. On July 27, the blue-clad troopers punctually broke camp and pointed their horses toward the enemy's country, passing countless streams and forests and miles of red clay. They also moved past Covington, Monticello, Hillsboro, and Clinton. As they rode, Stoneman resumed his old habits by dispatching detachments into the countryside to wreak havoc. In some cases, the Federal horse soldiers did not restrict their attention to items of military value. Provisions and horses and mules came into Federal hands, but so did whiskey and personal belongings. None of this satisfied Sherman, who believed that Stoneman did not focus on the real reason for the raid and instead reached for cheap glory. Rather than aim for the railroad, Stoneman rode for Macon and Andersonville. Sherman later charged Stoneman with disobeying orders.[26]

As Stoneman drew within sight of Macon and the Ocmulgee River, a modest force of militiamen, Home Guardsmen, and state reserves under Major General Howell Cobb barred the way. The raid ground to a disappointing halt in the summer heat. The Federals impotently shelled the town and tried to force an entry, but bad news turned their attention rearward. "Before I completed what I desired to accomplish," Stoneman later wrote, "I learned that a force of the enemy's cavalry was close upon my rear, and the only course for me to pursue to get out was to turn upon and, if possible, whip this force." This pursuing force—three brigades of Joe Wheeler's Confederate cavalry under the command of Brigadier General Alfred H. Iverson—cornered the New Yorker at Sunshine Church on July 31. Trapped, Stoneman gave permission for the bulk of his command to scatter and escape, while he stayed behind with a few hundred men to cover the retreat. "My own horse had been shot under me . . . and our chances of escape were so small that I consented to be taken prisoners of war," Stoneman reported.[27]

Colonel Charles C. Crews, commander of a brigade of Georgia horse regiments, did the honors. Riding up to Stoneman, Crews saluted and said that he had come to receive the Federal surrender. Stoneman demurred, hoping to surrender to Iverson instead, but the Confederate cavalryman insisted. Out of options and out of luck, the New Yorker gave up his sword, sat down on a log, and cried. Later, he would blame poor-performing Kentucky troopers and exhaustion from hemorrhoidal blood loss for his disaster. Whatever the cause, he now had the distinction of being the highest-ranking Union officer in Confederate hands.[28]

Now twice humiliated, the gruff, by-the-book Stoneman became the target of numerous critics. Complained one, "Stoneman couldn't command a company let alone a corps of cavalry." Another wag agreed and forecast that the New Yorker would botch any task. "I know Stoneman like a book," he quipped. "He will go to the proper spot like a cannon-ball, but when he gets there, like a shell, he'll burst." Fortunately, Stoneman had at least one admirer in Major General John M. Schofield, then commanding the Department of Ohio. In September 1864, after a humbled Stoneman was exchanged at Rough and Ready, Georgia, Schofield again came to the rescue. He gave Stoneman a chance for redemption by offering the New Yorker employment as his second in command, to the consternation of many observers.[29]

⚜

George Stoneman always had big ideas. Some were useless. Early in the war, hoping to create a distinct esprit de corps in the cavalry, he campaigned to outfit his men in scarlet jackets and caps and pea green trousers. While this concept fortunately died, he also generated more plausible proposals. One emerged in November 1864. Eager to prove himself in his new post, Stoneman presented his scheme to Schofield. "I propose by a rapid and forced march," he wrote, "to concentrate all the cavalry . . . , reach Bristol[, Tennessee,] before the enemy can, and thus cut him off from Saltville[, Virginia], and force him across the mountains into North Carolina, and maybe destroy the salt works. Should he get the start of us we can drive him up the valley, and North Carolina is thus opened up to us, and, for that matter, South Carolina too. Four days' march would take the cavalry to Salisbury, from which point we could act north or south, according to circumstances." It was a bold plan. The outcome of the war remained somewhat in doubt, with Federal armies dueling stubborn but weakening Confederate opponents in Virginia, Tennessee, Georgia, and elsewhere. Nonetheless, Stoneman had no qualms about riding into the enemy's country. "I owe the Southern Confederacy a debt I am anxious to liquidate, and this appears a propitious occasion," he told Schofield.[30]

Thirty-three-year-old John Schofield, also a New Yorker and West Pointer, liked the idea of pouncing on southwestern Virginia's saltworks. As one of only

Major General John Schofield believed in Stoneman when no one else did.
LIBRARY OF CONGRESS

two significant sources of salt still within Confederate lines, the wells around Saltville were an important strategic resource. The young nation desperately needed salt to preserve meat and other foods, to cure hides for leather goods, and to succor livestock, and Federal authorities knew it. In fact, the saltworks— the source of two-thirds of the South's wartime supply of salt—had already been the target of several Union expeditions, including two in 1864. The first, a spring affair led by William W. Averell, failed, but the second, in the fall, came much nearer to success. With Schofield's approval, Major General Stephen G. Burbridge led five thousand cavalrymen to the outskirts of Saltville itself before the Confederate defenses stiffened and repelled them. "Confound them salt works!" was the feeling shared by many Federals after these endeavors. In Schofield's mind, Stoneman's suggestion for another try was more than warranted.[31]

Schofield also liked and believed in George Stoneman, but the Salisbury part of his subordinate's plan was a stretch. True, the North Carolina town was an important Confederate supply point and contained a tempting prisoner-of-war camp. The problem was with Stoneman's reputation. Powerful critics had not forgotten the Georgia fiasco, and they wanted Stoneman's head. At the very least, that made Schofield's choice of Stoneman as his second in command controversial. Stanton, now Stoneman's leading critic, protested to Grant, "If you approve of his [Schofield's] so doing I am content, although I think him [Stoneman] one of the most worthless officers in the service and who has failed in everything entrusted to him." Grant agreed but deferred to Schofield. "I am not in favor of using officers who have signally failed when intrusted with commands in important places," he replied. However, Grant added, "as a general rule, when an officer is intrusted with the command of a department, he ought to be allowed to use the material given him in his own way."[32]

Grant relayed these messages to Schofield. Schofield, who would one day command the United States Army, reacted swiftly. He defended Stoneman, protested to Grant and Stanton, and took responsibility for his decision to give the New York cavalryman a job. He also decided to let Stoneman go ahead with the raid. There could be no mistake about it, though. This Saltville expedition would be Stoneman's last chance. If he failed again, his military career would be over. Schofield did not tell his new subordinate about these machinations yet; he simply gave his approval for the southwestern Virginia raid and hedged on the Salisbury idea. "I cannot decide as to further operations until affairs here take more definite shape, therefore do not undertake the other enterprise without further orders," he told Stoneman.[33]

If nothing else, George Stoneman was a soldier, and a good soldier did not question his orders. Tabling the Salisbury idea probably did not help his humor, however; wags characterized him as having dyspepsia, in view of his sometimes abrasive personality. Nonetheless, the New Yorker hastily gathered men for his raid.[34] Reporting directly to him would be two men who also had scores to settle. The first was Burbridge, who held few fond memories of his first trip to Saltville. Given his knowledge of the area, however, Burbridge was a logical choice. A former Kentucky lawyer and a veteran of Shiloh and Vicksburg, he had few friends because of his harsh administration of the District of Kentucky. On this raid, the thirty-three-year-old general would command eight regiments containing forty-two hundred men, most from his Fifth Division of Kentucky Cavalry.

The second of Stoneman's immediate subordinates was Brigadier General Alvan C. Gillem, commander of Tennessee governor Andrew Johnson's personal guard. A career army officer from the Volunteer State, Gillem had lost a disastrous battle at Bull's Gap, Tennessee, less than a month earlier. As a result, Stoneman found Gillem's command in a shambles. Officers were at each other's throats, and the men in the ranks followed their example. Supplies were scarce and mounts broken down. Observers might have questioned Stoneman's choice, but the undaunted New Yorker forged ahead. He quickly infused a new spirit into the troopers, provided new equipment, and rounded up fresh horses. Before long, Gillem's Eighth, Ninth, and Thirteenth Tennessee cavalry regiments, fifteen hundred men strong, were ready. Assembling at Bean Station, Tennessee, in early December, Burbridge's and Gillem's troopers steeled themselves for the challenge ahead.[35]

The raid was a success. Despite modest Confederate resistance and frigid temperatures, Stoneman's troopers laid waste to the saltworks at Saltville, the lead works around Wytheville, Virginia, and the ironworks at Marion, Virginia. The lead mines would be out of action for three months. Confederate facilities in neighboring towns such as Bristol and Abingdon and key bridges in the vicinity suffered at Federal hands as well. Their mission accomplished, the raiders returned triumphantly to Tennessee. They reached Knoxville on December 28 after a long, arduous trip back in weather cold enough to freeze boots in stirrups.[36]

Much acclaim awaited them. Major General George H. Thomas, Schofield's superior, congratulated Stoneman on his "complete and splendid success, and for which you richly deserve, and I have earnestly recommended you receive, the thanks of the War Department." Schofield added his kudos. "I have seen your report . . . of your late operations, and congratulate you most heartily upon your complete success and vindication of your reputation as a general," he wrote. Truly, Stoneman had performed well. In three weeks, his forces had navigated 870 miles of harsh, mountainous terrain in cold, wet December weather. Along the way, Stoneman had reduced the war-making capacity of the enemy by capturing over five hundred prisoners, nineteen artillery pieces, fifteen caissons, more than one thousand stands of arms, over twenty-five thousand rounds of ammunition, and several hundred horses. His forces had also captured the lead mines

Major General George Thomas, Stoneman's superior officer, specified the final strategy of the raid.
LIBRARY OF CONGRESS

and disrupted the East Tennessee and Virginia Railroad by destroying facilities, locomotives, and as many as twenty-eight railroad bridges. And his raid had not only rendered Saltville virtually impotent for the rest of the war but also cleared East Tennessee of Rebel forces.[37]

At last, the much-maligned Stoneman had his career back on track—or did he? Schofield decided to tell his subordinate about Grant's and Stanton's efforts to relieve him of command. "I may now inform you," he wrote, "that . . . while you were preparing for your late expedition, I was ordered by General Grant and the Secretary of War to relieve you from command, on the ground of your failure in Georgia. This order was revoked upon my earnest protest and the assumption of the responsibility for the result."[38] This dispatch cut George Stoneman deeply. Obviously, it would take more than one raid to make his critics forget the Georgia debacle. Another opportunity waited, straight ahead.

⁓

Major General William T. Sherman ached for action. By early 1865, the armies of the forty-four-year-old Ohio native occupied Savannah, Georgia, after their successful march to the sea. But rather than bask in his glory, "Cump" Sherman considered his next move. He offered his ideas to Grant, his friend and commander. "I feel no doubt whatever as to our future plans," he wrote. "I have thought them over so long and well that they appear as clear as daylight." Sherman proposed to march his army north through Columbia, South Carolina, to Raleigh, North Carolina. En route, he noted, he could break up railroad systems and cut off Charleston. He also wanted to "punish South Carolina as she deserves," as he had Georgia. Best of all, Sherman thought, the movement would help Grant's campaign in Virginia. Grant originally wanted Sherman to sail to Virginia, but he warmed to Sherman's proposal. The idea of Federal soldiers dining on the vitals of the Carolinas had great appeal. Grant approved Sherman's plan.[39]

Before he disappeared into the interior, Sherman left instructions for the forces under his command that would not join his march. He ordered Major General George H. Thomas to push his army into Alabama. To deflect attention from Thomas's advance, Sherman wanted Stoneman to take a small cavalry force on a modest feint. Sherman thought the horse soldiers should advance from Knoxville and follow the French Broad River into North Carolina. Seeing these orders, Grant decided to keep Thomas on the defensive. In his opinion, Thomas was "slow beyond excuse," so Grant wanted him on a leash. The cavalry raid was another matter. Instead of discarding the idea, Grant molded the raid to better purposes and ordered Thomas to execute it. "I think . . . an expedition from East Tennessee under General Stoneman might penetrate South Carolina well down toward Columbia, destroying the railroad and military resources of the country, thus visiting a portion of the State which will not be reached by Sherman's forces," Grant told Thomas. "He might also be able to return to East Tennessee by way of Salisbury, N.C., thus releasing some of our prisoners of war in rebel hands." Whether or not Salisbury was a feasible target would be up to Stoneman, once he finished his work in South Carolina. Either way, this would be a unique raid. "As this expedition goes to destroy and not to fight battles, but to avoid them when practicable, particularly against anything like equal forces, or where a great object is to be gained, it should go as light as possible," Grant wrote. "Stoneman's experience in raiding will teach him in this matter better than he can be directed."[40]

From a broader perspective, Sherman's march and Stoneman's Raid, as adapted, would fit perfectly into Grant's planned multi-column campaign to end the war. Some of the columns, including Stoneman's, would march with objectives of seizing or destroying places and things. Already, a combined Union army-navy force was assaulting Fort Fisher and Wilmington, North Carolina. Furthermore, Major General Edward R. S. Canby was instructed to reduce Mobile, and Major General James H. Wilson had orders to march his cavalry corps into Alabama to invest Selma and Montgomery and then continue into Georgia. Major General Phil Sheridan was also to play a role in the final act by striking from the Shenandoah Valley toward Lynchburg. Finally, the Union's key armies would renew their efforts. While Sherman's force marched into the Carolinas and sought to combine with troops surging inland from Wilmington, Major General George G. Meade's Army of the Potomac would again attempt to pry Lee's army out of its Petersburg, Virginia, trenches. The combined efforts of these Federal forces, Grant thought, would "leave nothing for the rebellion to stand upon."[41]

If Stoneman was to help kick the footstool from under the rebellion, much had to be done. February quickly arrived, and the campaigning season loomed, so Grant told Thomas to get ready. "Let there be no delay in preparations for this expedition," he wrote. To save time, Grant also relayed these orders to Stoneman. Eager at the thought of a raid on the Salisbury prison, Stoneman wanted to be sure his boss understood Grant. He had known Thomas since before the war and understood his character. "Please get me off as soon as possible," he wrote Thomas.[42]

Grant's and Stoneman's fears were not entirely misplaced. As it turned out, the smallest part of Grant's offensive would be among the most difficult to launch. The problems began at the top, with the man nicknamed "Old Slow Trot." Born on July 31, 1816, in Southampton County, Virginia, George Henry Thomas was an 1840 graduate of West Point. A veteran of the Seminole and

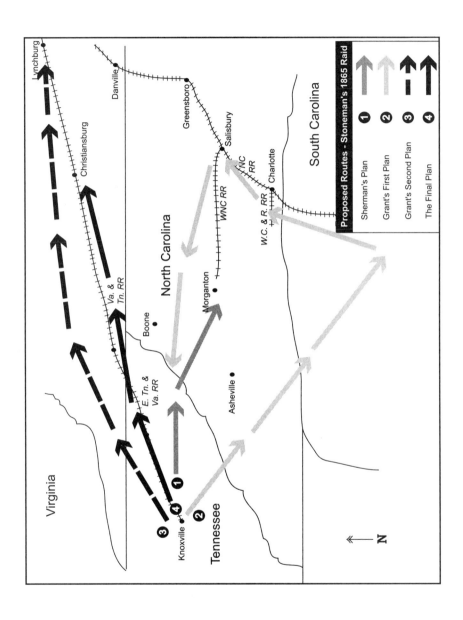

Mexican wars, he had risen through the ranks in the present conflict. After fighting in the Shenandoah Valley early in the war, Thomas was promoted to brigadier general and transferred to the Western Theater. Victory at Mill Springs in January 1862 earned him a promotion to major general. Thomas went on to perform superbly in many battles, including Corinth, Stones River, and Chattanooga. His most glorious moment came at Chickamauga, where his shattered Union forces conducted a legendary stand on Horseshoe Ridge, earning him the moniker "Rock of Chickamauga." Afterward, Thomas commanded the Army and the Department of the Cumberland during the Atlanta campaign. At Franklin and Nashville in late 1864, he again demonstrated his deliberateness, but once he attacked he virtually annihilated the Confederate army of John Bell Hood. Standing six feet tall and weighing about two hundred pounds, Thomas was an eccentric man, but no one doubted his fighting abilities. Though his thorough ways would not help speed the start of Stoneman's mission, other obstacles would have more to do with the delays to come.[43]

Given the size of his current command—which included the Districts of Middle Tennessee, East Tennessee, West Tennessee, and the Etowah and encompassed Major General David S. Stanley's infantry corps, the Artillery Reserve, the Signal Corps, and miscellaneous infantry and artillery units—it is a wonder that Thomas focused at all on East Tennessee. But he gave the raid the attention Grant wanted. Thomas appointed Stoneman commander of the District of East Tennessee, and then the two men turned to their first order of business: building the raiding force. In Grant's opinion, Stoneman would need only about three thousand cavalrymen to accomplish his mission. Many of them were already available from Stoneman's old Saltville force. In the District of East Tennessee was Brigadier General Alvan C. Gillem's Governor's Guard. On February 6, 1865, Stoneman told Gillem about the upcoming raid: "I have just received orders from General Grant directing a movement, in which your fine body of Cossacks is to play a very important part, and I would advise you to put them in condition to take the field as soon as possible." Stoneman hoped that Gillem would be able to furnish about two thousand men, but the Tennessean's force was still depleted from the southwestern Virginia raid. Ultimately, Stoneman secured only part of the Eighth Tennessee Cavalry Regiment and part of the Thirteenth Tennessee Cavalry. Thomas made it official a few weeks later when he applied for and received Governor Johnson's permission to use the Governor's Guard.[44]

Grant thought that the rest of the raiding force could be raised in the Department of Ohio without significantly reducing other commands. He recommended sending the two Kentucky cavalry regiments that had participated in the Saltville raid. The commanding general admitted that these two regiments needed reorganization, but Stoneman's familiarity with them made them good candidates. Following Grant's lead, Stoneman asked Thomas for reinforcements from Burbridge's command, but he wanted more than the Kentucky regiments. Whereas Grant had simple hell-raising in mind, Stoneman envisioned glory. He asked Thomas for not only the Eleventh Kentucky and Twelfth Kentucky cavalry but also the Eleventh Michigan and Twelfth Ohio cavalry regiments. On February 14, Thomas ordered all four regiments to report to Stoneman.[45]

Stoneman designated Knoxville as the marshaling point for his force, but gathering the various regiments there proved difficult. It was easy for the Eighth and Thirteenth Tennessee cavalry regiments, since both were already stationed in Knoxville, but the other regiments were widely scattered and poorly equipped. For example, the Twelfth Ohio Cavalry was dispersed at various outposts in Kentucky. The troopers first hopped a train to Louisville, where they assembled and reported to Stoneman. But before they could go any farther, the Twelfth Ohio needed reorganization. A week passed while the Twelfth re-equipped and remounted. The men took advantage of the break. Happily, their Louisville camp sprawled on a common near a German beer garden. "The week passed gaily away, the men bartering their ample rations for the beer and pretzels and odorous cheese . . . and the officers busy with the work of drawing and issuing clothing, horses, and such arms and equipments as were necessary to restore the losses of the year," noted a reveler. Finally, the time came to leave for Knoxville. It was a beautiful March day, and the prospect of an assignment other than chasing guerillas thrilled the men. Twenty-two-year-old Joseph Banks recorded in his diary how the Ohioans let out "chear after chear" when they heard they would "join our Comreads at the front."[46]

On March 1, the Twelfth Ohio Cavalry boarded five steamers and sailed up the Ohio and Cumberland rivers to Nashville. One horse soldier remembered this trip as perhaps the most pleasant of the war. Springtime began to work its wonders along the waters, and the regimental band provided able accompaniment. As the tiny fleet sailed past historic Fort Donelson and dozens of little river towns, the men relaxed, played cards, read, wrote letters, and told stories. On Sunday, March 5, the well-rested troopers disembarked at Nashville. The next day brought even more lax duty as the men took in the sights of the state capital. On the morning of March 7, the regiment marched to Murfreesboro by way of the Stones River battlefield. Then the command again took to the rails, riding via Chattanooga to Knoxville. On March 11, the Ohioans pulled into the station, took their horses off the cars, and marched about a mile outside town. They camped in a beautiful cedar grove.[47]

The other regiments took similar but less enjoyable routes. Like the Twelfth Ohio, the Eleventh Michigan had been scouting in eastern Kentucky when its orders arrived. As early as February 21, the unit began its journey to Knoxville. Traveling by road, rail, and steamer via Lexington, Louisville, and Nashville, it completed the trek on March 14–15. Meanwhile, the Kentucky regiments made their way southward. Both had been operating against guerillas in their home state when Thomas's orders came through. On February 27, the Eleventh and Twelfth Kentucky took a train at Lexington that chugged through Nashville and Chattanooga to Knoxville. The horses and men of the Eleventh Kentucky Cavalry rode the first train, their companion regiment following on a second train. Both units arrived on March 9.[48]

Another arriving raider was impressed by Knoxville. "A real pretty place," opined trooper Allen Frankenberry after taking in the town's sights. Frankenberry ("Frank" to his friends) was a newcomer to the smallest of Stoneman's units, its Signal Corps detachment. Lieutenant Theodore Mallaby, Jr., commanded the signalmen, who would play an important role on the raid by facilitating communications. On March 20, Mallaby reported to Gillem and formally began his new assignment as chief signal officer for the District of East Tennessee.[49]

An impatient Stoneman pushed hard to achieve even these slow results. In February, he sent a staff officer to the Bluegrass State to hasten the assembly of his raiding force. A few days later, he reminded the staffer to send the regiments on as fast as possible. The New Yorker then visited Louisville personally and learned firsthand the difficulties facing his troopers.[50]

These four regiments did not yet satisfy, so Thomas and Stoneman continued to expand the raiding column. Over the next few weeks, the command grew stronger with the addition of two more regiments and some artillery support. One regiment, the Tenth Michigan Cavalry, was at hand, having been stationed in Knoxville since December as part of the Fourth Division of the Twenty-third Army Corps. It also occurred to the raid's planners that artillery support might be necessary, so Stoneman cast about for a candidate. The most convenient and familiar unit was Battery E of the First Tennessee Light Artillery, officially part of the Artillery District of Nashville. Fortunately, the gunners had no trip to make, having been stationed in Knoxville since Gillem's Bull's Gap debacle.[51]

The final piece of the puzzle, the Fifteenth Pennsylvania Cavalry, had some distance to cover. Word of the raid first came when the regiment was resting at a "delightful" cotton plantation in northern Alabama. When officially transferred from the Cavalry Division of the Military Division of the Mississippi on March 6, the regiment was marching through the Cumberland Mountains en route to the Chattanooga area. After a pause in what Colonel William Palmer called "a not very agreeable" campground at Wauhatchie, Tennessee, to refit, the regiment received movement orders on March 11. Five days later, the troopers boarded a train for Knoxville. In contrast to their Ohio comrades, they found little to recommend the endeavor. "The journey by rail was a slow and tedious one, our poor horses suffering keenly for want of food and water," complained a Pennsylvanian. Another remembered that a car ran off the rails and overturned en route, which forced the men to disembark and push it from the tracks before they could continue. Despite these obstacles, it proved a short trip; at two in the morning on March 18, the trains rumbled into town. The troopers disembarked and camped in a nearby orchard for the night.[52]

How to organize these disparate units was another important question. Stoneman decided to place the gathering regiments into a division of three brigades. The first, commanded by Colonel William J. Palmer, contained the Fifteenth Pennsylvania, Twelfth Ohio, and Tenth Michigan cavalry regiments. The second, under the care of Brevet Brigadier General Simeon B. Brown, was comprised of the Eleventh Kentucky, Twelfth Kentucky, and Eleventh Michigan cavalry regiments. Colonel John K. Miller led the Third Brigade, which consisted of the Eighth Tennessee Cavalry, the Ninth Tennessee Cavalry, and the Thirteenth Tennessee Cavalry, although the Ninth would not ultimately go on the raid. Finally, Lieutenant James M. Reagan commanded Battery E of the First Tennessee Light Artillery. All told, the division contained about four thousand men.[53]

Another organizational question had to do with district leadership. One key would be those men who helped execute Stoneman's will—his staff officers. The general chose them carefully. The first choice was the easiest. Major Myles W. Keogh, who had been at Stoneman's side for over a year as aide-de-camp, would serve as senior aide-de-camp. Stoneman considered Keogh "one of the most superior young officers in the army," a man who offered "devotion to the cause . . . gallantry, zeal and intelligence and . . . fine soldierly bearing." The two men had shared much together; now, they would share Stoneman's final raid. Next, Stoneman selected Captain Robert Morrow, a veteran of East Tennessee campaigning, to be his assistant adjutant general. Although quite young, Morrow was intelligent and mature beyond his years. To round out his staff, Stoneman secured Major Gustavus M. Bascom, an experienced assistant adjutant general in the head-quarters of the Department of Kentucky, to fill the same position.[54]

Since he was responsible for the entire District of East Tennessee, Stone-man needed a commander for his new cavalry division. True, he would personal-ly accompany the division on the raid, but the force also needed an independent commander. That would free Stoneman to return to East Tennessee as condi-tions warranted. In the veteran cavalryman's mind, the choice was easy. By this late stage of the war, few officers boasted as much experience in rugged, wild, and politically divided East Tennessee as Brigadier General Alvan C. Gillem. Stone-man had known Gillem for years and thought highly of him. In fact, when the war began, Stoneman had asked the War Department to assign the Tennessean to his command. That did not work out, but Gillem had impressed Stoneman during the southwestern Virginia raid. On March 17, he offered Gillem the po-sition. The appointment became official the next day when Gillem accepted.[55]

While the men assembled, Stoneman and Thomas turned to an even more difficult problem—horses. Army-wide, there was a crisis, with the cavalry short by more than twenty-seven thousand horses in all theaters. Every command needed remounts. That was true locally, as the Saltville raid had truly depleted the horseflesh in Gillem's and Burbridge's commands. For example, the Elev-enth Michigan was particularly challenged, more than three-fourths of the unit having been dismounted during the raid. As a result, Thomas estimated that Stoneman would need between one thousand and two thousand fresh horses for the upcoming effort. On February 9, he sent a dispatch to Major William P. Chambliss, special inspector of cavalry for the Military Division of the Missis-sippi, the man responsible for Thomas's horse supply. Stoneman needed horses, Thomas wrote, "to fill a pressing and immediate emergency." He gave this request top priority. When Chambliss did not respond immediately, Thomas even asked the army's chief of staff, Major General Henry W. Halleck, to intervene. Hal-leck's help proved unnecessary. Chambliss had missed Thomas's inquiries simply because he was out of town. Thinking another voice would help, Stoneman also tracked Chambliss down and increased the request to three thousand horses.[56]

Chambliss's ability to fill the need was limited. As of February 16, his Louisville office reported only three hundred horses in reserve. Worse, the division's regular flow of horses had stopped. Chambliss had not received a single horse in almost a month because the War Department had given priority to Canby and his Mobile campaign and also to Major General Grenville Dodge at Fort Leavenworth. Nonetheless, Chambliss promised to do his best. He could not say exactly when he would deliver enough horses, but an educated guess put the time at about twenty days. His telegraph operator quickly tapped out an appeal to the War Department to resume delivery of horses to the Military Division of the Mississippi.[57]

The picture became clearer a few days later, but the news remained bad. Gillem met with Chambliss on February 18 and spelled out his need for fifteen hundred horses for his Governor's Guard. That brought the overall requirement for the division to thirty-five hundred horses. The delivery of horses to Chambliss had resumed, but in a trickle, not a flow. A daily average of a mere one hundred horses arrived at Louisville from Cincinnati, Columbus, and Indianapolis. At that rate, Chambliss estimated, it would take thirty-five days to mount Stoneman's command. Hopes for a quick start faded as February ended and March began.[58]

Somehow, Chambliss delivered a decent supply of horses over the next few days. The Fifteenth Pennsylvania Cavalry, for example, secured a few hundred fresh horses that one beneficiary described as "the best we have ever drawn." To collect these mounts, Colonel Palmer ordered Sergeant William F. Colton and a companion to Louisville. Colton's mission was to get the horses to camp in as good a condition as possible. Arriving in Louisville at three in the morning on February 17, Colton went to the Louisville Hotel to bed down for the night. He found a full inn and ended up sleeping on a cot in the parlor. The next day, after a late breakfast, Colton arranged for a proper room and then reported to the Cavalry Bureau. He presented a letter of introduction to one of Chambliss's subordinates, to no avail. It was almost a week before Colton was able to ship the horses to his comrades.[59]

Other units received an infusion of horses, too, as saddler Abraham Conger could attest. Conger served in the Twelfth Ohio's Company A. He drew a fresh horse at Lexington, Kentucky, in February, and named him Frank. An unbroken colt about five or six years old, Frank turned out to be a remarkable steed. While many of these new horses would not survive the rigors of the raid, Frank would

George Stoneman later served as governor of California.
WEST POINT MUSEUM OF ART COLLECTION,
UNITED STATES MILITARY ACADEMY

make the entire journey and live to a ripe old age. In later years, he acted like an old soldier as much as any veteran. When he saw the Stars and Stripes unfurled, Frank would trot up to it and stand in its shadow like a guardian. After the horse's death in 1886, surviving veterans of the regiment raised a monument in his memory.[60]

The horse-poor Eleventh Michigan likewise drew fresh beasts while traveling to Knoxville, including a supply of thirty-nine on March 6. Horseflesh problems continued to plague the regiment. Detraining in the city on the Holston River, trooper Henry Birdsall saw a distressing sight. "Our horses were all loose roaming about the country," he complained. "They were taken off the cars in the night and got loose. We found about one half of our horses." Fortunately, the Michigan men recovered more of their horses the next day.[61]

Try as he might, Chambliss could not pull horses out of thin air. By the raid's launch date in late March, several parts of the command remained unmounted, so a number of good men had to stay behind. These included Companies C and D of the Eighth Tennessee Cavalry, a detachment of the Thirteenth Tennessee under Major Patrick F. Dyer, a detachment of the Eleventh Kentucky Cavalry, the entire Ninth Tennessee Cavalry Regiment, and more than five hundred men of the Tenth Michigan. Several men had to stay behind for legal reasons as well, among them Colonel Samuel K. N. Patton of the Eighth Tennessee, who was arrested under "various charges of a serious character." His court-martial would wait until after the raid. And more than a few officers and men from the Thirteenth Tennessee Cavalry could not go because they were ill. They were posted either to the hospital or to the Invalid Camp under Major J. H. Wagner.[62]

Chambliss was also responsible for arming Stoneman's raiders. Because of its portability, its ability to load through the breech, and its medium range, the carbine was the desired weapon for horse soldiers, and the model of choice was the repeating Spencer carbine. Thomas and Stoneman wanted Spencers for the men. A lever-action .56-caliber weapon capable of firing eight shots—seven from the magazine and one from the chamber—before reloading, the Spencer was durable, serviceable, and probably the most advanced carbine to see action during the war. That made it almost as hard to come by as horses. January's supply of Spencers had failed entirely, and few of the coveted weapons had arrived since then. This created competition among commands. For example, James Wilson protested when Thomas ordered the Eleventh Kentucky Cavalry supplied with Spencers. The regiment's term had nearly expired, Wilson pointed out, so shouldn't the weapons be sent to his men? Thomas's orders held, however.[63] Troopers in the Tenth and Eleventh Michigan cavalry regiments also garnered a supply, but not every one of Stoneman's units was equally blessed. Officials had to scrounge for substitutes. Stoneman personally arranged for five hundred Sharps carbines for Gillem's Tennesseans, to add to the Enfields and Springfields already in their possession. The Sharps was not a bad alternative; a single-shot weapon, it was the most widely used carbine in the cavalry. The Sharps was advanced in its own right because it did not require a priming cap to fire it. Later, the Sharps would become buffalo hunters' favorite weapon because of its stopping power.[64]

The Fifteenth Pennsylvania's experience demonstrates the difficulty of procuring weapons. During his horse-seeking trip to Louisville, Colton also tried to get some Spencers. He found Chambliss to be obstinate. "The Bureau is in no hurry and I cannot get the carbines for several days," Colton confided to his diary. Finally, the Philadelphia cavalryman went to Stoneman and asked for an order to hurry up the carbines. Colton presented the order to Chambliss, and that got results. On February 21, Colton received 650 Spencers and sent them on to the regiment.[65]

All of this took time—too much time, in the opinion of U. S. Grant, who was impatiently awaiting the start of the raid. The first red flag appeared in mid-February, when Thomas asked about adding some Missouri cavalrymen to Stoneman's command. Grant told him to forget about reinforcements and start the raid immediately. Old Slow Trot did not budge. He simply reminded the nation's first soldier that he had done everything he could. "I have taken measures to equip General Stoneman as rapidly as possible," he assured Grant.[66]

As February passed, Richmond newspapers reported Federal activity in western North Carolina. Naturally, Grant assumed Stoneman had caused the ruckus. He wired Thomas, "When did Stoneman start on his expedition?" The answer shocked Grant: Stoneman had still not started. "You may judge my surprise," Grant later wrote, "when I afterward learned that Stoneman was still in Louisville, Ky., and that the troops in North Carolina were [Colonel George W.] Kirk's forces." Frustrated, Grant told Thomas to limit the raiding force to three thousand—as originally ordered—and to get started. Thomas explained that difficulties in gathering horses had slowed matters down, but guessed that the force would leave around March 1.[67]

Something else dawned on Grant. Because of the delay, a change of plans would be necessary. Sherman had now passed through South Carolina, eliminating any need for a raid into the Palmetto State. "I think now his course had better be changed," Grant ordered Thomas on February 27. "It is not impossible that in the event of the enemy being driven from Richmond they may fall back to Lynchburg with a part of their force and attempt a raid into East Tennessee. It will be better, therefore, to keep Stoneman between our garrisons in East Tennessee and the enemy. Direct him to repeat his raid of last fall, destroying the railroad as far toward Lynchburg as he can."[68]

Thomas, perhaps sensing his commander's growing exasperation, passed these orders to Stoneman and then apologized to Grant. He cited a lack of time as the key reason for the delay. Stoneman also assured Grant that the raid would have been well on its way if not for insurmountable obstacles. "You cannot be more anxious to have me get off than I am to go," he wrote. "The delay has been due entirely to the difficulty in collecting together these troops, which were very much scattered over Kentucky, and to the deficiency in horses to replace those entirely broken down and lost on their last trip into Virginia."[69] Still, problems with horses, men, and time, although legitimate, did not placate the commanding general.

March 1 came and went, and still no raid; none of the regiments had arrived in Knoxville. Stoneman personally hurried there and was welcomed warmly. "General Stoneman is an able officer—an experienced Cavalry officer—has been almost twenty years in the saddle as an officer of the regular army—and still looks to be in the prime of life, with an excellent constitution," *Brownlow's Knoxville Whig* noted. But neither his skill nor his constitution helped preparations. Then the weather intervened. For much of the country, 1865 turned out to be one of the wettest years in recent memory, and the month of March brought a key period of moisture. For example, the weather station in Washington, D.C., measured 5.6 inches of rain in March, the most since 1851. In Clarksville, Tennessee, observers recorded almost 8 inches, the most there in a decade. And a North Carolina newspaper reported an "unusual amount of rain for some weeks past." That same precipitation pounded East Tennessee. As Stoneman's raiders converged on Knoxville, a heavy storm crashed artillery-like across the countryside. It must have reminded Stoneman of the rains that had delayed the start of his Chancellorsville raid. This storm swelled streams and turned roads into a muddy morass. Worse, the bridges at Stones River and Lookout Creek were swept away, and part of the railroad bridge at Bridgeport, Alabama, was also gone, forcing troopers to unload horses from the train and lead them across the remnants of the span one by one. "The country is flooded with water," a witness marveled, "and we appear to be passing over a lake." On March 6, Thomas told Grant about the weather problems but optimistically predicted that the balance of Stoneman's force would reach Knoxville by March 11 and start from there immediately.[70]

The extra days gave Grant time to again rethink the strategy of the raid. On March 7, he ordered the New Yorker to bypass the railroad until he reached Virginia unless he saw a chance to cut off rolling stock to the west, away from the Confederacy's main forces. Sherman, in Fayetteville, North Carolina, on March 11 after a triumphant march through South Carolina, added his thoughts. "Let Stoneman push toward Greensborough or Charlotte from Knoxville," he wrote. "Even a feint in that quarter will be most important. The railroad from Charlotte to Danville is all that is left to the enemy, and it won't do for me to go there on account of the 'red clay' hills, that are impassable to wheels in wet weather." Finally, Thomas made sense of all these orders by directing Stoneman to march from Tennessee to Christiansburg, Virginia, via the New River Valley. From there, Stoneman was to destroy railroad tracks and drop key bridge spans, threaten Lynchburg, and, as Sherman had suggested, perhaps even move on Danville, Greensboro, or Charlotte. Both Thomas and Grant guessed that the Army of Northern Virginia, if driven from Petersburg and Richmond, might retreat toward East Tennessee via Lynchburg, so destroying the railroad and military resources of southwestern Virginia and central and western North Carolina could prove critical. Grant approved the plan. But in the end, he didn't care where Stoneman went as long as he did two things: start right away and threaten Lynchburg. "He will not meet opposition now that cannot be overcome with 1,500 men," Grant wrote.[71]

Also solidified at this time was the second part of Stoneman's plan. Back in his original January orders, Grant had recommended that a small division of infantry follow the raiders and hold the upper part of the Holston Valley and key mountain passes in East Tennessee and western North Carolina, thus retaining control over the region Stoneman's cavalry claimed. This concept remained alive in March, but Grant amended the plan by directing the force to repair the East

Tennessee and Virginia Railroad as it advanced. Above all, Thomas decided, the force should be prepared to "cover Stonemans rear & give him support should he be forced back by superior force."[72] At last, Stoneman's District of East Tennessee had its final marching orders.

With that issue settled, March 11 approached. But despite Thomas's forecast, the raiders were still not ready. The waters had fallen, communications had been restored, and the regiments had begun to trickle in, but Stoneman still had much to do. The New Yorker had arrived in Knoxville only on March 8 and formally assumed command of the District of East Tennessee the next day. Asking his staff to push the rest of the raiding force onward, Stoneman turned his attention to making sure his Tennesseans were properly prepared.[73]

Stoneman also asked his new First Brigade commander, Colonel William J. Palmer, to inspect the regiments to ensure their preparedness. Palmer did so and directed some changes. Company commanders in the Twelfth Kentucky Cavalry received instructions to turn over all unserviceable horses to the quartermaster. The Eleventh Michigan, Twelfth Ohio, and Eleventh and Twelfth Kentucky got approval to requisition anything they needed to complete their field equipment. Another regiment received a host of fresh accouterments: revolvers, sabers, bridles, currycombs, horse brushes, saddles, saddle blankets, nose bags, and more. All of this added up to a more battle-ready division.[74]

Slowly, it all came together. Stoneman told Thomas that he would start on March 18—but only if all his units arrived. Thomas did not communicate this delay to Grant, so again the impatient commanding general, at his City Point log-cabin headquarters, was left to fend for himself. On March 14, for the third time in two months, Grant checked on his subordinates. "Has Stoneman started on his raid?" he asked Thomas. This pressure filtered downward. "Gen. Grant getting in a hurry," wrote one of Gillem's officers. Finally, thanks to the tremendous progress Stoneman had made during March, a confident reply emanated from Knoxville. The New Yorker's March 18 prediction did not pan out, but it proved close. Thomas, who came to Knoxville in person to monitor events, told Grant that Stoneman would start the following Monday.[75]

That, too, turned out to be inaccurate, but it was near enough. Stoneman missed the official start by only one day. On March 21, he announced the happy news. "I have the honor to report," he told Thomas and Grant, "that my whole command is on the road, and that the advance will be at Morristown, fifty miles from here, today. It is a long, rough, bad road where we are going, and every precaution and care has been and must continue to be taken in order that our horses may not be broken down in the first part, which is over a country destitute of subsistence. I will keep you advised as long as I am within range of the telegraph or courier communication."[76]

At last, thousands of blue-clad cavalrymen wound their way eastward. Time would tell if the raid would do the Union war effort any good.

Chapter 2

A Column of Fire

Tennessee: March 14–27, 1865

The muse of history sang in the final days of March 1865. At Bentonville, North Carolina, General Joseph E. Johnston's makeshift army assaulted Sherman's force but lost. Near Petersburg, Virginia, General Robert E. Lee's besieged Confederate army readied a last-ditch surprise attack to break Grant's death grip. At City Point, President Abraham Lincoln and his leading generals contemplated the future of the war and the nation. Miniscule against this backdrop, George Stoneman unleashed his long-awaited raid.

Despite Stoneman's dramatic March 21 announcement, parts of the new Cavalry Division of the District of East Tennessee had in reality already begun to move. Its brigades had yet to marshal, so it looked more like a grim game of leapfrog than a division advancing in concert. The Kentucky troopers took the first step eastward on March 14 with a short ride to Strawberry Plains, a strategic outpost and railroad bridge about fifteen miles northwest of Knoxville. There, they awaited further orders.[1]

A few days later, Stoneman sent the Eleventh Michigan after its Kentucky comrades. When trooper Henry Birdsall arrived at Strawberry Plains on March 17, he was plagued by a severe headache. Birdsall blamed hunger, but the regiment's lack of shelter was another reason for worry. The Eleventh Michigan carried mostly old, worn tents—the same ones issued when the regiment was organized in 1863—that offered scant protection against the elements. But it was too late for amenities. The regiment camped for a day and then moved to Mossy Creek on March 19. Pitching their tattered tents in a large oak grove, the men settled in to await the rest of the division.[2]

On March 16, the camps of the Twelfth Ohio were nestled on the slope below Fort Sanders, where Lieutenant General James Longstreet's Confederates had come to grief in a November 1863 attack on Knoxville. The refrain of "Boots and Saddles" sent the men scrambling. After packing up and mounting their newly shod horses, they embarked for Strawberry Plains. Rain soaked the troopers' new uniforms. When the Twelfth reached its destination, the unit camped on a rocky hill shaded by cedar trees.[3]

The official start date of March 21 rang truer for other units. Knoxville bustled with activity that Tuesday as the rest of the division left town. Intent on success, Stoneman personally supervised the beginning. One cavalryman described the thin, tall district commander as "a powerfully-built man, standing six feet four, with a face that showed the marks of long and hard service in the field." His gaunt and sad appearance reminded some of the long-dead abolitionist John Brown and others of Abraham Lincoln. A hard-swearing, sour, and brusque man who looked older than his forty-two years, Stoneman was confident about the challenge before him. When he saw new Spencers slung over the shoulders of his men, he bragged, "We ought to be able to go anywhere with our seven-shooters."[4]

The camps of the Fifteenth Pennsylvania, which sat along the East Tennessee and Virginia Railroad about two miles northwest of Knoxville, came alive early. To the trumpeted notes of "Boots and Saddles," the Pennsylvanians saddled up and began what one trooper called "the long march." It was about nine in the morning when the Fifteenth Pennsylvania took the position of honor in the division's vanguard. However, it was not a pleasant day for a journey, nor was it an auspicious beginning. Ominously, the weather raged just as it had at the start of Stoneman's Chancellorsville and Macon raids. Rain fell and thunder rumbled as the troopers navigated Knoxville's muddy streets. The road to Strawberry Plains sucked at hooves, wheels, and boots. By evening, hail fell thickly from the dark sky, pelting the men in blue. Company H's H. K. Weand, a native of Norristown, Pennsylvania, never forgot it. "We started from Knoxville in an

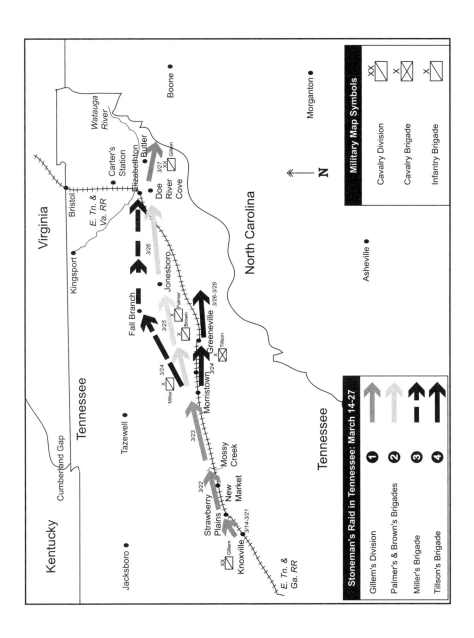

ordinary rainstorm, which increased in intensity during the day, and at night had developed into a furious hailstorm," he wrote. The Pennsylvanians managed to swim through for about thirteen or fourteen miles before camping two miles short of Strawberry Plains. It was about three-thirty in the afternoon when they halted.[5]

Stoneman's other Michigan regiment marched directly behind the Fifteenth Pennsylvania on the gooey Strawberry Plains road. However, to this unit, the worsening storm seemed comparatively insignificant. Detroit native Luther S. Trowbridge, freshly promoted to command the Tenth Michigan after serving as provost marshal of East Tennessee, was in the midst of a challenging first day on the job. Discipline problems appeared immediately when some men "liberated" private property. Worse, the commander of Company D, Captain Archibald Stevenson of Bay City, Michigan, got drunk. The Federals left him behind, but Stevenson decided the regiment needed him. He reappeared at about eleven at night and sought shelter in a farmhouse, where he attempted to rape a young girl. Fortunately, several officers arrived and stopped him. Flustered, Colonel Trowbridge unwisely ordered Stevenson to rejoin his command. As Trowbridge later explained, Stevenson had sobered up, "and the night and roads being awful, [the mission] required the care and services of every officer." Stevenson returned to his company but disappeared again an hour later. The Tenth Michigan made it to Strawberry Plains with no further incidents, but Archibald Stevenson would be back.[6]

Colonel Miller's two-regiment Third Brigade followed. Days before, the brigade had impressed *Brownlow's Knoxville Whig* in a stirring review. "Their clothes were clean. The horses were in good condition, and well curried, while the carbines and sabres were as bright as a silver dollar," a reporter wrote. Now, guiding their horses eastward, the Tennessee regiments began what a member described as a "long and tedious raid" with a short, wet ride to Strawberry Plains. Elsewhere in Knoxville, another Tennessean, twenty-nine-year-old first lieutenant James M. Reagan, ordered Company E of the First Tennessee Light Artillery to limber up. Its four guns and caissons were soon sloshing along the road. Last of all came the Signal Corps unit of Lieutenant Theodore Mallaby, Jr. The signalers left Knoxville at noon and camped at Strawberry Plains seven hours later. Frank Frankenberry was tickled to be part of this; he had learned of the raid just a few days earlier and had done his best to join it. "I offered $95.00 to get to go along but I fear there will be no chance for me," he told his journal. Frankenberry did not give up and kept asking. Finally, an officer allowed him to join a supporting unit, and then another officer transferred him to Mallaby.[7]

Fortunately, little encumbered Stoneman's raiders as they struggled eastward through the rain, hail, and mud. For that, they could thank Grant, who had wanted the raiders to march light, and Stoneman, who made Grant's vision a reality. According to a published circular from headquarters, each company was allowed only two pack mules—one for ammunition and the other for the officers' mess and company cooking utensils. Neither officers nor men could bring extra baggage except for necessities such as overcoats. Arms and equipment were the top priorities. Each man was to carry sixty-three rounds of ammunition, two horseshoes, and nails. Other essentials included kitchen utensils, a canteen, and horse-grooming tools.[8]

One company commander found out early that the cavalrymen would travel light, without government provisions to slow them down. Before the raid began, the quartermaster's depot loaded supplies onto the company's two pack mules. It stocked one mule with carbine ammunition and the other with picks and shovels. No sugar, bacon, or hardtack was to be found. Captain Frank Mason, a company commander in the Twelfth Ohio, never forgot these expectations. "The long distance to be traversed and the work to be done precluded all superfluous equipage," he wrote. Mason remembered carrying only a haversack filled with bacon and coffee, an extra set of horseshoes and nails, and a package of "Lone Jack." He did push the rules a little by packing one hundred cartridges for his carbine. After all, Mason had been out of a prisoner-of-war camp for less than a month. He had no interest in returning.[9]

That dreary Tuesday, the final piece of Stoneman's plans—the infantry division that was to repair railroad tracks and hold captured terrain and mountain passes behind the raiders—also marched. The forty-five-hundred-man, two-brigade division, officially the Fourth Division of the Department of the Cumberland, was formed from various infantry and artillery units in the District of East Tennessee. Brigadier General Davis Tillson, a thirty-four-year-old Maine native, commanded the unit. Tillson brought a solid background to the task. As a young man, he had attended West Point until losing a leg in a tragic accident. Turning to politics, Tillson held various state offices before returning to his nation's service when the war began. Instrumental in raising a Maine artillery battery, he went on to fight in the Battles of Cedar Mountain and Second Manassas in 1862. His movement through the ranks was simultaneous, first as chief of

Brigadier General Davis Tillson commanded the Fourth Division of the Department of the Cumberland, which protected Stoneman's rear by holding key mountain passes.
MASSACHUSETTS COMMANDERY MILITARY ORDER OF THE LOYAL LEGION AND THE UNITED STATES ARMY MILITARY HISTORY INSTITUTE

artillery for Brigadier General James B. Ricketts's division and then as a staff officer under Major General Irvin McDowell. Commissioned brigadier general in 1863, Tillson commanded the Department of Ohio's artillery and subsequently took charge of Knoxville's defensive works. Early in 1865, after the resignation of Jacob Ammen, Tillson had assumed temporary control of the district. Now, with Stoneman in charge, he was responsible for most of the district's artillery and infantry—five infantry regiments and seemingly enough artillery to blast the Blue Ridge into rubble. On March 21, Tillson began moving his First Brigade, comprised of the First Ohio Heavy Artillery, the Second and Third North Carolina mounted infantry, the Fourth Tennessee Infantry, the First United States Colored Heavy Artillery, and a handful of artillery and engineering detachments, along with the district's trains. In the coming days, the Maine general would lead the brigade in concert with Gillem's cavalry division, repairing the railroad and supporting the raiders with supplies. Finally, Major General David Stanley's Fourth Corps of the Department of the Cumberland would advance into East Tennessee to protect Tillson's rear and guard the construction corps as it repaired the railroad.[10]

When the cavalrymen and infantrymen camped that evening, the elements refused to relent. That made life miserable. It "blowed very hard," recalled one drenched trooper. At Strawberry Plains, some men erected tents as protection, but even the best ones proved useless. Wrote signalman Frankenberry, "In the evening we had a terrible storm with thunder and lightning. I saw a beautiful sight just before the sun went down[. T]he clouds parted and the sun shone in the storm clouds lovely[, but t]he wind blew fearfully and came near blowing down my tent."[11]

All the raiders could do was endure the water and mud and try to rest. Sergeant Angelo Wiser was an exception. As a member of Palmer's staff, he had plenty to do, even though dampness did not agree with his primary task. Since leaving Huntsville, Alabama, in early March, Wiser had carefully recorded his route in a small field notebook once owned by a Confederate treasury officer. This day, Wiser sketched the First Brigade's movements. "Camp in woods—¾ mi from Plns," he penciled above his crude map.[12]

⁓⁂⁓

Despite one of the wettest months on record, roughly half of the District of East Tennessee's forces were now on the move. In Knoxville, there was celebration. Already, Stoneman had eased local trade and movement restrictions, and now the division's purpose drew praise. "We are not in the habit editorially, of telling the enemy what our forces are, and what they are about," the *Knoxville Whig* crowed, "but if they can profit by what we say, we tell them the whole universal Yankee nation is now in East Tennessee—that they intend to hold the country and the roads—that they intend to crush out this rebellion in 1865— and that rebels in arms or in skulking deeds, had better leave here 'in double quick,' for parts unknown."[13]

In charge of the district's Cavalry Division was Tillson's fellow division commander Alvan C. Gillem. In the field, district and Cavalry Division leaders would ride side by side just as George G. Meade and Ulysses S. Grant were doing in Virginia. However, Stoneman and Gillem enjoyed a mutual trust and respect that was often absent in the Grant-Meade partnership. In fact, Stoneman and Gillem would often share a tent during the raid.[14]

Gillem was born in Gainesboro, Tennessee, on July 29, 1830. Chief among his early obstacles were the town's educational limitations. After their son milked what he could from a little log-cabin school in Jackson County, Gillem's parents sent him to Nashville to upgrade his learning. Gillem would never forget his parents for what they did to ensure his success, and in gratitude he cared for them in their later years. The liberal education he received in Nashville paved the way to the next level—a military education courtesy of the United States government. In 1847, Gillem headed for West Point. Although not the healthiest of cadets, the young Tennessean proved an intelligent, hardworking student. He graduated eleventh in the forty-two-member class of 1851.[15]

Commissioned brevet second lieutenant in the First United States Artillery, Gillem spent the next decade at various outposts. His first assignment—battling Seminoles in Florida—was probably his most dangerous. Then, from 1853 to 1858, Gillem shuttled among various Eastern duty stations including Fort Monroe, Virginia, and Fort McHenry, Maryland. Rising to first lieutenant, he next found himself at frontier posts in Texas.[16]

*Alvan C. Gillem commanded the Cavalry
Division of the District of East Tennessee.*
COLONEL DICK GILLEM

One of those duty stations was Fort Brown, where in early 1861 Gillem shared Stoneman's first experience of the Civil War. When General Twiggs decided to surrender all Federal military facilities in Texas, Gillem joined in the successful exodus. Being actors in this scene brought Gillem and his comrades unexpected notoriety. "Gillem and myself were quite a curiosity . . . when it became known that we were of the party that Twiggs betrayed in Texas," recalled comrade James W. Scully. At times, their fame proved annoying when admirers pressed them with endless questions.[17]

Gillem's next post was Fort Taylor. Few American forts were as isolated as the new, trapezoid-shaped bastion. Only about five dozen men from the First Artillery manned the fort, which sat deep in Southern territory at Key West, Florida. At that distant outpost, Gillem and his fellow gunners learned of the surrender of Fort Sumter. The event was especially galling because two sister companies and the First Artillery's band garrisoned the South Carolina fort. Soon afterward, Gillem declined a promotion to captain in an infantry regiment, only to accept the same rank with the First Artillery. But while his loyalty rested with the First, his heart burned for home. "I am ready at any time to go to the assistance of the loyal citizens of my native State," he wrote Andrew Johnson, a close friend, prominent antislavery Tennessean, and future vice president who would assume the presidency after Lincoln's death. "There can be but one nation on this continent. This is the first opportunity which has ever occurred of testing the strength of our government & unless this rebellion is put down in such a manner as to *awe* the evil disposed—we are a ruined people," Gillem declared.[18]

This appeal and a second one later that year came to naught, but the Tennessee soldier soon found more desirable employment. Although a candidate for chief of artillery in Kentucky, he instead was appointed quartermaster for George W. Thomas's brigade in the Department of the Cumberland. Gillem inherited an office in shambles. Undaunted, he tackled the challenges and soon squared everything away. As Thomas rose to command a division, Gillem advanced to division quartermaster. To one observer, Gillem became nothing less than Thomas's right-hand man.[19]

On January 19, 1862, Gillem fought in the Battle of Mill Springs, Kentucky. The engagement developed when Thomas's division, now part of the Army of the Ohio, advanced to recover eastern Kentucky from Major General George B. Crittenden's Confederates. Crittenden, hoping to defeat Thomas before reinforcements could arrive, attacked first, but Thomas answered with strength. A vigor-ous advance crushed the Confederate left. As the battle swirled in rainy weather, Gillem demonstrated promise. "Capt. Gillem was 'man of all work' in the fight," a witness wrote. "He was sometimes directing the movements of some of the regiments, at another time getting up ammunition and seeing to his train; at an-other directing the fire of the Batteries; but his chief attention (next to his duties as Qr.M. [quartermaster]) was directed toward the Tennessee Regiments, who of course he was most interested in. He brought them up twice leading them himself." In his official report, Thomas mentioned Gillem as one of the staff of-ficers who "rendered me valuable assistance in carrying orders and conducting the troops to their different positions."[20]

Having proved himself in both staff work and combat at the brigade and division levels, Gillem next vaulted to an army-level job. That spring, he became quartermaster of Major General Don C. Buell's Army of the Ohio and drew extra duty commanding Buell's siege artillery. The increased responsibility came at a momentous time, as the Army of the Ohio captured Nashville and then marched to Shiloh to join Grant's Army of the Mississippi. Gillem was proud of his role but longed to command troops in action. This feeling could only have been exacerbated during the Battle of Shiloh, which Gillem missed while en-suring the timely arrival of troops on the field. In his report, Buell commented, "Capt. A. C. Gillem, assistant quartermaster, is entitled to great credit for his en-ergy and industry in providing transportation for the troops from Savannah."[21]

Directing the siege artillery at Corinth, Mississippi, did not extinguish Gil-lem's desire for regimental command. And it was not just any regiment he want-ed. Although he had been hoping for a command for months, Gillem declined an offer to lead a Kentucky regiment. Nothing less than a Tennessee regiment would do. Tired of waiting, he again appealed to Johnson, now the military gov-ernor of Tennessee. Johnson would wield influence on his friend's behalf often in the months to come. For example, he would even help shield Gillem's wife from the criticism of neighboring Confederate supporters. Learning that Johnson was organizing troops, Gillem asked for a regiment. "I should be highly gratified to have the command of a Regt. I do not pretend to have any particular claim to such distinction," he wrote, then went on to describe his loyalty and his "good for-tune" to have served at Mill Springs and Shiloh. In addition to Johnson, Gillem recruited other prominent Tennesseans to lobby for him, including newspaper editor William G. "Parson" Brownlow and Congressman Horace Maynard.[22]

Gillem's efforts finally bore fruit and gave him an outlet for his growing hatred of the enemy. In May 1862, he was promoted to colonel and awarded command of the Tenth Tennessee Infantry. "I am anxious to serve my own state. . . . I desire to go to the aid of those Tennesseans who have suffered more than any, or all other people from the tyranny of the traitors[. A]mong the oppressed are my father & brother," he told Johnson. Before he could do so, however, Gillem had to fix problems within his regiment. In the opinion of one historian, he did so successfully, remolding the Tenth Tennessee so that it "vied in discipline with veteran troops." Three months later, he accepted extra duty as provost marshal of Nashville. Abuses had transpired in the office, and it needed reorganization. This job ended badly in December 1862, when he was relieved of his provost duties. He later speculated that the change was made when he failed "to obey an order from a Citizen who signed himself 'William Truesdale Colonel and Chief of Police.'"[23]

Gillem did not relinquish leadership of the Tenth either then or when he received his next assignment. On June 1, 1863, Andrew Johnson arranged yet another role—adjutant general of Tennessee—for his friend. During the rest of the war, Gillem would be tested not only by military problems but also by the domestic challenges connected with establishing a Union government in a seceded state. According to most accounts, he handled the job well. "By his stirring industry, close attention to every detail, and high organizing facilities, he soon brought order out of chaos," wrote an observer.[24]

Promoted to brigadier general to rank from August 17, 1863, Gillem brought his bolstered authority to these multiple tasks. He worked to recruit and reorganize various Tennessee units. He also found employment guarding the Nashville and Northwestern Railroad from guerillas while workers extended it to the Tennessee River. The idea was to provide a less vulnerable line of supply for the Armies of the Ohio and the Cumberland, which were then wintering in East Tennessee and northern Georgia. He accomplished the job, though not without trouble. A power struggle over the building of the road ensued, and slanders against both Johnson and Gillem surfaced. According to one charge, Gillem and Johnson were getting ready to take a trip to Chattanooga but postponed it after learning that Confederate and Federal armies were fighting along Chickamauga Creek. Critics and citizens on Nashville street corners whispered, "Where were you[,] General Gillem, at the battle of Chickamauga[?]"[25]

Having no such reservations about Gillem, Johnson also arranged his

*Alvan Gillem and staff. Major Sterling Hambright, the
Cavalry Division's provost marshal, is on the far right of the
front row.*
COLONEL DICK GILLEM

friend's next post. As military governor, Johnson had the authority to raise and
direct troops to use in Tennessee. That included his own personal force, a "Governor's Guard," to strengthen his authority. The force was limited to brigade
size, but it was Johnson's to direct and control. No one—not even Lincoln or
Grant—could touch the unit without Johnson's permission. Johnson tapped
Gillem to take command of the Governor's Guard at its organization. In August
1864, with two artillery batteries and the Eighth, Ninth, and Thirteenth Tennessee cavalry regiments, Gillem led the guard into the field for the first time. As
Johnson defined it, the unit's mission was to "kill or drive out all bands of lawless
persons, or bands which now infest" East Tennessee. The march began trium-

phantly with victories at Blue Springs, Morristown, and elsewhere that pushed the foe back into the mountains. Among the dead was the feared Confederate raider John Hunt Morgan. For his leadership in Morgan's final defeat, Gillem received a message of thanks from Abraham Lincoln.[26]

The Confederate forces of Major General John C. Breckinridge finally ended Gillem's party. When the Tennessee Unionist learned that Breckinridge was on his way with a large force, he withdrew to Bull's Gap. The Confederates followed and attacked Gillem on November 12. Pressed by the enemy, scraping the bottom of the barrel for food and ammunition, and unwilling to sacrifice his command's horses, Gillem decided he could do no more and ordered his Tennessee Federals to evacuate Bull's Gap. That was all the encouragement Breckinridge needed. Sending his men in pursuit, he struck the Federal rear guard hard on November 14. The Federal protectors, Gillem later recalled, "got into disorder and fled." Then the entire column panicked and stampeded. "All efforts of myself & their officers to rally them were fruitless," Gillem recalled. The cost was high—160 men and a battery were lost. It was, he admitted, a "terrible reverse." It would not be the last Gillem would endure in his military career.[27]

Like Stoneman, Gillem repaired his reputation in the southwestern Virginia raid. On December 13 at Kingsport, the Governor's Guard had the satisfaction of recapturing the wagons it lost at Bull's Gap. Three days later, it recovered the lost artillery battery. As a result of his work at Marion, Virginia, Gillem was awarded a regular army brevet to lieutenant colonel. Despite his success, he would never forget the trials of the campaign. "This raid was the most severe service I have ever experienced during my military life; Constant marching day and night and the latter part of the time amid snow and ice," he wrote. Soon after the raid, Gillem reorganized and remounted his command, only to have the political arena distract him. He was called to serve as vice president of a state convention to revise Tennessee's constitution and reorganize its government. He was also elected to the state legislature in March 1865.[28]

Personally, Gillem was a hard man to know. Among close friends, he could be caring. James W. Scully had known the Tennessean for a long time and thought well of him. "I could not begin to tell you how he treats me," Scully bragged to his wife in an 1861 letter. "He is like a brother—we always have the same room—and several times the same bed." Indeed, Gillem spared nothing in caring for Scully, who spent much of the war serving on Gillem's staff. Gillem bought a horse for him, helped him pay bills, expressed concern about Scully's wife, and even hired "a colored man" to wait on them. Gillem "acted the part of an everlasting friend to me," Scully testified. But Gillem's opinionated ways often led to conflict with those outside—and sometimes even inside—his intimate circle. For example, Scully and Gillem had a falling out and parted company in 1864. Gillem also had a running feud with Union brigadier general Jacob Ammen. Later, during the Modoc War, Gillem's temper would alienate his officers and men.[29]

His personality included other traits that belied his profession, including a ready sense of humor and a lively temperament. But in other ways, he was every inch a military man. Intelligent and practical, with a reputation for efficiency, he also looked like a soldier. Gillem was a tall man with a chiseled face, piercing eyes, a long and narrow nose, and a bushy beard. His hair, parted on the side, suggested a receding hairline. Duty was paramount to him, and his physical endurance was impressive. Detail oriented, strong willed, organized, a solid planner, and knowledgeable in the ways of politics, law, and government, he was also a man of refined tastes. Fairness in leadership was important to him, but he was not the kind of man who could naturally inspire others to follow him. Gillem was also conservative. In fact, he had been so troubled by the Emancipation Proclamation that he urged Lincoln to exclude Tennessee's occupied areas from the act.[30]

This was the man George Stoneman invited to command the Cavalry Division of East Tennessee—and Alvan C. Gillem jumped at the opportunity. After all, Gillem's first love was the cavalry. At the war's beginning, his desire had been to serve as a horse soldier. Now, thanks to Stoneman, he could continue his work in the saddle and get another chance to make amends for Bull's Gap. Quick as a flash, Gillem found himself in command of a column of raiders on the march.[31]

The rain and hail having tapered off overnight, the morning of March 22 opened fine and beautiful at Strawberry Plains. Roll call came before sunrise for some because foraging duties beckoned. The rest of the division stirred soon afterward. By eight o'clock, Stoneman's men had left their soggy camps behind. The division took up a line of march paralleling the East Tennessee and Virginia Railroad, a strategically important line that had once borne supplies to Confederate armies in Virginia. Stoneman and Gillem did not plan to push the men this day; they wanted to cover only about fifteen miles to Mossy Creek, where they would marshal their forces and instill their organization. By midafternoon, the column passed through Friends Station and New Market and bivouacked in the Mossy Creek area. There, the Cavalry Division of the District of East Tennessee took shape for the campaign ahead.[32]

The value of marshaling the division at Mossy Creek, which was still close to Federal lines, had much to do with the political situation in East Tennessee. The region was thick with opposing sentiments and bloody guerilla conflict, so the raid's leadership wanted the men well in hand for any problems that might arise. At the bottom of the region's struggles were tradition and history. Most residents of East Tennessee had little interest in and little to do with the slavery-centered power base in the western part of the state. Indeed, East Tennesseans had expressed an on-again, off-again desire to carve the area into a separate state. This also explained the region's later disaffection with the war, to the point that many called it the "Switzerland of America." When 1861 rolled around, few East Tennesseans supported secession, even after Lincoln's call for volunteers turned others reluctantly against the Union. On the contrary, the arrival of Confederate forces sparked a strong reaction in support of Lincoln's government. In November 1861, Unionists burned five important railroad bridges between Bristol and Chattanooga. It only got worse under the April 1862 Conscription Act, which made white males between eighteen and thirty-five subject to military service. Confederate authorities came down hard, and loyalists resisted by running, hiding, and sometimes fighting. Those who ran lived to fight another day. By one count, more than thirty thousand East Tennesseans enlisted in the Union army, some in the Cavalry Division of the District of East Tennessee.[33]

The geographic center of the Confederacy, East Tennessee had further strategic value. The region was the gateway to Kentucky and the Ohio River Valley beyond. East Tennessee also guarded the flanks of Confederate strongholds in Virginia, western Tennessee, Georgia, and Alabama. And it was a fertile region that could supply the needs of thousands of soldiers with the help of the East Tennessee and Virginia Railroad. Wrote one Confederate officer, "The country . . . contains as fine farming lands and has as delightful a climate as can be found. . . . Cattle, sheep, and swine, poultry, vegetables, maple-sugar, honey, were all abundant for the immediate wants of the troops." In recognition, main-force armies had occasionally trod the banks of the Holston and French Broad rivers in hopes of securing East Tennessee. Lieutenant General James Longstreet's was the last Confederate army to visit.[34]

The big question was the raid's objective, since Stoneman had made no formal announcement about his plans. "We are evidently going on a very extensive expedition," wrote a horseman from the Eleventh Michigan, but he had no idea where. Cavalryman Charles F. Weller, hearing premature rumors that Lee had evacuated Richmond, weighed in. "The object of the expidition is not yet known but I think we are going for the Sunny South R.R. which is now Lees only outlet from Richmond," he wrote. If that was merely a guess, the twenty-year-old son of a Methodist minister knew one thing for sure: "We will in all probability have some hard servace to perform during the comeing six months[. T]hey have not given us good horses & Spencer Carbines for nothing." Ohioan Joseph Banks, also eager to know the destination, listed the Shenandoah Valley, Lynchburg, Richmond, and Saltville as possible targets. Another Michigan man hesitated to guess because he knew the division's leadership didn't want him to know. "The object of the expedition was kept a profound secret," he complained. "If any one but General Stoneman knew it, the knowledge was not allowed to get to many of the subordinate officers." Trooper Paul Hersh came a little nearer the truth: "Of course, I can say nothing as to the destination, but rumor has it that we will . . . raid into North Carolina, where we will form a junction with a cavalry force from the coast. Time will 'tell the tale.'"[35]

Lieutenant Nathaniel Sample, commanding Company L of the Fifteenth Pennsylvania, already knew what to expect. Before the raid began, Sample had been invited to transfer to another unit as a staff officer. Thinking that the position would probably be safer, he decided to accept, but Colonel Palmer cornered Sample before he could act. Palmer confided that the regiment was about to join an expedition into the heart of the Confederacy. "I know you would not want to miss this trip for anything, so I shall notify General Johnson that I am short of commissioned officers and it would be very difficult to let you go at this time in view of our expected movement," he said.

"Oh, certainly Colonel," stammered a secretly disappointed Sample. "I would not miss that trip for anything."[36]

At about four o'clock in the morning on March 23, the strains of cavalry bugles sounding reveille echoed through "the hills and vales" of East Tennessee. Frank Frankenberry got up, fed his horse, had breakfast himself, and then saddled his mount. "The bands play, the bugles sound and all is lovely. . . . Pull out and are away," he wrote. The raid had now begun in earnest.[37]

Elements of the Cavalry Division left Mossy Creek as early as seven o'clock, and the bulk of the division was on the road within the hour. Despite a swirling wind, the day started with promise; the skies again dawned clear, and the road was good underfoot. Setting a leisurely pace, Stoneman steered the cavalry and Tillson's infantry and artillery toward Morristown, Tennessee, where he planned to supply the division. The trip was easy and picturesque, through a rolling agrarian landscape. "Move on over a very pretty country," Frankenberry noted. In the distance, low hills shadowed the column, while closer at hand occasional dwellings and cultivated fields bordered the road. In between, streams obstructed the way, but they were easily forded. By early afternoon, Morristown came into view. Barely one year had passed since Longstreet's army wintered around this key crossroads town. Remembering the hardships the Confederates had wrought, the citizens reacted warmly to Stoneman's raiders. "Had a cordial, hearty welcome from the loyal citizens," wrote a raider. "These people came from all the surrounding country to see us, and while perched on their rail fences greeted us with smiles and many a ludicrous expression."[38]

Equally welcoming were the rations and forage distributed at Morristown from Tillson's trains. Each man also received ammunition, four horseshoes, and nails. Most appreciated this bounty, but H. K. Weand presciently worried that it had "a smack of a hard campaign in it." And not everyone was quite so lucky. In Tillson's Fourth Tennessee Infantry, Thomas F. Hutton did not get to draw rations because he was on picket duty.[39]

Mundane activities claimed the rest of the day. The Tennessee brigade camped north of town. Elsewhere, in the bivouac of the Fifteenth Pennsylvania Cavalry, Frederic Antes took a few horses out to graze. Lieutenant Mallaby unfurled his flags and tried but failed to establish signal communication with Federal forces to the east. At least two signalmen wrote letters home; Frank Frankenberry included three pictures of himself. Other horsemen, warned to be ready to march early the next morning, simply relaxed and rested or talked. A camp rumor stated that Confederate president Jefferson Davis had resigned; another, more accurate rumor suggested that the armies of Sherman and Schofield had joined in North Carolina. Among those paying social calls that night was Sergeant Colton, who had helped gather carbines and horses for the Fifteenth Pennsylvania. Stopping at First Brigade headquarters, he sat by a campfire with his friend Colonel Palmer and talked about minerals.[40]

The pleasant evening gave way to an equally pleasant March 24. Long before the bugles sounded, Frank Frankenberry rose from his bedroll, which was close by his horse. He found some water, made coffee, and then packed up. The rest of the raiders did likewise and moved out at about seven that morning. Stoneman and Gillem again set a casual tempo, probably to help the men adjust to campaigning. After all, many had not been in the field since 1864. A thirteen-man detachment of the Fifteenth Pennsylvania remained in Morristown to wait for a following party and escort it to the regiment. George W. Madden, a member of the Tenth Michigan, also stayed behind. Stricken with a worsening illness, Madden was to be transported back to Knoxville for treatment.[41]

The day brought the raid's first disturbing news: an enemy force was reported around Jonesboro (now Jonesborough). Although still more than thirty miles away, Jonesboro sat squarely on the raiders' projected route. To deal with this possible threat, Stoneman resumed his old habits and divided his command. Once the column passed through Russellville and reached the old Bull's Gap battlefield, Stoneman sent Colonel Miller's all-Tennessee Third Brigade—accompanied by a telegraph operator to help with communications—riding rapidly toward Bristol. While Gillem's division continued to Jonesboro and Tillson followed the main road to Greeneville, Miller was to march to the East Tennessee and Virginia Railroad between Jonesboro and Carter's Station. If Miller could reach that point, he would be squarely behind the enemy. His action would also confuse Confederate defenders about Stoneman's true destination.[42]

It was Palmer's First Brigade that had the campaign's first brush with Rebel defenders. As they led the way on the Babb's Mill road toward Jonesboro that Friday morning, advance riders encountered a small enemy force. The Confederates scattered, but the raiders managed to collar a handful of enemy soldiers. Under close questioning, the Confederates identified themselves as members of the Sixty-first Tennessee, a mounted infantry regiment serving in Brigadier General John C. Vaughn's brigade. Routine returned as the journey continued through increasingly hilly terrain. At about five o'clock that afternoon, Palmer's and Brown's brigades bivouacked several miles east of Bull's Gap near Lick Creek.[43]

Across the countryside, troopers settled in for the night. Frank Frankenberry prepared supper and put up a tent. He then turned to his diary but had to set it aside when duty called. After stopping by Colonel Palmer's tent to pick up a guard, he and the other signalmen rode up a high hill to establish communications with Greeneville. Reaching the top, Frankenberry climbed a tall tree and saw the light he was looking for. Afterward, the signalmen returned to camp, picking up a straggler on the way. A large supply of hay awaited the signalers and their horses.[44]

To the accompaniment of music from the bands, Saturday, March 25, brought another early start. The First and Second brigades broke camp around seven o'clock and resumed the procession to Jonesboro. The Fifteenth Pennsylvania, a regiment that knew the area well, took the lead. The journey turned out to be as boring as usual, but at least the scenery was pleasant. A later visitor remembered East Tennessee this way: "It is a country of pleasant hills, bounded and broken into mountains. . . . A few first-class farmers have comfortable painted or brick houses, while scattered everywhere over the country are poverty-stricken, weather-blackened little framed dwellings and log huts." The sharp eyes of cartographer Angelo Wiser did not fail to note the surrounding woods either.[45]

Frank Frankenberry enjoyed this land of plenty. He spent the day in charge of the pack train and marched between brigades, just behind Reagan's battery. Stopping by the roadside, Frankenberry bought a chicken for twenty-five cents. That night in bivouac on a Rebel farm, the signalman made chicken soup for supper. He washed it down with a glass of cold milk, then grabbed a bar of soap to wash away his own dirt.[46]

The day was eventful in other ways. That afternoon as the Federals neared Babb's Mill, about sixty Confederates from Vaughn's brigade materialized. The Federals attacked immediately. Weand later remembered the result with satisfaction: "Company E of our regiment had the advance, and charged with such spirit that they [the enemy] were driven off, leaving four prisoners in our hands." Other witnesses claimed the capture of as many as nine "Johnnies" in the skirmish. Whatever the actual total, the Federals suffered little. Only one Union horse went down, pitching its rider headlong into a ditch. Later, Company F also encountered the enemy while scouting. The Federals pursued, but the four enemy troopers escaped.[47]

⌀

While the cavalrymen continued toward Jonesboro, Tillson's men followed the railroad as it trailed off toward Greeneville. Three days of uneventful traveling brought them there. On Wednesday, March 22, the brigade logged twenty-one miles. The

bulk of the men concentrated at Morristown, then continued through Russells-
ville before bivouacking two miles from Bull's Gap. Thursday required much
less effort; Tillson moved the brigade only into the gap itself. Friday's journey
was simply monotonous, as the soldiers left Bull's Gap and put one foot in front
of the other. Occasionally, something broke the boredom, as one artilleryman
remarked at a reunion thirty-four years later. "Do any of the boys remember,"
he said, "the toothless old maid, whose modesty and loyalty were as absent and
decayed as her teeth, who stood on her porch on the hillside, and made unkind
remarks at the boys? Yes. Well, then do you remember some of the things you
said back at her?"[48]

Around noon on March 25, the Fourth Division's First Brigade reached
Greeneville. Named for Revolutionary War hero Nathanael Greene, the home-
town of Andrew Johnson did not look like a presidential cradle. According to
one observer, "the mud came up to the very doors of its old, dilapidated, unpainted houses." Perhaps it was fitting that Johnson had worked as a humble tailor
there. Longstreet's men had done nothing to improve the town's appearance; in
Johnson's honor, they had looted and damaged his former home and tailor shop.
Greeneville was also famous as the site of John Hunt Morgan's demise, courtesy
of Alvan C. Gillem. Although most of Tillson's men would leave Greeneville the
next day, their arrival meant that enemy forces would do no more damage to it.
Federal soldiers would return soon to make it a base of operations.[49]

⚶

In the cavalry column, cartographer Angelo Wiser mapped the passage
through Babb's Gap and across Sinking Creek and Chalky Creek, as well as the
approach to Mill Creek. This was horse country, and the raiders easily logged
about twenty miles before Stoneman called a halt. It was still early, however, so
the men had extra time to attend to their horses and themselves. Three Michigan soldiers ended their raid here; they were ordered back to Knoxville, probably
because of poor health. Elsewhere, cavalryman Frederic Antes and his comrades
set up camp, cleaned their horses, and saw to their supper. Henry Birdsall of the
Eleventh Michigan set up his own tent and went straight to sleep, while around
the bivouac other horsemen foraged for their mounts but found next to nothing.
Apparently, only the Signal Corps detachment's horses fared well. They got to
dine on corn, hay, and salt and to spend the night in a stable.[50]

While most horses went hungry, the men reaped a bounty when Stoneman brought up Tillson's trains one last time before cutting loose from his line of supply. Queuing up, the First and Second brigades drew eight or ten days of rations. Coupled with the rations, ammunition, and horseshoes they had received in Morristown, the troopers now had saddlebags bulging with supplies. Yet while that was good news for the men, it was a different story for the horses. Michigan trooper Steven Thomas complained that it "made a tremendous load for the horses." Stoneman and Gillem realized the danger of overburdening the men and their mounts, so they decided to strip down the column for the mountainous journey ahead. Orders went out to discard anything that could slow progress. When the process ended, ten ambulances, one wagon, and four guns with their caissons were the only wheeled conveyances left. Tillson would follow with the rest of the trains, but his and Gillem's commands would operate independently after this day.[51]

An independent operation deep in enemy country presented temptations of excess. Even Unionist citizens in the environs of Knoxville had suffered from scofflaws, so Stoneman set his expectations for behavior. Issued in a circular on March 22, they reached the men of the Fifteenth Pennsylvania three days later in their camps along Mill Creek. Stoneman stressed that no soldier or officer, unless a representative of the Quartermaster and Subsistence departments, would be authorized to take private property. In all cases, Union troopers were required to give proper vouchers for any seized property. In theory, the superior officer of the person taking the property had to approve the voucher. The claimant, in turn, would present the voucher to the district quartermaster for reimbursement or approval for later payment. Any depredations were to be reported in writing to headquarters, and the amount of damage would be subtracted from the pay of the guilty regiment. In the worst cases, a court-martial would be the penalty.[52]

Gillem seconded the order; during his 1864 advance into East Tennessee, he had been careful to issue vouchers when property was seized for government use. Both men also were wary about some of the units in their command. The Twelfth Kentucky, for example, was known to be troublesome at times. On one occasion, an officer from the regiment had taken a horse from a Tennessee lady, prompting her husband to request compensation from the department. Other members of the Twelfth relieved a citizen of two horses and three mules, valued at one thousand dollars. And who could forget Archibald Stevenson, the drunken captain? He actually reappeared as the raiders made their way through East Tennessee, upon which Colonel Trowbridge immediately ordered his arrest. The Michigan man would accompany the regiment as a prisoner. He would later be dishonorably discharged.[53]

But if Stoneman's circular was supposed to minimize the requisition of civilian property, it actually posed more questions than it answered. What was the exact definition of private property? After all, anything that was useful for the soldiers—such as food, beverages, horses, and even fence rails—would be fair game. And there was an even larger question: would the order be enforced? Only the coming days would tell.

~⚘~

March 26, 1865, was a Sunday. The air was chilly and the ground white with frost, but the Union cavalrymen did not take time to either warm up or observe the Sabbath. Rations were still being distributed from the trains. Frank Frankenberry received coffee and sugar. Other men tended their horses. Already, some mounts were showing the wear and tear of the journey, so two Pennsylvanians from Company K of the Fifteenth were sent back to Knoxville with all the unserviceable horses. The rest of the mounts were fed, the men drew rations, and then the streamlined division headed into the rising sun, leaving the comfort and security of Tillson's troops and trains. Some troopers left as early as four that morning, and the entire column lurched into motion over the next several hours. Parts of the Eleventh Michigan were among the last to leave, finally putting hoof to road around ten o'clock. The morning slipped away uneventfully as the Federals rode through Leesburg, crossed a high ridge, and approached Jonesboro around midday. Now undefended, Jonesboro, one of the state's oldest towns, was as uninviting as most East Tennessee hamlets. They "look like Northern villages that have set out to travel and got stuck in the mud," one traveler noted. "Has been a pretty town, but shows the effect of war," added a raider. Soon, Jonesboro was behind them, and the afternoon passed away. Bored, the men had nothing to do but ride, talk, and enjoy the scenery. Pennsylvanian Septimus Knight was the exception. He drew the extra duty of shepherding the growing mass of blacks—mostly escaped slaves—now following the column. The hobbled condition of Knight's horse, which had been kicked the night before, made his job even harder.[54]

Thirty miles of ever-harsher terrain slipped away. Pennsylvania troopers from Company A surprised and captured four enemy soldiers, but that was the extent of the day's excitement. Between nine o'clock and midnight, the troopers camped in a broad area extending from Buffalo Creek to Dry Cove and Doe River Cove near the North Carolina road. The men were worn out, but their horses still had to be fed. Gillem and Stoneman spread out the division's camp-sites to make foraging easier, but it didn't help. "As we get nearer to the mountain forage becomes more scarce, and to-day our horses went hungry," a cavalryman lamented.[55]

The horses didn't go hungry for lack of effort on the part of their riders. Each day, men searched local residences for horses, mules, food, and anything of use to sustain the march. These visits were sometimes traumatic for the locals. Not far from Doe River Cove lived a typical East Tennessee family that knew only too well the hard hand of war. One son lay in a cold grave, killed at Spotsylvania. Two more had been wounded in other battles but remained in the army. Still, the night Stoneman came, no fewer than ten people were at home. The man of the house was seriously ill. His aging wife waited at his bedside. Their three daughters were also on hand to help, as were four servants. A Confederate soldier on furlough rounded out the home's occupants.

Rumor had preceded the raiders. "'Stoneman! Stoneman!' was the dread name on every lip," one of the daughters, Matt, remembered years later. The raiders appeared at midnight, cloaked in an eerie, rainy darkness. "A heavy wind moaned through the tree tops and drove an unintermitting patter of rain against the windows—a typical March night, an ideal opportunity for mischief," remembered Matt. Suddenly, deep voices and the heavy thumps of booted feet came from the front porch. Someone knocked loudly on the door. Hearts pounding, the daughters jumped to their feet and whispered urgently to each other. Julia, the eldest, finally went to the door, trembling as she walked, a young servant girl at her side. "Who's there?" she called weakly.

After a long silence, a muffled answer came from the other side of the door. "Cavalrymen from Stoneman's army."

"What—what do you want?" Julia asked.

"Supper and—O, just anything," replied several voices. The girls knew that meant anything they could lay their hands on—food, loot, or worse.

The door opened a crack. A tiny beam of candlelight streamed in, revealing armed shadows on the porch. Helpless, Julia opened the door wide, and the soldiers came in. Matt watched from a corner. "They tramped ponderously in, the shadows, uniformed in dark Northern blue, dripping with rain and clanking their spurs and scabbards, two dozen or more—tall, powerful men, principally well drilled and toughened by countless sleepless nights in the saddle," she wrote with understandable exaggeration. A few men walked toward the closed door of her father's room, which was also the refuge of the family's Confederate friend. Quickly, tears welling in her eyes, Matt stepped in front of the door and appealed to the officer in charge. "O, please don't let them enter this room! It is my father's room, and he is terribly sick, and the sight of all—all these blue uniforms, I—I fear, would kill him. Surely there is nothing in there you want. O, anything else—but to kill my father! Please keep them back."

The unshaven officer, a tall, handsome man, sized up the young lady. "There, there, Miss," he smiled, patting Matt on the head. "Don't cry, Miss. I will not let them come in; they shall not harm your sick father. They merely suspect that you might be concealing a Confederate soldier. It is all right now, however; cease crying." Turning to his men, the officer ordered them to steer clear of the room but to search the rest of the house. The troopers eagerly tramped into every corner, opening doors, peeking in drawers, moving furniture, and picking through china and cooking utensils. They told crude jokes and laughed as they worked.

But the tall officer returned his attention to the door. To Matt's horror, he opened it. Inside, he saw Matt's mother asleep in a chair, Matt's father lying on the bed, and a man, apparently the doctor, holding her father's wrist with one hand and a spoon and a bottle of medicine with the other. A shawl and the uncertain light from a tallow candle and the smoldering fireplace logs concealed the "doctor's" Confederate uniform. Matt breathed a sigh of relief as the officer, satisfied, closed the door.

Throughout the house, the looting continued. Given its long experience with bushwhackers, the family had carefully hidden many valuables, but the girls still had to plead for some possessions. In the kitchen, a trooper walked over to the oven. Julia, who had hidden her favorite riding bridle inside, tried to distract him. "Stop! What in the world are you looking for?" she cried.

"I'm looking for mules," came the irreverent, laughing answer. "D'ye reckon I'll find any in here?"

"Dear me!" Julia said. "How ingenious you are, and what a very excellent joke! Looking for mules in a cookstove oven! Bless my soul!"

The ruse failed, and in a flash the Federal soldier opened the oven door.

Out tumbled the bridle. The troopers in the kitchen roared in laughter as the red-bearded treasure hunter observed, "Not a mule by a long shot. No, not by a jugful, but the next thing to it, by cracky."

The raiders emptied the kitchen of food and then moved outside. From the barn, they liberated corn, wheat, rye, a half-dozen horses, and harnesses. Finally, the cavalrymen moved on, followed by at least one of the family's servants. But the little house had not seen the last of Stoneman's cavalry. The next morning, the same troopers returned and rounded up a few chickens. As Matt remembered it later, their exit was welcome and abrupt: "Slinging the feathered trophies quickly across their saddle bows, they sprang nimbly upon our horses, plied their merciless spurs, wheeled in a trice, took the fence at a bound, and away they sped up the clay road, out of sight forever."[56]

Matt did not say whether or not the "visitors" left a voucher in return for the property they seized. However, as traumatic as the visit was, at least the raiders apparently limited their requisitions to items they needed. Other cavalrymen ignored the circular Stoneman had issued and took advantage of "foraging" to relieve locals of valuables. That night, Gillem learned of an indiscretion committed by a corporal in the Tenth Michigan and ordered the man reduced in rank.[57]

While the men foraged for their horses or themselves, Stoneman concentrated on other matters. John J. Wickham, a future Pennsylvania Superior Court judge, reached Doe River Cove that night and met Stoneman. An expert telegraph operator, Wickham had ridden all day to catch the raiders. When he reached their scattered campsites, Wickham asked for directions to Stoneman's headquarters. He was pointed to a cabin where the general and his staff were spending the night. Deciding to announce his arrival, the Pennsylvanian went inside. He entered a room lit only by a candle. "The others were sleeping, but he [Stoneman] was sitting there planning and doing a little swearing," Wickham recalled. As he picked his way among the slumbering forms, the telegraph operator accidentally stepped on staff officer Myles Keogh. Keogh rose angrily from his sleep, and the men exchanged words. Fortunately, the spat ended as quickly as it began. Wickham and Keogh lay down beside each other and soon fell asleep. The general kept right on planning and swearing.[58]

Stoneman's choice words stemmed from worry. He might have been proud of his progress to date. After all, according to one diarist, the Cavalry Division had now covered 121 miles from Knoxville, and Confederate defenders had surrendered East Tennessee, clearing the raiders' path out of the state. Better yet, the Federals had suffered no battle casualties and had lost only a few men and horses to illness and wear and tear. But the lack of forage sparked his concern, and the dispositions of Confederate defenders around Christiansburg remained unknown. In the camps of the Tenth Michigan, trooper Steven Thomas realized what it all meant. He later remembered March 26 as the point when "the Excitement[,] novelty and the hard work of the trip commenced." For the next four weeks, Thomas told his wife, the men would be in the saddle twenty hours a day.[59]

Now about a day behind and moving a few miles south of the raiders' path, Tillson's First Brigade continued to shadow the advance of the Cavalry Division. On March 26, the brigade marched to the vicinity of Brabson's Mills, where it would remain for the next three days, while Stoneman scaled the mountains and moved into North Carolina.[60]

The raiders' presence probably helped confuse the area's now-alerted Confederate defenders. Before even one blue-clad trooper left Knoxville, Confederate brigadier general John Crawford Vaughn suspected he was in the path of a Federal movement. A forty-one-year-old native of Roane County, Tennessee, the former merchant and politician commanded a nine-hundred-man brigade covering the countryside between Greeneville and Bristol, Tennessee. Having endured combat from Mexico to First Manassas, Vicksburg, and the Shenandoah Valley, Vaughn recognized the value of intelligence. Although Stoneman tried to mask his plans, Confederate scouts had spotted his preparations and divined their purpose, and other sources provided confirmation. On March 20, warnings went up the ladder: a large cavalry force under Stoneman was preparing for an advance; infantry was expected to follow, since two or three trains loaded with foot soldiers were arriving in Knoxville daily; and General Thomas himself was expected to arrive in Knoxville soon. Vaughn's March 24 and March 25 encounters with Stoneman's raiders near Babb's Mill confirmed his fear that a powerful Federal column was slicing through East Tennessee. Suddenly, cavalry and infantry were "scattered up & down the R.R. from Bulls Gap to Knoxville," a Confederate wrote.[61]

How should the Confederates on the scene respond? That was the difficult question facing Vaughn and his superior officer, Brigadier General John Echols. Echols, who had just celebrated his forty-second birthday, commanded the Department of Southwest Virginia and East Tennessee. That department encompassed a huge area stretching from White Sulphur Springs, Virginia, to Greeneville, Tennessee. It was an important command because it contained what Echols called "the most valuable mineral interests left to the Confederacy." When Vaughn's reports suggested that Federal forces would menace Bristol, Echols made his decision. He ordered his command to concentrate along the Virginia-Tennessee border and moved his headquarters from Wytheville to Abingdon, where he could be closer to the anticipated scene of action. Echols was determined to protect Virginia's vital mineral resources.[62]

Vaughn's Brigade began withdrawing toward Bristol, as did the other forces that comprised Echols's command. Brigadier General Basil W. Duke's five-hundred-man cavalry brigade marked time in Abingdon, awaiting the return of its horses from North Carolina. Brigadier General George B. Cosby's cavalry brigade, Colonel Vincent A. Witcher's cavalry detachment, and Colonel Henry L. Giltner's cavalry brigade came up. Ned Guerrant, a staff officer in Giltner's command, recorded the day's work in his diary: "Somewhat of an exciting day . . . Another telegram from Gen. Echols, announces more threatening movement of enemy in E. Tenn. & *ordering our command immediately* to some point in six hours march of Bristol & Abingdon. Great urgency for prompt movement &c. &c."[63]

A few other units filled out Echols's command, including a scattered infantry division under Brigadier General Gabriel C. Wharton, Colonel Robert T. Preston's reserves, and Major Richard C. M. Page's battalion of four artillery batteries. All told, this force boasted around thirty-five hundred men and officers on paper. In reality, it left much to be desired. In a postwar report, Echols described the condition of his command as "very distressing." The winter fight against Stoneman's Saltville raid had left the men "thinly clad and needing everything to perfect their outfit and equipment," Echols complained. His command had improved recently, but Echols—a lawyer who had seen his share of combat—knew it was no match for Stoneman's fresh, well-equipped cavalry force.[64]

Actually, it didn't matter what condition Echols's men were in—not for the moment, at least. Stoneman was on his way to North Carolina, not Virginia. Vaughn's withdrawal, courtesy of Miller's Third Brigade, created an undefended vacuum. As ordered, the Tennessee brigade had marched northeast on March 24 to Fall Branch. From there, the Eighth and Thirteenth Tennessee cavalry regiments rode to the East Tennessee and Virginia Railroad. Encountering communities like Rheatown and Johnson City en route, they met little resistance. It was as if the area's Confederate defenders had simply vanished. Outriders reported that the Confederates had fallen back, leaving only stragglers and deserters in their wake, so Miller moved his brigade southward in two columns. One marched along Buffalo Creek toward Doe River Cove. The second aimed for Elizabethton in Carter County, arriving on Sunday, March 26.[65]

Elizabethton had endured its share of wartime violence from Unionists and Rebels alike, but for Colonel John K. Miller, commander of the Third Brigade, this was a homecoming. Miller, thirty-six, was a resident of Elizabethton who, despite a lack of formal education, had been the sheriff of Carter County when the war began. Since 1861, he had openly displayed his Unionist beliefs, first by participating in the celebrated East Tennessee bridge burnings and later by helping to organize the Thirteenth Tennessee Cavalry. Miller was not alone in his happiness. At least five companies of the Thirteenth hailed from Carter County, and several troopers from the Eighth also called the area home. So the clean-shaven, lanky colonel—known among his men as "brave and competent" and "patriotic, kind and generous"—charitably allowed his men to disperse and visit family and friends as long as they promised to rejoin the regiment the next day. To Stony Creek, Gap Creek, Taylor Town, Valley Forge, Doe River Cove, and a dozen other communities they went on French leave. For many, the temptation to return home and stay was great, but most returned to duty.[66]

⁂

On the morning of March 27, Stoneman issued orders based on the plans laid the night before. His goal: a rapid push across the Watauga River and into North Carolina, which would reunite his division in the process. At about eight o'clock in the morning on March 27, a clear, warm Monday, the First and Second brigades left their camps. For a few miles, their route paralleled the Watauga. Behind them, the Iron Mountains passed into the distance; ahead loomed the Stone Mountains, the last obstacle between the raiders and North Carolina. Frank Frankenberry called it a "romantic road. Mountains on each side . . . and a small stream by the road side." About five miles down the road, at a crossing of the Watauga, officers called a halt. After a three-hour pause to rest and feed the hungry horses, the march resumed. Only a few homes lined the rugged route; a lonely wood road that trailed off into the wilderness was the only intersecting route they passed. That afternoon, the Federals stopped to feed again. Stoneman, wisely taking precautions to ensure that he knew what—or who—awaited, sent a company ahead to scout.[67]

This was the second patrol of the day. At eight-thirty that morning, Sergeant William F. Colton had taken one hundred men from the Fifteenth Pennsylvania's First Battalion up the Stone Mountains to secure a key gap. The veteran sergeant endeavored to execute the orders with his usual efficiency, but en route he stopped to feed the contingent's horses. Palmer had ordered him to do just that, but it proved the wrong thing. By one-fifteen, the chore was finished and the men were ready to continue, but Stoneman appeared as the troopers were moving out. Asking what Colton's orders were, the general probed, "Were you ordered to feed?" Colton answered that he was. "Well, sir, either you have disobeyed your orders or my orders were misconveyed to you. You can halt here and report to Colonel Palmer." With that, Stoneman abruptly rode off, apparently to find another force to complete the task. A chastened Colton later confided to his diary, "It was cutting, but what could I say?" A few minutes later, he received other orders and was unable to complete the mission. Colton could only hope for an opportunity to redeem himself for not immediately carrying out Stoneman's orders.[68]

Around noon on March 27, Miller's Tennesseans left Elizabethton on Gillem's orders to follow the rest of the division into North Carolina. They rode southward through Valley Forge, found Stoneman's winding column at Doe River Cove, and fell in. They made it as far as what is now Butler before camping for the night. Once again, some Tennessee troopers scattered to visit friends and family in the vicinity, but others gave military needs a higher priority. Stoneman's troopers fortified Fort Hill, located near Butler, and established a post to relay signals from the North Carolina mountains back to Tennessee.[69]

At the front of the column, the Fifteenth Pennsylvania led the way, followed by the Tenth Michigan and the Twelfth Ohio. Stoneman and Gillem marched with the Second Brigade. The road, although narrow, winding, and steep, was a good one. Some citizens showed their colors and turned out to help, building fires and standing watch at fords and tricky places in the road. A local named Henderson Smith grabbed a torch and guided the Fifteenth Pennsylvania over the unfamiliar route. Palmer sent orders back for the cavalrymen to pitch in and build fires, too. Yet despite all these precautions, nighttime marching on a mountain road was still dangerous. At one troublesome spot, an artillery caisson tumbled over an embankment and into the depths, lost forever. A few horses and mules also fell to their deaths. An ambulance followed the caisson and fell into the blackness, and three men were hurt on the treacherous road. One of them was probably Henry Birdsall of the Eleventh Michigan. "I turned a somersault off my horse backward," he wrote. "Hurt me considerable but I got over better than could have been expected."[70]

The march was both surreal and beautiful. Wrote one veteran, "Looking back as we toiled up the mountain, the scene was grand and imposing as the march of the column was shown by the trail of fire along the road. Occasionally an old pine tree would take fire and blaze up almost instantaneously, looking like a column of fire. It was an impromptu illumination, and the sight of it repaid us for the toilsome night march." Another veteran described it even more vividly: "The fires were lighting up everything about, and the troopers looked like mounted specters, moving silently along. On the one side were the troopers, taking up nearly the whole road; on the other was the dark ravine below, with the tree tops coming up nearly on a level with the road." Another cavalryman wrote, "There were places on the western ascent where it was necessary for men and horses to scramble almost perpendicular cliffs, and the memory of that cold night on top of the mountain is very vivid yet."[71]

And so the march continued. "We kept moving along, walking and leading our horses, stealing a little rest when the column would stop," wrote a veteran. In the darkness, the extra horseshoes the men had received at Morristown clanked annoyingly against each other. Some tired of the noise and tossed the extra shoes aside. Finally, when the division's lead elements cleared the pass at the top of the mountain, Stoneman and Gillem relented. Between midnight and five in the morning, depending on their location in the long column, the exhausted raiders paused. One trooper remembered, "I was unfortunate in having to stop where the road was narrow and badly washed in gutters. I crowded up the bank to the side of the road, gathered a few crooked sticks, laid them across the gutter and lay down with my horse standing beside me. My feet extended over the path at the side of the road. I was disturbed several times by orderlies passing over my feet, but soon got used to that." But if rest was scarce that night, progress was evident. Angelo Wiser marked the First Brigade's headquarters at the Reese home, a mere two hundred yards from the North Carolina line.[72]

The Tennessee phase had ended successfully. Confederate defenders were back on their heels. Before the raiders lay new objectives and obstacles. The next chapter of Stoneman's Raid was about to begin.

Chapter 3

WE ARE GETTING ALONG VERY WELL
Boone to Mount Airy: March 28–April 2, 1865

George Stoneman had been to North Carolina before. Prior to the war, he had courted a young lady from Warrenton. Gillem had his own connections to the Old North State. His father, Samuel J. Gillem, was born in North Carolina around 1800.[1] But as day eight of Stoneman's Raid dawned, the two cavalrymen probably had other concerns on their minds.

March 28 broke fair as the troopers of the District of East Tennessee's Cavalry Division wearily tumbled out of their bedrolls. Some had gotten only a couple of hours' sleep after the treacherous mountain crossing, but there was nothing to be done about it. The horses were tired, too, and they also had to face the day hungry because no feed was to be had. Beginning at six o'clock, the cavalrymen resumed the eastward trek on the turnpike that led from Tennessee into Watauga County, North Carolina. To the rear, still down the mountain, the Tennessee brigade began its day like those at the front of the column. Appropriately enough, Miller's men would be the last to leave the Volunteer State. They announced their arrival in North Carolina by burning some cotton mills near the state line.[2]

Lead scout William McKesson "Keith" Blalock had been waiting for this moment for years. Born on the slopes of Grandfather Mountain on November 21, 1837, he was the son of a War of 1812 veteran. Having grown up in western North Carolina, Blalock was an able marksman and skillful hunter who, at the start of the war, had reluctantly joined the Confederate Twenty-sixth North Carolina Infantry. His wife, Malinda, disguised herself as a man and joined up as well so she could stay near Blalock. Though Malinda, called "Sam" by her unsuspecting comrades, and Keith proved to be good soldiers, they both found a way out of the service. Sam was discovered after being wounded near New Bern, and Keith feigned illness and secured a discharge.[3]

It was better that way, since neither Keith nor Malinda thought much of the Confederacy. They just wanted to be left alone. But authorities at home thought Blalock looked too healthy for a discharged man. Straight away, they began persecution and harassment in the name of conscription. The Blalocks answered with their own personal war. For the next three years, Keith and Malinda fought back. They hid in the mountains, attacking local Home Guardsmen and Southern sympathizers. They helped deserters and escaped prisoners. Keith Blalock also kept Federal officials informed about conditions and happenings in the mountains. In June 1864, Blalock became an official member of the Tenth Michigan Cavalry. He was given the independence to pilot recruits from North Carolina to Tennessee and to serve as a captain of scouts. The mountaineer proved his value, reportedly meeting often with Stoneman to provide information. Stoneman trusted that data.[4]

Keith and Malinda Blalock would not have missed the chance to raid their old stomping ground for anything. With the Blalocks and another Tar Heel Unionist, Jim Hartley, leading the way, the cavalry column pushed into North Carolina. About ten o'clock in the morning, word came that a meeting of the Home Guard would take place in Boone, the Watauga County seat, that very day. Stoneman and Gillem responded aggressively. They sent Major Myles Keogh, Stoneman's aide-de-camp, and a detachment from the Twelfth Kentucky Cavalry ahead to investigate. The Blalocks and Hartley guided the advance.[5]

Formed in 1862 at Caseyville and Owensboro, Kentucky, the Twelfth Kentucky brought a raiding-rich background to its task. Its first year of duty was marked by a couple of brushes with Brigadier General John Hunt Morgan. Morgan's July 1863 raid through Kentucky, Indiana, and Ohio brought the Twelfth

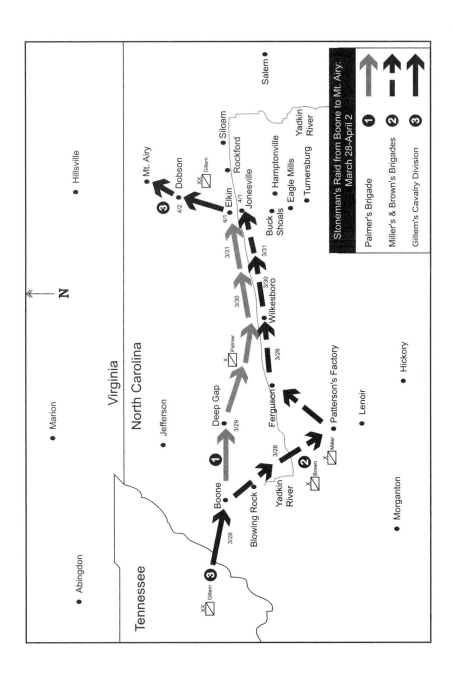

Stoneman called his aide, Major Myles Keogh, "one of the most superior young officers in the army." Keogh remained in the cavalry after the war, only to die with Custer at Little Bighorn.
MONTANA HISTORICAL SOCIETY

the opportunity to help in the pursuit and capture of the famous Confederate raider. Afterward, the regiment was posted to East Tennessee, where it participated in the siege of Knoxville and, boasted a veteran, "bore its full share of the fighting." In 1864, the regiment's twelve companies were consolidated into eight to make room for four companies from the Sixteenth Kentucky Cavalry. Thus strengthened, the Twelfth joined Stoneman in the Atlanta campaign and later the Saltville raid, with Major James B. Harrison in command.[6]

Harrison's Kentuckians had a poor record for behavior. In 1864 at Strawberry Plains, complaints surfaced that they had taken down houses and outbuildings without the owners' consent, probably to fuel campfires. On another occasion, an officer observed that the men were in the habit of "insulting and otherwise doing violence to peaceable citizens," including throwing stones at houses and stealing private property. At one point, a guard had to be placed around the Kentucky camp—not against attack, but to prevent anyone from leaving without authorization. Not surprisingly, it seems that the regiment's leadership was unconcerned about improprieties. Recently, the Twelfth had restored ten deserters to duty and given them back pay.[7]

Such behavior may have played a role in the raiders' visit to the home of Jacob Mast Councill that morning. The elderly Councill, who lived along the road to Boone, was known as a friend to everyone and a man who generally kept his opinions to himself. It seems that Councill should have been the last to suffer the wrath of the raiders, but the old man had one mark against him. According to his nephew Keith Blalock, Councill owned a slave. Exactly what happened that Tuesday remains a mystery. Councill and his slave, a woman named Phoebe, had been plowing the fields. He was either in the fields or putting away his harness in his barn when a Union trooper appeared. Councill protested— one source says he pleaded for mercy—but the trooper shot him dead. Why? Writing fifty years after the event, the county's historian offered no explanation. Phoebe later said Council was shot because he was an "infernal rebel." Whether those were the raider's words or hers is not clear. Another story suggests that Phoebe ran to the approaching cavalrymen and asked them to free her. The most reliable source is Angelo Wiser, the First Brigade mapmaker; on his map, he described the victim with one word: "Council—rebel." However, another family along the road escaped a similar fate even though it had three sons serving in the Confederate army.[8]

Regardless of what happened, few could argue that the Twelfth needed discipline. After all, Gillem had never liked volunteers, and that was probably why Myles Walter Keogh accompanied the regiment to Boone. Keogh could also fight. Few cavalrymen had served with as much distinction as the Irishman. "He was as handsome a young man as I ever saw," one admirer wrote. "He rode a horse like a Centaur. He had a fresh Irish complexion like the pink side of a ripe peach—more like the complexion of a 16-year-old girl than of a cavalry soldier. His uniform was spotless, and fitted him like the skin of a sausage, and if there had been any more of the man or any less of the uniform it would have been a misfit." Keogh's polished appearance did little to endear him to veterans. "I wonder if his mother cuts his hair?" and "What laundry do you think he uses?" were two of the taunts that came his way. All such thoughts vanished, however, when the six-foot-and-a-quarter-inch Keogh, blue eyes flashing, rode into battle.[9]

Keogh was born March 25, 1840, in County Carlow, Ireland. One of John and Margaret Blanchfield Keogh's thirteen children, he was educated at St. Patrick's College in Carlow. Keogh first donned the uniform of a soldier in 1860 when he joined other Irishmen in the service of the pope. He quickly earned a promotion to second lieutenant, but his first command experience was unsuccessful, as a rival Italian force roughed up the papal army. Dissatisfaction with the conduct of the Papal States prompted Keogh to resign his commission in the Company of St. Patrick. But rather than go home, he decided to offer his services to the Union.[10]

The Irishman arrived in New York on April 1, 1862. America quickly captured his heart. "This is a great country . . . for a man of *intellect[,] energy & Capital,*" he would later write. Keogh first offered his sword to Brigadier General James Shields, receiving an appointment as a staff officer. During the 1862 Valley Campaign, he enjoyed no more success under the Union flag than he had under the papal banner. After Stonewall Jackson humiliated Shields, Keogh became a staff officer for Brigadier General John Buford, who would prove to be one of the Union's best cavalrymen. Keogh thought the world of his new leader. He described the Kentuckian as "quite a handsome fellow" and "a very gallant soldier." With Buford, Keogh braved some of the Army of the Potomac's toughest battles, including Second Bull Run and Fredericksburg. A brief stint on McClellan's staff introduced him to the inner workings of high command and also to a man he would later serve—George Armstrong Custer. But Keogh's place was mostly at Buford's side during some of the Union cavalry's most critical moments, including Chancellorsville, Brandy Station, and Gettysburg. A rising star, he was brevetted major for his service during the Gettysburg campaign.[11]

Keogh's career with the Army of the Potomac took a severe turn on December 16, 1863, when Buford died of typhoid fever in his arms. As fortune had it, Buford breathed his last in the Washington home of his friend George Stoneman. For Keogh, this led to an opportunity; when Stoneman later left the Cavalry Bureau and returned to the field, he offered Keogh a staff position. The Irishman accepted. Promoted to major in April 1864, Keogh went on to serve with Stoneman during the Atlanta campaign and even shared Stoneman's captivity with him. In fact, the Irishman grew so attached to Stoneman that he turned down an opportunity to join a regiment in Custer's division. Stoneman was glad to have him. He thought Keogh intelligent, gallant, and "one of the most superior young officers in the army." Gillem agreed: "He is unsurpassed in dash, has admirable judgment—is peculiarly fitted for a Cavalry officer—is highly Educated and accomplished."[12]

Eleven years later, Keogh would die near the banks of the Little Bighorn River. Legend says he fought harder and more valiantly than anyone, and that his horse, Comanche, was the sole survivor of Custer's Last Stand. But that was in the future; today, Keogh had his eyes set on Boone and its Home Guardsmen.

Rumors preceded the raiders suggesting that a force of ten, fifteen, thirty, or even sixty thousand was on its way. In preparation, residents of Boone toted their hams to mountain pastures, set them on boulders, and covered them with moss.[13]

Although nestled deep in the mountains and distant from any front, Watauga County and the rest of western North Carolina had witnessed untold strife. In fact, East Tennessee and western North Carolina mirrored each other. When the war began, many residents of western North Carolina supported the Confederate cause. About twenty thousand men from the region flocked to the Confederate banner. But as in East Tennessee, mounting hardships bred Unionism. Casualties at the front, the depredations of foragers from both sides, the Conscription Act, inflation, and the Confederate government's tax-in-kind policy—which required farmers to turn over one-tenth of their crops to the government—left many mountain residents hungry and destitute. Wives begged their soldier husbands to come home. As dissent grew, western North Carolina became the dominion of guerillas, deserters, and raiders. This was an ugly internal war, and both sides had blood on their hands. Unionism peaked around the time George Stoneman arrived.[14]

For the balance of the war, Watauga County was better prepared than most places to deal with such internecine conflict. The local Home Guard, Major Harvey Bingham's Eleventh Battalion, was uniquely able. Bingham, a Caldwell County native in his twenties, was a twice-wounded, discharged veteran of the Thirty-seventh North Carolina Infantry Regiment. Invited to take command of the local Home Guard, he wisely recruited other discharged veterans wherever possible to lend backbone to his force. He ultimately raised two Home Guard companies from Watauga and neighboring Ashe County and stationed them at Camp Mast. Although an unimpressive array of Mexican War surplus tents, shacks, and works, Camp Mast became one of the Confederacy's few secure positions north of Asheville. Bingham kept one company on alert constantly, while the men of the second company stood down and went home. This system proved effective. Bingham made his presence felt in battling Keith Blalock and other Unionists. In February 1865, however, the tide turned. About one hundred Unionists surrounded, hoodwinked, and captured Camp Mast, ejecting a Home Guard company from the war and sending the local force into disarray.[15]

The Home Guard meeting in Boone on March 28 was an effort to regroup in the wake of the Camp Mast debacle. This was not just a gathering of green teenagers and old men beating their chests. Many of those present were furloughed, paroled, or recuperating Confederate soldiers home from the front. Organizationally, the men wisely emphasized experience and elected new leaders with that in mind, including Lieutenant Elijah J. Norris, a twenty-one-year-old veteran of the Eighteenth Tennessee Infantry who bore scars from five wounds. The men agreed that the reconstituted company's task was to keep order and prevent depredations. The first opportunity for the unit—officially Company B of the Eleventh Battalion of North Carolina Home Guards—came all too quickly.[16]

Boone was a town of several log cabins, a handful of larger homes, a courthouse, an inn, and a general store, surrounded by tree-covered hills and high mountains. It was about eleven in the morning on March 28 when Keogh and his men rode into town. At that moment, about one hundred Home Guardsmen were drilling at the muster grounds near the courthouse. More men watched from the upper story of the home of Jordan Councill, another Home Guard captain.[17] Suddenly, gunfire erupted. According to one account, it started when someone accidentally fired his weapon. However, it is more likely that the surprising sight of blue-clad cavalry in town sparked a deliberate reaction. Some of the Home Guardsmen had been off-duty when Camp Mast surrendered. Some had escaped the surrender. Others were just Southern sympathizers ready to serve. All were still smarting from the rough handling they had taken. They resolved not to be beaten this time but did not realize the power of the force headed their way.[18]

Some Confederates opened fire. As bullets flew past the head of the Federal column, Major Keogh ordered a charge. At the Irishman's command, horses' hooves pounded and sabers flashed in the midday sun. The skirmish became, a Kentuckian later recalled, "hotly contested." None of the dusty raiders called for surrender; instead, they brought up their carbines and fired back, shooting at anything that moved. One Boone resident, Mrs. James Councill, heard the racket and wondered what was happening. Her child in her arms, she stepped onto her porch to investigate. As she did, a volley of balls splintered the wood around her, missing her and her child. She ducked back inside, lucky to be unhurt. But Boone and its would-be defenders did not escape the withering gunfire. As Malinda Blalock later recalled, the column blasted away at windows and "pretty near shot up the whole town."[19]

To the would-be defenders, it was now frighteningly obvious that their enemy was more than just bushwhackers. Lieutenant Norris realized it and told his father, Ephraim, to run. The rest of the Home Guardsmen followed Ephraim's lead. Out of town and through the surrounding fields they fled, some aiming for the supposed safety of Howard's Knob. En route, a few Home Guardsmen fell with wounds in their backs. Calvin Green was but one example. When a knot of Federal troopers chased him, Green tried to surrender, but the Federals kept shooting, so he decided to resume the fight. It didn't last long. Green managed to shoot a Federal in the arm, but the raiders gunned him down and left him for dead. Meanwhile, Warren Green met his end while holding up his hands to surrender. Keith Blalock supposedly put a bullet into Warren Green's heart. The Unionist mountaineer also may have had a hand in Calvin Green's wounding.[20]

Casualties mounted. William W. Gragg, a veteran of the First North Carolina Cavalry Regiment at home on furlough, was shot. Thomas Holder, who stood beside Gragg, received wounds in the hip and groin. John Brown broke his ankle while trying to get away. And Lieutenant Norris's father didn't make it. He grabbed a horse and bolted for cover, but blue-clad troopers saw him. The Meat Camp native was shot in the back and killed.[21]

Private Eber Hendricks, one of the raiders, may have been the man who killed Ephraim Norris. Hendricks was a member of Company K of the Tenth Michigan Cavalry, which rode behind Keogh and the advance guard. In his arms rested his Spencer, loaded and ready. Hendricks thought highly of the weapon, "which I can shoot 8 times quicker than I can load Dad's gun," he wrote. The nineteen-year-old native of Mason, Michigan, wielded his Spencer with skill in the streets of Boone. He wrote that the Rebels "ran so like the old cat[. W]e could not hardly get a sight of them but thanks that my good horse can run like a streak of lightening and I made out to get about a dozen shots at them and I think I emptied one of their saddles."[22]

A handful of Home Guardsmen including A. J. McBride, the sheriff, continued to resist. "The fight got real hot for a few minutes, and a lot of us took shots at the Blalocks. I do not know how they came out alive," he recalled. McBride's fight ended when a bullet struck him in the chest, followed along a rib, and lodged in his spine. Fifteen-year-old Steel Frazier was another participant. As a squad of Federals bore down on him, Frazier ran, hurdled a fence, hid behind it, and waited. When the Federals drew near, he opened fire, then ran again. Pausing to load while a friend covered him, Frazier turned and threw more lead at the raiders. When the odds grew worse, the teenager ran again and somehow escaped unhurt, even though balls whistled past him. In the confusion of the fight, Frazier thought he had hit two bluejackets.[23]

The so-called Battle of Boone ended quickly. As the firing died down, the chore of collecting prisoners began. Major Gustavus M. Bascom, assistant adjutant general on Stoneman's staff, claimed one of the highest-ranking prisoners of the day in Captain Andrew J. Critcher, a twice-wounded company commander from the Thirty-seventh North Carolina Infantry Regiment. Critcher was one of the sixty-plus Confederates captured, who were soon on their way to imprisonment at Camp Chase, Ohio.[24]

The victors' other tasks were to treat the wounded and bury the dead. The Federals set up a hospital and morgue in the Councill house, where the division's medical staff attended to the wounded of both sides. Although Gillem reported no Federal casualties, the raiders did not emerge from the skirmish unscathed. Three reliable Northern sources listed one wounded trooper, a period newspaper related that "several men" had been wounded, and a Southern source claimed that one Federal suffered a broken arm and a second absorbed a head wound. Calvin Green claimed he had shattered a Federal cavalryman's arm so badly that it had to be amputated. Even so, it is clear that Stoneman's cavalry suffered little in the affair. The story was different for the Home Guardsmen. Stoneman's surgeon mended McBride's wound, reportedly without anesthesia, while the lawman lay on the floor. The Federals also treated Calvin Green, Holder, Brown, and Gragg, all of whom survived. Norris, Warren Greene, and Jacob Councill found early graves.[25]

Both Stoneman and Gillem gushed over the day's events. Reporting the capture of Boone, Stoneman wrote, "We arrived here this A.M., the Twelfth Kentucky in the advance, captured the place, killing 9, capturing 62 home guards and 40 horses." He added, "We are getting along very well." Stoneman also thought the populace had not expected the raiders. In his official report, Gillem later echoed Stoneman's tally of killed, but he inflated the prisoner total to sixty-eight. Whatever the count, both men ensured that the glory of the operation would go where it belonged. "Much credit is due Major Keogh and the gallant officers and men of the Twelfth Kentucky Cavalry engaged in this affair," Gillem reported. He would later recommend Keogh for promotion, in part because of his work that day. Northern papers trumpeted the raiders' success. The *Chicago Tribune* gave the capture of Boone nearly as much prominence as the Battle of Five Forks. "Stoneman's command is now well into North Carolina and will be heard of soon in the heart of the rebellion," the paper predicted.[26]

As the *coup de grâce*, the raiders left their mark on Boone by burning the town's jail. Reports of the raid are silent on the matter, but according to one early source, Stoneman rebuked Gillem for it. One thing was certain about the loss of the jail and the county records inside: it made for quite a show. "For the first time in my whole life I saw a building burn[. I]t was the jail and made a splendid fire," trooper Steven Thomas told his wife.[27]

⚜

As the black smoke from the Boone jail curled into the early-spring sky, the rest of the raiding column approached from the west. After its early start, Palmer's brigade had enjoyed an uneventful march into Watauga County. Around one that afternoon—moments after the skirmish in Boone ended—the Fifteenth Pennsylvania halted at Sugar Grove to feed. The column resumed its march later that afternoon and reached Boone that evening. Colonel Miller's Third Brigade was the last to arrive.[28]

While the division concentrated in the county seat, the commanders of the District of East Tennessee set up headquarters in the Jordan Councill house and attended to business. One item on the agenda was Stoneman's encounter with the Fifteenth Pennsylvania's Sergeant Colton. After Stoneman had chewed out Colton for supposedly disobeying orders, a Tennessee major had relieved the Pennsylvanian. Colton then rode after his regiment, passing over the mountains and into North Carolina. He finally caught up with the Fifteenth around midafternoon and reported to Colonel Palmer. Palmer took up the matter with Stoneman in Boone and apparently cleared the air. His reputation restored, Colton would prove himself repeatedly in the coming days.[29]

The chief matter facing Stoneman and Gillem was the lack of forage. Stoneman summoned several Watauga Unionists and pumped them for information. Blalock and others knew of no threats now that Bingham's force was defunct, but they verified the forage problem. The mountain communities, impoverished by the war, could offer little for man or beast to eat, especially a division of several thousand mounted men. That presented a dilemma. Thomas's orders specified Christiansburg as Stoneman's goal, but the road there led through the mountains. Even fewer foraging opportunities lay in that direction. That was an unacceptable risk, so Stoneman decided to take another route. "I shall be compelled to alter slightly from the proposed route on account of the great scarcity of forage and subsistence for the men," he wrote Thomas that evening. To the east lay the fertile valley of the Yadkin River. Stoneman decided to point his column there. "We shall, with ordinary luck, be out of the mountains tomorrow," he wrote. Thomas received Stoneman's dispatch on April 1 and complained to Halleck, "This is an entirely different route from the one I directed Stoneman to take before starting out." But "Old Slow Trot" had no grounds for complaint. Thomas had granted Stoneman discretion in his movements, and he admitted as much; the "Rock of Chickamauga" was simply worried that a move along the Yadkin River would leave Danville unthreatened. In truth, Stoneman altered his route only temporarily to meet the needs of his command. He had every intention of striking Christiansburg and threatening Danville.[30]

But first the raiders had to tap the Yadkin Valley's precious resources. For the second time during the raid, Stoneman decided to divide his command. He planned to lead Palmer's First Brigade through Deep Gap and down the mountains to Wilkesboro. Gillem, with the other two brigades and the artillery, drew the task of marching southeast into Caldwell County. Just north of Lenoir, Gillem was to make a hard left and ride northeast into Wilkes County along the Yadkin.[31] It amounted to a pincers movement on Wilkesboro, with one column north of the Yadkin and the other south of it. This would accomplish several purposes. First, it would give the men a wider territory in which to forage. Second, it would create the opportunity to destroy an important cotton factory. And finally, it would confuse the enemy.

His plans settled, Stoneman was finally able to unwind. Mrs. Jordan Councill, despite being a devoted Southern woman, treated her high-ranking guest well. Even though the raiders had made short work of her pantry, Mrs. Councill managed to prepare supper for Stoneman and also saw to his breakfast the next morning. The general particularly enjoyed her fine mountain butter. He asked Mrs. Councill if she had any more of it. Her answer was direct; a firkin of butter was about the only thing his men had left her. Stoneman nevertheless took that last firkin with him.[32]

On the evening of March 28, Gillem directed Brown's brigade to proceed without camping. Miller's brigade and Mallaby's Signal Corps detachment, which were still making their way to Boone, would bivouac that night atop the Blue Ridge and follow in the morning. So, too, would Gillem, who decided to remain in the mountains and give his "personal attention" to the artillery.[33]

Men from Brevet Brigadier General Simeon B. Brown's brigade again took the lead, turning south toward Caldwell County and the Yadkin River. Born

Simeon B. Brown commanded the Second Brigade, which contained one Michigan and two Kentucky cavalry regiments.
Massachusetts Commandery Military Order of the Loyal Legion and the United States Army Military History

on March 1, 1812, in Bridgewater, New Hampshire, Brown was a former merchant, farmer, and hotel proprietor from St. Clair, Michigan. He began the war
as a major in the Sixth Michigan Cavalry and joined that regiment in many
fights, including Gettysburg. Soon afterward, Brown accepted the colonelcy of
the new Eleventh Michigan. Stoneman's latest raid did not, however, represent
his first brigade command. Among other temporary postings, he had commanded a small brigade in the District of Kentucky for about two months. Saltville
had been Brown's shining moment. In that raid, a witness attested, "he showed
the 'true metal' and handled his brigade so skillfully that General Burbridge sent
his name to the War Department with the recommend[ation] that he be appointed a brigadier general for brave conduct and skillful management." Brown
accordingly received his brevet in January 1865.[34]

Good management also marked his march into Caldwell County. Brown's
brigade pounded southward past the seasonal mountaintop resort of Blowing
Rock and trotted through Watauga Gap. At nine in the evening, Brown reached
the foot of the mountains and cast his attention toward Patterson's factory. A
concern that converted cotton into yarn, the factory was built around 1850. It
had operated intermittently throughout the war, providing products for the new
Southern government and also for East Tennessee Federals, and was at work
even as the Second Brigade approached. It was tucked away alongside the Yadkin, which at that point was only a modest stream, its source being just a short
distance up the mountain. Around the mill sat the homes of some employees,
which gave the complex the appearance of a small community.[35]

Night fell. The blue-clad troopers came suddenly, without warning, and
flooded the factory and the community. In minutes, Federal guards surrounded
the place to prevent anyone from escaping to sound the alarm. The rest of the
troopers dismounted and camped. At least one witness was impressed. "They
were equipped in the very best manner, & under the severest discipline & were
not allowed to plunder to any great extent or commit any acts of violence," he
wrote.[36]

Other troopers examined their prize. Inside the factory, the cavalrymen
happily found what Gillem later called "an ample supply of corn and bacon."
They also chased a man named Clem Osborne. A regular at the factory, Osborne apparently came to pick up thread. Unaware that the facility had been
captured, he began unloading his wagon as usual until his dog started barking.
Osborne turned, saw someone climbing into his covered wagon, pulled out his

pistol, and opened fire. The interloper ran away, and a trooper cried, "A d___ rebel has killed one of our men." Osborne fled to the bell tower atop the factory as bullets nipped at him. Cornered, he gave the Masonic sign, at which a fellow Mason in blue stopped the pursuit. Other sources say that Osborne pretended to be drunk, or that he stammered when speaking, due to a disability. Something must have calmed his captors, since Osborne made it home with his team, wagon, and load. Gillem himself is said to have approved Osborne's release. But Osborne was so shaken that he would not return to Patterson's factory for twenty years.[37]

The mill superintendent had a similar experience. Again, accounts differ on the details. In one story, the man ran to a window and flashed the Masonic sign. In another account, troopers collared him as he descended the factory steps. When he asked for a Mason in the Federal ranks, an affirmative answer restored his hope for survival. Both accounts reported that he was treated well, as were all civilians that day. Osborne and the superintendent became the first of many in the coming weeks who would purportedly seek protection through Masonic connections.[38]

The manager of the cotton mill was handsome, respected thirty-four-year-old Rufus Lenoir Patterson. A graduate of the University of North Carolina, "Colonel" Patterson had dabbled in a variety of pursuits. He first studied law but then moved to Greensboro, North Carolina, where he took up banking. Finally, Patterson moved to nearby Salem, where, with his father-in-law's help, he opened a mill that worked flour, cotton, and paper. He also became involved in politics, serving as a delegate to the convention that ratified North Carolina's Ordinance of Secession. When his first wife died in 1862, Patterson sold his Salem property and returned to Caldwell County. His ties to Salem flourished anew two years later when he wed Mary E. Fries, the daughter of a Salem industrialist. The new family put down roots in Caldwell County, but the growing danger from refugees and deserters prompted Patterson to send his family to stay with her parents in Salem.[39]

Rufus dealt with the uninvited guests in the absence of his father, Samuel F. Patterson. In fact, as the troopers bivouacked around the mill, General Brown made his headquarters in Rufus Patterson's room. The two men got along fine. Brown treated his host with kindness. According to some sources, he assured Patterson that the mill would not be harmed on the authority of Stoneman himself, but this is apocryphal. Instead, Brown painted a frank picture of

Palmyra, home of Samuel F. Patterson
THE PATTERSON SCHOOL

the raid's objectives. He also predicted that secessionists downriver would fare much worse.[40]

Meanwhile, despite Brown's precautions, news of the raid sped to nearby Lenoir. But Gillem had no intention of approaching the town—at least not yet. The division commander, the Signal Corps detachment, and the artillery arrived at the factory at seven o'clock on Wednesday, March 29. Gillem and his contingent spent the morning feeding their horses and resting. "Plenty of girls and a pretty place," wrote Frank Frankenberry. "Eat supper[,] breakfast and dinner all together in the street of Patterson. Have apple butter, ham, and corn cakes." Finally, the column moved out at eleven. It took along at least one civilian as insurance. Only a rear guard remained to watch over the mill and supplies until Miller's brigade arrived. When the Tennessee brigade reached Patterson's factory, it also paused to enjoy the supplies the Second Brigade had captured. At about three that afternoon, the Third Brigade marched on toward Wilkesboro, but not before Gillem told Patterson that the United States government had been "too lenient" and that Southerners must "look out for the consequences." Two companies of troopers stayed behind to destroy the remaining supplies and then set fire to the factory's machinery and main building, as well as the company store, the warehouse, the granary, the oil mill, the tanning yard, a small office, and some other property. Rufus Patterson could only watch as his community went up in flames.[41]

That moment would always haunt him. He struggled with dyspepsia and lost considerable weight in the coming months. Hoping to get away from the depressing ruin that was his factory, Patterson decided to rejoin his wife in Salem. He never dreamed that he would encounter Stoneman's raiders again.[42]

Their work finished, the two companies rode after the Second and Third brigades. As darkness fell, the rain poured in torrents. In Lenoir, residents slept in their clothes, still expecting the Federals. But morning came and the roads into town remained empty. Finally, a lady by the name of Susan Sherrill arrived. She had been among those civilians detained at the factory. The mill was a charred heap, she said, and the Federals were gone. They had left nothing behind except for a note a cavalryman wrote for his brother. What the note said remains a mystery.[43]

⁕

"Some of the happiest moments of my life," George Stoneman once wrote, "were those I have enjoyed as seated upon the most elevated peak of some lofty mountain[,] its sides covered with the waving pines & its base washed by the roaring t[o]rrent."[44] The experiences of late March 1865 were enough, perhaps, to change his mind. Crossing the mountains into North Carolina had offered obstacles aplenty; vaulting the Blue Ridge into the Yadkin River Valley now brought fresh challenges. Making the journey worse was the weather. March and April in northwestern North Carolina are months of transition from brown to green and from winter to spring, a time characterized by a wild and unpredictable mix of rain, wind, cold, and warmth. Both the mountains and the weather would affect Stoneman's operations in the coming days.

Beginning around noon on March 28 and continuing overnight—as Brown's brigade marched for Patterson's factory and Miller's brigade followed—most of Palmer's brigade rode a couple of miles east of Boone and camped along the New River. There, it brought consternation anew. Part of the command bivouacked at Joshua Winkler's house, and the Watauga County resident found himself contributing mightily, if unwillingly, to the Federal cause. A miller and farmer, Winkler owned a twelve-hundred-acre farm. Blue-clad troopers picked it clean, relieving Winkler of seven hundred pounds of bacon, fifty bushels of corn, twenty-five bushels of potatoes, and thirty chickens. The troopers also dismantled about four thousand fence rails to build fires. Winkler complained so loudly that Gillem—who had not yet left for Patterson's factory—ordered a soldier to escort Winkler to the quartermaster to get a voucher. Somehow, the soldier lost the disgruntled farmer, who never got his voucher. He and several other neighbors would be reimbursed for their troubles after the war by the Southern Claims Commission.[45]

Winkler and his neighbors could have taken some solace in the confusion their mountainous country created. For Colonel Luther Trowbridge and the Tenth Michigan Cavalry, it was probably hard to imagine being any farther from Grand Rapids, the regiment's birthplace. Since its inception in the fall of 1863, the Michigan regiment had spent most of its career in East Tennessee. Its baptism by fire came when a company was escorting a drove of cattle to Knoxville; the incident proved an embarrassment. As Colonel Trowbridge recalled, "A superior force of the enemy relieved them of the further care of the cattle, and they were appropriated by the enemy's commissary." Afterward, the Michigan men learned their trade in numerous fights large and small, including battles against John Hunt Morgan and at Bull's Gap. Throughout, veteran leadership guided the unit. Most of its field officers had served in other regiments and applied that experience well. To most observers, it came as no surprise that the Michigan regiment ultimately proved itself worthy. Confederate major general Joe Wheeler reportedly once told a prisoner from the regiment, "If I had 300 men such as you, I could march straight through hell."[46]

As March 28 closed, an orderly brought Trowbridge instructions. He learned that he was to lead his regiment about a mile down a side road to find forage for the horses. He was to be ready to march by five o'clock the next morning. Trowbridge asked if the orderly also had the morning's order of march. "No," the man said, "you will receive the order in the morning." With that, the Michigan men bivouacked, fully expecting to be on the move early.[47]

March 29 began badly for the Michigan men, especially Private Hendricks and Colonel Trowbridge. When Hendricks and his comrades rose early to cook breakfast, a trooper knocked over a coffeepot. Its scalding contents burned Hendricks's foot. Nonetheless, by five o'clock, Trowbridge's men had eaten breakfast and saddled their horses. Then the colonel's problems began. When an hour passed and no orders came, Trowbridge sent someone to investigate. The man returned and reported the other camps quiet, with no signs of movement. Trowbridge resolved to wait but gave up at nine o'clock. He sent an officer to headquarters. The officer came back and said that everybody had gone, that the other regiments' camps were deserted, and that the roads were empty. Confused, Trowbridge ordered his regiment to march. It found a road that had recently been used by a large body of men and followed it.[48]

Someone had forgotten to notify Trowbridge. The Twelfth Ohio and Fifteenth Pennsylvania were already on the road. The two regiments left their New River camps between six-thirty and eight-thirty and moved west, passing a few homes that did not go unnoticed. About nine that morning, the first troopers approached the home of Smith P. Green. A farmer and blacksmith, Green owned fifty acres about two miles from Deep Gap. He was also a self-proclaimed Union man, so he watched with some interest as the column passed. Noting Green's blacksmith shop, Stoneman himself rode over and recruited Green to shoe his horse. Green agreed and was soon hard at work. But when his back was turned, someone made off with his bay mare. Stoneman told an officer to give Green a voucher for it, but he never got it.[49]

There were few other houses along the road to distract the raiders. On the column rode, up to the crest of the Blue Ridge and through Deep Gap, then downward into the Yadkin Valley. It traveled on a surprisingly good mountain road and enjoyed what the country had to offer. "Our travel has been mostly over mts & through coves. Mts well timbered—calculated good forage country," a First Brigade staff officer observed. Sergeant Colton, ever an admirer of nature, agreed. "Passed some beautiful marbles. The country is very piney," he wrote.[50]

The men of the Twelfth Ohio Cavalry, their Spencer repeaters at the ready, led the way down the mountain. Organized near Cleveland in late 1863, the regiment had started its war guarding the prison camp at Johnson's Island. Most of its subsequent service came in the Department of Kentucky. A veteran raiding force by 1865, the Ohioans had participated in both Burbridge's and Stoneman's Saltville expeditions. And like the Twelfth Kentucky, the Ohioans had battled Kentucky guerillas and the feared John Hunt Morgan, displaying particular gallantry at Mount Sterling and Cynthiana in June 1864. Currently, the regiment was dealing with command vacancies. Two company commanders had been dismissed for being absent without leave. In addition, Lieutenant Colonel Robert H. Bentley, not yet thirty, was substituting for Colonel Robert W. Ratliff, who was absent on court-martial duty. That unit tended to be more disciplined with Ratliff present, but overall the Twelfth was a good outfit. "Sufficient to say they were the real thing, and feared no noise," wrote an observer some years after the war. Another trooper echoed that sentiment: "Rebel bullets never broke our ranks, boys, our dis[c]ipline was too perfect, but the crow of a rooster would or a sweet potato patch beside the road."[51]

The Twelfth Ohio Cavalry crossed the Yadkin River at Holman's Ford and pointed its mounts toward Wilkesboro. Although it had done its share for the Confederacy, Wilkes County was no longer a bad place for Federal soldiers. Its hills had sheltered deserters and escaped Federal prisoners. Its people were prone to displaying their Unionists leanings in quite public ways, including fighting. In fact, according to a man who hid there after escaping from Salisbury, Wilkes was "so strong in its Union sentiments, that the Rebels called it 'the Old United States.'"[52]

It was wet and nearing dusk when the Ohioans approached the village. Evening came early because of the dark rain clouds overhead; the heavy precipitation that characterized March 1865 throughout the South had found the raiders again. Despite the weather, some young locals, fearing conscription, had spent the day plowing vigorously in the fields. In town, a new conscription officer and some three dozen Confederate soldiers went about their business. Forty-year-old Calvin J. Cowles, a local herb dealer, had just finished writing a letter when the Federals "came dashing into town and turned everything upside down. . . . They came in with a yell and ran completely through the place frightening a small body (36) of Confederates out of their wits and out of the place. In about half an hour they entered my yard . . . and they met me pistol in hand pointing threateningly at my breast commanding me to open my store which I did as quickly as possible. They 'prowled' the store but did not take my money—burned the Gray House and all my fence convenient to the road—took half my corn and all my fodder—took 4 mules and Nat and the mare—took Nels and Jim [unknown, probably slaves] off with them. . . . The boys took the . . . Gilbert saddle and rode off right before our eyes not even saying 'goodbye.'"[53]

Wilkesboro was the home of Lieutenant Colonel J. A. Hampton's Sixty-eighth Battalion of Home Guards. Hampton and his men never had a chance; according to Cowles, the Ohioans rushed in "like an avalanche." Local tradition suggests that a skirmish broke out on Barricks Hill between the Twelfth Ohio and the Home Guardsmen. If it did, the fight did not amount to much. One cavalryman, Major E. C. Moderwell, recalled only that the Federals rounded up a few prisoners and some commissary stores in Wilkesboro. Another Ohio trooper recorded that the town had been evacuated when the troopers arrived. Only Gillem, who was not present, dramatized the event when he reported that the cavalry "drove the enemy" from town. As darkness fell on March 29, the Twelfth Ohio Cavalry firmly held Wilkesboro. The regiment would remain in town for the night.[54]

A few miles away, the Fifteenth Pennsylvania continued its now-downhill trek to Wilkesboro, following the Twelfth Ohio. As the day lengthened, the weather worsened, extinguishing whatever light remained. Streams, hills, dales, and both Lewis Fork and the Yadkin River barred the way. Finally, around ten that night, the regiment halted at a plantation about four miles from Wilkesboro. In the heavy rain, it camped in a freshly plowed field. But if the weather was miserable, the fine plantation offered a cornucopia. The unit's worn-out horses got their first feed of grain since crossing the state line. The hosts, the Gray family, welcomed the raiders pleasantly and expressed a hope for peace. The night's work was not done for Howard E. Buzby, however. Buzby, a member of Colonel Palmer's escort, rode off to find Stoneman, applying his Texas spurs to his horse, Camelback, and pitching into the blackness. When he found the commanding general, he reported that "[Colonel] Palmer sends his compliments, etc." Stoneman offered no orders, other than instructions not to get too far ahead. Buzby returned to camp, delivered this message to Palmer, and then promptly fell asleep on his blanket.[55]

Last of all came the frustrated Tenth Michigan. Trowbridge's men marched all day to overtake their missing comrades, but only wildlife kept them company. "I do not remember that we saw, during the whole day, a single person of whom we could make a guide or from whom we could gain any information as to the country," the colonel wrote. As the day ended, his dilemma worsened. "Night came on, and it was so dark we could scarcely see our horses heads," Trowbridge complained. One of the men in the column testified to the difficulty of the rainy march. "This was the worst night march I ever experienced. The rain poured in torrents[,] dark as Egypt in a mountain region[,] the road frequently lying on the verge of awful precipices where to have gone off would have been instant death to both rider and horse," he wrote.[56]

About ten o'clock that night, the regiment approached the Yadkin, which Trowbridge described as a broad, swift, and deep stream. The Michigan men could see lights and hear voices across the water. Deciding to cross, Trowbridge managed to find a ford. A violent storm harassed them, but somehow the Michigan men reached the opposite bank with the aid of only sputtering torches to cut into the blackness. There, they found Reagan's artillery, fresh from Patterson's factory, stuck in a "narrow cut." To get past the Tennessee gunners, the regiment had to navigate steep, slippery banks on either side of the road. "Slipping and floundering along, many horses falling, we finally succeeded," Trowbridge remembered. The rear battalion, confused by the delay at the front of the column, turned back and camped on the other side of the river.[57]

At last, a courier found Trowbridge in the blackness and offered long-awaited orders. Like the Fifteenth Pennsylvania, the regiment was to return to and bivouac on the opposite bank by marching a few miles downriver and crossing the rising stream again. "Weary, wet and hungry, this was not the most agreeable news," the colonel grumbled, "but like good soldiers we moved on, and at two o'clock in the morning we again forded the river, were conducted to a piece of woods, and told that we could make ourselves comfortable for the remainder of the night." At least he did not have to order out any pickets, since the other regiments had already done so. When Trowbridge was satisfied with his regiment's disposition, he sat on the root of a large tree, leaned his head against the trunk, and fell asleep. With that, both the Tenth Michigan and the Fifteenth Pennsylvania had reestablished themselves north of the Yadkin River, while the Twelfth Ohio remained in Wilkesboro.[58]

The courier who relayed orders to Trowbridge was signalman Frank Frankenberry, who had spent the afternoon of March 29 riding from Patterson's factory. "I rode with the advance guard today and had a hard ride. . . . March down the Yadkin River and cross it often." Fortunately, traveling with the vanguard had its benefits. At one spot, he dickered with a local to buy two chickens and a canteen full of sorghum molasses. Hiding away the birds and molasses for later use, Frankenberry reined in at a house along the road. As a cavalryman should, he first saw that his horse, Charlie, was fed. Then he sat down to a supper of cornbread and milk with the homeowners. Happily, the family had three young girls for Frankenberry to flirt with while he ate. Afterward, the day went downhill. The signalman stopped by Gillem's headquarters, and the Tennessee general ordered him to carry orders to Brown's brigade and the artillery. "Have a dark ride and at last do as ordered. Rain pouring down in torrents, dark and the road is in awfull condition," he recorded.[59]

Behind Frankenberry, Gillem's men found much to enjoy along the meandering valley road from Patterson's factory to Wilkesboro. Full granaries and well-stocked smokehouses waited along the Yadkin River. Farmers plowing in their fields unwillingly gave up their fat horses to the Federals. Fortunately, some residents managed to save their possessions when they received advance warning of the raiders' approach. Fifteen-year-old Lee Ferguson sounded the alarm. He was riding a mule a few miles west of Wilkesboro when he saw the Federals. Somehow, Ferguson coaxed his mule into a rapid pace and began to warn his neighbors. Cavalrymen saw him and opened fire. "He could hear the crack of rifles, and the whizzing of bullets all about him and he thought every minute would be his last," a descendant testified. Realizing his mule could not outrun cavalry horses, the boy hid his mount in the woods. Bareheaded, he began working on a rail fence. Federal troopers saw him and asked if he had seen a "damned little rebel on a mule." No, Ferguson said, "I've been fencing here all day." The quick-witted youngster thus escaped.[60]

Late that afternoon, the column discovered the First Brigade's trail near Holman's Ford, west of Wilkesboro. Stoneman had passed just a few minutes earlier. The river was beginning to rise in the rainy weather, which made the ford tricky. One unconfirmed source reported that a cannon and caisson capsized in the river and were lost. The troopers followed the path until dark and then camped. It was about seven o'clock. Somewhere along the road, the artillery got stuck in the mud, where Trowbridge's Michigan men found it. Last of all, and farthest from Wilkesboro, Miller's brigade also bivouacked. Doubtless, every man was ready for a good night's sleep.[61]

꧁꧂

Thursday, March 30, 1865, dawned with the Cavalry Division camped around Wilkesboro. The torrential spring rain continued, soaking everything. Water trickled inside Colonel Trowbridge's coat and awoke him, so he began making breakfast. This did not ease his misery. "If you would have a picture of some of the minor discomforts of a cavalry raid," Trowbridge wrote, "imagine . . . sitting on a log in the woods, near a sputtering fire, with a tin plate on [your] knees, a tin cup of coffee . . . on a stump . . . , making a breakfast of fried bacon and corn pone, while the breakfast was fast being cooled and the coffee rapidly diluted by the incessant rain." Fortunately, an officer appeared and rescued him. "Why, Colonel, what are you doing here? They have a good warm breakfast for you down at that farm house. There are about thirty of the fellows there and they are keeping a place for you," the man said. The grateful Trowbridge wondered if the man was an angel.[62]

After breakfast, the Tenth Michigan stayed put on the north side of the Yadkin. Besides keeping dry, Trowbridge's main objective for the day was to collect the men who were still missing from the previous night. Lieutenant Colonel Charles M. Betts's Fifteenth Pennsylvania Cavalry exerted only slightly more effort. Despite the storm, the troopers marched at about eight o'clock. "Raining and roads very heavy," read Company A's morning report. Three or four miles down the road, the troopers approached the Reddies, a tributary of the Yadkin. Finding a very deep ford, they waded across. Betts ordered his men to camp on the other side, still north of the Yadkin at a point roughly opposite Wilkesboro.[63]

Stoneman's objective that Thursday was to reunite his part of the division with the Fifteenth Pennsylvania and the Tenth Michigan north of the Yadkin. Once joined, the division could resume its journey toward Christiansburg. Colonel William J. Palmer took the lead and ordered his brigade's last regiment, the Twelfth Ohio Cavalry, across the river to join the other two regiments. Palmer marched with the Twelfth as it headed for the nearest ford. Trooper Howard Buzby, astride Camelback, followed Palmer. Buzby had campaigned with Palmer often and knew him well. When deep in thought, Palmer would press one or both heels in toward his horse's flanks, as if trying to squeeze out an idea or a plan, yet without touching the horse. As the column passed through Wilkesboro—which Buzby called "quite a village"—he saw Palmer doing just that with both heels. Something apparently had disturbed his boss. Soon, Buzby understood. The Yadkin River, Buzby said, was "running wild" and was fast becoming a dangerous obstacle. As the Ohioans braved the river, Palmer ordered Buzby to stay on the south bank and guide the other two brigades to the ford.[64]

Buzby watched the Ohioans struggle across. It was still early; the column stretched back into Wilkesboro. The rain showed no sign of letting up. Private Joseph Banks, who described the storm as "powerful," noted with alarm that the river was rising fast. Soon, the crossing became a ford in name only, forcing some men to swim their horses, no easy task. "Almost any horse can swim, but you must let him have his head, ease up off the saddle and swim a little yourself," wrote Buzby. "Some never reached the other side. . . . It was a fearful sight." A few men may have drowned in the attempt, but the Twelfth made it across. Once on the north bank, the exhausted Ohioans bivouacked and searched for forage.[65]

The First Brigade was now reunited. Alone and wet, Buzby rode back into Wilkesboro to find shelter from the rain. The town was quiet and seemed deserted except for a few frightened children peeking from windows. Finding a blacksmith shop with a shed in front, Buzby rode under the shed and dismounted. While Camelback sniffed around, Buzby sat on a log, took off his boots, and emptied them of water. Occasionally, he peered down the road, where nothing moved. An hour passed. Finally, he saw the rest of the Cavalry Division approaching. Buzby jumped on Camelback and trotted out to meet it.[66]

Gillem and Stoneman led the way, followed by Reagan's Tennessee battery (finally freed from the mud) and Miller's Tennesseans. These men had started early and were already miserable. Lieutenant Theodore Mallaby's Signal Corps detachment was also nearby, looking at the cresting waters.[67] Buzby rode up to Stoneman, saluted, and offered to guide them. The two commanders agreed with Buzby's proposal, and the raiders followed him down to the river. Buzby noticed that Palmer had occupied a large house on a hill across the river. He saw men moving on the veranda, watching for their approach. Nearer to hand, he saw that the raging river was at least a foot higher than when Bentley's men crossed. "How long has it been since they crossed?" Stoneman asked.

"Easily an hour and a half," Buzby replied. Stoneman let loose a string of curses and then ordered a staff officer to try the river. The officer failed, barely making it back to the south bank.[68]

Seeing that, Stoneman and Gillem canceled the crossing. Stoneman quickly realized his predicament. Under most wartime scenarios, he would have faced a serious problem, as an army divided by a river is extremely vulnerable to defeat. Fortunately for the Federals, the rules did not apply in the backwater of the Confederacy. Noted one of Palmer's men, "We were on this side alone, but in no danger, unless the enemy should come at us in boats." The reduced danger did nothing for Stoneman's humor; swollen rivers had plagued him before. The New Yorker's wrath boiled over. "He fairly roared like a lion," Buzby recalled, "and in his roaring would say, 'Palmer on one side of the river with those Pennsylvania boys and me on this side!'" The New Yorker decided to take his anger out on Gillem. "Gillem, I am going to see what you have," Stoneman said. And so began one of the strangest reviews in military history.[69]

Partaking of some hyperbole, Buzby described what happened next:

> The very heavens had opened their floodgates, and the water was coming down in sheets, which accounted somewhat for the appearance of the troops on the outside, and several whisky stills, which had been struck back of the Ridge, accounted for their appearance on all sides. The number of "wounded" was startling, and a good many were "dead," for corn whisky is fearful stuff. With the rain coming down in torrents and the mud knee-deep, and the stuff warm in the stills, our brave allies were driven to drink. Stoneman blamed the officers for this, and was calling them down. . . .
>
> All the carriages and omnibuses along the route had been confiscated. There was a carriage of the George Washington kind, filled with soldiers, their boots sticking out in all directions. Here was the stage coach, which in times of peace had run between Rutherfordton and the Blue Ridge, filled to its capacity, with some on top. If my memory serves me right, this caravan of carriages and buses reached a mile or more. All the different kinds of carriages were there. General Stoneman . . . would stop the parade occasionally and make a general reduction of Captains and Lieutenants. But when the "wounded" came along in the carriages he said something like this: "By—if—I—I'll—you—can it—where in—this—beats—they ought—to be—be killed—if I don't—."
>
> A halt is ordered, and they are all tumbled out of the carriages, and ordered to dump into camp wherever they choose, and to go no farther. All this time Palmer was signaling on the other side of the river with flags. . . . Stoneman's headquarters wagon came up and his tent was unloaded. The staff tried to pacify him, but he was mad at them, and blamed them for the condition of things.[70]

No other source describes this spectacle, although another trooper confirmed that "some of the troopers have too much brandy and are almost drunk." Whatever the truth, Stoneman and Gillem were helpless until the waters receded and could only inch their separated brigades down the river. Virginia would have to wait for another day. Fortunately, the heavy rain finally stopped around ten o'clock in the morning. The afternoon brought clearing skies and a hot sun, which helped dry the soggy troopers.[71]

As the division moved, squadrons and battalions spread out to scour the countryside. This was standard procedure, but Wilkesboro bore more than its fair share of pain, thanks to the cresting Yadkin. One local historian termed it nothing less than a time of "robbing and plundering everything in sight leaving [in] their trail a howling wilderness." Another writer noted, "Small parties scoured the country, carrying off all the horses and mules, and burning the factories. There seemed to be no systematic plan of destruction; for while some mills and factories were burned, others in the same neighborhood and quite as easily accessible were spared. Much depended on the personal character and disposition of the commanding officer of these detachments." Some of this was an exaggeration, but the Federals did enjoy the benefits of an extended pause. As one officer recalled, they "feasted for a few days on the contents of numerous large warehouses filled with supplies intended for the rebel armies, and destroyed what remained."[72]

Henry Birdsall and his comrades in the Eleventh Michigan wanted tobacco, so they stopped in Wilkesboro to find it. Finishing their search by one in the afternoon, the Michigan men camped in the vicinity of the town. They fed their horses and rested for the remainder of the day. Frank Frankenberry and his comrades also found tobacco in Wilkesboro, as well as a large supply of brandy and some local Unionist sentiment to boot. Noticing three ladies watching from a house, Frankenberry unfurled a Union flag and asked one how she liked it. "O . . . I cannot tell how much I love it," the lady exclaimed. "My heart leaps with joy. May God bless such a noble banner."[73]

Other troopers made at least one resident a prisoner and also went inside the man's home and "took every thing he had," as his niece described it. Perhaps Mollie Sackett had the right idea. She saved her horse by holding the reins in one hand and a pistol in the other. E. M. Welborn was another local landowner who lost supplies to blue-clad visitors, but he fared better than most. A quartermaster left him a receipt for 130 bushels of corn, and Stoneman himself gave Welborn an additional note of protection. "The bearer, Mr. E. M. Welborn is authorized to retain his bay horse unmolested and no one of this comd. will interfere with it," the general wrote.[74]

North of the Yadkin and opposite Wilkesboro sat one tempting target: Oakland, the home of Brigadier General James B. Gordon, a Confederate cavalryman who had died in 1864. Stoneman's troopers thoroughly searched the large house, but the residents were prepared, having hidden the family's silver in a riverbank cave along the Reddies. They concealed other valuables and supplies beneath some loose pine floorboards; to protect that hiding place, they stationed a young girl and her dolls above it. Gordon's horse, stabled at his brother-in-law's house, did not escape, however, since Palmer had chosen that house as his headquarters. When a Federal trooper blew his bugle, the horse pranced as only a good military mount can. The Federals seized Gordon's horse and paraded it in front of Oakland for a few hours, as if to celebrate the defeat of the Confederacy. At least the owner of the house where Palmer made his headquarters was able to escape. While Mrs. Martha Finley played the parlor piano loudly for her guests, her husband slipped out an upstairs back window.[75]

Calvin Cowles did his best to stop the plundering, asking Stoneman to protect public and private property. Cowles restated his appeal when he encountered some Federals preparing to burn the tithes the Confederates had collected in an old building north of the courthouse. He persuasively argued that the provisions could be used to feed poor Unionist women and children. The soldiers agreed to delay burning the provisions until they discussed the matter with Stoneman. The tithes apparently survived, and so did Wilkesboro's jail and courthouse.[76]

While the troopers scoured the countryside, Stoneman continued to fret about his divided command. Fortunately, Mallaby's signal flags brought encouraging news; Palmer confirmed that the First Brigade was in no danger. Slowly, Stoneman regained his composure. Around midday, upon reaching some hills overlooking the Yadkin about four miles east of Wilkesboro, Stoneman decided to camp for the night. The general's staff began pitching his tent, and the New Yorker helped. When the camp was finished, Stoneman and Buzby got along so well that Buzby finally crawled into the general's tent and fell asleep. But the day's excitement was not yet over. That evening, some bushwhackers opened fire on the Fifteenth Pennsylvania's picket line. No one was hurt.[77]

⌁⁘⌁

In Raleigh, less than 150 miles to the east, General Pierre Gustave Toutant Beauregard took pen in hand and wrote to his superior, General Joseph E. Johnston: "My preference is to remain with you at present, for I could scarcely expect at this juncture to be furnished with a force at all commensurate with the exigency or able to make head against the enemy reported advancing from East Tennessee and Southwest Virginia." Unfortunately for the forty-six-year-old Creole, the message to Johnston changed nothing. According to reports from the field, the beleaguered Confederacy had a new problem on its hands: Stoneman's Raid. The problem now became Beauregard's.[78]

Although many other high-ranking officers were available, Beauregard was the best man for the job. While the hot-tempered general was not one to inspire confidence with his physical appearance—he stood five-foot-seven and weighed about 150 pounds—he was every inch a soldier. A native of St. Bernard Parish, Louisiana, Beauregard had a background that included a stellar record at West Point and a distinguished career in the prewar army. Commissioned a second lieutenant in the coveted Corps of Engineers, he went on to fight in the Mexican War

General P. G. T. Beauregard reluctantly took overall command of Confederate troops in western North Carolina, southwestern Virginia, and East Tennessee.
Courtesy of The North Carolina State Archives

*Joseph E. Johnston had direct responsibility for the area
Stoneman targeted. He delegated his second in com-
mand, P. G. T. Beauregard, to stop the raiders.*
COURTESY OF THE NORTH CAROLINA STATE ARCHIVES

and was twice brevetted for gallantry. In 1861, he cast his lot with the Confederacy and became the upstart nation's first military hero. That April, he presided
over the capture of Fort Sumter; in July, he played an important role in the Confederate victory at First Manassas. Promoted to full general, Beauregard next
went west after he fell out of favor with President Davis. There, he struggled.
When the highly regarded Albert Sidney Johnston died at Shiloh, Beauregard
assumed command of the Army of Tennessee, only to be defeated on the battle's
second day. He subsequently abandoned Corinth, Mississippi, to the besieging
Federals. Thereafter, illness sidelined him, and army command shifted to Braxton Bragg. When the Louisianan returned to duty, he was sent back to Charles-

ton, where he ably defended the vital coastal port against Federal threats in 1863 and 1864. Later, during the Petersburg campaign, Beauregard again displayed his flair for the defensive counterstroke. Could he once again pull off a defensive miracle, in North Carolina?[79]

Beauregard began at a disadvantage because the Confederacy simply lacked the troops needed to stop Stoneman. Over a week before, Brigadier General John C. Vaughn had predicted a Federal force would penetrate East Tennessee and western North Carolina. Vaughn's skirmishes with Federal troops on March 24 and 25 supported that prediction, and local commanders heeded the warning. Brigadier General James G. Martin, commanding the District of Western North Carolina, was very worried. His command was in disarray. "I regret to say I have nothing to report but disobedience of orders, neglect of duty, demoralization of the people, and desertion of both officers and men," he wrote. Realizing that his forces, even if combined with Vaughn's, could not stop the raiders, he asked for troops to protect the North Carolina Railroad. Brigadier General Bradley T. Johnson, Salisbury's post commander, heard Martin, recognized his own command's weakness, and appealed to General Joseph E. Johnston. Johnston turned to Robert E. Lee, general in chief of all Confederate armies.[80]

Lee was well aware of the danger lurking to the west. From his trenches at Petersburg, Lee feared that Grant planned to concentrate all his armies in Virginia and overwhelm the Confederacy. On March 20, he passed on to the War Department a dispatch from Lieutenant General Richard Taylor, commanding the Department of Alabama and Mississippi, who "thinks Genl Thomas is moving the 4th Corps and possibly part of his cavalry to East Tennessee." Unfortunately, Lee realized, "there is nothing to engage the attention of Thomas' troops at the south that I am aware of, & it will be a great object of the enemy to destroy the salt works[,] lead mines &c, & to concentrate all these troops in Virginia." Lee therefore proposed that Taylor launch a diversion into Tennessee. The War Department agreed with Lee's idea but noted a fatal flaw. Secretary of War John C. Breckinridge wrote, "I fear however that the danger from East Tennessee is immediate. . . . If no troops can be sent to South West Virginia, I fear we shall soon lose the salt works and lead mines, not to mention danger to Lynchburg and the loss of the supplies now obtained from the productive region of the Southwestern part of the state." That left Lee with only those resources at hand. On March 21, he ordered Echols's brigade to Lynchburg to ward off the expected "advance . . . from Knoxville."[81]

*Though confronted by many threats, the general in chief
of all Confederate armies, Robert E. Lee, was well aware
of Stoneman's tiny raid.*
LIBRARY OF CONGRESS

By March 30, no one could deny that Vaughn had been right. As Stone-man's raiders left Wilkesboro in the rain, Confederate telegraphs tapped out warnings that estimated three to four thousand raiders had entered western North Carolina. That posed a threat to Joe Johnston. As commander of the Army of the South, the Department of North Carolina, and the Department of South Carolina, Georgia, and Florida, the Virginia-born general already had his hands full. His makeshift army, licking its wounds after its defeat at Bentonville, was poised to oppose Sherman's advance on Raleigh. As Johnston was planning to reorganize his force into a new Army of Tennessee, Stoneman's incursion materialized. Johnston delegated the problem of stopping the raid to his second in command, Beauregard. "Please communicate with General [Bradley T.] Johnson, and if necessary, go to the point to direct measures for meeting this expedition," Joe Johnston ordered.[82]

Lee agreed with the idea and went a step farther. He decided to construct a command to assume the responsibility of warding off the raiders. "Can General Beauregard be spared for command of Western Virginia and East Tennessee? Would the duty be agreeable to him?" Lee asked Johnston. Lee's inquiry must have given the Creole pause. As Beauregard later exclaimed through the pen of Alfred Roman, this "new and unfor[e]seen danger" was "an additional complication in our grave and perilous situation; a crisis requiring, it was thought, the greatest promptitude, skill, and energy." It also prompted Beauregard's unqualified response: "I could scarcely expect . . . to be . . . able to make head against the enemy." Johnston sent Beauregard's negative reply on to Lee, but the commanding general apparently ignored it. The next day, Lee empowered Beauregard to take command of any troops from western Virginia and western North Carolina who came within his jurisdiction.[83]

Since Beauregard's new command included the Department of Southwest Virginia and East Tennessee, Lee ordered John Vaughn—and by implication Vaughn's superior, Brigadier General John Echols—to obey Beauregard's orders. Once a lieutenant of Stonewall Jackson, Echols had served in the Shenandoah Valley and western Virginia for most of the war. A large man at six-foot-four and 260 pounds, he suffered from heart problems. The events of late March only strained Echols's health more. After Vaughn's East Tennessee fights and his subsequent withdrawal toward Bristol, the Confederates lost track of Stoneman. On March 27, unofficial reports placed the enemy around the Watauga River, heading east. Echols also worried that Stoneman would strike toward the valuable lead mines in Virginia, so he ordered Henry Giltner's Brigade to Grayson County, Virginia. Echols told Giltner to scout into North Carolina, too.[84]

Since Tillson's Federal forces continued to demonstrate toward Bristol, Echols maintained his other brigades in the Bristol-Abingdon area. On March 28—the day Stoneman occupied Boone—Echols learned that an enemy contingent had been in Jonesboro en route to Taylorsville, Tennessee. Two days later, a small enemy detachment reportedly captured Taylorsville. Echols began to rest easier when news came that Stoneman had passed through Wilkesboro and was still marching east. After all, the farther east the Federals moved, the less likely it

became that they would penetrate Virginia. Giltner's brigade was having difficulty finding forage near Grayson County's lead mines, so Echols ordered it to
move back from the state line into Wythe County. Still, Echols realized that he
would not be out of the woods until Stoneman's force, estimated at forty-two
hundred men, clearly showed its hand.[85]

Beauregard apparently decided that Echols had his department under control, so he spent his time on other defensive matters. As luck would have it,
roughly thirty-five hundred effectives from the Army of Tennessee were within
easy reach. Those men, under Stephen D. Lee, were en route from Augusta,
Georgia, to reinforce Johnston. At thirty-one, Lee was the youngest lieutenant
general in the Confederacy and a veteran of campaigns in both the East and the
West. Over a thousand of Lee's men were unarmed, but surely the South Carolinian's infantry and artillery could beat off cavalry. On March 30, Beauregard
alerted Lee at Chester, South Carolina. "General Bradley Johnson reports from
Salisbury enemy's raiders (about 4,000 strong) at Lenoir. General Johnson will
keep you advised of enemy's movements and if necessary, you will stop a part
of your forces at or about Salisbury to meet or defeat him," he wrote. Later, the
Creole decided it was a necessity. He told Lee to "repair forthwith with all dis-
posable forces to Salisbury, for its defense and that of such other places as may
be threatened by Stoneman's raiders."[86]

For his part, Joe Johnston did not completely drop the matter. He asked
Martin to cooperate with the troops near Salisbury, and Lee affirmed those orders. But Martin could not help. He had only about fifteen hundred men who
were deep in the mountains and too far away to be of assistance. Johnston also
requested General Braxton Bragg's cooperation. Bragg, a forty-eight-year-old
North Carolina native, was a former Army of Tennessee commander who most
recently had led the Department of North Carolina. Now without a job, he
gladly offered advice and assistance. First, Bragg asked North Carolina governor
Zebulon Vance to order out cadets from the Hillsborough Military Academy
and the state's Home Guard. Unfortunately, this was a step of dubious value.
The cadets never made it; they ended up guarding prisoners in Raleigh. The
other possible option, the Guard for Home Defense, had been created in the
summer of 1863. An unpaid force of companies, battalions, and a few regiments
based in each county, the Home Guard was comprised of men between the ages
of eighteen and fifty who were not subject to conscription. In theory, the Home
Guard's purpose was to defend against invasion, hunt down guerillas, guard

bridges, arrest deserters, maintain order, and enforce the law. In practice, it was an unreliable force that proved difficult to rally in an emergency. Would these men fight well-armed, battle-tested Federal cavalry? With the possible exception of Bragg, nobody thought so, from Governor Vance on down. A western North Carolina resident probably summed it up best. "Home Guard no account," he wrote.[87]

Since the Home Guard had obvious limitations, Bragg sought reinforcements in the reserve artillery commanded by Colonel Ambrosio J. Gonzales. A one-time Cuban revolutionary, Gonzales had recently overhauled his seven four-gun batteries. Now, they sat quietly in Hillsborough, horseless but otherwise ready for action. Bragg asked Gonzales to send a battery to Salisbury. The chosen unit was apparently Bachman's South Carolina battery of four twelve-pound Napoleons. Robert Herriot, a member of the battery, remembered the moment when fresh orders reached the Hillsborough camps in late March. The battery moved west.[88]

Next, Bragg cabled to Asheboro, where Lieutenant Colonel Alexander C. McAllister commanded a 267-man detachment from the Army of Northern Virginia. McAllister had led his units into the state in late February to round up deserters. Salisbury became the detachment's next stop. McAllister's command consisted of the Seventh North Carolina and elements of at least eight other Tar Heel regiments. They took the train and arrived on April 1.[89]

There were not enough hours in the day for the defenders to adequately prepare. On March 30 and 31, the news was confusing at best. Some reports placed the enemy raiders at Wilkesboro, but rumors made that uncertain. "Reported raid all bosh," insisted a message from Salisbury. "Special engine just in from west and scouts report that excitement grew out of a foray by band of tories and deserters at Patterson's Factory." Beauregard nevertheless decided to ignore the rumors. Orders continued to flow from the Creole's desk as if the threat were real. It was a smart move, since Beauregard had to deal with several contingencies. If a raiding force was indeed at Wilkesboro, it could strike Salisbury, Greensboro, or Danville. Beauregard knew he had to protect all those places.[90]

Along the North Carolina Railroad, Beauregard continued to grab troops en route to the Raleigh area. One such unit was Brigadier General Winfield Scott Featherston's brigade. "Old Swet" Featherston, age forty-four, was a former lawyer and Mississippi congressman who had combat in his veins. On March 31, the man considered a "matchless general" by his men chugged into Salisbury on a train from Rock Hill, South Carolina. To defend the town, he had two brigades—his own and a collection of other troops he had led north from Augusta, Georgia. He also expected an artillery battalion and a cavalry regiment to join him on April 1. Beauregard directed "Old Swet" to defend the vital railroad bridge northeast of town. "Be careful enemy do not destroy railroad bridge across the Yadkin. Protect it with field works," he wrote. The clean-shaven general replied that he would begin building fortifications at the bridge the next day. McAllister's detachment arrived on April 1 and joined Featherston's men at the bridge.[91]

Meanwhile, to protect Greensboro, Beauregard advised Stephen D. Lee at Salisbury to keep a wary eye in that direction in case Stoneman marched there instead. Beauregard also arranged for more artillery. He told Gonzales to dispatch a second battery to either Greensboro or Salisbury, depending on events. A third battery was to be ready to move at a moment's notice. Johnston also tapped the artillery battalion of Major John W. Johnston. The battalion had left Augusta for North Carolina in mid-March, bound for Joe Johnston's army. When the gunners reached Salisbury, Beauregard ordered them to halt and camp on the edge of town.[92]

Beauregard wondered where else the Confederates might find defenders. Johnston advised him to summon Brigadier General Samuel Wragg Ferguson, who was on the march from South Carolina. Beauregard knew Ferguson well from early in the war, when the young man had served on his staff. A thirty-one-year-old West Point graduate and scion of a wealthy Charleston, South Carolina, family, Ferguson was a blooded veteran who had led a horse brigade through numerous Western Theater campaigns. His reputation was that of a fighter. But not everyone was enamored with him. Joe Wheeler thought Ferguson a spoiled, insubordinate troublemaker who led a desertion-riddled unit. Beauregard, however, was happy to get Ferguson's cavalry brigade, which would acquit itself well in the coming days.[93]

Meanwhile, for Greensboro's defense, Beauregard told Major J. C. Holmes, the post commandant, to stop any passing troops and press them into service. An official with the state's reserves also worked to furnish two regiments. Still, these forces were insufficient, so Beauregard asked Johnston if some cavalry could be sent from Raleigh. And Brigadier General Collett Leventhorpe's command was summoned and divided among Salisbury, High Point, and Lexington.[94]

In a short time, by grabbing infantry, cavalry, and artillery units wherever he could find them, Beauregard established a modest line of strong points—some clearly stronger than others—stretching along the railroad from Chester, South Carolina, to Danville, Virginia. Whether by design or accident, it was like a 250-mile-long sickle hovering over what remained of the Confederacy. Chester was the bottom of the sickle. Salisbury, along the handle, was the best-defended point, with a strong force on the scene and reinforcements on the way. Greensboro, High Point, and Lexington, farther up the handle, would shortly be secured. Echols manned the blade, which stretched from Bristol, Tennessee, to Wytheville, Virginia; his several brigades were in position to obstruct northward advances from either East Tennessee or western North Carolina. Only where the blade and handle joined—from Danville westward into Carroll County—were defenses weak or nonexistent. Beauregard was not worried about that area, however. He was preoccupied with more immediate questions. Could he rely on his patchwork force? What were Stoneman's true intentions? Were there other measures he should take? Having done all he could from a distance, the Creole general decided to visit the most threatened points personally. That evening, Beauregard and three staff officers boarded a westbound train, which chugged beneath a darkening sky toward the elusive foe. He arrived in Greensboro late on March 31.[95]

George Stoneman remained stymied by the Yadkin River. Indeed, of all the geographic obstacles the Cavalry Division of the District of East Tennessee would face on the raid, the Yadkin posed the greatest challenge. This was not the first army the river had frustrated; eighty-four years earlier, during the American Revolution, Cornwallis's British army had struggled across it en route to Guilford Courthouse. Today, March 31, Stoneman's planned move into Virginia remained frustratingly impossible, but the return of good weather promised to make the Yadkin passable again. "The rain had ceased and the afternoon was bright, having the appearance of Spring," recalled a Thirteenth Tennessee man. This fine day, Buzby added, meant that "everybody was in better humor. The 'wounded,' after a good night's sleep, awoke quite refreshed." The Pennsylvania trooper could not resist sharing the experiences of the previous day. Hopping onto Camelback, Buzby somehow made it across the river and described the review to Colonel Palmer. "Palmer rarely indulged in a good laugh, but did this time," Buzby recalled.[96]

After a leisurely breakfast, Mallaby's signalers established communications between the separated columns. Frank Frankenberry and two comrades paddled across the river in a dugout and set up a signal station on the porch of a house overlooking the river. By midafternoon, Palmer was ready to report to his superiors. "No enemy to be seen this [side] of the river," he signaled. With his way clear, Palmer suggested that he move the First Brigade past Roaring River to Hickerson's plantation, about six miles from Elkin. From south of the river, Stoneman and Gillem signaled back to affirm Palmer's plan and pointed the Second and Third brigades eastward as well. Sliding the division in that direction would position it for a quick northward march. Stoneman also signaled that the two brigades on the south bank would march on Jonesville. They expected to capture the town on April 1, while Palmer would take Elkin, opposite Jonesville. There, he was to camp and secure forage.[97]

With that, the march resumed at an easy pace. Since the rainy, muddy days had spread out the Second and Third brigades, the leisurely march allowed the column to close up. The raiders also scooped up the area's abundant forage. Thus, despite the obstinate river, Stoneman's Yadkin Valley detour was a success. The troopers even took time for other duties—specifically, an inspection. The division's inspector general reviewed the arms of the Eleventh Michigan to ensure readiness for anything that might come its way. The early halt also gave the men time to ponder their leaders' strategy. Like Beauregard, Johnston, and Stephen D. Lee, Stoneman's men assumed they would strike Salisbury, which was now within reach. Instead, Stoneman merely sent a few detachments toward different points on the North Carolina Railroad to create confusion.[98]

One such group, which included three companies of the Eleventh Kentucky Cavalry, rode into southern Yadkin and northern Iredell counties to burn the factories located along Hunting Creek. This was the industrial center of the region. Several cotton factories, including the Eagle Mills, Buck Shoals, and Troy facilities, went up in smoke, along with eight hundred bales of cotton and one thousand bushels of wheat at Eagle Mills alone. It was a lightning attack; the machines at Buck Shoals were still running when the match was applied. The troopers did pause long enough to share cloth with the workers before lighting the fire.[99]

Only Wilfred Turner's Turnersburg cotton mill escaped, even though the Kentuckians may have ridden within a half-mile of it. The reason for its safety is uncertain. According to one account, Turner asked Colonel S. A. Sharpe, commander of Iredell's Home Guardsmen, for help. Sharpe posted his men on a hill along Rocky Creek. The Home Guardsmen built breastworks and stacked cotton bales for protection, and this position may have dissuaded the Federals from making an attack. Another explanation has it that a local took a group of slave children to the raiders. "See these children?" he reportedly said. "If you burn that mill, you will take the bread out of their mouth." Yet another source claims that the Masonic ties of the defenders and the attackers saved the Turnersburg mill.[100]

North of the river, the First Brigade inched along the main Wilkesboro-to-Salem road. A local citizen by the name of John Wadkins guided it. A free, literate black man who owned property, Wadkins was a rare breed, but he was not exempt from confiscation. When some troopers took a horse from him, he complained to Palmer, who made a deal with him. If Wadkins would guide the raiders for a few days, he could have his horse back, or at least one of equal value. Wadkins agreed, so the march proceeded apace. The Tenth Michigan waited until about two in the afternoon to start and then moved twelve miles before camping. The Twelfth Ohio formed the rear guard and simply stayed in camp. The Fifteenth Pennsylvania covered about ten miles until reaching the Roaring River, another Yadkin tributary. Palmer hoped to press on, but the turbulent river lived up to its name. The Pennsylvanians were forced to bivouac on its banks. Frederic Antes spent the rest of the clear, pleasant day on picket duty. It passed quietly.[101]

Homeowners in the division's path reluctantly provided the needed supplies. James Gwyn, who owned a plantation between Wilkesboro and Elkin north of the river, was one example. He lost four mules, a mare, almost all of his cattle, and some corn and oats. A neighbor lost four oxen, a few other cows, and a handful of horses and mules. Fortunately, the Federals behaved well toward the locals. "I kept out of the way thinking I might be taken off a prisoner, but I need not have gone off, they would not have molested me," one man recalled. If the blue-clad raiders treated anyone poorly, it was the area's Unionist residents. They suffered as much as, if not more than, their Southern-sympathizing neighbors. Some of the "good Union folks in this Country . . . have had enough of Yankeys," Gwyn wrote.[102]

At Mallaby's signal station, the locals actually enjoyed the Federals' company. While the division marched east, the signalers stayed behind to keep communications open. They were happy to do so. "Two young ladies come down to the station and take a look through the field glass," Frankenberry wrote. "Think it is a lovely thing. The ladies are lovely, noble . . . and true to the dear old flag." The ladies, apparently motivated less by Unionist politics than by the prospect of getting a Northern dress, later invited the men to supper. The troopers accepted eagerly and were ushered into an environment that now seemed alien to them. First came the luxury of a washbowl. Then they sat in chairs and pulled up to a table covered with a clean tablecloth. On top of the table waited ham and eggs, sorghum molasses, butter, milk, and coffee with sugar and cream. It was like a dream. Indeed, although the men returned to work and kept the station open until eleven o'clock, they were invited to sleep on real beds for the night. The beds seemed awfully soft to the veteran campaigners.[103]

⁓⁓⁓

Back along the Tennessee–North Carolina state line, the other part of Stoneman's plan unfolded. Davis Tillson, his mind set on firmly plugging the key mountain gaps behind the raiders, put his men in motion the day after Stoneman secured Boone. Leaving Brabson's Mills, Tennessee, the Maine native steered his column toward the mouth of Roan Creek. From that strategic point about twenty-five miles from Boone and thirty miles from Jonesboro, Tillson could secure the approach routes to northwestern North Carolina from the interior of Tennessee and from Virginia. He arrived in early April.[104]

Meanwhile, in Palmer's camp, the sound of "Boots and Saddles" broke the early-morning stillness on April 1, 1865. Colonel Betts began day twelve of the raid by ordering his Pennsylvanians to once again test the Roaring River. This time, the raging stream proved fordable. Pickets were called in—one, Frederic Antes, was relieved at about nine that morning—and the eastward procession began anew. The day was pleasant and warm, the sky was clear, and the countryside made a favorable impression. Betts described it as "a very woody country, with few houses" and "a very barren country with but few inhabitants." H. K. Weand was particularly taken by the terrain: "On April 1st we marched through an immense pine forest. It was the finest piece of timber land I ever saw."[105]

By four o'clock, the Federals had put about ten miles of empty countryside behind them, and the quiet streets and modest buildings of Elkin were at hand. The town impressed one horseman as a "small but thriving" community that, fortunately for the raiders, was not thriving with Confederate defenders. On Big

Elkin Creek, a tributary of the Yadkin that flowed through town, sat the only structure of military value—the Elkin Manufacturing Company, a small cotton mill that had been in business for almost twenty years. Owned by the Gwyn family, it employed about sixty people, mostly young single women who boarded with local residents. The mill had manufactured Confederate uniforms for most of the war and so was conceivably a legitimate target.[106]

Forty-year-old Richard Ransome Gwyn managed the mill. A frail man who had not fought in the war, Gwyn tried to protect his operation. According to tradition, he met the Federals at the mouth of Big Elkin Creek and offered the hospitality of his home. He also offered to secure food for his guests. Palmer accepted and established his headquarters in Gwyn's home, which sat on a hill near the factory. The Pennsylvanian was apparently pleased by Gwyn's gesture and also by the fact that he was a fellow Mason. To this day, some say that Palmer placed a guard around the cotton mill to prevent its destruction.[107]

The men enjoyed their visit to Big Elkin Creek, particularly the opportunity to fraternize with the factory's female employees, who welcomed the visitors with "quite a reception." Flirting became the main pastime at the mill. Meanwhile, the men found ample supplies inside the factory, the local general store, and a nearby gristmill. Quartermasters lost no time in seizing and distributing bacon, flour, butter, honey, lard, molasses, chestnuts, and tobacco. It was a case of perfect timing, since rations had not been issued in a week. The only problem was finding the time to prepare the food. A Pennsylvanian wrote, "We miss our 'hard-tack' very much, now that it is all gone. In place of it flour and cornmeal are issued, which usually is mixed with water and fried, but if we stop long enough the colored women bake it for us, and how good it tastes!"[108]

Palmer recognized that the haul at the mill would not satiate his ravenous brigade, so he sought other food sources. He found a couple of other mills in the area, put them to work, and soon had three mills grinding meal. His troopers also added about five hundred bales of cotton to the list of captures.[109]

Thanks to these foraging successes, the people of Elkin suffered comparatively less than their neighbors in Wilkes and Watauga counties. Old man Dickie Gwyn, Richard's father, was one of the few who made an unwilling contribution to the cause. Federal troopers took all the corn, fodder, and straw from his home, Cedar Point, which sat on a hill west of Big Elkin Creek. The raiders did not molest Gwyn's bacon or horses, and his cattle escaped as well. Thus satisfied, the Federals camped for the night in and around Elkin.[110]

Mallaby's Signal Corps unit, still divided by the river, did its job and kept communications open. The signalers south of the Yadkin left the Wilkesboro area at seven-thirty and reached Jonesville around noon. Meanwhile, across the river, the flagmen said goodbye to their lady friends, but only after enjoying a good breakfast and picking up horses to replace the ones they had left on the other side of the river. These cavalrymen also followed the Yadkin River eastward, crossed the Roaring River at a deep ford, and finally caught up with the Tenth Michigan. By one o'clock, the two detachments were able to raise their flags again and start sending messages. When suppertime rolled around, Frankenberry took a break. Camping beside Palmer's headquarters near the Elkin factory, the Pennsylvanian tore into a supper of fried meat and a large biscuit. As he ate, he listened to the mill grinding away and admired the hundreds of bales of cotton stacked nearby.[111]

Also below the Yadkin, Stoneman's Second and Third brigades mirrored Palmer's march with their own eastward jaunt. The Thirteenth Tennessee's regimental history records the day's march: "April 1st we passed through a fine section of country and remembered that a year ago we were in Middle Tennessee, and now we were in the land of pine and tar, 'of cotton seed and sandy bottom.' It was 'All Fools Day' but we had no time for foolishness. We passed through Jonesville, but did not see Mr. Jones,—suppose he 'had gone and runned away.'" As Miller's and Brown's regiments camped around Jonesville, they found the area rich with food and forage. "We have plenty to eat now," commented an Eleventh Michigan trooper.[112]

Although few cavalrymen actually stayed in town, some nevertheless paid a visit to Jonesville. Incorporated in 1811, Jonesville was one of the oldest towns in western North Carolina. In 1860, about 200 people had lived there, not including the 125 or so students attending the Jonesville Academy. Federal troopers gravitated to the school, where they gathered food and also broke a few chandeliers and fixtures and destroyed or scattered some lab equipment. They even searched for the headmaster, who was nowhere to be found. Some observers believed that the academy's decline began when Stoneman came calling.[113]

Otherwise, all was quiet around Jonesville. Most of the cavalrymen probably spent their free time resting. They had ample reason; two hundred miles or more lay behind them, and many more lay ahead. The Tennesseans felt confident that their next stop would be Virginia. They were dead right. The river was showing signs of letup, and hopes rose that it would be fordable by tomorrow. After lunch, Gillem ordered Palmer to march to Rockford beginning at seven-thirty the next morning. The remainder of the division would follow. At nine o'clock that night, Stoneman directed Palmer to stretch a ferryboat rope across the river so it could be tried at dawn. He also ordered a cavalryman to attempt the river, but the horse floundered and was slow to recover. Stoneman furiously ordered the man out of the river, shouting that the damn fool would have drowned his horse. There would be no river crossing that night.[114]

Lieutenant Colonel Charles Betts thought that the plan of the campaign changed dramatically on Sunday, April 2. According to the Pennsylvanian, a minister shared information straight from Richmond suggesting that Robert E. Lee planned to give up the Southern capital and march to Pennsylvania. This, Betts recalled, prompted Stoneman to strike at the rail lines in southwestern Virginia instead of marching east to join Sherman. This story, however, has no basis in fact. As Ohioan Frank Mason recalled, not even Stoneman's brigade commanders understood their leader's plans. The only change that occurred on April 2 was that the Yadkin River finally became fordable. At last, Stoneman could carry out George H. Thomas's March 18 order directing him to capture Christiansburg. From that point, Stoneman could destroy railroad track and drop bridges on the East Tennessee and Virginia Railroad and even threaten Lynchburg.[115]

The division therefore went to work. Per Gillem's instructions, Palmer dispatched men to Rockford early on April 2. Extant records do not say how much of his brigade went, but there is no doubt that the town felt the presence of Union troopers that day. Septimus Knight of the Fifteenth Pennsylvania Cavalry was probably among the group. According to his field diary, he left Elkin at eight o'clock that morning. The march began like any other; as the column wound its way toward Rockford, the men kept their eyes open for anything that could help their cause, including replacement horses.[116]

A ride of about eleven miles brought the Federals to Rockford. Formerly the proud seat of Surry County, the once-prosperous town had played host to the likes of James K. Polk, Aaron Burr, and Andrew Jackson. But Rockford was now in decline; fifteen years earlier, the county seat had moved to Dobson. Only Rockford's location along the Yadkin made it important to Stoneman. While the division turned northward, a strong presence in Rockford would provide a strategic bulwark against any threats to the Federal rear and flank. A rumor suggested that the Rockford Home Guard tried to defend the town, but this was false. The only action the locals took—as was true throughout much of Surry—was to hide animals and bury valuables.[117]

Federal outriders also made their way to Siloam, another Surry County community, where violence erupted. Lieutenant Colonel William Luffman, commander of the Eleventh Georgia Infantry Regiment, was recuperating from a wound at the home of Major R. E. Reeves, another Confederate veteran. Early on April 2, the Spring Place, Georgia, native was taking a bath when he and his host heard a ruckus in the yard. Luffman looked outside and saw a knot of Federal troopers. "Great heavens, Major, the Yankees are upon us!" Luffman yelled. Grabbing his carbine, the colonel ran outside and saw a Federal sitting on Luffman's own horse.

Ordered to surrender, Luffman declined, pulled the trigger, and shot the man dead. The other Federals in the yard opened fire, as did Reeves, who had joined Luffman. The two Rebels were quickly outgunned. After emptying a carbine, two double-barreled shotguns, and four revolvers between them, Reeves and Luffman retreated through a back door. They managed to escape by hiding in the Yadkin River, leaving only their nostrils exposed above the water. As a consolation, the troopers did capture eighteen-year-old John Hardy, another resident. They also threatened to burn the Reeves home but relented when Mrs. Reeves promised to bury their comrade. The man's final resting place was atop a nearby hill.[118]

Dobson was the objective of the rest of the Cavalry Division, but Brown's and Miller's brigades had to get across the Yadkin first. Using the ferryboat rope strung the night before, the separated regiments carefully pushed into the obstinate river. The waters were almost too deep for the troopers' horses, but the Tennessee, Kentucky, and Michigan men crossed without incident. The river remained too high for the artillery and ambulances to ford, so some enterprising scavengers impressed a few boats. It took time, but before the morning expired the division was reunited for the first time since March 28.[119]

The rest of the division marched for Dobson as well, but in a more leisurely fashion because it did not have to cross the river. The journey was not pleasant, however. "In the Woods generally all day[.] Very poor country for forage," one man noted. In the Twelfth Ohio, Joseph Banks complained about wet weather, mountainous roads, and his horse, which "fell on me and hurt me badly." Stoneman himself may have had trouble on the trip as well. According to local legend, the New Yorker rode in a buggy because of his hemorrhoids. This is neither corroborated nor discounted by Federal sources but cannot be ruled out, since Stoneman's malady plagued him on every raid he led during the war.[120]

The cavalrymen were unimpressed with Dobson. As a member of the Thirteenth Tennessee remembered, it was "not a very pretentious village." However, that did not keep some troopers from making mischief. According to local tradition, Federal horse soldiers rode into town and demanded money and records from the county clerk. When the man refused, they decided to have a little fun by donning clothes belonging to the clerk's wife. Thus attired, they marched around the courthouse, doubtless to the catcalls and insults of their comrades and the horror of the locals. Another man dissuaded the Federals from visiting his home by telling them that his children were sick with scarlet fever. The raiders, unwilling to test the truth of this claim, rode on. It is also said that the Federals dumped a wagonload of silver and other valuables into the Fisher River because they needed the wagon for forage. For years, residents dug silverware out of the river.[121]

Mount Airy, nestled along the North Carolina–Virginia line, was the division's final goal for the day. Notable as the home of the famous Siamese twins Eng and Chang Bunker, Mount Airy added another important chapter to its history on April 2. Federal cavalrymen began arriving after dark and continued to come all night long. They rode into town along Main Street and soon found, to their chagrin, that cautious residents had hidden their horses and valuables. One family buried a silver candlestick in the stable yard. The Federals never found it, although they came close and dented it when horses trampled over the burial spot. A local youth rashly bragged about the residents' clever preparations. He told the horse soldiers that they could not find his daddy's liquor "cause he had it hid!"[122]

Like Dobson, Mount Airy struck the observant Pennsylvanian Weand as a "very ordinary" village. Even so, the men sought some unusual diversions. A few troopers amused themselves by raiding the post office and reading the "liberated" letters. Others paid a call on the Siamese twins. Born on May 11, 1811, near Bangkok, Siam, the two had spent much of their lives as entertainers, gaining worldwide fame in the process. During their travels, the twins had fallen in love with western North Carolina and now lived there. In an attempt to shield the twins, Stoneman ordered his men to leave the Bunkers' property alone. At least one trooper disobeyed by grabbing a Bunker daughter while the twins and their children sat on a porch. The young lady slapped her captor, and the trooper sheepishly released her while his comrades laughed at him.[123]

With Mount Airy now secure, the column was closed up except for the Tennesseans, who did not arrive until daylight the next morning. The Cavalry Division bivouacked, its camps stretching from Mount Airy to about three miles outside town. In one camp, word was passed that the march would resume at two in the morning, so the men snatched what sleep they could.[124] Some fared better than others; Frank Frankenberry put his horse in a barn and then got a room at the local hotel. The troopers remained in camp the next day. Some would stay until Monday evening at sundown.[125]

The day's work was not yet done for some cavalrymen. The Federals learned that a Rebel wagon train bursting with supplies had left Mount Airy at three o'clock that afternoon, bound for Hillsville. Palmer could not ignore a plum like that, so he ordered a detachment to capture the train. Captain C. J. Mather took sixty men from Company F of the Fifteenth Pennsylvania Cavalry and rode northward in pursuit.[126]

About fifty miles to the east, the hospitality of Greensboro did not distract General Beauregard, who spent the early days of April trying to guess the raiders' intentions. News from far and wide placed them in spots as varied as Jonesville, Mount Airy, Hickory Station, Huntsville, and even Wytheville. There was even a rumor that famed cavalryman Benjamin Grierson was involved. The countryside was filled with uncertainty. "Considerable excitement naturally pervaded this community, and at this writing . . . we know nothing definite of the whereabouts of Stoneman's forces," reported the *People's Press*, a Salem newspaper. Still, the editor had a good grasp on the Federals' progress. He accurately traced them as they moved east from Caldwell County, the bulk of the force operating south of the Yadkin and a few hundred men on the north side. Finally, word came that the raiders had left Mount Airy bound for Hillsville.[127]

Beauregard considered the reports unreliable and wished he had cavalry to peer through the haze. But the Creole realized he had to make an educated guess. "Enemy will probably move on this place [Greensboro] and Piedmont

Railroad or on Danville, keeping north of Dan River," he wrote. That assessment called for a change in his dispositions, but therein lay a problem. "I have not sufficient force," he told General Lee, "to guard well at same time this place, Salisbury, and Danville." The only solution was to shift his strength where it was most needed. On April 1, Beauregard ordered Featherston's brigade, two light artillery batteries, and the newly arrived brigades of Brigadier Generals Charles M. Shelley and Daniel C. Govan to Greensboro. Shelley and Govan had about one thousand men each. Just in case, Beauregard instructed Featherston to "push up troops rapidly as possible, and look out for him [Stoneman] on way to Greensborough." If necessary, Featherston could stop at Lexington or High Point if those towns appeared threatened. McAllister's detachment was also ordered to Lexington to bolster its defenses. Beauregard even worried about the North Carolina Railroad repair facilities at Company Shops east of Greensboro, so he asked Governor Vance to summon troops to defend them. At Smithfield, Joe Johnston did what he could to help his subordinate. "I am sending all I can to meet Stoneman," he wrote Beauregard.[128]

Troops now began to leave Salisbury as quickly as they had arrived. As a precaution, about three thousand men remained. Construction also continued on defenses around the Yadkin River bridge.[129] Even so, Salisbury was now vulnerable. The strategic implications of uncovering the town in favor of points northward would not become apparent for another eleven days.

Greensboro benefited from the weakening of Salisbury's defenses. The city was an important supply depot and the junction of the Piedmont Railroad, which connected Greensboro with Danville and Richmond, and the North Carolina Railroad, which linked Greensboro with Raleigh and Charlotte. These were the last rail lines serving both Lee's and Johnston's armies. Greensboro also housed state and Confederate storehouses containing important quartermaster and ordnance supplies, military hospitals, and commissary stores. It was a town the Confederacy had to save. By April 2, three infantry brigades and two artillery batteries arrived and Beauregard began to devise a "system of light defensive works" on the city's outskirts. Just in case, he ordered Greensboro's post commander to be prepared to evacuate.[130]

Danville was equally valuable as a rail center and lifeline, principally for Lee's embattled army. Its importance grew when crushing news came on April 2: Robert E. Lee was evacuating Petersburg and Richmond. Jefferson Davis and other Confederate government officials left the doomed Confederate capital that night on a special train bound for Danville. Alarmed, Beauregard took steps to reinforce the weak garrison there. He directed Shelley to take his infantry brigade to Danville and requested three artillery batteries from Hillsborough, but he was not sure they would arrive in time.[131]

The news from every quarter was bad. Nowhere did the Confederacy have the resources to respond to multiplying crises. Stoneman was running loose in western North Carolina, Sherman was threatening Raleigh, and Richmond had fallen. "When this sad news reached General Beauregard . . . he was bitterly grieved; all the more, because he saw what the necessary result must now be," wrote his nephew and biographer, Alfred Roman, who served on his uncle's staff. Yet Beauregard determined to "uphold the cause until the last hour."[132]

By all measures, he did just that, and did it remarkably well with the resources at hand. No one could have done more. Had the raiders attacked Salisbury, Greensboro, or Danville in late March, they would have met stern resistance. But George Stoneman had other targets in mind.

Chapter 4
Glory Enough for One Day
Virginia: April 3–9, 1865

Thirty-eight-year-old Edwin T. Clemmons, his servant Ike beside him, rode through the gathering gloom. The owner and operator of a Forsyth County stagecoach line, Clemmons normally transported mail and passengers throughout western and central North Carolina. On this day, however, he was traveling home from Wytheville, Virginia, where he had purchased horses and goods. His coach creaked and his draft horses puffed under a heavy load of salt, leather, and other commodities. Suddenly, just north of Mount Airy, drab routine vanished in a cloud of dust as Captain Mather and sixty mounted warriors surrounded Clemmons's stagecoach. Ignoring the contents of the wagon, the troopers exchanged some of their played-out mounts for Clemmons's comparatively fresh horses. The Federals also tried to persuade Ike to join them. They even tempted him with a wagon, horse, saddle, bridle, and weapons, but Ike declined. "I knew Masse Ed but I didn't know de soldiers, so I stuck to the boss," he later explained. In parting, the Federals boasted that they would be in Salisbury in about two weeks. Then they left the two stunned men, their loaded wagon, and the spent horses on the side of the road.[1]

Mather and his raiders kept riding, hoping to catch the tempting Rebel wagon train, as Palmer had ordered. However, when they reached the top of

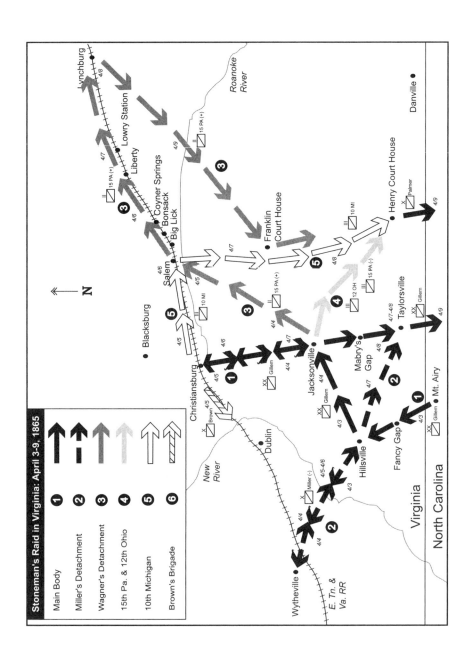

the Blue Ridge at Fancy Gap, Virginia, the captain decided to stop and wait for the rest of the division. Perhaps the detachment's horses could go no farther. Perhaps they could not trace the fleeing train in the darkness. Why they halted remains unclear, but Mather would come to regret his decision.[2]

A red sun announced the dawning of April 3, 1865. Behind Mather, the Blue Ridge Mountains barred the way of the Cavalry Division of East Tennessee. The column got an early start—some men marched at two o'clock—and left Mount Airy for the thin air and high country. The direction of the march surprised Michigan trooper Steven Thomas. He wrote his wife, "It soon became apparent that we were not going to Salisbury at present for we struck out in the direction of Virginia."[3]

It was about six-thirty in the morning when Betts led the Fifteenth Pennsylvania Cavalry across the state line. "Pass the Virginia line and now we are on the sacred soil," wrote one trooper. The raiders ascended to Fancy Gap without incident. At about ten o'clock, Betts encountered Mather's recalcitrant detachment roughly four miles from Hillsville. Betts was furious that Mather had not captured the train. "His conduct in not capturing a wagon train is inexcusable and he was placed under arrest," the angry colonel reported.[4]

To finish what had been left undone, Betts ordered Lieutenant Samuel Phillips after the train. Phillips took Companies G and E and galloped off. They met with speedy success. Near Hillsville, the Federal troopers spotted and cornered the wagon train. After a brief fight, the blue-clad raiders captured the prize. "I had charge of the advance. We killed one rebel," trooper Antes wrote in his diary. The number of wagons captured remains uncertain. Most Federal sources claim twenty-two, but Gillem's report cited only seventeen wagons and one forge. Regardless of the total, the conveyances furnished a much-needed supply of forage. The troopers burned the empty wagons and turned over the animals to the quartermaster.[5]

After navigating Fancy Gap, the column stopped to feed and then set its sights on Hillsville, the seat of Carroll County, Virginia. April 3 marked the first time that an organized body of Union soldiers had penetrated this part of Virginia, and the locals trembled. "There was much apprehension and alarm among the citizens as to the treatment they might receive at our hands," a veteran recalled. As advance guard, the Fifteenth Pennsylvania introduced the locals to Mr. Lincoln's army.[6]

Described by the raiders as a "little village" and a "quiet inland town,"

Hillsville did not welcome the cavalrymen warmly. A young disabled man by the name of Burnett, mounted on a gray mare, met them outside town, gun in hand. He came determined to fight, but one look at the fearsome, dust-covered warriors changed his mind. Burnett kicked his mount's flanks and tried to get away, but a Pennsylvanian shot his horse. Now dismounted, the young man crawled into a culvert under the road. He held his breath and hoped to avoid discovery, but the Federals found his hiding place. The troopers pulled the young man out and ordered him to lead the advance.[7]

Other local defenders waited at Hillsville itself. On May 14, 1862, the General Assembly of Virginia had passed an act authorizing citizens of each county to form Home Guard companies. These men generally served as local policemen and arrested deserters. Like North Carolina's Home Guardsmen, they were unpaid but exempt from front-line military duty. They even furnished their own weapons. One such defensive force was waiting at Hillsville when Federal troopers arrived about one o'clock that afternoon. The untested Virginians did not realize the power of the approaching enemy force. When a sharp skirmish erupted, two Virginians died before the Home Guardsmen "got out of the way," as one Federal described it. The retreating guards left behind a healthy supply of flour, butter, tobacco, and other goods—a welcome haul for cavalrymen with empty stomachs. Some Kentuckians also captured a printing press and made sure it would not be used to promote the Confederacy again.[8]

James Wilkinson, a Confederate quartermaster who was in town to buy supplies and return paroled men to their commands, had a different opinion on how to deal with the invasion. When word of the raid came, Wilkinson counseled residents to stay at home. He assumed that the raiders would be interested only in horses and food. Many followed Wilkinson's advice; even the proprietor of the gristmill kept grinding on April 3. But A. M. Hale, the clerk of the circuit court, chose to do otherwise, loading the court records and deed books into a wagon and fleeing. Some Pennsylvanians captured him and destroyed the wagon and its contents. At least that is what the locals later told John W. Eckman, one of Stoneman's cavalrymen. After the war, Eckman purchased property in Carroll County and endured constant litigation because of the missing records.[9]

Stoneman and Palmer arrived at Hillsville after Betts's men. They stopped at the well in the center of Main Street to quench their thirst. Then Stoneman made his headquarters at Wilkinson's home, next to the courthouse, and considered his next move. The New Yorker was determined to fulfill his orders to the

letter, so Christiansburg remained his primary objective. Nearby secondary objectives—those suggested by Thomas, Sherman, and Grant—included the lead
mines near Wytheville; the depots, bridges, culverts, and tracks of the East Tennessee and Virginia Railroad; and Lynchburg and Danville. To threaten these
many targets, Stoneman resumed his practice of sending detachments in every
direction. Each fragment was to do as much damage and create as much terror
as possible—and to do it quickly because other targets, including Greensboro,
Salisbury, and Charlotte, still beckoned.[10]

Soon after setting up his headquarters, Stoneman dispatched his first detachment, ordering Colonel Miller to take five hundred men from the Eighth
and Thirteenth Tennessee to Wytheville. Their goal was to cut the railroad,
demolish key bridges around the town, and destroy the lead mines. Doubtless
pleased to receive detached duty for the second time during the raid, Miller
quickly gathered his men. They left at dusk.[11]

As the Tennesseans filed northward in the twilight, a few units, including
part of the Fifteenth Pennsylvania and the entire Tenth Michigan, camped for
the night around Hillsville. The rest of the division headed for Christiansburg.
From Hillsville, the men rode northeast toward Jacksonville, some at a gallop.
Most troopers did not stop until well after midnight. A few incidents kept the
march lively. "Shortly after dark," Gillem reported, "our advance came upon a
force of rebels, which was charged and driven several miles." Later, troopers
found a factory and destroyed the machinery but left the building intact. Elsewhere, several companies passed by the home of a man named Chopin. The
drunken man stumbled out of his house and ordered the Federals to halt. When
they ignored him, Chopin pulled a gun, but he was shot down before he could
open fire. A few men dismounted and carried him inside. He later recovered.[12]

Late in the day, a fresh spring rain drenched the men. "It rained in torren[ts]
and became so dark that we were compeled to stop in the road," Private Banks
recalled. Lieutenant Colonel Charles Betts recorded the time of the halt as 2:00 A.M.
Having logged over forty miles, the tired and hungry troopers dismounted at
last, sought shelter, and broke out their bedrolls and food. Even their horses got
a treat when somebody discovered a Rebel depot filled with hay.[13]

⚓

Though relatively small-scale, Stoneman's Raid was growing in impact.

Every soldier Beauregard posted along the railroad from Chester to Danville was one denied to the severely undermanned Army of Tennessee. Far to the rear, George Thomas was still puzzled by Stoneman's detour to Wilkesboro. He complained more to Henry W. Halleck but speculated that something good would come of it. "I think," Thomas mused, "it will have an important effect on Johnston's movement." Stoneman's subsequent move into southwestern Virginia also complicated the projected retreat of the Army of Northern Virginia from Richmond and Petersburg. Lee wanted to join Johnston in North Carolina, but the presence of enemy cavalry on his flank in southwestern Virginia endangered such a move.[14]

For his part, Beauregard had no choice but to juggle his forces in response to the fluid situation. Following the fall of Richmond and the evacuation of the Confederate government, Danville became the new focus of his efforts. Jefferson Davis and his cabinet arrived there late in the afternoon on April 3 after a long, slow train ride from Richmond. A town of about five thousand residents, Danville was a cotton and tobacco center. It was also the junction of the Richmond & Danville Railroad and the Piedmont Railroad and the site of a Confederate arsenal. Davis learned that nearby telegraph lines had been cut, Stoneman was approaching, Sherman was threatening Raleigh, and Grant was pursuing Lee westward through Virginia. Yet he remained defiant. He decided to establish his capital at Danville, hoping to assemble Lee's and Johnston's armies nearby. He ordered troops to work on the city's defenses.[15]

Davis also ordered Beauregard to Danville to personally supervise construction of its defenses. Although the Creole never made it there, he recognized the growing danger to the city. He therefore ordered to Danville Shelly's Brigade from Greensboro and a battalion under Colonel Matthew R. Hall, as well as Ferguson's Brigade of cavalry from Salisbury. Beauregard also ordered General Featherston to send his "best organized Brigade" by rail to Danville. To replace Featherston's men, Beauregard sent a fresh contingent to take a position "immediately in front of the Enemy under Stoneman, and seize all transportation for public use that is likely to fall into the hands of the enemy. For the present you are confined to Stokes, Rockingham, Guilford, and Forsyth Counties." Colonel McAllister's detachment also left its Yadkin River bridge position and rode by rail to Danville.[16]

A worried Jefferson Davis kept the telegraph lines hot, asking Beauregard about the status of the enemy and General Lee. However, Beauregard was beginning to feel confident in his defense. "I consider railroad from Chester to Danville safe, at present," he wrote. The problem was that Stoneman's intentions remained unclear. "The reports in regard to raiders very contradictory," Davis complained.[17] "No definite information of Stoneman's movements. Reports thus far vague and unreliable," Beauregard agreed. He wanted cavalry reinforcements to penetrate the fog and therefore asked Major General Joseph Wheeler to bring his cavalry corps to Danville. Beauregard later decided that was overkill, since Sam Ferguson's cavalry brigade was on the way. However, one additional horse regiment was dispatched to Danville—the Sixth Tennessee (First Tennessee) Cavalry, commanded by Colonel James T. Wheeler. Beauregard ordered Colonel Wheeler to place his regiment "on the right flank of the enemy, between his column & Danville."[18]

<hr/>

April 4 dawned dry and clear. "Boots and Saddles" brought the Federals tumbling out of their blankets at daybreak. They had no time for breakfast; officers ordered everybody into the saddle immediately. Stoneman wanted to get to Jacksonville, a village about forty-five miles northwest of Danville, as quickly as possible.[19]

At about six o'clock that morning, the weary cavalrymen began the third week of the raid. Fortunately, the scenery helped some to forget their empty stomachs. "Beautiful country through this valley," Septimus Knight noted. Not everybody in the column was comfortable, however, especially the Tenth Michigan's Eber Hendricks, whose foot was still sore from the coffeepot accident back at Deep Gap. "It is with great discomfort [that I] keep my place in the ranks," he complained.[20]

Rumors of the approaching raiders swept the countryside. In response, blacks ran away and whites hid their valuables. Everyone chattered or whispered nervously. At his Jacksonville home, young Waitman Stigleman realized something was wrong when his father passed him in the hall without noticing him. "He was very pale and had a look on his face which frightened me," Stigleman recalled. Entering the room his father had just left, he found his mother crying. She ran to her son and held him close. "The news has been brought to your father that the Yankees are coming," she said. "They will burn up the town and take everything we have. They are welcome, if they just spare my husband."[21]

The boy's father, Colonel William Stigleman, was the highest-ranking officer in Floyd County. He planned to meet the raiders and formally surrender Jacksonville. Unfortunately for the locals, there was a complication. As some Federal cavalrymen approached the town, a dozen young men fired on them. "This had inflamed the Yankees. They were terribly incensed," young Stigleman recorded. The angered troopers returned the favor, killing Confederate lieutenant James Madison Howard. The rest of the Rebels retreated, chased by the Federal contingent. In town, Unionist citizens trembled.[22]

Their concern proved unfounded. According to a Pennsylvanian, the Federals found their encounter with the peace delegation "rather an amusing experience." He explained, "We were met by two professional men, a lawyer and a doctor, with a flag of truce, to surrender the town to us. It looked rather ridiculous, as we were asking no favors. They and their people were very agreeably disappointed when they found we were not doing as their papers had told them we were."[23]

But there was still the matter of the retreating bushwhackers. Jacksonville braced for the anticipated storm. Men, women, and children gathered atop the hill before the courthouse. Lookouts stationed at the courthouse dome and the church steeple scanned the horizon with telescopes. Soon, they sounded the alarm. "Ah, well do I remember that fearful sound! Soon all heard the clanging of the courthouse bell, followed by the ringing of all the church bells," wrote Stigleman. Then they saw an awesome sight: "The great army was first seen two miles west of town, coming down Bishop's hill. In the fields on each side of this long line of troops were scattered bodies of men on foot. These were the camp followers, deserters, runaway negroes, thieves and robbers. They were setting fire to hay stacks, barns and fences, burning homes and all buildings where the owners were absent or could not pay the heavy ransom. They were trying to destroy the last vestige of sustenance of the almost starving people. Silently, for no sound at that distance came from the advancing hosts, like a great black serpent, the long lines of the army slowly crept along."[24]

Onlookers could mark the enemy's approach by the columns of smoke rising above the hills and woods, as well as by more obvious indicators. "Several young men of the Home Guard, running for their lives, dashed through town, spurring and urging their horses to greater speed," Stigleman recalled. "They were followed by Yankee soldiers lying low on their horses and firing their carbines at the fleeing youths, their tired horses plunging through the deep mud." Federal cavalryman Frederic Antes of the Fifteenth Pennsylvania led the pursuit. "I charged through the town with 8 men but did not capture any one," he wrote. More cavalrymen followed. According to Frank Mason of the Twelfth Ohio, his regiment "swept through the town like a whirlwind."[25]

Afterward, Antes's contingent and those that followed took a break in the pretty village to feed their horses. The ladies of Jacksonville came out and treated their guests with kindness.[26] Spellbound, young Stigleman took all this in; no other source verifies his recollections, but they ring true despite being romanticized. The boy saw an old man holding a long staff with a large white flag on it. He saw his father emerge from his office, mount his horse, and take the flag from the old man. The elder Stigleman's sword hung at his side, but his head was bowed and he looked sad. "My father rode up the street, holding the flag aloft. It waved from side to side grandly, glistening," the boy recalled. As he rode, Stigleman told passing citizens to go home and stay there.[27]

Jacksonville was soon occupied in force, as described by young Stigleman: "Blue men, brass buttons and horses. The town was alive with them. . . . A broad dense array of blue cavalry, the tramping horses, the noise of marching hosts, the military trappings and trimmings, and steel and brass, the waving plume and red stripes, and over all, the flags, and in front the great white flag . . . As they came to our alley that blue mass of men divided half and half. Down the center they rode, and in their pomp and pride following their General, they rode up our alley. Fences were broken down, and soon our stable lot, garden clover lot and back yard were filled with men and horses."[28]

Stoneman and his staff stopped at Stigleman's house to eat. The boy remembered Stoneman as "a large man covered with gold lace and military decorations, a white plume flowing from a broad brimmed hat." A commanding presence, the general walked into the parlor, took off his belt, and laid his pistols on the center table. He remained undisturbed there until a servant complained about some stolen property. Stoneman ordered guards placed both outside and inside the house.

Frank Frankenberry thought Jacksonville a pretty place and enjoyed the chance to see the "lovely daughters of the Old Dominion." More mundane affairs had to be attended to, however, so he dismounted at a house to feed his horse, have his coat mended, and get breakfast. While a comrade took their rations inside to cook them, Frankenberry guided their horses to the stable. He was headed for the corncrib when a more interesting sight caught his eye: freshly churned earth. Since the spot was too small for a grave, Frankenberry started digging. He found a small tin box containing the record book and money of the local Confederate tax collector.

Frankenberry went inside, where an elderly lady and her two not-so-young daughters were preparing breakfast. The women mixed their own cornmeal with water and baked it. They also fried the ham and boiled the potatoes the Federals had brought. A pot of coffee completed the fare. When everyone was full, Frankenberry produced his newly found treasure and offered the ladies Confederate bonds for their trouble. This failed to impress his hosts. "We'uns don't like that ar money, but we'uns likes you'ns money the best," the elderly lady said. Lacking the preferred greenbacks, Frankenberry sheepishly handed over more Confederate bonds and left with his comrade.[29]

Other citizens had similar encounters with the raiders. Elijah W. Hylton, who lived with his children on his six-hundred-acre farm near Jacksonville, was a Dunkard who had harbored deserters and given information to Federal forces. That did not stop the raiders from taking what they needed from his farm. Stopping at the stable, two men abandoned their worn-out horses and put their saddles on a pair of Hylton's mounts. A soldier told Hylton that the army was obliged to have the horses. The raiders also took two hundred pounds of bacon and thirty bushels of corn, whereupon someone at last identified Hylton as a Dunkard and a Union man. An officer ordered the cavalrymen out of the house, posted a guard, and then advised Hylton to hide what he could. The guard remained from sunup to two that afternoon.[30]

Throughout the morning, Stoneman's units streamed into Jacksonville. Some, including the Signal Corps detachment, spent the afternoon there before resuming the march. Reagan's artillery also arrived and camped until after dark. Others including the Twelfth Ohio Cavalry followed the Christiansburg road a few miles beyond town. Trooper Joseph Banks was not with the Twelfth, however. His day began with misfortune when his horse gave out, forcing Banks to walk. A comrade, Phil Barch, found himself in the same predicament. The two men were soon far behind the division. They began to worry about bushwhackers, especially after they found the corpse of Lieutenant Howard at the site of the skirmish just outside town. "About 10 A.M. my companion and I were walking along the side of the road and driving our Horses before us (for they could scarcely carry us at all)[. W]e suddenly came upon the form of a *dead reble officer* which had not been dead long and whose pockets were all turned rong side out,"

Banks wrote. Fortunately, they reached Jacksonville safely and found the command "snugly incamped" just beyond town. After feeding their horses, Banks and Barch enjoyed a supper of pork, slapjacks, and molasses.[31]

The break was all too brief, as fresh objectives awaited. Gillem and Stoneman had most of the troopers back in the saddle again by seven that night. Before the march resumed, Stoneman designated another detachment for separate duty. This detachment would be the smallest of all, yet it faced the most daunting task. Taking 230 men, Major William Wagner was to march to Salem, Virginia, and destroy the railroad as far east as possible. Wagner would head toward Lynchburg, a large, well-guarded town that appeared to lie in the path of the retreating Army of Northern Virginia. He started immediately. As the brave band rode off, some in the main column wondered if they would ever see Wagner and his men again.[32]

Less Miller's and Wagner's detachments, the rest of the division continued north. Christiansburg had seemed so distant when the units left Knoxville fifteen days ago, but it was now just eighteen miles away.[33]

Stoneman and Gillem pushed on through the night. The march must not have been very memorable; in the Tenth Michigan's morning report, the regimental clerk wrote only that the raiders were "on the march." At First Brigade headquarters, Angelo Wiser noted a bit more detail in his map book. It was unfamiliar country, so the troopers drafted citizens to guide them in the darkness. Nonetheless, the black night and exhaustion made the trip a challenge. Recalled a Pennsylvanian, "It was a most miserable nights march and I was asleep fifty times."[34]

Joseph Banks probably enjoyed the march more than anyone else. Thanks to some forage and a few hours' rest, his horse had recovered, enabling Banks to fall in with his comrades. He boasted that his mount "carried me nobely through mud and I was in good spirrits all night [f]or I had a Canteen of whiskey at my side (*Apple Jack*)." Another Twelfth Ohio cavalryman, Frank Mason, had a more sober reaction to the journey. "The march, though exciting to the last degree, had been a weary and trying one," he wrote. By his calculation, the men had marched more than six hundred miles—roughly twice the actual distance from Knoxville.[35]

Established in 1792, Christiansburg rested on a plateau of rich limestone soil two thousand feet above sea level. The mountains that surrounded the town like sentries proved unable to obstruct the advance guard's entry. Lieutenant Charles S. Hinchman commanded the lead detachment from the ubiquitous Fifteenth Pennsylvania. As Christiansburg's defenders slumbered, Hinchman's men made their way quickly and quietly to the telegraph office, located inside a freight car. An operator was working there. Hoping to gather intelligence, the Federals broke in and captured the Rebel. Hinchman then turned the show over to John J. Wickham, the young telegraph operator who had stumbled over a sleeping Myles Keogh in Tennessee. Forcing the Confederate operator to continue working, Wickham engaged in a lengthy conversation with the operator at Lynchburg. When he asked about Rebel forces in the area, the truth dawned on the operator at the other end of the line. "I'm talking to the Yankees now," he typed. A barrage of curse words followed. Wickham accepted the dressing down in stride but bristled when the Lynchburg operator condemned the captured Christiansburg operator. "But here Wickham stopped him and wired back that he should not blame him, as a fellow with a pistol at his head is apt to say just what the fellow who holds the pistol wants him to say," a regimental historian recounted. Then the line went dead, and the operator thanked Wickham for coming to his defense.[36]

One of Stoneman's staff officers recalled this event differently. As Federal forces dashed into town, the staff officer recalled, Stoneman himself went to the telegraph office. Finding it abandoned but in perfect order, he had someone take over the key and began dictating messages. The Lynchburg operator quickly became suspicious. "How are you, Yanks?" he asked.

"You must be drunk, there are no Yanks anywhere about here," Stoneman replied.

"What has become of the Yankees you have been telegraphing about all day as approaching?" Lynchburg asked.

"Oh that was nothing but country rumors, and were found to be false," Stoneman answered.

In reply, the Lynchburg operator lectured the Christiansburg station about spreading rumors. He concluded by transmitting several messages of some importance. One stated, "During the day it has been reported through town that Sheridan was coming this way, but no one believes it now." Another message aroused Stoneman's interest even more, since it described planned Rebel movements to the west. Soon, the line went dead.[37]

These accounts are difficult to reconcile. Exactly what happened in the telegraph car will never be known. However, the accounts and the testimony of other witnesses make it clear that a telegraph exchange occurred. It is doubtful that Stoneman learned much of value, but the event probably helped sow confusion among Confederate defenders.[38]

Between midnight and three in the morning on April 5, the rest of the division entered town from the west. Although sleepy citizens peeking out of curtained windows may have been shocked, Federal cavalrymen had been to Christiansburg before. In May 1864, raiders under Brigadier General William W. Averell had come to town and torn up some railroad tracks, burned several buildings and a water tank, and destroyed supplies. Stoneman's 1865 visit simply reinforced the longstanding interest of Federal war planners in Christiansburg, a central depot on the East Tennessee and Virginia Railroad. Built in the 1850s, the railroad had served as a wartime conduit for moving men, supplies, and weapons east and west. In the view of Abraham Lincoln, the railroad was the Confederacy's "gut." Since mountainous terrain shielded it, Union commanders had sent only small, fast-moving units to try the railroad. Stoneman's force would be the last.[39]

According to William Bushong, a member of the Twelfth Ohio, the small garrison in town was completely surprised by the Federals. Blue-clad troopers overpowered the Confederates, and Christiansburg was captured within minutes. Afterward, the Federal troopers bivouacked, largely on land belonging to the R. D. Montague family. Stoneman established his headquarters in the Montague home, while Palmer and his staff chose quarters in town. As they fed their horses and bedded down, the men happily learned that they would remain in Christiansburg to damage the railroad.[40]

⁓

At dawn on Wednesday, April 5, the main body of the Cavalry Division of East Tennessee focused its destructive power on the East Tennessee and Virginia Railroad. One of the best-constructed and best-maintained roads in the South, it had a well-ditched roadbed. Stone ballast supported every joint along the rails. However, it would not stay that way for long, since Stoneman and Gillem planned to destroy as much of the line as possible. Gillem ordered Palmer's brigade to burn bridges and railroad ties and to destroy stores east of Christiansburg, while Brown's brigade wrecked tracks and rail facilities west of town. As these parties ranged along the road, a reserve was established in town. This force probably included most of the Third Brigade, already weakened by the detachment of Miller's men.[41]

The task began at daylight. Christiansburg, a pretty town with a "fine seminary," felt the hard Federal hand first. Commissaries had the town's black women bake bread, while unit surgeons moved their patients into Confederate hospitals. Meanwhile, Federal soldiers discovered and destroyed quartermaster's stores and burned some loaded railroad cars. "We took our first lessons here in destroying railroad tracks," recalled one veteran. The Christiansburg depot was torched and the adjoining tracks wrecked.[42]

Ohio cavalryman E. C. Moderwell explained that the process for ruining a railroad track was simple but also hard work. "We usually took all the fence rails from *both* sides of the track and piled them on *one* rail of the rail road, forming a continuous pile, then set the fence rails on fire," he wrote. "The heat in a short time, by expansion, distorts the rail into all sorts of shapes, and the fire burns off the one end of the ties. To one who has never seen a rail of iron subjected to this treatment the effects are truly wonderful. The rail very often assumes a zigzag shape, resembling a letter Z. . . . A regiment of men could in this way destroy from three to five miles an hour."[43]

Meanwhile, Brown's brigade marched west. Its objective was Central Depot, a small town that housed key railroad facilities, including a roundhouse that usually contained several engines and cars. Even more crucial was the nearby bridge over the New River. Known as the New River bridge or Long Bridge, the seven-hundred-foot span was covered by a tin roof and supported by metal piers sunk in the riverbed. In May 1864, Union troops had burned its wooden frame but left its metal piers intact. Within five weeks, the bridge had been rebuilt with fire-resistant green timber. Destroying it would pose a formidable challenge to Brown's raiders.[44]

Major Frederic Slater's Eleventh Kentucky Cavalry, forming the tip of Brown's sword, rode for the railroad bridges and ferries over the New River. Some of the men disabled the New River bridge "by cutting away two bents" but were halted from doing further damage by orders from headquarters. Other Kentuckians destroyed several lesser bridges and some railroad iron and crossties between Christiansburg and the New River bridge. A skirmish that erupted during the day did not hinder Brown's men in their work of destruction. Gillem later reported that the Kentuckians "performed the duty assigned them promptly and effectually." There was also a residual effect; Slater's men did not venture past the New River bridge, but their presence spread panic in neighboring Pulaski County.[45]

The Federals also worked east of Christiansburg, a portion of the Fifteenth focusing on the railroad tracks there. Pennsylvanian Charles F. Weller, who was among those tearing up rails, began his day at three in the morning with reveille and breakfast. After establishing a new camp about two miles from town, Weller and his comrades went to work. Frederic Antes was one of the lucky Pennsylvanians; he joined the bulk of the Fifteenth Pennsylvania in reserve that day. "Got up this morning at 7 A.M. and got our breakfast and cleaned our horses," he wrote in his diary. Afterward, Antes relaxed in camp before joining an expedition to gather corn.[46]

The Twelfth Ohio spent all day laying waste to tracks, telegraph lines, and bridges, destroying more than ten miles of the important road. The work was difficult, so Joseph Banks was grateful when the day finally ended. "We went into camp about Sunset to take a good nights rest after a [hard] days work," he wrote. At least the sweat and the sore muscles were for a purpose. "At Christiansburg, while ripping up the track of the Virginia railroad, the whole scheme was suddenly revealed to us," Ohioan Frank Mason recalled. "We were cutting the last avenues of escape that lay open to Lee, and we were a part of the machine by which the last great army of the Confederacy was to be hopelessly ensnared. Grant was at Petersburg playing his pieces in the final combination against Lee, and Stoneman was the hand with which he had reached out to move the pawns. From this moment, every soldier in Stoneman's Division felt that the end was near. The collapse was approaching, and we, every man of us, would be in at the death."[47]

Meanwhile, the First Brigade's Michigan regiment pushed northeast along the Roanoke River. It met no opposition while riding to one of the most vulnerable spots on the entire railroad, a twenty-mile stretch east of Christiansburg where the tracks crossed the Roanoke six times within six miles. The Michigan men destroyed six bridges that measured a combined thirteen hundred feet in length. It was a solid military achievement, though some later wondered if it was the right thing to do. After the war, Colonel Luther Trowbridge bemoaned the loss of the "six large beautiful bridges, five of them covered, a destruction which

would have been avoided could the events of the next ten days have been for-
seen." Enlisted man Steven Thomas thought the raiders had destroyed as many
as fifteen bridges by day's end, but regimental reports confirm Trowbridge's estimate of six. The Tenth Michigan's handiwork earned Gillem's praise in his after-
action report.[48]

While laying waste to one bridge, Union troopers boarded and searched a
stranded train. In a car, they found an April 4 Lynchburg newspaper with a stunning headline: Richmond had fallen! The men brought the paper to Trowbridge,
who ordered a courier to mount the regiment's fastest horse and carry the news
to Stoneman. "I . . . was thus fortunate in giving him the first information that he
had of the fall of Richmond," Trowbridge boasted. In truth, the courier first
delivered the newspaper to Palmer, after which Palmer carried it to Stoneman.
According to a rumor—which Trowbridge gave little credence—Stoneman

*Colonel Luther Trowbridge led the Tenth Michigan
Cavalry Regiment.*

celebrated by drinking a toast. "Well, Colonel," he exclaimed, "bring out the delicious juice of the succulent jack apple. If you can't get that, some of Vernor's ginger ale will do just as well, if it has plenty of sediment in it."[49]

The news of Richmond's capture raced through the command like a cannon shot. When Trowbridge announced it to the Tenth Michigan, the men shouted with joy. Word also spread to the other regiments. It was thrilling; a great celebration erupted in Christiansburg that night.[50] Finally, the end was near, and the raiders believed they were playing a key role in the North's final victory.

Although a Michigan officer thought Stoneman had changed his strategy after learning about Richmond's fall, April 6 looked much like April 5. The division continued to damage the railroad, and it did so with fresh purpose. "Never were troops in better spirits, and never did men work with a heartier will at the labor of destruction," noted one of Stoneman's staff officers. "Every stick added to the blazing fires, which were fast contorting the iron rails into all sorts of fantastic shapes, each falling bridge, each flaming storehouse hurried on the destruction of Lee's army, hastened the day of peace, and the return to the home fireside; so the work went on with shout and cheer, and gladsome song." It was, the staff officer concluded, "glory enough for one day."[51]

As April 6 progressed, the railroad work ended and the units prepared to resume the march. One concern was the division's ambulances. All ten had broken down by the time they reached Christiansburg, so Stoneman's medical staff was left scrambling. Other troopers saw to their personal needs. Frank Frankenberry washed his clothes and baked biscuits.[52] The Tenth Michigan received orders to stay in its Salem bivouac pending further orders. To ensure readiness, Trowbridge sent men to look for horses. They returned with far more. "One afternoon I was sitting under a tent fly enjoying the rest, the delicious air and the charming scenery, when I heard a commotion on the road," Trowbridge recalled. "Looking up, I saw one of my parties returning from their hunt after horses. The party was preceded by an elegant coach, drawn by a pair of cavalry horses, clad in resplendent silver-plated harness and on the driver's seat sat Corporal Delaney, as happy as a lord." Behind the coach came an equally amusing sight: a knot of campaign-hardened, dirty cavalrymen carrying ladies' clothing. The proud troopers claimed the carriage and clothing as legitimate captures, but

Trowbridge ordered them to surrender the loot after explaining that they were not warring against women and children. As the colonel returned the property to its rightful owners, a black man approached and asked if he could have a remnant of bright calico for his wife. "Why should I give that to you? It does not belong to you. It belongs to Mrs. White," Trowbridge said.

"Now see here, boss," the man answered. "I think that belongs to me more than it does to them. Fact is, I'se been workin' for dat family all my life and never got a cent for it and not one of them ever struck a lick of honest work in all their lives. I think I'se earn't it mor'n they has." Trowbridge let him have the calico.[53]

The Federals also had more troublesome matters to deal with. At their camp near Salem, a Tenth Michigan clerk reported the hard-drinking, rebellious captain Archibald Stevenson as absent without leave. Stevenson had apparently escaped from his jailers, gotten drunk, fallen into the hands of some guerillas, and

Captain Archibald Stevenson, who commanded Company D of the Tenth Michigan Cavalry, got drunk and tried to rape a young girl as the raid began. He was later arrested.
MASSACHUSETTS COMMANDERY MILITARY ORDER OF THE LOYAL LEGION AND THE UNITED STATES ARMY MILITARY HISTORY INSTITUTE

escaped again. But he had not yet reported for duty. During the short pause, the case of Captain C. J. Mather of the Fifteenth Pennsylvania also surfaced. Only three days had passed since the Pennsylvanian failed to capture the Confederate wagon train near Hillsville, but Mather had tired of incarceration and wanted to repair his reputation. Taking out a sheet of paper, he offered to personally explain his actions to General Stoneman. Betts endorsed and forwarded the proposal to brigade headquarters, where Palmer pondered it. Because Stoneman was planning to put the command in motion again, Palmer decided not to bother him with it. Instead, Palmer ordered Mather released and restored him to command of his company.[54]

Mather's opportunity was not long in coming. Division headquarters issued a circular describing the railroad destruction work as a complete success. The rails, trestles, bridges, culverts, and telegraph lines between the New River bridge and Salem would be of no service to the enemy for some time to come. Fresh objectives now beckoned, so division headquarters ordered the men into the saddle. Bugles blew in the darkness, and slowly the column snaked southward along the Jacksonville road. A long night of mountain marching lay ahead.[55]

⌒⁄⌒

In Greensboro, P. G. T. Beauregard was relieved to learn of the latest reports indicating that Stoneman was moving on Wytheville and the Virginia and East Tennessee Railroad. Even so, Wilkesboro, Jonesville, Madison, and other North Carolina towns were not beyond danger, and citizens as far south as Charlotte were worried. The Federal force was "commiting depredations on its way, and threatening the railroad from Salisbury to Danville, *via* Greensboro; hence great alarm was felt in all these towns," Beauregard's biographer wrote. However, the threat to North Carolina was apparently diminishing. Every mile Stoneman marched northward put him deeper into Virginia. Beauregard recognized that the Army of Tennessee urgently needed men to fend off Sherman.[56]

As a result, Johnston instructed Beauregard, "If there is no longer danger from Stoneman please send on our troops rapidly [to Smithfield]. It is important to consolidate." Beauregard complied. He relieved a battalion of furloughed men at Greensboro and countermanded an order to seize stock in that town, since the defenders no longer needed it. Beauregard also released a contingent of men from scouting duty at Shallow Ford in Yadkin County.[57] The Creole ordered Featherston to move his command by rail to Smithfield and report to Johnston, and he directed Colonel Ambrosio Gonzales's artillery back to Hillsborough. Other artillery left Salisbury, among it the battalion of Major John W. Johnston, which departed for Yorkville, South Carolina, to graze its horses. More than fifteen hundred soldiers marched away, too. At Johnston's behest, Beauregard returned to Raleigh on April 7 and devoted his "greatest energy" to moving troops to Smithfield to oppose Sherman.[58]

Stoneman had utterly deceived the Confederate high command in North Carolina. Some credited him for this. "The strategy was well-planned and effective," wrote one of the raiders. In reality, the raid's ebb and flow had more to do with foraging and geography than any grand design, but the result was the same. Whenever Stoneman's movements had threatened key points such as Salisbury and Greensboro, the Rebels had hurried troops there. The raiders' pause along the Yadkin and their detour over the mountains into Virginia finished the job and "completely mystified" Confederate commanders, wrote a contemporary observer.[59] The Confederacy would pay for this misjudgment.

At dusk on April 3, a detachment from Colonel John K. Miller's brigade consisting of five hundred men from the Eighth and Thirteenth Tennessee peeled off to destroy railroad tracks, key bridges, and lead mines around Wytheville. Although these Tennesseans had sometimes proved unreliable, Miller believed they could handle the job. Once half-naked ruffians bearing antiquated arms, the Tennesseans now enjoyed a reputation as the killers of John Hunt Morgan.[60]

Organized in the fall of 1863 at Strawberry Plains, the men of the Thirteenth Tennessee at first knew nothing of war. The regiment was given monotonous duties and even had its horses taken away at one point. According to one of its officers, many of the men were guilty of "some of the most outlandish depredations imaginable." But incessant drill and active duty in Kentucky and East Tennessee, mostly with Andrew Johnson's Governor's Guard, had taught them well. By mid-1864, Gillem thought they needed only a "little more experience to make excellent soldiers." The Thirteenth earned that experience the hard way at Bull's Gap, then saved the day at Saltville, where Stoneman reported that the regiment and its commander "acted the most conspicuous part." David Moss, a Republican from Cherokee County, North Carolina, captured the regiment's

Colonel John K. Miller commanded the Tennessee cavalry brigade.
Scott and Angel, *History of the Thirteenth Regiment Tennessee Volunteer Cavalry, U.S.A.*

patriotic spirit best. "I fought for my gov[ern]m[e]nt and I vote the way I shot," he wrote.[61]

The Eighth Tennessee Cavalry Regiment was far more worrisome. Created from a merger of the Fifth and Tenth East Tennessee cavalry regiments, the unit began forming in the summer of 1863 and finally took the field in February 1864. The regiment served in several campaigns in East Tennessee, including the siege of Knoxville, but it had not earned a good reputation. "The troops of the 8th Tenn Cavalry are new and not fit for duty," complained one Union general. "I have no use for them." The regiment was rife with desertions and office selling. Samuel K. N. Patton, the regiment's commander for most of its existence, had few admirers. "I do not entertain a high opinion of his abilities," Gillem wrote. This proved prophetic when Patton was arrested in March 1865 on "various charges of a serious character." Lieutenant Colonel Andrew J. Brown, a far better soldier in Gillem's view, probably led the regiment during Stoneman's final raid.[62]

The soldiers of Miller's brigade bore a deep-seated grudge. The Thirteenth contained not only Tennesseans but also many other Southerners, including about 150 North Carolinians and a few Virginians.[63] Many of these Southerners had paid a heavy price for their loyalty. According to an observer from another regiment, this was an insurmountable handicap: "In the beginning and during most of the war they had suffered terrible cruelties at the hands of the rebels. They had been hunted and shot down as unworthy of any humanity being show them. Their homes were burned and their families driven away, and all because they were loyal to the flag, but now that the tables were turned and disloyal families were at their mercy, they repaid what they had suffered by an indiscriminate pillage. The result was a demoralized command, out of which little military duty could be had, and their General knew they were in no condition to fight an organized force, no matter how small."[64]

Although that overstated the case, the Thirteenth Tennessee nevertheless suffered from uncertain discipline. Gillem once wrote of the Thirteenth and another regiment, "Their officers seem to have but little control over them, nor do they seem to endeavor to obtain any."[65]

Small wonder that George Stoneman called these men Cossacks, after the irregular pastoral cavalrymen that served czarist Russia. What did Miller expect from his Cossacks on this raid? He would soon find out. About eight miles from Wytheville, near Poplar Camp Gap, a drunken citizen by the name of Alexander Chaffin decided to stop the advance single-handedly. As the Federals passed his house, Chaffin opened fire, but in his stupor he managed only to wound a horse. A Federal trooper shot Chaffin, after which another trooper jumped off his horse, drew his saber, and grimly advanced to finish him off. But fortune smiled on Chaffin. An old slave threw himself over his master to ward off the saber, and an officer stopped the trooper.[66]

Beyond Chaffin's home lay the New River. Despite its name, it was one of the oldest streams on the North American continent, having first been encountered by European explorers in 1671. The New River was not new to Stoneman's men, who had already contended with it in North Carolina. Simply wanting to find Porter's Ford, Miller's men pounded on the door of George Gray, a foreman at the lead mines. Gray, who didn't think much of the raiders' invitation to guide them to a suitable crossing spot, tried to escape, but the Federals were persuasive, telling him that they had just shot one damn fool and would just as soon shoot him as well. The foreman wisely agreed to guide them.[67]

Under Gray's reluctant guidance, Miller's mounted band arrived near Porter's Ford about midnight on April 4. But where was the ford? The river was surging from the recent rains. Somehow, Gray managed to pilot a squad across. Once the cold, soaked men gained the opposite bank, they built a fire to point the way. The Thirteenth Tennessee followed, Lieutenant Colonel Barzillah P. Stacy leading the way. The twenty-eight-year-old Stacy was a Pennsylvania native, an Ohio resident, and a veteran of the Seventh Ohio Cavalry. He swam the raging New River with his first squad, leaving his adjutant and future brother-in-law, Samuel P. Angel, on the opposite bank. As the rest of the column came to the river, Angel showed each man the way, yet it remained a hazardous crossing despite his guidance. Company A's William Jenkins rode a mule and swore he would not try it, but he eventually realized he would be left alone if he did not cross. He made it, but others were not so fortunate. Miller's orderly probably would have drowned had the colonel not saved him. According to local tradition, at least one trooper succumbed to the waters. He was buried on the river-bank, where relatives later retrieved his body.[68]

Leaving the river behind, the troopers adopted a brisk pace that brought them quickly to Wytheville. As the sun peeked over the horizon, they looked down on the sleeping town from the surrounding mountains. Miller ordered an advance. Wythe County's local defense force consisted of little more than a single company of Home Guardsmen, but they were ready. When Miller's men dashed into town, a sharp skirmish erupted. The rattle of musketry briefly echoed in the streets, and then the fight was over. The raiders now controlled Wytheville; at roughly the same moment, Stoneman's main body was approaching Jacksonville.[69]

Miller's raiders wrecked the town's large railroad depot and the supplies stored there. They burned four cars full of salt and ten thousand pounds of powder. The horse soldiers also destroyed harnesses, corn, hay, cotton, cloth, and wagons. According to a staff officer, the men scattered hundreds of bales of "fine Kinnikinick tobacco" in the streets. Although few supplies escaped undetected, the vital court records of Wythe County had wisely been removed to Grayson County "for safe keeping during the present raid of the public enemy."[70]

Miller's cavalrymen also wrecked railroad track and bridges. East of town, the Tennesseans burned the depot at Max Meadows and destroyed some track and five bridges. The depot agents offered no resistance, but the Federals "thoroughly subjugated" them anyway. One agent lost four slaves and five horses, while another appeared to have reached the "latter end of an ill spent life." Cavalrymen laid waste to an old train of boxcars, the salt house, the log-cabin guardhouse, and some wagons and supplies. They also blew up a large amount of ammunition and ten thousand pounds of gunpowder, causing a frightening explosion that was heard for miles. "Soon we heard what we took for the boom of cannon in the direction of Wytheville," a witness who lived in distant Cripple Creek recalled, "and naturally concluded that some of our forces had come upon the enemy and engaged them in battle. And so rapid and thunderous was the firing that, having heard cannon in battle before, I concluded it was the clash of arms in close artillery duel."[71]

Other Tennesseans worked west of Wytheville, firing both the railroad and highway bridges at Reed Creek. By late afternoon, huge clouds of black smoke billowed above town, signaling the Federals' success. Miller's men had taken Wytheville out of the war.[72]

Colonel John Miller's carefree jaunt abruptly turned deadly when a regular Confederate force—Colonel Henry L. Giltner's Brigade of 546 horsemen—appeared in his front. According to Ned Guerrant, a twenty-seven-year-old staff officer, the brigade had been shuttling to and from Wytheville for several days, thanks to numerous false alarms.[73] The most recent movement had begun when General Echols learned that Federal raiders had reached Mount Airy and that Grant had ejected Lee from Richmond. Echols decided to march "eastward with all my command for the purpose of dislodging Stoneman should he attempt to obstruct by his presence communications between [General Lee's] command and my department." He had to keep the supply lines for both subsistence and lead open.[74]

On Tuesday, April 4, Giltner's Brigade reached Wytheville. The men trod a familiar road. Brushy Mountain loomed to the north, Glade Mountain rose from

The forces of Brigadier General John Echols, commander of the Department of Southwest Virginia and East Tennessee, were the first to face Stoneman's raiders.
Library of Congress

the south, and the Middle Fork of the Holston ran beside them. The specter of low morale haunted the troops. "Things mighty blue this morning—Dreadful blue. Bluer than I ever saw them before," a Confederate wrote. "The soldiers seem depressed, that is, those who can see the countenances of the knowing officers. The citizens are bluer than indigo." The soldier's sad reverie was interrupted when a messenger galloped up and reported that four hundred enemy soldiers were in Wytheville. This was no false alarm, Giltner decided, so he pressed ahead with the Fourth and Thirteenth Kentucky and an artillery battery. The rest of the command followed close behind. It was about three in the afternoon when they drew near Wytheville.

As the afternoon shadows lengthened, the butternut cavalry encountered a trail of destruction west of town. Red flames leaped from the bridges over Reed Creek. Giltner ordered his men to find the perpetrators; one regiment and the battery halted at the creek while others splashed into the fords by the two bridges. As the Kentuckians crossed, a soldier in the advance unit spied the enemy. "The first they knew of the rebels was a volley & a yell, & then a race to town," Guerrant recalled. "They [the Yankees] ran furiously, pursued by a dozen of 4h. [Kentucky] & the clatter of their horses hooves could be heard a mile." On the outskirts of town, the Rebels struck a Federal line of battle. The Federals counterattacked, some on horseback and others on foot. During the melee, a Confederate soldier was shot in the head and fell mortally wounded. Meanwhile, Giltner deployed his brigade, and the Confederates opened up. The firepower of more than five hundred Enfield rifles proved too much for the defenders, who were compelled to backpedal.

Down the road, Giltner's Brigade ran into another Federal line. In order to break it, Giltner deployed his forward regiments. He ordered the Thirteenth Kentucky to dismount and posted it on the left. The Tenth Kentucky deployed on the Thirteenth's right. Then, together, the two Kentucky regiments charged. Miller had no plans to stay, so he withdrew his men "in hurried gait." The Tenth Kentucky, coming up from behind the other regiments, nearly cut the Federals off. "Our boys charged wildly thro' the town on the heels of the fugitive Yankees, amid the waving of handkerchiefs & acclamations of the women & girls (for all the men were gone)," Guerrant bragged. "The Yankees took to the mountain & ran their horses nearly to the top, where some of them dismounted, but were driven off by 64 Va."[75]

Miller had planned to leave Wytheville at nightfall anyway, but the butternut attack caught many of his men off-guard and disrupted his timetable. As his pickets withdrew in good order, his delaying actions bought the chance the raiders needed to escape. It required a solid performance from Miller's often unreliable Tennesseans. "We crossed Walker's ridge by a circuitous route and had to hold the enemy in check by forming on the spurs of the ridges and fighting and falling back alternately," a Tennessee veteran wrote. Still, it was a near thing. The same raider admitted the result might have been different if the fight had taken place earlier in the war.[76]

Miller managed to break off the engagement around four-thirty that afternoon. The raiders later blamed their rout on superior numbers, but in reality the opposing forces were roughly equal. Since the Federal leadership had not intended for the raiders to get into a battle, Miller felt comfortable with the withdrawal. Around nightfall, the raiders recrossed the New at Porter's Ford. The river had receded somewhat and proved more easily fordable. Some Confederates exchanged shots with the Federals, but Giltner made no attempt to follow. Having crossed to safety, Miller's detachment camped for the night on the banks of the New.[77]

In the day's skirmishing, the Confederates suffered one man killed and one wounded and lost a half-dozen horses. Miller's losses were far worse: thirty-five killed, wounded, and missing, with at least three horses dead. It would be the highest Federal loss of any day of the raid and also one of the force's few tactical setbacks. Echols even bragged that the Federals had done no "material damage" at Wytheville, but that was patently false. Though bloodied, Miller rode away with a strategic victory, thanks to the destruction his men had wrought around Wytheville. He now sought to expand his success by wrecking Wythe County's lead mines.[78]

The lead mines, deep in a south-bank bluff overlooking the New River, were among the most critical assets of the Confederacy. They had produced ammunition for George Washington's Continental Army and continued to operate after the Revolutionary War. In 1860, the Union Lead Mines Company assumed control. Its name notwithstanding, the company continued to produce lead and shot for the Confederate government. In fact, Wythe County's mines provided as much as three and a half million pounds of lead, or about one-third of the quantity consumed by the Confederacy.[79]

Federal forces had targeted the mines before. In May 1864, the Battles of Cloyd's Mountain and New River Bridge resulted from incursions against the mines. Of all such attempts, Stoneman's raid the previous December had done the greatest damage, halting production until March 22, 1865. Since then, the miners had worked around the clock to smelt mined ore into lead and haul it by wagon to Max Meadows, where it was shipped to munitions factories and made into bullets. To defend the mines, the Confederacy relied on the area's rugged terrain and its ability to shuttle troops along the railroad. Two Home Guard companies, sometimes reinforced with artillery, served as the last line of defense. Unfortunately for the Confederacy, the Home Guardsmen and artillery had been sent elsewhere, and George Cosby's Brigade failed to halt Miller's advance. Miller's men therefore destroyed the hastily rebuilt lead-mining facilities, leaving untouched only a store of food because they were told it was all the locals had to eat.[80]

Miller's detachment spent April 5 at Porter's Ford, either wrecking the mines or resting. Miller also dispatched a courier to Gillem with details of his activities, and the latter replied with fresh orders. Gillem directed his fellow Tennessean to return to Hillsville and then march to Taylorsville in Patrick County.[81]

After Miller's withdrawal from the lead mines, Echols shifted his command back to the New River. Giltner's victory over Miller proved hollow, for it had failed to save the lead mines or Wytheville's rail lines and highway bridges. Wrote staff officer Guerrant, "The deepest clouds that ever hung over our prospects cluster about them now, and the very sky is darkened over our heads."[82]

⌇

Little in William Wagner's personality marked him as a warrior. Quiet, even-tempered, and congenial, Wagner "not only enjoyed good company and a good story, but he was ever ready himself to illustrate a point with aptness and tasteful humor," a friend recalled. In fact, Palmer thought Wagner "the wag of the Reg[imen]t," no pun intended. Nevertheless, Wagner possessed enough magnetism that his fellow officers would honor him and his promotion to major after the raid by giving him a gold watch. By then, the major had proven that he also possessed the command skills to lead a tiny force on a remarkable excursion deep into enemy country.[83]

The journey began at six in the afternoon on April 4, when Wagner left the main column near Jacksonville. His force consisted of 230 men from a half-dozen companies of the Fifteenth Pennsylvania Cavalry. Their job was simple: to wreak havoc along the East Tennessee and Virginia Railroad as far east as possible. The rails led through difficult terrain deep into the Confederate rear. Their objectives included the depots at Salem and Big Lick, thirty miles away. Beyond the Blue Ridge and another thirty miles up the line was Lynchburg, a major Confederate supply center and the probable destination of the retreating Army of Northern Virginia. South of Lynchburg and near the state line was Danville, now the nominal capital of the Confederacy. Wagner was to threaten or even capture these objectives and then rejoin the main column. If necessary, he could withdraw northward and join Federal forces there.[84]

The roads the raiders trod were bad. A downpour drenched the men and horses, but at least it helped conceal their progress. The storm also brought other benefits. "The good horses of the farmers," noted a trooper, "instead of being run off and secreted, were kept in their stables, where we found them, and traded our played-out ones, without the usual dickering, which goes along with a horse trade." The rain fell all night, so Wagner called a halt at about two in the morning on April 5. The warriors camped in a plowed field. After resting for about two hours, they resumed the march as dawn approached.[85]

April 5 proved a rainy and eventful day. After descending steep Bent Mountain, Wagner and his men splashed across the chilly waters of Back Creek. During their crossing, the alarm was raised: enemy scouts were ahead! Wagner sent a squad in pursuit and managed to capture two or three Rebels; some of the scouts probably escaped to warn of the Federals' approach. Wagner's column continued northward, then halted about seven miles from Salem. It was ten o'clock, and the wet, hungry troopers would at last eat breakfast after their all-night march. Wagner did not allow his men to tarry long, however. "Bridle up and move on the town," came the order, and they resumed the advance.[86]

At two that afternoon, the town of Salem came into view. Captain George W. Hildebrand and his Company B led the column. As they approached the town, an unexpected sight greeted them: a flag of truce carried by several representatives of Salem. Hildebrand and Wagner accepted the surrender and sent troopers ahead to occupy the town. Nonetheless, the Federals still had to drive out a handful of diehard Confederates. Wagner was also disappointed to discover that all rolling stock had been removed from Salem.[87]

After a brief rest, Wagner's men left Salem and continued east along the railroad. However, the citizens of Salem had not seen the last of Stoneman's raiders. Sergeant William F. Colton, commanding Wagner's rear guard, rode into town about three that afternoon. He ordered his company to follow the column to Big Lick but decided to remain in town a bit longer himself. Joined by Captains Hildebrand and James H. Lloyd of Company A, Colton enjoyed dinner at the Salem Hotel. Apparently unconcerned about the enemy, the men stayed in town until about five-thirty. Later, the First Brigade's Tenth Michigan arrived and camped for the night, fresh from its destructive work along the Roanoke River to the west. The locals assumed that a horde of Federals was plaguing the countryside, but of course Salem was merely the common destination of small detachments on separate missions.[88]

East of Salem, Wagner's men captured and burned eight wagons loaded with hay. An even better opportunity materialized as they neared Big Lick, for they learned that a trainload of provisions was about to leave, apparently bound for Lee's army. Wagner's column dashed into town, but the thunder of hooves gave it away. The train crew heard the men coming and somehow managed to get up enough steam to escape before the pursuers could overtake it. Still, other targets remained. The Federals captured and burned the Roanoke River bridge and the railroad bridge across Tinker Creek. As dusk fell, flames and smoke filled the cloudy skies.[89]

Near Tinker Creek, Wagner paused to update his superiors. He reported that Salem and Big Lick had fallen and that Rebel scouts and locals stated that Lynchburg was unguarded. Wagner therefore planned to continue eastward. He also relayed the exciting news that Lee's army was on the run and had reportedly been defeated near Burkeville Junction. This news fueled Wagner's detachment with fresh purpose. After passing through Bonsack in the darkness, the troopers reached Coyner Springs, where they captured an express car full of tobacco—a welcome find for the cavalrymen—and other provisions. The Federals stuffed their pockets and saddlebags with all they could carry. The remainder went to "the negroes, who were always our friends and naturally gravitated to us," a trooper recalled. Finally, the raiders burned both the car and the depot. The fleeing Army of Northern Virginia would not receive these desperately needed supplies.[90]

Despite a driving rain, the Federals marched on, pausing only to damage the railroad by burning ties and bending rails on the bonfires. Just beyond Coyner Springs Station, Wagner encountered bushwhackers, who opened fire on the column as it passed through "a flat gap in the Blue Ridge." Several bullets zipped alarmingly close, but the Federals suffered no casualties and were only briefly delayed. "While we were under fire all the time, no particular attention was paid them, nor did they succeed in hitting any of our men or of stopping the march of the column," a Unionist recalled. After the bushwhackers were driven off, Wagner called a halt. It was about three o'clock in the morning when the weary cavalrymen dismounted and bivouacked at Buford's Station.[91]

Dawn on Thursday, April 6, revealed a magnificent scene; north of the railroad loomed the twin forty-two-hundred-foot Peaks of Otter. After enjoying the scenery and breakfast, Wagner's column resumed its eastward march. Beneath the horses' hooves, the ubiquitous tracks trailed ever eastward. By midafternoon, the column was within a mile of Liberty, a community named in honor of the Revolutionary War victory at Yorktown. Bearing a white flag, the mayor and the town council came out and surrendered the town. The solemn ceremony merely amused the men in the ranks, who still regarded themselves as unstoppable and entitled to plunder whatever they wanted. Nevertheless, the formal surrender probably gave the locals a feeling of self-importance for having done their civic duty, one trooper decided.[92]

A blue-clad soldier found Liberty "a very pretty town." It remained that way, for Wagner's men found no military stores to destroy. Most of the column moved on after a two-hour halt, leaving behind a provost guard under Sergeant Colton. The detail paroled about 130 sick and wounded Rebels from Liberty's military hospital. The men found it a welcome duty. Colton noted that the Confederate surgeons were likewise "very pleasant gentlemen." His detachment finished its work late that afternoon and then followed Wagner's column down the Lynchburg turnpike.[93]

The Federals rode a few short miles to the east, where the Little Otter and Big Otter rivers flowed across the Lynchburg road. Near Lowry Station, several railroad bridges crossed the two streams. One of Wagner's men remembered the spans as "very long and high railroad bridges . . . of splendid construction, one of them being 600 feet long and 100 feet high; the other 600 feet long and 150 feet high." The bridges were roofed with highly flammable dry pitch pine. Their destruction would halt western rail traffic to and from Lynchburg.[94]

To maximize damage, Wagner divided his forces. Captain Lloyd took three companies to the Big Otter bridge, and Wagner rode to the Little Otter bridge with the rest of his command. While pickets protected them, the troopers scoured the countryside for fences, tore them down, and carried the rails to the bridges. They filled each bridge with fence rails to serve as kindling. The task took about four hours. By about nine that night, both bridges were ready for the torch. However, Wagner was not yet prepared to light the fires. As the news of Lee's retreat had demonstrated, the strategic picture was rapidly changing. Wagner wondered, with the war almost over, if it was necessary to destroy the bridges. Hoping for specific instructions from brigade or division headquarters, he ordered his men into camp.[95]

On April 7, they remained encamped around the bridges. It was a welcome change. While most of the men rested, Wagner sent out scouting parties to search the countryside for horses, signs of the enemy, or even Stoneman himself. Two men went looking for horses but did not return. Another squad of twelve under Sergeant John Anderson reconnoitered the approaches to Lynchburg. They exchanged shots with a few Rebels along the way but did not encounter a large enemy force. After riding to a point within eleven miles of Lynchburg,

Anderson turned back, carrying news that the road to town was open. That welcome information was tempered, however, by a subsequent report that about fifteen hundred Confederates held Lynchburg itself.[96]

Back at the bridge, Wagner pondered the reports of his patrols. Lacking new orders from Stoneman, he had some decisions to make. First, should he burn the bridges? Second, should he turn south and try to rejoin the Cavalry Division? Or should he threaten Lynchburg and Danville, as his orders suggested? Rather than make these important decisions alone, Wagner called a council of war. He and his subordinates settled on a compromise; they would burn the bridges and proceed toward Lynchburg but avoid attacking the town itself. The work of firing the bridges began about eight o'clock that night. Within three hours, the framework of both spans was in flames.[97]

At midnight, Wagner's column resumed the march toward Lynchburg. His plan was to approach the town early on April 8 and, if possible, surprise the defenders before turning south. Taking the Forest road, the Federals spent the rest of the night riding east. Around daybreak, they passed Forest Station. One man went missing as they rode.[98] Lynchburg was only seven miles away.

Nestled among hills overlooking the James River, Lynchburg was the gateway to southwestern Virginia. At the war's outset, it had been a thriving tobacco-producing center. It was also an important crossroads; the James River and Kanawha Canal, six major turnpikes, and the East Tennessee and Virginia, Orange and Alexandria, and South Side railroads all converged there. A Confederate commissary, medical storehouses, and military hospitals were also in town. All of these features made Lynchburg an inviting military target. In fact, Federal forces had threatened it the previous spring.[99]

In early April 1865, Lynchburg was beset with rumors. "Well we heard every day that they [the raiders] were getting nearer & nearer, every thing was in excitement," recalled Janet Cleland, a Lynchburg kindergarten teacher. "Some said they had an overwhelming force which would soon overcome our handful of militiamen, & others that they had only 250 but [George] Thomas was coming behind him with a large army. Day after day we were kept in suspense for I could not work or think[,] nothing but ask & tell what was the news!" On April 6, fugitive state legislators and officials, followed by stores, munitions, and machinery, came down the canal, all on the run from Grant. The furor reached Grant, who was with the Army of the Potomac near Farmville, about forty miles away. "I think there is no doubt but that Stoneman entered that City [Lynchburg] this morning," he wrote. At that moment, Grant may have thought that Stoneman's tardiness was at last paying dividends.[100]

Forty-one-year-old brigadier general Raleigh Colston, a French-born VMI graduate, commanded the post of Lynchburg. He knew that raiders were nearby and looked to Lee's army for help. "Will any reinforcements be sent here to enable me to hold this place?" Colston asked Lee. "I have no troops—the Enemy are at Salem & advancing—all General Echols forces were above [Wytheville] when last heard from." The message found Lee in full retreat near Farmville. "Can send no reinforcements," he replied. "Try to defend Lynchburg. If you cannot, send all the provisions you can get to Farmville, or as far in that direction as possible." Raleigh Colston would have to fend for himself.[101]

Although chilled by this dispatch, Colston resolved to stand firm. He received timely reinforcements from Staunton in the form of a cavalry brigade under Colonel George W. Imboden. Colston also persuaded Lynchburg's male citizens to start carrying guns and recruited sick and wounded soldiers from the hospital. Among the sickbed soldiers was Lieutenant Colonel George Alexander Martin, who was recovering from a fever. "It has just been reported at Headquarters that the enemy in strong force is advancing on Lynchburg," Martin wrote, "and I have volunteered to assist in repelling them, and Gen. Colston has just directed me to organize and command the regulars in his department." From the hospital, Martin helped sort out and equip the furloughed soldiers moving into position around the city.[102]

On Friday, April 7, while Wagner's men destroyed the Otter bridges, Martin emerged from his ward. He spent the day arming and equipping men, forming a staff, and establishing a proper camp. By day's end, the resourceful Martin had organized ten companies; his makeshift command even had a band. Even so, Lynchburg remained poorly defended. All told, Colston's force numbered only four hundred defenders. Fortunately, Lynchburg's fortifications were strong. "Nature so assists the work of art that a few men could successfully resist a large number of assailants," Martin confidently predicted.[103]

At four o'clock in the morning on April 8, Wagner's detachment passed Forest Station and encountered a Rebel picket post—Lynchburg's initial line of defense. The pickets opened fire, and the Federals returned the favor. According to a Union soldier, "one of our boys was killed by one of our advance who thinking him a reb halted him and on his attempting to draw his pistol shot him through the body." The dead Federal's comrades partly avenged his death by driving back the enemy pickets and capturing two Rebels.[104]

Turning off the Forest road, the column stopped at Clay's Mill. Tired after their tense nighttime ride and depressed by the early-morning skirmish, the troopers ate breakfast, fed their mounts, and buried the dead soldier. The mill was only about six miles from Lynchburg, and this pause so close to the city seemed unnecessarily bold to one trooper. It was as if Wagner were challenging the enemy to attack him. But the major had something else in mind. During the break, he sent an eight-man scouting party under Corporal Vance C. Gilmore toward town. "From information gained from prisoners[,] contrabands and civilians of the defence of Lynchburg I considered it hazardous to proceed to that place," Wagner later reported. At seven in the morning, "Boots and Saddles" sounded. The column bridled up and headed south, away from Lynchburg.[105]

Wagner was not yet out of danger, however. After about an hour's southward march, the column reached the Lynchburg pike. Barring its way was a force of at least forty gray horsemen spoiling for a fight. Wagner's advance guard quickly dispersed them into some nearby woods but then ran into still more Confeder-ates. "Then we had a fight at Lynchburg, and some twenty-four of us on advance guard were shelled in the woods, and some of us got in a fight with a Kentucky regiment," a Federal recalled. "The Rebel infantry we encountered near Lynch-burg was too much for us," another trooper admitted, wondering at the time if the men had found Lee's army. Regardless of the enemy he faced, Wagner knew better than to fight so near Lynchburg and therefore quickly disengaged. The Federals suffered one casualty, Corporal William J. Currin, who was wounded in the chest. Behind them lay one dead and one wounded Confederate, the major reported. Meanwhile, in Lynchburg, Colston again sent a warning to Lee. "Enemies van guard, about three hundred strong, within six miles," he wrote. "Main body said to be this side of Salem. Will hold this place to the last." Fortunately for the defenders, Wagner had no intention of testing their resolve.[106]

As it developed, Robert E. Lee received Colston's dispatches while contem-plating the surrender of the Army of Northern Virginia. Veterans of Wagner's detachment went to their graves believing they had hastened the surrender of the Army of Northern Virginia, which occurred the next day at Appomattox Court House. As trooper Nathaniel Sample wrote, "The presence of a large cav-alry force from the Army of the Cumberland appearing in Lee's rear no doubt had much to do with the surrender of the Rebel Army."[107] The Fifteenth Penn-sylvania Cavalry's regimental history agreed, claiming that "the movement of

Major Wagner's battalion around Lynchburg was of much greater importance than we had at that time any idea of, as it was a factor in bringing about the surrender of the Army of Northern Virginia, on April 9th, at Appomattox, less than 20 miles off."[108] Even Ulysses S. Grant conceded the impact of Wagner's diversion. "The only possible good that we may have experienced from . . . [the raid] was by Stoneman's getting near Lynchburg about the time the armies of the Potomac and the James were closing in on Lee at Appomattox," he later wrote in his memoirs.[109]

In truth, Wagner's activities had only an indirect impact on the Appomattox campaign. Wagner did not prevent the Confederates from sending many supplies to the starving Army of Northern Virginia; the credit for intercepting most of the Confederate supply trains belongs to Phil Sheridan's cavalry. Nor did Wagner help bring Lee's army to heel; Grant's forces needed no outside assistance in trapping Lee at Appomattox Court House. However, Lee did know that Federal cavalry menaced his western flank. News of Wytheville's capture reached the Confederate commander on April 4. Over the next four days, Colston sent Lee more messages appealing for help and reporting enemy movements. News of this unexpected threat meant that another obstacle menaced Lee's westward avenue of retreat, which certainly did nothing to bolster his faith in ultimate success. Lee nonetheless attempted to fight his way to Lynchburg, but the last-ditch effort failed. Hemmed in by Federal forces, he surrendered at Appomattox Court House on April 9.[110]

Ignorant of these momentous events, Wagner's blue column rode southward and away from Lynchburg on April 8. Over the following days, the troopers made their way toward the North Carolina border to find Stoneman, encountering both bushwhackers and friendly citizens as they rode.[111]

Brigadier General Davis Tillson's division guarded mountain gaps as it followed the Cavalry Division of East Tennessee. On April 3, Tillson's men finally reached Roan Creek, Tennessee. Leaving one regiment at Roan Creek, Tillson sent the Fourth Tennessee Infantry and a battalion of the First United States Colored Heavy Artillery to Taylorsville, Tennessee. They found little to do, an Ohio trooper later lamented, because "the scoop of Lee's entire army was so complete that there were no detachments to escape."[112]

On April 4, Tillson sent another contingent, made up largely of "Home Yankees"—North Carolinians who had fled their state to join the Union army—toward Boone. The column, which consisted of Major Andrew J. Bahney's Second and Colonel George W. Kirk's Third North Carolina mounted infantry regiments, proceeded under the command of Colonel Kirk.[113]

A native of Greene County, Tennessee, Kirk was the son of poor Scottish immigrants. At first indifferent to the war, the young back-country farmer soon turned firmly against the Confederacy and joined the Union army. By 1865, the bold, stubborn Kirk had risen to the rank of colonel, having led numerous raids in East Tennessee and western North Carolina. While most Confederates regarded him as little more than a bushwhacker, Union men respected him as an able guerilla leader. Reaching Boone on April 7, the controversial Kirk established his headquarters in the Councill home. This time, however, the Federals were far more destructive, tearing down fences, trampling flowers and shrubbery, and littering the yard with trash. The raiders even locked Mrs. Councill in her bedroom. They also foraged the countryside.[114]

Tillson helped Kirk select five key spots in Watauga County and ordered "rough but formidable field-works" built at each location. The first stronghold was at Boone, where Union soldiers converted the courthouse into a fortress with gun ports. Bahney's Second North Carolina Mounted Infantry built a palisade fort in Deep Gap, east of town on the Wilkesboro road. South of Boone, Major W. W. Rollins and the Third North Carolina Mounted Infantry occupied Watauga Gap and built Fort Rollins. Barricades at State Gap and Sampson Gap completed the dispositions. Only the road from Banner Elk remained uncovered because sentiments in that direction remained favorable to the old flag.[115]

Tillson now covered the countryside from the South Branch of the Holston River to Watauga Gap. The cautious Thomas filled the vacuum behind Tillson and Stoneman with "a strong support for General Stoneman's cavalry column in case it should find more of the enemy than it could conveniently handle and be obliged to fall back." This support consisted of the Fourth Corps of the Department of the Cumberland, commanded by Major General David S. Stanley, a former comrade of Stoneman's in the Second United States Cavalry. Stanley moved his twenty-thousand-man corps up from Huntsville, Alabama, to hold key points in East Tennessee and to protect parties repairing the East Tennessee and Virginia Railroad. In early April, he also dispatched a brigade to Asheville to divert attention from Stoneman.[116]

On the night of April 6, George Stoneman's main column was on the move again. Leaving Christiansburg around six o'clock that afternoon, the cavalrymen retraced their route toward Jacksonville and began arriving there around ten the next morning. After a brief pause, the raiders resumed the advance around one in the afternoon. Except for Palmer's brigade, the column passed through Mabry's Gap in the Blue Ridge. "We march down the Blue Ridge and follow the road leading between high hills or mountains. Here was some grand scenery," recorded one of the marchers. With flags flying, the cavalry's advance guard reached Taylorsville at about ten that night, having traveled forty miles in just over twenty-four hours. The rest of the column, including the Eleventh Michigan and Reagan's Tennessee artillery, would not arrive in Taylorsville until the next morning.[117]

On April 8, Stoneman and the Second and Third brigades rested in Taylorsville, which was also called Patrick Court House. It was, a horseman wrote, "a fine section of the country. The houses are beautiful. Tobac[c]o is so plentiful that all are smoking very fair cigars." The Federals burned the jail, gathered horses and provisions, and captured some potential recruits of the Confederacy. They forced at least one prisoner to walk alongside the mounted column. Somehow, he kept up deep into North Carolina until he was finally sent to Camp Chase, Ohio. The man apparently replaced another captive, N. J. Agnew, who escaped into the darkness. A veteran of the First Virginia Cavalry, Agnew had just been exchanged after a long hiatus in a Yankee prison.[118]

Many Patrick County residents lost possessions to the raiders. Among the victims was Hardin Reynolds, the county's wealthiest planter. The Reynolds family lived on an eight-thousand-acre estate called Rock Spring. One of Reynolds's sons was future tobacco tycoon Richard Joshua Reynolds. Fifteen-year-old "Dick" saved the plantation's horses by hiding them in the woods, but he could not prevent the raiders from looting Rock Spring. The cavalrymen also made off with some livestock, and Hardin's slaves followed the raiders to freedom, rejoicing as they left. Among the odds and ends the troopers left behind was a rifle that remains at the Reynolds Homestead today.[119]

Frank Frankenberry was one of the beneficiaries of Taylorsville's bounty. The signalman noted that "the place was almost deserted but we found plenty of forage and brandy." He also amused himself by rummaging through some courthouse records and even found a deed with Patrick Henry's handwriting on it. "All is lovely and gay," Frankenberry wrote. Other cavalrymen reflected on their journey through Virginia. Henry Birdsall of the Eleventh Michigan wrote, "We have had no fighting yet. I think it rather strange having been in a Rebel Country."[120]

April 8 also marked the end of Miller's odyssey, as his brigade reached Taylorsville after a two-day march from Porter's Ford. The journey had not prevented the troopers from raising a little hell. One soldier noted that "some of the men found two barrels of brandy and after the 'spirits' went down the men's spirits went up and many men and officers began to get merry but the fun was spoiled by Col. Stacy having the heads knocked out of the barrels and the contents emptied."[121]

The First Brigade rejoined the division as well, doing so via an alternate route. In the crepuscular light of April 6, Palmer left the Jacksonville road and headed for Cannady Gap in the Blue Ridge. Gillem had ordered Palmer to send the Tenth Michigan from Salem to Henry Court House, thinking that a move in that direction would threaten Danville and the adjoining rail lines, but Palmer misunderstood and sent his entire brigade.[122] The move involved much of the Fifteenth Pennsylvania and the Twelfth Ohio. If there was a direct road to Henry Court House, the two regiments were unaware of it. They soon found themselves in "a verry rough, barron Country," but at least they discovered plenty of forage and fresh horses. The journey was nonetheless confusing. "If Stoneman's purpose was to deceive and confuse the enemy, he was remarkably successful," one cavalryman recalled, "for his own officers and men were kept in ignorance of the object of the expedition."[123]

The two regiments reached Henry Court House the afternoon of April 8.[124] Wreathed in the smoke of battle, the troopers of the Tenth Michigan Cavalry were there to welcome their comrades.

While the Second and Third brigades left Christiansburg, the Tenth Michigan was preparing to march south. Its enjoyable two-day stay in the "beautiful valley" of the Roanoke was now over, a stark reminder that the war awaited. "I suppose it was in anticipation of the attempted junction of Lee's and Johnston's armies that it was thought that our division could do some more effective work on the railroad running from Richmond through western North Carolina," Trowbridge wrote. Orders arrived at one in the afternoon on April 7 directing the regiment to move "by the shortest and best route" to Rocky Mount and Henry Court House. The goal was to reach Henry Court House by nine in the morning on April 8 to rejoin the rest of the brigade. To trooper Steven Thomas, writing home on paper normally reserved for muster rolls, this marked the start of the long-anticipated march on Salisbury.[125]

With just over twenty-four hours to cover thirty-six miles, the Michigan colonel set a quick pace. Trowbridge's troopers were in the saddle by four in the morning, riding up and over the Blue Ridge, then down into the Dan River Valley. Despite the darkness and the rugged terrain, the column made good time, reaching Jones Creek north of Henry Court House early on April 8. It halted at Rough and Ready Mill.[126]

At that moment, three mounted Confederate soldiers—Joe King, Samuel Martin, and Hairston Watkins—were riding from Smith's River toward Jones Creek, looking for signs of the approaching raiders. Near the mill, the soldiers encountered and questioned a black horseman. When the man claimed to be ignorant of the troopers' whereabouts, they let him go. They soon discovered their mistake. When the black rider suddenly changed direction and galloped back, King spotted a United States brand on the horse. "Shoot, Hairston! Shoot him!" King shouted. "He's on a Yankee horse and is going to betray us!" But it was too late; the man escaped. The three Confederates followed, passed a bend in the road, and ran into the Federal camp near Jones Creek. When Michigan pickets spotted them and ordered them to halt, the Southerners refused. King and Martin galloped away, and Watkins started to follow but dropped his hat and paused to recover it. When his horse began to rear and plunge, common sense took over, and Watkins made a run for it. Somehow, the three Confederates escaped.[127]

Most likely, the Rebels slipped away because the Federals had weightier matters on their minds. Lieutenant Frederick N. Field, one of Trowbridge's company commanders, felt as if he had been marching nonstop for a week. Rarely indeed had the men stopped long enough to feed or unsaddle their horses, and today was no exception. Field's company had just dismounted when the regimental adjutant rode up. Between four and five hundred Rebels were in town, the adjutant said. Trowbridge wanted Field's company to charge them with sabers. Company M would follow with drawn pistols. Thinking this "a very bad way of charging," Field nevertheless ordered his company to saddle up. As a precaution, he asked Lieutenant Thomas Kenyon, Company M's commander, to caution his men about firing their pistols, since Field's company would be in front.[128]

Field was not fond of Luther Trowbridge. In his opinion, the colonel had shown favoritism toward other men at Field's expense.[129] Yet he had no choice but to execute Trowbridge's controversial order, and thus began the largest fight Henry Court House ever saw. "Forward, trot, march!" yelled Field, at which his troopers advanced toward Henry Court House. The lieutenant maintained a marching pace until they approached the edge of town and saw a knot of ten or fifteen Confederates. When Field ordered his Company D men into a gallop, the startled Rebels fired a volley and fled. It was about six o'clock in the morning on Saturday, April 8, 1865.[130]

Lieutenant Fred Field commanded a company of the Tenth Michigan Cavalry. He was wounded at Henry Court House.
BENTLEY HISTORICAL LIBRARY, UNIVERSITY OF MICHIGAN

As Company M thundered into town from the west, it saw no sign of the enemy. When the Federals drew near the town square, Field cautiously stopped the charge. Captain James H. Cummins and his battalion, which had been ordered forward in support, joined Field after routing some Confederates themselves. Cummins told Field that Trowbridge wanted him to press on until finding the enemy. Once again, Field was convinced that his company would be cut to pieces, but he obeyed and flung the men forward at full speed. Those with the fastest horses led the pack, and Field's was as fast as any.[131]

Back at Rough and Ready Mill, Trowbridge and the rest of the regiment heard the firing, saddled up, and formed a line of battle.[132] But they could not help Field, who was now nearly a mile outside town. Field moved ahead of his company and overtook a fleeing Confederate. When the lieutenant ordered the man to surrender, the Southerner turned in his saddle and raised his weapon. Field was faster. He skewered his opponent and left him for dead beside a fence.

Farther on, Field and his men saw more Confederates. The enemy horsemen veered off the road and into some woods, and Field followed. What happened next astonished him: "I found myself opposite a rebel camp of four or five hundred men. At the same time glancing over my shoulder I perceived that my men were fifteen or twenty rods back. I called to them to *come on* as it would not do for me to rush into the camp by myself and being unable to stop my horse at once as he was going at full speed I kept straight on some ten or fifteen rods and succeeded in stopping him just as I came face to face with a rebel interior picket dismounted in the road."

A double-barreled shotgun was trained on Field, but the owner was apparently too stunned to pull the trigger. Field grabbed his revolver and called three times for the man to surrender. Fortunately for Field, the shotgun-toting Rebel gave up, even though he had ample time to blow the lieutenant into oblivion.

Field had stumbled into the camp of Colonel James T. Wheeler's Sixth Tennessee Cavalry. The 420-man regiment had arrived at Henry Court House on April 7 to glean intelligence and shield Danville from Stoneman. Comprised of green recruits and veterans from the First or Second Tennessee cavalry regiments, the unit had served under such leaders as Nathan Bedford Forrest and Joe Wheeler. James Wheeler was himself a game fighter, having been wounded twice in the war. As Field was about to discover, the Sixth Tennessee Cavalry was a worthy adversary.[133]

The exact location of Wheeler's regiment that morning is unknown. Some sources place the Confederates at Jones Creek, but that is unlikely. Another account places the regiment on the west side of the road leading to Shady Grove. The best guesses come from Trowbridge and Angelo Wiser, who marked the enemy camp about a mile east of town. In any event, the Confederates were cooking breakfast when Field ran into the shotgun-brandishing picket. The Southerners sought cover in a hilltop pine thicket just beyond a creek. It was about seven o'clock.[134]

Behind Field, Company D also saw the enemy camp and tried to halt its momentum. Dust swirled and shouts echoed as the Federals drew rein. Across the way, the Rebels were surprised as well, and many began to withdraw. Seeing the enemy's confusion, Field ordered a charge, but his men balked, believing the enemy position was too strong to carry. In his heart, Field understood, but he had a mission to perform. He begged his men to obey, but few listened. Among them was Lieutenant Kenyon, saber in hand, who rode to the front with a handful of his men. This proved to be the last order Kenyon ever carried out, for he was immediately shot dead. Two of his men also fell lifeless by his side. Field now faced a superior enemy force with only a dozen or so stalwart troopers in support.[135]

The Tenth Michigan was in a fix. "I do not know that I ever found the time when it was exactly pleasant to come unexpectedly upon a superior force of the enemy," Trowbridge later wrote, "but if there is any time which is more unpleasant than another, it is in the early morning after a continuous march of twenty-four hours when men and horses are thoroughly fatigued." This was the situation facing Fred Field. Twenty-five or thirty Rebels, now mounted, rushed out of the camp and cut off Field's line of retreat as more of his men fell under heavy fire. But Field was not finished. The Michigan lieutenant fired three more rounds with his revolver, two of which struck home, or so he thought. He then ducked his horse behind a tree, closely followed by a Confederate volley that riddled the trunk.[136]

Alone and outgunned, Field realized he was trapped and decided to surrender. As he began to unbuckle his belt, he noticed that some of his men had managed to rally and form a line across the road. Moments later, as the combatants exchanged fire, a ball shattered the lieutenant's left elbow. The wound led Field to dismount and collapse behind the tree. Meanwhile, the Federal fire forced the Confederates to fall back. Field could only watch as the Confederates left him behind, taking his weapons, while bullets struck all around him.

Once the Michigan men ran low on ammunition, their fire slackened. The Confederates sent up a Rebel yell and prepared to charge, but then the distinct sound of rapid-firing Spencers heralded the arrival of reinforcements. The outgunned Confederates began to withdraw. Field was ecstatic: "At this change in the program *my heart jumped right into my mouth*, and in the excitement of the moment I jumped onto my feet and staggered into the middle of the road by the assistance of my horse which had stood by me." Field shouted to his company, "Come on, give them hell!"[137]

Led by Captains Cummins and William H. Dunn, the Tenth Michigan drove back the Confederates. The Rebels took refuge in a ravine, where they "huddled together . . . [and] formed an excellent target for the Spencer carbines of Captain Dunn and his plucky boys," Trowbridge recalled. Eventually, Wheeler's men extricated themselves from the ravine and retreated toward Danville, leaving Henry Court House to the men from Michigan.[138]

Five Federals lay dead, and one man was missing. The Federals also lost four horses and four sets of arms and accouterments. Both Trowbridge and Gillem claimed that the enemy's losses were far greater, but Confederate histories list only several wounded and one man killed.[139]

After the fight, Colonel Trowbridge and Major John H. Standish stopped by a makeshift Federal hospital, but neither man paid his respects to the wounded, according to Field. The disgusted lieutenant decided that "they were ashamed to show themselves as the whole affair had been badly managed *and they knew it*, for if it had not been managed as it could have been, most every reb might have been taken prisoner without a shot being fired." Field had a point. Instead of conducting a proper reconnaissance, Trowbridge had thrown tired men pell-mell against a force of unknown size. He might have counted on shock to carry the day, or perhaps the relative ease of the raid to that point had bred overconfidence. In any event, only valor and Spencer firepower saved the day at Henry Court House.[140]

The skirmish achieved little except to deceive the Confederates as to the raiders' destination. That night, Wheeler warned Beauregard about the enemy's probable intentions. "They tell citizens they will advance on Danville in the morning," he reported. Both the townspeople and the fleeing Confederate government braced themselves for a Federal onslaught.[141]

After falling back another three miles, Wheeler's troopers noted the arrival of a large Federal force. It was Colonel William J. Palmer with the Fifteenth Pennsylvania and Twelfth Ohio. Late in the day, the First Brigade camped in town and turned its attention to what Henry Court House had to offer. According to a local historian, the cavalrymen were polite and respected private property, taking only what was necessary. Wheeler was surprised. "As yet no buildings have been burned in town," he wrote, expecting that to change. The reality was that the raiders had other things in mind. Fred Antes of the Fifteenth Pennsylvania was one who needed little because he had picked up fresh mounts while on the march. Other troopers just wanted food. Many had eaten nothing for the past twenty-four hours.[142]

Nevertheless, when some cavalrymen found more bacon than they could carry, they loaded the excess and additional items onto wagons and burned them. Other indiscretions took place as well. "We are now in the Yankee Lines and power," a local woman wrote. "The raiders have been at Jeff Penn's—burn the Gov't meat & all their clothes, everything but what Catherine [Penn] had on was burnt—their trunks were in the woods where the Bacon was hid & they set fire to it & burnt all. . . . They are a terrible foe." At Hordsville, a two-story brick house built in 1836, a charred spot remains on a second-floor ceiling to indicate where raiders allegedly held a torch.[143]

Setting up headquarters in the house that also served as his hospital, Colonel Palmer discovered that his hostess, Ruth Redd, was a feisty Rebel. Mrs. Redd told the colonel that his presence was "very obnoxious and that she did not want him on the premises." Palmer ignored her, however, because he had work to do. Several headquarters tents popped up in the front yard, and staff officers were soon copying and distributing Palmer's reports and orders. One dispatch to Stoneman announced the repulse of three hundred Rebels at Henry Court House. The enemy, Palmer erroneously stated, had retreated toward Lynchburg.[144]

Palmer also received orders to march to Danbury, North Carolina. The next day—Sunday, April 9—the First Brigade marched southwest via Horse Pasture Store to Sandy Ridge, North Carolina. Meanwhile, at Taylorsville, the Second and Third brigades set out for North Carolina as well.[145] Wagner's detachment would have to catch up with the main body later.

Behind them, roughly one hundred miles of East Tennessee and Virginia Railroad track lay twisted and torn. Nearly every railroad bridge and trestle of any importance—thirty-three, by one estimate—had been destroyed or disabled. Depots were in ruins. Countless supplies and stores were destroyed. Virginia towns and outposts from Dublin to Danville cowered. Bragged Thomas, "A railroad was never more thoroughly dismantled than was the East Tennessee and Virginia from Wytheville to near Lynchburg." In short, George Stoneman's raiders had fulfilled their orders to the letter.[146]

Before them awaited new challenges. "After a few hours rest we turned our faces south towards Saulsbairy," wrote a Tennessee trooper.[147]

Chapter 5

YONDER THEY COME
Danbury to Salem: April 9–10, 1865

On Palm Sunday, the Cavalry Division of the District of East Tennessee vanished into North Carolina like a ghost. Echoes of its passing lingered for days in Virginia. The Confederate treasury, just arrived from Richmond, was evacuated from Danville because of rumors of an enemy cavalry threat. Reserves dashed to Danville's weak works. "Raiding parties were careering around us in various directions, robbing and maltreating the inhabitants, but none of the thieves ventured within reach of our guns," complained one of Danville's defenders.[1]

The uproar spread. In Lynchburg, "gloom and sadness con[su]med the entire community," according to a witness. In Christiansburg, the grim news from Appomattox Court House shook John Echols's command. "If the light of heaven had gone out, a more utter despair and consternation would not have ensued," wrote one man. The command began to fall apart. Grasping for any hope, Major General Lunsford Lomax suggested that he and Echols combine forces and march to Johnston's aid. Around blazing campfires, Echols called for the opinions of his officers. Could and should the command join Johnston? After much debate, the officers decided to furlough the infantry and take only Vaughn's and Duke's horse brigades to North Carolina. Speed was required and muddy mountain roads lay ahead, so they also decided to leave their artillery and trains behind. The Confederates spiked their guns and gave goods from the trains to needy citizens. Duke's men, their horses still foraging in North Carolina, mounted the animals that had once pulled their guns and wagons. The mounts were still too few, and many lacked proper equipment, but it was the best they could do. On the afternoon of April 12, Duke's and Vaughn's ragtag remnants started for Fancy Gap.[2]

"The rain was falling in torrents when we prepared to start upon a march which seemed fraught with danger," Basil Duke recalled. "The men were drenched, and mounted upon mules without saddles, and with blind bridles or rope halters. Everything conspired to remind them of the gloomy situation. The dreadful news was fresh in their ears. Thousands of men had disbanded around them; two Kentucky brigades had left in their sight to go home; they were told that Stoneman held the . . . gaps in the mountains through which they had to pass." The troopers rode in silence, picking up a few men from other brigades along the way.[3]

Other North Carolina–bound refugees included Jefferson Davis and the Confederate cabinet. An unbowed Davis had hoped to remain in Virginia, but Lee's capitulation ended the government's authority in the state. Resolving to find Johnston and his army, the Confederate leaders evacuated Danville near midnight on April 10. Their train lumbered through the darkness along the Piedmont Railroad toward Greensboro.[4]

⁓ⱴⱪ⸰

In contrast to their neighbors to the north, North Carolinians were somewhat at ease. When Stoneman left Mount Airy a week earlier, most Tar Heel residents assumed they had seen the last of Federal cavalrymen. The weather was turning docile, too, which was welcome after March's wetness. All of this boded well for George Stoneman, who wanted to strike quickly at the strategic points of Greensboro, High Point, and Salisbury.[5]

John Goolsby could have warned his fellow North Carolinians about Stoneman. Goolsby, normally a slave at a Davie County plantation, was in Stokes County on an errand. His master, Peter Hairston, had sent him to hide the silver at the family's Stokes plantation. Goolsby put the silver in a chest and buried it

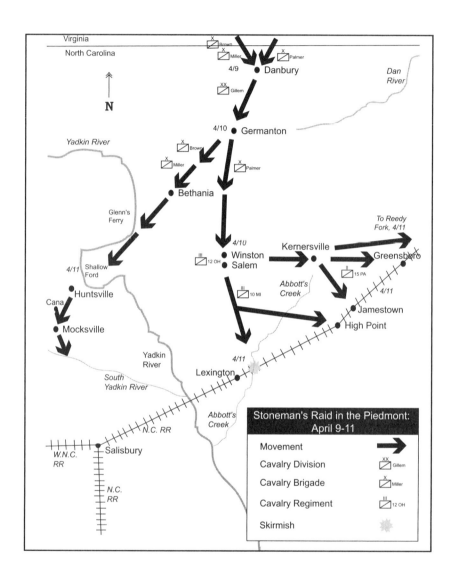

in a vegetable garden before the raiders arrived. But according to family legend, someone betrayed him. On his way back to Cooleemee, he ran into about one hundred Federals. The soldiers threatened to hang him, but Goolsby did not give up the silver. At length, the raiders rode off. A frightened Goolsby hid for two weeks.[6]

As Stoneman's column moved into North Carolina that April 9, the first goal was to reunite the division. The First Brigade came from Henry Court House, where "Boots and Saddles" sounded early. According to Frederic Antes, the Pennsylvanians left at five o'clock and crossed the South River. A quiet but full day's march awaited. "We had no fighting to do today," Antes wrote. Other troopers left later. Selden L. Wilson marched at nine o'clock and marveled at the countryside around him. "The homes of the aristocratic Virginia tobacco plant-ers. The houses and yards were beautiful. Tobacco was so plentiful that we were all smoking fine cigars. We captured some fine horses, for although all the stock had been run off in the woods, the negroes told us where they were and if we had time we got them," he wrote.[7]

Matters were more troubling for Trowbridge and the Tenth Michigan be-cause they had to make a difficult decision. The regiment had wounded who could not travel and had to be left at Henry Court House. Lieutenant Fred Field, one of the wounded, did not think much of the idea, worried as he was about being abandoned deep in enemy territory. But a black boy volunteered to care for the wounded. The youngster did his job well. Three weeks later, Field and Sergeant Smith were able to make their way to Federal lines.[8]

At least the day was shaping up well. Eber Hendricks of the Tenth Michigan remarked on the fine weather. Accordingly, the brigade made good time. Joseph Banks of the Twelfth Ohio Cavalry remembered crossing the state line about noon. "We passed a country church and they broak serves [broke service] and came out to see us pass[. T]hey seemed to be delighted with ou[r] appearance[.] Our band played 'The Read[,] White And [B]lew' while passing," he wrote.[9]

Meanwhile, the Second and Third brigades pushed south from Taylorsville. They encountered a more rural setting in their early-morning march. "This is the holy sabbath day yet I see but very little to remind me of its holy clothes," a horseman wrote. Nothing but "barren country" was around them, the sole land-mark worth mentioning being the Dan River. A Tennessean saw only a "rough, poor country" where forage was scarce. Thanks to the lack of distractions, the two brigades set a brisk pace. According to one of Brown's Michigan men, the column crossed the state line around noon. That placed it on the same pace as its sister units to the east.[10]

During the afternoon and early-evening hours, the two columns reunited at Danbury, the seat of Stokes County. Stoneman led the way, reaching town around four o'clock. He and his officers set up headquarters in a two-story hotel and tavern. Nathaniel Moody, the owner, watched helplessly as men camped in every corner of his house and yard. "I saw the soldiers in the porch of the hotel and all about the house," wrote a witness. About 115 or 120 men enjoyed both supper and breakfast there, costing Moody about one hundred dollars' worth of food and trouble. Troopers also took Moody's saddle and bridle, his surgical tools, three horses, two mules, thirty-five bushels of oats, seventy-five bushels of corn, and even a telescope. The oats and corn were used immediately; cavalrymen carried the forage outside in buckets and baskets and poured it on the ground for the stock.[11]

The arrival of the raiders was surprising to the Joyce family, enjoying Sunday dinner at home with a guest. Their mealtime conversation included the subject of Federal raiders; the Joyces wondered if they were in harm's way. Their guest, Captain John Eudy, the manager of the Moratock Mining and Manufacturing Company, said that no Yankees were within fifty miles of Danbury. "Just then," recalled Hamilton Joyce, "my mother looked out toward the river and said, 'Well, Captain, yonder they come.'" Eudy tried to escape, but Federal troopers caught him and took his jewelry and beaver hat. The Joyces also lost honey and meat and suffered a few shot-out windows. The family's horses were saved, however, because they had been hidden in a thicket.[12]

Stoneman's entire division hit Danbury simultaneously. "The whole place was full of cavalry and they were in every corner almost," a witness recalled. Mallaby's Signal Corps detachment, marching with Miller's and Brown's brigades, halted in Danbury at about four that afternoon. Upon its arrival, the Eleventh Michigan cavalry camped, posting one company on picket duty. The other regiments in the brigade did likewise. Palmer's First Brigade arrived soon after, threw out pickets, and camped wherever the men could find a good spot. Many found resting places in and around Danbury. A hill one mile north of the courthouse was a popular location. Others were reported farther out of town, beside the Dan River.[13]

Before turning in, the Federals searched for food, horses, and valuables. At a plantation on the north bank of the Dan, seventy-two-year-old James Davis, a widower and father of thirteen children, watched at the white picket fence around his yard as a rider approached. The rider—according to legend, it was Stoneman himself—asked if any weapons were there. After Davis surrendered his muzzleloader, the cavalryman bashed the weapon over a gatepost and handed it back.

Next, the raiders searched the property. For the most part, Davis was ready for them. Slaves had hidden cornmeal and silver and had even stashed hams under the canopies of high poster beds. Horses and cows had been hidden in a plum thicket with pieces of cloth tied around their noses and mouths to keep them quiet. But the family could not save everything. Cribs and granaries were emptied, and slaves were ordered to bring out the meat from hogs and cows killed the previous fall. Troopers also exchanged their broken-down horses for Davis's fresh, healthy mounts. They named one of the horses "Old Stoneman."[14]

Davis's home was comfortable, so some officers established headquarters there. Enlisted men spread out across the plantation. To the Davis family, the officers' main goal seemed to be eating in the dining room, not doing paperwork. Servants were put to work fetching food from the kitchen, which sat a few yards from the house. Unfortunately for the hungry officers, soldiers grabbed food from the servants. Finally, someone posted a guard to ensure that the food arrived safely.[15]

Frank Frankenberry discovered a bounty in Danbury. "We capture a vast amount of corn, bacon, and we get a lot of beans and cook them," he wrote. "The town is small and lies in the mountains." The corn, it turned out, had been collected for the Confederacy. Other men looted the McNally place, built by a Revolutionary War hero in 1785. Legend has it that the Federals looted but did not burn the house because both McNally and Stoneman were Masons. This story rings false, however, because the raiders rarely burned private homes.[16]

Some cavalrymen rode farther afield. One party burned the outbuildings and closed the Moratock Iron Furnace, which had been supplying the Confederate government. Other troopers cornered a wagon train full of food and supplies near Dalton. They confiscated the food and horses, then piled up the vehicles and burned them.[17]

It was a long night for the people of Danbury. No doubt George Stoneman had a long night, too. According to a community history, Stoneman and his aides visited the courthouse, after which he retired to his headquarters tent to consider the next day's work. To help formulate his plans, residents and slaves were rounded up and taken to the courthouse for questioning. Salisbury and its hated prison were one day closer, and so was retribution for Stoneman's past failures.[18]

୬୬

Simeon Brown's Second Brigade led off early the next morning, April 10. The goal was Germanton, a small settlement in southern Stokes County. By noon, Brown's troopers captured it with ease. "Charged the Town of German-ton. Rebs all gone," declared Henry Birdsall of the Eleventh Michigan. After-ward, the men camped and ate, then prepared to continue the journey. By five that afternoon, the brigade resumed the march along the Salisbury road.[19]

John Miller's Tennessee brigade followed. A Thirteenth Tennessee man lost a horse near Germanton for unknown reasons, but otherwise the visit was routine. At least the town was interesting; an observant Tennessean thought it must have been "a nice prosperous place before the war." Like their comrades in Brown's brigade, the Tennesseans paused to eat before moving on.[20]

Gray skies hung low over the raiders the entire day. Near first light, Penn-sylvanian Smith Cozens took about twelve men on picket duty. Presently, it began to drizzle, so the troopers pulled on their rubber coats. Around seven, bugles sounded "Forward," and the Fifteenth Pennsylvania Cavalry and the First Brigade took their places in the column. Rain fell all morning as Palmer's men wound their way to Germanton. They arrived around midday and stopped to rest, but the weather did not change. "It was still quite cloudy and occasionally drizzled a little," Cozens complained. To some, Germanton was unremarkable. "It was without paint or whitewash and laziness was apparent all over it," a cav-alryman wrote.[21]

As usual, the experience of the Tenth Michigan was worse. It had some problems with broken-down horses, two men were reported absent without leave, and a third apparently went missing. One of these men, it developed, died at the hands of bushwhackers.[22]

Frank Frankenberry and the signalmen also marched near seven that morn-ing, at the tail end of the column. His charge for the day was the division's mod-est wagon train, which bumped along behind Reagan's artillery. Arriving at Germanton around noon on April 10, Frankenberry found nothing to impress him. "Come into Germanton[,] a rather deserted town," he wrote. He did get to fill up his canteen with sorghum, and he fared well against the weather, thanks to his overcoat. "Raining but my gums keep me dry," he noted.[23]

Behind Frankenberry was a growing problem: hundreds of former slaves following the column. Stoneman's Raid had freed them. They had nowhere else to go, so they were following the Federals to safety. Reported General Gillem, "The number of negroes who were following the column had increased to such an extent as to endanger the safety of the Command in case it should be closely engaged with the enemy." Ultimately, Stoneman and Gillem sent about four hundred blacks, along with a guard to protect them, to East Tennessee. After the freedmen arrived safely, more than one hundred went on to enlist in the 119th United States Colored Troops.[24]

Although Stoneman did not plan on tarrying in Germanton, he had to attend to other matters. One task was to gather intelligence about the surrounding roads. He probably sent out scouts, and he also asked local citizens like Samuel Stoltz, a farmer and former justice of the peace, to help. Stoltz lived on a 213-acre plantation near Bethania, a community about ten miles to the southwest. According to Stoltz, he "had a right long conversation with [Stoneman]." The New York general questioned the farmer closely. "I tried to get him to wait a while and I would send my sons to him and let them join his army but they were not at home, and he (the Gen) did not have time to wait," Stoltz testified. When Stoneman told Stoltz that the horsemen were headed to Salisbury to release the prisoners, Stoltz shared all he knew about the best route.[25]

Fully armed with intelligence, Stoneman again divided the division. From Germanton, raiders could move easily to either Salem or Shallow Ford on the Yadkin River. The former was the gateway to Greensboro and the North Carolina and Piedmont railroads; the latter was on the direct road to Salisbury. Accordingly, Stoneman ordered his division to capture both. Palmer's brigade received the Salem assignment. "I detailed Palmer's Brigade to destroy the bridges between Danville and Greensborough, and between Greensborough and the Yadkin River, and the large depots of supplies along the road," Stoneman reported. Palmer was "to destroy the large factories engaged in making clothing for the rebel army," added Gillem, "and thence send out parties to destroy the railroad south of Greensborough, and that one party should attempt to cut the road between Greensborough and Danville, and after executing these orders to withdraw across the Yadkin at Shallow Ford."[26]

While William J. Palmer and his brigade streamed off toward Salem,

Brown's and Miller's brigades and Reagan's artillery, with Stoneman and Gillem in command, pushed on for Shallow Ford and Salisbury. They would march by way of Bethania. It was near four in the afternoon on April 10 when the column lurched into motion along the Salisbury road and entered Forsyth County.[27]

According to Samuel Scott and Samuel Angel of the Thirteenth Tennessee, the country was fine. It was the same old story; Stoneman's troopers took food, feed, horses, and mules as they found them. About three miles north of Bethania, the Federals came across the fifteen-hundred-acre plantation of Dr. Beverly Jones. One of the family's slaves was a young girl named Betty, who was about ten years old at the time. "Yes'm we saw Yankee soldiers," she later recounted.

> They came marchin' by and stopped at the house. I wasn't scared 'cause they was all talkin' and laughin' and friendly but they shore was hungry. They dumped the wet clothes out of the big wash-pot in the yard and filled it with water. Then they broke into the smoke-house and got a lot of hams and biled 'em in the pot and ate 'em right there in the yard. The women cooked up a lot of corn pone for 'em and coffee too. Marster had a barrel of "likker" put by an' the Yankees knocked in the head an' filled their canteens. There wasn't ary drop left. When we heard the soldiers comin' our boys turned the horses loose in the woods. The Yankees said they had to have 'em and would burn the house down if we didn't get 'em. So our boys whistled up the horses an' the soldiers carried 'em all off.[28]

Not everything that disappeared had military value. Near Bethania, two soldiers took a watch with fob from a citizen. It was a distinctive piece bearing a large gold seal with red and green sets. Forty-seven years later, the owner was still trying to get the watch back. He published an appeal in a veterans' magazine; it is not known if the ad was answered.[29]

At last, the long column arrived in Bethania, one of several Moravian communities in Forsyth County. Organized near Prague in the 1400s, the Moravian Church was a persevering body. Persecution nearly extinguished the church, but it revived in the 1720s on a German estate. The grateful Moravians recommitted themselves to spreading the gospel. Some took the message to the New World, where they settled in Pennsylvania. In 1753, Moravians made their way to North Carolina and purchased a large tract of wilderness they named Wachovia. There, they started the towns of Bethania, Bethabara, and Salem.[30]

Bethania was no stranger to armies. During the Revolutionary War, Cornwallis had passed through on the way to Guilford Courthouse. On the Monday evening when Stoneman arrived, most residents were packed into the Moravian church attending an Easter week service. Hearing a ruckus, the congregation streamed out to find the streets full of enemy horsemen. "It was an astonished congregation that left the church that night," wrote a historian. "Houses that had been locked were broken open and drawers and closets were ransacked. No resistance was offered, hence no overt act, such as burning buildings, occurred. But there was so much plundering and thieving that the inhabitants of modern Bethania felt, after Stoneman's troops had gone, as did the inhabitants of Bethania of old when Cornwallis and his army took their departure." Indeed, despite the words of the historian, the cavalrymen behaved as well as they had elsewhere. Most of the plundering was confined to horses and food. Still, shaken church leaders decided to cancel services for the rest of the week.[31]

While the raiders ate, rested, and searched for supplies, Stoneman established temporary headquarters in the home of Elias Schaub. Not everyone, however, made it to Bethania in time to partake. Frank Frankenberry, still with the trains, expected to march all night to catch up with the column, but he had to stop at midnight and camp by the roadside in the pines not far from Old Town. At some point, there was even a minor skirmish with bushwhackers, but it was forgotten as soon as it happened.[32]

Stoneman had Salisbury on his mind. He allowed a pause of only about three hours at Bethania. By midnight, the column returned to the road. The Yadkin River was about nine miles ahead.[33]

⌒ᾒᴄ⌒

Shallow Ford was an important crossroads. Its popularity as a river crossing stretched across the centuries, from early Native American usage to the 1700s, when European immigrants came from the North. A sand-and-gravel bar sat just beneath the surface near a bend in the river, making a firm low-water highway for travelers. Warriors had fought here, too; in 1780, a skirmish near the ford claimed the lives of more than a dozen men. But April 11, 1865, was like no other day in the ford's history. When dawn broke, its light revealed thousands of dust-covered, well-armed cavalrymen led by Alvan Gillem and George Stoneman. They splashed into the Yadkin around seven o'clock.[34]

From Stoneman's perspective, Shallow Ford had a strategic purpose. By crossing the river there, he gained access to the least-defended route into Salisbury. The route also offered security for his flank and rear. Between Shallow Ford and Salisbury, the Yadkin River followed a winding but generally north-south line parallel to the Salisbury road. Thus, the river would protect his left from Confederates around Greensboro and Lexington. Controlling Shallow Ford would also ensure rear protection. Palmer's troopers would handle that once they finished with Salem and Greensboro.

Confederate forces also recognized the ford's importance. Days earlier, news of raiders at Patterson's factory and of "disguised men . . . lurking along the Yadkin" had caused "great consternation" in Salem. At a public meeting, Lieutenant Colonel Alfred H. Belo, a Confederate officer home on furlough, proposed "that if the citizens would provide me with good horses, I would gather together the soldiers home on furlough and keep the town informed of their movements." The idea was well received. In short order, Colonel Belo and Home Guard commander R. F. Armfield assembled about 230 men on the west bank of Shallow Ford in "a little breastwork." From his headquarters at the R. C. Puryear home, Belo also established a line of couriers between the river and Salem. These troopers eventually warded off a few of Stoneman's outriders, but that was it. When Stoneman detoured into Virginia, most of the ford's defenders were released. Only a few Home Guardsmen still manned the trenches the morning Stoneman arrived, and the Federals dispatched them with ease. "The detachment of the enemy guarding the ford were taken by surprise, made but a feeble resistance, and fled, leaving upwards of 100 new muskets in our hands," Gillem reported. The Federals also captured a mail rider near the ford, but he was freed. Johnston and Beauregard soon heard of Stoneman's whereabouts.[35]

Some warning had preceded the raiders. About two in the morning, someone knocked on the door of R. C. Puryear's home in Huntsville, a village about a mile from the ford. The visitor brought a message from a man who lived a few miles away: General Stoneman and a Federal army were on the way. The former congressman roused his children. "Dressing as rapidly as possible we packed trunks with the most valuable things—negroes made wagons ready and things were sent out to be concealed in the woods." The Puryears hid the family silver in a corner of the icehouse, under blocks of ice and straw. Brigadier General Thomas Clingman, an Army of Northern Virginia veteran who was at home after being wounded near Petersburg, and a few other soldiers on leave also took the chance to escape. Those who stayed behind crossed their fingers and made ready.

"Just at that time without any degree of procrastination every body 'got busy' and for awhile there was 'something doing,'" recalled a local citizen. "Those who had horses hustled out to hide them, and the men proceeded to make themselves scarce about town."[36]

For the raiders, crossing the river was not as easy as expected, due to the recent rains. A traveler noted a few days later, "The name given to this Ford is evidently a misnomer or ironical, for I found it very deep." Once across, the vanguard traced the old stage road a short distance to Huntsville. About a mile beyond that point, it stopped to feed and rest. It took some time, however, for the full column to pass the ford. Frank Frankenberry with the trains and Mallaby's Signal Corps detachment did not arrive at Huntsville until about ten that night. According to Frankenberry, the column had been fired on—the threat being mere potshots—at some point that morning. Meanwhile, the scenery noticeably improved. "We are now in a better country," he wrote. Huntsville, which Frankenberry described as "a small village," was the perfect place to fall out, eat breakfast, and prepare for the next stage of the journey. Frankenberry did so by having a shoe put on his horse.[37]

Meanwhile, troopers roamed the countryside. On the north side of Huntsville, the cavalrymen found a large warehouse containing government corn, flour, meat, and more. They gladly consumed those goods. They also discovered the "White Store," a building about one hundred yards east of the warehouse. The raiders burned it, along with the stock of goods, guns, and ammunition inside.[38]

Elsewhere, encounters between Federal soldiers and North Carolina citizens numbered in the dozens. One group of blue-clad horsemen captured a Home Guard officer who had a commission in his pocket. The Federals hauled the man before Stoneman, who ordered him placed under guard and marched on foot in the van of the column. For the next three days, the man would be forced to keep pace with the raiders, part of the time at the run, and entirely without food. Simeon Brown decided to release him, remarking that he saw no point in "dragging such prisoners through the country." A local historian has surmised that Stoneman's experience with Home Guardsmen in Georgia fueled this incident.[39]

Another resident, Teen Blackburn, had served as a bodyguard and body servant in the Confederate army. In later years, Blackburn testified that Stoneman's men came through Huntsville "riding three abreast and burning everything along the way." That was an exaggeration, but Federals did burn the White Store and a house near Huntsville and also took livestock from slaveholders.[40]

Clingman's presence did not go unnoticed either. Soon after the raiders arrived, a major rode up to the Puryears' back porch. The man said he had heard a Confederate general was in the house and explained that Stoneman had sent him to "protect" the general. A family member countered that no Confederate officer was present; that was true, as Clingman had left. The officer refused to accept the explanation, so the family invited him inside to look for himself. At that moment, a group of soldiers arrived and announced, "General Stoneman has sent [us] to arrest General Clingman and take him to his camp." Hearing that, the major wheeled his horse, jumped the fence, and galloped away. The puzzled Federals who had just arrived searched the property and found no general.[41]

Margaret Elizabeth Hauser, a widow, farmer, and mother of two Confederate soldiers, lived on a five-hundred-acre farm nearby. Around breakfast time, two officers—one of whom had a sister living nearby—and a squad of troopers arrived. Explaining that they had orders allowing it, the troopers collared two of Mrs. Hauser's horses, despite her complaints. They also took 320 pounds of bacon, five bushels of corn, 20 pounds of dried beef, and five gallons of molasses. Then the raiders ushered Mrs. Hauser's two daughters into the kitchen, where they cooked so much food that they went through 200 pounds of flour. One officer wanted something more stout, so Mrs. Hauser produced a bottle of apple brandy and a tumbler. Once the officer drank a "modest dram," he told her to store the liquor where the men could not find it. The women ended up rolling an entire barrel of brandy behind the smokehouse to hide it.[42]

Another Yadkin County widow, Sarah Dalton, was in her seventies. Never in her decades of living on her three-hundred-acre farm had she experienced such a day. It started about seven o'clock on the morning of April 11 when an officer from Miller's command appeared on her doorstep and asked "in a very respectful manner" for breakfast for fifteen officers. "I went to work and prepared breakfast for them as quick as possible," she noted. Fifteen turned out to be a low estimate because the Federals kept coming. By four that afternoon, about one hundred officers and men had eaten in her house, while many more Federals camped outside. Miller's command also fed copiously from her corncrib and used 1,440 of her fence rails for campfires. By day's end, she would also lose five mules, one horse, 350 bushels of corn, 25 bushels of oats, 325 pounds of bacon, one barrel of flour, and two sets of harnesses.[43]

Thus did Huntsville and Shallow Ford feel the hard hand of war. The visit seemed long to the locals, but in truth bugles sounded after only a few hours. That afternoon, Brown's Kentuckians and Michiganders and Miller's Tennesseans turned south toward the prize of Salisbury.[44]

～

To the east, at the same time the rest of the division moved on Bethania, Palmer's First Brigade trotted along the Germanton road toward Salem. The Fifteenth Pennsylvania, Tenth Michigan, and Twelfth Ohio faced a difficult mission.[45] Fortunately for the Cavalry Division of the District of East Tennessee, the right man was leading the brigade.

At twenty-eight, William J. Palmer was one of the Union army's youngest generals, even if it was by brevet. His men thought the cigar-puffing Palmer was tough; some said he had "very little of the milk of human kindness in his composition." That missed the point. *Determined* was a better description. According to a newspaperman, Palmer was "bold, heroic, and adventurous," as well as a man of few words. A friend portrayed him as "one of the most reticent of men; modest and reserved by nature, he is a gentleman of elegance and refinement and superior scientific attainments. He has a long and rather angular face with a slightly projecting chin. His forehead is high and his eyes gray in color and set wide apart. There is great determination in my friend's face, but it is determination in repose rather than in action."[46]

All of this added up to a rich and powerful personality and superior leadership skills. As one of his men wrote, "Palmer had a way of hypnotizing everything he looked at, and everything about him in his command moved like clockwork." Perhaps the best illustration of his aptitude for military management was his attitude toward fencing. The sport was, he declared, a "manly art" that offered "the best exercise in the world" and had "room for any amount of brain in it."[47]

Born September 17, 1836, in Kent County, Delaware, Palmer was raised a Quaker. When he turned five, he and his family moved to Philadelphia. His father was originally from that city, so the move was a homecoming. Palmer's early education took place in the city of the Declaration of Independence. As a young man, Palmer was sickly, but in keeping with his Quaker upbringing he was never too ill to help others. One day, he bought a bag of candy. When he left the store, he saw a black child who could not afford sweets. Taking pity, Palmer immediately poured half his candy into the child's hat. He was also known to have walked several blocks one cold night to give change to a beggar.[48]

At seventeen, Palmer selected what would become a lifelong avocation. Joining the engineering staff of a Pennsylvania railroad company, he fell in love with both the railroad and the mountains. "I find car-travelling quite tame now and one can certainly get tired in half the time boxed up in a long passenger car, that he would on the engine, watching the flame in the furnace or the black smoke wreathing out of the chimney and talking with the engineer and fireman of the wonderful machine which they control with such facility." The mountains that the train conquered boasted scenery "of unabated magnificence" and weather that was "cool and invigorating."[49]

Palmer also came to admire coal, the lifeblood of the railroad. In 1855, the young businessman journeyed to England to study railroads and coal mines. Upon returning to the States, he became secretary of the Westmoreland Coal Company. Coal, he decided, was the fuel of the future, the catalyst that would drive the rails westward. "What a terrible thing this coal is," he wrote. "The foundation of the material prosperity of our State rests in a great measure thereupon." The lure of the rails was stronger, however, and in 1857 Palmer accepted a job as secretary of the Pennsylvania Railroad.[50]

Aside from the business of transportation, the political questions of the day interested Palmer. He was an active member of the "Wide Awakes," a group of young Republicans who wore oilcloth caps and capes and carried torches while marching to political meetings. Along with a friend, Palmer even sponsored an antislavery lecture series in Philadelphia. If the series was educational and thought provoking, it also bred tension. During one meeting, proslavery factions threw bricks, heckled the speaker, and tried to stop the lecture. City leaders questioned whether or not the series should go on, but Palmer and his friend were not deterred.[51]

When war came, the young Pennsylvanian faced a tough decision. Palmer clearly believed in the Union, abolition, and the Republican Party, but the idea of war was at odds with his Quaker religion. Ultimately, he chose duty. He decided to raise a cavalry unit because "that is now most needed by the Government, because I am a fair rider and because there is something about the Cavalry that accords more with my spirit than other arms," he wrote.[52]

A planner with an eye for detail, Palmer carefully plotted a recruitment strategy for a unit he called the "Anderson Troop." Designed to serve Brigadier

William J. Palmer commanded Stoneman's best cavalry brigade during most of the raid. He later assumed overall direction of the raid during its pursuit of Jefferson Davis.
MASSACHUSETTS COMMANDERY MILITARY ORDER OF THE LOYAL LEGION AND THE UNITED STATES ARMY MILITARY HISTORY INSTITUTE

General Robert Anderson as escorts, bodyguards, and scouts, the troop would contain only "young men of respectability" from across the state, among them many Palmer knew from the railroad business. He also mandated that his recruits be intelligent, of good character, patriotic, and acquainted with horses. Each man was even expected to abstain from drinking. Beginning in September 1861, Palmer began to build this ideal unit at Carlisle Barracks, Pennsylvania. By December, all was ready.[53]

Heading west, the Anderson Troop saw service on the staff of several generals, including Don C. Buell, William T. Sherman, and William S. Rosecrans. Its performance was solid. "This company is composed of superior men, many of them well qualified for officers," Buell wrote. Since the need for good cavalry was equally high, Buell decided to expand the troop to a battalion. Palmer was sent back to Pennsylvania to recruit. By August 1862, he had mustered about twelve hundred men, mostly from the eastern and central parts of the state. Not a few were also of Quaker descent. Instead of the battalion that Buell envisioned, Palmer built the Fifteenth Pennsylvania Cavalry Regiment.[54]

As he had with the Anderson Troop, Palmer set high standards. Recruits were required to pass a physical and furnish letters of recommendation. Prospective officers had to enlist as privates and earn promotion. Despite these requirements, the men were still greenhorns who struggled to learn soldiering. One of the hardest things for the city boys was getting out of bed early. They also looked funny when they donned ill-fitting, baggy clothes. And they had to practice with arms and equipment that were often quite old. Fortunately, Irishmen from the regular army drilled the volunteers relentlessly. The training was hard work, but it would serve the men well later.[55]

In September 1862, the Army of Northern Virginia interrupted Palmer. When General Robert E. Lee's army invaded Maryland, Pennsylvania's nervous governor called out militia and recruits. Palmer came with his "half-organized" cavalry companies, which were not yet fully equipped and still lacked noncommissioned and commissioned officers. Some of the men had not even ridden a horse yet. Nonetheless, the green troopers divided into small squads to scout and picket. Alexander K. McClure, a militia officer and newspaper editor, posted Palmer along the Hagerstown-Chambersburg pike. According to McClure, Palmer "proved to be a host within himself, as he entered the Confederate lines every night for nearly a week under various disguises, obtained all information possible as to the movements of Lee's command, and . . . attached his instrument to the first telegraph wire he struck and communicated to me all movements of the enemy." On one occasion, Palmer even spent a night in the camps of Confederate brigadier general Howell Cobb's division. Any news Palmer gathered was ultimately passed on to General George B. McClellan, commander of the Army of the Potomac.[56]

One important piece of information came to Palmer when he camped opposite Lieutenant General James Longstreet's corps near Hagerstown. A reverend named J. J. Stine saw the rear guard of Stonewall Jackson's corps crossing to the south side of the Potomac River near Williamsport in a prelude to Lee's attack on Harpers Ferry. Palmer telegraphed the intelligence to McClure. The next morning, further reconnaissance verified the move on Harpers Ferry and a companion enemy advance toward South Mountain. The sound of guns rolled across the countryside as the armies converged on Sharpsburg.[57]

McClure saw Palmer next during the Battle of Antietam. After complimenting him for his work, McClure cautioned Palmer against sneaking behind enemy lines again. Palmer ignored the warning.[58] In fact, when McClellan decided to send a spy across the Potomac after the battle, Palmer jumped at the chance. The goal was to determine if Lee's army was about to retreat. "I decided in a fit of injudicious patriotism to cross the Potomac myself . . . and endeavor to procure this important information, on the possession of which I thought the fate of the rebel army of Virginia and its possible complete destruction might hinge," he wrote.

On the moonless night of September 17, 1862, Palmer and two comrades approached the Potomac and hailed a ferryman. Once across, Palmer attempted to contact citizens who were supposedly loyal to the Union. In the process, Confederate soldiers captured him. Palmer was wearing civilian clothes, having thoughtlessly discarded his uniform. Had he left his uniform on, he would have been a simple prisoner of war, but in civilian clothes he was a spy and subject to execution. Palmer claimed to be a citizen of Baltimore who had been caught between the armies while looking after mining interests, but his captors were suspicious and sent him to Castle Thunder in Richmond.[59]

Back in Pennsylvania, McClure grew worried about Palmer. After conferring with the president of the Pennsylvania Railroad Company, he placed dispatches in Pennsylvania newspapers announcing the arrival of William J. Palmer in Washington. McClure thought these articles misled the captors and saved Palmer from execution. Whatever the reason, Palmer was released in January 1863 after a harrowing stay at Castle Thunder.[60]

Returning to duty, he found his new regiment in a shambles. During his absence, the old Anderson Troop had been united with the new recruits of the Fifteenth Pennsylvania. It was like mixing oil and water. Many of the Anderson men, believing they had enlisted for special duty, declined to serve as ordinary cavalrymen. Rivalry and distrust flamed between the regiment's old and new elements. When orders to go to the front arrived, some refused and others obeyed, but everybody grumbled.[61]

Palmer saved the day. He weeded out mutineers, put men of his choosing into leadership positions, and molded the Fifteenth Pennsylvania into a first-class regiment. Realizing that the regiment was his first love, he decided to remain with the Fifteenth for the rest of the war. His leadership paid dividends. "I left it [the regiment] once to my sorrow, and it came near being ruined," Palmer wrote. "The blot its reputation then received has been so thoroughly effaced that I think if General Thomas were asked to day, he would say it is the best Regiment of Cavalry in his army."[62]

The reconstituted Fifteenth Pennsylvania joined the Army of the Cumberland as it advanced on Murfreesboro, Tennessee. On December 29, 1862, the Pennsylvanians conducted a gallant charge at Wilkinson's Crossroads. When the smoke cleared, they counted their first casualties, including two dead. Later, at Stones River, Anderson men helped capture a Confederate banner that boasted, "Death Before Subjugation." This brought praise from Brigadier General David Stanley, the chief of cavalry. "Tell the Anderson Cavalry I am extremely pleased with their behavior today," he said.[63]

The regiment went on to turn in one of its best performances of the war in Alabama, just after the 1864 battles outside Nashville. Given temporary command of parts of four other cavalry regiments, Palmer was ordered to pursue Confederate general John Bell Hood's retreating army. Ultimately, his men cornered and captured over three hundred wagons, five hundred mules, a pontoon bridge, and about 150 prisoners. He also ruined more than one Confederate unit, including the command of Brigadier General Phillip D. Roddey. Thomas described the raid as "another of the very valuable services rendered by Colonel Palmer, and I most heartily recommend him again for appointment as a brigadier-general of volunteers." The troopers followed this up by bagging Brigadier General Hylan B. Lyon, commander of the Department of Western Kentucky, in January 1865. Lyon escaped, but Palmer got revenge. "I do not think Lyon's command will give much more trouble as an organization," he reported. Palmer was later awarded the Medal of Honor for his service in Alabama. As the spring of 1865 arrived, he was so well thought of that one officer said he was worth a whole brigade of cavalry.[64]

Thus, William J. Palmer and his men embarked on Stoneman's final raid as the best leader and the best regiment in the Cavalry Division. Palmer learned about the mission in February 1865 during a visit to George Thomas's Nashville headquarters. Palmer held a high opinion of "Old Pap," whom he considered the "chief instrument in winning all the west." He had only one complaint about the Virginian's military abilities: "I might wish to have him a little faster." But he believed Thomas was a tactician without peer. "With Sherman to plan the campaign, and Thomas to fight the battles, I would feel the confidence almost of assured success," Palmer wrote.[65]

Palmer knew Thomas as a cool, thoughtful, and dignified man who "is well known never to say anything but what he means." In their February 12 meeting at Nashville, Thomas did just that. Thomas asked how the Fifteenth was getting along, then turned the conversation to Palmer. Thomas said he had recommended Palmer for promotion to brigadier general three times. Unfortunately, no action had been taken, so Thomas decided that political influence was needed. Palmer balked, but Thomas pressed until the Pennsylvanian identified a well-connected friend. "I don't claim to be particularly modest, but there are certain things which I don't think a man ought to beg for," Palmer wrote. "The only thing a soldier has the right to beg for is a chance to distinguish himself in the field." Thomas ignored these sentiments and pressed ahead. Palmer subsequently received a brevet to brigadier general before the raid began.[66]

Thomas told Palmer why his promotion was so important. "A long and important expedition" was planned, he said, and Palmer was to help lead it. "He has picked out our Regiment specially to go because he says I can find the roads—he wishes me to command a Brigade on the expedition, and hence apparently his haste about the confirmation matter," Palmer wrote. Personally, Palmer was worried about the whole idea. "Large expeditions of cavalry are very apt to be mismanaged—so that I do not much care to go along with it," he complained.

When the orders for brigade command came through, Palmer promoted Charles M. Betts, the regimental major, to command the Fifteenth, then put together a staff for himself. Every man came from his beloved Fifteenth Pennsylvania. Dr. J. W. Alexander, who was "as brave, efficient, and faithful a surgeon as ever lived," was assigned as brigade surgeon. Captain Henry McAllister, Jr., was made assistant adjutant general. Lieutenant Charles S. Hinchman became commissary of subsistence. Lieutenant J. W. Johnston was assigned as assistant quartermaster, and Lieutenants Anthony Taylor and John F. Conaway became Palmer's aides. It was an able group, Hinchman being possibly the brightest star. Palmer once said of him, "He is just as well able to take care of five thousand horses as one thousand."[67]

As they rode during the late afternoon on April 10, 1865, William J. Palmer, his staff, his old regiment, and his brigade prepared to face perhaps their greatest test of the war.

ᴄ𝑀ᴄ

Salem, a town of some importance to the region, was Palmer's goal. The town had several hundred residents and a diverse economy that included shoe-makers, gunsmiths, saddlers, coopers, painters, printers, and even a toy merchant. In the summer, its three hotels were popular destinations for lowlanders escaping heat and disease. The town was also the home of the Salem Female Academy, the largest institution in the South devoted to educating women.[68]

Salem had sent as many as fifteen hundred soldiers to fight for the Confederacy, but the spirit of disunion was elusive in the community. As the Moravian Church's administrative center and principal settlement in the South, the town instead manifested the peaceful teachings of Christianity. Word of Stoneman's antics at Patterson's factory and other points stirred the population. Edwin Clemmons told of his encounter with the raiders at the state line. On April 1, hearing that Yankees were in Yadkinville, Carolyn Fries Shaffner "immediately commenced packing as we were certain that they would burn the factories and we feared the house would go also." Later newspaper reports added to the excitement, placing the raiders near Jonesville and Hillsville. News of the fall of Richmond and Petersburg added to the stress. The burghers of Salem and neighboring Winston met and agreed to surrender their towns to prevent their destruction. Colonel Belo's motley defenders watched Shallow Ford, warding off deserters and reporting the raiders' movements. Back in Salem, the night patrol was increased, but residents felt better when a small party of Confederate cavalrymen arrived and set up a line of couriers to Greensboro. When Colonel James Wheeler's Tennessee cavalry regiment came later, "the hills below town were soon bright with their camp fires." Although Wheeler's men stayed only overnight, squads of Confederate cavalry visited the town regularly in the uncertain days that followed. The residents waited in expectation that the raiders would appear at any moment.[69]

But the days passed quietly, the raiders disappeared over the mountains into Virginia, and the would-be defenders dissipated. Then Sunday, April 9, dawned. Late in the day, rumors that the raiders had pierced Stokes County reached Salem. April 10 was a court day, but only the sheriff, attorneys, and a few jurors turned out. The bench was empty because of the rumors. All across Salem, citizens made fresh preparations. Wrote John Blackburn, the clerk of court, "I procured some sacks; & in a hurry & threw the most valuable papers, into them that was in the office. Sent off the Dockets, to different houses, in town for Safe Keeping." Other citizens hid cotton and cloth. Horses were stashed; two black ones ended up beneath the main hall of Salem Female Academy. School officials and students hid money, jewelry, papers, and other valuables. A sunken spot in the cellar floor of the principal's house, concealed by a stone, proved a good hiding place. Sitting-room floorboards were also used to conceal valuables.[70]

"This [news of the approaching raiders] caused a sensation," declared a Salem resident, "and men and women were busy hiding silver and gold, and valuable jewelry . . . in various ways." One resident cut off old pieces of boiler, hid gold coins inside, closed the pieces off at each end with a plug, and then buried the lot. Another poor soul even ventured into the church to hide valuables. While climbing to stash his possessions, he stepped in the wrong place and broke through the ceiling. Southern boys at home on sick leave also made themselves scarce. Some left town to hide on neighboring farms. According to legend, one or two Confederates even stuffed themselves inside the large metal coffeepot that stood outside town, but no contemporary evidence proves the tale. West of town along the Yadkin at the site of an old fort that had protected settlers during the French and Indian War, a little boy drove his father's cattle into the woods.[71]

Back in town, two young girls, Fannie and Louisa, lived with their mother in the "Salt House," where locals had once stored the precious preservative. They felt the excitement caused by the approaching raiders. The girls buried a little trunk containing their father's watch and silver spoons under a lilac bush in the garden. They also saw a neighbor enlist his servant's help. "Jess, go take the horses and hide them in the woods where the Yankees cannot find them," he said. Jess obeyed and rode away with the horses, never to return.[72]

As wagons creaked and rattled along Main Street in preparation, a half-dozen scouts left Salem around noon on April 10 to see if the raiders were indeed in Stokes County. Meanwhile, a few miles away, Palmer's First Brigade found the road to Salem quiet. Except for the pause at Germanton, Pennsylvanian Fred Antes had been in the saddle since seven that morning. There was no prospect of a halt until the men reached Salem. "Marched hard all day," he wrote.[73]

Corporal Smith Cozens, a Philadelphia resident in peacetime, commanded the brigade's twelve-man advance guard. As he rode, Cozens pondered his orders. The brigade commander did not expect to reach Salem until late afternoon, and he did not anticipate any resistance. His orders were simple; when Cozens spotted Salem, he was to halt. Company L would then come up and take the lead. The idea, Palmer had said, was to make "an orderly entrance into the town," then turn attention to the rails, bridges, factories, and supplies around Greensboro and High Point.[74]

Wearing a rubber coat against the dreary weather, Cozens enjoyed the ride. "It was a fine country through which we traveled, and the ride was without incident, although we kept a sharp lookout for the enemy," he wrote. Just in case, two men rode about one hundred yards ahead. The rest of the advance guard followed, ready for anything. "As I looked around at my little company, most of whom I knew intimately, I felt that if any emergency should arise there would be no laggards," Cozens noted.

It was late afternoon when the leading troopers topped a hill and saw the church spires of Salem in the distance. Cozens motioned to the men in front to halt. Another hill was just ahead, so someone suggested that they move there before calling for Company L. Cozens agreed. The column was still out of sight, so it made sense to make sure that the road was clear.

Onward they rode, but suddenly the Pennsylvania troopers were on the horns of a dilemma. "We reached the top of the hill, and right in front of us lay the town in plain view, about a mile and a half away, and at the bottom of a hill a rebel picket post of five or six men. We all saw them at once and they us. I can remember so distinctly [Joseph S.] Overholt's remark, 'Cozens, there's the Johnnies!'" Cozens debated what to do. He had Palmer's orders to consider, but there was also an unwritten rule in the regiment: if you saw the enemy, you were to pitch in. After a moment's reflection, he decided. "Come on, boys!" Cozens shouted, drawing his revolver.[75]

One account states that three men were at the bottom of the hill. John Fries, Captain Phillip D. Headley, and Albert Butner were citizens of Salem and members of the volunteer scout group sent to find the raiders. Headley looked up, wheeled his horse, and said, "Here they come." Fries shifted his gaze toward the Yankees. "I saw the heads of two men as they came to the top of the hill ahead of us, and by the time we could turn and start back, they were coming in a gallop, and shooting as they came. I do not know how often they shot, but I distinctly heard the whistle of two bullets. One of them must have passed between Headley and me for he said, 'By God, that was close'—the other probably passed me on the left, because Headley did not remark on it." Now the scouts were riding away full tilt, but Butner could not keep up. He turned into a stand of woods to escape.[76]

According to Cozens, the scouts resisted. As he saw it, most of them immediately retreated, but one placed his carbine over his horse's saddle and fired. Cozens heard the bullet whistle past. The man fired twice more and then rode off. Other accounts agree with Cozens, but they claim that a fourth Salem resident, H. F. Burke, was responsible for the shooting. A veteran who had lost a leg at Sharpsburg, Burke rode a fine black steed up Liberty Street, pistol in hand. When the Federals appeared, he fired his gun, possibly by accident.[77]

These accounts are difficult to reconcile. There is no doubt, however, that an exchange of gunfire took place on Salem's outskirts. It is also certain that the Federal pursuit was fast and effective. Charging about one hundred yards down the hill, Cozens caught one Rebel. "Halt!" he shouted, but the man kept going. Cozens's troopers told him to shoot, and the Philadelphian took aim with his pistol. Just then, the fugitive turned and looked back. He was a boy, fear etched on his face. Cozens put away his pistol, spurred his horse, and grabbed the boy's bridle and pistol. Apparently, Cozens had captured Butner, who was forced to give up his horse. Fries and Headley escaped, galloping to Salem and High Point to raise the alarm. When they reached Salem at four o'clock that afternoon, the news prompted the Confederate enrolling officer, his guard, and a few citizens to flee.[78] Burke also managed to outride his pursuers. The captured young man was released on parole and sent to Palmer, who generously discharged him as a noncombatant.[79]

Still charging, Cozens's advance guard neared town. Behind it, bugles sounded; the rest of the column was responding. Ahead, a new sight appeared. Twenty or thirty civilians were lined up across the road, holding up their hands to stop the cavalrymen. When he saw that the party was not armed, Cozens pushed his troopers right through with a shout. "On into the town we went, the people flying in all directions," he wrote. At some point, a trooper snatched one civilian's hat, which made the man the butt of a few jokes until a friend gave him a replacement.[80]

The man who lost his hat was the mayor of Salem, Joshua Boner. Fannie and Louisa had seen him ride past, wearing his high silk hat, just moments earlier on his way to meet the raiders. Fannie, hidden behind a gatepost while Louisa crouched in a corner of the yard, also witnessed several other important citizens with the mayor.[81] One was the Reverend Robert William de Schweinitz, one of the most popular and able administrators Salem Female Academy had ever had. De Schweinitz held a cane that had a white handkerchief tied to it in

The Reverend Robert de Schweinitz, administrator of the Salem Female Academy, was among the first Salem residents to meet the raiders. When the cavalrymen approached, he lifted a cane that had a white handkerchief tied to it.
COLLECTION OF
OLD SALEM MUSEUMS AND GARDENS

surrender. T. J. Wilson, the mayor of Winston, was also present to represent his constituents. So was Augustus Fogle, a prominent citizen, and Rufus L. Patterson, who had joined his wife in Salem after the adventure at Patterson's factory. These leaders, hearing of the raiders' approach, had ridden up Liberty Street and stopped in front of a house. They hoped to prevent destruction of their homes.

It was between five and six in the afternoon—to the northwest, the Second and Third brigades were securing Bethania—and the tension was thick. "Near sundown a small squad of soldiers rode up in full gallop, pistols in hand," wrote John Blackburn, Salem's clerk of court and a member of the party. When the civilians raised white handkerchiefs in submission, the troopers replied, "All right," but that failed to clear the air. Some Federals, angry over the shooting, asked about the men who had fired on them. According to legend, troopers grabbed the reins of de Schweinitz's horse, and Palmer pulled a pistol. When the principal defiantly called, "I am de Schweinitz," Palmer suddenly recognized him. Holstering his pistol, he said, "I had a teacher of that name when I was in school in Lititz." The truth of the matter is that Palmer was not present when this exchange occurred, and he did not attend school in Lititz either. Palmer, his staff, and other Federals arrived a few minutes later and defused the situation. Introductions were made. According to Blackburn, Palmer politely asked several questions. In the discussion, the Federals learned that Salem was undefended and assured the citizens that both they and their private property would be pro-tected. Finally, Palmer asked the company to walk with the Federals into town. They followed Liberty Street to Main Street.[82]

The de Schweinitz incident probably derived from the experiences of Na-thaniel Sample. Sample, who joined Cozens's advance guard, remembered see-ing about a dozen Confederates drawn up across Main Street. "They did not oppose to any great extent, but fired a volley and ran away," he wrote. Pursuing the Confederates toward Salem, Sample realized that the town reminded him of Lititz and Bethlehem, which were also Moravian communities. In fact, it was like a reunion between the Pennsylvanians and the Moravians, since both shared similar heritages. Sample met the principal of the academy:

> In following them [the Confederates] through the town (it was rain-ing), I noticed a man come out of a house, hoist an umbrella with a white handkerchief on top and advance to the sidewalk. I rode up to him and asked to what command the party that fired on us belonged; he protested they were boys that belonged to the homeguard. He was very nervous and seemed much interested in my appearance and finally asked me what the letters 15th P.V.C. on my hat meant. I explained it stood for the 15th Pennsylvania Volunteer Cavalry; his countenance changed at once and he said, "Why, I am from Pennsylvania!" I asked him what part; he said Lancaster County,—that he was principal of the girls' school here and had been detained in Salem by the war. I recognized him then as the principal of the girls' school at Lititz when I was attending the boys' school there. He asked me to protect his school, which I did by placing a safeguard about the buildings in which there was said to be 300 young girls from all over the South. We were the first Federal troops that Salem had ever seen, and when the people discovered we did not have horns or hoofs or forked tails and that some of us were from Lancaster County, Penna. and knew the Lititz people, they became very friendly and treated us to the best they had.[83]

Meanwhile, Cozens's advance led the charge into Salem "full tilt." The men encountered no resistance as the local militia, the Sixty-fourth Home Guard Battalion, retreated from its courthouse position. After rushing through de Schweinitz's party, Cozens's dozen Pennsylvanians dismounted at the post of-fice. Cozens dashed inside and seized a bundle of letters. Other men emptied mailbags in the public square and tore up some letters. Presently, Palmer arrived. Cozens saluted and gave a letter to one of Palmer's staff officers. Palmer returned the salute with a smile and ordered Cozens's company to picket the road until relieved. As he rode away, Cozens wondered what Palmer thought of his "orderly entrance" into town.[84]

By about six in the afternoon on Monday, April 10, Salem was teeming with Federal cavalrymen. "Before we could realize it," a Moravian church official wrote, "soldiers were seen at every corner of the streets, had taken possession of the post office, and secured our whole town." Hooves clattered as cavalrymen rode along Main Street and sized up their new surroundings. They were pleasantly surprised. Recalled Colonel Betts, Salem was "one of the prettiest places we had visited during the [last] two years." The girls' school impressed another cavalryman. "The grounds were very fine. It was a beautiful place," he wrote. The town's hospitality was even more surprising. "The citizens were mostly loyal and we were received with many manifestations of joy," wrote one trooper. According to another, "young & old, men, women, and children appeared in front of their houses and waved their Handkerchiefs as we passed. These spontaneous demonstrations were most refreshing to the tired soldiers heart, for we felt we were again midst friends, and the men of the 15th Pa Cavalry will ever cherish the kindest feelings towards the citizens of Salem for their cordial welcome." At least one young man provided the raiders with assistance of another kind, even though it was unintentional. Six-year-old George Hanes Rights, the son of town clerk C. L. Rights, yelled out of his window, "You can't get our horses! We got them hid in the cellar!"[85]

The cavalrymen found a warm welcome in Winston, too. "The two towns are separated only by a street, but are really one," recalled Selden Wilson. "Here was the first thing like a cordial reception we had received for a long time; not like we had been receiving. The ladies cheered us and brought us bread, pies, and cakes. The people showed much enthusiasm at the sight of the flag we carried. Old men wept like children and prominent citizens took off their hats and bowed to it. We could hear such expressions as 'Look at that old flag,' 'Let me kiss the flag,' 'Once more the flag goes through our town.'" Wrote another raider, "There are plenty of stores here, and in the center of the town one of the finest seminaries we have seen in the South. It was a charming place and they were good Union people, but we had no time just then to do more than just acknowledge it." Fred Antes smiled when he remembered the visit. "The people of Salem treated us very kindly. I drew rations from a rebels Commissary," he wrote.[86]

Academy students, from their vantage point facing the village square, offered a mostly warm welcome, too. "We found a very nice little town, with a female seminary in session," a horse soldier wrote. "The young ladies were at the windows, and at one of them a United States flag was displayed, which was greeted with cheers as we passed." Another story, unconfirmed by Federal accounts, claims that a Salem Female Academy student heckled the blue column. As troopers rode by the main hall, a girl from Alabama leaned out a window, waved a Confederate flag, and gave a Rebel yell. The young lady was pulled back inside and rebuked. But she was the exception; one helpful student baked pan after pan of biscuits for the soldiers.[87]

Brothers Edward and Levi Blum, who ran a print shop on Salem's principal street, watched events unfold. "While marching downtown, several overanxious citizens hung out flags of truce, and were only laughed at for their pains, and some quickly hauled down their colors," the Blums wrote. "At the sisters house the good sisters were considerably excited, and were out on the pavement, some gesticulating in their excitement, and showing their white handkerchiefs. A report was made to the General that the inmates of the woman's lunatic asylum were out on the streets and needed looking after. A general laugh followed, upon the explanation and [was] readily understood as several of the staff, as well as the General himself, were acquainted with the Moravian institutions at Bethlehem, Pa. The sisters were mortified, but soon saw the fun in the matter and laughed as heartily as anyone."[88]

The Blums also saw something more ominous: a throng of men marching behind the raiders. These men had been dismounted as a punishment for straggling. Immediately, the stragglers demanded food, but officers told the citizens to ignore their pleas because they would be fed at camp. Palmer also saw to it that strict discipline was enforced and depredations were minimized. In fact, after meeting with Cozens, Palmer went to the bank and posted a guard. He also established guards at other key spots and sent out patrols. Then he rode to Mayor Boner's house, a two-story brick structure just down the street from the girls' school, and established headquarters. Palmer's troopers set up camp and then secured provisions for their horses and themselves. Their tents went just south of town, across Salem Creek. The spot offered access to water, sat on easily defended high ground, and controlled a bridge over Salem Creek. For extra strength, cavalrymen surrounded the camp with a brush fence, then raised the

Stars and Stripes. It marked the first time in nearly four years that the flag fluttered over Salem.[89]

Palmer's guards did their job well and kept everything quiet, welcoming celebrations notwithstanding. As a church official observed, the cavalrymen's presence was marked with comparative silence. "Had it not been for the noise their swords and horses made it would have been scarcely noticed that as large a number of troops was passing through town. The strictest discipline was observed, guards rode up and down every street, and the violations of mild and gentlemanly conduct were few indeed." A few locals were taken prisoner as a precaution, but they were quickly paroled.[90]

With Salem well in hand, Palmer lost no time in moving on his next objective. According to one historian, the North Carolina Railroad was the Union's most important remaining strategic target, after Johnston's army. It was not the best line in the world; heavy rains and flooding, accidental fires, and Union operations had plagued it during 1865. Gauge differences between it and other lines made it inefficient. But at this stage of the war, it was the key supply and reinforcement conduit for Johnston's army, which was still facing William T. Sherman near Raleigh. The railroad also offered possibilities as a way of escape for Johnston. Palmer had to take the line out of play, as well as the Piedmont Railroad, which linked Danville with Greensboro and the North Carolina Railroad.[91]

He sent for Colonel Betts. About five thousand Rebels guarded Greensboro, Palmer told him, so the job would be difficult. He ordered Betts to divide the Fifteenth Pennsylvania into detachments. One detachment was to destroy a Piedmont Railroad bridge north of Greensboro. Another was to angle toward the village of Jamestown, a whistle stop on the North Carolina Railroad. The rest of Betts's regiment would march toward Greensboro, targeting North Carolina Railroad bridges along the way. Colonel Luther Trowbridge, commander of the Tenth Michigan Cavalry, received marching orders, too; part of his command was to destroy the North Carolina Railroad bridge over Abbott's Creek, between Greensboro and Salisbury, while the rest created havoc around High Point. Palmer would remain in Salem with the Twelfth Ohio Cavalry. Their orders given, the raiders streamed off toward the unknown.[92]

The odyssey of the First Brigade was under way.

Chapter 6

The Proudest Day in Our History
Salem to Abbott's Creek: April 10-11, 1865

In 1781, two armies fought a bloody battle at Guilford Courthouse, North Carolina. When the smoke cleared, the British had beaten the Continental Army, but the victory came at a price. The British suffered such heavy casualties that their army would never be the same again. It went on to defeat at Yorktown, Virginia. To honor their important battle, Guilford County citizens renamed their county seat after the Patriot commander, General Nathanael Greene.

Years of peace followed. Greensboro grew into a pleasant, peaceful hamlet of eighteen hundred residents. The railroad came, the town's economy expanded, and stately homes were built along the streets. Then the unthinkable happened: war came again, and everything changed. By the spring of 1865, "Greensboro was no longer the beautiful, quiet, delightful place of yore," wrote an observer. To one Confederate soldier, the town was now nothing more than a "little Union hole." Casualties from the Battle of Bentonville were crammed into churches and homes and even the county courthouse. The railroad through town bore a steady stream of freight trains carrying troops and supplies to Johnston's army around Smithfield. A line of hastily dug breastworks ringed the town, and watchtowers looked to the horizon, but they were forlorn hopes against two converging terrors: the ninety-thousand-strong army of William T. Sherman to the east and the four thousand raiders of George Stoneman to the west.[1]

Stoneman presented the more immediate threat. On April 6, the *Greensborough Patriot* announced that Yankee cavalry had raided factories in Caldwell and Iredell counties, leaving a trail of burning buildings and plundered citizens in its wake. "A number of negroes went with them [the Union cavalry]," the paper reported. The situation worsened on April 10. Beauregard informed Johnston that the enemy had appeared farther east, in Stokes County. Colonel James Wheeler confirmed the report, saying that the enemy had swept into North Carolina. "These movements indicate evidently a raid on Danville railroad, and probably on Greensborough," Beauregard told his superior. "Can you spare any cavalry for their defense? No time should be lost." But Johnston had Sherman to worry about. He ordered Brigadier General Samuel W. Ferguson's Brigade to Greensboro and lamely pointed out that another regiment must be nearby. But Johnston could do nothing else. "No other cavalry could reach that quarter in time," he wrote.[2]

On April 9, deciding there must be something more he could do, Beauregard boarded his mobile headquarters, which consisted of an engine and three boxcars. One car served as the general's office, bedroom, and dining room. The second housed his staff and the third his horses. The train whisked Beauregard and his staff westward from Raleigh. Arriving at Greensboro late on April 10, the cars rolled onto a side track, and the general and his staff immediately went to work. An observer noted that the general looked like a fox, but the Louisianan probably felt anything but cunning as he sized up the situation.[3]

Beauregard found a town in chaos. "The streets were swimming with mud, and the houses looked as if they sympathized with their deplorable condition," recalled a citizen. "'Tramp, tramp, tramp' was heard at all hours, day and night, as our infantry marched to their lines of battle. Horses and horsemen were dashing through the mud from street to street. The drum and fife and bugle were heard giving out their discordant sounds wherever a group of Confederates could be seen, and the nightly campfires sparkled and blazed from every hill-top and on every street in and around the town." Panic was in the air. A local textbook publisher whose books had a decidedly Southern slant buried his printing plates. Stragglers sacked homes and warehouses. Not surprisingly, the Confederate treasury, which had just arrived from Danville in the care of five dozen midshipmen, was moved to Charlotte for safekeeping.[4]

In the early-morning hours on April 11, a "leaky old car" pulled into the

Greensboro train station. It bore President Jefferson Davis and his cabinet, who emerged thankful after a quiet ride from Danville. The travelers knew that enemy raiders were on the loose; before the government party left Danville, scouts had reported a Federal cavalry force somewhere between that town and Greensboro. As he entered Davis's car, Beauregard thought the Confederate leaders looked utterly helpless. Still, they greeted the general cordially—until they learned how lucky they were to arrive safely. Shortly after the presidential train crossed a railroad bridge a few miles north of Greensboro, raiders had captured and burned the span. Davis was unmoved by the information. "A miss is as good as a mile," he quipped.[5]

Greensboro did not welcome the fleeing government warmly. The town had never harbored vigorous Confederate feelings. In 1864, residents had held several meetings decrying the condition of the South. Now that Lee had surrendered and Federals were on the prowl, it was obvious that the Confederacy was finished. Residents, fearing reprisals from expected Federal occupiers, invited few of the fugitive officials into their homes. Most of the Confederate leaders were forced to remain in the railroad cars. For his part, Davis moved into a simple abode with his nephew and family, under the care of a nervous landlord who feared Yankee retaliation.[6]

Meanwhile, Davis grilled Beauregard about the latest news. It was a bleak picture. Lee's army was finished. Sherman's army had been resupplied at Goldsboro and was pursuing Johnston. A cavalry raid was slicing through Alabama. Closer to Greensboro, Stoneman was carrying out his own raid. Beauregard assured Davis that he was doing everything he could, but he feared "every moment, to hear of his [Stoneman's] having broken these lines at some important point." Given this foreboding news, President Davis and his cabinet sat down to consider the dark future. Beauregard joined them for the discussion. So did Joe Johnston, whom Davis had summoned from Raleigh. Davis remained hopeful, but Johnston hoped to persuade him that the end had come.[7]

Beauregard did what he could to strengthen Greensboro. Troops were on the way from Danville following its evacuation. Realizing he needed cavalry to serve as scouts, Beauregard ordered Ferguson to speed his cavalry brigade from High Point. The Creole also tried to secure the much-traveled infantry detachment of Lieutenant Colonel Alexander C. McAlister, but the railroad agent at Danville was slow in providing transportation, so McAlister's men left town later than planned. They sat at Danville as Stoneman's detachments approached

Greensboro, and thus arrived too late to be of any service. Veterans of the unit believed that Stoneman had somehow bribed the agent.[8]

In mid-April, North Carolina governor Zebulon B. Vance came to Greensboro and sent out scouts to find Stoneman, "who was rushing through the mountain gorges of the Blue Ridge like a furious torrent intimidating that hitherto peaceful and retired country," the governor wrote. Meanwhile, Brigadier General Collett Leventhorpe, an English Confederate who had been wounded at Gettysburg, marshaled his command of North Carolina Home Guardsmen. Johnston found more reinforcements. On the afternoon of April 11, twelve hundred soldiers from Brigadier General Edmund W. Pettus's Alabama brigade rode west from Smithfield. "These will make Greensborough safe," Johnston noted.[9]

The trickle eventually became a deluge. Lee's paroled soldiers began drifting in from Appomattox, closely followed by Johnston's entire army. They swelled Greensboro's population by some fifty thousand soldiers. Among them were a "host of heroes", including D. H. Hill, Stephen D. Lee, W. W. Loring, Matthew C. Butler, Alfred Iverson, Raphael Semmes, and Lunsford Lomax. "Our ranks were increased daily by incoming soldiers," Colonel Belo wrote. Unfortunately for the Confederacy, these men could do little to halt the raiders. Morale among them was low and the rate of desertion high.[10]

And Stoneman, it seemed, was everywhere. Colonel Belo, who served for a time in the Greensboro defenses, thought the growing Confederate presence there was effective, but in truth the defenders could not stop the raiders from doing what they wanted. "Foreboding bad news. Stoneman raiding around destroying the roads," a Confederate soldier wrote in his diary. "Enemy cut road between this place and Salisbury at High Point and Jamestown; also cut road between this place and Danville, about twelve miles from here, this morning. Hope to repair road at High Point and Jamestown in short time," Beauregard wrote. The mail rider who had been captured at Shallow Ford also raised the alarm, revealing that Stoneman's main body camped on the night of April 11 near the ford on the west bank of the Yadkin. Beauregard saw the danger. "May not this column now move down that river either to Yadkin Bridge (railroad) or Salisbury? Would it not be well to send, say, 500 men, under General B. T. Johnson, who is still here, to Salisbury?" he wrote. Accordingly, Beauregard sent Johnson to Salisbury with five hundred troops; another five hundred would soon follow. The Creole also alerted Ferguson. "Yadkin Bridge should be well guarded on both sides, especially on south side now," Beauregard cautioned. He must have wondered if his brave few would be able to stop the enemy.[11]

⁓⁌⁓

At eleven o'clock on the night of April 10—while Beauregard was arriving at Greensboro and Davis was en route from Danville—the discordant notes of "Boots and Saddles" echoed through Salem's cobblestone streets as hundreds of cavalrymen from the understrength Fifteenth Pennsylvania Cavalry stepped off. A guide led the way in the darkness. Occasionally, a few men left the column, a trooper recollected, and "considerable 'trading' was done during the night for better animals belonging to the citizens en route." At two in the morning, the Fifteenth reached Kernersville, where the regiment divided. One group of horse soldiers headed southwest, toward Jamestown. Five miles farther, another detachment turned northward. Colonel Betts and about eighty or ninety men kept straight on toward Greensboro. Betts's objective was to draw attention away from the other two detachments.[12]

A native of Bucks County, Pennsylvania, Charles M. Betts had spent his entire military career in the Fifteenth. After enlisting in Company E, Betts was commissioned a captain in May 1863. He vaulted to major in April 1864. On February 23, 1865, Betts was promoted to lieutenant colonel when Palmer assumed brigade command. The new colonel was known to be a disciplinarian and a "brave and gallant" fighter eager to prove himself.[13]

His men rode all night on the main road. Greensboro teemed with enemy infantry and cavalry, so the troopers advanced cautiously, carbines at the ready. Five men comprised the advance guard. Sergeant Selden Wilson commanded the six-man rear guard, which was under orders to stay on the heels of the main column. "We rode all the time with advanced carbines or drawn revolvers," Wilson wrote. "It was a very fog[g]y night towards morning, so thick we could hardly see the horses in front of us."[14]

At length, the raiders spotted the outline of a covered wagon parked beside the road. Sergeant William McGee, a member of the advance guard, trotted over to investigate. He found a black man on the ground near the wagon, sleeping beside a log. Inside the wagon, a white man was dozing next to a five-gallon keg of whiskey. An overjoyed McGee sent his men ahead with the liquor and waited for the colonel. When Betts rode up a few minutes later, McGee turned over the prisoners and then quickly excused himself. The sergeant and his men filled their canteens with whiskey and drank deeply to fortify themselves after their tense ride. "We then went forward, in high spirits, and were ready for anything that might happen," McGee recalled.[15]

While the Second and Third brigades approached the Yadkin and Palmer waited in Salem for news of his detachments, Betts's column reached a point about ten miles west of Greensboro, near Friendship and Sandy Ridge. Upon arriving at a crossroads, Sergeant McGee saw a black man. Spurring their horses, the soldiers of the advance guard chased the man, caught him, and took him straight to Betts. The man claimed he was simply on his way to the post office to mail a letter, but the cavalrymen did not believe him. They asked if he had seen or heard of any Yankees in the area. "I dunno mars'er but I spects you's Yankees," the man replied. It turned out that the man was a slave of Lieutenant Colonel Thomas Hewlett Johnson of the Third South Carolina Cavalry, part of which was camped less than a mile away. That regiment was searching for the raiders.[16]

The Third South Carolina Cavalry had seen only occasional combat while stationed around Charleston and Savannah for most of its career. Poor judgment was its hallmark. In 1864, a Federal force had surrounded and all but annihilated one careless company. On another occasion, the Third foolishly opened fire on a fleet of gunboats, barges, and steamers along the Broad River, only to be repelled by "a terrific fire of grape, shell, and musketry" from the vessels. In the wake of Sherman's advancing armies, three squadrons were in South Carolina while the rest of the unit accompanied Johnston into North Carolina. In later years, one of Betts's men was thankful that the Fifteenth Pennsylvania encountered the Third South Carolina that morning. "If we had run into one of General Wheeler's old regiments as we did into this one—well, I would not, in my seventy-fourth year, be sitting here writing this story," he admitted.[17]

Poor judgment once again haunted the Third South Carolina on the morning of April 11. Blue-clad scouts confirmed the captive's story and found the enemy camp ten miles from Greensboro. They also noted that the Confederates there were just waking up and cooking breakfast. The hungry scouts were near enough to smell the food. The best news, however, was that the South Carolinians had posted no pickets and were therefore vulnerable to surprise attack. After his scouts reported back, Betts huddled with his officers and reminded them of Colonel Palmer's lesson that a bold charge by a small body of men could overcome a larger force. Johnson's detachment was roughly equal in size to Betts's command, but Betts did not know that. He decided to charge anyway. Lieutenant Charles E. Beck and ten or fifteen men on good horses would lead the way. McGee and his troopers, who did not want to miss the excitement, received permission to join Beck. The advance was to locate the camp and then charge it, making as much noise as possible. The rest of the detachment would follow, except for fifteen or so cavalrymen on worn-out animals, who would guard the rear and flanks.[18]

Although morning had come, the fog still hung low, virtually concealing the warriors from view. Urging their horses into a trot, the Pennsylvanians entered a small valley. Like fireflies on a summer night, campfires winked on a hill to their left. It was the enemy camp. One hundred yards from the foot of the hill, the men slid their revolvers from their holsters. As they approached the camp, leather creaked, leaves and twigs crunched under hooves, and the tension mounted. Would they be discovered? Would the enemy resist? The bugler, astride a blind horse, put his instrument to his lips and blew the charge. Horses and riders leaped at the sound, galloping up the hill. "When we got to the place where we would leave the road and take the hill obliquely," recalled one Federal, "in looking around to see what was before us I saw a group of men standing by their camp fire some distance from the main camp and directly to our left. My first thought was that they would get away. I turned my horse out of ranks, went straight at them and fired two shots. By this time I was getting close enough to see that their arms were piled under shelter, so I dashed in between them and their guns and ordered their 'hands up,' which order was obeyed instantly. One big, fat fellow, a few feet up the hill above the others, was down on his knees behind a stump, and yelling at the top of his voice, 'I surrender! I surrender!'—long sound on the 'I.' Six men gave up."[19]

Moments before the attack, Adjutant Josiah Reiff rode back to explain the plan to Selden Wilson's rear guard. Wilson's men responded by closing in on the column. They barely had time to catch up when Wilson heard Colonel Betts shout, "Charge!" As bugle calls rolled down the hillside, the soldiers of the rear guard dropped their carbines, drew their revolvers, and joined the wild ride into camp. "It was dark and the road was rough but we rushed on[,] landing in their camp while they were cooking and eating their breakfast, and you bet we did not go in very quietly," Wilson wrote. "We were shooting and holloing like Indians. They were so surprised that very few of them got their arms or horses. Many got away in the dark."[20]

From his saddle, Betts sized up the enemy response. "We met with considerable resistance[,] the Rebels grasping their guns and firing at us from behind trees for some 10 minutes when we got them," he wrote. Among the defenders was Colonel Johnson, forty years old, who aimed at Adjutant Reiff but hit his horse instead. Johnson did not have time for a second shot. Reiff fired back and then swung his saber. His shot missed, but the sharp steel struck Johnson and persuaded him to surrender. Everywhere, the speed and shock of the attack and the demoralizing sight of blue warriors pointing revolvers and waving sabers were too much. Most of the South Carolinians surrendered or ran, some jumping into a deep ditch in a nearby meadow. They probably could have held out there for some time, but the Federals threatened no quarter, and the South Carolinians wisely gave up.[21]

Suddenly, it was over. In mere minutes, the Fifteenth Pennsylvania had annihilated Johnson's battalion. While some Federal estimates ran as high as eighty prisoners, Betts reported that his men killed one Confederate and bagged forty-eight more. The haul included one captain, two lieutenants, and Johnson. The raiders also captured as many as seventy-five horses, at least one wagon, thirty stands of arms, and some camp equipment.[22]

To the victors go the spoils, and so it was with the Pennsylvanians. Some one-sided horse trading placed the Confederates' fresh mounts in Federal hands. Unable to carry off all their prizes, the Federals cut the spokes of the enemy wagons and destroyed guns and equipment. The most popular prize of all was the South Carolinians' uneaten breakfast, which the Federals devoured. Selden Wilson considered himself the luckiest of all. He found a Dutch oven with a chicken pot pie inside, as well as a canteen filled with peach brandy. Wilson magnanimously shared the liquor and the pot pie with Betts and other troopers.[23]

After their meal, the Federals mounted their prisoners on worn-out horses and lined them up. The scene verged on the comical, for prisoners were almost as numerous as guards. Betts ordered his men to shoot any prisoner who tried to escape. The threat of escape was probably low, however, because most of the Rebels were awed. "Do you fight this way all the time?" a prisoner asked Sergeant McGee. "Yes, this is our style of fighting; how do you like it?" he answered. McGee, equally curious, asked why the South Carolinians offered only minimal resistance. The night before, a captive explained, the Confederates had sent out scouting parties. When the Federals appeared, the men in camp simply assumed that the approaching column was their own, so they were unprepared for the attack.[24]

For his part, Johnson was disgusted. Recalling the personal battle he and Reiff had waged, he rode up to Reiff and snapped, "Adjutant, allow me to congratulate you upon your bad marksmanship."

"The same to you, d___n you," the trooper shot back.[25]

Later, Palmer was effusive with praise. "The 15th sailed into a South Carolina Regt of Cavalry near Greensboro in a manner worthy of its best days," he told a friend, "capturing the Lieut Colonel Comdg and Everything they had. Adjutant Reiff chopped that Rebel Colonel a little with his sabre." In his after-action report, Palmer cited Betts for outstanding leadership and also praised Reiff for conspicuous gallantry. In 1892, Betts would receive the Medal of Honor for the rout of the Third South Carolina Cavalry. The citation would explain that Betts, "with a force of but 75 men, while on a scouting expedition, by a judicious disposition of his men, surprised and captured an entire battalion of the enemy's cavalry." The medal bore engraved words commending Betts for "distinguished conduct near Greensboro, North Carolina," but misdated the action to April 19. Betts did not care. He called it "one of the greatest honors of my life."[26]

But the laurels would come later. For now, Betts had a mission to accomplish. Leaving the smoldering camp, he led his men another mile closer to Greensboro, where they dismounted to feed their horses. Before returning to Salem, Betts wanted to be as conspicuous as possible. Surely, escaped Confederates would soon raise the alarm and draw attention away from Palmer's other detachments and directly toward Betts's highly visible presence on the main road.[27]

Nor was that all. As the horses ate, Betts summoned Sergeant Wilson. "Sergeant," Betts said, "I want you to pick ten of the best men and horses in this command—you know them all—and if a man you want does not have a good horse, and if a man you do not want has a horse you do want, I will see that you get what you want. Tell the men to eat quickly and get ready at once and you come back and I will give you your orders." Wilson quickly gathered ten dependable men and ten excellent mounts. He personally selected a horse from an officer of the Third South Carolina. The horse was ornamented with a heavy silver-plated bridle that bore the Palmetto State's coat of arms.[28]

Presently, Wilson and his ten men gathered around Colonel Betts. An elderly citizen recruited to guide the Federal troopers was also there. The men listened as Betts explained their task. About four miles outside Greensboro, the North Carolina Railroad crossed Buffalo Creek. Wilson was to go to that bridge. If it proved to be unguarded, he was to burn it and cut the telegraph wire. If the bridge was held in strength, Wilson could ignore it, but the wire had to be cut at all costs. Afterward, Wilson could either rejoin the brigade at Salem or Shallow Ford or latch onto other detachments, as circumstances dictated. "You know what horses can stand and make the trip on trot or gallop. You will be away from any other troops," Betts cautioned.[29]

With that, Wilson's squad rode away. Betts saw it off with some misgivings. "Knowing the man and the danger attending it I bade him good bye with slight expectation of seeing him again, but could not spare him any larger force," Betts told a regimental reunion years afterward. But if Wilson was troubled, he gave no hint of it. For two hours, the eleven cavalrymen headed east, following the guide. Their alert eyes scanned the landscape, but they saw nothing—no enemies and no civilians, only a quiet, empty land. The only signs of life were some distant puffs rising above trees and hills to the south. The tiny white clouds rose from a locomotive heading toward Greensboro from Jamestown, where another Federal detachment was doing its destructive work. The quiet was unnerving, and the apparent danger troubled the old guide. The man began to complain, but Wilson told him he could not be released just yet. He also warned his men to carefully note their route in case they were separated.[30]

At length, Wilson and his squad arrived at the bridge. Approaching quietly, they were relieved to find it unguarded. Only one young man was present; the troopers briefly detained him, then shooed him away. Then it was time to go to work. "When we came in sight of the bridge I told Jonas Cottrell to take one of the axes we had gotten along the road—a man would hold his horse—and for him to cut the telegraph pole," Wilson wrote. The rest tackled the eighty-foot bridge, which soon burst into flames. "It did not take much chopping of kindling as the roof and whole structure was made of pitch pine," the sergeant noted. The noise drew a farmer working in a nearby field. "Men, don't spoil my ax," the farmer said. "Let me have it; I will help you, for I am as good a Union man as God ever let live, but it is the first time I ever dared say so," he said. The farmer was allowed to help.[31]

Jonas Cottrell had a harder time with the telegraph pole. He was a strong man—something of a Samson, in Wilson's eyes—but the pole did not accept its fate meekly. The ground around the bridge was rough and stony, and the pole stood on a bank about twenty feet above its surroundings. Having no good place to stand, Cottrell managed only to knock the pole off its base. It remained stubbornly upright, suspended by the telegraph wires. Cottrell let out a string of curses and went at the pole again, ax blade flashing in the early-morning sun.

He finally succeeded in cutting the wires, thus silencing the telegraph line to Greensboro.[32]

Smoke from the burning bridge billowed into the April sky while, just a few miles away, Jefferson Davis and his cabinet debated the future of the Confederacy. Wilson's mission was complete, and none of his men had been lost. Now, he thought, "the thing to do was to get back." The sergeant released his guide. The man apparently had a change of heart and protested that the Federals would get lost, but Wilson preferred to follow his own star. During the march to the bridge, Wilson had surmised that he and his men could travel faster by cutting across a hollow and some woods, so off they went. It proved to be the right move, as the enemy was stirring. Near Buffalo Creek, the troopers saw a squad of at least fifty enemy cavalrymen fleeing Jamestown. The Confederates did not spot Wilson's men, and they also ignored the burning bridge. Within minutes, the contingent passed on toward Greensboro, and the troopers breathed easier, though they continued to keep their eyes peeled. "We kept a good lookout all around us but dodged everything of danger," Wilson wrote. The men next happened upon a country store where a crowd of men, women, and children had surrounded two barrels of applejack. The troopers asked Wilson if they could draw liquor from the barrels, too. Wilson agreed, but only if they would promise to abstain until they got back to their companies. Only one trooper, an Irishman, disobeyed. He got drunk and strayed but later made his way back to Federal lines.[33]

While Wilson's men destroyed the Buffalo Creek bridge, Betts withdrew the rest of his detachment toward Salem. Legend has it that the Federals turned away from Greensboro thanks to a telegraph operator's false answers to some inquiries; in reality, the raiders left because they had accomplished their objectives. Betts's chief worry was how to control his many prisoners while maintaining his combat power. His solution was to assign one man to guard every three prisoners. He also reiterated his orders to open fire if anyone tried to escape. Every other trooper was charged with defending the column. Ten men under Sergeant Lyman S. Strickler took the advance with orders to attack any force they encountered. A similar number brought up the rear. Thus organized, the withdrawal began.[34]

It was a disconcerting journey. Some enemy cavalrymen materialized in the distance, watching and waiting. Presently, a larger enemy force appeared on the Federals' left, but Strickler's advance guard chased it away. A still-larger contingent was spotted on the right. Again, the advance guard charged, possibly killing

Main Street in Salem, North Carolina, in 1866. On April 10–11, 1865, Palmer's brigade used Salem as a base of operations while detachments raided toward Greensboro, High Point, and Lexington.
COLLECTION OF OLD SALEM MUSEUMS AND GARDENS

one enemy soldier with a lucky shot. Colonel Johnson took heart from these developments. As the blue column descended a long, gentle hill, he glimpsed Betts's entire column. "Why Colonel Betts, where are your men?" he asked, surprised by the size of the detachment. He predicted that the Confederate prisoners and the Federal guards would soon exchange places. Privately, Betts knew the odds were against him, but he bluffed the South Carolinian. "There are others within supporting distance," he said.[35]

If the prisoners and the hovering Confederates were not enough to worry about, a courier atop a sweating horse brought new troubles. Reining in at Betts's side, the courier presented a hastily written message from Palmer in Salem. It stated that Colonel Trowbridge and the Tenth Michigan Cavalry were in trouble. Some twenty miles southeast of Betts's position, the Michigan troopers had run into more than a thousand enemy cavalrymen. "Col. T is falling back to

Salem, fighting them all the way, but is somewhat pressed by the rebels," Palmer wrote. "On receipt of this you will immediately start back at the trot to this place to re-inforce us. Start back with your reserve, and send for the detachments to follow you." To ensure that Betts got back quickly, Palmer told him to take the direct road. The only exception was Betts's detachment to the north, which could recross the Yadkin without going through Salem. "Keep a sharp lookout on your left (Western) flank as you return, and if you find you can help us by charging the right flank of the Rebels do so, otherwise go around to the right and join us at Salem."[36]

Suddenly, fortune seemed to be turning against the raiders. Where were Kramer and Garner with the other detachments? Betts wondered. And how had Trowbridge gotten into this mess?

~

While Betts marched on Greensboro, the detachment he sent from Kernersville pushed southwest on the Jamestown road.[37] Captain Adam Kramer, known to his comrades as "Dickory," commanded the detachment. Eighty-six troopers from Companies I, K, and L followed him. Although they were the best-mounted soldiers in those companies, even their horses were tired. The long ride had taken its toll, and this extra jaunt promised no rest. Captain Frank Remont called it "one of those all-night rides with which we had by that time become very familiar, but which we never learned to love." At least this weary march offered many Federals a chance to remount. "The men kept themselves awake by their anxiety to procure fresh horses from an 'unplucked' country, and the necessary exertion to obtain them and yet keep up with the little column, moving silently along the sandy roads through the midnight darkness," Kramer wrote.[38]

At five in the morning, the cavalrymen spied the village of Jamestown. The vista that lay before them was incongruous, as described by a later traveler: "County poor—houses small & dilapidated—women dirty. Sometimes picturesque—hills covered with verdu[r]e." Best of all to the raiders, tracks and buildings of the North Carolina Railroad stood before them. The mournful sound of a locomotive whistle drifted their way. Fog hung like a misty blanket, hiding Kramer just as it covered Betts's men to the north. As day reluctantly broke, Kramer ordered a halt. He wanted information before going farther. After a short delay, some troopers produced a "terrified and most unwilling guide." Once they felt suitably informed, the men snaked ahead. No enemy soldiers were in evidence, so Kramer decided to seize Jamestown without further delay. He ordered his men into "a lively trot" and then split his force. Remont and twelve men angled toward the depot, while Kramer and the rest, in the words of a participant, "plunged across the fields to the right at the gallop."[39]

The latter group aimed for the Deep River railroad bridge just outside town, a vital link in the North Carolina Railroad. With it, rail traffic traveled smoothly from Raleigh to Greensboro to Salisbury; without it, the shipment of troops and supplies from the south to Beauregard and Johnston would cease. Two Confederate guards materialized, but the troopers disarmed and captured them without firing a shot. It took only five minutes for Kramer to claim the prize.

Eighty-five feet long and thirty-five feet above the river, it was a covered truss bridge of highly flammable yellow pine. Near at hand was enough kindling to get a good fire started. The guard shack, made of loose planks, was easily dismantled with axes taken from inside. A nearby telegraph pole was brought down, too, and the telegraph line severed with it. Then the men piled the kindling on the bridge and added a straw mattress they found in the shanty. Distant whistles announced the approach of more trains and added impetus to the work. In less than fifteen minutes, the bridge was aflame; in thirty minutes, it was a wreck. "As it was composed of yellow pitch pine its destruction was wonderfully rapid and just as the little party left the [bridge] fell down with a loud crash," Kramer wrote. Thanks to the troopers' work, "competent engineers state that even with the best of facilities, it could not be rebuilt in less time than four weeks." Simultaneously, a troop train—probably the one that produced the puffs noted by Betts and his men—approached the bridge. When the engineer saw the blazing span, he stopped and backed away. Later, the troop train would return, too late to save the bridge. Its mission accomplished, Kramer's detail prepared to pull out of Jamestown once Remont returned.[40]

Meanwhile, Captain Remont and his party dashed for the Jamestown depot, spurred on by locomotive whistles. They found it about three-fourths of a mile from town and easily captured six enemy guards. The men also seized seven cars, four of them loaded with commissary supplies. Among the loot were several hundred weapons, along with large quantities of cotton, flour, grain, meat, cloth, salt, and molasses. After taking whatever they wanted, Remont's men applied the torch.[41]

While his troopers fanned the flames, Remont wisely posted pickets. One of them was Private George Alexander. When he was relieved, Alexander sought a replacement for his worn-out horse. Stopping at a farm, he tethered his horse to a fence and quickly located a suitable beast. A young lady begged him to leave it, however, so he gave up. Returning to the fence, Alexander stopped short. Several other horses were now tied beside his own. Arms and equipment leaned against the fence. Thirteen white and ten black men, wearing clothing of assorted colors and styles, were beside the horses cooking and eating. Eyeing one man rifling through his saddlebags, Alexander approached and ordered him to stop. Then he asked the stranger, "Have you seen the lot of rebels we captured in Jamestown?"

Up to that moment, neither man had guessed the other's identity. Alexander's dirty, greasy uniform concealed his Union blue, and the disordered Confederates wore enough blue to conceal their allegiance. The stranger answered, "You're one of Wheeler's men, are you not?"[42]

Suddenly, the truth dawned on Alexander. He grabbed his carbine, leveled it, and announced that the men were now his prisoners. Anybody who dared move would get shot, he added. The Confederates obeyed and watched Alexander ruin their rifle-muskets by bending the barrels against the fence. He then ordered the party to ride bareback toward Jamestown. A few minutes later, another Federal appeared to help. Soon, Remont had more than a dozen cursing, disgusted prisoners in hand. Other troopers brought in additional prisoners. Private Samuel E. Wampler captured three men.[43]

Back in Jamestown, Captain Kramer was growing impatient because of Remont's absence. The smoke pouring from the bridge and the depot announced the troopers' presence for miles around and deepened Kramer's concern. Scouts announced that they were in a more precarious position than expected. "I was now within five miles of Greensboro in which place from the best information there was a considerable force under General Beauregard," the Federal captain wrote. Kramer also learned that a Confederate cavalry brigade was camped just three miles away; enemy cavalrymen were visible on the surrounding hillsides. The captain posted his men on the incoming roads and sent a courier to hurry Remont. Fifteen tense minutes passed before Remont finally arrived. Slowed by the prisoners who were on foot, he had been further delayed by squads of Rebels nipping at his heels and even forcing an occasional skirmish. Now, the column began to leave, about sixty horses and mules and thirty-five prisoners in tow.[44]

The men did not simply ride away, given the other points of interest along the way. According to local tradition, the Federal raiders left one Jamestown mill intact after a persuasive miller claimed he was grinding meal for women and children. Less clear is the fate of the Jamestown Woolen Mill, which stood about a quarter-mile from town along the Deep River. About forty people in the two-story wooden building carded, spun, wove, dyed, and finished yarn for Confederate uniforms. The mill's fifteen looms, two sets of cards, and spinning jack were tempting targets. Stories as to its fate abound. Some local historians suggest that the mill went up in smoke and its workers were arrested and jailed. One gentleman recalled being held against a wall at gunpoint while the raiders struck matches. According to another tale, the Federals ended up at the mill by accident. When asked for directions, some flustered boys sent them there instead of to the arms facility the raiders really wanted. The truth remains elusive, for Federal accounts are silent and local accounts unsatisfactory.[45]

The fate of at least one factory is certain, however. Retracing their route to Salem at a rapid walk, the troopers reached the hamlet of Florence, where they found the North Carolina Armory. Under the direction of Captain Zimri S. Coffin, the armory was still in operation, unlike most of the factories in the area. About thirty or forty men worked there. Kramer described it as "a large structure in which rifles, carbines, &c were being turned out in large quantity for the Rebel army. This structure was mostly of wood, 3 stories in height, and from 70 to 90 feet long, together with its contents consisting of about 3500 stand of arms finished and in process of manufacture, and a large quantity of material and very valuable machinery of English make which could not be replaced." The Federals also discovered some ammunition and an apparatus for assaying and coining gold and silver, and even some of the coin. While Lieutenant Ed Smith and five men fired the armory, Kramer paroled some captured citizens and then mounted the remaining captives on horses.[46]

Now moving at a faster speed, the detachment resumed the march at about nine in the morning. Enemy soldiers were about, but none challenged the Federals. Reaching the Kernersville road without incident, the troopers paused to wait on Betts. "The rest of an hour, seemed rather to aggravate the fatigue of the men," a witness wrote. Around noon, Betts came into view from the east, on the way back from his Greensboro expedition. Kramer took stock of his raid for his boss. He reported that his troopers had ridden more than fifty miles in about twelve hours, accomplished their objectives, captured about three dozen prisoners, and replaced their mounts. Although the distance covered was closer to forty miles, it was still no mean feat. Only one man, Private Anthony Gibbons of Company K, was missing, having fallen into enemy hands while foraging. Kramer proudly reported, "The behavior of both men and officers was in the highest degree commendable." Palmer agreed. In his after-action report, he praised Kramer for his "skill and gallantry" in destroying the important Deep River railroad bridge, as well as arms, munitions, and trains.[47]

But praise would come later. For now, Betts was worried by the message from Palmer announcing that Trowbridge was in trouble. Kramer was now at hand, but where was Garner?

For once, their famished horses were satiated. Frederic Antes and his comrades of the Fifteenth Pennsylvania Cavalry saw to that before their all-night ride. It began an hour before midnight on April 10, as Lieutenant Colonel Charles Betts led dozens of dusty horsemen east from Salem. Five miles beyond Kernersville, Antes and ninety-nine other men, all under the guidance of Major Abraham B. Garner, turned north. Their objective was the Piedmont Railroad bridge over Reedy Fork, a tributary of the Haw River. Destroying the bridge would halt rail communications between Danville and Greensboro.[48]

Garner's nighttime ride was a difficult one. His target, northeast of Greensboro, was deep in enemy country, so the Confederate presence was thick in his path. That forced him to change his route so he could avoid a fight wherever possible. The rear guard got into a scrape near the railroad, but that did not stop the troopers' momentum. They arrived at the bridge without a scratch at eleven in the morning on April 11. (Meanwhile, to the southwest, Kramer was rejoining Betts's column. Thirty miles to the west, the Second and Third brigades were at Huntsville.) Before Garner stretched a new span built of stubborn hardwood that would not yield willingly to ax or flame. Undaunted, the men tackled the bridge with a will. "By two hours' hard work with axes and saws on the main beams it was put in condition for fire to do the balance of the work," Garner reported. Then the bridge gained a brief reprieve. "Before we burned the bridge, a train of freight cars came along and we stood on the bank guerilla style, and fired into the train, but they got away safely," another Federal wrote. The train was not the only threat. "While we were hacking at the trestles a rebel cavalry command which had been following us on the march attacked our skirmish-line. We dropped our axes, mounted and formed in haste, just as our skirmishers, led by Serg't Marshall, charged them, and we following with a genuine Yankee yell. [T]hey took to the woods, and we did not see nor hear of them again." When the excitement subsided, the Federals returned to their work. By early afternoon, the bridge was ablaze.[49]

The troopers consigned one ambulance and nine wagons to the flames and rounded up between forty and fifty mules. Confederate cavalrymen attacked the Federals a second time, but the results were the same. As Garner put it, the raiders were obliged "to drive off a force of cavalry, about our equal in number, after finishing the work." Another participant, Baldwin Colton, added that the scrum did not stop the men from performing their "laudable job" of bridge burning.[50]

Bathing in the firelight of their destroyed objective did little for Sergeant John K. Marshall's humor. He was a worried man. Marshall was in the thick of the fighting around the bridge and saw firsthand how the enemy was growing in boldness and strength. Intelligence suggested that the Confederates came from Wheeler's Tennessee regiment—the same one that had battled Trowbridge at Henry Court House—as well as an unidentified unit from Greensboro. Now that the time had come to withdraw, he wondered if the raiders would escape at all. When Lieutenant Theo Ramsey was ordered to lead the advance guard on the return trip, Marshall insisted on resuming his position with the guard. As the withdrawal began, enemy troops shadowed the raiders.[51]

The tiny party aimed for Shallow Ford at first, but plans changed upon the receipt of news of the emergency at Salem. Rather than risk getting mixed up with the pursuing Confederates, Garner decided to head for Glenn's Ferry, a Yadkin River crossing north of Shallow Ford. From there, he figured he could follow Stoneman toward Salisbury while avoiding any Confederates in the area. It turned out to be the right plan.[52]

Near midnight on April 12–13, the raiders safely reached Glenn's Ferry. It had taken thirty-six hours to cover forty-odd miles. Both men and horses were exhausted. They had been on the move for about forty of the past fifty hours. They allowed themselves a two-hour rest before crossing the Yadkin. Some made it across by boat and others on horseback. One trooper had no luck with either method until the enemy prodded him. "The mule he rode would not swim, and while he debated what to do the rebels came up and settled the question for him," a comrade recalled.[53]

Garner's detachment found safety on the far bank of the Yadkin and camped near Conrad's Ferry before resuming the march. Because his horses were in such bad shape, the major decided to take it slow for the next couple of days. The men would not rejoin the Cavalry Division until late on April 13. Whatever pace they adopted, they would be welcomed warmly for their performance. As Palmer later reported, Garner displayed considerable "gallantry and skill in having . . . his battalion of 100 men [destroy] the railroad bridge over Reedy Fork, between Danville and Greensborough[, and evade] superior forces of the enemy."[54]

Legend has it that a raider posing as a Confederate telegraphed Greensboro to ascertain Jefferson Davis's whereabouts and the strength of the Confederate forces in town. The operator at Greensboro replied that the president was not there but a large force was. That message supposedly caused Stoneman to turn away from Greensboro. In truth, he never planned to strike the town. At the same time, the raiders missed out on a history-changing opportunity. While the Federals were destroying the bridge, they learned that Davis and his cabinet were somewhere nearby. True enough, the Confederate leaders had traveled from Danville to Greensboro by train that same day and passed over the Reedy Fork bridge just hours before the Federals destroyed it. The close shave prompted Davis to make his "A miss is as good as a mile" remark.[55]

⌘

At ten o'clock on the night of April 10, 1865, a second column of cavalry emerged from the Moravian town of Salem. This was Colonel Luther Trowbridge's Tenth Michigan Cavalry Regiment. The Michigan men took a more southerly route than Betts's regiment, but their objective was the same: the North Carolina Railroad. Trowbridge's column split when it approached within seven miles of the railroad. While Trowbridge and two of his battalions headed for a railroad bridge over Abbott's Creek, the third battalion, under Captain James H. Cummins, rode for High Point. Its objective was to draw attention from Trowbridge's column and, as trooper Steven Thomas told his wife, burn "the Depot and Government property and tear up the [rail]road."[56]

Although a receding hairline, puffy cheeks, and a scruffy beard made Captain Cummins look like a teacher or a salesman, he was every inch a solider. Wrapping his legs around a fresh horse, Cummins led the High Point contingent through the night. The mount was a recent gift from his men, who had found the horse earlier that day at the Davidson County farm of Samuel D. Yokeley

about seven miles from Salem. An avowed Unionist who had helped men escape from the Salisbury prison, Yokeley could do little as the Federals relieved
him of his mare and a silver watch. The men told Yokeley that the mare looked
"smart and fast" and would suit Cummins "exactly." Yokeley went to Salem the
next morning to get his horse back, but he was too late. Cummins had already
left for High Point.[57]

Indeed, the battalion was busy in High Point even as Yokeley arrived at
Salem. The town was situated on the highest point of the North Carolina Railroad and had earned its name accordingly. As a railhead, High Point was a way
station for wounded awaiting transportation to the large Confederate hospitals
at Goldsboro, Richmond, and Petersburg. After the fall of those towns, they
were crammed into High Point's hotels, churches, and even the girls' school.
Local women nursed the sick and wounded and thereby created their own legends. The name of Laura Wesson is still held above all others. She nursed men
stricken with smallpox until the disease claimed her, too.[58]

Churning dust, Cummins's troopers entered the town at high speed. It was

*Captain James H. Cummins
commanded the battalion of the
Tenth Michigan Cavalry that
captured High Point.*

Massachusetts Commandery
Military Order of the Loyal Legion
and the United States Army
Military History Institute

just before breakfast on April 11 when fifteen-year-old Henry Sechrest looked up. (At the same moment, Kramer was reaching Jamestown, Garner was riding for Reedy Fork, Betts was routing the Third South Carolina, and the rest of the division was crossing Shallow Ford.) Sechrest's hands were caked with the dirt of his family's Main Street garden, but the approaching rumble from a column of blue-clad cavalrymen galloping toward the depot ended any thoughts of horticulture. The Federals captured two trains packed with supplies and torched the depot, warehouses, water station, and shed of the North Carolina Railroad. They also captured warehouses full of clothing and destroyed a small gun shop that made stocks and sold them to other concerns.[59]

More than one thousand bales of cotton piled alongside the tracks went up in smoke. The cotton belonged to Salem businessman Francis Fries, Rufus Patterson's father-in-law. When he heard the Federals were coming to High Point, Fries decided to save as much cotton as he could. He loaded two four-horse wagons with all they could carry, hid them in some woods along a creek outside town, and waited. The next morning, when passersby reported that Union cavalrymen were at High Point, Fries waited a bit longer. A day later, he decided it was safe to return. Upon his arrival, he realized his worst fears. In the ashes of the railroad station, Fries saw "what had been our accumulation of cotton, 1500 bales, piled up on the end of the depot lot, and covered with boards. I learned that the party of Stoneman's men who had wrought the damage, had only been a small scouting party. I heard that our mill had been burned and that Gen. Lee had surrendered the day before. Altogether it was a pretty blue day." Fries also lost a pocketknife to a roving band of ruffians. But at least he saved some of his cotton.[60]

Robert Alexander Jenkins, a member of Beauregard's staff since January, saw the burning cotton from his train window. Earlier, Beauregard had sent Jenkins to Salisbury to obtain supplies. The return trip to Greensboro was full of rumors of the raid. Soon, Jenkins found himself in the middle of it. "Coming to High Point, and running at a very rapid rate, we saw a troop of Federal cavalry coming into the town," he wrote. "One officer, riding a gray horse, rode up to a building not very far from the track, in which cotton was stored, and set fire to the building. This act of vandalism was being done just as our train flew past the station. I jerked a gun from one of the guards and fired at the officer, but never knew whether the ball took effect or not." Farther up the track, Jenkins witnessed Kramer's Deep River bridge actions, too. "Near Jamestown . . . was a small covered bridge which the engineer saw was burning, but as he had previous orders to ignore all obstructions, he dashed along and ran through the bridge safely," he wrote.[61]

Back in High Point, Cummins's firebrands got a bit carried away. According to local legend, some torch-bearing troopers eyed a warehouse, but citizens convinced them not to burn it. The warehouse was near the Barbee Hotel, and locals feared that fire would spread from the warehouse to the hotel and endanger the wounded within. The raiders compromised, moving the warehouse's contents into an open square and burning them there. Shoes, supplies, clothing, and medicine taken from the train were also fired. Despite the precautions, the flames soon threatened to engulf the hotel. Alert residents moved the wounded to a sweet potato field while bucket brigades fought the inferno.[62]

All in all, it was a thorough job of destruction. In the words of one man, Cummins "performed very creditably." Estimates placed the value of destroyed goods at $2 to $4 million. In his after-action report, Palmer cited Captain Cummins for capturing High Point and "destroying the track, telegraph, and a large quantity of supplies and railroad trains loaded with quartermaster's stores."[63]

Cummins did not linger with his detachment. Reports placing Stephen D. Lee south of High Point and Robert F. Hoke north of it prompted a speedy withdrawal, which indeed proved fortunate for the Michigan men. Shortly after Cummins's departure, Confederate cavalrymen arrived at High Point. We "got out just in time to save our bacon [as] 300 Rebel Cav charged into Town within an hour after we left," Thomas wrote. Later that day, Brigadier General Collett Leventhorpe reported the results of the raids on High Point and Jamestown to Governor Vance. "Very painful rumors from Virginia," he added, in reference to Lee's surrender.[64]

⁕

For all of Cummins's success, Trowbridge ran into trouble. In his own words, Trowbridge "came very near getting into a bad fix." At the start, however, the colonel's independent foray encountered no more difficulties than the four other Federal columns crisscrossing Piedmont North Carolina. After Cummins and the Third Battalion peeled off for High Point, Trowbridge continued with his two remaining battalions. No more than three hundred men were in his column. Their job was to destroy the railroad bridge over Abbott's Creek and then

*Captain James B. Roberts of
Ionia, Michigan, directed the
advance guard at Abbott's Creek.*
MASSACHUSETTS COMMANDERY MILITARY
ORDER OF THE LOYAL LEGION AND THE
UNITED STATES ARMY MILITARY HISTORY
INSTITUTE

proceed to Salisbury to cooperate with Stoneman.[65]

"Another all night march was before us," Trowbridge wrote. "It was desirable that the bridges should be destroyed before daylight." The mustachioed victor of Henry Court House sent two companies ahead at a trot while the rest followed at a leisurely pace. "All our information was to the effect that there was no force of the enemy in that vicinity," Trowbridge noted. "It seemed quite unnecessary, but as a matter of form, a small advance guard was sent forward although it was confidently expected that should there be any enemy on the road, timely notice would be given by the two companies which had gone on in advance." Captain James B. Roberts of Ionia, Michigan, commanded the advance guard.[66]

But Trowbridge was in for a surprise, thanks to Sam Ferguson's Confederate brigade. The homespun-clad unit, one thousand strong, arrived in Lexington at the same time Trowbridge left Salem. Its march from Augusta, Georgia, had been long and difficult, with starts and stops aplenty due to the fluid situation. On March 29, it reached the Saluda River; on April 3, Beauregard ordered it to Greensboro; it was later directed to Danville, then again to Greensboro. The editor of the *Carolina Watchman* thought it likely that Ferguson's cavalrymen would run into Stoneman, but Ferguson himself apparently did not. He was absent, escorting his wife to the home of a family member. In his stead, forty-seven-year-old colonel William Boyles commanded the brigade, which numbered five veteran regiments—the Second Alabama, the Fifty-sixth Alabama Partisan Rangers, the Ninth Mississippi, the Tenth Mississippi, and the Eleventh Mississippi. Although Federal observers reported the presence of infantry, that is uncertain.[67]

Boyles's men were more than enough to contend with. After passing through Salisbury on the morning of April 10, the Confederates camped for the night near Trowbridge's objective, the Abbott's Creek railroad bridge, which stood midway between Lexington and Thomasville on the North Carolina Railroad. In 1860, Lexington was a town of fifteen hundred inhabitants. Named for the Revolutionary War battle, it had not grown much since the North Carolina Railroad reached it in the mid-1850s. Passengers admired the "pretty village with some fine houses of brick &c & a court house" and the "rich soil red clay" valley.[68]

For the Federals, the night passed without incident. They stopped only once to feed their horses. At some point, an officer captured a telegraph office, where he discovered an erroneous message announcing the fall of Lynchburg.[69] At dawn on April 11, a Company B blacksmith brought the Federal colonel the grim news that he had nearly run into enemy pickets. Henry Court House had shown that Trowbridge was sometimes hasty in his judgment, and he was again this day. He ignored the blacksmith, assuming the man had simply seen the pickets of his own advance companies. By now, Trowbridge thought, his advance guard should be at the bridge. On the raiders went.

Captain William H. Dunn was the first to spot a covered wagon turning into the road and disappearing around a bend. When Dunn pointed out the wagon, Trowbridge permitted him to capture it. The Michigan men quickly surrounded the wagon and nabbed two Confederate officers inside. An interrogation produced some interesting intelligence. "They informed me," Trowbridge later wrote, "that a large force of Confederate cavalry was encamped some distance ahead on the road." Trowbridge dismissed this, just as he had the information minutes earlier, chalking it up to a Rebel ruse. Surely, his two advance companies would have informed him if the enemy lay ahead. The captives were turned over to the officer of the day, and the Federals moved on.[70]

Meanwhile, Captain Roberts's Federals reached the bridge. When Cornwallis passed through the area during the Revolutionary War, fearful locals had packed their valuables into a barrel and sunk it in the creek. Rumor had it that the spot was haunted, but Roberts's men ignored the ghosts and simply de-

Captain William H. Dunn commanded a company of the Tenth Michigan Cavalry. A fellow officer described him as "bright, jolly, and full of fun."
MASSACHUSETTS COMMANDERY MILITARY ORDER OF THE LOYAL LEGION AND THE UNITED STATES ARMY MILITARY HISTORY INSTITUTE

stroyed the 250-foot bridge at this critical spot. It was the third North Carolina Railroad bridge Stoneman's troopers had burned, in addition to the Reedy Fork bridge on the Danville road.[71]

Trowbridge at last realized he should have paid attention to the warnings. His men confirmed that a large enemy force was bivouacked just ahead. It was Ferguson's Brigade. Since Roberts's detachment was still afield, Trowbridge ordered a barricade thrown across the road. Dunn and his "reliable and plucky company" took a position behind it, and the rest of the column set up in strong positions nearby. Then they waited.[72]

At about six-thirty that morning, Trowbridge's small advance guard reappeared. The colonel saw it in the distance, at a dead stop. Puzzled, he galloped ahead to investigate. Roberts reported the destruction of the bridge and confirmed that enemy cavalry and infantry were nearby. "There is a large force about a mile down the road," he said. He and his detachment had slipped quietly past the enemy camp while returning from the bridge. Fortunately for the raiders, the Confederates had not spotted them. What to do? Trowbridge quickly calculated the odds and decided that the enemy outnumbered his own force four to one. "With fresh horses it would not have been difficult to make a sudden attack even against largely superior numbers with the chances of success greatly in our favor," he later wrote. "But with horses worn by a continuous march of twenty-four hours without rest, it seemed extremely hazardous to attack a force so largely outnumbering ours, and that force refreshed by a comfortable night's rest in camp." Another consideration also dawned on the colonel. A successful attack would drive the enemy toward Salisbury, where Stoneman was headed at that very moment. Pushing the Confederates there would only strengthen Salisbury's defenses, whereas drawing them away would increase the probability of Stoneman's success.[73]

The decision was easy. Trowbridge gave the order to withdraw in column, only to find it was too late. "No sooner was the movement commenced than we were attacked with great fury. I think I may be pardoned for saying that there then followed one of the most spirited and exciting, and in my judgment, one of the best fought minor engagements of the war," he wrote. To ward off the foe, the colonel organized a cautious retreat. The plan was for the Tenth to retire by alternate squadrons, thus ensuring that a solid front always faced the advancing Confederates. It worked simply but effectively. As the Confederates advanced, one Federal company would wheel out of column and into line of battle. While this line held the enemy back with blazing Spencers, its comrades pulled back to form a new line of battle. Then, once the new line was ready, the fighting company would wheel into column and fall back to form yet another line of battle. "Oh it was most exciting," Trowbridge wrote the next day. "When I would be forming a new line the enemy would be charging and yelling, and our men firing rapidly and steadily." Throughout, the colonel thought, his men and officers were brave, cool, and well disciplined. They moved as if they were on a parade ground, not pressed by a superior force far behind enemy lines.[74]

Trooper Eber Hendricks, a member of Trowbridge's force, never forgot the long road from Germanton to Abbott's Creek. It was an especially painful one for him, since his foot still throbbed from the coffeepot accident near Deep Gap. All that was forgotten, however, when the Federals "came to a stand by running against" Sam Ferguson's men. "As we were only a small detachment, we fell back. The rebels vigorously attacking. Many were killed on both sides as there was constant fighting over a space of six miles." Apparently, Keith and Malinda Blalock, the Unionist mountain scouts, were participants. They returned fire with their Spencers, shooting "not just a few" of the enemy.[75]

The fight proceeded according to plan, but Trowbridge could not help worrying, since the enemy force, though poorly armed, was so far superior to his own. When a courier reached Salem with the news near ten that morning, Palmer was prompted to summon Betts from Greensboro at a run.[76]

It was a wise move. Trowbridge was not only outnumbered but also hard-pressed by an equally smart Confederate strategy. "The enemy attempted to pass a column by each flank, while the attacks in the rear were made with a daring and courage worthy of a better cause," the colonel noted. The regiment's chronicler agreed. "We were furiously attacked and . . . the enemy [was] pursuing rapidly," he wrote. "This was the most trying attack in which the regiment has been engaged and nothing but the cool bearing of officers and men averted a serious disaster." The terrain—open Piedmont country of low, rolling farmland—was ideal for a cavalry action. But the enemy was never able to get the upper hand, and the Michigan men maintained good order. Indeed, the enemy continued charging for two or three hours across more than six miles until finally giving up.[77]

Afterward, the Federals estimated that the Confederates suffered between fifty and sixty casualties. They were also surprised to learn that none of their own men were hurt in the fight. Only two were missing, having been captured while trying to take horses out of a barn. "It seems very strange as the firing was very rapid & heavy," Trowbridge wrote. "The enemy must have suffered severely as we gave them some splendid volleys & saw many empty saddles." Confederate records provide no official casualty count to dispute the Federal estimate.[78]

If Ferguson had any thoughts about the fighting that raged in his absence, he did not mention them. Other news caught his attention. He arrived in Greensboro early on April 12 and later heard rumors of Lee's surrender. "Old soldiers could be seen by the hundreds, weeping as though their hearts would break, my feelings I cannot attempt to describe," he wrote. New orders came his way as a result. In a meeting with President Davis and Generals Cooper, Johnston, and Beauregard, Ferguson was ordered to take command of all the cavalry and pursue Stoneman. His men would encounter the Federal troopers again in the coming days.[79]

Trowbridge's command returned to Salem. One horseman estimated that the troopers had traveled ninety miles in forty hours with only two feeds, but the distance was actually closer to fifty miles. The men had plenty of laurels to anticipate. "The conduct of both officers & men was worthy of all praise, and it was the proudest day in our history," Trowbridge wrote. Palmer sounded a congratulatory note as well: "The gallant resistance thus made protected and covered the detachments of my brigade which were destroying the railroad at High Point, Deep River, and elsewhere." The brigade commander also praised Major John H. Standish, who fought gallantly, and Trowbridge for "efficiency as a commanding officer in steadily improving the discipline of his regiment from the time of its entering North Carolina."[80] The praise for the Tenth Michigan was richly deserved, but that for its commander was overly generous. For the second time, Trowbridge had gotten his men into an avoidable jam. Only sound tactics and hard fighting had extricated them.

~*~

Meanwhile, the cavalry was riding to the rescue. Fresh from their success against the Third South Carolina, Charles Betts and his troopers were now trotting urgently west in answer to Palmer's summons. Near Kernersville, they linked up with Dickory Kramer's men, who were bursting with tales of destruction and captured prisoners at Jamestown. The column did not wait for Garner or the Fifteenth's third detachment; those men were on their own. So was Wilson's tiny detachment, which had not yet returned from Buffalo Creek. Off they rode again, dust clouds trailing them. The drama continued awhile longer. Horses sweated, men swore, and officers wondered if they would arrive in time to rescue Trowbridge. Then a courier appeared with word that the Tenth Michigan had driven off the enemy and that Betts could return to Salem at a walk. The tension abruptly slackened, and Betts discarded the thought of striking Ferguson's right and rear.[81]

Betts's intrepid band reached town that afternoon. "It was with hearty satisfaction that they finally drew up for a halt in Salem," Kramer wrote. The men sorted out prisoners and prizes and asked what had transpired while they were gone. Salem had experienced a curious mix of quiet and mishap. When the Tenth Michigan and the Fifteenth Pennsylvania moved out on the night of April 10, the Twelfth Ohio had settled into the Moravian community and looked forward to a period of rest. "We drawed forrage for our Horses and flower and Meete for our Selves," an Ohioan recalled.[82]

Because of the Federal presence, worried officials of the Moravian Church decided to cancel a Holy Week service. That night saw a "good deal of riding to and fro in the main street," a local recalled. Many citizens lay awake with fear at the idea of Federal warriors in their midst. "It was a night of anxiety in many a home as in the mid-night hour, amid mad shrieks the commissary stores on Marshall Street were burned," recalled Fannie, the young girl who lived with her mother on Salt Street.[83]

Although the Marshall Street warehouse did not actually burn that night, it was certainly a beehive of activity. Throughout the evening, a hungry mob gathered to plunder the government stockpile there, "which was amply supplied with necessaries for men and horses." At last, the mob rushed the warehouse and took what it could until Palmer's cavalrymen stopped it. "A large barnlike warehouse on Marshall Street, containing government tithes of hay, meal, corn, fodder, and wheat, for the use of the Confederate Army, was also made safe by a guard, so that there was no material [loss], except for some cloth, thousands of yards of which was boldly taken from the Factory without leave or license, and not for the use of either army, but for the benefit of the people who had really not contributed anything for the boys in the Confederate army," wrote the publishers of *Blum's Almanac*. "I did not see the mob, but it was said . . . , as though it had sprung up out of the ground, to consist of all kinds of folks, reputable and disreputable,—men, women, and children," another witness added. Although it did not seem so at the moment, the warehouse was actually a boon to the citizens of Salem. Because of the stores, Federal soldiers required few provisions from the people.[84]

On the morning of April 11, the Ohio troopers remained at Salem. The regiment's commander, Robert T. Bentley, was a Mansfield, Ohio, resident and a veteran of the Thirty-second Ohio. He had served in the Shenandoah Valley, where Federal forces dealt harshly with civilians. Here, it was different. Rather than have his men terrorize residents and plunder or destroy property, Bentley busied his regiment. "We had been pretty near all day engaged in throwing up obstructions across the road," a trooper wrote. The result, contemporary observer R. L. Beall noted, "was a departure from the ordinary course of civilized warfare as practiced by the Federals—there was not the usual amount of pillage." While Beall overstated the case, he correctly pegged the raiders' conduct. A few weeks afterward, a local newspaper recounted that the raiders "strictly [respected] persons and private property."[85]

That did not mean Salem emerged unscathed. The Federals helped themselves to the government stores on Marshall Street, and a few raiders relieved residents of everything from bread to horses and mules. Even the horses belonging to Palmer and his staff were not safe. Just a half-hour after they were stabled, they were stolen by "camp bummers" who did not know who the beasts belonged to. "An orderly reported the theft, and a shout of laughter followed," an eyewitness wrote. "The orderly had to go to camp, where he found them hid in the bushes." A few material items also went missing. The editor of a secessionist newspaper lost several hundred dollars in gold coin, as well as his gold watch. But the Ohioans failed to discover that the basement of a local hotel contained a tailor shop stocked with Confederate uniforms and cloth. When the Federals arrived, the tailor locked the door and slipped out, and no one was the wiser.[86]

The experiences of two Salem citizens were typical. One local Unionist rode out to welcome the cavalrymen and proclaim his loyalty. The Federals smiled, took his mule, and sent him home on foot. Another man, John Butner, decided to transport a load of hay into Salem that Tuesday morning. Harnessing a mule and a mare to his wagon, Butner rode into town. Realizing something was amiss, he stopped at a friend's house. "John, you are in the Yankee lines," the man told him.

"Surely not," a skeptical Butner replied.

"Is that government hay?" someone else asked, pointing to the contents of Butner's wagon.

"No, it belongs to a private individual."

As Butner rode ahead, dozens of blue-clad cavalrymen came into view. One Federal saw Butner, rode across a field, and relieved him of his mule. Convinced at last, Butner unharnessed his mare and started for home, only to have another trooper stop him and take the horse as well. Two of his bridles and some sheep-skin also disappeared. An angry Butner walked to Palmer's headquarters at the mayor's house. A staff officer listened to the complaints and said he would give Butner an order to retrieve the animals but added that it was not worthwhile because the cavalrymen would soon be breaking camp.[87]

Palmer apparently had little interest in destroying local manufacturing concerns, of which there were several. Neither the "old factory" (a grinding company) nor the Niessen Wagon Works was damaged. The troopers did gut a large building on "government hill," mostly taking the government cloth stored inside. It was also widely assumed that Palmer would destroy the F & H Fries cotton and woolen mill.[88] The five-hundred-spindle mill normally ran day and night, making gray cloth for uniforms, blankets, tents, and coats. The workers, including several slaves, often put in eighteen-hour shifts. It was commonplace to see cloth tacked to fences around town so that the firm's employees could paint it with weatherproofing for transformation into tents and coats.[89]

On Tuesday, April 11, several soldiers broke down the doors of the Fries mill buildings and invited some citizens to follow them inside. A shopping spree ensued as men, women, and children—including many respected citizens— took whatever they wanted under the assumption that the raiders were about to burn the place. "An indiscriminate removal of every article that could be handled immediately took place," a disgusted Francis Fries later wrote. Everything from bobbins and spools to finished goods disappeared. The machinery was also damaged, the belts cut or stolen. But in the end, the soldiers started no fires. Local sources suggest that Palmer reacted swiftly. An eyewitness recalled that "Gen. Palmer placed a guard over the property immediately upon hearing of the breaking of the doors, and declared that it was an outrage." It is doubtful, how- ever, that Palmer was too upset over the looting, since the mill was producing goods for the Confederacy.[90]

A few days later, one of the mill's owners, Henry Fries, issued an appeal for the return of the stolen property. Although the goods were made for the Con- federate government, Fries had not yet been paid for them. The Fries family also sent a representative around town to collect what he could. Some of the prop- erty was returned without protest, the citizens saying they had taken it to save it from the expected fire. Most of the goods were never recovered.[91]

For his part, Palmer soon shifted his attention from the mill to the bad news from Abbott's Creek. He wisely determined to reconnoiter the countryside for the enemy. Scouting parties rode in various directions. It developed that a handful of Confederates was indeed scouting near Salem that afternoon. Hav- ing learned of the Federal presence in Salem, those enemy soldiers came from Lexington and Greensboro. The Confederates were not nearly strong enough to attack the Federals at Salem, so they threw up breastworks across the Greens- boro and High Point roads. Some skirmishing flared as the Confederates fired on foragers and patrols. One such incident came around two o'clock in the after- noon at the plantation of Sheriff John Masten when the Confederates spotted a vulnerable enemy party and attacked. "The Yanks broke and run, leaving their horses, which were hitched outside, followed by the scouts, who captured 3 or 4 on Sheriff Mastens plantation in full view of the homestead," a citizen noted. "One escaped and reported to head quarters." The four men the Confederates captured were from the Twelfth Ohio Cavalry.[92]

Later that Tuesday afternoon, Betts's troopers returned from their raid, as did Trowbridge's exhausted men. Several weary horsemen took a wrong turn and entered the Salem cemetery by mistake. The Federals were suitably respectful, removing their hats and leading their horses through the Moravian graveyard with its square white headstones resting flat against the earth, so as to face the heavens.[93]

Sergeant Wilson's detachment also appeared, much to the relief and surprise of its comrades. Though exhausted, sweating, and dirty, the troopers were flush with the success of their Buffalo Creek bridge expedition, aided perhaps by the applejack that filled their canteens. Wilson sent his men to rejoin the regiment, then rode to brigade headquarters. He found Betts and his adjutant sitting on a fence. The two men were so happy to see Wilson that they almost pulled him off his horse. "Here comes Wilson. Where are your men?" they cried.

"They have all reported back to their companies; both men and horses are all back safe," Wilson replied.

"Lose any horses?"

"No, sir."

"Did you burn the bridge?"

"Yes, sir."

"Did you cut the telegraph wire?"

"Yes, sir," the sergeant said.

"Wilson, I never expected to see all back again safe," Betts said. Palmer agreed, later citing Wilson in his official report for "great skill & gallantry."[94]

It was the final act in a dignified drama. Before dark, Palmer's brigade left Salem; the grand prize of Salisbury waited. As "Boots and Saddles" echoed through the cobblestone streets, the troopers mounted their horses and turned down Shallowford Street. In parting, Palmer offered Mayor Boner final words of wisdom. "Your town is surrounded by Confederates," he said, "and you must take care of yourselves, as there may be scattering thieves, who claim to belong to my command, but are nothing more than deserters from both armies."[95]

Palmer was right; problems developed even before the column left town. As the last of the blue-clad soldiers passed down Shallowford Street, a few deserters appeared and made for the Confederate commissary. Boner was ready. His Home Guardsmen came to the rescue, driving the deserters from town. They left with "a hang dog look" on their faces, noted one citizen.[96]

As dusk lowered that April 11, Palmer headed west toward the Yadkin River. The many accomplishments of the First Brigade in its odyssey were impressive. It had wrecked miles of the North Carolina Railroad and the Piedmont Railroad and destroyed several large bridges "in the most complete manner." The men in the ranks were proud of their work. "The same amount of damage, scattered over so large a territory, with so little loss was never accomplished by the same number of men during the Civil War," a trooper boasted. Stoneman bragged, "This duty was performed with considerable fighting, the capture of 400 prisoners, and to my entire satisfaction."[97]

For the relieved citizens of Salem, the Federal cavalry's exit meant the war was all but over. "We thanked God and took courage," one resident wrote. Some young men fired volleys into the air and celebrated with a cheer. Then the townspeople tried to put their lives together again. They started by reading the torn mail. The news was mostly sad. A student at the academy learned of her mother's death, and a church leader heard of a missing son. Meanwhile, over on Salt Street, Fannie and Louisa's mother beckoned to her girls. "Come, children," she said. "God has been good and we have been preserved from all evil—go down in the garden and dig up the . . . trunk."[98]

Chapter 7

THE GREATEST CALAMITY
THAT EVER BEFELL OUR CITY

Mocksville to Salisbury: April 12–13, 1865

From the shade of her porch, nineteen-year-old Elizabeth Frost Cain gazed toward the stable. She had no desire to step out into the hot April sun, but she had work to do. "I had just pulled on my bonnet," she recalled years later, "when I noticed a light a flashin' in the sun." A slave accompanied Elizabeth to the edge of the woods for a closer look. "Then we were able to discern a cloud of dust and realized it was some one or some people on horse back, and saw that it was a considerable group," she wrote. "I recollect my first thought: 'Company and the house in a mess.'" But Elizabeth's slave, Elminy, understood quicker. "Oh, good Lord Jesus, Miss Lizzy," she cried. "Dat aint no company. Dems . . ." Elminy didn't finish. Rather, she ran off yelling, "Git in dat house." Elizabeth lingered, her gaze held by sunlight glinting on polished steel.

When the spell broke, Elizabeth ran after Elminy. Reaching the house, which was located near Cana, North Carolina, she beheld a knot of Federal cavalrymen. "I recollect how the horses hoof[s] clop clopped across the stones, and the dust as the men trotted up into the yard, all bearded and dusty, and I recall how I thought, 'Why they look just like anyone else,'" she wrote. Three soldiers dismounted in the yard. Three others headed to the stables. Other raiders went into the house and ripped open a mattress, spilling feathers everywhere. One tow-headed trooper found some goose eggs and ordered Elminy to boil them. When the party finally left, Elminy started laughing so hard that tears came to her eyes. The eggs, she smiled, were rotten![1]

The foraging soldiers, members of either Brown's or Miller's brigades, meanwhile rejoined the cavalry column careering south from Shallow Ford. The troopers had left the ford on the afternoon of April 11 after resting a few hours at Huntsville. They were bound for Salisbury. Grant had anticipated this moment. "[After Greensboro, Stoneman] might also be able to return to East Tennessee by way of Salisbury, N.C., thus releasing some of our prisoners of war in rebel hands," he noted. Stoneman thought capturing Salisbury's prisoner-of-war camp would redeem his reputation.[2]

Gillem pushed the men hard. In 1862, he had led a sixty-mile march in thirty-six hours. Now, Stoneman wanted a similar pace. Still, the visit to the Cains was typical. As the column moved, troopers rode afield to find food, forage, and mounts. They would close up only as the column neared a fortified or garrisoned point. One of those points was the town of Mocksville, which the column now approached. Mocksville's citizens had recently debated the "condition of the country" and passed resolutions that reaffirmed their support for the Confederacy.[3]

Perhaps these resolutions led citizens to resist the raiders. More likely, it was an accident. On April 11, townspeople heard that a small squad of bushwhackers was lurking nearby. Major A. A. Harbin's Third Home Guard Battalion responded. Less than two dozen men, including a fifteen-year-old boy and several old men, took position on a hill outside Mocksville. Spotting Stoneman's advance, the Home Guardsmen fired several shots. When the raiders returned fire, the Home Guardsmen realized their mistake and scattered. Signalman Frank Frankenberry was riding with the division's advance guard. "Bang! Bang! That was a musket, and there came the sharp report of our own guns," Frankenberry recalled. "I was up near the front and away we went in a charge. The 'Home Guards' fled and we push[ed] on[,] came to Mocksville and charge[d] into the town." Gillem reported the incident, too. "When near Mocksville the advance guard came upon a small party of the enemy, which was at once charged and dispersed," he wrote.[4]

Some of the cavalrymen swore they would burn the village in retaliation,

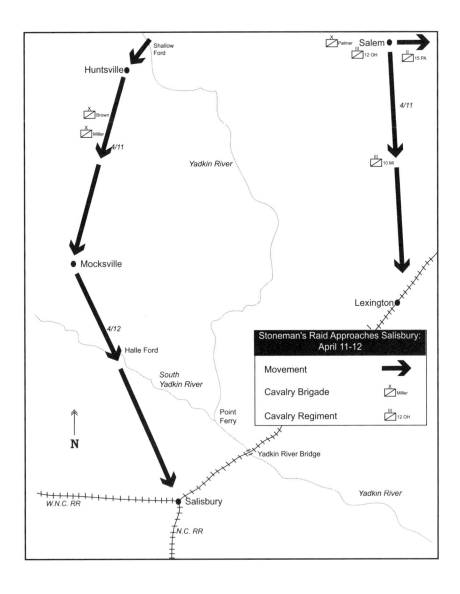

Shallow Ford

Huntsville

Brown

Miller

4/11

Yadkin River

Mocksville

4/12

Halle Ford

South Yadkin River

Point Ferry

N

Yadkin River Bridge

W.N.C. RR

Salisbury

N.C. RR

Palmer   Salem

12 OH

15 PA

4/11

10 MI

Lexington

Stoneman's Raid Approaches Salisbury:
April 11-12

Movement

Cavalry Brigade   Miller

Cavalry Regiment   12 OH

Yadkin River

but it proved a hollow threat. Only Thomas McNeely's cotton mill, which had not operated since the 1840s, went up in flames. Stoneman's troopers were more interested in finding food. They pressed the people of Mocksville into preparing meals. The women boiled shoulders and hams in a big iron wash pot and served officers in dining rooms and troops on the lawns. One black cook was so unnerved by the experience that she put too much saleratus, or baking soda, in her biscuits. They came out of the oven with an ugly yellow-and-green hue.[5]

That afternoon, the town fairly swarmed with Northern soldiers, some of whom misbehaved. "There were a dozen awful things that set did. Why recall them?" wrote a citizen. "There was so much sadness in the memory of those days that Mother seldom spoke of them."[6] Whatever the truth of the raiders' activities, Stoneman paused at Mocksville for only a short time. He was anxious to press on to Salisbury. Resuming the march late that afternoon, the column finally bivouacked around nine in the evening near Ephesus, just twelve miles from Salisbury. Signalman Frankenberry, who knew it would be a brief halt, had to take care of business. "I came to a darkey and told him to hand me the best horse or mule in the stable," he wrote. Later, Frankenberry bedded down. "To move at midnight [we would have] only 2½ hours to sleep[,] so let us be at it as I slept but little last night." The troopers camped along Whetstone Branch and wondered what the next day would bring. A member of the Eleventh Michigan predicted, "Expect a fight tomorrow morning."[7]

⁕

"I consider that the greatest man who ever lived was he who invented sleep," George Stoneman once wrote. But at midnight on April 12, Salisbury was more important to him than sleep. In a few hours, he would capture the prize and redeem himself. "I waked up just before midnight," signalman Frankenberry recalled, "and find the column moving out[,] saddl[ing] up and away we go to the front. Dark and muddy." Miller's Tennessee brigade took the lead. A moon just a few days past full lit the landscape.[8]

Some temptations lay between Mocksville and Salisbury. The juiciest target, the impressive Cooleemee Plantation, sat on the west bank of the Yadkin ten miles from Mocksville. It was the home of Peter Hairston, one of the largest slave owners in the South and a cousin of late Confederate major general J. E. B. Stuart. The raiders had already encountered Hairston's coachman, John Goolsby, in

Stokes County. This night, however, they ignored the plantation. Its only loss was a slave. A note in Cooleemee's records reads simply, "Henry ran away."[9]

The South Yadkin River blocked the raiders' approach to Salisbury. Gillem reported that the river was "a deep and rapid stream with but few fords." One such crossing was the Point Ferry, which proved to be a dead end. Raiders discovered that the ferry lines had been cut and that the water was too deep. That left the Halle Ford as the best way over the South Yadkin. Gillem assumed the river would be defended, but it was not. Approaching the ford, the raiders encountered a few enemy soldiers milling around the north bank, but they disappeared without firing a shot. The column then crossed the South Yadkin. While standing on a fence rail beside his horse, one Federal watched his fellow cavalrymen ford the river. When his turn came, it was easier than he expected. "Cross over and fail to get wet," he wrote. Then the advance resumed in earnest. "March lively," he wrote. It was about two o'clock in the morning.[10]

About a quarter-mile beyond the river, the raiders came to a fork. The main road was newer, better, and led directly to Salisbury. The other route, the old Mocksville road, offered a rougher, more circuitous course—and a tactical opportunity. Stoneman and Gillem suspected that defenders waited at Grant's Creek, the next natural obstruction en route to Salisbury. The two roads crossed Grant's Creek within a half-mile of each other, so the commanders decided to take advantage of the old road and launch a two-pronged attack. Gillem ordered one battalion of the Twelfth Kentucky Cavalry to take the old eastern road. Its job, Gillem reported, was "to make a determined demonstration of crossing Grant's Creek two miles from Salisbury, and if successful to attack the forces defending the upper bridge in the rear." D. H. Baker of the Twelfth Kentucky rode with the flankers, who moved after taking a break. "We dismounted, and the tired men and horses rested until near daybreak when we mounted and moved up near town," he wrote.[11]

The main body marched on. As daylight arrived—sunrise was at 5:53 A.M. that day—the blue column crested a gentle hill overlooking the valley of Grant's Creek. Advance troopers ran into enemy pickets and pushed them back. Once the pickets withdrew, the Confederate defenses were revealed; the Salisbury side of the stream bristled with the enemy in a position of strength rarely encountered on the raid. Confederate artillery and small arms opened up. The Battle of Salisbury had begun.[12]

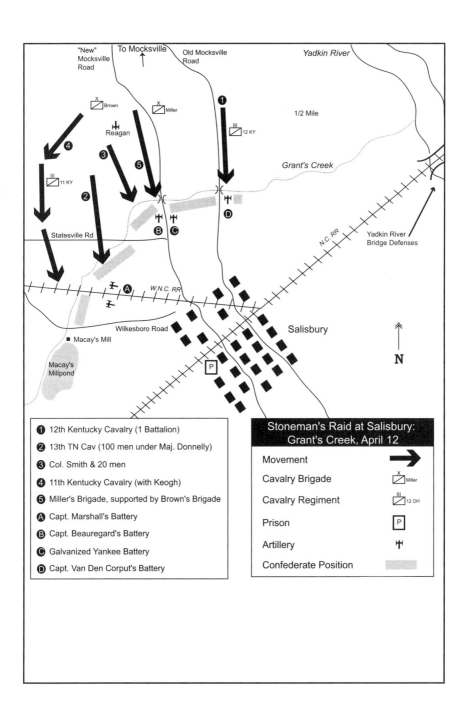

To Mocksville

"New" Mocksville Road

Old Mocksville Road

Yadkin River

Brown

Miller

1/2 Mile

Reagan

12 KY

Grant's Creek

11 KY

Statesville Rd

N.C. RR

Yadkin River Bridge Defenses

W.N.C. RR

Wilkesboro Road

Salisbury

N

Macay's Mill

Macay's Millpond

P

❶ 12th Kentucky Cavalry (1 Battalion)

❷ 13th TN Cav (100 men under Maj. Donnelly)

❸ Col. Smith & 20 men

❹ 11th Kentucky Cavalry (with Keogh)

❺ Miller's Brigade, supported by Brown's Brigade

Ⓐ Capt. Marshall's Battery

Ⓑ Capt. Beauregard's Battery

Ⓒ Galvanized Yankee Battery

Ⓓ Capt. Van Den Corput's Battery

Stoneman's Raid at Salisbury: Grant's Creek, April 12

Movement	➡
Cavalry Brigade	Miller
Cavalry Regiment	12 OH
Prison	P
Artillery	ⵙ
Confederate Position	

The seat of Rowan County, Salisbury was the fifth-largest town in North Carolina. It had a population of about twenty-four hundred in 1860. Another twelve thousand people, one-fourth of them slaves, resided in the county.[13]

Since 1861, the Civil War had ravaged Salisbury, killing fathers, brothers, and sons and ruining dreams. Inflation drove prices sky-high; in March 1863, a few dozen soldiers' wives waved hatchets at local merchants to persuade them to sell goods at affordable prices. As an important transportation center, Salisbury saw the trappings of war up close. At the time of Stoneman's Raid, military supplies were crammed into the town's warehouses, refugees filled hotels and boardinghouses, and many paroled Confederate prisoners awaited transportation there.[14]

The prison was by far the most significant feature of Salisbury. After it opened in December 1861, the first prisoners were placed in an old four-story brick building that had once been a cotton factory. Six small brick buildings and a small frame hospital soon joined the factory. They stood in a yard surrounded by a twelve-foot-high stockade wall bordered by a deep and wide ditch. The prison guards were mostly aging senior reservists. The inmates consisted of Union soldiers, disloyal Confederates, deserters, and criminals. They enjoyed tolerable conditions until 1864, when the Union and the Confederacy stopped exchanging prisoners. After that, the exploding population overwhelmed what the prison had been designed to handle. As food, medicine, and shelter grew scarce, illnesses and deaths became commonplace. Mass graves were dug in an old cornfield on a hill overlooking the prison. Salisbury citizens and local Confederates appealed to Southern authorities. "The evil is pressing and needs relevant remedy," complained one officer.[15]

The remedy finally came in early 1865, when the two sides resumed the exchange of prisoners. As a result, authorities decided to close the prison. On February 22, Salisbury's remaining three thousand prisoners—everyone except for a handful of men too lame, ill, or weak to move—shuffled out the gates. They reached Union lines in early March.[16]

Stoneman knew nothing of their evacuation. Fortunately for him, Salisbury contained other important military targets. One was the Salisbury Foundry and Arsenal, a manufacturer of weaponry and ammunition. By mid-March, Salisbury was also probably the largest supply depot in the Confederacy. It was the regional supply reservoir for the Fifth North Carolina District's Commissary of Subsistence. In addition, the advances of Sherman and Grant prompted authorities to ship a hoard of stores to Salisbury from various points in the Carolinas. "I can only say that the supplies were immense," wrote North Carolina governor Zebulon Vance. Enough material clogged the yards to fill 120 rail cars. Supplies overwhelmed Salisbury's warehouses and were stored wherever space was available.[17]

Salisbury was also the junction of the North Carolina Railroad, a 220-mile line from Charlotte to Goldsboro, and the Western North Carolina Railroad, a 70-mile route from Salisbury to Morganton. Both roads maintained numerous facilities in the area, not the least of which was the massive North Carolina Railroad bridge a few miles northeast of town. Salisbury's depot was especially busy because the track gauge changed there. Travelers and goods had to be transferred to different rolling stock before continuing their journeys. In short, Salisbury was one of the most important rail junctions of the ever-shrinking Confederacy.[18]

That was why Beauregard worked so hard to defend the town. Fortunately for Stoneman, the Confederate leadership responded to his movements by dispersing its forces and leaving Salisbury vulnerable. The post commander at Salisbury was Brigadier General Bradley Tyler Johnson. But on April 12, 1865, Johnson was at Greensboro and would miss the Battle of Salisbury.[19] In his absence, Brigadier General William Montgomery Gardner commanded the town's defenses. The forty-year-old father of seven had graduated from West Point with Stoneman and served with distinction in Mexico. Fourteen years later, while commanding the Eighth Georgia at Manassas, Gardner was felled by a projectile that shattered his leg. He took a year to recover and afterward was fit only for administrative duties. Promoted to brigadier general, he was eventually assigned to command the military prisons east of the Mississippi. In 1865, he assumed command of the post of Richmond, then fled to Salisbury after Richmond was evacuated. Gardner was assisted by the unlikeliest of defenders in Lieutenant Colonel John Clifford Pemberton. A native of Philadelphia and an 1837 graduate of West Point, Pemberton won two brevets for gallantry in Mexico. When the Civil War came, the Pennsylvanian cast his lot with the Confederacy. Rapidly promoted to lieutenant general, he commanded the important Mississippi River bastion at Vicksburg. After he surrendered to Grant on July 4, 1863, his career never recovered. Upon resigning his commission, Pemberton requested and received an assignment as lieutenant colonel of artillery. In January 1865, he became the army's inspector general of artillery and ordnance. Pemberton found himself in Salisbury after the fall of Richmond.[20]

Gardner and Pemberton realized they had a motley army to work with. It included several hundred prison guards, a few regulars, several hundred senior and junior reserves, about three hundred "galvanized" Yankees—foreign-born prisoners of war who volunteered to serve in the Confederate army rather than rot in prison—four hundred government employees, two companies of Home Guardsmen, and a handful of citizen volunteers. Small companies of invalid soldiers "hastily gathered" from the hospitals were thrown in for good measure. At most, Gardner commanded five thousand men, but the total was probably closer to half that. Most of them had seen little or no combat.[21]

Although John C. Pemberton is remembered chiefly for his role in the 1863 Vicksburg campaign, he also made an appearance during Stoneman's Raid, commanding Confederate forces at Salisbury.
Library of Congress

Gardner and Pemberton employed this untried force at two locations. A large detachment guarded the railroad bridge over the Yadkin, while the rest of the force was posted along Grant's Creek. That stream was one of Gardner's few advantages. It was deep, had steep banks, and covered the town's northern and western perimeter. Gardner failed to deploy along the high ground beside the creek, however.[22]

Major John W. Johnston's artillery battalion formed the core of the Grant's Creek defenses. Its batteries were veterans of several Western Theater campaigns. Their most recent battle was at Nashville, where the Army of Tennessee lost nearly half of its artillery. Upon the battery's arrival, Gardner and Pemberton directed the artillerymen to report to an unidentified engineering officer. "Put your batteries on the ground selected by the engineer," they were told. By eleven o'clock that night, the engineer completed his deployment. Captain Max Van Den Corput's Cherokee artillery dropped trail at the old Mocksville road, Captain René Beauregard's South Carolina battery—commanded by P. G. T. Beauregard's son—took position overlooking the new Mocksville road, and Captain Lucius G. Marshall's Tennessee battery set up to cover the Western North Carolina Railroad and the road to Wilkesboro. According to a member of Marshall's battery, the line was about four miles long; the actual mileage was closer to two. Corput's and Beauregard's batteries were only about a half-mile apart, but Marshall's guns were a mile and a half away. That posed a problem. "The enemy could easily lap around the left flank of the line of batteries and attack them in the rear, between the town and the position," recalled Marshall. The same was true of the right flank, where Corput waited. The terrain and the distance separating them also made it difficult for the cannoneers to see their neighbors. The gunners would not be able to work together.[23]

Some evidence suggests that the Confederates at Salisbury had a fourth battery. Galvanized Yankees from the notorious prison at Andersonville reportedly manned those guns. The battery was probably located in the center of the line, near Beauregard, where reliable Confederates could more easily monitor them. A cartographer on the scene later confirmed that the Confederates had eighteen twelve-pound guns on hand, so this galvanized battery was likely present.[24]

The lack of infantry canceled out any advantages gained through the artillery and the terrain. "We had plenty of artillery but no one to manage it," a local civilian wrote. According to one historian, the effective force along the creek was about 500 men, with no more than 150 at any one point. Other estimates of the force in front of Salisbury range from as few as 250 men to as many as 1,500. No official records exist, but it is likely that the Grant's Creek force contained about 1,000 men, based on the number of defenders captured on April 12. At best, only one man occupied every five to ten feet of line—far fewer than needed.[25]

Such was the force defending Salisbury that Wednesday morning as Stoneman's troopers arrived. Meanwhile, fear reigned in town. Anxious citizens hastily buried their valuables and hid their livestock. They secreted horses and mules away in a deep ravine west of town, tying the mouths of the mules shut with hemp ropes. The Dr. Josephus Hall family packed a wagon with valuables and its silver and sent it to a spot outside town. Another resident had her slave dig a trench and plant a row of grapevine cuttings along a fence. She then asked him to toss several old shoes into the trench. "Plant the vines now, Dorsey; they say old leather is the very best thing to make grapevines grow, and I saved these old shoes to put under them," she explained, not telling Dorsey her silver spoons were inside the shoes. This was a clever ruse, but a local doctor invented the safest hiding place. He asked toothless old Mrs. Kress to hide his gold watch in a stocking attached to the waistband of her skirt. Surely, no one would think to or care to search her.[26]

On April 11, trepidation increased as the raiders approached. News of Lee's surrender did nothing for morale. That night, fresh news spread: Stoneman was just twenty miles away. Men worked late loading ammunition onto trains for evacuation. A military court packed up and retreated to the Catawba River, leaving records behind in its haste. The town was abuzz with rumors. "Warning of the impending raid came a day or two before any of the enemy put in an appearance, and our local population was stirred with excitement and fear," a resident wrote. "The excitement in the little town was intense," agreed an artilleryman. "Whenever a party of officers rode through the streets, however late in the night, numerous and anxious inquiries would be made about the situation, especially by the women. No men—at least in citizen's dress—were visible."[27]

At midnight, sixteen-year-old Mary Eliza Currey, the daughter of the late post surgeon, was about to retire when a neighbor arrived and "told us some most alarming news," she wrote. The raiders were just eight miles away! They had been at Mocksville at five o'clock that afternoon and burned it. "We were very much excited of course, and I forth with went to packing," she recorded. "I do hope the Yankees will not burn and destroy as they have done at nearly all the towns they have been to."[28]

J. J. Bruner, the editor of Salisbury's *Carolina Watchman*, had prepared his readers for this day. In previous editions, he had announced the fall of Richmond and Petersburg. "The great crisis of the war is now undoubtedly upon us," he wrote, then warned of "raiding parties of merciless demons." The signs were obvious—the two o'clock mail train had not arrived, telegraph lines were down around Lexington, and the railroad had been cut at High Point. Yet Bruner's April 12 edition missed the mark. "Rumors were very abundant and extravagant yesterday in our streets. They produced a rather feverish state of public mind," he wrote. Clearly, Stoneman was no longer in the mountains. Rumors placed him near Salem or in the west. "Indeed we hear of Stoneman at several points, making him rather ubiquitous for an ordinary being," Bruner wrote. "Doubtless he is hovering somewhere not very distant north of the railroad between this point and Danville."[29]

The Battle of Salisbury is often dismissed as little more than skirmish. Less than a year afterward, a local citizen wrote, "As to the fight two miles and a half from Salisbury—'tis all a *myth*. . . . But little resistance was made—for it was so clearly of no avail. . . . Every one here falls into a giggle over the battle with the three thousand and the hosts of prisoners."[30]

The soldiers who fought that morning would have disagreed with the citizen's disparaging statement. At dawn on Wednesday, April 12, 1865, the men of the District of East Tennessee's Cavalry Division approached the valley of Grant's Creek. They advanced in two columns—one on the new Mocksville road, the other on the old one—toward their long-sought objective.[31]

On the new road, Alvan Gillem sized up the situation while enemy shells crashed about him. From his vantage point, the road sloped gently down to a bridge across Grant's Creek. "A close reconnaissance discovered the fact that the flooring had been removed from two spans of the bridge and piled on the enemy's side," Gillem reported. Southern artillery and infantry covered the bridge, and the creek defied crossing. Grant's Creek had "very high and precipitous banks and could not be forded," wrote a witness. "The only way to cross it was by a bridge, which was effectually commanded by the enemy's artillery." Another wrote, "The creek had steep banks, and was passable in only two or three places." From the bridge, the road continued through the Confederate barbican and up a slope toward the town just two miles away. Above the racket, Gillem could hear trains leaving Salisbury. An evacuation was obviously under way.[32]

George Stoneman knew the importance of speed and made his plans accordingly. "He may be considered as a safe rather than a brilliant man[,] practical rather than theoretical," an admirer once wrote. Stoneman's next moves displayed his pragmatism. Rightly judging Gardner's defenses to be undermanned with their flanks in the air, he decided on a flanking maneuver. Couriers sped off with his orders. Miller's and Brown's brigades were brought up. Another messenger sent one hundred men to ford Grant's Creek two and a half miles above and west of the main bridge. Their objective was to cut the railroad, perhaps capture a train, and "get in rear of Salisbury and annoy the enemy as much as possible," Gillem explained. They were to advance until reaching the Statesville road, which joined the new Mocksville road behind the main bridge. Gillem chose Slater's Eleventh Kentucky for the job.[33]

Stoneman also ordered Major Robert H. M. Donnelly of the Thirteenth Tennessee Cavalry to take one hundred men and cross Grant's Creek on Slater's left. The thirty-year-old Donnelly was a Virginia-born carpenter from Taylorsville, Tennessee. According to a comrade, he was "a brave, intelligent officer, and was often selected for duty when courage and firmness were needed." On April 12, Donnelly's qualities were much in demand.[34]

A detachment under Major Israel C. Smith aimed for a point on Donnelly's left. A member of the Tenth Michigan Cavalry serving on Gillem's staff, Smith was a Grand Rapids resident with wavy hair and a determined expression. Stoneman issued Smith's orders personally: "I want you to take twenty men armed with the Spencer carbine, cross this creek in some way, and flank those fellows out of there."[35]

Mallaby's signalers established an observation post near the new Mocksville road under enemy fire and watched the battle. It unfolded quickly. "As fast as the column came up," a staff officer wrote, "the troops were put in position, and immediate attack commenced, as Stoneman has great confidence in the theory of 'getting in first blow.'" Five separate detachments struck the defenders of Grant's Creek—Slater's, Donnelly's, Smith's, the Twelfth Kentucky Battalion, and the main body of Miller's brigade, supported by Brown's brigade. The last-named force would advance up the middle and attack once the other detachments crossed.[36]

However, it was the horse artillery that drew first blood. While the brigades closed up and the detachments deployed, Lieutenant James M. Reagan coolly unlimbered a two-gun section of Battery E in a position commanding the new Mocksville road bridge and opened fire. The raid had provided Reagan, a veteran of both the Second Iowa Cavalry and the Tenth Tennessee Infantry, few opportunities to employ his guns. "Upon First Lieut. J. M. Reagan, commanding Battery E, First Tennessee Light Artillery, devolved the laborious duty of commanding his battery," Gillem later reported. "His management of it, whether on the long and tedious marches with broken-down horses or in the battle-field, was such as to challenge the admiration of the entire command, and often elicited the praise of the major-general commanding." Reagan's other two guns may have joined the fray as well, but the effort was not enough. Beauregard's battery and the galvanized Yankee battery outgunned him, apparently concentrating their fire on the Tennesseans. Reagan did not receive a scratch—tragically, a fall from a horse would kill the lieutenant in June—but he lost as many as twenty men. Despite their best efforts, the Federal gunners were unable to dislodge the enemy.[37]

Miller's Tennesseans dismounted and deployed nearby but shared Reagan's lack of success. "Adjutant [Samuel P.] Angel was riding a white horse at the opening of this fight and was therefore a conspicuous target for the enemy," recalled a Tennessee trooper. "When the Regiment was dismounted before the charge across the bridge, and just as he was in the act of dismounting, a shell from the enemy's battery burst just over him[,] frightening his horse so badly that he fell, throwing the Adjutant to the ground, dislocating the middle finger of his right hand." The badly shaken Angel did not rush to remount.[38]

Because Reagan's artillery was so ineffective, it was up to the horsemen to win the day. Among the first units to make contact was the battalion of the Twelfth Kentucky Cavalry riding down the old Mocksville road against the Confederate right. According to trooper D. H. Baker, the battalion reached a point near Salisbury about two hours before daylight. Gillem's orders were to demonstrate along the creek, then get into the rear of the forces defending the upper bridge. Recalled Baker, "As it began to get light we went into position waiting for the signal. About sunrise we got orders to advance. The Confederates had been apprised of our coming, and were in position near our front, so we were not long in getting together. The contest lasted but a short time, and the field and all else was ours."[39] The valley of Grant's Creek was at its widest here, so the Kentuckians easily outflanked the Confederates.

W. O. Connor was a gunner in Van Den Corput's battery. The Rome, Georgia, battery had borne the brunt of the Battle of Lookout Mountain, only to end its long career at Salisbury fighting the Twelfth Kentucky, the same unit that had blazed a bloody trail into Boone. Connor blamed shaky infantry support for the loss of his battery. "Having no fortifications, of course this force offered but little resistance to the impetuous onslaught of Stoneman's disciplined cavalry. The 'galvanized' Yankees threw down their arms and refused to fight as soon as the Yankees made the charge on our lines, and they, with nearly all the rest of the command, were captured by Gen. Stoneman." Connor was collared, along with forty-five other members of the battery.[40]

Once across the creek, the Kentuckians pressed ahead. "As we made the advance we saw a train pull out from town, and it was passing in our front from right to left," Baker wrote. This was one of several trains on the North Carolina Railroad that tried to evacuate supplies and refugees from Salisbury. "Our left wing made a dash for a point on the railroad where there was a cut and where there was piled up for loading on cars a lot of crossties. Our men simply tossed the crossties on the track, and the train ran into it and stopped. It was loaded with citizens trying to escape, and we did not wish to fire on the train, and I do not think there was a single shot fired at it," Baker wrote. Other Federal troopers began pouring into town across Shober's bridge.[41]

Gardner's right had crumbled.

⁓

The Confederate left did not give quite so easily. Just minutes after Slater's Kentuckians wheeled right and rode away from the new Mocksville road, two staff officers, Morrow and Keogh, followed. Stoneman and Gillem probably thought the Kentuckians needed some additional leadership. The two officers overtook the column in short order.[42]

Though undisciplined, the Eleventh Kentucky was a hard-fighting unit. Battered on occasion, it had also doled out its share of punishment. Organized in the summer of 1862, the Eleventh was first called to duty upon Braxton Bragg's invasion of Kentucky. During the Perryville campaign, the unit spent its time drilling, picketing, scouting, and skirmishing around Frankfort and other towns. Indeed, the regiment saw much of its service within its home state. Brigadier General John Hunt Morgan, the notorious Confederate raider, was a frequent foe. Part of the regiment helped capture him. The Eleventh Kentucky had served in East Tennessee, where it played a supporting role in Ambrose Burnside's Knoxville campaign, losing more than two hundred men killed and captured in the process. The Kentuckians also rode with Stoneman to the gates of Macon. When he was cornered deep in enemy territory, the Kentuckians had to cut their way out. Subsequently, the Eleventh Kentucky raided Saltville on two separate occasions.[43]

On April 12, 1865, Myles Keogh rode at the head of the Kentuckians. Keogh had been on many fields himself. He had battled J. E. B. Stuart at Brandy Station and withstood the Confederate advance on Gettysburg's Seminary Ridge. He cut a dashing figure, brandishing a custom-made English pistol and wearing a conspicuous Catholic medal that the pope had given him. Salisbury's defenses held no horror for him. "Major Keogh led the regiment sharply forward, and made an attempt to cross [Grant's] creek," a staff officer wrote. "Major Keogh rode boldly down into the creek, but was met by such a fierce fire that he could not cross, and the steep bank preventing him from getting out, he had to ride for

Confederate artillery and infantry guarded the Western North Carolina Railroad bridge over Grant's Creek outside Salisbury until Myles Keogh and the Eleventh Kentucky Cavalry Regiment overwhelmed them.

ED AND SUE CURTIS

some distance up the creek, constantly exposed to a fierce fire."[44]

That fierce fire came courtesy of Captain Lucius G. Marshall's Confederate battery, which commanded the key crossings over Grant's Creek on the Confederate left. The gunners had bivouacked after dark with their horses still in harness and their guns pointing west, so the surrounding terrain was unfamiliar to them. Gardner's engineer had posted the battery in two sections, the left under Captain Marshall and Lieutenant A. T. Watson and the right under Lieutenant James M. Cockrill. Between the two sections ran the Western North Carolina Railroad. A deep cut bordered the railroad on both sides of the creek. To the left of the battery, a dirt road approached the creek and led to a bridge. The Confederates attempted to destroy the bridge to prevent the Federals from crossing. A millpond and gristmill stood south of the road.[45]

Along that sector were few trees to shade Grant's Creek, so the Confederate gunners could easily see across it at daybreak. In the growing light, they watched as their pickets fired a few shots to announce the Federal approach and then retired. One Confederate gunner glimpsed Federal horsemen "flitting about," probing the Confederate flanks. One of these was probably Keogh, riding along the creek. Captain Marshall ordered the left section to open fire, and the right section followed suit. "Very rapid firing was maintained about twenty minutes, the enemy meantime not showing themselves in front," a gunner recalled.[46]

Seventeen-year-old sergeant Sterling Cockrill, Lieutenant Cockrill's younger brother, served with the two-gun section on the right side of the railroad cut. At the first streak of dawn, he peered through the gray mist and spotted enemy cavalry. Cockrill watched as the dusty blue horsemen deployed from column into line of battle, then galloped at the Confederates through an open field. "We received them first with solid shot, then with canister, and, as they drew nearer still, with double charges of canister," the sergeant wrote. "When they reached the timber on the creek the line broke and retreated in a good deal of disorder to the opposite side of the broad field alluded to." Then the Federals re-formed and charged again. A man on a large white horse led them:

> The line showed signs of wavering earlier than at first; but, led on and encouraged as they were by the gallant leader on the white horse, they came to within about one hundred and twenty-five yards of the guns, wavered, broke, and fled pell-mell. Not so, however, with the rider of the white steed. There was no flight in him. As I look back . . . he seems grand-

er than a statue in bronze as he checked his charger in the very teeth of the guns, raised himself full height in his stirrups, and tried to rally and cheer on his men. At this juncture I could hear his words, when they were not drowned by the noise of our two guns, and . . . as his men deserted him, he then and there, for the time at least, lost his piety . . . stood tiptoed in his saddle, and showed himself a veritable trooper in swearing. But he railed in vain, and when he could do no more . . . he struck a gentle pace and re-tired as sullenly as a lion from his prey. But we were not lost in admiration of the scene, for both guns had been active, and both were now specially directed at the rider of the white horse. I myself sighted the first piece at him three times charged with canister. We literally harrowed the ground around him, and followed him with solid shot till he was out of range.

Sergeant Cockrill identified the gallant rider as Stoneman, but it was prob-ably Keogh.[47]

Meanwhile, across the creek, the Federals heard the unmistakable chug-ging of an approaching train. This was too tempting a prize to pass up, so they abandoned the creek and moved to the tracks of the Western North Carolina Railroad about two or three miles west of town. The engine was attempting to escape from Salisbury with stores and passengers. Quickly, the cavalrymen obstructed the tracks and forced the engineer to stop. When the train came to rest, a contemporary historian wrote, "a volley was poured into it without any demand for surrender." Some passengers were wounded. Inside one car, the Fed-erals discovered the widow and daughters of Lieutenant General Leonidas Polk, who had probably been visiting family in town. The troopers claimed Mrs. Polk's valuables, which included Polk's sword, uniform, papers, and other relics. "These things were all seized with great triumph, and though much that was taken be-sides was afterward restored to Mrs. Polk, no inducements could prevail upon the gallant Colonel Slater of the Eleventh Kentucky Cavalry to return to the widowed lady these mementos of her husband," an indignant writer noted. "He claimed them as 'taken on the battlefield,' and kept them." The Kentuckians burned the cars, along with all the remaining baggage.[48]

According to Lucius Marshall, two trains chugged down the Morganton line that morning. The first, a freight train, escaped. Twenty minutes later, a second train approached. This was the passenger train that Slater's troopers saw. Dr. L. B. McCreary, surgeon for Marshall's battery, ran to the edge of the cut, shouting and waving for the engineer to stop. The engineer did not see him, but some passengers did. As they called for the engineer to stop, the enemy's obstructions on the tracks forced him to do just that. The train came to rest in the cut on the Federal side of Grant's Creek. Its passengers spilled out and fled in all directions. Major Alphonso C. Avery was among the passengers and was captured. Others managed to cross Grant's Creek and return to Salisbury.[49]

To avoid hitting civilians, the Confederate battery once again stopped firing, but the train—now operated by a Federal cavalryman—started moving. That got Marshall's blood up. "The practiced gunners of the [Confederate] battery fired through and through the train, trying to dash the wheels, or some essential part, to pieces," he later wrote. "But they failed to disable the running apparatus, and the train, riddled with cannon-shot, slowly passed into the cut, where it stopped and soon burst into flames, as the captors had made a promising fire in every car."[50]

The train was now hidden in the cut, so the Confederate gunners began hurling shells all along their front. The battle had raged for ninety minutes, and thus far the Confederates had held their own. The men heard Corput's and Beauregard's pieces roaring as well, but that roar began to steadily diminish. Then a courier brought word from Gardner that the other batteries were withdrawing toward town, so Marshall was to retreat and tie in with them. "The left section was limbered up at once, pulled into the road, and moved at a trot toward town, all in plain view of the enemy," he recalled. Unfortunately for the Confederates, the Federal cavalrymen forgot the train and took advantage of the Southerners' withdrawal. Marshall watched as the Federals crossed the creek and galloped "down the opposite side of the ravine by the grist-mill as the battery passed over a slight elevation in the road."[51]

The Federal cavalrymen had finally made it across Grant's Creek, by way of a ford near the old Wilkesboro road. Once on the far bank, the troopers moved to outflank the Confederate artillery position. "Near a mill, a large number of rebels were concealed behind a fence, who greeted their approach with a deadly volley," recalled a Federal staffer. "Captain Morrow was struck just below the knee with a rifle ball, and Private Aldrich, orderly to Major Keogh, lost his leg. Major Keogh did not give them time to reload, but with a loud 'hi-hi,' dashed forward and scattered them right and left, and in a few minutes was up with the artillery, who were surprised and, for a time, evidently supposed them to be rebs, instead of hated Yanks." The Kentuckians charged gallantly. The fighting spread along the old Wilkesboro road to the site of what is now Livingstone College.

Macay's Mill was the scene of some of the heaviest fighting during the Battle of Salisbury.
ED AND SUE CURTIS

When the smoke cleared, Keogh and the Kentuckians had routed Gardner's left flank.[52]

On the opposite side of the railroad cut, the battery's right section held out a little longer, but it, too, was hard-pressed. Many Federals in that sector had crossed the creek on foot, and now those cavalrymen charged. Cockrill finally ordered his guns to withdraw once he realized his infantry support was useless. "The galvanized infantry that was left to support us made no effort at resistance. We were not much disappointed in this, for we stood in fear of their guns being turned on us," Cockrill wrote. "They were content, however, to hug the ground close until the cavalry occupied our position." The right section limbered up and galloped away.[53]

Marshall's retreating left section made its last stand about a half-mile from town. Trees to the front and high ground to the left restricted the field of vision, but it was the best position the men could find in their haste. The veteran gunners pulled down a fence and wheeled their cannons about. According to Marshall, the Confederates had to wait just fifteen minutes until the raiders "came dashing down the road as if from town in the rear, while the guns were playing to the front." The gunners initially thought the men approaching from the rear were galvanized Yankees. When they realized the truth, it was too late.

"They galloped into the battery from the rear while we were firing to the front," Marshall recalled. "We made them pay pretty well for the prize. The teams shied at the rush, and the gunners ceased firing without orders." The Federals quickly overran the battery and captured it. "The enemy were dashing about trying to fire their pistols, but they seemed to be all out of order or recently discharged, and, besides, these troopers had evidently been favored with heavy whisky rations," wrote one Confederate gunner. Lieutenant Watson of Marshall's battery tried to jump a nearby fence, but his horse refused. A blue-clad officer aimed his revolver at Marshall, but the weapon failed to discharge. "If you remain where you are you will not be hurt," the trooper said. Marshall could only answer, "You have the battery." After some tense moments, the Confederates were herded to the rear. "Thus fell in an obscure skirmish the old battery that . . . had, in short, seen more service than perhaps any other single field-artillery company west of the Alleghanies," Marshall wrote. In consolation, the gunners claimed the honor of firing the Army of Tennessee's last artillery round.[54]

The right section galloped away as well. On the retreat, Sergeant Cockrill rode beside the first piece and W. J. Pierson rode with the second. As the Federal cavalry closed in, Cockrill ordered the men to run for it. Pierson dashed to a rail fence, cleared it, and drew his revolvers. Suddenly, a Union officer galloped past, apparently riding for the head of the Confederate column. Several other Federals followed about one hundred yards behind the officer. For some reason, Pierson returned to the road and fired at the officer. The officer rode toward him, stood in his stirrups, and raised his sword. Pierson fired twice more and knocked his antagonist from the saddle. As more cavalrymen arrived, Pierson shot at them as well; he thought he hit a man and a horse. The Rebel then made his escape. Somehow, Lieutenant Cockrill and his noncommissioned officers also escaped, but everyone else was captured.[55]

Federal cavalrymen now occupied what had been Gardner's left flank. After the battle, Stoneman recommended that Morrow receive a brevet to lieutenant colonel for his work that day, which happened to be his twentieth birthday. Morrow "was severely wounded in the left knee while executing an order I had entrusted him to carry out Viz, leading a charge," Stoneman wrote. But the day really belonged to Myles Keogh, whose inspirational leadership moved Gillem to report that the staff officer had covered himself with gallantry.[56]

While Gardner's flanks were being turned, his center was likewise over-whelmed. Donnelly's detachment, downstream from Slater, crossed the creek, sliced through enemy defenses, and reached the railroad, probably at a point south of town. The Tennesseans captured a passenger train and several prison-ers. Farther downstream, Israel Smith's thirty dismounted men used fallen logs and trees to cross the stream undetected, then crept up on the enemy. Once the detachment was in position, the troopers gave a yell and delivered "some rat-tling volleys from [their] repeating carbines, when the whole force broke and fled." Noted one witness, "The effect was remarkable. Panic stricken[,] the whole force broke in greatest confusion." Another eyewitness agreed that the attack developed "in gallant style, putting the rebels to flight, leaving two of their pieces behind. . . . Smith, in person, captured the first piece of artillery." Gillem later recommended Smith for promotion to colonel by brevet.[57]

Meanwhile, at the new Mocksville road crossing, the Confederates began to give way, so Stoneman and Gillem launched the main attack. "As soon as a proper disposition could be made I ordered a general charge along the entire line," Stoneman reported. Gillem transmitted the order. "So soon as the parties sent across the river became engaged and the rattling fire of the Eleventh Ken-tucky Cavalry Spencer rifles announced that the enemy's left had been turned I ordered Colonel Miller to advance up the main road," he wrote. "The flooring of the bridge was found to have been taken up, but was laid by a detachment of the Eighth and Thirteenth Tennessee Cavalry, and Miller's brigade charged across. The enemy by this time was falling back along their entire line." Brown was ordered up to support Miller and press the enemy. "The retreat soon became a rout. . . . The pursuit was kept up as long as the enemy retained a semblance of organization and until those who escaped capture had scattered and concealed themselves in the woods," Gillem wrote.[58]

In leading the advance, Colonel Miller earned compliments in after-action reports and was recommended for promotion to brigadier general by brevet. Lieutenant Colonel Barzillah P. Stacy received plaudits as well. Under heavy artillery fire, his dismounted Thirteenth led the charge and replaced the miss-ing planks on the bridge. Other men from the Eighth Tennessee, also on foot, pitched in. "The engagement which ensued was fierce for a few moments," a sol-dier in the Thirteenth reported. "Lt Col Stacy was ordered to charge the bridge. He took position at the regiment's head. He gave the command and with one loud and long yell the bridge was carried."[59]

Gardner and Pemberton could do little to stem the rout. When the line began to collapse, Beauregard's and Corput's batteries were ordered to withdraw, which prompted the message to Marshall's gunners on the left. Although Union soldiers captured the cannons and gunners, Beauregard's Confederate battery went out in style. "The Confederate Artillery is said to have been handled effectively and the Artillery men fought gallantly until they were outflanked and compelled to leave their guns in the power of superior numbers," wrote the Reverend Beall. "Had they been adequately supported the result might have been different." As for the battery of galvanized Yankees, it simply fired its cannon over the heads of Stoneman's charging cavalrymen and greeted the victors with cheers. A few miles away, P. G. T. Beauregard was blissfully unaware of his son's fate. "Where is Capt Beauregard's Battery and how is the Capt?" he wrote shortly after the battle.[60]

Indeed, nowhere along the line did the Confederates hold out for long. The invalid soldiers from the hospitals were quickly pressed back. A few galvanized Irishmen fought well, but most went over to the enemy and thus abandoned the artillery. Some of the galvanized Yankees fired their guns into the air and gave three cheers for the Union. Once again, John Pemberton saw a disaster in the making. "I witnessed the capture of our last piece of arty. and narrowly escaped the same fate myself," he wrote. Less than three hours after the battle began, Johnston's veteran artillery battalion was *hors de combat*.[61]

One of the Confederates on the scene was Valentine Heerman, a wealthy New Orleans cartographer who had been making battlefield maps for the Confederacy for two years. The map of the battle at Grant's Creek would be his last. At the bottom of the map, he noted that the defenders briefly stood their ground but then "ran like the devil[,] whipped and ridden."[62]

All along the line, the defenders broke and fled with Stoneman's raiders in hot pursuit. "The Union Cavalry men drew their sabers and literally cut the entire rebel force to pieces," exaggerated one trooper. Confederates dropped their rifles and accouterments and ran into the woods. A few individuals or small bands made stands, but most simply scattered. Miller reached the intersection of the new Mocksville road and the Statesville road above Grant's Creek. Keogh and the Eleventh Kentucky came up from the Confederate left. A battalion of the Eighth Tennessee Cavalry under Major John M. Sawyers also arrived. It was nine o'clock in the morning. The junction of these forces marked the end of the fight at Grant's Creek.[63]

New Orleans cartographer Valentine Heerman sketched the Grant's Creek battlefield soon after the smoke cleared. He wrote that the Confederates "ran like the devil[.] whipped and ridden." *SALISBURY POST*

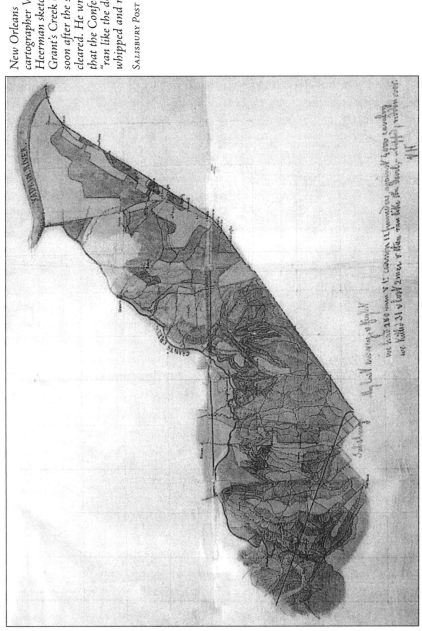

In the words of Alvan Gillem, the morning had already seen "some very hard fighting." A trooper echoed that sentiment, describing the battle as a "very spirited engagement."[64] But the struggle for Salisbury was not yet over.

For the people of Salisbury, it had been a long night and an even longer morning. According to a reporter, the raid was the "greatest calamity that ever befell our city. Our hills and valleys, for the first time in the memory of the oldest citizen, resounded the echoes of hostile cannon and death dealing shells. At day-break on the morning of the twelfth our citizens were aroused from their quiet slumbers by the loud detonations of artillery, which had been placed on commanding positions around the ill-starred city. The foeman was slowly but surely advancing. All was excitement, all was terror. Terror stricken women and weeping children were running from house to house, or secreting themselves in cellars." Stoneman's Raid would be far different from the visit paid by Hessian troops in Cornwallis's army during the Revolutionary War.[65]

The events of April 12 were unforgettable. Twenty-four-year-old Maggie Ramsey lived with her three children and some slaves at the corner of Monroe and Horah streets. "News, bringing horror and dismay, reached us each day telling of the contemplated attack of Sherman and the dreaded approach of Stoneman," she recalled. Maggie prepared accordingly. "Night after night, the young surgeons who room at my house helped me shell corn, bag it and store it, together with wheat and flour in the attic," she wrote. Still, she was not as ready as she thought. The sounds of gunfire along Grant's Creek brought "cold terror."[66]

Residents traced the progress of the battle by its sound. "At day light on the morning of the 12th the first sound we heard was the boom of cannons," wrote one young lady. "Nearer and yet nearer through the long hours the sound of the guns came, showing that the little force of Confederates was being steadily forced back by overwhelming numbers," noted another witness. Another resident recalled how "the boom of continuous combat noised the swift approach of General Stoneman's cavalry," who came "by every dirt road that stemmed from the Blue Ridge Mountains." But if the noise of battle was frightening, something unexpected followed. "The deafening din of battle suddenly ceased," a citizen wrote. "On the night air fell the hush of silence like a deep sigh breathed of absolute repose."[67]

To sixteen-year-old Mary Eliza Currey, the fading sounds along Grant's Creek meant that a new stage of the battle was about to begin. Soon after dawn, the young lady got dressed, said a prayer, and wrote in her journal, "Oh! Could I write all my thoughts I would soon have this volume full. Aunt Nellie came in about day light and said that they were fighting about two miles from here. By the time I got dressed the fireing had ceased." Mary then joined her family for breakfast, and together they waited.[68]

The wait was not long, for the victorious raiders entered Salisbury shortly after nine that morning. They seemed to come from all directions. Cavalrymen rode into the public square, a witness related, "with drawn swords in their hands and oaths in their mouths." The mayor greeted the Federals with a flag of truce, but a trooper cut the flag down. Another soldier, blood streaming down his cheek, yelled at the top of his lungs as he galloped into town. Other cavalrymen stopped to let their horses feed on corn that was "poured out on the pavements of every street in town." Many cavalrymen stopped and dismounted, hitching their horses along Innes, Fisher, and South Long streets. "They were just a lot of skinny old nags, fit for little if anything," a local recalled.[69]

The leadership of the Cavalry Division reined in at the Mansion House. The clerk pulled out the hotel's register and presented it to the officers. Using pen or pencil, several scratched their names in the book. These initial names were legitimate, but clerk Bell would have cause to complain in the days to come about the "unprincipled dogs" who jotted down fictitious names such as N. B. Forrest, Stonewall Jackson, and Robert E. Lee.[70]

The atmosphere remained fearsome on the streets outside. On West Innes Street two blocks from the town square, Mrs. Mary Ellis and her four daughters tried to carry on normally. They sat down to breakfast with a houseguest, but eight-year-old Harriet could not ignore the appearance of Federal soldiers. "Suddenly the sweet air of April was rent by an uproar of war whoops, the rhythmic beat of galloping hoofs," she recalled. Mrs. Ellis grew frantic. "The Yankees! The Yankees have taken the town!" she cried. In a flash, the family butler set his serving tray down and ran outside to lock the front gates. The ladies dashed to the parlor and peered out the front window. Along Innes Street the troopers came. "The roadway was jammed with a surging mass of mounted soldiers and rampant horses spurred to breakneck speed," Mrs. Ellis wrote. "It was frightening, curiously thrilling to see the capless cavalrymen standing erect in their stirrups as they rode, brandishing bared sabres in hand as they let

Souvenir of Old Mansion House,
Burned November 8th, 1907.
The Wood to which this Card is Attached is Part of a
Hewn Sill of the Original Building.
THE MANSION HOUSE CORNER, 100 YEARS AGO
MOST NOTED INN IN WESTERN NORTH CAROLINA.
SALISBURY, N.C.

After capturing Salisbury, Stoneman established his headquarters at the Mansion House Hotel on Innes Street. He, Gillem, and a few staff officers signed the hotel's register.

ED AND SUE CURTIS

out earsplitting yells." They came marching in for hours, some at top speed, others more deliberately.[71]

Fresh fighting broke out between pursuing Federals and retreating Confederates. "Then what a rout through the streets and way beyond the town," Union trooper Frankenberry recalled. One skirmish began at the arsenal, where Rebel captain Frank Y. McNeely was shot and then beaten. He later died of his wounds. Once the arsenal was secured, General Gillem ordered Frankenberry to raise the flag above it. "I carried it through the streets and soon the stars and stripes floated over the city," the signalman recalled. Frankenberry then paused to feed his horses and himself. It was about nine-thirty. Other United States flags went up, including one hung from a rope stretched across Innes Street. A defiant little girl reportedly cut the rope holding the flag. That act earned her no friends among the raiders, but her age saved her from retribution.[72]

J. I. Shaver, a boy who lived on East Innes Street, saw some of the fighting close at hand. "It was an occasion that I shall never forget," he wrote. "There were only a few Confederate soldiers here, too few to put up much resistance.

However these men did what they could. . . . Being a youngster I was filled with excitement and ran about all over town. I distinctly remember some of our soldiers chopping the spokes out of a cannon's wheels which had to be left behind. After this task was accomplished . . . I found that the soldiers had overlooked the powder and shot in the caisson. We hid this before the Yankee troops arrived." A bit later, more fighting erupted when the Federals chased some Rebels over an old covered bridge above the Innes Street tracks. "Mother and I were in the front door when we saw the first of the troopers come through the bridge. These were cavalrymen," Shaver wrote. He watched as a Confederate and a Federal officer crossed swords. "Both were mounted. They cut and slashed at each other, cutting up one another right sharp. Before help came to the Yankee, his opponent got the better of the combat and escaped down the road toward Town creek." Presently, another Rebel officer galloped down the road and shot two Federals with his pistol.[73]

Some of the defenders retreated through town in good order, battling as they withdrew. One was Lieutenant Bradley Stokes. A Confederate soldier since he was eighteen, Stokes had ridden with Brigadier General Turner Ashby in the early days of the war. After Ashby's death, Stokes joined the staff of Brigadier General Bradley Johnson. He remained with Johnson for the rest of the war and came to Salisbury with the Marylander in late 1864. Stokes was a handsome, unforgettable young man, an admirer wrote. Entering town with the last of the Grant's Creek defenders, he stopped at Johnson's headquarters at the corner of Main and Bank streets to get his favorite horse and grab some important papers. When blue-clad cavalrymen appeared, he mounted and rode deliberately toward the square on Main Street. The enemy troopers were so surprised that they only stared at him. But then several Federals started shooting. Stokes fired back, hitting more than one enemy soldier. A Federal officer charged him, but Stokes did not budge. He simply drew his pistol, waited until the officer was at point-blank range, and shot him. Next, the Confederate spurred his horse on until another raider caught up. Stokes suddenly stopped his horse, let the surprised raider pass, and shot him from behind. Finally, the lieutenant managed to escape from Salisbury.[74]

The Ramseys watched the skirmishing from their second-story bedroom. "The missiles were flying thick and fast around and upon the house," Maggie Ramsey recalled. Meanwhile, a particularly wrenching scene unfolded out front when a galvanized Irishman—one of the few who actually fought—was shot in the lungs. Despite the wound, the man kept loading and firing until he collapsed on the Ramseys' piazza. Maggie's mother refused to let him die there. "Though the balls fell thick about him, and she was alone with her little children, she went out to him and managed to get him inside the house," Maggie wrote. The soldier, pale and drenched with blood, told his rescuer, "They have killed me, but I die a brave man; I fought them as long as I could stand." The persistent Mrs. Ramsey called for a doctor anyway and did what she could to mend his wounds. A local physician came, removed the "missile," and took the soldier to the hospital. He survived and came back a fortnight later to thank her.[75]

As the fighting ended, the troopers began searching the town's homes and businesses, which brought them into close contact with citizens. One such encounter occurred in the empty offices of the *Carolina Watchman*. In addition to printing proclamations, several troopers decided to report the latest news of Stoneman's Raid by finishing a story begun by the newspaper. "Some wag of a typo among our cavalry got up a small extra, and continued the editorial, showing the different stages of uncertainty, fear and final exit of the editor," a cavalryman recalled. The troopers then put the *Watchman* out of business, wrecking the presses, burning the files, and throwing out the type.[76]

The Ramseys had an alarming brush with the raiders as well. "Then plunging their horses over the fence, some of the soldiers rushed into the hall and up the steps, demanding of me, 'the damned rebel who lives here,' " wrote a family member. "Downstairs the men were ransacking, pillaging, wielding their swords among the terrified servants and shouting, 'Make me some coffee! Fry me some meat! Make me some bread or I'll cut you in two!' "[77]

Mrs. James C. Kerr had an especially agonizing morning. When she saw a man riding her husband's horse—James Kerr had fled that morning—she approached and inquired about her spouse. The soldier, "with great glee, told her he had captured the rebel and left him dead on the roadside," wrote a historian. "She, of course, suffered agonies until her husband appeared a few days after—sound and well—he had been taken a prisoner." Mrs. Ramsey probably best summed up the attitude of Salisbury's people. When an officer saw her mahogany piano, he asked her to play a song. "I cannot play," she replied. "There is no music in my soul today."[78]

Mrs. Colonel Folk, whose mother, Mrs. Jordan Councill, had lost her last firkin of butter to George Stoneman in Boone, encountered Federals who possessed more decorum. When some officers rode up to the house where she was staying, they tried to calm her fears. "We are Yankee soldiers, but we are gentlemen," one officer said. "Don't be alarmed." Reassured, Mrs. Councill asked about Boone. "No madam," a cavalryman said. "Gen. Stoneman's soldiers are above doing anything mean, but you have some home Yankees under Kirk. We prepare the way for them, and they follow us and do the dirty work."[79]

To some degree, the cavalry column's commanders ensured good conduct, prompted by residents such as Mrs. Ellis, who reached her boiling point and decided to confront Stoneman in person. Young Harriet, the family's houseguest Mrs. Barringer, and Mrs. Ellis put on their bonnets and drew their shawls about them. They marched through the throng of horse soldiers along Innes Street and stopped at the Mansion House Hotel, where Stoneman had established his headquarters. They found him sitting with several officers at a table on the brick veranda. The soldiers were imposing in their blue uniforms covered with red dust, but Mrs. Ellis was not intimidated. She approached an orderly and said, "I wish to speak to the gentleman who is in authority here."

The solider dutifully passed along her request and returned. "Madame, General Stoneman will listen to what you have to say," he announced. When the ladies were introduced, they bowed. Stoneman stood and touched the brim of his plumed hat. His officers did likewise.

"General, will you kindly assign a guard to protect my dwelling house from violent entry, and my household from malicious annoyances?" Mrs. Ellis began in a steady voice, a smile on her face. "Our personal safety is endangered by the devilish conduct of your looting soldiers. I shall appreciate the civility most sincerely, I assure you."

"Madame, your request for the protection of your dwelling is granted," Stoneman answered. "A guard will be detailed immediately to attend you to your home."

Thanking the general, the ladies returned home with their guard. Unfortunately, the man was drunk, so Stoneman had him arrested and assigned another. The second guard, a Michigan man, proved better. He paced the sidewalk in front of the house for the rest of the day, leaving his post only to eat and take a nap. He also briefly returned to headquarters and came back carrying the Confederate flag that had flown over the prison. He fastened the flag to a pole outside the Ellis home.[80]

Fearing Salisbury would be destroyed because of the prison, many other citizens appealed to Stoneman for help. Not even the gunfire still echoing along

Innes Street kept them away. Among them were local leaders who happened to be fellow Masons. They begged Stoneman not to burn the town. The New Yorker promised personal protection to everyone who asked for it, repeatedly stating that the raiders were not making war on noncombatants. As his orders directed, he was interested only in destroying government property. "Salisbury was not unduly incensed against General Stoneman," remembered a local, who went on to hint that the general was apparently suffering a flareup of his hemorrhoids. "He obeyed his orders and destroyed the stores, but also he gave guards to all who asked for them. He restrained looting, and little unnecessary havoc was made in the dwellings of the town. Although he was a sick man while he stayed in Salisbury, he found the means to prevent such burning and destruction as took place so wantonly in Columbia, South Carolina, and with impunity in many other less important places."[81]

By midday on April 12, 1865, Salisbury was firmly in Federal hands. That meant Stoneman and Gillem could turn their attention to other matters.

꜅ഄꜟ

The wooden railroad bridge spanning the Yadkin River was 660 feet long. Each end clung to a bluff towering more than 100 feet above the river, which was almost wide enough there to pass for a lake. "We always called it 'The River,' as if in all the world there was but one," remembered one woman. "The river was always colored reddish-yellow by the soil of its bed, and sometimes it ran thick as soup when heavy rains swelled its volume." Another local resident wrote that the "Yadkin is beautiful & the country broken & picturesque. Large forests— red clay." "The river is deep . . . with high banks at the bridge," explained another man. The spot was not only majestic, it also smacked of history. "The bank on the Davidson county side of the Yadkin rises precipitously from the water, and twenty-five or thirty feet above it, and then ascends backwards, forming a steep hill, high-overlooking the Rowan Bank of the river," wrote a reporter after the war. "The 'noble Yadkin' sweeps past with a rush and a roar, splitting in two, the two foamy halves racing around Hedrick's island to see which will beat to the heights of Gowery, a mile below the bridge, where Gen. [Nathanael] Green[e] crossed and escaped Cornwallis in the Revolutionary War."[82]

The bridge loomed over the Trading Ford, once an important Yadkin River crossing. Everyone from Indians to Spanish explorers to European settlers had used the ford. Greene and Cornwallis even fought a skirmish over it; Greene's army survived to fight at Guilford Courthouse the following month. The Trading Ford was not the only way across; several fords and ferries were nearby, although only the Trading Ford could accommodate heavy wagons. There was even a road bridge, the Beard bridge, built in 1818. It rested on five stone pillars within sight of the Trading Ford but was in disrepair around the time of the Civil War.[83]

The impressive railroad bridge, built in 1855, was crucial. By spanning the Yadkin at this most difficult spot, it made the North Carolina Railroad possible. It linked Salisbury, five miles southeast, with Lexington, ten miles northeast. It connected western North Carolina to eastern North Carolina. It joined south to north. And it represented hope of supply and escape to the harried Confederate soldiers of the Army of Tennessee.

The people of Salisbury recognized the bridge's importance and feared it would draw enemy soldiers. "The people are looking for Stoneman to come here; his object seems to be to burn the bridge," wrote one citizen. "I suppose there is some truth in it for they have taken all the troops from here over the river—I don't know what they mean leaving Salisbury so unprotected but I suppose Generals know best."[84]

Indeed, the Federals had coveted the bridge since Kirk's 1864 raid but had not managed to reach the span then. Now, they were interested in it more than ever. Confederate authorities grasped the danger and built defenses on the Davidson County side of the river. Construction began as early as 1864, but the work of fortification started in earnest at Beauregard's behest. In late March 1865, he ordered Brigadier General Winfield S. Featherston to build field works around the bridge. "Be careful enemy do not destroy railroad bridge across the Yadkin," he warned. During visits to Salisbury, Beauregard personally supervised construction. From other posts, he telegraphed ideas such as positioning a light artillery battery south of the Yadkin and constructing *têtes-de-pont* at the bridge and nearby fords.[85]

Wielding only picks and shovels, men dug into the rocky soil. Slowly, on a hill 120 feet above the river, an hourglass-shaped, fifteen-acre defensive system emerged. The strong point, today called Fort York, was well sited. From its vantage point, the fort dominated either end of the bridge and the approaches to it. It was large enough to contain as many as three thousand men. A mile of breastworks, organized into separate inner and outer lines, circled the fort

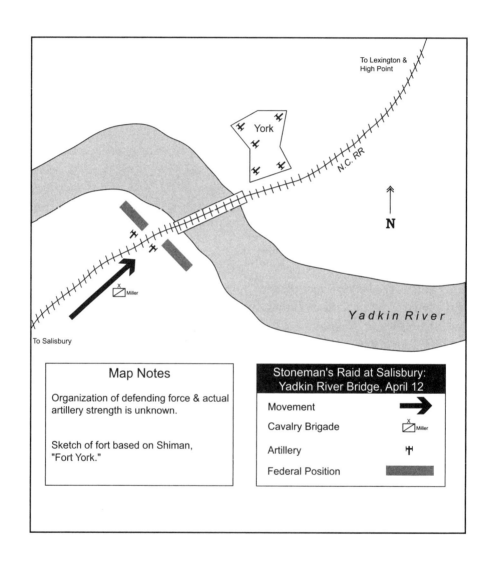

To Lexington &
High Point

York

N.C. RR

N

Yadkin River

To Salisbury

Miller

Map Notes

Organization of defending force & actual
artillery strength is unknown.

Sketch of fort based on Shiman,
"Fort York."

Stoneman's Raid at Salisbury: Yadkin River Bridge, April 12

Movement

Cavalry Brigade   Miller

Artillery

Federal Position

to provide protection against threats from any direction. The workers carved out embrasures for seven artillery batteries as well. Although the Confederacy boasted stronger and better-designed works, the terrain and the river made this position truly formidable.[86]

While some sources estimate the fort had as many as ten thousand defenders, only between four hundred and twelve hundred soldiers manned it on April 12. Their makeup was similar to the force that had defended Grant's Creek, as it included a mixture of Home Guardsmen, militia, galvanized Yankees, regulars, and senior reserves. But unlike the Grant's Creek defenders, these men enjoyed the protection of the fort, with its well-placed cannons covering the approaches to the bridge. Though the number of cannons inside the fort that day is unknown, at least four guns were in place, probably a mix of light- and high-caliber types. According to a local citizen, Beauregard had given the men "strict orders to hold the bridge . . . as the post was of the highest importance to Johns[t]on's army."[87]

Brigadier General Zebulon York commanded the fort. A veteran of the Army of Northern Virginia, York was a native of Avon, Maine. Born October 10, 1819, he had studied at Wesleyan Seminary in Maine and Transylvania University in Kentucky and later matriculated at the University of Louisiana (now Tulane University), where he received a law degree. After settling in Vidalia, Louisiana, York became a successful attorney and cotton farmer with six plantations and seventeen hundred slaves to his name. When the war began, he organized a company of the Fourteenth Louisiana Infantry Regiment. Rising through the ranks, he was promoted to brigadier general on May 31, 1864, and took command of a brigade of Louisiana troops. His service in Virginia ended on September 19, 1864, when a shell shattered his left arm, which had to be amputated, giving rise to his nickname, "Old One Wing." How York came to command the fort on April 12 is unclear. Beauregard may have assigned him the duty because of his experience or simply because he was available. Traveling from Charlotte on the night of April 11 with three companies of galvanized Yankees, York stopped at Salisbury to obtain equipment and ammunition, then continued to the Yadkin River bridge.[88]

York had several able subordinates at the bridge, including Captain Frank Smith of Alabama and Lieutenant Henry Clement, a native of Rowan County, North Carolina. Then there was the "torn and tattered" Confederate who offered his services. "He told York that he had gotten separated from his command," recorded the *Carolina Watchman* years later. "'Old One Wing' asked him what he could do. He answered that he was a gunner, and offered to prove it if York would allow him the use of one of the guns for a few minutes. York assented and the gunner, whose name cannot be ascertained, directed the attention of the soldiers who had gathered around to a plumb bush away up the river. Then after sighting along the gun, he fired at it, and the plumb bush which was then covered with white blossoms, was immediately broken off and floated down the river."[89]

The gunner's demonstration and the well-fortified position must have filled York with confidence, as he reportedly sent word that he could hold his position against ten thousand Yankees. He would have to face only a fraction of that number on April 12. After the Federals captured Salisbury, Gillem and Stoneman dispatched Miller's brigade to destroy the railroad east of town. Knocking out the bridge would be an important part of that task. "Command was then sent 4 [miles] East to the Yadkin River to burn the railroad Bridge," wrote one of Miller's men. The Federals arrived at the bridge around two in the afternoon and opened the second phase of the Battle of Salisbury. When gunners at the fort greeted the raiders with artillery and small-arms fire, the cavalrymen realized they had stumbled into a hornet's nest. Within the hour, the Federals brought up artillery pieces they had captured at Salisbury to answer York's guns.[90]

Back at Salisbury, a local resident visiting Stoneman's headquarters overheard the order sending reinforcements to Miller at the bridge. The man was talking with an officer when another officer dashed up and stated that reinforcements were needed. According to the Salisbury resident, the first officer responded, "Take five hundred men and secure the bridge if it cost the lives of every one of them." In the end, the reinforcements did little good, and Miller failed to capture the bridge. The Confederates' position was simply too strong. Their guns threw solid shot at the approaches to the bridge, and their fire was accurate enough to draw blood. One Union officer attempted to approach on horseback. "The officer was promptly shot off his horse, which no doubt served to discourage similar rash action on the part of other Union officers," recalled an eyewitness. C. D. Simmerson, a boy who lived nearby, thought the Confederate cannon fire was remarkable. He watched two of the largest cannons, which were placed to command the approaches to the bridge. Noted Simmerson, "These big guns mowed down trees on the Rowan side of the river as the invaders attempted to approach the bridge." York's galvanized Yankees fought well, and apparently so did the ragged Confederate gunner who had volunteered on April 11.

He was said to be responsible for the accurate artillery fire.[91]

A Federal trooper who was there called it "a sharp fight." Fortunately, the flying lead hit few combatants. Only a few Confederates were wounded and one or two killed at the bridge. Sixteen bluejackets were reportedly killed or mortally wounded, though official records indicate no more than two Union soldiers died.[92]

The lack of Federal casualties before this strong position reflects Stoneman's strategy for capturing the bridge. The best way to seize a bridge is by attacking both ends at once. Plus, the weak spot of the fort was its northern side, in Davidson County, where the terrain offered some cover to an advancing foe. Accordingly, Stoneman planned to attack the bridge from both Rowan and Davidson counties. Across the river, Colonel Palmer apparently dispatched the Tenth Michigan Cavalry to aid the attack, but Sam Ferguson's Confederate cavalrymen foiled the plan on April 11 at Abbott's Creek. Other evidence bolsters this case. Miller's brigade was not Stoneman's best unit, and it is doubtful that he would have sent second-rate troops to capture a first-rate objective. Moreover, there is no indication that Miller's men ever tried to outflank the position via nearby crossing points, which were available, though defended. His effort was half-hearted at best.

Without any additional support, Miller had little hope of reducing the fort. Fortunately for the Federals, they did not need the Yadkin River bridge. The raiders had already ruined three North Carolina Railroad bridges and miles of track above the Yadkin, as well as more rails and facilities around Salisbury. Between the bridge and Salisbury, Federal troopers bent rails over fires made of crossties. Additional bridges and track would be destroyed in the coming days. Since Stoneman had stopped rail traffic in central North Carolina, he decided to abandon the bridge. Rumors of enemy reinforcements approaching from Greensboro may have contributed to his decision. At dusk on April 12, after a full afternoon of cannonading, phase two of the Battle of Salisbury ended with a whimper when Miller quietly withdrew his brigade. "We were compelled to retire without accomplishing the work," wrote one Tennessean. "Camp near the city for the night." The fight at the bridge was a black eye for Stoneman and Gillem. After all, it was one of the last engagements in North Carolina. It was also one of the last Southern victories of the war, though it availed the Confederates little besides bragging rights. Neither Union general mentioned the action in his report.[93]

Miller's brigade returned to Salisbury after dark, its men sullen and silent. They left behind shattered caissons and limbers and dismounted field pieces, including one that had apparently been struck in the mouth. The withdrawing Federal cavalrymen "gave it up and hurried off—passing through this town just before night—I saw them all [as] they passed just by my door," wrote one resident. "The stir of excitement pervaded the ranks of idle riders, their unsaddled horses stabled at the curbstone," added another eyewitness. "Stoneman's pursuing cavalry was coming back to Salisbury after a battle lost. But no wild cheers, no war whoops of victory marked their return to town. General Beauregard's defenders had saved the Yadkin River railroad bridge."[94]

⟋⟍

April 12, 1865, was a day of contradictions for George Stoneman and his raiders. The capture of Salisbury was the raid's ultimate objective, but Stoneman's success was incomplete. Not only were the Federals defeated at the Yadkin River bridge, but they also learned that the Salisbury prison was empty. On the other hand, they had consolations such as the discovery of some of the prison's former inmates. These were the wretches who had been too ill or weak to travel when the prison was evacuated. "Many of the unfortunate men, wasted to skeletons by privation and disease, became delirious from the excitement and joy of their sudden release," Ohioan Frank Mason recalled. So few prisoners were left that many Union accounts fail to mention their presence. But Frank Frankenberry saw them, as did a Tennessee trooper who encountered three when the column withdrew. At least 245 galvanized Yankees also were considered liberated Union soldiers. They, too, celebrated their release, despite the stigma that came with their service to the South. "These men had never been armed until that day and when the fight commenced, took the first opportunity of throwing down their arms and going in our lines," Charles Betts recalled.[95]

Many curious raiders inspected the notorious prison. "I went to the prison pen and was all over it. I shall not forget it," wrote Frankenberry. "I saw the . . . holes in which our men lay and suffered." Trooper Frank Mason saw "the frowning stockade, the dirty enclosure honey-combed with dens and holes . . . and the long line of narrow graves in which lay more than twelve thousand [*sic*] brave men, dead from hunger and suffering, or shot at the fatal 'dead line.'" Mason thought the scene proved "that the worst that had been told of Salisbury's horrors were more than true."[96]

Another consolation was the discovery that Salisbury was jammed with supplies. Signalman Frankenberry was in awe when he described the "vast quantities of stores, ammunition, clothing, rations, coffee, sugar, meat, flour, corn, etc. etc.," that the troopers seized. "The sight that met the eye beggars description," another witness wrote. Gillem ordered his provost marshal, Major Sterling Hambright, and a staff officer, Major George F. Barnes, to "ascertain the locality and amount of stores, with a view to their destruction."[97]

What they found was staggering:

> * Four large magazines containing ten thousand small arms and accouterments
> * One million rounds of small-arms ammunition
> * Ten thousand rounds of artillery ammunition
> * Six thousand pounds of powder
> * Seventy-five thousand to one hundred thousand gray uniforms, plus uncounted caps, shoes, and hats
> * A quarter-million army blankets of English manufacture
> * Twenty thousand pounds of harness leather
> * Imported medical supplies valued at $100,000
> * $15 million in Confederate currency
> * Seven thousand bales of cotton
> * Ten thousand bushels of corn
> * Fifty thousand bushels of wheat
> * Six thousand pounds of bacon
> * Thirty-five thousand pounds of cornmeal
> * Ten thousand pounds of saltpeter
> * Twenty thousand pounds of sugar
> * One hundred thousand pounds of salt
> * Twenty-seven thousand pounds of rice
> * Eighty barrels of turpentine
> * More than seventy-five thousand complete rations and a variety of foodstuffs, including hams, molasses, whiskey, wine, pork, mackerel, and beef[98]

Major William R. Tracy, the Cavalry Division's quartermaster, guessed that the supplies could have easily sustained seventy-five thousand men. Others estimated one hundred thousand men. The supplies were sorely needed by the fleeing armies of the Confederacy, so George Stoneman and Alvan Gillem decided to destroy them.[99]

Major Barnes assembled a detachment of six hundred men to accomplish the job. Their work began at noon on April 12. "All kinds of goods, wares, and merchandise were carried out into the middle of the street and piled up," a citizen recalled. "They are breaking open the commissary stores, and throwing them out in the street," added another. "It is not very far from here[,] only one square, and if they blow it up, I am afraid some of the pieces will fly over here." The pile grew until it filled four squares, including a stretch from the main square to the courthouse. Main and Innes streets and several adjoining roads were also filled. It was an unforgettable sight. "Out of every storage warehouse in Salisbury had been carted wagon loads of army blankets, army overcoats, army shoes, army underclothing, in fact every oddment listed in the military stores, and then were heaped in piles on the roadway of Inn[e]s Street," a resident wrote.[100]

As the men piled up the supplies, they and their horses ate heartily for the first time since leaving Tennessee. The Federal cavalrymen also confiscated medical supplies and other needed items. Nathaniel Sample replenished his wardrobe with a pair of English-leather cavalry boots. The raiders also showed charity. "The soldiers took what they wanted and gave some of what remained to such civilians as were standing about," an observer recalled. The poor were among the beneficiaries. They received rations "regardless of race, color [o]r previous condition of servitude," a reporter wrote. As the throng grew, the orderly distribution degenerated into a free-for-all. "The negroes and the poor are gathering it up and carrying it off as fast as possible," wrote one citizen. "As soon as the word was given for the needy to help themselves," agreed another witness, "every one—black and white—went to work carrying off as much as they could well manage, and in several hours everything in the commissary was thrown out and for miles around people could be seen carrying off plunder." Some fortunate souls made off with a year's supply of meat and flour.[101]

Yarn, cloth, and clothing from the Quartermaster Department were also in demand. People stacked coats, shirts, and other articles on horses and rode away. A few enterprising scavengers even carried off huge bolts of gray cloth. "The whole day was consumed in pilfering, and the troops and the lower class of citizens mingled quite freely together," a witness wrote. Another observer never forgot how the poor and the blacks chanted "weird hallelujahs" while they climbed over the mound of goods and carried off their plunder. For the next few days, the scene was repeated countless times. An ex-Confederate soldier passing through several weeks later met "many country people bearing off the remnants of half ruined articles, such as pieces of machinery, half burnt cotton, wool, etc."[102]

By late afternoon, Federal troopers began to clear the streets, until only the soldiers on guard duty remained. Some cavalrymen marched about three miles outside town and camped. Others pitched tents across Town Creek on what is now Herrington Heights. A striking change came over Salisbury as citizens hunkered down to await the expected conflagration. "The stillness in the town was death-like," one man recalled. "Not a sound to be heard except the clinking of the sentinel's sword as he walked his round, and now and then a stray shot would cause a shudder, as the people would imagine that some loved one had probably been the victim of the bullet." The Salisbury newspaper called it "the hour of sadness and suspense. Not a citizen was to be seen—every door was closed, and the inmates were in momentary expectation of a demand to render up their houses to the flames."[103]

Now a prisoner, Confederate gunner Lucius Marshall saw the first flames at nightfall. "After dark the large pen or building in which the Confederate prisoners were held was set on fire," he wrote, "and when the whole neighborhood was lighted up with the burning the inmates were ordered out." The happy task of firing the prison fell to a detachment of the Twelfth Ohio Cavalry. The prison, the barracks, and the surrounding buildings, along with the books and records of the prison hospitals, went up in smoke. "No one was sorry," a citizen stated, "when the Yankees made a bonfire of the evil-smelling empty, dolorous prison, the scene of so much unalleviated suffering and so many deaths."[104]

A nearly full moon shone upon the cavalrymen as they did their destructive work. After the war, a traveler who inspected the old prison grounds found only stumps and empty holes where the fence had once stood. The walls of the old factory building still stood, but the roof, floors, and windows were gone. Rusty knife blades, coat buttons, and pieces of pipe were strewn about. Oak trees inside the stockade were either dead or dying and surrounded by ugly weeds. The holes the prisoners had lived in were partially filled. In striking contrast to the ruins in the prison yard, the mass graves were surrounded by a plain but sturdy board fence carefully built by Stoneman's men. As he took in the spectacle, the traveler saw a black man and mentioned the awful destruction. "Does ye call dis yer horr'ble?" the man said. "I calls it beautiful since Stoneman polished it up."[105]

At about eight in the evening on April 12, the Federals set the massive pile of goods in Salisbury's streets on fire. Other Confederate facilities in town—

including the arsenal, the old garrison, several hospitals, machine shops, the pur-
veyor's office, a steam distillery, a foundry, and four large cotton factories—were
put to the torch, too. Within moments, the buildings were blazing furiously.
Shells exploded at the arsenal, scattering debris up to two miles away. Fortunately, no one was hurt. Most private buildings escaped serious damage, except for
a tannery that burned down. The fires consumed buildings valued at $500,000
and public stores worth $7 million. Records were also lost, including the papers
of a fleeing military court and the books of the Confederate tax agent.[106]

A reporter for the *Carolina Watchman* commented on the scene a year later.
"The destruction of property was immense," he wrote. "The glare of the flames,
and the explosion of shells at the arsenal were seen and heard 15 and 20 miles in
the country. These days will long be remembered by our citizens as the saddest
and most distressing in our history." The explosions at the arsenal reminded one
man of continuous thunder. Others far away thought that "a fierce battle was
raging," as noted by one eyewitness. "There was no hallooing by the soldiers—no
shouts—only the crackling of the flames and the bursting of shells. Now and
then a mounted troop swept through the streets, the horsemen in profound silence, the lurid flames from the burning distillery making their rough faces look
ghastly enough, while the buttons and other mountings of their equipments
sparkled in the firelight. No one thought of sleep that night, not even the children." The explosions and flames created "one of the most terribly grand sights I
have ever witnessed," a Federal officer recalled.[107]

A foul odor arose from the conflagration, caused by burning wood, powder, shells, and other debris, including a few barrels of balsam. The smell would
linger for weeks. "Tongues of fire shot in and out of scorched leather, and the
charred woolen garments that broadcast a dense smoke-screen, that set adrift
intermingled acrid smells of the hospital drugs," observed a Salisbury resident.
The sights and smells were awe inspiring even to men accustomed to war. "All
night last night the depot and arsenal and all public buildings were burning,"
wrote one Federal. "The explosions were heard all the day and last night and
today."[108]

The troopers also destroyed railroad facilities. Miller's brigade continued
working on the tracks to the east, while other units fired the facilities in town
and tracks and bridges to the south. The cavalrymen did their work well. "This
Corporation has been a great sufferer by war," reported officials of the Western
North Carolina Railroad. In Salisbury, the firm sustained nearly one hundred

thousand dollars' worth of damage to its headquarters building, passenger depot and shed, machine shops, workshops, roundhouse, and water tank. Damaged rolling stock included ten boxcars, three flatcars, two passenger coaches, one second-class car, and three locomotives. The North Carolina Railroad was also devastated. Ten miles of track were burned, along with several warehouses, the water station, and a shed.[109]

Postwar railroad inspectors were aghast at the devastation. "Reaching Salisbury we find all the splendid and convenient buildings, erected at a great cost, a mass of ruins," one reported. "The beautiful edifice used as an office and reception room, and the shed attached, equal to any thing of the kind in the Southern States, have both disappeared under the inexorable hand of war. The machine shop and foundry is entirely destroyed, the walls crumbling and worth nothing except for the brick." Fortunately, engineers thought they could repair much of it, given time and money. For example, the engine Catawba, although a burned wreck, was back in service by 1866.[110]

Fires burned throughout the calm, clear night of April 12–13. The darkness gave the scene an ominous cast. "As night drew near, the sky was red from the firelight," recalled a citizen. "I took my maid and went into the yard to watch and wait. A soldier passed by and remarked, 'Madam, before the dawn of the day, this town will be laid in ashes.'" Anxious residents could only watch and wait. "What an awful and grand spectacle it is! It reminds me of the siege of Knoxville, where every night several buildings were burned," a citizen wrote. The red sky was visible for miles. Mrs. John Rice of Woodleaf saw it and called to her children. "Look out the window," she said. "The Yankees are burning Salisbury."[111]

⁓⁂⁓

Beneath the red skies of Salisbury, the men of Palmer's brigade returned from their three-day mission late on April 12. The brigade had performed superbly. "We have had a great time & I think have struck some telling blows for our good Govt," affirmed Colonel Trowbridge. Although their success came at a price, the men believed it was well worth it. "You can't make an omelette without breaking eggs," a Pennsylvania cavalryman wrote.[112]

The night of April 12–13 was indeed one of reunions for the Cavalry Division because Wagner's 250-man detachment also returned. His command had been absent since April 4. From Lynchburg, the troopers bypassed Henry

Court House, reentered North Carolina, crossed the Yadkin at Shallow Ford, and rode through Mocksville. The location of Stoneman's command was soon obvious. "We can hear the explosions of the shells and see the light of the conflagration at [a] distance of 12 or 14 miles," a trooper wrote. In the rainy early-morning hours on April 13, Wagner's worn-out cavalrymen finally caught up with the main column just outside Salisbury. The rest of the Fifteenth Pennsylvania rejoiced to see them safely returned. "Hearty cheers and happy hellos greeted Major Wagner and his little band as they rejoined us on the march, after an absence of some ten [*sic*] days riding through the enemy's country," recalled a veteran.[113]

Reporting to Palmer and Betts, Major Wagner related the story of his amazing eight-day, three-hundred-mile journey. The detachment had lost only one man killed, two wounded, and three missing. Wagner had achieved "the destruction of a number of bridges on the R.R. west of Lynchburg[,] . . . the capture of 130 sick & wounded Rebel[s] in [the] Hospital at Liberty who were paroled, and on the return march almost constant skirmishes with the enemy[,] several of whom were killed & wounded & many captured who were paroled." Palmer later recognized Wagner "for skill and good conduct in having with his battalion of 250 men destroyed the Virginia Railroad from thirty miles east of Christiansburg to within three miles of Lynchburg, and thence succeeding in withdrawing his command in the face of a superior force."[114]

On the morning of April 13, "Salisbury wore a very f[o]rlorn appearance," recalled an eyewitness. Major Barnes reported the job of destruction finished, even as one last "terrific explosion" rocked the town. Gillem was proud. "From the preceding afternoon, up to this time the air has been constantly rent by the reports of exploding shells and burning magazines," he wrote. "For miles around[,] the locality of the city was marked by a column of dense smoke, and at night by the glare from burning stores." The fires would smolder for weeks. People came from miles away to pick through the ruins and salvage what they could.[115]

Gillem could also have pointed to his casualty list with some pride. Although they were the attacking force, the Federals lost only an estimated three killed, thirty wounded, and a few captured (who were probably deserters). The Federal casualties included Angel, a member of the Eighth Tennessee Cavalry shot through the arm, Morrow, and Aldrich. A captured artilleryman saw some "desperately wounded men" in a field hospital west of Grant's Creek. Some of them probably belonged to Reagan's battery, which suffered twenty casualties, more than any other unit. The dead included a Tennessee soldier and Captain John Edwards of the Eleventh Michigan Cavalry, the highest-ranking officer killed on the raid.[116]

The Confederates lost only about one killed and a half-dozen wounded. These included two men from Marshall's battery who were wounded when their gun fired prematurely due to a dirty barrel. Most of the Confederate losses came instead in captured soldiers. One source lists 364 Confederates missing. Gillem claimed that the Federals captured around 1,300 enemy soldiers. While other estimates vary widely, Gillem's rings true. The Federals also scooped up 8,000 sick and wounded Confederates from local hospitals.[117] There may have been more casualties. After the war, United States authorities moved more than 300 bodies from makeshift graves around town to the new Salisbury National Cemetery. The cause and timing of those deaths are unknown.[118]

Gillem collected many trophies at Salisbury, including at least a dozen stands of colors and an old United States banner. He reported that his men seized eighteen artillery pieces, although other sources claim the Federals captured anywhere from thirteen to twenty-two guns. The cavalrymen sent most of the captured pieces to Knoxville; the rest they destroyed, abandoned, or took along. One of the guns was most unusual. The "pepper box," as a Kentucky veteran described it, was a highly polished brass piece mounted on the carriage of a six-pound howitzer with eighty-four small holes bored through the barrel. It was apparently a Gatling gun that Queen Victoria had given the state of North Carolina, albeit sans ammunition. This curiosity eventually wound up in Washington, D.C.[119]

◦᷍ᵒ

In Greensboro that same afternoon of April 13, 1865, Generals Beauregard and Johnston, President Davis, and the Confederate cabinet met to debate the future. The situation was bleak. Johnston's army still survived, but it was outnumbered, and the government was short of cash, arms, and ammunition. Davis, ever defiant, wanted to keep fighting. "We can whip the enemy yet," he said, then wove an incredible tale of resurrecting the army with deserters. Joe Johnston disagreed with brutal honesty. Since Lee's surrender, Johnston knew the time had come to open negotiations to lay down arms. "It would be the greatest of human crimes for us to attempt to continue the war," he said. Beauregard supported Johnston. Among the cabinet members, only Judah Benjamin sided with the president. The time had come, the majority pleaded, to open negotiations for peace.[120]

So the wheels began to slowly turn. Meanwhile, back in Salisbury, George Stoneman was ignorant of such discussions. Instead, he had more raiding in mind.

Part Two
Gillem's Raid

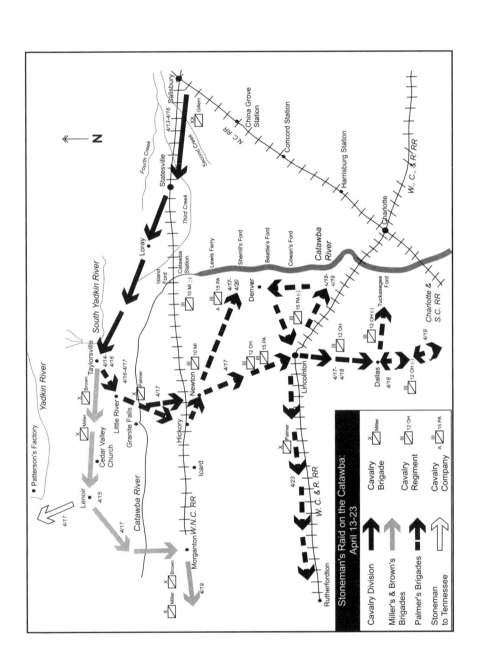

N

Patterson's Factory

Yadkin River

Fourth Creek

Statesville

Loray

South Yadkin River

Third Creek

Second Creek

Salisbury

4/13-4/16

Gillem

China Grove Station

Concord Station

N. C. RR

Harrisburg Station

Charlotte

W., C., & R. RR

Catawba River

Lenoir
4/15

Cedar Valley Church

Little River

Granite Falls

Icard

Taylorsville
4/14-
4/16

4/16-4/17

Miller

Brown

4/17

Palmer

4/17

Hickory

Newton

10 MI

Island Ford

Catawba Station

10 MI (-)

15 PA
A

Lewis Ferry

Sherrill's Ford

Beattie's Ford

Cowan's Ford

Catawba River

4/17-
4/20

Denver

12 OH
15 PA

4/17

15 PA (-)

4/18-
4/19

12 OH

Lincolnton

4/17-
4/18

Dallas
4/18

12 OH (-)

Tuckasegee Ford

12 OH (-)
4/19

Charlotte & S. C. RR

Rutherfordton

4/23

Palmer

W. C. & R. RR

Morganton

W.N.C. RR

4/17

4/17

4/19

Miller

Brown

4/19

Miller

Brown

Stoneman's Raid on the Catawba:
April 13–23

Cavalry Division

Miller's & Brown's
Brigades

Palmer's Brigades

Stoneman
to Tennessee

Cavalry Brigade
Miller

Cavalry Regiment
12 OH

Cavalry Company
A   15 PA

Chapter 8

THERE ARE BAD MEN IN ALL CROWDS
Salisbury to Lenoir: April 13–17, 1865

Standing in the ashes of Confederate Salisbury, George Stoneman asked himself, What next? April 13 was the twenty-fourth day of the raid. The Federal cavalrymen had accomplished virtually every task specified in their orders, from destroying rails and supplies in Virginia and North Carolina to threatening Lynchburg, Danville, and Greensboro. The only target left was Charlotte, about forty miles to the south.[1]

After that, the Cavalry Division could presumably return to Knoxville, dealing with secondary targets en route, such as the Western North Carolina Railroad. Chartered in 1855, the line was a dream come true for residents of western North Carolina, who had long crusaded for a railroad to spur growth. When the war brought construction on the line to a halt in 1861, the rails stretched only from Salisbury to a point ten miles west of the Burke County line. Stoneman's orders did not mention this rail line, but it loomed as a valuable supply artery. Farther south was the Wilmington, Charlotte, and Rutherford Railroad. The line itself was unimportant, but its bridge across the Catawba River was worth seizing. So were the river's fords, which withdrawing Confederate forces would likely need. Several North Carolina towns west of the Catawba such as Morganton, Lincolnton, and Asheville were also potential objectives. Hedging his bets, Stoneman decided to "move to the south side of the Catawba River, and be in a position to operate toward Charlotte or upon the flank of any army moving south." From there, he could withdraw toward Knoxville as events or fresh orders dictated.[2]

With that decision, the raid was about to undergo a striking change. During its first twenty-three days, the Federal cavalrymen had traveled more than five hundred miles across three states. The operation was characterized by speed, hard strikes, and generally good behavior among the men. The next twenty-three days would see the raiders travel a similar distance across three more states, but amidst multiple changes in unit leadership and mission and against the chaotic backdrop of the war's end. The result would be a breakdown of discipline among some of the units, much to the chagrin of the local population.

The division began leaving Salisbury around midafternoon on April 13. For the next several hours, the Federals rode in a northwesterly direction on the Statesville road. Eleven captured Confederate guns bounced along, the rest having been destroyed or abandoned due to a lack of animals to pull them. One last wagonload of captured small arms also went with the column. Two men from the Tenth Michigan did not join the column, however; they were sent back to Knoxville, probably due to illness.[3]

The residents of Salisbury watched the raiders assemble, saddle up, and leave town. "Roll of drums, the blare of bugles caused the lounging soldiers, the prancing horses to debouch from the side streets, to rejoin the . . . brigades in marching order along the Salisbury thoroughfares," wrote Harriet Ellis. Although angered by the raiders' work in Salisbury, eight-year-old Harriet was still impressed by the procession. "In the yellow glow of the late afternoon sun the Yankee columns swung round the corner of Main Street at the Mansion House Hotel, and General Stoneman and his officers rode into view," she wrote. "I noticed that they checked their horses to a slowing pace as they passed our house. Behind the general and his officers jogged the jaded cavalrymen with swords eased in the scabbards and the holster straps released."[4]

Rear guards withdrew in the following hours, leaving Salisbury free of Federal forces by dawn on April 14. The townspeople breathed a collective sigh of relief. "What good news I have to write in my journal this morning!" noted sixteen-year-old Mary Eliza Currey. "The yankees have left, [and] are going in the direction of Charlotte and Statesville."[5]

⟨⟩

Although Palmer's brigade had returned from its raid and Wagner's detachment was back from Virginia, the Federal cavalry column that marched westward through the night of April 13–14 was still missing one contingent. Major Abraham Garner's ninety-man detachment, which had ridden for the Reedy Fork bridge early on April 11, remained absent. Stoneman and Gillem hoped they would soon hear from Garner's men. In the meantime, they pushed their horse soldiers onward.

A hard rain fell on the column as it left Salisbury. Cavalryman Septimus Knight counted himself lucky to be part of the procession. "I caught a mule in the road which I rode about ten miles," he recalled. Later that day, he turned the mule over to the quartermaster, which fell far short of replacing the eight horses a company of the Fifteenth Pennsylvania abandoned near Salisbury. After covering fourteen miles, Betts's troopers camped at ten o'clock that night at Fleming. Garner's detachment caught up with the Fifteenth Pennsylvania there, concluding its journey from Glenn's Ferry.[6]

Steven Thomas of the Tenth Michigan recalled halting around midnight. Dismounting in the woods, he lay down beside the road and went to sleep, his bridle looped over his arm. "During my sleep I was blest with one of those visions of home and happiness which so frequently break in upon the slumbers of true soldiers, and it made so vivid an impression upon my mind," he wrote his wife. "I had in imagination finished my military career[,] had thrown off the uniform and was at home in the enjoyment of its comfort. . . . You were pleased to see me[,] the children were delighted[,] I was wild with joy[,] but the first blast of the bugle brought me instinctively to my feet. I was lost for several moments[,] could not realize where I was[,] but the spell was broken and I soon became conscious that I was a soldier yet."[7]

Signalman Frank Frankenberry was in the Statesville-bound column, too, but the rain did not dampen his spirits. Sugar and meat hung from his saddle. New clothes, thread, and socks were packed in his saddlebags. And best of all, Frankenberry had a full stomach. That morning, he had enjoyed a nice breakfast in camp, topped off by coffee. Later, he had dinner with some citizens and promised to call on them again if he ever got the chance. Then the long ride began. For Frankenberry and the other signalmen, it continued all night.[8]

Along the way, the raiders did not neglect their duty, for the road they traveled ran beside the Western North Carolina Railroad. The cavalrymen spent

Sergeant Angelo Wiser drew crude maps of the raid in a small field notebook once owned by a Confederate treasury officer. He added a sketch of the Fifteenth Pennsylvania Regiment's commander, Lieutenant Colonel Charles M. Betts.

much of their time "destroying railroad depots, &c., on the route," a trooper reported. They destroyed the railroad bridge over Second Creek and the depot and buildings at Third Creek, and they may have damaged or wrecked the bridge at Third Creek. The troopers also destroyed a water tank. Thanks to the Federals, the Western North Carolina Railroad between Statesville and Salisbury suffered at least eleven thousand dollars' worth of damage. The destruction would have been worse had it not been for the quick thinking of the line's chief engineer and superintendent, James W. Wilson. "By recrossing the river and running down to Third Creek, while the army was crossing above," he reported, "I was enabled to save three engines[. T]he other two, though seriously injured, can be repaired, when we have the necessary shops."[9]

It was tiring work. "We were engaged in distroying rail road all day and forrageing until sunset when we went into Camp," wrote Private Banks of the Twelfth Ohio. "At 10 P.M. 'Boots & Saddles' sounded and we mooved out again verry mutch displeased as we were verry sleepy[. W]e marched all night—sleeping in our saddles."[10]

✂

April 14, 1865, was Good Friday, but nothing good came of it. In Washington, D.C., John Wilkes Booth assassinated President Abraham Lincoln at Ford's Theatre. The shooting not only added yet one more tragedy for the nation to mourn, it also stole headlines from other events. Booth's act pushed the raid of George Stoneman deeper into obscurity. That was not the case, however, in parts of North Carolina. "Few persons here at the time will ever forget" the day Stoneman came to Statesville "at the head of an army with banners," wrote the editor of the *Landmark*.[11]

On the maps of Angelo Wiser, Statesville was a major crossroads leading to Concord, Charlotte, Mocksville, Wilkesboro, and Taylorsville. The Western North Carolina Railroad passed through Statesville en route to Morganton. The Catawba River was also nearby. Statesville's proximity to the river and its role as a transportation center gave the town some strategic value.[12]

In April 1865, the people of Statesville had Stoneman's raiders on their minds. "For weeks past we have been kept in a painful state of excitement— threatened with the approach of Stoneman's Army from E. Tenn., and terrible company of raiders under the command of Kirk," wrote a Statesville schoolteacher. "We have packed up and sent to the country a few valuable articles, but

274 There Are Bad Men in All Crowds

we feel that it is almost useless to attempt to save anything." Anticipating little help from the government, Statesville's people held daily prayer meetings, alternating between the Presbyterian and Methodist churches. "We feel utterly unprotected and helpless[,] having no earthly protector[,] but we are still busy and cheerful, trusting in God and endeavoring day by day to 'cast all our cares upon Him, who careth for us,'" the Statesville teacher explained.[13]

The earthly protection Statesville did have dissipated the closer Stoneman came. In an account written two decades after the fact, S. W. Stevenson remembered that the town was packed with Confederate cavalrymen, including a battalion of Kentuckians "recruiting up their horses." The men had two to three horses apiece and drew supplies from Statesville's tithe stores, which had been gathered for just such a purpose. The soldiers camped on the south side of the "tanyard branch" about three hundred yards below the street leading to the depot. Around sunset, two local men scouted east and saw the enemy near Salisbury. Alarmed, officials stationed pickets at the edge of town. Stevenson and two other men were among them. They took position at a "branch in the corner of a fence near Sharpe's tanyard, on the east side of the road, with orders to allow no one to pass either way."[14]

Stevenson carried an English rifle and only two cartridges. His comrades toted double-barreled shotguns. Together, they spent the night along the fence and saw no one except a country doctor returning from a house call. The next morning, the Kentucky battalion left for Mocksville, only to return at the double-quick about one that afternoon. "They were excited and asked how far it was to Beattie's Ford; said they wanted to cross it that evening," Stevenson wrote. "Someone told them it was too far; they could not reach it that soon. They said they must and went on, and have never been heard from since."[15]

If the departure of the Kentuckians was not enough, other signs made it clear the Federals were on their way. "The town was full of rumors as to Stoneman's approach. We saw the lights of the fires made by the burning of houses in Salisbury and it was certain he was approaching," Stevenson explained. Another citizen wrote, "For several days there had been ominous rumors; it was noised about that 'the Yankees were coming,' but there was no confirmation of these rumors until about dark on the evening in question when Messrs. T. A. Watts and J. S. Miller, who had gone scouting down the road toward Salisbury, 'rid like madmen' through the streets of Statesville even as Brutus and Cassius are said to have passed through the gates of Rome." Watts and Miller had found the raiders about six miles from town. "Their return, with the news that they brought, was the signal for a general movement of the male population toward the friendly forests. Such a packing up of valuables for immediate transportation was never known before," the citizen wrote.[16]

Samuel Wittowsky somehow missed Watts and Miller's warning, but he did not need it. The future father of North Carolina building and loan associations, Wittowsky went to the top of the three-story Simonton Hotel to verify reports that Stoneman had captured Salisbury. Looking east, he saw the ominous glow of distant flames and heard faraway explosions. Believing he had to do something, Wittowsky the next day joined Colonel S. A. Sharpe and about twenty-five other men, some of them sixty years old. Armed with shotguns, rifles, bowie knives, and pistols, the band rode out to meet the enemy. The men stopped at a railroad crossing three miles from Salisbury and sent out scouts. When the scouts came back empty-handed, the men decided that the Federals would not risk a nighttime journey through the unhealthy swamps of Second and Third creeks. Satisfied, Sharpe's party went home.[17]

Back in Statesville, Wittowsky knew the reprieve was temporary, so he hid his valuables. He stashed some possessions in the brick wall of the Simonton Hotel and others under his hearth. He even "saved" a barrel of apple brandy by having a servant spill its contents into the backyard. Finally, Wittowsky decided he should look his best for the raiders. Exchanging his old clothes for a brand-new, Richmond-made thirty-three-hundred-dollar suit, he awaited the raiders.[18]

Statesville's tense wait ended shortly after dark on April 13 with the arrival of Stoneman's advance guard. According to one source, the occupying unit was a regiment commanded by a Colonel Smith—probably Lieutenant Colonel Charles E. Smith and the Eleventh Michigan Cavalry. A member of that regiment, Henry Birdsall, noted that his unit pushed hard that night, as if it was indeed in the lead. "Marched all night without stopping[,] passed through S[tatesville] about three o'clock and camped at daylight," he wrote. The entry was not uneventful. As the cavalrymen sauntered into town, they noticed a darting figure and fired a shot. The bullet winged a lawyer, C. L. Summers, who was trying to escape into the woods. The cavalrymen took him prisoner.[19]

A desultory skirmish broke out as the Michigan men approached the public square. Several Confederate soldiers on leave who had gathered there took a few potshots at the Federals before fleeing on horseback. One of the raiders, probably in response to this challenge, fired two shots down Depot Street. One bullet lodged above the door of a nearby house, while the other slammed into a tree in front of a hotel.[20]

The escapade of T. A. Watts generated more gunfire. Watts was in the public square when the cavalrymen appeared. When he tried to escape, the Federals gave chase and cornered him between two storehouses and a picket fence. Thinking quickly, Watts climbed over the fence and disappeared. Cavalrymen fired a volley at him, but the bullets missed, striking the fence behind him. The troopers consoled themselves by capturing Watts's revolver, horse, and gray shawl.[21]

Then all was quiet. Colonel Smith set up headquarters at the home of Dr. R. L. Bogle on East Broad Street. He also posted pickets all over town. Anyone who tried to pass was subject to arrest, as a local lawyer discovered. A. W. Jamison was on his way to a meeting at the courthouse when a picket stopped him. The Federal cavalrymen, sitting on their horses, sent him to headquarters, where he was detained for several hours. Jamison was later released, but not until he showed the enemy where some Confederate supplies were stored.[22]

Later that night and into the early morning on Good Friday, the main body of raiders began to arrive, marching down Broad Street. Even though most of the troopers pushed on without stopping, they made quite an impression. "The town was now literally swarming with troops," a citizen noted. "They were in every yard and house." Frank Frankenberry was among the arrivals. "March all night and at 2 A.M. came into Statesville having marched 28 miles," the signalman wrote. The Thirteenth Tennessee reached town at daylight on April 14 and continued toward Taylorsville.[23]

The column that streamed into Statesville was a motley one. "The army was accompanied by a number of prisoners who were taken at Salisbury and elsewhere, and also by many Federals who had been released from the Salisbury prison," an eyewitness wrote. The prisoners included several of Salisbury's Home Guardsmen. "For hours the streets resounded with the tread of this army, numbering about 5,000. It struck camp in the college campus, which was soon ablaze with the light of camp-fires, made principally of the palings which surrounded the grounds." Mitchell College thus became the site of the main Federal camp. Troopers also bivouacked in vacant lots and along Fourth Creek two miles north of town.[24]

The arrival of the Cavalry Division made Statesville hold its breath. One of the first things the raiders did was destroy the town's railroad. "At Statesville

Private Allen D. "Frank" Frankenberry served in the Signal Corps detachment on the raid.

THE RICHARD K. TIBBALS COLLECTION AT THE UNITED STATES ARMY MILITARY HISTORY INSTITUTE

sad havoc was made by the raiders of the buildings belonging to the Company; the walls of the Depot are however good and should be immediately covered to protect them from the frosts of winter," explained a Western North Carolina Railroad Company report. Two depots and some large sheds were burned, along with government provender and sixty bales of cotton. A large supply of tobacco burned inside one depot; one young man remembered walking barefoot through the ashes. Officials calculated that Statesville's rail facilities suffered damages totaling forty-five hundred dollars.[25]

In their ongoing search for food and horses, the raiders canvassed seemingly every home, smokehouse, and stable. They broke store windows and showcases with their carbine muzzles, cracked open safes, and swapped jaded animals for fresh mules and horses. But Colonel Smith vowed to the people that their property would be safe, and the raiders generally kept that promise. "There is a decent way of doing a mean thing, and to do them justice the soldiers generally did not behave badly toward the people," attested a citizen. "The citizens were of course much terrified at their approach," explained another, "and expected to witness such scenes of horror as had been enacted in various other places but they passed steadily and quietly through, large bodies of their troops making no halt at all. And they did comparatively little damage here to private property." The Federals even distributed some of the goods they found to needy blacks. Perhaps the actions of a few determined women kept the soldiers in line. The women took up hatchets and axes, dashed to the depot, and smashed the kegs of liquor stored there.[26]

Many officers kept a close watch on their men, but the raiders nonetheless remained enemies in the eyes of Statesville citizens. "Companies of Yankees were passing through town all day[. A]bout ten oclock a General (reported to be Gen. Stoneman) came through, they were very handsomely dressed," Annie Donnell wrote in her diary. "The Gen. Who is a foreigner, and one of his staff, a New Yorker[,] seeing the girls in the yard jumping rope, and, I suppose, thinking we looked very lively to have the enemy constantly passing, rode up in the yards, where we were very politely asked if we were disturbed by their troops the night before." A trooper even offered to carry letters to Northern boyfriends. One girl appeared interested until she realized the cavalrymen would read it. The conversation then returned to the raid. "They had the impertinence to say they would occupy this country [e]ntirely before a great while[,] that they had large forces coming on, both infantry and cavalry, and rode off saying the sooner we lay down our arms the better," Annie Donnell wrote. "If I had had a pistol I should have shot him from his horse."[27]

As the officers feared, some of their men were guilty of misconduct. Wittowsky met the raiders soon after the first units appeared in town. He was still hiding valuables when he heard firing from the direction of the public square. Then he heard a knock on his store door. "Who is it?" he asked.

"A friend, open the door," came the reply.

Wittowsky complied, but he saw no friends, only six mounted Federals pointing their weapons at him. They asked Wittowsky what he was doing and if he had any arms. Wittowsky denied possessing any weapons and explained that he lived in an apartment behind the storehouse. Without further discussion, the six horsemen rode right through the doorway. Disappointed to find nothing of value, they asked for the local watchmaker, an East Tennessee refugee working from a room in the Simonton Hotel. Wittowsky took the soldiers there but learned that the watchmaker had left town. The Federals broke into the watchmaker's room anyway, despite Wittowsky's offer to produce a key.

Outside, some soldiers discovered the brandy barrel Wittowsky's servant had broken. "Boys, I smell liquor," a passing trooper said. When he learned the brandy's fate, the trooper railed, "Some one has knocked the head off the barrel. If I knew I'd kill the _____ in a minute." Fortunately, the Federals did not vent their anger on anyone, but they nearly burned down a building. The barrel had come to rest beside a warehouse, which the angry cavalryman and his comrades decided to burn on the assumption the barrel had come from there. "As soon as they left," Wittowsky recalled, "I and [a] slave went out and asked such of the soldiers as were then in the store robbing it of what the others left, permission to put out the fire, which they gave us, and we thus saved the store and perhaps the whole block."

Back at his storeroom, Wittowsky found more trouble. "Three big Irishmen" barged in and took everything in sight, including the old suit of clothes he had taken off. The problem was that Wittowsky weighed only 118 pounds and the Irishman who took the suit was much heavier. Discovering that the old suit was too small, the Irishman proposed a swap. The Statesville resident "did not think it healthy to refuse." Fortunately, an officer walked in and asked the men what they were doing. When Wittowsky explained that he was being robbed, the officer ordered the Irishman to take off the stolen clothes and leave. Hastened by the flat of the officer's sword and a few choice words, the three Irishmen scurried away. Wittowsky thanked his savior. "We are not a lot of robbers," the officer told him. "We make no war on private citizens. We are soldiers of the United States, fighting for our country."

Wittowsky had not seen the last of his Irish friend. The man came back at three in the morning to retrieve his forgotten pistols. "Mishter, Mishter, hand me my pistols," the man whispered into Wittowsky's window. When the merchant explained that the officer had taken the pistols with him, the Irishman decided to look for new pistols rather than risk the officer's wrath.

Another drunken cavalryman stumbled into Wittowsky's room about midnight. "Hello, Brother!" the man said, recognizing Wittowsky as a fellow Mason. While a prisoner at Salisbury, the soldier had been allowed to attend the local Masonic lodge the same night Wittowsky visited. Agreeing to Masonic confidence, the two men went to the cellar, where the soldier confessed that he had cut the throats of several Rebels in Salisbury. The man was lying, but he nevertheless gave Wittowsky two horses he had captured on the way to Statesville. One was pregnant and died a few days later. The other belonged to a man from Third Creek.[28]

Bill Watts fared even worse at the hands of the raiders. A jack-of-all-trades, Watts repaired clocks, clerked in stores, called witnesses at the courthouse, and sometimes served as deputy sheriff. A squad of troopers arrested him and made him double-quick through town. Finally, Watts stopped and told his persecutors that they could kill him but he would "be burned if he would trot another step." The Federals let him go. Then there was Frank Bell. According to Southern sources, Bell "was cruelly beaten and tortured to make him disclose the hiding-place of gold which they suspected he possessed." But Bell had no treasure to disclose.[29]

While Bell suffered the most severe physical injuries among the residents of Statesville, the Drake family sustained the greatest property loss. E. B. Drake and his son edited Statesville's newspaper, the *Iredell Express*, an ardent supporter of the Confederacy. Even the Drakes' press had a long association with rebellion, having printed the Mecklenburg Declaration of Independence during the Revolutionary War. The very day the raiders arrived, the *Express* placed Stoneman in Virginia heading for the lead mines and saltworks. It urged its readers never to submit to the "Northern despot, and his band of thieves and murderers." Frightened by news of the raiders' approach, E. B. Drake tried to save the press by dismantling it. After several hours' work, he managed to remove the framing, but that was as far as he got.[30]

Once the raiders arrived, a squad of nine soldiers came to the printing office. Some citizens guessed their purpose and begged them to spare the office. They feared for the Drakes, but they were also afraid that once the *Express* building went up in flames, the rest of the town would follow. When the officer in charge ignored the entreaties, a Mr. Andrews asked if the citizens could tear the small newspaper office down and move it into a vacant square across the street, where it could be burned safely. The officer refused Andrews's request. The troopers then ignited a bale of cotton on the first floor of the office. Within moments, the building was aflame. The home of Dr. Y. S. Dean soon caught fire as well. Bystanders managed to rescue Dean's furniture, but they could not save his home, office, or outhouses. According to a local historian, the fire left a "worthy gentleman with a family of children . . . homeless and utterly prostrated." Fortunately, the winds blew the flames away from town, and no other structures were lost.[31]

Rumor had it that Stoneman's raiders piled up and burned records at the courthouse. But that ends the litany of destruction in Statesville. In truth, good behavior on the part of the Federals was the rule, as the first family of North

Carolina could have attested. While Governor Zebulon B. Vance attended to state business in Raleigh, his wife, Harriet, and their four sons searched for a safe haven from the enemy. After stopping at Asheville and Morganton, they came to Statesville—right in Stoneman's path. Hearing of the raiders' approach, Mrs. Vance sent off some large trunks filled with clothing, silver, and gold that a bank had entrusted to her. She did not have time to move the furniture from the governor's house, which Vance had also sent to Statesville for safekeeping. Mrs. Vance's efforts went for naught. Other Federal troops later seized the furniture, while Stoneman's cavalrymen captured the trunk. According to one source, the raiders "rejoiced exceedingly over this finding of spoil, more especially as belonging to the rebel Governor Vance." Fortunately for the family, Palmer learned of the trunk, ordered its contents recovered, and sent it back to Mrs. Vance with his compliments. The Federal troopers behaved well toward the Vances. "Mrs. Vance was treated with respect and entirely unmolested," observed a North Carolina historian shortly after the war.[32]

Annie Olympia Donnell never forgot the raid, which occurred shortly before her nineteenth birthday. "The Yankees came in town this morning with a very large force about one oclock, and came in the College yard, to camp, built about fifty fires, and cooked their sup[p]er or breakfast," she wrote in her diary. "I do not know which they intended it for[. T]hey cooked their bread and batter-cakes in pieces of tin that blew off the house a few days before, and cooked some meat, and ate some raw, after having broken open Mr. Caldwell's smokehouse and taking all his meat and corn. What a beautiful sight it was to see their fires[,] there being so many, but one I never want to see again, under the same circumstances." Annie estimated that nine hundred men camped at the college. She added that the only crime they committed was stealing money from a servant. Perhaps the absence of students helped, as the college had closed under the threat of the raid. "We all enjoyed ourselves very much, after we saw they were not going to disturb us," Annie wrote.[33]

Many raiders would doubtless remember Statesville because it was there that they first heard the news of Robert E. Lee's surrender at Appomattox Court House. Colonel Trowbridge picked up rumors on April 13. Kramer's battalion heard the same glad tidings during its jaunt to Eckel's store the same day. Homeward-bound veterans of Lee's army, including two cavalrymen carrying a white flag, told the same tale. "We meet now plenty of returning Confederates, and they give interesting accounts of the fall of Richmond and Lee's surrender," wrote a Pennsylvanian. "They say it was Phil. Sheridan and his cavalry that did the mischief. They never saw any fighting equal to what our cavalry did on that campaign." One of the returning Confederates was Marshall H. Walker, a resident of Statesville and a veteran of the Sixth North Carolina. Arrested by a squad of Federals shortly after his return home, Walker was taken to Stoneman. Upon hearing the news of Lee's surrender, an overjoyed Stoneman sent Walker home with a guard for protection. Colonel Betts recalled that the news "fully stunned us with its importance and it took us several days to realize the fact." Official confirmation would arrive in a few days.[34]

While his men gathered supplies, Stoneman dismounted at the Bogle home. Still suffering from hemorrhoids, he had ridden into town in a carriage that once belonged to a Salisbury lawyer. The general had not updated General Thomas on his progress since March 28, so he went inside and wrote a report. So far, he wrote, the raid had been an unqualified success. Since March 20, the division had marched five hundred miles, crossing Stone Mountain once and the Blue Ridge Mountains three times. Nowhere, Stoneman claimed, had the enemy been ready to oppose him. "The rapidity of our movements has in almost every instance caused our advance guard to herald our approach and made the surprise complete," he boasted. The division had also been successful in keeping its men well mounted. "I can say that we are much better mounted than when we left Knoxville," he wrote. Stoneman praised Keogh, Morrow, and Bascom, then inserted a lukewarm compliment for Gillem, "the immediate commander of the division, who is entitled to a full share of whatever is due." Thomas received Stoneman's dispatch a few days later. He passed it on to Halleck "for the information of the Secretary of War and the lieutenant general," noting especially "the importance of the work performed by General Stoneman, who in spirit fully executed the orders given him before starting on the expedition." Stoneman had not freed the prisoners at Salisbury. He had not grabbed glory or big headlines for his raid because other events had overtaken him. But in the eyes of his superiors, George Stoneman had at last redeemed himself.[35]

One last tragedy remained to be played out in Statesville. No one was more aware of the war's continuance in North Carolina than General Sam Ferguson's Confederate troopers. On April 12, in a meeting with President Davis and Generals Samuel Cooper, Johnston, and Beauregard, Ferguson was ordered to pursue Stoneman. Fresh from its victory over Trowbridge at Abbott's Creek, the Rebel brigade sent out scouts to find the Federals. One scouting party became involved in a deadly skirmish, the details of which remain unclear. All sources, however, agree that it occurred late on April 15. One account suggests the incident began when some of Palmer's troopers rode out North Main Street, camped at the George Watt place, then slid over to the Taylorsville road along a country way. Another source indicates that the fighting broke out when Palmer's rear guard left town. Even the exact location of the incident is uncertain, but it probably occurred a few miles northwest of town near or along the Taylorsville road.[36]

The skirmish involved Lieutenant A. B. Coffee, "a fine specimen of a man" from Mississippi who served with Colonel T. C. Flournoy's Confederate scouts. Coffee led a small detachment that found the raiders. According to an 1882 newspaper account, "in the dim light of early morning, [Coffee] ordered a charge upon the Federals, and was shot dead in the road." The brave lieutenant charged because he thought he faced only a small enemy force. He was wrong and paid with his life. Shot through the mouth, Coffee was taken to a home in Statesville, but he was past saving. Shortly after he uttered his last words—"My gracious"— and expired, citizens prepared his body for burial in a fresh suit of clothes. On April 16, Coffee was laid to rest with Masonic rites in the old Fourth Creek cemetery. Annie Donnell was one of the college girls who helped. "He was a brave looking soldier," she wrote.[37]

Coffee's death brought down the curtain on Stoneman's Raid in Statesville, with one exception. Even as Confederate troopers mourned the fallen lieutenant, a Federal soldier paid the ultimate price. Private George S. Hysinger of the Eighth Tennessee Cavalry died after being shot by Captain Landon Carter of the Thirteenth Tennessee Cavalry "under a pretence of insubordination." Unlike Coffee's death, Hysinger's passing was a harbinger of worse behavior to come from the ranks of the raiders. At six-thirty in the evening on April 15, 1865, the last of the raiders saddled up and left town. After their day of rest, the cavalrymen were as fresh as they had been for some time. But an all-night march lay ahead. Betts ordered his men to take only good roads as they made their way to Taylorsville.[38]

As the cavalrymen disappeared into the darkness and dust, "the people then gathered themselves together to look over the wreck and compare notes," recalled a citizen. "Those who had received, the night before, assurances from Col. Smith that property would be protected, looked upon the scene which the Federals had left behind them and thought unutterable things. After the departure of the troops the town became very quiet and few persons were seen on the streets except of the colored race; but they were moving about quite briskly and generally with a good quantity of supplies." The raiders left much evidence of their passing—burned fences, wasted provisions, unused bushels of corn, a half-stack of hay, several hams, a few broken-down horses, and even a dozen dirty old socks. "We walked over their camp after they left and found several little things, such as cartridges[,] spools of thread and some other things. I found a very nice gimlet," Annie Donnell wrote. Stoneman's mark would remain on Statesville for some time, as a veteran of the Army of Tennessee who passed through later attested. "The Stoneman raid had burned the Depot and some other buildings a few weeks ago," he wrote.[39]

From Statesville, the vanguard of the Cavalry Division aimed for Taylorsville. This move marked a northwestern shift away from the Western North Carolina Railroad because Stoneman did not want to use the Island Ford, the most direct route across the Catawba River. According to Angelo Wiser, it was a "very rough ford—not advisable to ford at night unless well acquainted with ford." Turning to Taylorsville would allow the division to skirt the Catawba but remain within striking distance of the main river crossings and the Western line.[40]

On April 14, the vanguard reached Taylorsville, the seat of Alexander County. Mallaby's signalers arrived at noon, along with the Thirteenth Tennessee. They settled in for the night. Faithful diarist Henry Birdsall and the rest of Colonel Smith's Eleventh Michigan reached Taylorsville on April 14, too, fresh from their charge into Statesville. That was a busy day for Birdsall, who served on a detail collecting horses. "Did not get any," he wrote. "Captured one Reb. Paroled him. Attempted to cross the River but saw too many Johnnies." Trailing the column were the Confederate prisoners captured in Salisbury. They were placed under guard in the courthouse square, where citizens were allowed to bring water and food to them.[41]

The Federal entrance into Taylorsville was unopposed but not without incident. When the raiders' advance guard galloped into town, the men called loudly for everyone to surrender. At that moment, eighteen-year-old James Taylor McIntosh was outside near the jail. Unfortunately for McIntosh, he was wearing a Confederate uniform. The cavalrymen arrested him and took him to an old storehouse for safekeeping. Later, McIntosh managed to slip away and change coats. He had no further trouble with the Federals. Another eyewitness, a young boy, noted that his "earliest recollection of anything military was standing on the old store porch that bright Sunday morning, listening to the band play in the street, and watching the long line of horsemen go by."[42]

The commanding officer—locals thought it was Stoneman but it was probably Brown or Miller—established his headquarters at the Alexander C. McIntosh home, which stood on the corner opposite the courthouse. The commander and his staff stayed the rest of the day and all night. "I have distinct recollections of the men as they came to the table for meals, and what they had to eat was somewhat different from what we children could get at the time," wrote a resident. "I remember the steady and solemn tread of the sentry, as he paced before the door and under the large flag which was on a pole at the front gate."[43]

The rest of the cavalrymen in Taylorsville had to scrounge for food. Frank Frankenberry stabled his horses, then put his well-practiced foraging skills to work. "I cook dinner and change clothes," he wrote. Other cavalrymen took food from Taylorsville homes. Dr. John M. Carson was among the victims. Carson was able to get a guard, since he claimed to have voted against the Ordinance of Secession in 1861, but his protector came too late. The Federals relieved Carson of 200 pounds of bacon, 35 bushels of corn, 500 bushels of fodder, 110 bushels of oats, 70 pounds of lard, a buggy, a fat hog, and a barrel of flour. In an affidavit, Carson attested that about 100 men were "engaged in taking property," and that the quartermaster was present. Carson's buggy was confiscated to bear a sick soldier, perhaps the hemorrhoidal Stoneman himself.[44]

The troopers also searched for fresh horses to replace their exhausted steeds. In addition, Taylorsville suffered limited looting. Barging into one home, a cavalryman stopped in a bedroom, removed the bedspread, and spread it on the floor. While a young girl who lived there watched, the man opened a bureau drawer and began to empty it. Clothes, pillowcases, sheets, and more went onto the bedspread. The contents of the top drawer, however, stopped the man short. When he saw a Masonic apron inside, he ordered his comrades out of the room and closed the door. He turned to the young girl and asked, "Where is your Daddy?"

"Working for Jeff Davis," she said.

"Aren't you afraid of a Yankee?" he asked.

"No, sir," she answered.

That ended the conversation. A guard appeared soon afterward, ending the search.[45]

At least two incidents sent flames and black smoke curling into the skies above Taylorsville. At one point, somebody threw a lit match into some loose cotton. The cotton burst into flames, and the breeze carried it in every direction. Some bystanders managed to put out the fire.[46]

If the first incident was an accident, the second certainly was not. It happened at the courthouse, where some troopers carried records outside, piled them in the yard, and set them on fire. At least one source claims the raiders also torched the courthouse. Only the deeds were saved. According to tradition, that was because Alexander County's register of deeds, Lanson Herman, liked to play checkers. He kept the deed books at home, preferring to work at night and play checkers all day at the courthouse.[47]

Luckily for Taylorsville, Gillem decided to ride on the next morning. It was April 15 when John Miller and Simeon Brown pointed their brigades toward Lenoir, the next significant town to the west. Taylorsville was not unoccupied for long, however. Under rainy skies, William J. Palmer's brigade arrived several hours later, fresh from the fight that killed Coffee. The Tenth Michigan Cavalry reached Taylorsville late that Saturday, and the Twelfth Ohio Cavalry—still in the saddle after a nonstop ride—rode into town near midnight. The Ohio men camped in and around the courthouse. Those of the Tenth Michigan camped with slightly thinner ranks. During the march from Statesville, bushwhackers had ambushed and killed Private Orlour J. Brackett. The speed of the movement also cost the regiment two stragglers, who later rejoined their comrades at Knoxville.[48]

Last of all came the Fifteenth Pennsylvania, which did not reach Taylorsville until the early-morning hours of April 16. Its journey from Statesville was anything but quiet. "There was considerable firing at us by rebels on the march, but it was harmless, so no attention was paid to it," a Pennsylvania trooper wrote. Camp rumors were of greater interest to the men. One had it that they were returning to Tennessee, since the main objectives of the campaign had been achieved. A poor road, however, made the journey to Taylorsville uncomfortable. Faithful mapmaker Angelo Wiser described a "march made at night, very

woody & bad road generally." Some of the troopers nonetheless managed to enjoy the ride. Sergeant Colton and his men, serving as the regiment's rear guard,
halted at eleven o'clock in the morning on April 16 to eat. Colton discovered
some fresh eggs and boiled them. His company also probed toward the Catawba
River, then camped for the night.[49]

Meanwhile, in Taylorsville, Palmer emulated other commanders and
stopped at the McIntosh home. "My father took the General and showed the
small quantity of grain which Stoneman's men had left and a guard was at once
placed around the house and there was no further trouble," a resident of the
home recalled. "These troops remained only a short time." Failing to find much
food at the McIntosh home, Palmer's men appropriated two cribs of corn from
a neighbor. The lady of the house—at home alone because her son had fled with
their three mules—was treated with respect. No troops were allowed inside.[50]

Palmer's men were much less destructive than their predecessors. The next
morning, they prepared to renew the march. One task was to impress a civilian
carriage to carry a wounded officer. The horsemen fixed it up to make the officer
more comfortable. (The carriage, later found broken down in the mountains,
was returned to its owner. It remained in the family for years.) The troopers then
assembled and left town. A number of citizens, including an old man and his
granddaughter, came to watch the cavalrymen depart. One soldier, probably an
officer, welcomed them and showed them a cannon. At last, the bugles blew and
the raiders exited. "I was sitting on the steps watching the crowd go by when an
officer rode up to the gate and asked me for a bunch of lilacs," the little girl later
remembered. "I gave it to him but had to stand on tiptoe. He thanked me, raised
his cap and rode off."[51]

It was Easter Sunday morning, April 16, 1865.[52]

⚬⚮⚬

Easter Sunday also found Jefferson Davis on the move again, in part because
conditions in Greensboro had rapidly deteriorated since his arrival on April 11.
"The town was in a perfect uproar," recalled James W. Albright, "the Yankees
expected every minute." Brigadier General Alfred Iverson observed the "almost
entire desertions of their troops with the exception of some five hundred men
on duty in town." The latter men mentioned by Iverson were close to bolting,
too. Outside town, another witness saw "a scene of desolation . . . all the public

stores having been plundered the day before. The vultures [were] scouting their prey for ten miles around," he wrote.[53]

Davis left Greensboro reluctantly. Conditions notwithstanding, the president still wanted to fight. He even ordered supply depots established on Johnston's expected route of retreat. Neither his cabinet nor his remaining generals shared his optimism. They urged Davis to authorize Johnston to seek surrender terms from Sherman, and the president grudgingly agreed. Since the probable surrender of the last Confederate army east of the Mississippi would only increase their personal danger of capture, Davis and his cabinet abandoned Greensboro. On April 15, Brigadier General George G. Dibrell's Tennessee cavalry escorted the group southward toward Charlotte. The slow journey along muddy roads was made all the harder because of Stoneman's Raid. The route took the group right across the raid's path, to Jamestown, High Point, and Lexington. The raid's passage was unmistakable and dictated their mode of travel. Since the raiders had left the rails and rail bridges below Greensboro in ruins, the once-proud government officials and their baggage were relegated to ambulances, carriages, wagons, and horseback.[54]

As they neared Salisbury on April 17, Davis and his cabinet saw more evidence of the raid. They crossed the Yadkin River on the bridge Zebulon York and his men had defended just five days earlier. Signs of fighting were evident, including damage to the bridge itself. The government leaders hesitated to enter Salisbury, presumably because they now had a healthy respect for the raiders, whose whereabouts were unknown. In town, the rubble still smoldered. Somehow, Davis remained upbeat, as a South Carolina soldier noted. "He was sitting gracefully erect on his horse, and courteously returned our salutes," the soldier wrote.[55]

At Taylorsville, the Cavalry Division once more separated into detachments. Stoneman and Gillem and the brigades of John Miller and Simeon Brown continued westward toward Lenoir on the morning of April 15. The next day, Stoneman sent Palmer's brigade south from Taylorsville to watch the crossings of the Catawba River.[56]

For Miller and Brown, the march was short, slow, and tense. The thirteen hundred prisoners captured at Salisbury followed the main body on foot, slowing its progress. A throng of black refugees also trailed, seeking freedom and new lives. The rain that fell on horsemen and pedestrians alike only made matters worse. At one point, unseen assailants opened fire. No casualties resulted, but the scene did nothing to bolster the spirits of Frank Frankenberry. The signalman rode out to find horses, captured a Rebel straggler instead, and returned unimpressed with what he described as "a very poor country."[57]

Caldwell County was better prepared for the raiders than most of the places Stoneman visited, thanks to the presence of a strong Home Guard contingent. Three infantry units and one cavalry company were guarding the county, mostly against robbers and Unionists. One infantry contingent contained able-bodied men who were exempt from conscription. The other infantry units were less reliable, consisting of men physically unfit to serve in the Confederate army. Each company alternated on duty every ten days, with the cavalry company held in reserve. Captain Nelson A. Miller commanded the cavalry, and Captains W. A. White, R. R. McCall, and Fin Shearer led the infantry. The units comprised the Seventeenth Battalion, commanded by Major Alphonso Avery, who had been captured at Salisbury. Avery was a former staff officer under General John Bell Hood.[58]

Caldwell County's first brush with Stoneman's raiders came when Gillem struck Patterson's factory. Hearing of the Federal raid, Captain White rode to Lenoir to take charge of his company, which was scheduled to go on duty. En route, White met Captain Shearer, who had just completed his ten-day tour. The two men decided to keep both companies on duty. As if to confirm their decision, "a horseman came riding at a great rate" when the two captains entered town "and reported that a detachment of Yankees . . . was approaching Lenoir from that direction, while the main army was coming in on the Patterson Road and would be soon pouring down North Main Street." To avoid capture and to verify the story, White and Shearer rode to a hilltop within sight of the courthouse. They waited expectantly, but it turned out to be a false alarm. The raiders had moved on to Wilkesboro. Lenoir was safe for the present.[59]

Colonel George W. Kirk's April 7 appearance in Watauga County introduced a new threat to Lenoir's security. Kirk's force was less than twenty miles away. A scout confirmed the news, which spurred local authorities into action. While Captain White posted pickets, Major Avery asked Bradley Johnson at Salisbury for reinforcements, then headed to Lenoir to study the situation. Deciding to launch a night attack on Kirk at Watauga Gap, Avery went to Salisbury to follow up on his request for more men and equipment. It was this mission that put Avery in the Grant's Creek railroad cut west of town during Stoneman's attack on Salisbury.[60]

Meanwhile, the people of Lenoir waited anxiously. They knew that Kirk was nearby, that Davis Tillson was in the mountains, and that Stoneman was within striking distance. "Of course we expected them every day and hour, and made preparations accordingly, living in constant suspense," a local woman wrote her uncle. Needless to say, Lenoir's citizens hid their valuables while they were able.[61]

Rumors spread as the day of Stoneman's second visit to Caldwell County approached. Unfortunately, the Home Guard failed to locate the raiders because it searched the wrong road. Other Home Guardsmen did find the enemy at Little River, a township about halfway between Taylorsville and Lenoir, but they could not act. It was April 15, and Major Harvey Bingham, Watauga County's luckless Home Guard commander, was in Little River visiting Jacob White. Fellow Home Guard commander Fin Shearer was there, too. Hearing of the Federal approach, the three men walked to the Lenoir-Taylorsville road to verify the news. Suddenly, Federal cavalrymen trotted around the corner and fell on them like lightning. Shearer raised his rifle to his shoulder, shouted "Halt!" and fired at the first horseman. The ball appeared to hit the man in the arm, and the raiders fell back. Bingham, White, and Shearer knew their victory would be short-lived. "Form! Form! Charge!" a voice in the distance cried out, and in seconds the raiders came galloping back "like a thunderstorm." The three Confederates fled. Bingham escaped by hiding on Bald Knob Mountain, and White got away by hiding in a brook, but Shearer was captured.[62]

Word of this skirmish failed to reach Lenoir in time, so Captain Miller led Company B toward Taylorsville on a reconnaissance that same morning. Pausing at Cedar Valley Church about seven miles west of Little River, the company sent a small detachment forward. A mile from the Alexander County line, the Home Guardsmen encountered two Federal cavalrymen with a prisoner. The Home Guardsmen captured the two Federals and freed the prisoner, Catawba County man W. L. Payne. Satisfied, they withdrew. The liberated Payne foolishly hid alongside the road to watch the raiders pass. He was soon recaptured.[63]

To the east, Gillem's raiders realized two of their men were missing, so they sent two parties ahead on different roads. As they marched, these cavalrymen took whatever they needed. "They captured all the horses they could get, took almost everything that could be found in the shape of provisions, and rummaged people's houses[,] carrying off whatever their whimsical fancy might dictate whether it was valuable or otherwise," wrote an onlooker. The Federals marched west, the low Brushy Mountains looming on their right.[64]

Sandwiched between Gillem and Lenoir, Nelson Miller's Home Guardsmen welcomed their comrades back. After sending their two prisoners to Lenoir, they unwisely decided to eat at Deal's mill. William Deal, an attorney and the owner of the mill, was their host. It was possibly the quickest meal in Caldwell County history. The part-time soldiers had not even started eating when the raiders materialized. The Home Guardsmen "ran to their horses, mounted quickly and formed a line of battle," recalled an eyewitness. The veteran Federal cavalrymen were too much for the Rebels, however. The raiders swung in behind the Home Guardsmen to the north of Deal's house and forced a retreat. Miller's soldiers withdrew a short distance up the road, then formed a new line of battle.[65]

Union accounts do not mention this action, but according to a local source the Home Guardsmen managed a fighting withdrawal. "As soon as the Yankees were within gunshot, both sides began firing," an observer claimed. "Several Yankees were wounded, but it is not known that any were killed." Still, Miller's men could not stop the blue tide; the unit began to disintegrate. Some men disappeared into the thickets of Hibriten, a spur of the Brushy Mountains. The rest galloped for Lenoir, halting occasionally to form a line of battle but rarely standing for long.[66]

The unit Nelson Miller fought was the Eleventh Michigan, Stoneman's advance guard. The Michiganders were followed closely by the Thirteenth Tennessee, Stoneman's carriage, and the guns of Battery E of the First Tennessee Light Artillery. The veteran cavalrymen easily pushed through the Home Guardsmen and reached Lenoir in midafternoon on April 15. Some Federals arrived ahead of Miller's men and gathered near the home of J. C. Norwood a group of the retreating Home Guardsmen crossed Lower Creek. The bluejackets opened fire, prompting Miller's Home Guardsmen to wheel about and ride for the mountains. Some of the raiders pursued but did not catch their quarry. While none of Miller's men were hurt, the raiders managed to free their comrades who had been captured earlier.[67]

Lenoir resident Louisa Norwood heard the firing. Dashing to her front door, she "saw a long column of blue coats . . . and the evening sunshine lighting up the stars and stripes." As it passed, the column gobbled up the Norwoods' horse. At the same time, the family also spotted some local men, unaware of Stoneman's arrival, galloping toward town. Louisa ran outside to warn them. "The Yankees are in town!" she shouted. This brought the approaching riders up short. Realizing their mistake, they changed direction and attempted to escape, but several raiders saw them and opened fire as the men rode away. No one was hurt. The riders made a clean getaway, thanks to Louisa Norwood.[68]

More riders appeared in due course, and the Norwoods again raised the alarm. These men, however, proved to be Federals. They had some fun at the ladies' expense. "Oh, yes, you thought we were rebs and you tried to save us, eh?" the men laughed.

"If I had a known you were Yankees, I wouldn't a tried to save one of you," Louisa replied.

This comment prompted several threats. The raiders "ripped and cussed and offered to burn the house if we didn't tell where Pa was with the mules," Louisa recalled. The horsemen also emptied the corncrib and smokehouse and plied the servants with offers of watches and money. When that did not work, they even tried pointing their guns at the servants, but the blacks were uncooperative. The cavalrymen found little else before a guard came and sent them off.[69]

By day's end, two brigades of Gillem's cavalry had bivouacked in Lenoir. Disagreement exists over how destructive the raiders were. According to a local history published in 1956, "most of the buildings and homes in Lenoir were ransacked," while another history states that "there occurred heart-wringing experiences that haunted Caldwell citizens for time untold." A more reliable contemporary account states otherwise. "They [the Yankees] did very little damage in Lenoir," wrote a Statesville resident. Despite some claims to the contrary, Davenport College was ultimately plundered and vandalized, and the boarding-house at Finley High School was burned. Much of the damage was probably the handiwork of stragglers.[70]

Those citizens who secured guards generally experienced little trouble. One man "obtained a guard for his house and they were not molested," according to an observer. Unfortunately for the people of Lenoir, guards were not easy to obtain. When some citizens asked Stoneman to stop plundering, he explained that he "could not furnish guards for corn-cribs and smoke-houses."[71]

Mrs. George W. F. Harper, wife of a Confederate infantry officer, agreed that guards made a difference. "At sunset, the Yanks rushed in on us. We obtained a guard about our house after they came in, and fared better than some others.

Did not undress or sleep all night." Getting the right guard was also important. One woman asked General Gillem to protect an iron safe containing the personal papers and money of some orphans. Gillem sent a guard, who proceeded to break into the safe. Though the man's actions were within earshot, the general was oblivious to the sounds of safecracking. When the woman called Gillem's attention to it, he ignored her.[72]

Mrs. John C. Vaughn, the wife of Brigadier General Vaughn, was another lucky resident. She was living in Lenoir while her husband was off fighting. Vaughn and Gillem had known each other before the war and had apparently agreed to care for each other's families if the opportunity arose. Gillem fulfilled his obligation and placed a guard at her house. Unfortunately, the man later disappeared, and ruffians broke in and demanded Mrs. Vaughn's watch. She pulled a pistol on them, but they wrenched it away and convinced her to hand the watch over. Neither was a guard present when raiders barged into a room where a woman was giving birth. The doctor kicked them out "with difficulty."[73]

Mrs. Laura Pruett Cochran, who was eighteen in 1865, never forgot her brush with the raiders. "As Eastertime drew near the little ones gathered up the eggs. But alas, that Easter was a day long to be remembered," she wrote. "About 4 P.M., April 15, 1865, we fully realized what we had long dreaded. We heard pistol shots we knew meant something. We ran to the front—what a sight! Soldier after soldier on every street[,] volley after volley, high in the air sounded the pistol shots. . . . Ours was a little village. . . . We watched the enemy take the town as if a deed in fee had been signed up. We dared claim nothing save the dresses we had on, and that numbered our wardrobe, two, three, or four. I had on three, and the top was a calico." As it later developed, young Laura's family received a guard. "A fine body of staff officers rode up to our gate and a servant opened it," she wrote. "Father saw, and trembled. They strode in, and the Captain said, 'we are staff officers and only want your barn and feed for horses. We will send you a guard for your house.'" The guard protected the family members while they fed hungry soldiers that night and all the next day.[74]

Other citizens experienced firsthand what the lack of guards meant. Cavalrymen looted the property of a sick woman, Mrs. Boone Clark, even dragging her out of bed and snatching her watch from her bosom. Elsewhere in town, the Reverend Jesse Rankin, sixty-three years old, endured curses and threats when he told hungry raiders that all the food he had to spare was going to the prisoners.[75]

In general, the residents of Lenoir withstood Stoneman's cavalry. "I was proud of the way Lenoir acted," a citizen wrote a few days later. "All stuck together and the Yanks said they liked us better than any people they had met, but it was the d____est little rebel town they ever saw."[76]

By dark on April 15, Lenoir belonged to the Cavalry Division of East Tennessee. As the troopers settled in for the night, Stoneman made his headquarters in the Episcopal rectory at the end of Rectory Street. Gillem took residence in an old log house. Before going to bed, the officers sat down and ate their supper, prepared by a local resident.[77]

Easter Sunday, April 16, dawned bright and warm. In Lenoir, Mrs. Harper wondered what the day held for her. "But Oh! How unlike the Holy Sabbath, excitement, confusion, and hurry all day," she wrote. It was just the contrary for cavalryman Frank Frankenberry. He awoke and enjoyed a fine breakfast of ham, coffee, cakes, and honey. He also received official word that the Army of Northern Virginia had surrendered. "A lovely day. All quiet," he jotted in his journal. Frankenberry spent the rest of the day at the home of William M. Priest. "I enjoyed myself finely. Had a good supper and then a long chat with the ladies." Satisfied, the signalman went to bed at ten that night.[78]

Frankenberry was lucky, for most of Miller's and Brown's men had to work on Easter Sunday. One resident thought that Stoneman stayed overnight because he was waiting on something, but the reality was that work remained to be done. Lieutenant Mallaby tried but failed to establish communication with General Tillson, who was now at Boone and still holding the gaps in the mountains. On Sunday afternoon, scouts combed the countryside as far as Granite Falls near the Catawba River. Back in Lenoir, other troopers readied the captured artillery and prisoners for transport to East Tennessee. They had been slowing the column, and Lenoir was a good place from which to send them back. The Tennessee state line was easily accessible via Boone, and friendly forces were close at hand in that direction. A guard would escort the motley band and see that the prisoners went on to Camp Chase, Ohio.[79]

The departure could not have come too soon for the thirteen-hundred-plus prisoners. Lenoir was simply unable to accommodate them. Colonel Miller had direct responsibility for the prisoners, but the best he could do was cram them in and around St. James Episcopal Church, just down the street from Stoneman's rectory headquarters. Rebel officers were kept inside the church and enlisted men in the churchyard. A strong guard watched the captives. Gillem ordered the guards to shoot anyone who attempted to escape. "[I] would rather have ten men shot than one escape," he reportedly said. Even had they wanted to attempt a breakout, most of the prisoners were in no condition to test Gillem's directive. The march from Salisbury had utterly exhausted them. Few of the prisoners had ever tramped so far in one day, especially at the double-quick. The blisters on their feet proved it had been a hard march. The prisoners were also famished. They did not receive rations until Easter Sunday. The locals gave them what little food they could spare.[80]

Louisa Norwood was one of those who came to the prisoners' aid. Two of her cousins, A. C. Everett and Major Avery, were among the captives. "Sunday morning we went up to see the prisoners," she recorded. "They arrived Saturday evening, after a very hurried march (some of the men falling dead by the way from sheer exhaustion) with blistered feet, and almost famished." The sight that awaited her at the rectory was unforgettable. "Imagine the scene, and remember that it was Easter Sunday! Of course we paid the poor fellows all the attention we could, taking them all the provisions we could save from the Yanks, and they seemed very grateful—said that the people between here and Salisbury had been afraid to even look at them." From chatting freely with the captives, Louisa Norwood learned they had not even been allowed to drink from the creeks they passed.[81]

The prisoners were thankful for the kindness of Louisa Norwood and other citizens. "Whenever any of the townspeople carried any thing to the prison, the scene was said to have been most piteous, so many men begging for just one morsel of dry bread," noted R. L. Beall, a Lenoir resident and historian of the raid. "All accounts agree that the prisoners were treated hardly." Another witness wrote, "Our poor prisoners seemed almost starved." Indeed, the feelings of twenty-three-year-old private Albert Stacey Caison were probably universal. A member of the Twenty-sixth North Carolina, Caison had been wounded and captured on the third day at Gettysburg. Released from Point Lookout just a month before, he had been recaptured by the raiders in his own yard. Caison said that he "had rather have died" than become a prisoner again.[82]

Prisoner maltreatment stemmed from the personal feuds that marked the war in western North Carolina. The raid presented the opportunity for "Home Yankees," earlier made to suffer for their Unionism, to take revenge on their

Confederate neighbors. "There seemed to be a spirit of bitterness and cruelty toward the prisoners among the men generally, and sometimes the officers," wrote one observer. Major Sterling Hambright, the Cavalry Division's provost marshal, was just such an officer. A Tennessean, Hambright was dashing and popular with his men but was said to be "especially insulting to citizens, and cruel to prisoners." The case of Dr. J. A. Ballew, an ill and feeble resident of Lenoir, demonstrated Hambright's cruelty. Upon his arrest, Ballew was taken to headquarters. He sat on the porch steps to catch his breath, but Major Hambright ordered him to go straight to the rectory. When Ballew did not move fast enough, the major kicked him in the rear end. According to a postwar account, Ballew did not survive captivity.[83]

Ballew probably did nothing to deserve his tragic fate aside from being in the wrong place at the wrong time. The same could not be said of Major Avery, whose ruthless campaigns had earned him the hatred of North Carolina Unionists. The Home Yankees riding with Stoneman had sworn to kill Avery, but thus far none knew he was among the prisoners. Avery could thank Sidney Deal for his anonymity. Deal, a friend of Avery's, had been captured in Lenoir while home on furlough from the First North Carolina Cavalry Regiment of the Army of Northern Virginia. Realizing Avery's life was in danger, Deal decided to disguise the major. Deal had been the sheriff of Watauga County when John K. Miller was sheriff of Carter County, Tennessee, so he approached Miller and asked for his help. Strangely enough, the Union colonel agreed to help Deal and Avery. With Miller's blessing, Deal took Avery into the church vestry on Easter Sunday morning. He exchanged Avery's Confederate clothes for a new hat and suit and took a razor and scissors and clipped off Avery's whiskers, leaving only an imperial and mustache. The disguise made Avery virtually unrecognizable.[84]

On April 17, the procession of guards, captured artillery, prisoners, and ex-slaves left Lenoir. As the column toiled up the mountain toward Blowing Rock, William "Keith" Blalock, one of the Unionists who had joined the raiders earlier, moved among the prisoners. He threatened, robbed, and sought out personal enemies—and also found longtime friend Sid Deal. That night, Blalock slept under the same blanket as Deal and the disguised Avery. He even talked about how badly he wanted to kill Avery without knowing his quarry slept just inches away.[85]

After a long and difficult march, the Federals eventually steered their prisoners to Camp Chase. Gillem admitted that some men died along the way. To a man, they were former Salisbury prison inmates still in old Confederate uniforms. "That gave rise to an unfounded report that my command had killed prisoners," Gillem wrote. He denied the accusations.[86]

⌐⋎⌐

George Stoneman joined the column of prisoners streaming up the mountain toward Blowing Rock. Having fulfilled his orders—and considering his continued health problems—he decided that it was time to return to Knoxville and attend to the other business of the District of East Tennessee. The New Yorker turned over the reins to Alvan C. Gillem.[87]

With Stoneman gone and Palmer raiding elsewhere, the people of Lenoir believed they now had ample reason to worry. Indeed, local observers thought that among the present commanders only Simeon Brown could be trusted. "General Brown is represented as a humane gentleman. When informed of outrages, he would check them promptly," wrote an early historian of the raid. (Later events would prove this contention questionable.) In contrast, John Miller, with his East Tennessee background, had already demonstrated that he could be ruthless. And Gillem denounced Lenoir as a "rebellious little hole." His actions reflected his words. Locals returned the sentiment. "Gen. Gilliam [sic] deserves a special notice," testified one postwar account. "Concurrent testimony represents him as supercilious, insulting, and unfeeling."[88]

In a conversation with Mrs. Albert Hagler, Gillem denounced the Confederacy for starving Union prisoners. Mrs. Hagler disagreed, suggesting that the Union might have prevented much suffering by continuing prisoner exchanges. Gillem reportedly was so angered by her retort that he allowed his men to plunder the nearby homes of Mrs. Hagler's married daughter and niece. At the home of the married daughter, Mrs. Hartley, the raiders broke open and emptied barrels of sorghum onto the floors and over the wheat in the granary. They also smashed furniture and crockery. At the home of Mrs. Boone Clark, Mrs. Hagler's niece, raiders chased off Dr. Clark, a disabled Confederate veteran who was raising recruits for home defense. The Federals came in waves, repeatedly turning the home upside down in search of weapons and valuables.

Mrs. Clark at last broke down and wept, begging the raiders to stop. They answered her by calling her names and cursing her. "What are you trembling for? . . . Are yer cold? . . . What yer crying for? . . . Are yer sick?" they asked. A soldier grabbed her by the throat, cursed her, and struck her. He even ripped a gold watch from around her neck. That was the last straw. Mrs. Clark grabbed her child and ran to Mrs. Hagler's.

When asked to intervene, Gillem waved off the request. "There [are] bad men in all crowds," he said. An outraged Mrs. Hagler also asked Gillem to protect Mrs. Hartley, but he turned his back on her. Mrs. Clark appealed to Lieutenants Jerome B. Rice and Mallaby, who took pity on her. One of the lieutenants arrived at her house just as the last offender ran out. Shocked at the man's actions, Mallaby had him arrested and then asked Mrs. Clark to identify him. The soldier denied coming near her house, but she had him cold. "Why, that is a piece of a silk dress of mine round your hat now," she said.

"Is it? Well, then, you may have it back," the man said, and handed it to her.

"This was in the presence of General Gillam [*sic*], for whom, by the way, it was generally observed, the men seemed to have no respect," an onlooker explained. General Brown sent a guard to Mrs. Clark's house, but he arrived too late to save anything.[89] It is unknown whether the men who committed these acts were stragglers or soldiers still under the authority of their commanding officers. Regardless of their status, the perpetrators tended to belong to Miller's and Brown's brigades, rather than Palmer's.

Fortunately for the people of Lenoir, the Federal cavalry had orders to move out. "After the invasion of East Tennessee by General Burnside, Ash[e]ville, North Carolina, had been used as a base from which expeditions constantly invaded Tennessee," Gillem explained. "I was directed to attack and disperse any force in that section of the state." Accordingly, on the morning of April 17, Miller's and Brown's troopers packed up and trotted southwest toward Burke County and Morganton, the county seat. "Making ready to move at 6 A.M.," Frank Frankenberry wrote in his diary. After giving his address to his hosts, shaking hands, and promising to write, the signalman joined the column as it rode down the Morganton road.[90]

The people of Lenoir had to endure one last thing: the stragglers who remained behind, robbing and destroying indiscriminately.[91] The next morning, some of Vaughn's Confederate cavalrymen trotted into town, driving off the last stragglers. Lenoir's menfolk came out of their hiding places, pulling their horses and mules after them. Near Bald Knob Mountain, a passerby found an abandoned Federal bivouac "literally covered with things curious, valuable, and otherwise," including "corn, oats, meat, hats, shoes, brass cartridges, run down broken firearms, old clothes, some books, an old violin, and all manner of trinkets and curiosities." It was a treasure trove for war-weary citizens, who happily carried off the leftovers. However, few celebrated the passing of Stoneman's cavalry because the people of Lenoir realized it was their neighbors' turn. The sound of gunfire was now clearly audible from the direction of Morganton.[92]

Chapter 9

Watch on the Catawba

Taylorsville to Morganton: April 16–22, 1865

On Easter Sunday, April 16, while the rest of the division made short work of Lenoir, Colonel William J. Palmer's brigade left Taylorsville. Stoneman's parting thought was for the command to assume a position from which it could either advance on Charlotte or harass the flanks of an army moving through the Carolinas. Palmer would play the key role. Stoneman sent him to Lincolnton, where Palmer would establish headquarters and "scout down the Catawba River toward Charlotte." According to Colonel Charles Betts, the scouting assignment meant guarding the "lower turn of the Catawba River to prevent any of Johns[t]on's army from crossing" as well as "picking up and paroling the disabled men of Lee's army." Palmer's mission also included menacing Charlotte, a growing crossroads town near the South Carolina border. Stoneman did not mention railroads in his orders, but they were also important targets. A southward march from Taylorsville would allow Palmer's men to once again strike the Western North Carolina Railroad and also draw near the stretch of the North Carolina Railroad between Salisbury and Charlotte. The latter served as both Johnston's supply line and his line of retreat. It, too, had to be cut in more places.[1]

So the journey continued. Private Banks of the Twelfth Ohio recalled that the brigade's final act at Taylorsville was destroying "by fire a frame building con-

Lieutenant Colonel Charles M. Betts led the Fifteenth Pennsylvania Cavalry Regiment for most of the raid. He was later awarded the raid's only Congressional Medal of Honor.

MASSACHUSETTS COMMANDERY MILITARY ORDER OF THE LOYAL LEGION AND THE UNITED STATES ARMY MILITARY HISTORY INSTITUTE

taining reble coutton." Palmer then took a circuitous route, jogging west toward Lenoir and then turning south near Barrett Mountain. The Federal cavalrymen next crossed the Middle Little River, passing the spot where Gillem's men had run into Bingham and Shearer. This was not the most direct route to Lincolnton, but it would take the raiders near Western North Carolina Railroad facilities at Icard's, Hickory Station, and Newton.[2]

Despite the brigade's early start, the zigzag route slowed progress. The Fifteenth Pennsylvania left Taylorsville at eight o'clock. After stopping to feed their horses at Harrison mill, the troopers moved toward Lovelady Ford on the Catawba River. They found the countryside full of Confederate deserters who, one trooper decided, had "slid out, as the jig is up." The raiders had to deal with each one. "Captured some of Lee's disbanded soldiers who corroborated the important news of the surrender," a trooper wrote. The brigade bivouacked about seven that evening four miles from the Catawba. "First nights rest we have had for a long while," wrote Septimus Knight, who shared some "very nice" molasses with a comrade. It was close to midnight when the Twelfth Ohio bivouacked. Private Banks stretched out on his blanket in a patch of woods along the road to snatch a few hours' sleep.[3]

According to Charles Weller, Monday, April 17, began with a party of engineers repairing the bridge over the Catawba near the Horse mill. (At the same moment, Stoneman was leaving for Tennessee and Miller's and Brown's brigades were marching for Morganton.) The rest of the regiment followed around eight that morning. Within two hours, the bridge was strong enough to support the horse soldiers, although Septimus Knight thought it was still "very shaky." The troopers reached the opposite bank safely. By Knight's count, the regiment had now tallied 623 miles on the raid.[4]

Once across the Catawba, Palmer split his brigade. The Tenth Michigan headed for Newton. The Federals soon awakened the sleepy village, riding up the "old Laurel Hill road" into Newton "yelling, shooting, and swearing." Chaos ensued. The students of Catawba College were dismissed, and the Beard family lost a cow, hogs, and chickens. The family matriarch, Nancy Hewitt Beard, approached an officer and begged for the cow so she could get some milk for her small children. The cow was returned. Matters got worse with the killing of Charles F. Connor. Some claimed that Connor was shot without provocation. Others said the Federals shot him when he hopped on his horse and tried to escape. In any event, Connor was dead, and a three-year-old girl was now fatherless. The raiders also evicted prisoners from the jail and then burned it down. They next set fire to a Confederate commissary warehouse. "Large supplies of food was stored in the Commissary and hungry children stood by crying as burning molasses ran down the side of the hill," a local historian wrote.[5]

The citizens derived little comfort from the fact that the raiders destroyed mostly supplies of use to the military. Nor did they enjoy the presence of the Tenth Michigan, which bivouacked in and around Newton. P. C. Henkel, who lived north of town, looked on helplessly as the Michiganders camped in his yard and confiscated his grain. The Michiganders found Newton a simple "little village." As a previous observer commented, "Newton . . . is a small, quaint town, of rather a German origin, with which the traveller will have but little to do."[6]

Elsewhere, the Fifteenth Pennsylvania carried out its scouting mission. One company separated from the regiment a half-mile below the Catawba and followed Trowbridge to Newton. After stopping for forty-five minutes, it rode east toward the river. The rest of the Fifteenth Pennsylvania went to Hickory Station, a whistle stop on the Western North Carolina Railroad. Charles F. Weller recalled that most of the troopers simply camped, but locals found the incursion quite disruptive.[7]

Before the enemy arrived in Hickory, many residents managed to hide their possessions. "Families around Catawba have passed down many stories, all of them similar in cause, effect, and plot, about the day the Yankees came," wrote a historian. "The most retold usually involves burying the family valuables and hiding livestock in the woods." In some cases, the preparations were too thorough. Major E. M. Todd, a Confederate commissary officer, realized he could not move the heavy bales of cotton, sacks of salt, and barrels in his care. Panicking, he knocked the heads out of all the barrels, sending a stream of molasses, vinegar, and brandy down the railroad tracks toward a mineral spring. Then he set fire to the commissary building and its contents, including a large amount of cotton. The fire resulted in a total loss except for some scorched salt. The people of Hickory never forgave Todd. They urged Governor Vance to punish him, but Todd easily escaped censure.[8]

The Union cavalrymen agreed that Todd's act of destruction was senseless. "In a military sense it was wise to destroy stores that might be of use to us, but to burn their cotton was rank foolishness," a Pennsylvanian wrote. "We cannot use it and have no way to transport it North, where it is selling at seventy-five cents per pound. Everyone recognizes that the rebellion is on its last legs, and that in a short time they could realize from a waiting market an amount of money which could go far to make up for their losses, but a madness seems to make these people believe that in so despoiling themselves they are hurting us."[9]

The raiders arrived after Major Todd had done his worst. Noted citizen George Pope, "They came up yelling, shooting and swearing. They then began to ransack the town."[10] J. L. Latta thought the cavalrymen "a horde of myrmidons, from God-knows-where." The raiders reminded others of characters "out of the wild west" who shot up towns and "burned homes, barns, drove off cattle they didn't kill and generally made themselves rude and unwanted." Although this was an exaggeration, Sarah Link was prepared for the worst. She grabbed a pitchfork when a Federal officer and two enlisted men came to her plantation to get horses. Link had told other soldiers she had no horses, but these new men saw a mount at her side. "So you have a Cavalry mare after all," one of the Federals said. "We have come for her!"

Sarah Link was not afraid. "Moll, see to the horse," she told the old white woman who lived on her plantation. Moll did not listen, but rather grabbed a stick and with a yell started hitting the raiders' horses instead. The spooked horses kicked up dust and started backward. The soldiers yelled, "Don't let a damn woman run you off!" Link then grabbed a pitchfork and went after the officer. "You come one step nearer and I'll run this thing clean through you. Now Git!" she cried, and the soldiers obeyed. Link saw no more of the raiders until she visited Hickory to get some salt, when they ran her off and shot a hole in her salt bag, emptying the contents. Link's experiences were unique, however, as Palmer's troopers generally restricted their interest to items of military value. In fact, the tables were turned on the raiders at one house. When a Union cavalryman stopped at the Wilfong home to eat, family members stole his pistols. They remain in the family today.[11]

Strangely enough, the Federals left most of the Western North Carolina Railroad facilities in the area intact. No depots or buildings at Hickory Station, Newton, or nearby Catawba Station were disturbed. Perhaps Palmer decided he had already done plenty of damage at Salisbury, Statesville, and other points. The only exception was Icard's, a stop on the railroad west of Hickory. There, Federal soldiers destroyed some cars, the depot, a gristmill, and a brand-new steam-powered sawmill. The sawmill and gristmill were valued at $3,100, which brought the total losses of the Western North Carolina Railroad to $111,000 at prewar prices.[12]

After finishing their business in the Hickory-Icard's area, the Fifteenth Pennsylvania rode on toward Lincolnton, about twenty miles away. In fact, some of the troopers, including Fred Antes, simply rode through Hickory Station without stopping. The Twelfth Ohio did likewise.[13]

Palmer's progress was not unopposed, however, for Brigadier General John Echols and the horse brigades of Brigadier Generals John C. Vaughn and Basil Duke were nearby. These Confederates had entered North Carolina via Fancy Gap on April 12 astride draft horses and mules because their regular mounts were foraging in North Carolina. The news of Appomattox hung over them like a pall. They also knew about Stoneman's raiders and wondered how they would fare against them. North Carolina citizens hoping to be rescued were disappointed by their would-be saviors, since the undersupplied Confederates were forced to take food and forage from the locals much like the Federals did. Only John Echols found something to admire. "For the conduct of Gen. Duke's Kentucky Brigade I can never sufficiently testify my admiration and respect," he reported. "Mounted upon mules and horses without saddles, they turned their faces from their homes, and executed a march which even under the most favorable circumstances would have been an extraordinary one."[14]

From Fancy Gap, the column meandered south through Surry, Yadkin, Iredell, and Davie counties, crossing the Yadkin River on April 14. Evidence of Stoneman's passage was everywhere, unmistakable, and ominous. Reaching Salisbury, Echols learned that Stoneman's raiders had moved west toward Statesville. Unsure of the situation, the general telegraphed Joe Johnston for guidance. Johnston, who had little understanding of Stoneman's intentions, ordered Echols to cover Salisbury and Charlotte.[15]

On April 15, Echols pushed his troopers to Statesville, following in Stoneman's wake. They arrived soon after Palmer's soldiers had left for Taylorsville. "About four thousand of our men passed through that night about nine o'clock," recorded a Statesville resident, who miscounted the size of the force. "Gen. Duke was their Commander, following after the 'Blue Coats.' I hope they will meet with great success." In actuality, the Confederates' prospects for success were grim at best, but Echols did what he could. He sent Vaughn's brigade toward Morganton and Duke's brigade to Lincolnton, then rode off to report to Johnston personally. In Echols's absence, both brigades would have a chance to fight the enemy, but Duke's mission was the more critical. Lincolnton was where Colonel Thomas Napier had taken the brigade's horses to winter. For Echols's men to have any hope of success, they had to retrieve those mounts. The problem was that William J. Palmer was headed for precisely the same place as Duke.[16]

The stage was set for a collision. As Duke's Confederates marched for Lincolnton, the Catawba was the first obstacle they encountered. "We were compelled to cross the Catawba River by marching on top of the covered railroad bridge, a tedious and somewhat hazardous undertaking, especially when attempted with mules," Duke recalled. Reaching the left bank safely, the horsemen learned from scouts that the Fifteenth Pennsylvania and Twelfth Ohio cavalry regiments were also on their way to Lincolnton. "I was anxious to be first there [in Lincolnton], fearing that, if the enemy anticipated me, [our] horses and [the] detail guarding them might be captured or driven completely beyond my reach," Duke recalled. "In an hour or two I discovered that the Federal cavalry was marching upon another road leading to Lincolnton, parallel with that on which I was moving and some three miles to the west of it."[17]

It was a race the twenty-seven-year-old Kentucky general had to win, but his brigade's obstinate mounts failed him. Somewhere in the roughly twenty-mile space between the Hickory-Newton-Icard's area and Lincolnton, fighting flared, the Federals and Confederates skirmishing all afternoon. The Confederates got the worst of it. "I soon found, to my great disgust, that my men were not holding their own as well as they had been accustomed to do in that style of fighting," Duke wrote. "When I inquired the reason, every fellow said it was the fault of his 'infernal mule,' which could not possibly be induced to behave reasonably in action or conduct himself creditably under fire."[18]

Duke somehow managed to reach the Lincolnton area about the same time as the enemy, but he did not find the brigade's horses, as they had been withdrawn. Thus disappointed, the general was forced to continue toward the Catawba River. With luck, he might still be able to find the horses and ward off the enemy. Palmer's escort, a squadron of the Twelfth Ohio under Lieutenant Robert J. Stewart, captured Lincolnton. "Just as the rear guard of the brigade was entering the town, a force of four or five hundred rebel cavalry was seen leisurely approaching by a parallel road," an Ohio trooper recalled. "Colonel Bentley ordered the third battalion of the Twelfth to charge them with the sabre. An exciting horse race of three or four miles ensued, but most of the rebels escaped."[19]

⸎

By dark on April 17, Lincolnton was firmly in the grasp of the Fifteenth Pennsylvania and the Twelfth Ohio. The victors surveyed their new surroundings and discovered what a journalist described as a "small country town with a fine row of Linden tre[e]s and a large court House. Houses unpainted and shiftless looking." Joseph Banks of the Twelfth Ohio thought better of the place. "Linco[l]nton is a beautifully [s]ituated town," Banks wrote. A Pennsylvania trooper agreed, explaining that it "was a very nice town of about 1,000 inhabitants, rather above the ordinary."[20]

The raiders' arrival was a shock for five-year-old William Sherrill. "When I saw that long procession of 'blue coats' ride down the streets in front of our home, not knowing what it all meant, I was filled with fear and amazement," he recalled. "Why did all that host come to feed upon a people who had no bread to spare?"[21]

As they rode into Lincolnton, the Federals met with a hostile reception. "The [Fifteenth Pennsylvania's] advance guard entered the town without any disturbance, but when the column appeared a half hour after, with . . . Palmer at its head and the buildings of the town in sight, one shot was fired from the side of the road in front which came near to ending [Palmer's] career," explained the Fifteenth's regimental history. "The orderlies . . . dashed forward, followed by Company E, which was the leading company that day. The bushwhacker running across the field was in plain sight, and in a few moments our men were across the fence and had him surrounded." The would-be assassin proved to be only about sixteen years old. Palmer ordered the boy brought to his headquarters, whereupon his mother intervened and begged for his life. Palmer released the boy into her custody.[22]

With that, the Union cavalrymen settled down for the next few days. The Ohioans camped two miles to the southeast and the Fifteenth in town. Palmer and his staff and escort established brigade headquarters at the home of Colonel John Peiffer on West Main Street. They began their occupation of Lincolnton on a tragic note, however, when some Confederate officers approached the Federals under a flag of truce, carrying word of Lincoln's assassination. The news did nothing for the raiders' humor, as a local man discovered. When Lincoln's death was announced at the large brick house where the Fifteenth Pennsylvania established its headquarters, Peiffer, whom one Federal described as "an insignificant little man calling himself a lawyer," was within hearing. He indiscreetly uttered the same phrase John Wilkes Booth had after shooting the president. The words *"Sic semper tyrannis"* were too much for Lieutenant Weand. Drawing his pistol, Weand ordered the man to get on his knees and apologize. "It is safe to say," the lieutenant later wrote, "that if any citizen of Lincolnton had expressed himself in sympathy with the assassin, it might have resulted in the destruction of the town and many of its inhabitants."[23]

Better news came from the patrols and pickets Palmer began sending into the countryside. "We were visited by three Confederate officers under a flag of truce, bearing dispatches from General Sherman announcing . . . an 'armistice' between his forces and those of General Johnston," a trooper explained. One of the messengers was the editor of the *Louisville Journal*. "There will be no further need for my services in this war, but in case of a foreign one I am a United States man," he said. Sherman and Johnston had signed a preliminary surrender agreement on April 18 at the Bennett farm near Durham Station. Word was rushed to Stoneman's raiders. Davis's cabinet had urged the Confederate president to sue for peace, and now its wish appeared to be fulfilled. The raiders had no idea that Washington would reject the preliminary agreement. It now remained for Palmer to determine his course of action.[24]

But that was difficult because the same picket post also received conflicting orders. One set came directly from General William T. Sherman. Stoneman's district formed part of the Army of the Cumberland. But since the army's commander, George Thomas, was so far away, Sherman decided he should direct Stoneman's movements. After all, the Department of the Cumberland was part of Sherman's responsibility. "General Stoneman is under my command," Sherman assured Johnston, "and my order will suspend any devastation or destruction contemplated by him."[25] His April 18 dispatch informed Stoneman that "General Johnston and I have agreed to maintain a truce in the nature of status quo by which each is to stand fast till certain propositions looking to a general peace are referred to our respective principals. You may therefore cease hostilities, but for supplies may come to me near Raleigh. Keep your command well in hand and approach Durham's Station or Chapel Hill, and I will supply you by our railroad. As soon as you reach the outer pickets report to me in person or by telegraph." A pass from Joseph E. Johnston was enclosed with Sherman's dispatch: "The march of Major-General Stoneman's command . . . is not to be interfered with by Confederate troops."[26]

Palmer received more messages as well. One note, from Thomas, directed the raiders to march to Greeneville, Tennessee, and camp near the railroad, while Gillem was to personally report to Thomas at Nashville. Another message, this one under a flag of truce from Confederate general Echols, contained additional confirmation of the armistice. Finally, Palmer received yet another order, this from Gillem himself, directing him to move the brigade to Rutherfordton. The colonel now faced a dilemma: which order should he obey? Palmer decided the cease-fire made it proper to suspend the confiscation of horses and provender, and he issued orders to that effect.[27] Otherwise, Palmer needed positive orders from his immediate superior, Gillem, before he could abandon his watch on the Catawba. "As neither Stoneman or Gillem are here," wrote one of Palmer's men, "we await the action of Gillem." So Palmer sent an acknowledgment to John C. Breckinridge, the Confederate secretary of war, in Charlotte. He also sent a seven-man party under Lieutenant Charles E. Beck toward Morganton to find Gillem. Until Palmer heard from Gillem, he would continue business as usual.[28]

Palmer's Ohioans, Pennsylvanians, and Michiganders therefore paused for five days in the Lincolnton area. The Federals gave the locals little to complain about, besides occasional impressments of horses. Mary Carpenter was victimized; even though she was a widow and had nine children under the age of sixteen, troopers relieved her of two horses on April 18. A paralyzed man named George Ditherow lost one horse to the raiders, while the Sherrill family lost a white pony. Dr. Samuel Lander asked Palmer to return the pony, and he did so. Lander later fancied himself as having saved the town from harm, thanks to his supposed Masonic ties with Palmer and his own "courtliness and diplomacy." In truth, the armistice and Palmer's firm hand had far more to do with the good order that prevailed in Lincolnton.[29]

The Union cavalrymen enjoyed their stay in spite of the town's obvious allegiance to the Confederacy. In fact, four Confederate generals—Robert F. Hoke, Stephen D. Ramseur, John H. Forney, and Robert D. Johnston—hailed from Lincoln County. "This is a pretty town, of about 1000 inhabitants; they are extremely rebellious—bitterly so—but with it all are refined and intelligent," wrote a Pennsylvanian. "They have hardly felt the ravages of war, and we are the first 'Yankee invaders to pollute their soil.'" Nonetheless, Lincolnton offered the invaders some old-fashioned Southern hospitality. Invitations to dinner came regularly. One trooper added that "the colored people are eager to help us by baking biscuits and cakes for the men." Many ex-slaves refused to work for their former masters and instead lounged around the streets, ready to alert their new bosses about any hidden horses or food they might discover. A trooper observed, "Cigars are plentiful, too, and for a time the pipe is discarded and we revel in some of the best the town affords." One of Betts's men summed it up: "Lincolnton was a pleasant place to be in."[30]

Palmer kept his men busy, assigning some to guard duty in camp and others to provost duty in town. To maintain discipline, he held several inspections and a dress parade every evening. Regimental bands played martial airs to boost morale. These exercises gave Palmer an opportunity to have general orders read. Each event was, a cavalryman boasted, a "fine display for 'raiders.'"[31]

In the countryside, Palmer's raiders pressed Duke's men back and captured and immediately paroled straggling Rebels. As a result, Lincolnton fairly bulged with paroled Confederates. Some of them stayed at the home of General Ramseur's widow. "I had about twenty-five rebel officers, of all ranks from captains to major-generals, lying on the floors of the house," recalled a Federal cavalryman. "It was very amusing to me to sit and listen to them telling of the break-up of

Lee's army." The courthouse was another spot where parolees were gathered. "One of the largest rooms in the court-house was used for this purpose," a cavalryman wrote, "and one of the companies of the Fifteenth was detailed to make out the papers and administer the oath of allegiance. It ought to have been a solemn affair, but instead it was amusing and jolly. When told to 'kiss the book' the smack was given with a gusto, and one enthusiastic rebel said 'he was so glad that if necessary he would eat the book.' Instead of attending to each one separately, which was slow, they paroled them in squads. The rebels said the politicians had fooled them into going to war, but would not acknowledge being whipped, only overwhelmed. Between jokes, handshaking, speeches and cheers many of the paroles were not made out correctly, and later on the process had to be gone over again." All told, Palmer's brigade captured and paroled as many as two thousand Confederates during its occupation of the Lincolnton–Catawba River region.[32]

Palmer's success in capturing Confederates was due to his strategy of covering the countryside with a combination of patrols, raiding parties, and stationary picket posts. Every day at almost every hour, cavalrymen trotted in and out of Lincolnton in "a long line of battalions and squadrons moving by different paths and roads." These patrols sometimes encountered bands of enemy soldiers, some of them eager to fight. When that happened, each man knew what to do. "Orders were in all cases to charge immediately with the saber, no matter where the enemy was found nor the apparent disparity of forces," recalled an Ohio trooper.[33]

The raiders scoured all points of the compass. One patrol, comprised of men from the Tenth Michigan and the Twelfth Ohio, searched along the Wilmington, Charlotte, and Rutherford Railroad. A scout from the Fifteenth Pennsylvania searched for horses on the Rutherfordton road but came back empty-handed. Only Charles Weller succeeded in capturing "a fine horse" as veterans from "Lees Army passed thro our lines on there way home."[34]

Yet another sortie encountered the wife of Thomas J. "Stonewall" Jackson, Stoneman's West Point roommate. Following her famous husband's death in 1863, Anna Morrison Jackson had retreated to the family homestead, Cottage Home, near the Lincoln County–Gaston County line. The two-story, twelve-room house situated on two hundred acres was a tempting target. According to one account, a "full regiment of Yankee cavalry . . . passed us and took all the mules and horses on the place," including a horse and some mules that had belonged to Stonewall. Hoping that her husband's friendship with Stoneman would mean something, Mrs. Jackson sent a young man with a letter to the Federals asking for the return of the animals. "When I got there, a mile or more away," the young man later recalled, "I asked for General Stoneman and was told that he was not with the raid; that Colonel somebody else was in command, and to go to a certain tent and present my note. The note was sent in and the Colonel came out, really excited. He asked me if I would know the horses and I told him that of course I would, as I had ridden them many times. We walked over together to a temporary corral and there I saw 'Fancy' at once." The officer allowed the young man to retrieve Fancy—also known by his better-known moniker, Little Sorrel—as well as some mules. In addition, the colonel gave the young man an army bridle and a note of apology for Mrs. Jackson and sent him on his way. Three soldiers went, too, under orders to guard Cottage Home.[35]

Most of the patrols scouted toward the crossings of the Catawba River. Company D of the Fifteenth Pennsylvania rode out to Lay's Ferry. Fred Antes and his comrades "went out on a scout with 25 men on the Charlott[e]ville Road," he recalled. "We rode very hard all day but didn't see any wild Jonny. We got plenty to eat and drink." Elsewhere, Palmer's men were more productive. Antes noted that two hundred prisoners were brought in on April 19. Lieutenant Weand confirmed the success: "Many officers & men of the Rebel army came in today and were paroled."[36]

One of these patrols resulted in the Fifteenth Pennsylvania's last battlefield fatality. On April 18, Major Abraham B. Garner's battalion searched for some Confederate horses that were said to be about ten miles from Lincolnton. The detachment found no horses and managed to lose one of its own mounts in the process. Corporal George French, a blue-eyed, sandy-haired, twenty-one-year-old Philadelphian, was ordered to retrieve the stray horse. Instead of finding it, French and two other men discovered enemy soldiers about one mile from Lincolnton. In a brief exchange of gunfire, French fell badly wounded.[37]

His comrades rushed him to camp but could do nothing for him. He expired shortly afterward. "Before he died he sent this message," French's messmate Selden Wilson recalled. "'Tell mother and sisters that I die like a brave man and my comrades carried me from the field.'" French's death hit the regiment hard. "He was the last man killed in the regiment and never was there a better one," wrote a friend. "His gentlemanly manners had endeared him to all, and the loss was felt deeply." Betts sadly recalled French as "a young and gallant soldier."[38]

He was buried with military honors the next day in Lincolnton's Episcopal graveyard. It was a sad, poignant scene. The local ladies decorated French's coffin and grave with flowers, an act they would repeat every Memorial Day for years to come. Then fresh dirt was tossed on the grave of the young man who was due to be mustered out in only two months. Selden Wilson would never forget his friend. For years, he treasured a fine linen towel that French had captured from General Duke's baggage. In honor of French, Wilson used the towel to cover each of his newborn children when they were weighed.[39]

✥

Near Newton, Colonel Trowbridge's Michiganders were among the first raiders to clamp down on the Catawba River. Their haul of prisoners included some Georgia artillerymen from the Army of Northern Virginia who hoped to continue the war in the West. Since leaving Appomattox Court House, these Rebels had met with few obstacles, but crossing the Catawba proved a different matter. "The river at that point [Island Ford] was wide and the ford led across an island," the major in command later recalled. "I had no difficulty in getting my men to the island, and then with all our eyes we scanned the south bank for some signs of the bluecoats. Not discovering any I sent two men across with instructions to signal to us if they found the coast clear." The two soldiers crossed easily, rode up the opposite bank, and then disappeared. Their comrades waited for what seemed an eternity, but the two failed to return. The major at last decided to make a personal investigation. When he reached the opposite bank, he realized too late what had happened. Before him was a rifle pit, out of which a low voice barked, "Halt." Seven Federals lay flat on the ground, pointing seven carbines at him.

"All right, Jonnie, come in out of the wet," another unfriendly voice said. "You can just throw down for the present what arms you have and ride over to the bank. You will be in good company and we will treat you well, but don't try to signal to those men on the island. If you should, don't you know, it would be a bad day for you." The rest of the artillerymen were captured in short order.

That evening, the Federals escorted their captives to Newton. For a few moments, the war seemed far away, the commander of the Federal detachment, Captain William H. Dunn, and the Georgia major enjoying a pleasant conversation. When they reached Trowbridge's headquarters, Dunn presented the major to the Federal commander. The Confederate artilleryman asked if his men could spend the night with friends in the neighborhood. Much to the major's surprise, Trowbridge agreed. In fact, he did not even bother to send a guard along. Upon returning the next morning to receive his formal parole, the major asked if the Federals could provide the Georgians with some fresh horses, their own having given out. Trowbridge complied and wished them Godspeed. Such kindnesses went a long way toward reconciling the Confederates to defeat.[40]

So it continued for the next five days, with the Tenth Michigan headquartered in Newton and its detachments watching the Catawba east of town. In addition to Island Ford, the regiment monitored Catawba Station, where the Western North Carolina Railroad crossed the river, as well as other crossings to the northwest. According to the superintendent of the Western North Carolina Railroad, the Michiganders did little damage to the "expensive and splendid" bridge spanning the Catawba there, aside from ripping up "a small portion of the covering" near the middle. The days were filled with paroling Confederate stragglers and patrolling the countryside. The regiment also tended to official business. Captain James Roberts, the commander of the Second Battalion, was arrested on unspecified charges. Steven Thomas replaced him.[41]

The next unit downstream from the Tenth Michigan was Company A of the Fifteenth Pennsylvania Cavalry. These men had initially followed Trowbridge into Newton on April 17, then peeled off to reach their objective, Sherrill's Ford. William F. Colton commanded the company, which was led by a local guide. During their ride, the Federals "came across about twenty rebs who fled in great confusion," Septimus Knight wrote. "There was only five of us [in the advance guard]. But they did not stop to see our number. We captured three of them and did not stop to keep them thinking the company would come up and take them[.] But the company was so far behind that they did not hear the firing." According to Colton, the force the command encountered contained forty men from Basil Duke's brigade. The Federals ultimately captured ten enemy soldiers, who confirmed that the Confederates had crossed the Catawba at eleven in the morning and that Vaughn's brigade was not far behind. Both were marching on Lincolnton. Colton forwarded the prisoners and information to Colonel Trowbridge at Newton, and the company continued its journey.[42]

Knight and the advance guard reached Sherrill's Ford at ten that evening without any further trouble. Colton arrived thirty minutes later. He bivouacked the men in Mrs. Sherrill's yard and used her home as his headquarters. After sending a picket down to the ford—Knight was a member of the detail—

Colton got supper, then went to sleep in a feather bed.[43]

April 18 proved as pleasant as the previous days. Colton even had the chance to enjoy a swim in the Catawba. Meanwhile, Colton's pickets scooped up more prisoners and forwarded them to Colonel Trowbridge. They also confiscated a wagon carrying five trunks that belonged to Mrs. Harriet Vance, the governor's wife. She was escorted by two Confederate officers and the cashier of the Bank of the State of North Carolina. One trunk held the assets and "all the specie papers and books" of the bank, including gold, bonds, and a large quantity of treasury notes. Another trunk contained clothing, jewelry, silver plates, and a caddy with two pounds of fine green tea. The remaining trunks contained Mrs. Vance's wardrobe. After confiscating the tea for his men, since it was "an article of Commissary stores," Colton sent the trunks to Palmer, who entrusted them to prominent citizens in Lincolnton. The trunks were eventually returned to Mrs. Vance.[44]

The Pennsylvanians remained at Sherrill's Ford for two more days, watching the crossings of the Catawba and scouring the countryside. They also continued to bring in horses and food. Early on April 20, a dispatch arrived at the ford ordering Company A to join the regiment at Lincolnton, twenty miles away. "Strike out for that place which we reach early in the afternoon," Knight wrote.[45]

The cavalrymen also guarded Beatty's and Cowan's fords, the next crossing points south of Sherrill's Ford. Major William Wagner's battalion of the Fifteenth Pennsylvania covered these points, as well as two bridges over the Catawba farther south. Wagner's ride began early on April 18 and ultimately became a day-long, forty-two-mile foray. His mission included the pursuit of Duke's Confederates, who were retreating from Lincolnton.

Leaving Lincolnton, Wagner's men traveled southeast into a region of iron mines and forges. Passing Rehoboath furnace at six o'clock in the morning on April 18, the cavalrymen found a deserted Confederate camp a half-mile beyond. From all appearances, it had been evacuated only minutes earlier. The enemy's rear guard fired on Wagner's troopers when they appeared.

Wagner followed the retreating Confederates to the Catawba. Reaching a plank bridge over the river about two that afternoon, the dusty blue cavalrymen found more enemy soldiers. After another quick skirmish resulted in a Union victory, Wagner occupied the bridge. "We forced the rebels across the river and in crossing the bridge they tore the planks off," recalled W. E. Reppert of Company C. "I was one of the party detailed to go down and fix up those planks. . . . We forced the rebels back and drove them; and I was saying to Captain Hamilton to-day, the longest shot that we ever made I believe I made there when I killed a horse which was 2,000 yards off. He said he did not think I could do it, but I did." After driving the enemy away, Wagner destroyed the span "very effectively."[46]

One Federal report stated that the Fifteenth Pennsylvania was occupied in "dispersing the advance of Basil Duke's command of cavalry, who was in the vicinity for horses, previous to joining Johnston's army." A morning report for Company B of the Fifteenth Pennsylvania Cavalry estimated that the First Battalion skirmished with four hundred Confederates before driving them across the Catawba. It also burned a bridge and destroyed a section of the Wilmington, Charlotte, and Rutherford Railroad. Colonel Betts wrote of the action in his diary as well: "Advance skirmished with some Rebel cav of Dukes command." No casualties were recorded.[47]

Basil Duke fell back from Lincolnton because the enemy had already taken the town and was about to attack him. "I was unwilling to fight," Duke recalled, "and knew that to countermarch would be ruinous. Fortunately an officer had . . . mentioned that a small road turned off to the left two miles from Lincolnton, and led to other traces and paths which connected to the main road to Charlotte." Seeing this as an opportunity to withdraw, Duke deployed a blocking force to protect his rear and moved out. With the help of some local guides, the command crossed a Catawba River bridge shortly before the pursuing Federal cavalry arrived. Duke noted that the enemy destroyed the bridge to prevent the Confederates from returning. Back in Statesville, rumor had it that Duke and his cavalry had been captured, but such was not the case. The two groups were reunited on the Charlotte road. The only course left open to Duke was to obey Johnston's orders and retire to cover Charlotte. Lincolnton and the crossings of the Catawba River were firmly held by Colonel William J. Palmer's brigade.[48]

From the bridge, the Federals rode six miles toward the Wilmington, Charlotte, and Rutherford Railroad bridge spanning the Catawba. At four-thirty that afternoon, Wagner's raiders arrived and found the bridge unguarded. Wagner thought it was a "fine structure," but he burned it anyway. In a half-hour, this bridge was engulfed in flames. The battalion then rode to Beatty's Ford, arriving at two in the morning on April 19.[49]

By now, the horses of Wagner's battalion were exhausted, but this was no time for rest. Wagner assigned Company B to guard Beatty's Ford. The unit did a brisk business paroling former Confederate soldiers. Guarding the ford required vigilance because no fewer than six roads converged at that point. Beatty's was not a pretty spot, but it had some distinctive features. "Country poor but broken & punctuated with growth of oak & pine—soil red clay," a traveler later wrote of the area. "Abundance of wild fruit & strawberry, plum, blackberry."[50]

Fords above and below Beatty's, including Cowan's Ford, came under Wagner's watchful eye. "Details from the battalion were sent in all directions, hunting up the enemy, but they had fled from the vicinity," wrote the regimental historian. "Our troops were the first Federals the citizens had seen, and it seemed comical to us to witness the fear they had of being killed or robbed by us."[51]

At last, Wagner marched the balance of his battalion to a point between the ford and Vesuvius furnace on the Lincolnton–Beatty's Ford road to await orders. The men had plenty to do. While George Neil of Company D fired up the furnace, his comrades received and forwarded dispatches.[52] For his part, Wagner could only worry. Under orders to cover numerous river crossings in his sector, he knew he could furnish only sixteen men per crossing. Reports from Confederate prisoners stated that a regiment from Vaughn's Brigade was planning to cross the river, and that about one hundred Rebels were already on the near side. Wagner thought Vaughn was already west of the Catawba, and he knew Ferguson's Brigade was also nearby. He therefore watched the river fords closely. At daylight on April 19, a dozen Confederates started across the river. When they reached the middle, Wagner's pickets hailed them, and the men turned around and headed back. The pickets thus repulsed the Confederates without firing a shot.[53]

The Confederates attempted another crossing at nearby Rozzell's Ferry. Confederate brigadier general Robert D. Johnston was at his mother's Lincoln County home recuperating from a wound suffered at Petersburg. A graduate of the University of North Carolina and the University of Virginia's law school, Johnston was only twenty-eight but a veteran of many battles. A neighbor interrupted his convalescence with news that Stoneman's cavalry was heading toward Charlotte. Ignoring a sprained ankle, Johnston mounted his horse and rode toward the town to see if he could help. He crossed the Catawba at Rozzell's Ferry and encountered a Tennessee cavalry regiment, probably belonging to Vaughn's Brigade. Johnston persuaded the regiment's commander to detail a company to protect the bridge at Rozzell's Ferry.[54]

Johnston led the company to the bridge. Captain Joseph G. Morrison, a one-time member of Stonewall Jackson's staff, joined him. Morrison had been present at Jackson's death. Now, he was witnessing the death of the Confederacy. Several other men rode up as well. "I posted them, dismounted, on the South side of the bridge and took my position on the hill just in their rear and in front of the Rozzell House," Johnston recalled.[55]

Here the war found Johnston again. "When the enemy appeared on the hill across the river they opened fire on us and sent a detachment down to destroy the bridge," Johnston wrote, "no doubt thinking I had a brigade of infantry, as they could tell from my uniform that I was of the infantry. We sat on our horses expecting that the company I had posted at the bridge, would open fire and drive them back. I found to my dismay that the command at the bridge had been withdrawn without firing a shot. The enemy's fire became exceedingly warm, and just as I stated to the officer with me that I thought we had best retire, a bullet struck me on my left side, just over my heart. The shock was so severe that it sickened me, and I fell on my horse's neck, thinking it had passed through my body." Fortunately, the bullet only bruised the general. It actually struck his purse and flattened out against a half-dollar. But the enemy now possessed Rozzell's Ferry.[56]

Of all the small raids executed by Palmer's brigade during its occupation of Lincolnton, none equaled the one led by Erastus Cratty Moderwell. A native of Bucyrus, Ohio, Moderwell was born on March 6, 1838. After graduating from Pennsylvania's Jefferson College in 1859, he ran private schools in Elkhorn, Kentucky, and Fairmount, Virginia. When the war closed his school, Moderwell enlisted in the Union army. His first command was with the Eighty-sixth Ohio Infantry, which he served as a captain until the unit's term of service expired in 1863. Afterward, Moderwell joined Company A of the Twelfth Ohio Cavalry and was quickly elected captain once again. All agreed that he had developed into a fine officer. He had three wounds to prove his bravery. The most grievous one occurred at Mount Sterling, Kentucky, in June 1864, when a bullet carried a piece of a gold pen into Moderwell's body. That shard of metal would trouble him for the rest of his life. "He was a man of high character, public spirited, companionable, and popular," an observer wrote. Later promoted to major, Moderwell was thought capable of independent command.[57]

That was precisely what Palmer entrusted him with at ten o'clock on the night of April 17, 1865. He ordered Moderwell to take 250 picked men from the Twelfth Ohio Cavalry and ride into South Carolina. The goal was the Charlotte and South Carolina Railroad bridge over the Catawba River near Nations Ford. The bridge, about thirty-five miles south of Lincolnton, was an inviting target for three reasons. First, it was another link in Joseph E. Johnston's supply line. Many of Johnston's recent reinforcements had traveled over that bridge. Second, the span was less than twenty miles from Charlotte, so an attack there would appear to threaten that town. Third, the bridge was the most southerly Catawba River crossing the raiders would strike, so the operation would cover Palmer's flank. Moderwell wasted no time in executing his orders. By midnight, he recruited two guides and had his men in the saddle. Joseph Banks was among them. He and his comrades did not depart until two o'clock in the morning. "We packed up and moved out in a South Easterly direction," Banks wrote.[58]

From Lincolnton, Moderwell set a deliberate pace. "Owing to the large force of the enemy in the vicinity it was necessary to move with great caution," recalled the major, aware of the presence of Vaughn's, Duke's, and Ferguson's brigades. The wisdom of this was soon borne out, for the column found the enemy—or rather, the enemy found it. "At Dallas we had a skirmish with Vaughn's and Duke's Brigades but evaded them," Moderwell recalled. The Federals captured thirty-five Confederates before they extricated themselves from the fight.[59]

Because he was two hours behind the advance, Joseph Banks missed the skirmish. He reached Dallas at seven in the morning on April 18. "We went into Camp in a seeder [cedar] grove adjoining town[. W]e ate breakfast and fed our Horses," Banks wrote. Afterward, the Ohioans resumed the cavalcade toward South Carolina, less one man. John Knolds, a member of Banks's company, had to be left in Dallas for unspecified reasons.

The passage below Dallas was quiet. Challenged no more, the column stopped to feed its horses and eat at dusk. Shortly after resuming the journey, the men were reminded that they were far from Union lines. "In the night we passed a reble wagon train but did not disturb it," Banks wrote. Ominously, an Irishman named Pat McGee from Company B also disappeared. In the blackness, the men could only wonder if he had been captured by the enemy. (In truth, McGee fell asleep during the battalion's halt below Dallas and was overlooked when the march resumed at dusk.) They crossed the state line and entered York County, South Carolina—site of the Revolutionary War battles of Huck's Defeat and Kings Mountain—and turned in a more easterly direction.[60]

Shortly before daylight on April 19, the raiders approached the Catawba near Rock Hill. Banks's Company B took the lead. The closer the men got to the river, the more enemy soldiers they encountered. The raiders gobbled up two enemy outposts. The first one, comprised of five men, surrendered to the Ohioans before dawn. The second group, a stronger picket post about a half-mile from the bridge, surrendered at about eight that morning "without fireing a shot," as Banks boasted. Moderwell's troopers disarmed their prisoners and destroyed their guns and in the process learned that the bridge was fortified. "We proceded to the Bridge and found it defended by about 60 men & 2 peaces of Artillery," Banks wrote. Another trooper, Frank Mason, assumed that the Confederate force was as large as Moderwell's battalion.[61]

The Confederates, however, had neither artillery nor breastworks. Moderwell realized he lacked the strength to assault the bridge, so he decided to try a ruse. Putting on gum overcoats, he and Captain Franklin DuBois cast themselves in the leading roles of a one-act drama. Moderwell would play Stoneman, while DuBois would play Gillem. Stepping to within earshot of the captured picket commander, the two men began to speak. "General Gillem," Moderwell told DuBois in his most commanding voice, "order Captain Hill to put his battery in position and open fire on the bridge."

Moderwell's ruse worked. When the lieutenant heard them, his eyes opened wide. "I do not think it is necessary, General," he piped up. "The Major commanding will surrender, if you make the demand."

The "general" accepted the Confederate lieutenant's proposal and sent Captain DuBois with the captured picket officer to the bridge under a flag of truce. DuBois carried a note that read,

> Headquarters U.S. Cavalry Corps
>
> To the Officer Commanding at the Catawba Bridge:
>
> Dear Sir:
>
> In order to prevent unnecessary shedding of blood, I demand the unconditional surrender of the forces under your command.
>
> George Stoneman, Major General,
> Commanding U.S. Forces

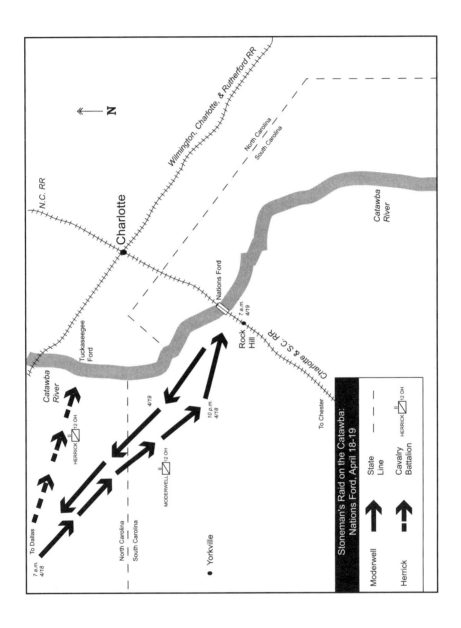

Stoneman's Raid on the Catawba: Nations Ford, April 18-19

Major E. M. Jones, the Confederate commander at the bridge, received the Federal flag of truce. DuBois, still posing as Gillem—the real Gillem at that moment was marching on Asheville—handed over the note and explained how futile it would be to try and hold the bridge. The captured Confederate lieutenant confirmed that the Federals had a powerful force and that Stoneman himself was in command. The interview and the note threw Jones into a fury. He railed and cursed about the performance of his pickets. It did not dawn on him that this could be a trick. "Sir," he finally wrote in reply, "Owing to the cowardly surrender of my picket post and in consequence of the vastly superior force of your command, I surrender this garrison with its military stores."[62]

All of this happened quickly, Private Banks attested. "Major Modderwell [*sic*] demanded the uncondecinal [unconditional] Surrender of the bridge and amediately the White flag was raised," he wrote. At that point, the Federals paroled the defenders and destroyed their arms and ammunition. Estimates vary on the number of prisoners taken. Banks counted 75, while other sources estimated between 230 and 325 men, along with 200 horses.[63]

The bridge was the greatest prize of all. One Federal described it as the finest structure of its kind in the Confederacy. The defenders had already removed its trestlework, but its tin top still gleamed proudly in the sunlight. With enthusiasm, the troopers lit a fire at its north end. "It was a superb structure, eleven hundred feet in length, supported by ten stone piers which towered many feet above the water, and, once destroyed, was beyond the power of the Confederacy to replace," a cavalryman wrote. Since the Federals could not carry off the captured artillery, they destroyed it along with the bridge. According to an observer, "the two pieces of artillery were spiked and run on the bridge, which was fired, and in less than thirty minutes had burned from end to end." Moderwell later noted, "The bridge (of which I sent you a photograph) was a splendid structure—1,150 feet long and 50 feet above the water."[64]

The fire also had unfortunate consequences for the Federals because it became a beacon for Confederate cavalry in the area. "The smoke was seen thirty miles off," Moderwell explained. Minutes after the bridge was burned, Sam Ferguson's cavalry brigade appeared on the north bank of the river, between the raiders and Charlotte. Gunfire rang out. "We skirmished with them for a couple of hours and prevented them from crossing," Moderwell wrote. "The bridge had just give way when a brigade of reble Cavalry maid their appearance on the opiset side of the river," Banks added. "But they were a little too late to see the fun." Although the skirmish concluded in the raiders' favor, Moderwell prudently decided to withdraw. Shortly before dusk, the Federal cavalrymen rode away, except for fifty men who remained as a rear guard. The destructive work left Confederate authorities groping for ways to resume the flow of men and supplies across the river.[65]

Moderwell's worst fear was that the Confederates would pursue him to exact revenge. On the morning of April 20, before either horses or men had been fed, that fear proved all too true when an enemy officer approached the Ohioans' picket lines under a flag of truce. Moderwell's men assumed that the officer carried a surrender demand. They steeled themselves, a trooper recalled, for "a fight or a flight." Imagine the men's relief when they learned that the enemy officer bore instead an appeal from Ferguson to Stoneman for a five-day cease-fire, perhaps as a result of the truce between Sherman and Johnston. Figuring the enemy forces outnumbered his own, Moderwell accepted the proposal. Thus unhindered, the men remounted and rode on to Dallas, where they arrived that afternoon. There, Banks recalled, "we found our old Comand encamped anxiously awaiting our return[. W]e took our old position on the Left Wing and encamped for the night."[66]

Moderwell's raid ranks with Wagner's Lynchburg raid as the most successful of the campaign. In two days, his Ohioans had ridden more than eighty miles, captured and destroyed one of the most important railroad bridges remaining in the Confederacy, and returned to their parent unit without a casualty. One participant boasted, "This [was] a brilliant exploit, in which the major, by a clever ruse, captured the bridge guard of seven officers and two hundred and twenty-three men, with two guns, destroyed the immense bridge, eleven hundred feet in length, and returned to camp without the loss of a man." Palmer was so impressed by the exploit that he had photos taken of each man who participated. Moderwell's raid even impressed historian Benson J. Lossing, who called it "one of the most gallant little exploits of the war" in his three-volume history, *Civil War in America*.[67]

⌐∿⌐

While Moderwell was absent, the rest of the Twelfth Ohio Cavalry marched to Dallas, then the seat of Gaston County, to establish a base of operations. From there, Major John F. Herrick, a native of Cleveland, Ohio, led a battalion of the regiment toward Tuckaseegee Ford, downstream from Cowan's Ford and ten miles west of Charlotte. This Catawba River crossing was valuable not only as a transportation route but also because the Confederacy operated two factories nearby. One was a powder mill and the other a plant that produced wet cell batteries for telegraphs. Herrick's men probably destroyed these factories soon after capturing the ford. They were also tested by some of Wheeler's cavalrymen, who tried to force their way across. The Ohioans held their own with no trouble.[68]

Back from its raid into South Carolina, Moderwell's battalion was directed to secure yet another river crossing. On April 21, the battalion left Dallas and moved toward Armstrong's Ford between Dallas and Charlotte. The unit accomplished its mission but in contrast to the South Carolina raid found it a dull affair. "After we had marched about 10 miles we fell in line of battel to fight our own rear guard[, t]hinking it was a reble Comand," Private Banks wrote. "We discovered our erer before any thing cerious occurred[,] and we proceded to Armstrongs Ford on the Catoba river, where one company stoped to guard it while others went on[,] and our Company (B) went back one mile to a forks in the road and was Stationed for picket." At least the picket line was productive. While at Armstrong's Ford, Moderwell's troopers scooped up several returning Confederate soldiers, disarmed them, and sent them to Dallas to be paroled.[69]

The next two days were equally busy for the Ohioans. According to Banks, the cavalrymen spent April 22 capturing and paroling more Confederate stragglers. "They do not apeer to Show mutch disposetion for fight—They all seem to be going to Mississippi," he wrote. On April 23, Banks received permission to ride out and search for horses. Joined by three other men, he enjoyed himself immensely. "We went about 10 miles in to the country and At noon we stoped at an overseers house on a large plantation where we got our Dinners and our Horses feed," Banks recalled. "We only got one Horse which I fell Heir to[. W]e joined our Company about Sunset and found them prepareing to leave. We mooved about Dusk and joined our Comand again at Dallas about 9 P.M. [and] went into Camp."[70]

⁓⁓

The combined operations of the Twelfth Ohio also threatened Charlotte, just as Thomas, Sherman, and Stoneman had hoped. For weeks, the people there had been on edge as the war crept ever closer. The town commissioners had not met since March 24. Sick and wounded Confederate soldiers packed Charlotte. Meanwhile, state and Confederate officials sent books and papers and even the assets of the Bank of North Carolina away for safekeeping. "No hotels are open and our footsteps echo through the silent streets as we pass along, and awaken in our own breasts hollow feelings of desolation and woe," recalled one Confederate soldier. "Stoneman's raiders are said to be nearby and are expected in the town before day break. If so, the sleeping townsmen are not much concerned at his near approach, for they are sleeping so soundly that we are unable to gain admission into any home, not even Mr. Kerr's hotel."[71]

Colonel William J. Hoke certainly was worried about the raiders. A Gettysburg veteran nicknamed "the greatest old granny," Hoke commanded the post of Charlotte with its one-thousand-man garrison. One of the first things he did to prepare for the raid was to decide what to do with the large quantity of cotton bales on hand. Hoke did not have the resources to move the cotton but did not want it to fall into enemy hands, so he decided to burn it. His men fired the bales just outside Charlotte, which caused some anxious moments as the burning cotton embers endangered the town.[72]

Another concern for Hoke was the Confederate treasury—that is, what was left of it. On April 8, sacks and boxes containing about half a million dollars in gold and silver coins, bricks, and nuggets had been off-loaded from a wagon train and stored in the Charlotte Mint. Captain William H. Parker, former commandant of the Confederate States Naval Academy, and about sixty midshipmen escorted the shipment. Once the money was secured, Parker went to the telegraph office to notify Secretary of the Navy Stephen R. Mallory. The effort proved futile because the raiders had cut the lines. When Parker could not get word to Mallory, he feared Stoneman might learn of the treasure and attack Charlotte, so he decided to move it farther south.[73]

Meanwhile, the raiders left their mark on the Charlotte region. A Federal cavalryman who passed through the area a few weeks later reported seeing the burned remnant of a bridge that had once spanned a "deep creek" and several miles of destroyed telegraph poles and wires. Tremors were felt over the border in South Carolina as well. When a journalist traveling with a South Carolina infantry regiment stopped at a railroad station in Chester, he found a town alive with the news of approaching United States troops. Soldiers and civilians alike were panicking and even looting.[74]

Into this charged atmosphere came Jefferson Davis and his entourage.

Riding into Charlotte on April 19, the party found a chilly welcome because residents had heard that Stoneman would burn the home of anyone who housed the president. Only one man—Lewis F. Bates, a bachelor from Massachusetts—was willing to invite the fugitives in. Bates lived in a "very shabby looking house" at the southwest corner of Tryon and Fourth streets, but it sufficed.[75]

General Echols met the group outside town and escorted it to the Bates residence. Winding their way through the city's streets, the travelers saw throngs of refugees, straggling soldiers, and even some escaped officials from Richmond. In return, those men and women could not help noticing the large, unusual column and especially the distinguished figure at its head. Eventually, a crowd gathered outside the Bates home and called for a speech. Davis obliged. After expressing thanks for Charlotte's hospitality, the president admitted that the Confederacy was in deep trouble. Still, there was no surrender in Jeff Davis. "The cause is not yet dead," he said. "We may still hope for success." Upon finishing his impromptu speech, Davis had turned to go inside when a telegraph operator handed him a wire from Breckinridge. The message stopped him cold: President Abraham Lincoln had been assassinated. When the telegram was read to the crowd, one or two listeners cheered, but most of those present, including Davis, were stunned into silence.[76]

Settling in at Charlotte, Davis set up a temporary office in the Bank of North Carolina building. For the next six days, only despair came across his desk, including news of the fall of Mobile and other Confederate cities and word of Johnston and Sherman's negotiations toward an armistice. In and around Charlotte, the remaining soldiers of the Confederacy were deserting with distressing frequency. Working closely with Echols, who still commanded Confederate troops in the area, Davis tried to establish some semblance of order. Fully aware of the presence of Stoneman's raiders west of the Catawba, Echols concentrated his men between Charlotte and the river. Some of them headed for the Charlotte and South Carolina Railroad bridge over the Catawba, but they arrived too late to stop the Twelfth Ohio from destroying the bridge near Nations Ford.[77]

While Charlotte felt the pressure from Palmer's work along the middle and lower Catawba River, Gillem, leading Miller's and Brown's brigades, secured the upper Catawba. April 17—the day Palmer occupied Lincolnton—found the

Tennesseans, Kentuckians, and Michiganders moving southwest toward Burke County. Before the day's end, they would stumble into a fight audible as far off as Lenoir.[78]

In issuing his final orders before departing for Knoxville, George Stoneman had set the objectives of Gillem's march. In ordering Gillem to Morganton, the terminus of the Western North Carolina Railroad and the seat of Burke County, Stoneman had two goals in mind. First, he wanted Brown's brigade to establish its headquarters there and "to connect with Palmer down the Catawba River." Second, he wanted Miller's brigade to continue to Asheville to "open up communications through to Greeneville[, Tennessee]." Those dispositions, Stoneman thought, would enable the Cavalry Division to "obtain forage and to intercept and disperse any bands going south, and to capture trains &c." It was also Gillem's understanding that he was "to attack and disperse any force in that section of the state" because Asheville had served as a base for raids into East Tennessee.[79]

Morganton came first. Named for Revolutionary War hero Daniel Morgan, it was one of western North Carolina's largest towns. A mountain gateway and commercial center, it was also one of the region's oldest communities, having been established in 1784. Its founders laid out a rectangular street pattern centered on the Burke County Courthouse. A passing Confederate soldier described Morganton as "an old looking town." He was far more impressed with the surrounding countryside: "The mountains were piled in awful grandeur on either side and in front of us, and their lofty peaks seemed to struggle in the distance as to which of them should be the first to kiss the clouds."[80]

Morganton was certainly desirable to the Union army. George W. Kirk's Federal cavalry had raided the area the previous summer. Now, ten months later, the people of Morganton shuddered at the news that another Federal force was heading their way. When Stoneman's raiders hit Patterson's factory, only about twenty miles away, a sixteen-year-old Morganton resident wrote that the population was "very much excited." Everybody expected Federal cavalry to charge into town at any minute. Fortunately, the raiders turned east down the Yadkin River, and the locals breathed easier—for the moment.[81]

Three weeks later, the Federal raiders returned with the suddenness of a summer thunderstorm. A handful of local and Confederate military leaders decided to defend Morganton. Colonel George T. Walton, commander of Morganton's Eighth Home Guard Regiment, was ostensibly in command but had experienced advisers close at hand. Lieutenant Colonel Samuel McDowell Tate, a veteran of the Sixth North Carolina Infantry, was home recuperating from a wound. Captain George West, a New Orleans man who had once served on Major General D. H. Hill's staff, was also in town. The ranking officer on the scene was Major General John Porter McCown, a forty-nine-year-old West Point graduate and decorated Mexican War veteran. McCown had commanded a division in the Army of Tennessee until Braxton Bragg made him a scapegoat for the defeat at Murfreesboro. Since then, he had been relegated to military backwaters. In March 1865, McCown came to Morganton to visit friends.[82]

Although these officers initially posted defenders east of town at the terminus of the Western North Carolina Railroad, they quickly realized that the Catawba River was the key to Morganton. Located less than two miles north of town, the Catawba at that point was not as wide and deep as it was near

Major General John P. McCown, a West Pointer and veteran of the Army of Tennessee, briefly brought Gillem's column to a standstill at Morganton.
LIBRARY OF CONGRESS

Lincolnton, but it still presented a formidable barrier. Any force approaching Morganton from Lenoir would have to cross it. The Confederate officers accordingly placed troops at Rocky Ford on the Lenoir-Morganton road. A low bridge crossed the river there, but its flooring had been removed. The ground around the ford rose sharply, and the Confederates took advantage of it, placing their lone artillery piece on a bluff high above and about 250 yards away from the ford. In preparation, West drilled a squad of young men on the gun, while others dug earthworks. "All day Sunday [April 16] . . . a few hundred old men and boys, known as home guards, worked digging rifle pits along the south bank of the Catawba river at the old Rocky ford, preparing to give the Yankees a warm reception," recorded an eyewitness. A smaller force under Captain Will Corpening trotted to Fleming's Ford to defend the right flank. Soldiers worked all night building breastworks there as well.[83]

While the defenders prepared their positions, a patrol rode across the river to locate and size up the approaching raiders. According to an eyewitness, the men saw "an overwhelming force, numbering several thousands, and covering a mile or two," camped only four miles away. Because the enemy was so close, the Confederates had no time to build additional defenses or plan other stratagems; they would simply have to hold Rocky Ford. In the final hours before the battle, the authorities at Morganton appealed to neighboring towns for help. A few reinforcements appeared, among them some citizens and soldiers on furlough and twenty-six men from Major Alphonso C. Avery's Seventeenth Home Guard Battalion under Captain W. L. Twitty. These men took position atop the hill in support of the cannon and in the rifle pits lining the riverbank. Even with the reinforcements, the Confederates still had far fewer than one hundred men on hand.[84]

Gillem's cavalrymen broke camp at seven o'clock in the morning on April 17 and filed into the Lenoir-Morganton road. Having discovered that the bridge over the Catawba on that road was impassable, Gillem planned to cross the river at Rocky Ford, beside the bridge. While some officers expected to encounter stiff resistance at the Catawba, the men in the ranks simply whiled away the time. Taking in the view, Frank Frankenberry noted "a very good country and indications of wealth."[85]

From Morganton, General McCown sent out more scouting parties to follow the raiders' progress. The scouts found the enemy at John's River, only a half-mile from town. Captain West, one of the scouts, barely managed to return to Rocky Ford to line up the artillery piece before the Federals arrived. "The head of the column had nearly reached the foard," explained an eyewitness, "when a shell from our Howitzer, directed by Capt. West, exploded just in front of them[. F]inding [defenders] in their path, they wheeled to the right in double quick time." Twitty's men were under orders to hold their fire until the enemy tried to cross.[86]

It was about ten in the morning, and the fight was on. From their position on the bluff, West and his novice gun crew fired at the approaching Federals. The defenders could plainly see enemy officers directing their troops in response to the shelling. The Federal officers included Lieutenant James Reagan, who un-limbered his battery and opened fire. Frankenberry watched the action develop. "They are on the south side of the Catawba River and have a good position. Our guns come into position and send them a few shells," he wrote.[87]

Presently, Twitty's Confederates and the Home Guardsmen began shooting their Enfield rifles at the enemy. The Federals tried several times to cross but were unable to in the face of the heavy fire. "The advance of the cavalry came dow[n] on the other side of the river," Twitty wrote. "We opened fire upon them and drove them back. They made from two to three advances and were repulsed each time, in fact they never crossed the river there at all until we left the ford. I do not know whether any were killed or not." Another eyewitness agreed: "These kept up a continuous and effective fire on the Federal troops when they ap-proached the river and prevented their efforts to cross." For the moment, Twitty added, many of the boys fought like veterans. A lack of cover around the ford also hindered the Federal advance. On one charge, the head of the column reached the river before Twitty's fire emptied several saddles and sent the Federals reel-ing in retreat once more. Gillem's troopers finally dismounted and took position on a thickly wooded hill opposite the ford four hundred yards away. A battalion of the Eighth Tennessee Cavalry, also dismounted, found a protected position close to the bridge. The resistance was strong enough to persuade Gillem that the defenders had about three times their actual strength.[88]

Although the defenders briefly held the upper hand, they could not match the volume of carbine and artillery fire that now roared at them. Residents who lived nearby were terrified by the sounds of battle; one cannonball sailed over the Catawba and plunged into the front lawn of Bellevue, a hilltop house. Un-der such a galling fire, the tide began to turn against the defenders. West ran short of both shells and friction primers. A picket reported that a strong Union

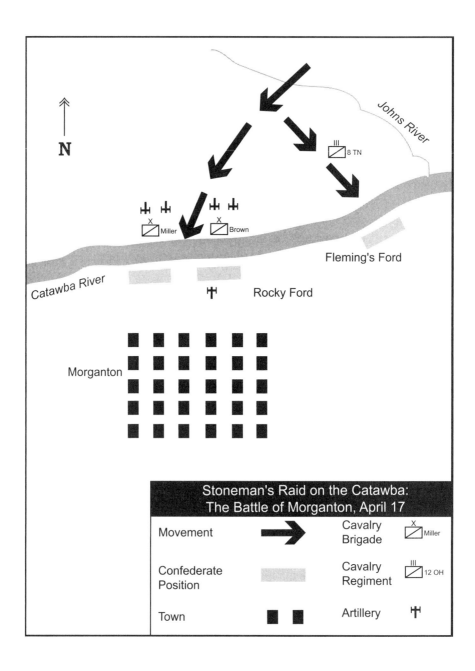

Stoneman's Raid on the Catawba:
The Battle of Morganton, April 17

force had arrived at Fleming's Ford, and that the defenders there could not hold. This was Gillem's response to the failed Rocky Ford attack. Rather than attempt more frontal assaults, he sent Major Christopher C. Kenner and the rest of the Eighth Tennessee Cavalry to outflank the defenders. Thus, while Reagan and the dismounted cavalrymen kept the Rocky Ford defenders busy, Kenner's Tennesseans easily crossed at Fleming's, a half-mile east of Rocky Ford. According to the Eighth's regimental records, the action there was "a short fight[,] whipping the enemy."[89]

"No hope was then left us, further resistance on our part was deemed useless," recalled a defender. But the Confederates were not quite ready to withdraw. West and his crew served their gun as long as they could. Twitty's soldiers in the trenches and the citizens on the hill held on as well, "blazing away, in defiance of the storm of shot &c & shell poured upon them from the enemy." But Colonel Walton knew the time had come. He ordered a retreat as West's gunners fired some parting shots. The crew "cooly & deliberately loaded, and discharged the gun 4 times, having fired the very last shell in the caisson," an eyewitness recalled.[90]

Much to his chagrin, West was unable to save his gun. Some sources say the Confederates forgot to chock the wheels and the cannon rolled down the bluff, but in truth Reagan's battery disabled the enemy gun. Not long after the fight began, the Federal lieutenant sighted West's piece with the help of Union signalmen. The Confederate cannon sat unprotected in an open field, making it an easy target. A Federal shell dismounted the gun by breaking an axle and knocking a wheel off.[91]

Federal small arms drove away West's gunners as well, as Captain Twitty discovered. When the cannon suddenly fell silent in the heat of battle, the Home Guard commander decided to investigate. "I left the Company . . . and went myself[. A]s soon as I started the federals commenced firing at me and cursing me. Some-times the bullets struck near me but none of them struck me." Reaching the cannon, Twitty saw that the gunners had abandoned their piece. The crew members blamed their retreat on overwhelming enemy fire.[92]

Now that West's gun was silenced, the Federals turned their artillery on the Confederate infantry. This time, however, Reagan failed to find the range. His case and canister crashed around the hill overlooking the ford, but most of the shot sailed six or eight feet over the defenders' heads. Retreat orders from the various Confederate commanders, not Reagan's fire, ended the determined stand. With the Federals across the river at Fleming's Ford and now entering Morganton, the defenders were ordered to run for their lives.[93]

Alvan Gillem delivered the *coup de grâce* by sending his men across Rocky Ford. Major William J. S. Denton's dismounted battalion of the Eighth Tennessee Cavalry led the charge, pushing across the stringers of the dismantled bridge. Other cavalrymen rode through the ford. "The advance crossed over and away we went for the town on a great charge. I had the train and led them on a charge for a mile," Frank Frankenberry stated. Reagan's guns added a final salvo. Lieutenant James Atkinson was credited with pulling the lanyard.[94]

The attack had the desired effect, scattering the Confederates "to the four winds." Most of the defenders found refuge in the woods and mountains surrounding Morganton. Among those who escaped was Colonel Tate. "When news came that the flanking party from up the river was taking us in the rear," one of Tate's men recalled, "our cannon already being rendered useless . . . our troops at Rocky Ford were withdrawn and Colonel Tate and I rode off just in time to prevent being caught in a *cul de sac.*"[95]

Other accounts describe the chaos that ensued as the defenses collapsed. "When [the Confederates] were flanked and had to run, [one soldier] did not hear the order and was . . . soon perfectly surrounded by Yanks ordering him off his horse and shooting at him," a witness wrote. "He couldn't make his horse run so jumped off and took off on foot—ever so many firing at him all the time. Finally he got into the woods and thought himself pretty safe and went to a spring to get a drink, when a big Irishman raised his gun and ordered him to lay down his arms." The soldier refused to comply, remounted his reluctant horse, and this time managed to gallop away. The Irishman chased him, firing, but the soldier apparently escaped.[96]

The fight for Morganton was over. Casualties were light, although both sides maintained that their foe had suffered mightily. Citing tales of bodies in the river and fresh graves in the woods, local historians claimed that the Federals lost as many as twenty-five killed and wounded. Historian Cornelia P. Spencer later quoted one of Gillem's staff officers to the effect that the Federals suffered eleven killed and seventeen wounded. But Federal records indicate that only one man, a member of Company E of the Eighth Tennessee Cavalry, was wounded, while two horses were killed. The Federals captured about fifty prisoners plus West's damaged cannon, which they repaired and took away. The Federals believed they had killed several enemy soldiers, but they, too, were mistaken. At most, the Confederates lost several men wounded and a few horses killed. The injured included one of Twitty's men, who received a flesh wound in the right arm, and a Burke County man named Hill. Most of the Confederate casualties occurred as the defenders withdrew.[97]

The defenders later boasted of their heroic stand at the Catawba River. Captain Twitty argued that the fight passed "beyond the dignity of a skirmish." Another participant bragged, "We held Stoneman's vastly superior force in check till his flanking force had crossed the river above and were ready to take us in the rear."[98] While this may have been true, there was never any question that the Federals would triumph. The Confederates simply lacked the manpower to prevent the enemy from occupying Morganton. In the final analysis, the skirmish at Morganton was a noisy affair that had minimal impact on the outcome of Stoneman's Raid, other than to demonstrate that the population remained defiant. Perhaps harsher measures would be required to persuade the Confederates of western North Carolina that the end had come.

Gillem's raiders next struck Morganton itself. "Soon drove the Rebs and entered the town," a cavalryman wrote.[99] A handful of retreating Confederates made a brief stand in Morganton, but the Federals "put to horses and hasty flights were made." One citizen never forgot how the Union cavalrymen "dashed furiously through our streets, cursing and swearing vengeance on the 'damned rebels.'" The town appeared deserted; doors were closed and windows darkened and shuttered. The only people to be seen were a few curious slaves along the road. The blacks quickly discovered that the raiders were in ill humor. "Hail, Columbia, Happy Land! If I don't shoot a nigger, I'll be damned!" a trooper yelled. According to one source, the soldier raised his carbine and shot one of the blacks. The rest ran away.[100]

General Gillem arrived with the column, riding a horse that had once belonged to Confederate cavalryman John Hunt Morgan. He stopped at the home of Annie Lizzie Pearson, who watched the men guide their horses uncomfortably close to her front door. "I hope you are all gentlemen," she said. The soldiers replied that they were. When an officer asked for something to eat, Annie gave him a platter of cold chicken, over the protest of a family member. Gillem failed to convince the Pearsons that Lee had surrendered. "These men were pleas-ant, tiring of war and eager to return home," Annie noted. Gillem made his headquarters at the Pearson house and asked the women to cook some of his provisions.[101]

Meanwhile, Miller's and Brown's brigades rode into town and made quite an impression. A Morganton resident named Jimmy Moore, who had lost a leg in the war, watched a squad ride past. The cavalrymen, squirrel tails hanging from their caps, held their revolvers at the ready and scanned the windows for threats. Henry Birdsall and his comrades rounded up at least five "disbanded rebs" in town. Once they determined that the town was clear of the enemy, the troopers bivouacked at various places, including Law's store on the old Morganton road. Birdsall camped in town, fed his horses, and then relaxed. To pass the time, the Michigander managed to collect some books, including a French-English dictionary and *Don Quixote*. In another camp, a Tennessee trooper caught up on lost sleep. He fondly recalled Morganton as the first place he enjoyed a full night's rest since crossing the Blue Ridge.[102]

Ever the social butterfly, signalman Frank Frankenberry found much to en-joy. "Morganton is a rich, pleasant place," he wrote. He found a home where some young ladies lived. After leaving his horses and packs in the stable, he re-turned and introduced himself. At first, the Tate family refused to speak with the Federal interloper. They became friendlier, however, when they learned that Frankenberry was from Pennsylvania, as they had family ties there as well. By the end of the evening, the Tates shared conversation and dinner with the caval-ryman, who promised to take a letter to Pennsylvania for them. "They were very kind," he wrote.[103]

Most of Gillem's cavalrymen had to gather food and horses by force. With-in a half-hour of their arrival, the raiders began to ransack homes, barns, and smokehouses. "The streets were full of blue coats, and the air resounded with the shouts, yells, & terrible oaths of the enraged soldiery," a citizen recalled. Al-though guards were promised and provided to many homeowners, they some-times proved worthless. Gillem later reported that the raiders found a large supply of corn and bacon at Morganton. "By nightfall almost every house in the village had been entered by the vandals, (under the pretence of examining for firearms) and nearly everyone deprived of their supplies in the way of provisions, some to a greater, & some to a less extent," a historian observed.[104]

Colonel Walton, the Home Guard commander who fought at Rocky Ford, lost all his meat, meal, flour, and livestock to the raiders, who also damaged or destroyed carpeting and curtains inside his house and even took some of his clothes. The depredations ceased only when Lieutenant Colonel Stacy of the Thirteenth Tennessee arrived and drove the offenders out of the house. Though bitter over their losses, the Waltons never forgot Stacy's kindness. When six-year-old Hugh Walton ran into the house crying, "Oh, Mother, don't let the Yankees take my colt!" Stacy promised, "You shall have your colt back[,] my little man." But the boy never saw his colt again, and the Waltons never received compensation for their losses.[105]

At another Morganton home, Louisa Norwood wrote, invaders "tore everything to pieces . . . and put pistols to the ladies' heads, drove them out of the house and took what they liked, guided by a negro boy." Other cavalrymen cornered a slave who had hidden his master's jewelry and silverware. They whipped the slave to force him to tell where the jewelry was, but he did not betray his master.[106]

Although Gillem's men left the large brick railroad depot untouched, they burned property more freely in Morganton than they had in other towns. The home of Dr. Felix Dula was one of the first to burn. Soldiers removed deeds and other records from the courthouse, tossed them in a pile, and burned or otherwise mutilated them. Down the street, ruffians entered the local bank only to discover that the safe had already been emptied. They contented themselves with destroying the ledger and other records. Troopers also demolished the post office. Property owners in the countryside did not escape either. Former sheriff John H. Pearson, who lived eight miles from Morganton, lost meat, corn, and meal to the Federals. Cavalrymen also burned his mill lumber room and gin house. The raiders swore they would torch his house if he did not bring his animals out of hiding. Fortunately, they did not make good on the threat.[107]

In a few cases, cavalrymen such as Frank Frankenberry rescued private property. On April 18, the raiders' second day in Morganton, Frankenberry arose, had breakfast, and returned to the Tate home to flirt with the daughters. It was "a lovely pleasant day," he wrote. But upon his arrival, he learned that raiders had intercepted some valuables the Tates had sent away in a buggy for safekeeping. The chivalrous Frankenberry rode past the pickets and found the buggy three and a half miles from town. Many articles were missing, but at least the signalman managed to salvage something for the Tates. "I drove the buggy lively and at dusk we arrived at the house of Dr Tate and was welcomed by the smiles of the ladies," Frankenberry wrote. The grateful Tates invited him to dinner. "Soon we are seated at a long well spread table and all was happy as circumstances would allow," he continued. After supper, Frankenberry sat on the porch and had a pleasant conversation with Laura Tate, whom he described as "a Christian woman if a little rebellious in spirit." When it was time for him to leave, the cavalryman promised to call again. "Laura said to me, 'Mr. Frank[,] if you are [ever] a prisoner and can only let me know it we shall do all in our power to make you happy[,] and if you ever in the future pass through Morganton you *must* call and see us.'" Bidding the ladies good night, Frankenberry returned to camp and "was soon in the arms of Morpheus and away in happy dream lands dreaming of a lovely sweet future."[108]

Contrary to Frankenberry's dream, the future promised only more raiding. Gillem decided there was no need to remain at Morganton. He had yet to receive news of the preliminary Sherman-Johnston agreement, so he turned to his next task, which was to reach Asheville and open communications with Federal forces at Greeneville, Tennessee. On April 19—the day Jefferson Davis arrived in Charlotte—Gillem departed with Brown's and Miller's brigades. At six o'clock that morning, the column began marching westward toward Marion and Asheville. "They took with them every 'nigger' that would go and every horse and mule that they could find," a resident wrote. On the way out of town, Frankenberry stopped at the Tate home one last time. Laura Tate gave him a lovely little white flower. "I bid them 'good day' and was soon away," he wrote.[109]

Most residents were grateful to hear the sound of the bugle and "the hurried tramp of horses hoofs," which "proclaimed that the joy full hour had come." The bad news was that stragglers were on their way. The departing cavalrymen warned the locals to beware. Indeed, plunderers visited a number of homes shortly after the main body left.[110]

At length, the ruffians moved on. According to one estimate, Morganton suffered several hundred thousand dollars' worth of damage at the hands of raiders and stragglers. "The county was left almost destitute in the way of provisions for man, or beast," a resident wrote. "Immense tithes of corn and grain were consumed or destroyed, and hundreds of horses, mules, &c. carried off." Another local claimed, "They scoured the country as if with a fine tooth comb."[111] The citizens of Morganton had paid dearly for lying in the path of Stoneman's raiders.

Chapter 10

God Only Knows
What Will Be the End of this
Marion to Mooresboro: April 19–30, 1865

Although Corporal W. E. Reppert was exhausted, his day was far from over. "Men and horses had been put to their utmost endurance," he recalled. It was the evening of April 21, one long month into the raid, and Reppert was at Lincolnton. A member of the Fifteenth Pennsylvania Cavalry, he had arrived with his company the previous night after driving Duke's Confederate cavalry across the Catawba River and burning a few bridges. Unfortunately for Reppert, he would have no time to rest. Two couriers delivered fresh orders, one from Sherman directing the raiders to cease military operations and join him because of the armistice, the other from Thomas recalling the Cavalry Division to Tennessee. Adding to the confusion, Gillem had ordered Palmer to Rutherfordton. Not knowing what to do, Palmer decided to seek Gillem's advice. That's where Reppert came in. "At about dark, while eating supper," he wrote, "I received orders to take six men and report to Lieutenant Beck in Lincolnton." Beck explained that they would find Gillem and the other two brigades near Morganton, thirty miles away. An all-night ride lay ahead for Reppert and his detachment.[1]

It was eight o'clock when the party left Lincolnton. "The night was exceedingly dark, with not even a star to guide us," Reppert recalled. "Anyone who has traveled country roads, even in daylight, knows how perplexing it is to always keep the right road." After two hours of groping blindly in the dark, Beck impressed an "old citizen" to serve as a guide. The citizen was "very much scared and reluctant to go with us," Reppert continued. "We lost half an hour getting him out and mounted." When the man claimed to know little about the countryside, the troopers let him go and trusted their own sense of direction. It remained slow going, however, thanks in part to several seemingly unfordable streams that barred their way.[2]

Riding a horse captured from a South Carolina cavalryman, Reppert struggled through the long night. At last, just before dawn, the riders reached Morganton. Unfortunately, they discovered that Gillem and the other brigades had left town three days earlier, so Beck's party was forced to continue its westward journey. After an hour's rest, the cavalrymen rode another fifteen miles to Marion, arriving before noon. There again, they were disappointed to find that Gillem had marched on toward Asheville. Reppert's trip continued with no end in sight. Miles away, Gillem and the brigades of John Miller and Simeon Brown rode on, unaware of the most recent orders of Thomas and Sherman.[3]

⟶⟵

Leaving Morganton on April 19, Gillem's raiders entered the Confederate District of Western North Carolina. Created in September 1863 after Union Major General Ambrose Burnside occupied East Tennessee, the district stretched from the Blue Ridge Mountains west of Morganton to the Tennessee line. Brigadier General James Green Martin had commanded the district since August 1864. He was General Lee's personal choice. Born on Valentine's Day, the forty-six-year-old Martin hailed from Elizabeth City, North Carolina. An 1840 graduate of West Point, he joined the First United States Artillery, saw service on the Canadian border, and went on to lead a battery in the Mexican War. At Churubusco, Martin's right arm was shot off; turning his guns over to Thomas J. Jackson, he took his empty sleeve in his teeth and rode off the field. Afterward brevetted for gallantry, Martin was given the nickname "Old One Wing" in honor of his missing arm. He somehow managed to overcome his disability and remain in the army. When the Civil War began, he threw in his lot with his home state and quickly demonstrated leadership qualities that have not received their due. Appointed state adjutant general, he rendered bril-

*Brigadier General James "Old One Wing" Martin was
Robert E. Lee's choice to command the Confederacy's District
of Western North Carolina.*
COURTESY OF THE NORTH CAROLINA STATE ARCHIVES

liant service in raising and equipping more than forty regiments in ten months.
Another of Martin's contributions was the idea for the state's highly successful
blockade-running enterprise. He even proposed the creation of the foreign-born
prisoner-of-war units that Stoneman had faced at Salisbury. Later transferred
into the field at his own request, Martin fought in North Carolina and at Petersburg. But when his health broke down, he asked for another transfer. Assigned
command of the District of Western North Carolina, the exhausted Martin
established his headquarters at Morganton.[4]

A few months later, Old One Wing had nearly 3,000 men on the district's
rolls, but only 1,535 were ready for action. John Palmer, who had remained in
the district despite being superseded, commanded a unit of just 421 effectives.
Although essentially a battalion, the unit actually contained parts of the Sixty-
second, Sixty-fourth, and Sixty-ninth North Carolina infantry regiments. A bat-

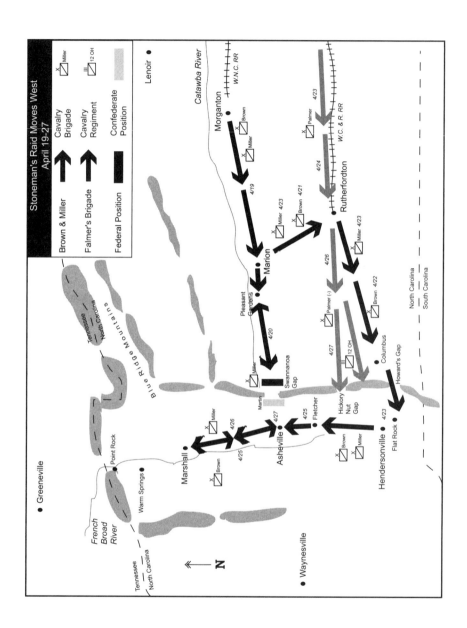

talion of senior reserves was present as well but contained only 74 overage men. The Macbeth Light Artillery, fielding six guns and about 100 men, gave Martin his only real firepower. Colonel William "Little Will" Thomas's Highland Legion formed the core of the force, counting more than 1,000 able-bodied men. The legion included an infantry regiment led by Lieutenant Colonel James R. Love, an infantry battalion under Lieutenant Colonel William W. Stringfield, and an unsteady one-gun artillery battery commanded by South Carolinian James Barr. It was best known for its Cherokee Indian battalion, which boasted a largely undeserved reputation for scalping and other forms of savagery. Martin had little faith in his Cherokees. Neither could he place much reliance on the Home Guardsmen, though he did have some cause for hope thanks to the Home Guard regiment of Alphonso Avery, which had fought Stoneman at both Lenoir and Morganton.[5]

The resourceful Martin moved his headquarters to Asheville and did what he could, but by March 1865 he had failed to work his old magic. The independent-minded mountaineers in his command showed more interest in feuding with each other than in fighting the enemy. Supplies were scarce, the men had not been paid in over a year, morale was plummeting, orders went unheeded, and desertion was rampant. Martin begged for reinforcements—and warned that he was helpless to stop the inevitable. "I am fearful of serious consequences to the welfare of the district," he wrote. "The present force cannot hold it against any determined effort."[6]

It was equally clear to General Martin that just such an attack was coming from East Tennessee, so he sounded the alarm. Ordered to concentrate his command and support Salisbury's defenders, he was proved right when Stoneman launched his raid. Old One Wing breathed a sigh of relief when the raiders headed north into Virginia. Unfortunately for Martin, a second threat to his district materialized in early April. This time, the menace came from Davis Tillson's infantry division, which occupied Watauga County's mountain gaps to protect the raiders, as well as Major General David Stanley's Fourth Corps of the Department of the Cumberland, which was advancing into East Tennessee to support Stoneman. On April 3, Stanley dispatched Colonel Isaac M. Kirby's First Brigade up the French Broad River to capture Asheville—ironically, along the same route Sherman had originally envisioned for Stoneman's Raid. "The object of the expedition was principally to make a demonstration in favor of General Stoneman," Stanley wrote.[7]

From Greeneville, Tennessee, Kirby led nine hundred soldiers and about two hundred partisans and former Confederates to Asheville. Martin was not ready for him. In fact, Stoneman's movements had drawn Martin and most of his troops away, including Thomas's Legion, which was depleted because of expiring enlistments. Only about three hundred troops—many of them old men and boys—were on hand to defend Asheville. They filed into some makeshift trenches on Woodfin's Ridge a mile and a half northwest of town, and the Macbeth Light Artillery unlimbered in support. When Kirby arrived, both sides opened fire. Five hours later, Kirby retreated to Tennessee, having failed to rout the defenders. According to Stanley, Kirby "drove the enemy into his works, but being unprovided with artillery [which he had left at Warm Springs], and being but little superior to the rebels in point of numbers, very properly decided not to assault the position, the enemy being protected by two inclosed field works." That evening, Asheville celebrated Kirby's abrupt departure. Kirby may have intended to join Stoneman, but the encounter at Asheville changed his plans.[8]

The fight also had more significant consequences. Kirby's defeat sealed Martin's vulnerable Tennessee flank for the time being. The pressure from Davis Tillson's division also eased when Stoneman directed Tillson's command to concentrate at Greeneville. With both Stanley and Tillson pulling back, General Martin decided to concentrate his forces against Gillem. He sent Confederate soldiers east to plug the gaps in the Blue Ridge Mountains between Asheville and Morganton.[9]

After leaving his raiders on April 17, George Stoneman made his way back to Knoxville to attend to other business of the District of East Tennessee. He spent the first night of his journey in Boone with the Jordan Councill family, with whom he had stayed in March. The Councills had enjoyed little respite since the raiders' departure. Colonel Kirk had made their house his headquarters, confining Mrs. Councill to her room while the mounted infantry made short work of the place. As a witness described it, "The fencing [was] gone—the flowers and shrubbery trampled bare, the yard covered with beef hides, and sheep skins, chicken feathers, and pieces of putrid meat and all manner of filth." Surveying Kirk's handiwork, Stoneman said, "Well, Mrs. C., I suppose you hardly know whether you are home or not."[10]

At three in the afternoon the next day, Stoneman arrived in Carter County, Tennessee. After attending to their prisoners, the general and his staff camped. One staff officer, identifying himself only as "NEMADIA," sat down and wrote an account of the raid that would appear in the *Cincinnati Daily Commercial* on May 10, 1865. The next day, the party arrived in Jonesboro, where Stoneman paused to update Thomas. "The condition of things in Western Virginia and Western North Carolina is truly deplorable," he reported. "The people are in a starving condition and the country is overrun by bands of disbanded Confederate soldiers, who rob and plunder indiscriminately while making their way south." Already, Stoneman suspected that Confederate forces in the East would head for the Trans-Mississippi. "I hope my cavalry will be able to intersect [intercept] them," he wrote.[11]

Reaching Knoxville a few days later, Stoneman formally resumed command of the district and then trumpeted his success. On April 22, he reported, "There is now no organized force in Southwestern Virginia claiming to belong to the Confederacy." He found the same to be true in East Tennessee, where he noted that the "most perfect quiet exists . . . , except now and then a private difficulty." Stoneman added that he had not heard from Gillem but expected news once his subordinate established a courier line from Asheville to Greeneville.[12]

Alvan Gillem was indeed marching on Asheville, just as Stoneman thought. Departing Morganton on April 19, he led Miller's and Brown's brigades and Reagan's artillery along the Asheville road. Passing through Marion, the column camped at Pleasant Gardens, a village nestled against the upper Catawba River.[13] Pleasant Gardens was the site of the Carson home, a popular stop on the Morganton-Asheville stagecoach line. Built around 1780 by Colonel John Carson, the large log house with double verandas sat among boxwoods at the end of a long driveway. "This is a lovely spot," a traveler wrote. Jonathan Logan Carson and his family occupied the house now, sharing it with a private school for young women. The teacher was twenty-six-year-old Emma Lydia Rankin, whose father had met the raiders in Lenoir. A gifted woman, Miss Rankin was said to have both a "strong character" and an equally "strong intellect."[14]

Aside from the usual privations and concerns about friends and loved ones in the service, the war had hardly touched this McDowell County community— that is, until now. "We had thought it highly improbable that a blue-coat would ever be seen in our secluded region," Emma Rankin wrote. The last winter of the war changed that, with Union soldiers such as Colonel George W. Kirk raiding nearby. Emma started setting her valuables beside her bed so she could quickly grab them in case of an emergency. By early spring, nearly everyone expected the Federals to enter Pleasant Gardens, and they were right. While spending the night with a friend, Emma woke to the sight of her friend standing by her bed, a candle in one hand and a letter in the other. "I shall never forget the ghostly picture," Emma wrote. "The tall figure with face as pallid as the night dress she wore, the dim blue light, and the whole foreshadowing of evil." The letter announced that Stoneman's raiders were on their way. "It is impossible to realize now the dread terror with which we received these tidings," Emma wrote.[15]

Emma reached her home in time to join "the biggest burying I ever attended," as the Carsons dug holes and hid hams and valuables, including a box big enough for a piano. The servants pitched in, burying valuables and driving livestock into the woods. Emma personally buried a container of Confederate money. "It was only a foot and a half long and about half as wide and deep," she recalled, "but I thought I would never get the hole deep enough, and I chose a soft place too." She also hid some clothing in a decrepit cabin off the road, think- ing the raiders would not search such a humble dwelling. Afterward, Emma and the others hid in the bushes and waited.[16]

Around noon, a squad of Confederates trotted past. They were members of Asheville's defensive force on patrol. The Confederates soon came galloping back with the dreaded news that the Yankees were across the Catawba. Carson and the slaves scattered, leaving Emma, Mrs. Carson, and the children behind. The Confederate scouts stayed, deploying near the front gate to ambush the enemy.[17]

Although it may not have occurred to the ladies, the Confederate soldiers posed a grave danger to their safety. The sudden arrival of Federal cavalrymen saved them. The bluejackets appeared along a path beside the creek, rather than on the main road as anticipated. The Confederate squad leader realized that the Federals had turned his flank and rendered his position untenable, and that he was heavily outnumbered. The captain "lifted his cap and called to us that he had concluded not to fire from that place lest the enemy should burn the house," Emma recalled. As the Confederates wheeled and rode away, the Federal cavalrymen spotted them. The two forces exchanged shots, but no casualties resulted.[18]

"By the time the little skirmish was over the horrid blue coats were swarm- ing in and through and around the house," Emma wrote. At first, the raiders burst through the front door and rushed past the frightened ladies and children, but soon they were entering through every door in the house. "Every office and out house seemed to be full of them, and still they came," Emma recalled. "It seemed to us that there were about a million of them, but I suppose there were only a few hundred in the yard." Helpless against a sea of men in blue, Mrs. Carson and Emma sat on the porch and waited for the storm to subside.[19]

The raiders did not allow them to wait in peace. "They went through their usual program of plunder and insulting the ladies," wrote R. L. Beall. One trooper spotted a breast pin on Emma's dress and asked to see it. When she refused, the cavalryman promised to return it. Emma grudgingly gave it to the man, who looked at the pin and then headed for the door. "I've got a good mind not to give it back to her," he said. But Emma reminded him of his pledge, and he returned the pin. Another interruption came when an officer—reportedly Gillem himself—ordered Mrs. Carson to cook dinner for him. She protested; most of her food was gone, and her cook had vanished, too. "You cook it yourself," the officer said. "I intend to have my supper, and if you don't get it, I will turn my men loose in your house." It was a hollow threat because dozens of cavalrymen had already tramped through. Mrs. Carson held her ground. The soldiers managed to find only some sorghum and corn batter cakes to appease their hunger.[20]

An hour or two later, the road and the house finally emptied. While the Federals settled into camps nearby, the ladies went inside to survey the damage. It was far worse than they had imagined. Bedding and other belongings were scattered everywhere. Bureau drawers were smashed. Property was missing, and molasses had been spattered over the furniture. Worst of all, their food was gone. "The pantry was as bare as old Mother Hubbard's cupboard," Emma wrote. The smokehouse and the springhouse were also empty. The Federals left only a few dirty scraps of meat and some headless turkeys sitting on their nests. As night fell and a dark thunderhead formed in the west, the dejected ladies put the children to bed and settled in to keep watch. It proved unnecessary, as heavy rains kept the raiders away. One thing was obvious, however: discipline in Miller's and Brown's brigades was falling apart.[21]

When April 20, 1865, dawned, Mrs. Carson and Emma Rankin returned to the porch and watched yet another Union regiment trot past. Suddenly, a soldier left the ranks, galloped over to the house, and asked for Miss Rankin by name. "If his Satanic majesty had called for me, I could scarcely have been more astonished," Emma recalled, "but I stepped to the edge of the porch, and announced that I was Miss R." The soldier explained that he had guarded her father's home in Lenoir. Handing over a letter from the Reverend Rankin, the trooper told Emma what had happened there and rode away.[22]

The first trooper had barely departed when a young lieutenant rode up, bowed, and asked for a drink of water. Impressed, Emma told the officer about the behavior of his comrades and asked him for protection. The man was Harrison F. Davis of Company F of the Eleventh Kentucky Cavalry. Granting Emma's request, Davis stayed as long as he could. The lieutenant admitted his shame for serving in such an undisciplined command "and tingled at the outrages they had committed ever since they started from Tennessee." All too soon, Davis had to leave because the cavalrymen were about to resume their westward march. He warned the ladies that stragglers would soon arrive and that they would be worse than the men who had already passed. He gave them permission to use his name, since he was officer of the day. It did little good. When the stragglers came, they cursed Davis's name, searched the house yet again, and even threatened to burn it.[23]

꙳

Leaving Pleasant Gardens, the cavalry column once more wound its way up the Blue Ridge, beneath a torrential downpour.[24] The Asheville road led through Swannanoa Gap, which was plugged firmly by Lieutenant Colonel James Robert Love's Sixty-ninth North Carolina. Recently promoted to full colonel, Love had been ordered to hold the gap against the Federal cavalry marching from Salisbury. He was soon joined by General Martin, who moved his entire command up in support. Love's soldiers took position along Mill Creek and felled trees across the roads to Swannanoa Gap and Lakey's Gap. The Confederates also placed at least one artillery piece in Swannanoa Gap. "We succeeded in making a barricade that no cavalry force could soon cross or clear away," a Confederate recalled.[25]

On came the Federals, trotting up the mountain from Pleasant Gardens. Home Guardsmen from Avery's battalion watched from the surrounding hills, hoping to ambush small groups. In the gap, the defenders waited impatiently. "Time hung heavy on their hands," a solider recalled. They believed their barricades and weapons would stop the enemy.[26]

Suddenly, gunfire echoed through the mountain hollows and against the peaks; Gillem's cavalrymen had collided with Love's infantrymen. "Cross creek three or four times and start up the mountain," Frankenberry recalled. "Bang! Bang! [g]o the guns of the rebs." It quickly became obvious to the Federals that they could not easily dislodge their opponents. As Gillem explained, "I found it [the gap] effectually blockaded and defended by about 500 men with four pieces of artillery." He ordered a reconnaissance to find an undefended way through the gap, but the patrols discovered none.[27]

At the outset of the fight, the Federals surprised about thirty Confederates who had been working on the road; Gillem released the prisoners soon afterward. The Federals also suffered a few casualties; a member of the Eighth Tennessee sustained a flesh wound in his jaw, while two members of the Thirteenth Tennessee were killed. However, records disagree on the fate of these men, and a lone Union grave in the woods near the gap only deepens the mystery. Two stones mark the spot. One reads, "A United States Soldier," and the other reads, "Bill." Is this the grave of a Federal killed in the skirmish, as one account suggests? Or does it hold the body of a deserter who was summarily executed near the gap on another occasion, as other sources claim? More than 140 years later, these questions remain unanswered.[28]

The success of the Confederate stand at Swannanoa Gap is clear, however. As Martin later reported, Love's men repulsed the raiders "without difficulty." For Alvan Gillem, the solution to this military problem was obvious. If he could not force Swannanoa Gap, the raiders would have to use other Blue Ridge gaps to outflank the defenders. Leaving Miller's brigade at the gap to keep Love occupied, Gillem withdrew Brown's brigade to Marion, where it camped late on April 20. From there, Gillem planned to march south to Rutherfordton and then west to Howard's Gap. Reagan's artillery and Mallaby's Signal Corps detachment accompanied Brown, the signalers camping six miles from the gap. "We cannot go up at this place so we 'Right about wheel' and go back towards Marion, camp, and get supper," Frankenberry wrote.[29]

The raiders thus returned to Pleasant Gardens, much to the chagrin of Emma Rankin. It was dusk on April 20 when the long cavalry column reappeared. A soldier told Emma and Mrs. Carson that the enemy had blocked the gap by cutting down trees and piling up stones. "It would take a month to clean out the road," he explained, adding that the Federals were going to cross the Blue Ridge through another gap to the south. The ladies feared that the return of the raiders meant more abuse, so they were relieved when Lieutenant

Davis's regiment camped outside their door and Davis's superior officer made the Carson house his headquarters. Davis introduced the ladies to the officer, who expressed his regret at their losses. His sincerity was doubtful, however, since he allowed his men to use fence rails on the property for firewood. The Carsons suffered more losses after Davis left, and so did some neighbors.[30]

On April 21, Gillem's and Brown's men marched at seven in the morning. Their objective was Rutherfordton, about twenty miles south of Marion. They began filing into the town at eight o'clock that evening. After camping in a field, signalman Frank Frankenberry went into town to get some corn. He found Rutherfordton to be "a very pretty town" but was too tired to linger. The next morning, the raiders headed west, passing Columbus Court House and beginning their ascent of the Blue Ridge. As the sun drooped to the horizon, the troopers approached Howard's Gap.[31]

As the way grew steeper, signalman Frankenberry dismounted and led his horse by the reins. He was struck by the sight of "a lovely grand mountain water fall . . . hundreds of feet above us" and found the surrounding mountains no less beautiful.[32] Frankenberry and his comrades were soon brought back to earth by what Gillem called "slight resistance" at Howard's Gap. When the shooting stopped, Frankenberry became embroiled in a war of words with a local resident. "I gave him as much as he wanted for his talk," the signalman later wrote, "and told him a few things."[33]

The resistance could have been worse. Anticipating Gillem's maneuver, General Martin ordered Colonel John B. Palmer's brigade to the gap. However, Palmer's men refused because it was clear that the war was all but over. They had heard of Lincoln's assassination and Lee's surrender and hastened to inform the Federals. Soon after daylight on April 22, as the raiders stirred in their Rutherfordton camps, a squad of Confederates approached with the news from Ford's Theatre and Appomattox. "The information of these two events," wrote a Tennessee cavalryman, "the one so sad, filling our hearts with the greatest sorrow[,] left little room for the joy that would otherwise have filled our hearts over the good news that the war was virtually over."[34]

Upon the refusal of Palmer's men to fight, Asheville now lay undefended against Gillem's column. Martin remarked that things looked a "little squally." He was right, for the news from Appomattox did not change Gillem's plans. Leaving Howard's Gap during the cold and windy early-morning hours of April 23, the raiders arrived in Hendersonville at first light. They discovered three hundred stands of arms and learned that enemy artillery had left the town the previous afternoon for Asheville. "I immediately ordered . . . [Major Frederick] Slater, commanding the Eleventh Kentucky Cavalry, to pursue, attack, and capture this artillery at all hazards," Gillem reported. The Eleventh Michigan rode in support. By midday, Slater captured four pieces of enemy artillery and seventy infantrymen. Gillem cited him for gallantry in the incident.[35]

More good news reached Gillem at Hendersonville. "At 3 p.m. I received a flag of truce from General Martin at Asheville," he wrote, "stating that he had official notification of the Sherman-Johnston truce. Later in the evening another flag of truce informed me that General Martin would meet me next morning." At eleven o'clock that night, the dispatches Colonel Palmer had entrusted to Lieutenant Beck arrived as well. Eight hours earlier, after riding 110 miles in twenty-two hours, Beck, Reppert, and their comrades had caught up with Miller, who forwarded the dispatches from Sherman and Thomas by a fresh courier. "I believe we made the longest march that was ever made by the regiment," Reppert wrote.[36]

The official confirmation of the truce was cause for celebration. "All right[,] boys[,] we are all gay," Frankenberry wrote upon hearing the news. "Happy and in the best of humor." He proceeded to celebrate by drinking more than he ever had in his life. For Gillem, however, the truce presented a dilemma: whose orders should he obey, Thomas's or Sherman's? The division commander's immediate reaction was to postpone the attack on Asheville and to accept Martin's invitation. After some reflection, he also resolved to follow Thomas's orders. "Being thoroughly convinced that the order had been given by General Sherman in the belief that the Cavalry Division was at or near Salisbury," Gillem wrote, "when in fact it would have required a march of about 200 miles to have reached Durham's Station, and but sixty to our base at Greeneville, Tenn., after mature consideration I determined to march to the latter place." Gillem then reaffirmed his previous orders and directed Palmer to establish his headquarters at Rutherfordton, where he could cover either Howard's Gap or Hickory Nut Gap. "I regarded the possession of one of the gaps of the Blue Ridge as being absolutely necessary to the safety of my command," Gillem explained.[37]

While Gillem considered his options, his roaming cavalrymen relieved several citizens of foodstuffs and animals.[38] Troopers were also drawn to Flat Rock, a popular resort community in Henderson County. Wealthy plantation owners had been spending their summers at Flat Rock for years, fleeing the heat and pests of the lowlands for the vistas and cooler temperatures of the highlands. Many built fabulous homes there, such as Rock Hill, erected by Christopher Gustavus Memminger in 1838 at the foot of Glassy Mountain. The first Confederate secretary of the treasury, Memminger resigned from the cabinet in June 1864 due to poor health. He retired to Rock Hill, but the war caught up with him even in that remote locale. Frankenberry was among the blue-clad visitors to Rock Hill. Noting its fountain, pond, costly furnishings, and gorgeous landscape, the signalman was impressed. He picked a bunch of flowers from the front yard before returning to camp.[39]

On April 24, Miller's brigade joined the Eleventh Michigan and the rest of Brown's brigade at Hendersonville.[40] They bivouacked at various points near Fletcher, including Calvary Episcopal Church. As the raiders bedded down for the night, they were struck by the beauty of the six-year-old church. The commanding officer—an incorrect local tradition says it was Stoneman himself—forbade any vandalism and directed his men to mind their language. But the church's red carpet proved too tempting to resist. The next morning, the men persuaded their commander to let them take the carpet for saddle blankets.[41]

⸺

April 22 found Colonel William J. Palmer's cavalrymen still ranging along the Catawba River and awaiting orders from Gillem. This marked the fifth day of the brigade's occupation of the Lincolnton and Newton areas. (At that moment, Jefferson Davis was in Charlotte, Johnston and Sherman had agreed to a cease-fire, Stoneman had reached Knoxville, and Gillem was marching on Howard's Gap.) During their stay, the cavalrymen had secured or raided at least eleven crossing points along a fifty-mile stretch of the Catawba. They had also destroyed two key bridges and paroled as many as two thousand Confederates. In the process, Palmer's raiders clogged the westward route of escape for Joe Johnston's Army of Tennessee and also cut a key supply line by destroying the Charlotte and South Carolina Railroad bridge at Nations Ford.

While his men conducted business as usual throughout Lincoln and Catawba counties, Palmer continued to ponder his dilemma. He still had not heard from Gillem, and Beck's party had left only the day before. Whose orders should he follow, Gillem's, Thomas's, or Sherman's? At least one thing was clear: the brigade would have to leave Lincolnton soon, especially after the news of the armistice and Lincoln's assassination. Deciding to follow Gillem's most recent orders, Palmer instructed his brigades to march the next morning. The wisdom of this was borne out when Gillem's confirmation of the orders arrived the next day.

Early on April 23, 1865, the men of the Tenth Michigan, Fifteenth Pennsylvania, and Twelfth Ohio cavalry regiments struck their tents. Their objective was Rutherfordton, forty-five miles to the west. It was an uneventful march under blue skies through a "poor country." The next day, Palmer's brigade occupied Rutherfordton. This was the third time in as many days Federal troopers had descended on the town, Brown's brigade having spent the night of April 21–22 there and Miller's brigade having passed through on April 23. A crossroads town, Rutherfordton possessed strategic value. Situated near several Blue Ridge gaps, it was a good location for guarding Gillem's rear, and it served as a springboard for future operations. Arriving at nine o'clock in the morning, the brigade camped in and around the town.[42]

Miller's and Brown's cavalrymen had left their mark on Rutherfordton. "It is a very ordinary town, and the two days' stay of the Tennesseans did it no good," claimed a Pennsylvania trooper. "They stole everything they could carry off, put pistols to the heads of citizens, persuaded them to give up their pocketbooks, and even took the rings from ladies' fingers. The sympathy we used to feel for the loyal Tennesseans is being rapidly transferred to the enemy." A Pennsylvania cavalryman blamed Unionist Tennesseans out to avenge years of persecution by their Confederate neighbors. "There were some Tennessee (Union) troops that were so badly demoralized they were no use as soldiers and a disgrace to the name," he wrote. "They stole everything that was loose and some things that were not loose."[43]

⌒*⌒

As sunlight splashed across the now-greening valleys and misty peaks of the Blue Ridge on Monday, April 24, 1865, Alvan Gillem mounted his horse. It promised to be another warm, lovely spring day. Riding northward on the Asheville road with his staff, a flag of truce waving overhead, Gillem was en route to a meeting he hoped would end the raid. Meanwhile, Confederate general James Martin rode south from Asheville toward Hendersonville. The two parties met about five miles south of Asheville, near Busbee. A roadside tree stump served as their table. By all accounts, the men were cordial as they quickly agreed to observe the armistice. Then Gillem made a proposal. "I announced to him [Martin] my decision to march to Greeneville," Gillem recalled, "and at the same time suggested to him that it would be a great relief to the people if he could supply me with three days' rations, and thus avoid the necessity of stripping the citizens of their scant supplies." Martin liked the idea and agreed to furnish Gillem nine thousand rations but was unable to offer any forage. In return, Martin asked Gillem to return the artillery unit Slater had captured, since it was taken while the Sherman-Johnston agreement was in force. "Of course I declined restoring the battery," Gillem wrote. The two men nevertheless parted on a positive note, agreeing to dine together that night.[44]

With peace at hand, Gillem ordered Palmer to march westward. Martin rode off to gather cornmeal and meat. When the citizens learned of Martin's requisition, they thought it "almost impossible" but somehow managed it. "No doubt Gen Martin collected them [the rations] with less inconvenience to the inhabitants than my troops would have caused in helping themselves," Gillem wrote. That evening, Gillem and his staff joined Martin for supper. Martin rode off afterward with the understanding that the Federals would pass through Asheville the next day on their way to Tennessee. He also believed that Gillem had agreed to honor the truce, including the provision that the Federals would give forty-eight hours' notice if it became necessary to resume hostilities. Gillem left with a different understanding. "I do not remember having heard the question raised concerning forty-eight hours notice in case the truce should be ended," he later explained.[45]

The next morning went as planned. The Federals rode peacefully into Asheville, the most important town in western North Carolina. Established in 1795, it was a rapidly growing town largely known for tourism. Each summer, visitors from across the South flocked to Asheville and neighboring Hendersonville, Warm Springs, and Waynesville to enjoy the beauty of the mountains, the cool climate, and the area's numerous mineral springs. The war brought many refugees, including the families of some well-known Confederates, to these resort communities. Despite the town's remote location, the war was all too present for Asheville and its fifteen hundred inhabitants. The town was the center of Rebel sentiment in western North Carolina. Andrew Johnson called it a "damned secession hole in the mountains." Asheville and the surrounding area had contributed twenty-one companies, sixteen colonels, and two generals to the Confederacy, not to mention Governor Zebulon Vance. The town had once hosted a Confederate armory, and it remained the site of a Confederate hospital and four training camps, making gray a common color around town.[46]

"They [the Federals] passed thru our little village very quietly on the 25th," wrote an Asheville resident. Another noted, "A large force of Yankee cavalry passed through as quietly as if they were not on hostile soil." However, a few moments of tension occurred once the Federals and Confederates came face to face. "The enemy had stacked arms in accordance with the truce and rebel soldiers lined both sides of the streets, the soldiers on both sides guying [ridiculing] each other," wrote the historian of the Thirteenth Tennessee. Although some Federals and Rebels traded insults, guards from both sides, standing at posts throughout town, managed to maintain order. The Union cavalrymen were ordered to keep moving and remain in formation; they paused only to draw twelve pounds of cereal and ten pounds of meat apiece. Even so, the men could not help noticing the town's fortifications and rebellious spirit. General Gillem concluded that capturing it would have been easy. After the Federal soldiers disappeared, an eerie calm fell over Asheville. "A *sad quiet* reigned supreme," one of Martin's staff officers recalled. "A change in an hour from the busy, exciting scenes of a *besieged town* to a *quiet* that was almost painful because of its uncertainty."[47]

If the residents of Asheville breathed a collective sigh of relief upon the peaceful departure of Gillem's raiders, it was premature. Unbeknownst to the townspeople, the armistice Martin and Gillem had agreed to was about to expire. After Sherman and Johnston inked their agreement at the Bennett farm on April 18, a Union staff officer took a copy from Raleigh to Washington, D.C., for President Andrew Johnson's approval. The officer delivered it three days later, while the nation's capital was still mourning Lincoln's death. At Grant's suggestion, President Johnson and his cabinet met that evening, reviewed the agreement, and unanimously rejected it. They were outraged that Sherman had drafted a surrender document that delved into political as well as military matters. Secretary of War Edwin Stanton ordered Grant to travel to Raleigh and personally inform Sherman that his agreement was disapproved, and that Sherman was to offer Johnston the same terms Lee had received at Appomattox Court House. In the meantime, Sherman was to resume hostilities.[48]

Grant arrived in Raleigh early on April 24, the same day Martin and Gillem met outside Asheville. Pulling Sherman into a private conference, the general in chief delivered Stanton's orders. Sherman immediately sent dispatches to Johnston ending the truce and demanding his surrender under the Appomattox terms. He also notified Johnston that hostilities would resume in forty-eight hours and likewise informed subordinates elsewhere in his command, including Major General James H. Wilson and General Thomas.[49]

Thomas immediately notified Stoneman of the changed situation. Stoneman in turn transmitted a message to Gillem on April 24: "I have just received a telegram from Genl. Thomas, informing me that the terms of surrender of Johns[t]on to Sherman have been disapproved by the President and Sherman is ordered to push his military advantages. The cavalry under your command will do all in its power to bring Johns[t]on to better terms. For this purpose, the most strenuous efforts will be made to destroy his communications and all sources of supplies. Charlotte should be destroyed if possible, and also the Railroad from and including the R.R. bridge over the Catawba river, north of Greensboro, and the country east of the railroad and north of the Catawba river laid waste."

Stoneman also directed Gillem to establish his headquarters at Asheville and to assign Tillson's division to guard the approaches to town. He reserved Gillem's Cavalry Division for field operations. Stoneman also took the opportunity to make the third command change of the raid. "I am directed by Genl. Thomas," he told Gillem, "to give you a leave of absence to go to Nashville to attend the session of the Legislature." William J. Palmer would assume command of the Cavalry Division.[50]

It would take time for Stoneman's message to reach Gillem near Asheville. Meanwhile, Gillem's Cavalry Division continued marching west on April 25. From Asheville, the column crossed Bull Creek and various other streams, riding along what Frankenberry called a "rough road leading among the mountains." It bivouacked for the night about ten miles north of Asheville. The next morning, the Federals trotted into Marshall, the seat of Madison County. There, the war found them again. Reconnaissance showed the road by the French Broad River was blocked, so Gillem began looking for an alternate route. However, that became unnecessary when a courier arrived with Stoneman's orders. The news spread quickly. "Turned back," Birdsall wrote. "We hear that Gen. Vaughn had broken the armistice." Added a Tennessee trooper, "There was more or less disappointment at the idea of turning our backs instead of our faces toward

Tennessee, but we had become somewhat accustomed by this time to doing not what we pleased but what it pleased 'Uncle Sam' to have us do."[51]

Gillem had good reason to be frustrated with Stoneman's orders. Since his departure eight days ago, the district commander had clearly lost touch with the Cavalry Division. The raiders were now one hundred miles from Charlotte, well beyond striking range. Stoneman's order to destroy the railroad bridge over the Catawba River north of Greensboro was equally perplexing, for not only was Greensboro even more distant than Charlotte, but the Catawba ran nowhere near the area. Besides, the raiders had already destroyed the key bridges north of Greensboro. Perhaps Stoneman had confused the Catawba with another river. In any event, Gillem understood Stoneman's order to destroy Johnston's communications and sources of supplies. He would start with the town he had just left.

Before sending the division back to Asheville, Gillem ordered Lieutenant James Reagan's artillery battery to Greeneville with a company of the Eighth Tennessee Cavalry as escort. While the artillery's departure reduced the division's firepower, it enabled the column to move faster and respond quicker, which Gillem deemed necessary at that point. Gillem's part in the campaign also ended on April 26. In obedience to Stoneman's orders, he placed Brown in temporary command until Palmer could join the division. Then he rode to Greeneville. He was in such a hurry that he did not wait on Reagan's battery. Reaching Greeneville late that afternoon, well before Reagan's guns, Gillem wrote a brief report to update Stoneman and Thomas.[52]

Meanwhile, Brown turned the rest of the force around and sent it swooping down on Asheville. It attacked just after dusk on Wednesday, April 26. The soldiers, who had been spiraling out of control in recent days, now unleashed their frustrations on Asheville. They were out to avenge Lincoln's murder and finish the war once and for all. "Heard that Abe Lincoln was assassinated," wrote trooper Henry Birdsall. "Caused considerable excitement among the Soldiers. They feel more like fighting than ever."[53]

Asheville was about to become the scene of the worst episode of the entire raid. Brown's brigade led the way. The troopers surrounded the town, demanded its surrender, and then moved in when the demand was refused. Martin tried to hold, but the Union cavalrymen simply overwhelmed the Confederates. "No one was prepared for so speedy a return after seeing them [the Federals] pass through the day before[,] the 25th of April[,] under a flag of truce," Martin wrote. A few Confederates fought back, but it was token resistance. Federal cavalrymen, including two companies of the Eleventh Michigan, crushed the Confederate forces of Porter's battery. Among the charging Federals was Henry Birdsall, who had a rough ride. "My horse fell with me and sprained my knee severely," he wrote. Other would-be defenders sniped at the raiders near Mine Hole Gap. The amount of resistance varied from point to point; signalman Frankenberry wrote, "No resistance and only a few shots fired," while a Thirteenth Tennessee man thought the Confederates put up a stiff fight. "We opened fire[,] driving in his outposts," the Tennessee trooper recalled, "and after considerable skirmishing, our command passed back through the town." In the process of overrunning Asheville, the Federals reportedly captured seven artillery pieces.[54]

Once Asheville fell, the pillaging began. "We were surprised and almost panic stricken by their return as a devastating mob, to capture and sack our unprotected homes," one of Martin's staff officers wrote. Federal cavalrymen barged into homes, tearing plaster from walls and ceilings, ripping open mattresses, and rifling through clothing in a mad search for hidden valuables. A prominent local Unionist managed to obtain a guard, but the detail got lost and ended up protecting the property of a diehard Confederate while the Unionist's house was ransacked. Other homeowners sought guards but did not receive them in time. "Several private homes were robbed of everything," a local testified. He went on to praise the Eleventh Kentucky for guarding his end of town but warned that the Michigan regiments "stole every piece of gold and silver and watch in the village." While that was certainly an exaggeration, Asheville nevertheless suffered the most harrowing evening in its history. "Through the night pandemonium held sway," an eyewitness wrote, "and Asheville will never again hear such sounds and witness such scenes—pillage of every character, and destruction the most wanton."[55]

"I have heard of no worse plundering any where than was permitted in & near Asheville by General Brown—I believe no one escaped entirely," agreed General Martin. Martin himself was arrested and taken to Brown. Less than an hour later, he was allowed to return home under the care of a Federal officer. "When we reached the house," Martin wrote, "I found Mrs Martin & my daughter going into the house with a squad of Federal soldiers holding candles . . . for them to examine all the trunks &c for such things as they fancied & to such things they helped themselves. The officer ordered them out of the house immediately & they obeyed. The same men had been before or were immediately afterward detailed as a guard for my house, but the officer remained also till the troops left. This I believe was about the experience of all the houses in town, where the ladies remained and faced the US soldiers."[56]

Gunfire awoke Confederate staff officer James Ray, who had gone to bed early in an Asheville boardinghouse. Heading toward the town square to investigate, Ray ran into Dr. Walsh Morrison. "He told me the Federals had violated the terms of the truce and were shooting at everybody they saw," Ray recalled. "He advised me to save my horse, and with this in mind I started in the direction of Beaucatcher." Ray did not get far before he saw cavalrymen firing pistols and yelling. He turned his horse into some woods and made for the mountains. Hiding out through the night, he listened helplessly to the "appalling sound" of Federal soldiers in Asheville. "They made the night hideous with their yells," he wrote. Ray was one of only a handful of Confederates who escaped.[57]

According to Federal records, the cavalrymen captured several hundred prisoners, including two hundred by the Eleventh Michigan alone. Brown saw to that by placing a cordon of pickets around Asheville. Inside the picket line, troopers randomly arrested citizens and locked them up in two warehouses. "Such a time as the unprotected citizens of Asheville had! It is almost past imagination," a witness wrote. "Every home save one was inva[d]ed[,] robbed and some of them nearly torn to pieces. All men and boys of any size were arrested and put under guard in two stores. All were jammed together, abusively treated and neither age nor calling respected. Nor, in most cases, was sex shown consideration." The captives included the mayor and the Reverend Branch Merrimon. The elderly Merrimon spent the night in confinement, then was forced to march toward Knoxville the next morning with the other prisoners and the sick and disabled cavalrymen.[58]

Brown's men caught some legitimate prisoners as well, but under questionable circumstances. "They captured Col [John] Palmer and several of his officers with a flag of truce in their hands," wrote an eyewitness. "What do you think of such treachery?" The Federals also burned the armory and several adjoining structures. The homes of General Martin and the Reverend Robert H. Chapman may also have been destroyed, but sources disagree. One resident noted that the Federals "threatened to burn the whole town."[59]

Twelve-year-old George F. Robertson, son of a Confederate officer who had moved to Asheville from Greene County, Tennessee, never forgot that day. He saw that "an ominous cloud of dust was rising above the trees down the French

Broad River, north of town, and in a very short time we understood the situation." The cloud, of course, marked the hostile return of raiders who had been so friendly before. "They seemed almost to spring from the ground," Robertson wrote. "They were at every door at the same time, pounding for admission. When inside, they rushed all over the house, their sabers rattling against the floors with noisy clanging, their spurs rasping, heavy boots thumping like the stamping of horses in a livery stable, all conspired to make a bedlam." The Robertsons were luckier than most, as the cavalrymen took only some dried beef after a thorough search of their house. Fortunately, they did not find additional meat and flour, which were hidden in a closet behind the sifter, rolling pin, and kitchen table.[60]

Not surprisingly, the Federals also "concluded to take all the horses, mules, and buggies in town," according to a citizen. At one home, cavalrymen confiscated two animals and left two old, broken-down mares behind. Later, the owner of the animals heard a rumor that the Federals had decided to return all the stock taken after Johnston's surrender, which had occurred on the afternoon of April 26. The owner soon learned that was not quite true. When she found a Federal colonel riding one of her horses and asked him about the rumor, he told her he had decided to keep the horse because he captured it before hearing of the surrender. The colonel did return one of her mules but also decided to take the horse she was riding. On her way home, she met a cavalry squad carrying dispatches. Its men took her provisions and a bag of corn but fortunately left the mule alone. The mule later proved a boon to her farm.[61]

In the midst of these tragic scenes, some Federal soldiers performed acts of kindness. Four cavalrymen stopped at Martha Marlowe Sales's home and asked for water. "Though naturally tense and furtive in their manner, they proved not only harmless, but courteous and appreciative," recalled a local. One of the men even gave Mrs. Sales a pen as a token of gratitude. Frank Frankenberry was disgusted by the "plundering and robbing" of Asheville by "villains" in blue. The signalman refused to take part in his comrades' misdeeds, spending a quiet night instead at the home of a Dr. Hilliard. The next morning, he choked a "thieving" Eleventh Michigan cavalryman whom he caught raiding the stable where Frankenberry was having his mule shoed. Afterward, he posted a guard at the stable so it wouldn't happen again.[62]

The beneficiaries of the raid were the blacks, who now realized they were free. Most apparently decided to leave Asheville. "There were hundreds and hundreds of the freedmen and women and children in an almost interminable procession," recalled Robertson, "going by two's even as some of their liberators had gone not many days before but in a decidedly better organization." Some rode horses piled high with bundles of possessions. Most sang and laughed, including one old woman, her bonnet hanging carelessly over her back. She sang, "Glory, Glory! We's free, we's free! Glory, hallelujah!"[63]

During and after the occupation, the people of Asheville complained to authorities about their losses. One resident informed General Martin that Federal soldiers had taken all her silver and other valuables. Martin took her appeal to General Brown and asked that her property be returned. Brown agreed but did not deliver on his word. "Some very hard stories [are] told of Genl. Brown but I think I had better say nothing more," Martin wrote. Martin also suffered personal losses from the raid. He wrote to the District of East Tennessee asking that he either be compensated or that his property be restored. Martin included his staff officers in the request. A man named C. W. Polk joined the chorus, asking for the return of his horses. Gillem simply referred these inquiries to his subordinates and asked "whether or not Private Proppery was respected." No records indicate that any action was taken in these matters.[64]

To this day, the raiders' failure to give forty-eight hours' notice before attacking Asheville remains controversial. General Martin protested this oversight, but Gillem never admitted any fault in the matter. He had several good reasons for that. First of all, Brown did provide an advance warning to Martin, albeit a brief one. Second, the forty-eight-hour notice provision in Sherman's and Johnston's agreements technically applied only to them, not to their subordinate commanders. Third, the raiders actually attacked Asheville more than forty-eight hours after Sherman notified Johnston that hostilities were resuming. Thus, if anyone was to blame for a failure to give notice, it was Johnston, who should have informed other Confederate commanders that the armistice had ended. If the Federals had any culpability, it had more to do with the fact that they attacked Asheville after Johnston surrendered, an event both Brown and Gillem were unaware of at the time. Still, General Palmer held the opinion that the Federals had erred. "On further reflection," he told Martin, "I have come to the conclusion that our men should have given you, under all the circumstances, notice of the termination of the armistice, and that in honor we cannot profit by any failure to give you this notice." At Palmer's order, all the officers and men captured and paroled by General Brown on April 27 and 28 were released from their paroles.[65] His gesture offered scant consolation for the townspeople, since he did nothing to return private property.

Residents also found little solace in the modest Federal casualty list from the attack on Asheville. No Federal soldiers were killed or wounded. At least two bluejackets deserted during the attack, and two Federals from the Tenth Michigan Cavalry disappeared and were presumed captured.[66]

Fortunately for Asheville, the end of the ordeal was at hand. Colonel Palmer was about to receive orders that would completely change the purpose of the raid.

⁂

A week after he arrived in Charlotte, Jefferson Davis decided it was time to move on. Johnston's surrender of all Confederate soldiers in the Carolinas, Georgia, and Florida made flight inevitable. On April 26—the night Brown's cavalrymen returned to Asheville—Davis set out for the Trans-Mississippi via South Carolina and Georgia. Most of the cabinet members and a five-brigade cavalry escort commanded by Confederate secretary of war (and major general) John C. Breckinridge rode with the president. A long wagon train bounced along behind them carrying supplies, the Confederate archives, and part of the Confederate treasury. Brigadier General Basil Duke commanded part of the escort but was not sure what Davis had in mind. "It was perfectly manifest to every one else," he wrote, "that there was no hope of further successful resistance."[67]

From Charlotte, Davis's party marched toward a spot familiar to Stoneman's raiders. According to a rumor in the Federal ranks, Wheeler's cavalry had tried to capture the Tuckaseegee Ford and rail bridge so Davis could cross there. Major Herrick's First Battalion of the Twelfth Ohio Cavalry prevented the move by capturing the ford and destroying the bridge. In truth, Davis never planned to use the Tuckaseegee crossing. Instead, he crossed the Catawba River at Nations Ford—but on a pontoon ferry, since Moderwell's battalion of the Twelfth Ohio had destroyed the railroad bridge. "What a sight to see Jeff Davis and Breckinridge and the Cabinet standing on the pontoon," wrote an eyewitness. "The cause has gone up. God only knows what will be the end of this."[68]

The column pressed on to Yorkville, just over the South Carolina border. "We moved through South Carolina with great deliberation," recalled Basil Duke. After leaving Yorkville, the presidential column camped along the Broad River on the evening of April 28. The next morning, the party crossed the river and traveled to Unionville, where General Braxton Bragg joined it. During their passage through South Carolina, the fugitives were often greeted with cheers and given fresh milk and food. These gestures moved and even encouraged the president, but he also realized that Federal forces were in hot pursuit. As Davis's column crossed the Saluda River and kept marching, the Confederates expected Stoneman's raiders to attack at any moment.[69]

On April 27, George Stoneman received a startling telegram from General Thomas in Nashville. Thomas's message quoted a dispatch from Major General Henry W. Halleck in Richmond warning that Jefferson Davis and other "rebel chiefs" were moving south in wagons loaded with millions in specie. The telegram also included an order from Secretary of War Stanton directing the army to "spare no exertion to stop Davis and his plunder. Push the enemy as hard as you can in every direction." At the close of the telegram, Thomas added his own orders: "I want you to carry out these instructions as thoroughly as possible." A second telegram from Thomas clarified his intentions. Stoneman was to send three brigades of cavalry "across the mountains into South Carolina to the westward of Charlotte and toward Anderson," South Carolina, to catch "Jeff. Davis, or some of his treasure." The exception was Slater's Eleventh Michigan Cavalry Regiment, which Thomas ordered to Chattanooga. Finally, in keeping with Grant's instructions, Thomas directed Stoneman to obey orders only from himself or Grant, even though Sherman was Thomas's superior. This probably stemmed from Sherman's April 18 attempt to direct the Cavalry Division's movements, which had sown confusion to no advantage.[70]

George Stoneman wasted no time. He ordered Palmer to assemble the Cavalry Division at Asheville, cross the mountains into South Carolina, and follow the Saluda River to Anderson. From there, the division was to scout toward Augusta, Georgia. "The object of sending you to this point is to intercept Jeff. Davis and his party," Stoneman wrote. "If you can hear of Davis, follow him to the ends of the earth, if possible, and never give him up." If the separated brigades could not be quickly assembled, then General Brown was not to wait on Palmer and the First Brigade. Stoneman wanted him to push on with the Second and Third brigades. Palmer would catch up later. "Time is precious," Stoneman wrote. The only part of Thomas's orders Stoneman balked at was the Eleventh Michigan's transfer to Chattanooga. He told Thomas that he would send the regiment as soon as possible but that he needed it for now. Stoneman also ordered Davis Tillson to send his infantry to Asheville to "clear that region of all rebels" and to "push a portion over the Blue Ridge and keep up communication with the cavalry." Thomas approved Stoneman's dispositions.[71]

The new orders first reached the raiders at Asheville. On Friday, April 28, Miller's brigades departed town and began their pursuit of Jefferson Davis. "I was the last man to leave Asheville," Frank Frankenberry claimed. "We fired the arsenal and some villain fired the 'Female College,' a shame on the vandal." The cavalrymen marched south on the Howard's Gap road. "Everything seems to indicate that we are going into South Carolina," wrote Michigan trooper Birdsall. That evening, the cavalry column camped and enjoyed victuals near Hendersonville. Some of the men managed to stable their horses. The next day, Brown's and Miller's brigades marched to Brevard, which a cavalryman described as "the [Transylvania] county seat and not much town as yet." The South Carolina state line now lay within easy reach.[72]

At seven o'clock in the morning on April 30, Brown's and Miller's men left Brevard for Saluda Gap, a key pass through the Blue Ridge Mountains. From there, they would march to Pickensville. Brown expected to meet Palmer at Anderson. By Frankenberry's count, this was the fifth time the raiders had crossed the Blue Ridge. They were rewarded with a "lush magnificent view." The column soon entered South Carolina. A Tennessee trooper explained, "We did not at that time have many scruples about despoiling the country," given South Carolina's role as the "cradle of secession." Three miles below the state line, the troopers stopped at Caesar's Head, a 3,266-foot peak famous for its resemblance to a human head. In the shadow of the strange outcropping, the cavalrymen were paid for the first time in months. Frankenberry was pleased with both the greenbacks and the vista. "Halt on top of a rock called Caesar's Head and have the grandest[,] most magnificent view of the country and mts. I ever had. . . . Left the initials of my name on a rock with HdQrs Stoneman's Cav 30th, 65," he wrote. From there, the march continued downward into South Carolina's Piedmont. At seven that night, the raiders camped near Pickensville, where they were forced to leave a man after bushwhackers shot him.[73]

To the east, Palmer's First Brigade was the last unit to receive Stoneman's April 27 orders. In fact, Palmer had yet to receive all of the orders issued before that date. Until late on April 25, he was still operating under the assumption that he was to hold Rutherfordton and the nearby Blue Ridge gaps. Then Gillem's April 24 orders arrived. Reassured by his meeting with Martin that the raiders' rear was safe, Gillem ordered Palmer to march west down the Little Tennessee River toward Waynesville and Quallatown to "clear the mountains south of Asheville."[74]

Palmer's occupation of Rutherfordton thus ended on April 26. The Twelfth Ohio marched first, having been the rear regiment during the last movement. "The Sun arose clear and bright. And found us still in the pleasant grove," wrote an Ohio cavalryman. "We cooked our Breakfasts which consisted of Coffee[,] fried Ham & Slap Jack Molassesed." After the Ohioans filled their bellies and cared for their horses, orders arrived instructing them to be ready to march at ten that morning. They departed on schedule. In due course, the Federal troopers passed through Rutherfordton and continued west, halting at dusk after logging twenty miles. The Blue Ridge Mountains loomed, stark against the setting sun. Ahead lay Hickory Nut Gap, a mountain pass between Swannanoa and Howard's gaps.[75]

The Tenth Michigan Cavalry followed the Twelfth Ohio. The blue-clad riders were treated to a breathtaking vista along the Rutherfordton-Asheville turnpike. "Leaving Rutherfordton, the traveller begins to enter the mountains in reality," an earlier observer wrote. "The road winds along the banks of Broad River, crossing it several times,—the river foaming and boiling over rocks and rapids all along the course. Occasional glimpses are caught of the distant mountains, and every little while the road winds along the edge of a frightful precipice." The Fifteenth Pennsylvania brought up the rear, enabling Fred Antes to spend a leisurely morning in camp until orders to move arrived and the packing commenced. Mounting up, the Pennsylvanians left Rutherfordton beginning at one that afternoon.[76]

On April 27—the day Stoneman ordered the pursuit of Jefferson Davis— Palmer's brigade marched west to Hickory Nut Gap. The Twelfth Ohio Cavalry moved first, with the exception of Companies C and D, which had left two hours earlier to clear the road and repair bridges. The balance of the brigade followed around sunrise, the Fifteenth Pennsylvania and the Twelfth Ohio taking different roads. The Fifteenth's journey was memorable for the excellent road and some of the most remarkable scenery the men had seen.[77]

The road the Pennsylvanians followed was among the oldest in the Appalachians. The centerpiece was Hickory Nut Gap. Six miles long from its eastern end at Lake Lure to its western entrance in Buncombe County, the gap ranged in width from 200 feet to a half-mile. Looming above it was 2,280-foot-tall Chimney Rock. Nearby, Hickory Nut Falls sent cold, clear mountain water tumbling 400 feet down the mountain. Close by was Bat Cave, a dark and forbidding home to legions of bats. With hiding places galore, Hickory Nut Gap offered deserters and escaped slaves a safe haven.[78]

Since the local defense unit, Lieutenant Colonel C. L. Harris's Sixty-ninth Home Guard Battalion, was nowhere to be seen, Palmer's men took in the vistas at their leisure. "Warm and pleasant," wrote Sergeant Colton of the Fifteenth Pennsylvania. "Passed through Hickory Nut Gap and saw one of the most beautiful of scenes." Colonel Betts was equally impressed. "Hickory falls . . . a sheet of water falling from the top of the Mtn[,] was witnessed with much pleasure," he wrote. "Our march to-day was through the grandest scenery we have looked on through our term of service," agreed another Pennsylvanian. "It was so imposing that the usual chat of the riders was hushed, as they gazed with awe on the sight. As we rode we plucked the fragrant magnolia from the forest trees, and the wish of all was to stay longer with it."[79]

Having secured Hickory Nut Gap by early afternoon, Palmer allowed his men to bivouac. Campsites sprang up along the road. The advance halted near Asheville, some troopers camping at the foot of the mountain along the Broad River and others as far as the future site of Biltmore Estate. Meanwhile, the Twelfth Ohio Cavalry crossed the mountain safely and camped along Mill Creek six miles west of Hendersonville.[80] Some of Palmer's men reined in at Bedford Sherrill's farm and tavern, a popular stagecoach stop at Hickory Nut Gap's western entrance. When an officer rode his horse onto the porch to arrange lodging, the Sherrills were ready. They had hidden their hams behind a wall in the house and covered the fresh carpentry by hanging Mrs. Sherrill's hoop skirts on the wall. The Sherrills fed the raiders breakfast and reportedly gave the interlopers more than they bargained for. Local lore has it that "one of the daughters shook her stockings over eggs frying for the soldiers, saying, 'They can eat the dust off my feet and they'll think it's pepper!'"[81]

Around the campfires that night, there was consensus that the cavalrymen were going home. "The war is considered over!" wrote one Pennsylvanian. "Everyone rejoiced at the prospect of going back to Knoxville and perhaps, soon, home." Ohioan Joseph Banks agreed. "By this time we were convinced beyond a doubt that we were en rout for Knoxville Tenn and that we were within 3 days march of it," he wrote. "We were well mounted at this time and [had] provisions enough to See us over the rough looking Blew ridge Mountains which lay heaped before us." Others questioned the rumors. "We had more flying reports than would pack the Red Mill," wrote cavalryman Fred Antes.[82]

The skeptics were right. A courier found Palmer at Hickory Nut Gap and gave him Stoneman's outdated April 24 orders announcing the end of the armistice and instructing the cavalry to "do all in its power to bring [Johnston] to better terms." The news that the raid was not yet over "was some disappointment to the men," wrote a Pennsylvania trooper. "The greatest desire was to get letters from home, but to offset that, Stoneman was gone, and Gillem, who had asked for and received a leave of absence, had gone too, and our Colonel, as Brevet Brigadier General, commanded the whole division." Unaware that Johnston had surrendered to Sherman on April 26 and that Stoneman had already issued him new orders, Palmer began pondering how best to use his new command to destroy Confederate communications and supplies toward Charlotte and the Catawba River.[83] He completed his plans while bivouacked on the Esmeralda estate below Hickory Nut Falls. (The falls made such an impression on Palmer that he returned to the site with his daughters thirty-six years later.) Since the Twelfth Ohio had already cleared the Blue Ridge, Palmer decided to send the regiment straight to Yorkville, South Carolina, not far from Nations Ford. The Fifteenth Pennsylvania and the Tenth Michigan would meet the Ohioans there by retracing its steps eastward, then turning south. From Yorkville, the brigade could strike Johnston's supply lines at Charlotte.[84]

Palmer's expanded responsibilities also dropped a problem squarely in his lap. He was well aware that Brown's and Miller's troopers had not behaved well during the raid, so the general spelled out his expectations. "No property of any kind will be taken from citizens," he wrote. The only exceptions were subsistence stores, forage for animals, and the horses necessary to mount the command, in which case unserviceable animals were to be left in exchange. "You will be particularly careful, after entering South Carolina, that these orders are observed," Palmer ordered. "This is absolutely necessary in order to preserve the discipline of your command."[85]

Reveille sounded early in the camps of Palmer's brigade on April 28, 1865.

Mounting up, the cavalrymen turned around and marched back through Hickory Nut Gap along the Rutherfordton-Asheville turnpike. "Again on the War Path," a cavalryman wrote, but that was not quite accurate because the journey was uneventful and the troopers appreciated a second chance to see the gap. About sundown, they arrived at Rutherfordton and settled into their old campsites. Their arrival did not improve the humor of local residents. "So we returned to Rutherfordton where the citizens furnished horses and corn—not willingly," a Federal recalled. "They supposed we had left for good, and they had brought back from the mountains where they were concealed, and we got back in time to get them." The citizens also had to supply the cavalrymen with rations. "I got some bread baked at camp," one man wrote. Meanwhile, Palmer's staff made plans for the next day. Captain Henry McAllister, Jr., the brigade's assistant adjutant general, informed Colonel Betts that the raiders would move at six-thirty in the morning, the Tenth Michigan Cavalry in the lead and the Fifteenth Pennsylvania following.[86]

Down the mountain, the Twelfth Ohio moved south. Word of the change in plans was slower to reach the Ohioans, so when they tumbled from their bedrolls the men were still happily under the impression that Knoxville was their destination. After breakfast, Private Joseph Banks saddled his horse and mounted up, "filled with joy from the expectation of Soon arriveing at Head Quarters where we might not only receive a fiew days rest but the Idea of hearing from our friends again which we Had been deprived of for so long." As the men sat on their horses awaiting the order to move out, the news came that the armistice was canceled and South Carolina was their next destination. A few of "Stoneman's Uhlans"—a complimentary reference to the famous Polish light cavalrymen of the same name—even liked the idea of another mission. "They 'sullenly rejoiced' that the truce was broken, and that they could have another opportunity of avenging the foul crime at Washington," wrote the Twelfth Ohio's Frank Mason. "Carbines were reloaded, and . . . [the Twelfth,] again on a war footing," rode south.[87]

The Ohioans marched through Hendersonville and then crossed the mountains via Saluda Gap one day ahead of Brown and Miller. "We struck the foot of a mountain about 10 oclock," Banks wrote. "Assended it and on reaching the Summit we could gaise out over the deserted lands of South Carollinia as far as the Eye would carry and I must confess the Sene was most delightfull." As it marched back down the mountain, the regiment drew a crowd. "We presented a beautifull display to the wondering and amased Spectators at the foot of the mountain," Banks explained. "Our bright blew uniform and the flags Could be seen plainly winding around the Short Curves and among the dry brown clifts." Curious locals peppered the soldiers with questions such as "What regiment do youeuns all belong to?" and "How's the weather up there, Company E?" At two o'clock in the afternoon, the cavalrymen stopped, ate, and rested. Then they "pushed on at a swinging trot for many weary hours," Ohioan Frank Mason recalled. The eastward march finally ended at midnight. The troopers dismounted and collapsed beside a fence, carelessly leaving their horses standing in the road.[88]

Dawn on April 29 reminded the Ohioans just how rough the previous day's journey had been. "When day light appeared," Joseph Banks wrote, "our horses presented anything else th[a]n a pleasing Sight[. T]hey were Mud from there Hoofs to there Back bones." The animals and the men were as hungry as they were dirty, but Colonel Bentley's timetable did not allow for breakfast. Eastward the Twelfth Ohio rode, mostly through a pine forest that seemed to stretch endlessly. At ten that morning, the column arrived at the old Cowpens battlefield, where on January 17, 1781, Brigadier General Daniel Morgan's militia and Continentals had crushed Lieutenant Colonel Banastre Tarleton's British force in one of most lopsided battles of the Revolutionary War. The Union cavalrymen were captivated as they rode single file past the battleground's monuments. They then marched until sunset and camped on the west side of the Broad River at Smith's Ford. There, the cavalrymen captured ten Rebels from Davis's cavalry escort, who said that the Confederate president had the night before camped beside the Broad some twenty miles south at Pinckneyville Ferry.[89]

Marching east parallel to the Twelfth Ohio but still in North Carolina, the Fifteenth Pennsylvania and the Tenth Michigan cavalry regiments made progress on April 29 as well. The men left Rutherfordton at seven that morning and marched to a point near Shelby, North Carolina.[90] There, they learned that plans had changed again; Stoneman's April 27 orders initiating the pursuit of Jefferson Davis had arrived at last. Palmer immediately recalled the Fifteenth Pennsylvania and the Tenth Michigan to the Mooresboro area, telling them to "make all possible inquiry into the movement of Jeff Davis who without doubt left Charlotte last Wednesday." The orders found Sergeant Colton as he sat to enjoy a dinner of chicken and fresh vegetables from "an old rebel's" garden. "We just got well fixed for the night when boots and saddles sounded and to our disgust we moved out[,] taking the back track," Colton wrote.[91]

Back in their Mooresboro camps, the men learned why they had turned around for the second time in two days. Copies of a wanted poster were pressed into their hands:

$100,000 Reward in Gold

Headquarters, Cavalry Corps, Mil. Div. Miss.
Macon, Ga., April 28, 1865

One hundred thousand dollars reward will be paid to any person or persons, who will apprehend and deliver Jefferson Davis to any military authority of the United States. Several million dollars of specie reported to be with him will become the property of the captors.

J. H. Wilson, Major General[92]

It was Sunday, April 30, 1865. Stoneman's raiders marched southwest on their new mission.

Part Three

Palmer's Raid
and the End of the War

The chief executive of the Confederacy, Jefferson Davis, eluded Palmer's raiders for almost two weeks until another Federal unit finally captured him.

Chapter 11

We Would Have Liked to Spare Them

The End of Stoneman's Raid: May 1–November 25, 1865

Jefferson Davis was captured on May 10, 1865, but not by George Stone-man's raiders. It was not due to a lack of trying. The raiders started their pursuit in a great spot—right on the heels of Davis, who was fleeing southwest from Charlotte. They pushed hard, yet Palmer's men were not alone. In Washington, President Andrew Johnson announced a hundred-thousand-dollar reward for Davis's capture. Along the coast of Florida, Union naval vessels went on full alert. In the Deep South, Major General James Harrison Wilson's fifteen-thou-sand-man Cavalry Corps of the Military Division of the Mississippi turned its full attention to capturing Davis. Wilson was in the best position of all. He had just completed his own raid through Alabama and Georgia. When word of Davis's flight reached him, he deployed his horsemen on key roads in Alabama, the Florida Panhandle, and Georgia. Between Palmer's and Wilson's commands, about twenty thousand Federal cavalrymen were involved in the search.[1]

Wilson's cavalry played the role of waiting hunters, while Palmer's served as the pack of hounds driving Davis toward them. Generally, Palmer's division played its role well, but poor intelligence and decisions robbed it of any real chance of capturing Davis. Wilson's men bagged him instead. "It was a keen dis-appointment to [Stoneman's raiders] to know that the game they had chased so far had been captured by another command, but this feeling was only momentary," one trooper wrote. "The important thing was that the Confederate President was a prisoner and the long four years agony of war was at an end."[2]

At least the raiders gained more laurels. They added three additional Confederate states to their travelogue: South Carolina, Georgia, and Alabama. They captured a number of Confederate luminaries, including Braxton Bragg, Alfred Iverson, Alexander Stephens, Robert Toombs, Howell Cobb, and Joe Wheeler. The capture of Iverson and Cobb was as rewarding as any; both men had played a role in Stoneman's 1864 capture, and Palmer had personally spied in Cobb's camps back in 1862. The raiders also paroled another eight thousand Confederates and seized more than $4 million in bonds, silver, gold, and specie. Still, the pursuit of Jefferson Davis turned out to be another disappointment in a raid that brought its share of them. It also resulted in one last casualty with the death of Private David H. Morrison, Jr., of the Twelfth Ohio.[3]

The pursuit of Jefferson Davis even brought fresh accusations that George Stoneman had failed to obey orders. It started in Washington, where Edwin Stanton heard that Sherman had ordered Stoneman's cavalry to join him near Raleigh. Since those orders would have moved Stoneman away from Davis, Stanton thought they would allow the Confederate president to get away scot-free. The *New York Times* gladly reported the secretary's worries, and Sherman was furious when he heard about the story. "Mr. Stanton . . . is in deep error," he wrote. Pointing a finger at Stoneman, Sherman argued that if Stoneman had actually joined his army as ordered, chances are it would have already captured Davis. It would take a month for cooler heads to realize that Gillem's decision to obey Thomas and not Sherman was correct.[4]

⁓⁂⁓

Ten days after Davis's capture—the sixty-first day since the Cavalry Division left Knoxville—the raid finally and officially ended. It was May 20 when elements of Palmer's command reached the Tennessee River and met a gunboat that had orders from Stoneman aboard. The instructions directed Palmer to "immediately order the Fifteenth Pennsylvania Cavalry to this place [Nashville] and the rest of your command to . . . Knoxville, Tenn." Palmer replied that his troopers, who were "in very good condition except as regards clothing," would comply.[5]

Between May and November 1865, the various elements of the Cavalry Division returned to Tennessee and, with the war at an end, disbanded.[6] Leaving their comrades behind proved the hardest part of going home. "There were some sad partings among the officers and men, for a companionship of three years in camp and field cannot be sundered without separating many friends," one trooper recalled. On the other hand, the best part was being reunited with family and friends. Nathaniel Sample arrived at his mother's home in Lancaster County, Pennsylvania, one Sunday morning in early July. "I imagine there was never a happier woman than my mother that day," he recalled.[7]

Stoneman's Raid thus passed into history and legend.

⌒⋏⌒

Looking back at Stoneman's 1865 raid through the lens of a song, is it possible to find the spirit of The Band's Virgil Caine?

Stoneman's raiders returned to Federal lines with no sadness, only pride in the belief that they truly had been successful. "Of the conduct of the Cavalry Division while I was with it, and judging from what I have heard of its operations since I left it, I cannot speak in terms too high of praise," George Stoneman wrote as the raid wound down. "We were equally the surprise, terror, and admiration of the enemy wherever we went, and the results accomplished sufficiently attest the capabilities of the agents employed." In General Orders No. 8, Colonel Charles Betts hailed the raiders' "campaign of more than two months, during which time you have shared a prominent part in securing the grand result just attained in the suppression of the Rebellion. . . . Wherever you have encamped you have left a name eulogized by all."[8]

From the ranks came more chest-beating. "We have had one of the greatest marches on record," one cavalryman wrote. This "last and longest cavalry raid of the Civil war" was "the final thrust to the dying Confederacy," an Ohio veteran claimed. For Luther Trowbridge, the raid's success grew with the telling. Immediately after the raid, he told his girl, "We have had a great time & I think have struck some telling blows for our good Govt." Years later, he upped his claim: "It may be safely said that no similar enterprise in the history of the war accomplished so much of importance with so little public attention." The Tennessee legislature, presumably at the suggestion of new member Alvan C. Gillem, passed a resolution of tribute to the raiders.[9]

On the other hand, it is easy to find the spirit of Virgil Caine among the people who endured the raid. They believed Dixie had been crushed. In Statesville, eighteen-year-old Annie Donnell complained that her life had changed for the worse. "School out today at noon on account of the depreciation of the currency, and when will I get home, the railroads are so badly torn up it will take two months to repair them," she wrote. "What an awful state of affairs! Under a Yankee government! It makes me angry to think of it." In Salisbury, mournful breezes tumbled worthless, abandoned Confederate money down the streets. Throughout the town, twisted, ruined rails gleamed in the spring sun. Telegraph wires were strewn about, and news was scarce. "Everything wore a look of demoralization," a local wrote. Everywhere, residents struggled, as a man in Crab Orchard, North Carolina, recalled. "Money invisible, food and clothing scarce," he wrote. A fellow farmer found much the same thing: "The prospect for crops this year is gloomy indeed and the farmers are feeling much depressed."[10]

What can be said about the sixty-one-day raid Stoneman conducted across six states? Were the raiders or the civilians right?

‹∽

The truth is, from a military perspective, Stoneman's Raid failed in its quest to help end the Civil War.

The raid was a manifestation of evolving United States military policy. As historian Russell F. Weigley paints it, Union strategy at the outset of the Civil War did not bother much with civilians and their property. However, as the war lengthened, Union forces adopted a "harsher conduct . . . toward enemy property and liberties." Major General John Pope was one of the first to institutionalize punishment as an element of military strategy. He allowed his men to live off the country. Other generals copied Pope. Ultimately, Grant realized that victory could be achieved only if the Union destroyed the two main Confederate armies. But the war had also demonstrated how difficult that would be to achieve on the battlefield. Grant understood the Union would have to stretch the Confederacy's forces thin by simultaneously attacking multiple targets and by making war against its resources.[11]

From the outset, Grant, Sherman, and Thomas hoped that Stoneman's Raid would hasten the Confederacy's defeat by eliminating resources it needed to continue the war. The raid simply did not speed the demise of the Confederacy, however, so the only conclusion is that it was a strategic failure. The reason why is simple: action on other fronts ended the war before Stoneman's raiders had a chance to contribute much. Indeed, had the raid never been launched, its absence would not have affected the outcome of any battle on other fronts. However, if Stoneman had started his raid earlier with a smaller force, as Grant wanted, its strategic impact likely would have been greater.

In her book *Stoneman's Last Raid*, Dr. Ina W. Van Noppen suggested the opposite. "This raid was of great strategic importance," she wrote, "because of its impact upon the morale of the invaded areas and the immense destruction of war potential." Dr. Van Noppen has a point, but a big *if* must be attached to it. The raid would have had a better chance of achieving strategic importance if Lee's or Johnston's armies had somehow managed to escape the clutches of Grant or Sherman. Under that scenario, those Confederate forces could have retreated only into southwestern Virginia or western North Carolina. Thanks to George Stoneman, they would have found nothing there to help them—no transportation facilities, no equipment, little food, and dwindling popular support. As a Northern newspaper crowed, "Stoneman, we learn, has succeeded in cutting the railroad behind Johnston, between Greensborough and Salisbury. This, if true, will sadly embarrass the Rebel host in its plans of retreat."[12] Armies fleeing from superior forces simply cannot last long without help. Thus, Stoneman's Raid was an insurance policy against the war's continuation. In the end, the Union did not need that insurance.

Postwar historian Cornelia Phillips Spencer came to a similar conclusion. "Had the war continued, the capture of Salisbury would have been a stunning blow to General Johnston, and would have severely crippled his movements," she wrote. And so did a member of the raid, trooper Charles Weller, who understood the just-in-case nature of the raid. "Our principal operations were in the states of Virginia [and] South & North Carolina[. I]n the former state we insured the capture of Lees Army by effectually destroying all means of retreat. In the latter we effectual[l]y insured the surrender of Johns[t]on by cutting the communications in his rear at Salsburey."[13]

Even Ulysses S. Grant agreed, stating in his memoirs that Stoneman's Raid, like Wilson's and Canby's, was successful but came too late to do much good. "Indeed much valuable property was destroyed and many lives lost at a time when we would have liked to spare them," he wrote. Blaming Stoneman for the raid's death and destruction when Grant himself had ordered it and did nothing to stop it was unfair, but it showed how frustrated he was by the whole business. He had designed the raid to hasten the war's end, but that did not happen, so the cavalrymen rode to little purpose. "The war was practically over before their victories were gained," Grant went on. "They were so late in commencing operations, that they did not hold any troops away that otherwise would have been operating against the armies which were gradually forcing the Confederate armies to a surrender."[14]

So did the raid accomplish anything from a military perspective? The raiders could claim at least one minor strategic accomplishment; Wagner's hell-raising around Lynchburg affected Confederate decision making during the Appomattox campaign in a small way. Grant himself complimented Stoneman for this contribution. And Raleigh Colston certainly would have agreed with Grant.[15]

Stoneman's Raid was quite successful in the tactical sphere. As Dr. Van Noppen wrote, "From the standpoint of military tactics the raid was admirably conceived and ably executed. It did untold damage, achieved important military objectives, and demoralized the war efforts of a whole region. It was a knife thrust into the virtually undefended back of the South."[16]

Indeed, Stoneman's Raid offers much to admire. There is no question that the raiders hit the Confederate infrastructure hard and well, fulfilling Stoneman's orders. Railroads suffered the most. The raiders burned ties and bent rails across more than 115 miles of four different lines. They also destroyed at least six locomotives and cars and six depots. Culverts and bridges—particularly those on the rail lines—were important targets as well. Some sources affirmed the destruction of twenty-one bridges, while other witnesses claimed the demise of thirty-three in Virginia alone, which would bring the total to forty. "I think the best thing we did," Palmer wrote, "was the destruction of four bridges on the Railroad between Danville and Salisbury in rear of Johnstons Army. This was done by my Brigade—whose detachment accomplished the work in spite of meeting superior force of the enemy at every point."[17]

In addition, the cavalrymen ruined more than 30 buildings, including factories, jails, government offices, and two homes. The quantity of supplies they captured or destroyed is huge and uncountable, but it included small arms, ammunition, gunpowder, cotton, shoes, uniforms, blankets, medical supplies, foodstuffs, turpentine, and more, Salisbury's haul accounting for the greatest share. The Union column also destroyed many wagons and cut communications between Danville and Charlotte. In the process, the raiders fought dozens of small to medium-sized skirmishes, captured more than 20 pieces of artillery, forced the abandonment of 21 more guns, and also seized 17 battle flags. Confederate casualty reports do not exist, but a tally from various sources suggests that Stoneman's raiders inflicted on Confederate forces 17 men killed, more than 15 wounded, and more than 10,193 captured and paroled. They also gathered 1,000 "hale and hearty negroes" to Union banners. Finally, the raiders picked the countryside clean of horses and mules to keep themselves mounted. A witness described the animals taken as an "immense number." The impressment of at least 8,000 horses and mules may be estimated, assuming a modest two remounts per man.[18] Finally, the pursuit of Jefferson Davis added more laurels for the Cavalry Division, albeit not the one Stoneman hoped to achieve.

Despite the numerous changes in plans, the raid was also well conceived. Its length and breadth were amazing in an age when armies still relied on feet and hooves for movement. Indeed, the raid rivals any such march in American military history. Calculations vary widely, but most place the length at or well beyond one thousand miles. Some individual units likely covered twice that distance. "On this our final raid and our last active service in the field we had marched a distance of about 1000 miles," one veteran wrote, "passing through parts of five States and through numerous towns and cities, crossing the principal southern rivers, and crossing and recrossing the different ranges of the Allegheny Mountains a number of times." The most honest estimate comes from a morning report that suggested the distance would never be known, since the raiders were "very frequently cut up into many detachments for long, forced marches[. M]any more miles have really been traveled."[19]

A drive on modern highways along the rough route of the raid—from Knoxville to Boone, Elkin, and Wytheville; to Salisbury and Asheville; to Anderson and Athens; and finally back to Knoxville—totals 1,175 miles. Traveling curvy 1860s-era roads and tossing in additional excursions certainly added a few hundred miles. By way of comparison, no ground movement in World War II—neither the United States Army in its trek from Normandy to the Elbe River nor the Red Army as it rolled from the outskirts of Moscow to Berlin—went farther or faster. Certainly, the Germans provided significantly more resistance to the United States and Red armies than the Confederates did to Stoneman's raiders, but it was still quite an achievement. Cavalryman Charles Weller explained how they did it. "We have been almost constantly on the march and have moved at an average rate since that time of fourty miles per day," he wrote.[20]

Those many miles crossed some of the most challenging terrain in the South. "The field of operations was in the most rugged and inaccessible part of the country, and the season was the most inclement of the year; yet rapid marches were long continued over almost trackless mountains," an observer pointed out. One of Stoneman's staff officers cataloged the challenges; the column crossed Stone Mountain once and the Blue Ridge three times and forded the Yadkin, Dan, Catawba, and Roanoke rivers multiple times, all before it even left Lenoir. Later, the raiders crossed more rivers, including the Savannah, Chattahoochee, and Coosa, and faced the Blue Ridge and other mountain ranges again and again.[21] One veteran went so far as to describe "the crossing of the Great Smoky Mountains" as "a victory over time and nature."[22]

Making the distance covered even more incredible was the fact that the raiders pulled it off without a line of supply. In 1865, executing a military operation without the benefit of a supply line was not a new concept. General Winfield Scott had done it during the war with Mexico, and armies under Grant and Lee also went without supply lines in some of their campaigns. Stoneman's raiders did it with the same success as their predecessors, but again over a huge distance. Colonel Trowbridge explained, "We had been in the enemy's country since the 26th of March, living on what we could find in the country, except for the 2400 rations received from Atlanta." All told, Trowbridge judged that the raiders went fifty-eight days without supplies. Cutting loose from a supply line was perhaps the greatest risk Stoneman faced during the campaign.[23]

Tactically, the division benefited from the way it marched. Throughout the raid, the Cavalry Division rode hard and fast, zigging and zagging to reach its objectives, but never in a way that unmasked the expedition's intentions. This emasculated many Confederate defenses without a fight. "I cannot close this report without remarking on the complete surprise of the rebels at every point at which we appeared," Gillem wrote. "When the expedition crossed the Blue Ridge into North Carolina they were convinced that Salisbury was the point of intended attack. By turning due north from Jonesville the enemy were completely surprised and the Tennessee and Virginia Railroad at our mercy." This trend continued as the division marched south. "The enemy withdrew several thousand of their troops from Salisbury before they discovered the real point of attack[, and] Salisbury with its immense depots and magazines fell into our hands," the general wrote. The story was the same to the west, before the gates of Asheville. "Whilst all their available force and artillery was at Swannanoa Gap a brigade was passed to their rear, surprising and capturing most of their force," Gillem explained. Luther Trowbridge agreed. "From the beginning to the end, the expedition was managed with rare judgment and skill," he wrote. "While its movements were so directed as to constantly deceive the enemy as to the real point of attack[,] its quick and heavy blows were delivered in unexpected quarters, working immense damage to the waning hopes of the Confederacy." This was vintage Stoneman, and it was perfect for his final raid, even though geographic challenges and a need for food and forage, more than design, often led to these maneuvers.[24]

Benefits came on the human level as well. The way the raiders captured and paroled ten thousand Confederate soldiers, including several prominent officers, contributed in a small way to sectional healing. Indeed, in most cases, the Federal cavalrymen treated their former foes with respect and courtesy. By the same token, not a few citizens—particularly the region's pro-Union residents—appreciated the raid despite the hardships it wrought. These were the men and women who had remained faithful to the Union flag throughout the war, sometimes in the face of harassment and persecution from Confederate neighbors. After the war, a North Carolina citizen wrote Palmer, "Your soldiers of the Union who breasted the storm and flood riding the rough mountain roads by day and by night to restore the Old Flag to a people from whom it had been wrested by force and fraud can not ... forget the welcome ... you received at the hands of the people of the Yadkin. But for prudence I should have shouted for joy when your columns filed through our old village."[25]

For all these accomplishments, the raiders paid only a modest cost. No Federal casualty reports are extant, but it is possible to arrive at an estimate by piecing together various accounts. The raiders lost a confirmed 23 men killed, more than 40 wounded, and 21 captured. Records also list another 35 to 60 casualties without specifying whether they were killed, wounded, or missing. Combining these totals, it can be surmised that Federal casualties were between 119 and 144 men, or about 3 percent of the raiding force. Meanwhile, Davis Tillson's division suffered no casualties except for the capture of some cavalrymen.

The raid was not without mistakes, beginning with the men's failure to fulfill an important vision of Grant's. "This expedition goes to destroy and not to fight battles," he wrote before the raid, yet Stoneman's forces got into numerous scrapes. Grant's wisdom was borne out by performance on the battlefield. The raiders were soundly defeated on several occasions, particularly at Wytheville and Abbott's Creek. On fields such as Henry Court House, Morganton, and Swannanoa Gap, the raiders achieved victory, but only after changing their tactics and committing reserves. Only at Salisbury did they succeed in outmaneuvering and outfighting a well-posted enemy force. Ironically, Salisbury was one of the few places Grant would have approved of a fight because capturing the railroad town was "where a great object is to be gained."[26]

Another error involved the application of Brigadier General Davis Tillson's force. The idea of plugging the mountain gaps behind Stoneman with Tillson's division was wise, and Tillson performed well in carrying out his orders. However, his men failed to watch the gaps along the North Carolina–Virginia line. He was never ordered to do so, and that was a serious oversight. As events proved, Stoneman's rear was just as likely, if not more likely, to be threatened from Virginia. Holding those gaps would have saved Stoneman from fighting Echols's Confederate cavalrymen and would also have reduced the men available to serve as escorts for Jefferson Davis.

Alvan Gillem saw another error. "On this expedition, hundreds of horses were lost from a failure to provide horse shoes[,] the loss falling principally upon the troops who reported too late to be supplied," he wrote. "I always required each cavalryman to carry on his horse four shoes and prepared nails,—a hammer can generally be had. I would recommend that this should be required in all cavalry detachments leaving posts." Since most horseshoes needed replacement every one hundred miles, some cavalrymen used up as many as twenty horses on the campaign. Only a handful returned with the same horses they started with. "Our rapid and lengthy marches were very hard on our horses," a trooper wrote. Fortunately for the raiders, their farriers and blacksmiths performed small miracles. The troopers were also able to capture enough animals from citizens to remain mounted.[27]

Individual and unit performances during Stoneman's Raid were as varied as the raid itself. Some men—including George Stoneman himself—emerged with intact, if not enhanced, reputations. In fact, the best thing that can be said was that Stoneman executed his orders to the letter, fulfilling every task given to him. He overcame the expectations of detractors such as Stanton and did not deserve the criticism that Sherman placed on him as the pursuit of Davis began. The New Yorker's weakest moments came before the raid even began; his tardy start had more to do with the raid's failure to contribute strategically than did anything that happened during the raid itself. Once the long ride started,

Stoneman performed well. He led decisively and creatively and used his men in a manner that suggested he understood their strengths and weaknesses. The capture of Salisbury was his shining moment. He managed the battle with skill. In the end, Stoneman's biggest disappointment was doubtless the fact that he was not able to grab the glory, the redemption, and the headlines he dreamed about. Still, the general exonerated himself in a quiet manner that paved the way for a successful postwar career that may not have been possible immediately after Chancellorsville or Sunshine Church.

Federals and Confederates alike have been kind to Stoneman. One cavalryman was in awe of the way he managed the raid. "The roads were known to our General as well as if he had lived there all his life," the trooper wrote. "He had maps, and would hypnotize a colored man or a man too old to be with our illustrious Southern brethren, so his directions always carried us through." Even a Confederate observer offered praise. "All who came into contact with Stoneman and his officers were favorably impressed," wrote Captain A. G. Brenizer. Cornelia Spencer fairly heaped praise on the New Yorker. "General Stoneman must certainly be allowed to have accomplished his ends with a skill, celerity, and daring, which entitle him to high praise as a military leader," she wrote. "Add to this the higher praise of humanity, and the ability to control his troops, and he well deserves a higher niche than some who led grand armies on great marches."[28]

Stoneman's division commanders, Davis Tillson and Alvan Gillem, contributed to the success of the raid as well. Tillson performed solidly, carrying out his orders to the letter with aggressiveness and solid leadership. Gillem's performance was less consistent. Early on, he doubtless benefited from Stoneman's controlling hand, but he did command independently on occasion. After Stoneman left, Gillem fulfilled his orders in the short time he led the raiding column. He guided his men well during that period, moving the column toward and beyond the Catawba while winning skirmishes at Morganton and Asheville. He also chose well when confronted with conflicting orders. "General A. C. Gillem, who will be recollected from his defeat of John Morgan, gained greater reputation than ever," a staff officer stated. The fact that Gillem was afterward brevetted—largely for his work at Salisbury—underscores the officer's observation.[29]

At the same time, it must be concluded that something was missing from Gillem's performance. In his April 13 report, Stoneman wrote that the general was "entitled to a full share of whatever is due," an odd statement that suggests both good and bad things happened under Gillem's direction. It is also tempting to view Gillem's April 24 relief to attend the state legislature as a censure, but that probably had more to do with his political skills being needed at home. His involvement in the controversy over whether or not Asheville should have been given adequate warning of the end of the truce raises questions as well, but a look at the facts largely exonerates him. In truth, Gillem's worst fault was simply that he allowed discipline in his command to decline. His lax leadership was doubtless colored by his personal experience in the war, which was nothing like Stoneman's. After all, Gillem's wife, father, and brothers had been subjected to Confederate oppression, and he had personally witnessed the bitter internecine conflict in the Tennessee hills. Gillem considered Confederates traitors and villains and believed that "the rebels are not to be conquered by kindness[. T]hey must be made to feel . . . that every offence will be speedily punished."[30] It is not surprising that he turned a blind eye to indiscretions, blaming them on "bad men in all crowds." Fortunately, Gillem kept a tight enough rein so that wholesale pillaging never occurred.

Among the brigade commanders, William J. Palmer stands out. Gillem commended Palmer "for his uniform gallantry, zeal, and ability in the management of his brigade." One staff officer concurred. "Colonel W. J. Palmer," the officer wrote, "has added fresh laurels to his name during this campaign, and we predict that the 'star' will at length [be] bestowed upon them."[31] Indeed, Palmer was the single indispensable man in the entire column. Under his leadership, the First Brigade performed ably. More often than not, his brigade drew the most difficult detached duties, which became some of the brightest spots of the raid. These included Wagner's Virginia raid, the operations around Salem and Greensboro, and Moderwell's Nations Ford excursion. Only when he took command of the Cavalry Division did Palmer struggle. Although he generally performed well, he failed to solve the behavior problems in the Second and Third brigades, and he also misdirected the pursuit of Jefferson Davis.

Palmer's successes stemmed from the quality of his regiments and their leaders. The Fifteenth Pennsylvania was unquestionably the best regiment on the raid, adding a number of accomplishments to its banners. Colonel Betts deserves much of the credit. In his post-campaign report, Palmer cited Betts "for gallant conduct in charging [and] capturing a South Carolina Battalion of Cavalry" at Greensboro and for "thoroughly preserving the discipline of his Regiment on an active Campaign during which the troops were compelled to live exclusively off the country."[32]

The Twelfth Ohio also proved a solid, well-disciplined unit. Its best moment was Moderwell's Nations Ford raid, but it turned in even work throughout the campaign. Afterward, Palmer recommended Colonel Bentley for promotion, noting his "meritorious conduct and gallantry throughout the Campaign for keeping his Regiment at all times efficient and under good discipline." Palmer added that Bentley was ready for brigade command. Among the men in Bentley's regiment, none stood out more than Moderwell. Both Palmer and Gillem praised the major for his gallantry and skill in leading the raid on the Catawba River bridge.[33]

The Tenth Michigan was the brigade's weakest link. The unit and its commander were inconsistent, falling short of expectations more often than not. For example, Palmer praised Trowbridge "for skill and gallantry in resisting the attack of Ferguson's Brigade upon his regiment near Lexington, N.C.," and "for efficiency as a Commanding officer in steadily improving the discipline of his Regiment from the time of its entering North Carolina." He also recognized Trowbridge for his raid on High Point.[34] However, Trowbridge botched more than one march, especially that from Boone to Wilkesboro. The men in the ranks had little use for the way Trowbridge led, as Lieutenant Fred Field attested. Worse, Trowbridge struggled on the battlefield. The beating the Tenth suffered at Henry Court House would not have occurred had it been better led. In the final analysis, Trowbridge's postwar writings probably represent his greatest contribution to the raid.

Simeon Brown, commander of the Second Brigade, was the quiet man of the raid. Throughout, Brown was conspicuous by his absence. He figured little in many movements and battles, so it can be surmised that Stoneman, Gillem, and Palmer had little use for him, despite his Army of the Potomac experience. Perhaps Brown was handicapped by the poor units under his command. Yet his men were entrusted with difficult work on occasion. However, even in those cases, Stoneman typically assigned Keogh, not Brown, to escort them. Witness the Twelfth Kentucky Cavalry's advance into Boone—which still resulted in the tragic death of Jacob Councill—and the Eleventh Kentucky's attack on the Confederate left at Salisbury. The Twelfth Kentucky Cavalry also turned in yeoman's work on the Old Mocksville road at Salisbury, and Brown's men tore up track as well as anyone in Virginia. At only two points did Brown assume some responsibility, and those added nothing to his reputation. At Asheville, he was in command when the raiders committed the worst atrocities of the entire raid. He was also given independent command when the Second and Third brigades were separated from the First Brigade during the pursuit of Jefferson Davis. This independent command does not suggest that Brown was being rewarded; it says more about Palmer's washing his hands of two unruly brigades. Plus, Brown was not complimented in any raid report.

Miller and his regiments of Tennessee "Cossacks" in the Third Brigade had more positive moments than Brown. Probably because he was neither a proven brigade leader nor a professional military man, Miller enjoyed only a few opportunities for detached command. His first effort, which came while the column was still in Tennessee, was unremarkable except for his decision to allow his men to take French leave. In Virginia, Miller again left the main column and thoroughly destroyed the transportation infrastructure around Wytheville and the lead mines south of it, but he also lost the fight at Wytheville. The presence of superior officers typically brought the best out of Miller and his men. At Salisbury, for example, Miller earned compliments in after-action reports and a recommendation for promotion to brigadier general by brevet.[35] He also fought well during the skirmish at Morganton. His shortcomings, it seems, had to do with his inability to maintain discipline in the ranks.

If Stoneman's Raid failed to affect the Confederacy strategically, what did it do? From the perspective of the home front, it sadly succeeded in "driving old Dixie down." Indeed, the true legacy of the raid is that instead of helping end the war, it created conditions that retarded postwar recovery and Reconstruction.

According to Professor Van Noppen, Stoneman's Raid, combined with the simultaneous operations of Sherman and Wilson, were "something approaching total warfare." In truth, the raid did not come close to meeting that definition. Grant was the general who finally realized that it was necessary to destroy resources to beat the Confederacy. William T. Sherman took this idea even farther, conceiving a "deliberate strategy of terror directed toward the enemy people's minds." Stoneman's Raid was pure Grant—it existed solely to destroy the enemy's resources—but carried little of Sherman's brand of terror. In 1865, Stoneman's column did not strip the countryside clean, as Sheridan did in the Shenandoah. The raiders did not deal as harshly with the population or its property as Sherman's army did on its March to the Sea. They did not even shoot worn-out horses to deny them to the enemy, a typical practice of Union raiders that Stoneman himself had employed during the Chancellorsville campaign.[36]

"What we want to impress upon our readers," a postwar historian wrote, "is that while we were in the hands and at the mercy of an alien army, an army whose comrades were being shot to pieces by our fathers and brothers, they lived on subsistence, but made no attempt to terrorize us. There was not a home desecrated or burned; not a woman was violated; the fanes of our faith were left untouched, and the country was in no way devastated." Van Noppen agreed: "One of the outstanding conclusions to be drawn is that not all'd_____ Yankees' were absolute villains. Stoneman and Palmer were in the main gentlemanly, and they restrained their soldiers on numerous occasions."[37]

However well behaved they were, the raiders had an unavoidable and significant impact on the local population. "The condition of things in Western Virginia and Western North Carolina is truly deplorable," reported a Federal officer in the war's closing days. "The people are in a starving condition and the country is overrun by bands of disbanded Confederate soldiers, who rob and plunder indiscriminately while making their way south." Speaking of North Carolina Unionists, another man explained, "Many of those fellows have never recovered from the hard lick struck them first by the Rebels and last by 'Stoneman's Raid'—they got it both sides! Some who lost a horse have had to plow [an] ox ever since."[38]

Federal troops were largely to blame for this, as their requisition of food left many residents hungry and wondering where their next meal would come from. "My Division of Cavalry during this raid," Alvan Gillem wrote, "had not a single wagon, subsisting entirely on what could be found in the Country, and when nothing could be found, going without." This meant that the troopers took whatever they needed whenever they found it. "Our march was principally through a part of the Confederacy not devastated by either army, and there was abundant food for man and beast," wrote a raid veteran. "When in camp for a few days we would gorge ourselves, anaconda like, with stewed chickens, ducks and turkeys, having as a substitute for crackers and bread flap-jacks made out of cornmeal and flour mixed with water and fried in a skilletful of grease." Civilians were still reeling from the raid over a year later. "There are many families now," a Catawba County resident wrote, "heretofore comparatively independent, suffering for meat and bread."[39]

Impressments of animals also affected the population's ability to farm and to travel. As a Pennsylvania raider wrote, "On this expedition we were in the saddle almost every day for three months, frequently making forced marches by night and day, were compelled to live entirely off the country, and to confiscate all the horses and mules we could find, to keep mounted." A postwar observer explained, "They took many horses, but it was generally in the nature of a swap. They took a fat horse and left a lean one. Sometimes the one they [left] was as good as the one they took except that it was poor." Fortunately, the locals had some good news. "In most cases this was only a forced trade of our wearied animals for fresh ones, and in many cases after ours had been rested up they proved better than the ones we had taken," a trooper wrote. "Gen. Stoneman in passing through here last spring left the country very [bare] of stock," a Wilkes County native complained. "The citizens picked up worn out horses & succeeded in raising a part of a crop. Bearly a sufficiency for the county."[40]

Though the raiders were generally well behaved, some depredations such as stealing and plundering occurred. The excuse of one regimental commander was that it was difficult to control the actions of several thousand cavalrymen strung out in a six-mile-long column.[41] That is true, but the worst discipline problems tended to develop when either alcohol was present or the men had idle time on their hands. Whenever the raiders moved fast, the problems were few; where they lingered, problems mounted. The length of the raid also told. As the war wound down and the raiders were seemingly no closer to going home, discipline deteriorated.

Incidents of poor behavior came chiefly but not exclusively from members of the brigades of Brown and Miller, and particularly from the Home Yankees. The lack of discipline in these units was mostly to blame. But even Palmer's brigade was not entirely innocent. A speaker at a Fifteenth Pennsylvania Cavalry reunion said of the Tenth Michigan Cavalry, "You recollect those marauders." However, in many cases, the men who committed the worst acts were not cavalrymen under the purview of commanding officers but stragglers, hangers-on, and camp followers trailing the column. Citizens were unable to make distinctions among the groups. At the same time, Confederate forces were not innocent either. "It is said . . . Wheeler's [Confederate] Cavalry are the terror of the country. They are represented as being terrible desperadoes—utterly without discipline," a resident of Salem wrote.[42]

Responsibility for these acts belongs, of course, to the men who commanded the raid, beginning with Stoneman. In his March 22 circular, Stoneman attempted to set the tone by ordering his men to respect private property. Anyone who failed to do so would suffer from reduced pay or even a court-martial. However, little evidence suggests that Stoneman's good intentions were ever backed up with action. R. L. Beall related correctly that Stoneman was "gentlemanly in his deportment, and seemingly indisposed to harshness, but he must necessarily be responsible for much of the wanton outrages that were committed; for the expedition was under his command, and if he had enforced the discipline required alike by the laws of war and of humanity, the same amount of robbery and outrage could not have been committed on helpless non-combatants." Gillem deserves a large share of the blame as well. One witness to an outrage explained that it occurred despite Gillem's presence.[43] This was typical Gillem; he struggled throughout the war to gain the respect of his men and failed to do so later in his career as well, particularly during the Modoc War.

After the Civil War, citizens filed several civil suits against the raiders in North Carolina courts, prompting the United States Army to intervene. Complaints and requests for financial help also poured into the governor's office. "When Gen'l Stoneman came through here part of his command fed at my house and consumed every thing I had to support on and took my horses[,] 6 in number[,] leaving me destitute of subsistence and stock and almost without means," went one such request from Yadkin County. "You will oblige your citizen subject by letting him know if there is any chance to recover part of his losses."[44]

Whether militarily justifiable or illegal, the raiders' foraging and destruction brought the war up close and personal to dozens of communities that would not have tasted it otherwise, and this made Reconstruction all the harder. Indeed, as the raid and the war ended and Confederate authority collapsed, much of the countryside fell into disarray. Fields lay untilled and cribs and storehouses yawned empty. Livestock had been driven off or taken away. Property was in disrepair. Orchards were untended. Here and there, charred heaps of lumber and piles of rubble marked where buildings once stood. "Disaster was never more complete than when the Confederate cause was committed to the ages," a local historian wrote. "The fields were destitute of cattle, the homes mourning their dead, the larder empty and the stoutest hearts saw no dawn of a better day from out of the gloom." In western and Piedmont North Carolina, southwestern Virginia, and East Tennessee, many citizens knew whom to blame: George Stoneman and his raiders. The Yankees' "departure . . . left behind a destruction that promised a future resultant poverty, bitter indeed!" a Salisbury resident grumbled.[45]

The challenges left by the raid began and ended with money. By the summer of 1865, western North Carolina's economy was in shock. Banks were closed and money depleted; one man found that his account, worth $13,500 at the beginning of the war, now held a mere $513. Confederate money was worthless, and those who had hoarded Federal greenbacks still came up short because inflation sent prices skyrocketing. Bacon, for example, cost $7.50 a pound, while wheat flour went for $500 a barrel. Bartering was the only option for many. Some scholars have suggested that this economic decline would have taken place anyway because of changing population and land-ownership patterns and declining farm production, but the war and Stoneman's Raid undoubtedly made the situation worse. "These people . . . have no money and nothing that will bring money," a Catawba County resident wrote of his neighbors.[46]

Another factor that slowed recovery was the lack of ready labor. The war's heavy casualties and the end of slavery brought serious problems to the agrarian economy. In Davidson County alone, the population was reduced by more than one thousand men and women. The raid also liberated the region's slaves, who often exercised their newfound freedom by leaving their former owners' farms. Many farms were so short of workers that they failed. New stresses also appeared as former slaves sought land of their own and the population rebounded. Near Asheville, one man's slaves moved a short distance away into a new cabin. Their former master gave them his best cow, three hogs, and a large supply of bacon, corn, and some tools to help them get started. Few slaves enjoyed such a head start but were rather forced to compete for land.[47]

Businesses also struggled to resume operations in the raid's aftermath. This was especially true of the cotton mills in Stoneman's path, as the raiders had left many of them in ashes. Having operated their mills at full capacity during the war, thanks to robust demand, the owners were confident in the market for their products and decided to try again. Eagle Mills, for example, was rebuilt and back in operation in short order. It ran until 1894, peaking with thirty employees spinning four hundred pounds of cotton a day. Two fires eventually ruined the cotton mill and gristmill, and the site was abandoned. The Turnersburg mill, which narrowly escaped the Federal raid, continued in operation until 1910. The old mill produced as much as five hundred pounds of cotton a day before giving way to a new electric mill nearby. These and other facilities became the foundation for the textile industry of the New South—but only after they rose from the ashes of Stoneman's Raid.[48]

Economic recovery was not quick in any walk of life. Income levels in western North Carolina settled in at about half the national average for the next seventy-five years. Even when other areas of the South started to industrialize, western North Carolina lagged. Atlanta, Knoxville, and Charlotte—all towns with easy access to rail lines—enjoyed a resurgence, but Asheville, Morganton, Hickory, and other places Stoneman visited remained stagnant for years.[49]

The virtual collapse of transportation systems in the region—thanks to Stoneman's raiders and the war in general—exacerbated the situation. Highways were in sad shape, while the raiders saw to it that virtually all the railroads were unfit for use. Historians John C. Inscoe and Gordon B. McKinney argue that destruction of the railroads delayed economic expansion in western North Carolina by at least a decade. The same could doubtless be said for neighboring areas. Indeed, the cavalrymen had done a thorough job. Around Wytheville, the East Tennessee and Virginia Railroad was left with only the Glade Spring station still standing. Other stations such as those at Max Meadows and Rural Retreat lay in ruins. The entire line would not reopen until July 1865, and it was much later before crews were able to rebuild the destroyed stations. The North Carolina Railroad faced similar challenges. One observer estimated it would take at least four weeks to rebuild the Deep River bridge alone.[50]

The Western North Carolina Railroad, once a showpiece, was in worse shape. "This Corporation has been a great sufferer by war," company president Samuel McD. Tate wrote. Stoneman's raiders in particular ruined the company's shops and other buildings and burned machinery, tools, maps, surveys, papers, two engines, and cars. The raiders destroyed a train of cars two miles from Salisbury, plus the tank and adjoining building at the Six Mile post, the bridges over Second and Third creeks, and the depot and buildings at Third Creek Station. Statesville's and Icard's stations also went up in flames, along with more cars at Statesville, the station house and cars at Icard's, and a new steam sawmill five miles east of Morganton. Only the depots at Catawba, Newton, Hickory Tavern, and Morganton still stood. All told, the line suffered $111,000 worth of damage at prewar prices. Four years would pass before it resumed daily service. It was nearly the turn of the twentieth century before rail lines penetrated deeply into the North Carolina mountains, delivering the twin economic benefits of industrialization and tourism.[51]

Even the normal trappings of life emerged in a retarded state. In the wake of the war, North Carolina's school system remained closed for two years. Mail service was virtually suspended in the days and weeks following the raid, and the telegraph struggled to keep up. Few people could afford to travel any distance, leaving lodges and taverns—including the Mansion House in Salisbury—quite empty until summer. And luxuries such as real coffee and tea were unheard of, at least until sutlers followed occupation troops into the South.[52]

⸺∿⸺

The South also had another worry sparked by the war and exacerbated by Stoneman's Raid. While the war still raged, deserters began to flow into western North Carolina, East Tennessee, and southwestern Virginia. Whatever the motivation, the area was perfect. A man could hide in its hills and valleys, mountains and coves, forests and fields and never be found—unless he wanted to be. It was a place where an individual or even a large group could survive. Some chose to fight against the Confederacy. Anarchy erupted in the mountains as the worst of these renegades swept through the countryside sowing consternation, stealing, robbing, injuring, and killing. Eventually, the problem grew beyond the ability of Home Guardsmen to handle, so the Confederate government sent in troops.[53]

Confederate forces did not help the situation. "Not less a terror than the Yankees were the predatory bands of Vaughn's and Wheeler's Confederate cavalry which rode about the country for a few days after the entry of Stoneman's army, stealing all that the Federals had left," recorded a local newspaper. The motivation of these cavalrymen was typically survival, but the callousness bred by the war surfaced, too. One band of roving Confederate cavalry burned fifty bales of cotton near Statesville's depot just so nobody could profit from it.[54]

The guerilla war did not stop with the end of the raid and the surrender of Lee and Johnston. In fact, with the economy falling apart and the Confederate government and its armies collapsing, the situation deteriorated. Deserters came out of the mountains. Former soldiers "flooded [the countryside] going home— downcast, or still hopeful." They flowed into a vacuum where civil control no longer existed. Violence became commonplace, and the residents of Dixie paid the price. One citizen, C. C. Jones, was on his way to Lenoir when he was robbed of three hundred dollars in Confederate money. The road to Wilkesboro was equally dangerous; two ladies traveling alone with their children were robbed. Near Shallow Ford, a deserter murdered a man, while a family living nearby exchanged shots with other deserters.[55]

Stoneman's raiders saw this violence firsthand. One day, Federal cavalrymen came across some local citizens in distress. The family was mourning the loss of its father, husband, and breadwinner, who had been bushwhacked while taking a wagonload of grain to a mill. The grain, wagon, and oxen were gone, and the family members had no guarantee the bushwhackers would leave them alone, since the man had been a Unionist. Although the family's future looked frightening and uncertain, the horse soldiers could do nothing but ride on.[56]

Not every incident involved petty thieves. Gangs and groups of renegades terrorized some areas, particularly in western North Carolina and southwestern Virginia counties where Unionist feelings pervaded and Stoneman had raided. One group, the Adair gang, held Rutherford County, North Carolina, in its grip, stealing livestock and burning barns. In Virginia, Patrick and Henry counties had a gang led by a man in a Federal uniform who called himself Colonel Scott. One of Scott's favorite targets was George W. Hylton's home, which he relieved of horses, corn, meat, and fodder. On one raid, the gang even took quilts and bedding and then demanded that Mrs. Hylton and her sisters bring water from a distant spring and prepare dinner, despite the fact that Mrs. Hylton had just given birth to twins and her two sisters were frail. Mrs. Hylton died within the month, perhaps because of the stress Scott's raiders caused. Colonel Scott kept up his depredations until sixty-five local men, most of them Confederate veterans, cleaned out the bandits.[57]

Wilkes County, North Carolina, was the base for a renegade named Wade. His story reads like a bad Wild West novel. Wade appeared soon after Stoneman left Wilkesboro. He was likely a deserter who joined local renegades. Witnesses claimed he had served in one of Stoneman's Michigan regiments, and Federal records list one man meeting that description. On April 30, 1865, in Wilkesboro, one Michael Wade deserted from Company F of the Tenth Michigan Cavalry. Twenty-one years old, Wade was an Irish-born trooper and former laborer who had enlisted in Flint, Michigan, on September 17, 1864. He was a tall, "good looking and fairly intelligent" man, according to a witness; he stood just short of six feet and had a light complexion, hazel eyes, and brown hair. Another member of the Tenth Michigan, Sheof Lockwood, deserted with him.[58]

Wade gathered about twenty-five or thirty men, armed them with pistols and repeating rifles, and drilled them until they had the precision of a military force. For his base of operations, he chose a fortified log house near Holman's Ford on the Yadkin River. Called Fort Hamby after the disreputable woman who owned it, the house sat on a high hill overlooking the countryside for a half-mile around. "It would have been difficult to have chosen a stronger location both offensive and defensive, than this," a witness wrote.[59]

In short order, Wade's men carved out a reputation, if not a legend. "All the people of Wilkes County lived in constant dread of them—frightened by the bark of a dog or the rattling of the leaves," a local wrote. After gathering his force and settling into Fort Hamby, Wade "completely terrorized Wilkes and portions of other counties" with "frequent raids." By early May 1865, locals realized that government help would not be forthcoming. The people of northwestern North Carolina would have to stop Wade themselves. Former soldiers, including Major Harvey Bingham, Watauga County's former Home Guard commander, took the matter into their own hands. They attacked Fort Hamby twice and failed twice, leaving four of their number dead. Wade's rampage continued unabated.[60]

The third attempt was successful. On May 19, 1865, the strongest force of former soldiers yet surrounded Fort Hamby on three sides. Colonel George Washington Sharpe commanded the attackers, who besieged the fort for a day before finally driving the gangsters out by setting fire to the structure. In the confusion, many of the gang members—including Wade himself—managed to escape, but Sharpe's men did capture four of them. The victors tied their captives to stakes and shot them, then returned home to celebrate.[61]

The victory at Fort Hamby did not end the violence Stoneman's Raid helped spawn. Sympathizers of the Hamby gang managed to extract some revenge, while other groups of desperadoes continued to operate. These included a force led by C. W. Hayes, based in Purlear, a settlement about eight miles west of Wilkesboro. Hayes's gang, made up mostly of Confederate deserters, may have been larger than Wade's. "They were a terror to several counties in N.W.N.C.," a witness recalled. Nonetheless, the victory at Fort Hamby discouraged violence and robbing. It also inspired a book that in 1970 became the Walt Disney TV movie *Menace on the Mountain*.[62]

Wade and Hayes were not unique. Shortly after Lee's surrender, some young men from Floyd and Wythe counties in Virginia who had not served and a few veterans of the war formed a secret organization that aimed "to be revenged on General Stoneman." Their opportunity came when Stoneman was invited to participate in a grand review in Washington, D.C. On May 18, 1865, Stoneman took six thousand cavalry, ten thousand infantry, and twenty-three guns on a hundred-mile march from Knoxville over the mountains to the rail line at Christiansburg, where they would embark on a train for Washington. The secret group planned to ambush him en route. But before it could execute its plan, the entire group deserted except for three men. These three, emboldened by alcohol, opened fire and wounded several Federals before they died in a hail of gunfire.[63]

Violence, poverty, and isolation: these were the terrible, yet very real, outcomes of the end of the Civil War and Stoneman's Raid in particular. They thrived long afterward in the areas touched by the raid and even found their way into postwar literature, which helped create the hillbilly stereotype that endures in the mountains of Tennessee, Virginia, and North Carolina to this day.[64]

⤳

So The Band's Virgil Caine had it right after all. Just as the group's song was more about Vietnam than the Civil War, George Stoneman's last raid was more about a beginning than an ending. The raid did not help end the Civil War as intended, but it made the beginning of Reconstruction harder in those areas it touched. Had the war continued, the raid would have played a much more significant role, for George Stoneman ruined the infrastructure the Confederacy needed to survive. But that did not happen, so Stoneman's Raid stands as a tactical success and a strategic failure—a hedged bet against the end of the war. To borrow Dr. Van Noppen's phrase, it was a powerful knife thrust in the South's back. It was also an unnecessary one.

Having been driven down, Southerners started over as best they could. Bethania resident O. J. Lehman captured the attitude best. He came home from the war hoping for something better than a soldier's diet but ended up eating cornbread made with water, a little salt, brown cowpeas, and badly seasoned molasses and drinking coffee made from sweet potatoes and parched rye. "Under those circumstances, what was to be done?" he wrote. "It was root hog or die. We went to work the next day, and managed to make a precarious living."[65]

With such a spirit prevalent in the lands it ravaged, Stoneman's Raid could not, and did not, keep Dixie down forever.

Acknowledgments

I grew up in Wilkesboro, North Carolina, one of the communities raided by Stoneman so long ago. In 1988, while a student at the University of North Carolina at Chapel Hill, I wrote a paper about Stoneman's Raid for a history course. Not long after graduation, I moved to the Winston-Salem area, which was also hit by the raid. I've spent a lot of time in the years since learning as much as I could about the raid, but it has not been a lonely journey. I want to say thanks to the many, many people who helped make it possible.

I must begin with Mark Bradley, the accomplished historian who served as my primary reader and adviser. I can't say enough about his invaluable assistance. Thanks, Mark. Dozens of other individuals and institutions gave extremely valuable help, providing sources and photos, giving me tours, offering advice, debating with me, referring me to others, asking me to speak, and offering words of encouragement. If I miss anyone, I apologize, but you know who you are. These individuals include Dr. Gene Adcock; Dr. John G. Barrett; the staff of the Bassett Branch Historical Center in Bassett, Virginia; Stephen Birdsall; Wayne Boone; Jennifer Bean Bower; Ann Brownlee; Matt Bumgarner; Brad Bush; Chris Calkins; Kevin Carle; Pete Carmichael; Jerry Carroll of the Forsyth County Public Library; Steve Chandler; Tim Cole, formerly of the Forsyth County Public Library; Susan F. Cook; the staff of the Colorado Historical Society; Randall Crews; Ed and Sue Curtis; William B. Eigelsbach of the University of Tennessee Libraries; Marva R. Felchlin of the Autry Museum of Western Heritage; Jennifer Ford of the University of Mississippi; Ben F. Fordney of James Madison University; Dr. Gary Freeze, the professor who assigned and graded my first Stoneman's Raid paper; Colonel Dick Gillem (great-grandson of General Alvan C. Gillem) and his son, Colonel Richard Gillem; Nina Groce of the Yadkin County Historical Society; my late friend Peter Hairston; Darrell Harkey of Lincoln County, North Carolina; Lisa Hartley of the Patterson School; Maureen D. Heher of the Beinecke Rare Book and Manuscript Library; Kaye Hirst of the Rowan Museum; Steven Kaplan; the staff of the Kegley Library at Wythe Community College; Robert E. L. Krick; the Reverend Dr. Robert P. Lawrence; Boyd Lamberth, Jr.; Jo White Linn; Dr. and Mrs. Thomas P. Lowry; Horace Mewborn; the staff of the University of Michigan; the staff of the National Archives; Brent Nimno; Ken Norman; Old Wilkes; Genella Olker; Kimberly Parker and the staff of the Thomas J. Boyd Museum Resource Center; Hokie Tom Perry; J. D. Petruzzi; the late Brian Pohanka; Dr. Richard A. Sauers; Naomi Schultz of the Bancroft Library at the University of California-Berkeley; Tccj Smith; the staff of the Southern Historical Collection; Lonnie Speer; Janet H. Spoon of the Patterson School; Dan Slagle; Barbara Upright; Michael Veach of the Filson Historical Society; Gerald Via; the staff of the Virginia Historical Society; the late Wayne Whitman; Gino Williams; the late Mrs. Annie F. Winkler, for her gift of Van Noppen's book; Eric Wittenberg; Susan Wittenberg; John Woodard; and Steve L. Zerbe. To each and every one of you, thank you.

Since the publication of my first book, I've often been asked when I'll finish my next one. Well, I'm proud to say that this book has been delayed in large part because I'm a dad. I am blessed to have an incredible family. My wife, Laurie, is the love of my life—a smarter, more beautiful, more loving woman can't be found—and she and I have been a little busy the last few years with our daughters, Caroline and Taylor Ann. They are the best kids a parent could ask for. Girls, I am very proud of you. One of these days, you might even enjoy Dad's books. My own parents are my biggest fans, and they not only cultivated my interests but also set the example for us all. I am equally blessed to hail from a wonderful and loving extended family, from my sister, Rebecca Marion, and her family to my Connor in-laws.

Above all, I thank God and His Son.

Appendix A

Order of Battle

Organization of Union Forces[1]

Department of the Cumberland
Major General George Thomas

District of East Tennessee
Major General George Stoneman

<u>Cavalry Division</u>
Brigadier General Alvan C. Gillem

<u>First Brigade</u>
Colonel William J. Palmer

Fifteenth Pennsylvania Cavalry (Lieutenant Colonel Charles M. Betts)
Twelfth Ohio Cavalry (Lieutenant Colonel Robert H. Bentley)
Tenth Michigan Cavalry (Lieutenant Colonel Luther Trowbridge/
    Major John H. Standish)[2]

<u>Second Brigade</u>
Brevet Brigadier General Simeon B. Brown

Eleventh Kentucky Cavalry (Major Frederick Slater)
Twelfth Kentucky Cavalry (Major James B. Harrison)
Eleventh Michigan Cavalry (Lieutenant Colonel Charles E. Smith)

<u>Third Brigade</u>
Colonel John K. Miller

Eighth Tennessee Cavalry[3] (Colonel Samuel K. N. Patton/
    Lieutenant Colonel Andrew J. Brown/Major John M. Sawyers[4])
Ninth Tennessee Cavalry[5] (Colonel Joseph H. Parsons)
Thirteenth Tennessee Cavalry (Lieutenant Colonel Barzillah P. Stacy)

Artillery
Battery E, First Tennessee Light Artillery[6] (Lieutenant James M. Reagan)

Fourth Division
Brigadier General Davis Tillson

First Brigade
Colonel Chauncey G. Hawley

First Ohio Heavy Artillery (Major Timothy S. Matthews)
First United States Colored Heavy Artillery (Colonel John A. Shannon)
Second North Carolina Mounted Infantry (Major Andrew J. Bahney)[7]
Third North Carolina Mounted Infantry (Colonel George W. Kirk)
Fourth Tennessee Infantry (Major Thomas H. Reeves)[8]
Wilder Battery, Indiana Light Artillery (Captain Hubbard T. Thomas)[9]
Engineer Battalion
Band[10]

Second Brigade[11]
Colonel Horatio G. Gibson

Thirty-fourth Kentucky Infantry[12] (Colonel William Y. Dillard)
First Tennessee Infantry[13] (Lieutenant Wiley M. Christian)
Seventh Tennessee Mounted Infantry (Lieutenant Colonel James J. Dail)
Second Tennessee Infantry (Lieutenant Elisha Harbour)
Second Ohio Heavy Artillery (Major Daniel W. Hoffman)

Fourth Army Corps,[14]
Major General David S. Stanley

First Division
Brigadier General Nathan Kimball

First Brigade
Colonel Isaac M. Kirby

Twenty-first Illinois (Lieutenant Colonel James E. Calloway)
Thirty-eighth Illinois (Lieutenant Colonel Edward Colyer)
Thirty-first Indiana (Lieutenant Colonel James R. Hallowell)
Eighty-first Indiana (Lieutenant Colonel Oliver P. Anderson)
Ninetieth Ohio (Lieutenant Colonel Samuel N. Yeoman)
101st Ohio (Lieutenant Colonel Bedan B. McDanald)

Second Brigade
Colonel Jesse H. Moore

Ninety-sixth Illinois (Captain John K. Pollock)
115th Illinois (Lieutenant Colonel George A. Poteet)
Thirty-fifth Indiana (Colonel Augustus G. Tassin)
Twenty-first Kentucky (Lieutenant Colonel William R. Milward)
Twenty-third Kentucky (Lieutenant Colonel George W. Northrup)
Forty-fifth Ohio (Lieutenant Colonel John H. Humphrey)
Fifty-first Ohio (Colonel Charles H. Wood)

Third Brigade
Colonel Louis H. Waters

Seventy-fifth Illinois (Colonel John E. Bennett)
Eightieth Illinois (Captain James Cunningham)
Eighty-fourth Illinois (Lieutenant Colonel Charles H. Morton)
Ninth Indiana (Colonel Isaac C. B. Suman)
Thirtieth Indiana (Lieutenant Colonel Henry W. Lawton)
Thirty-sixth Indiana (Lieutenant Calvin C. Mclaind)
Eighty-fourth Indiana (Lieutenant Colonel Martin B. Miller)
Seventy-seventh Pennsylvania (Colonel Thomas E. Rose)

Second Division
Brigadier General Washington L. Elliot

FirstBrigade
Brevet Brigadier General Emerson Opdycke

Thirty-sixth Illinois (Captain Benjamin F. Campbell)
Forty-fourth Illinois (Lieutenant Colonel John Russell)

Seventy-third Illinois (Colonel James F. Jaquess)
Seventy-fourth Illinois (Lieutenant Colonel Thomas J. Bryan)
Eighty-eighth Illinois (Lieutenant Colonel George W. Smith)
125th Ohio (Lieutenant Colonel Joseph Bruff)
Twenty-fourth Wisconsin (Major Arthur MacArthur, Jr.)

Second Brigade
Brigadier General Ferdinand Van Derveer

100th Illinois (Lieutenant Colonel Charles M. Hammond)
Fortieth Indiana (Lieutenant Colonel Henry Learning)
Fifty-seventh Indiana (Captain John S. Summers)
Twenty-eighth Kentucky (Lieutenant Colonel J. Rowan Boone)
Twenty-sixth Ohio (Lieutenant Colonel William Clark)
Ninety-seventh Ohio (Colonel John Q. Lane)

Third Brigade
Colonel Joseph Conrad

Forty-second Illinois (Lieutenant Colonel Edgar D. Swain)
Fifty-first Illinois (Captain Merritt B. Atwater)
Seventy-ninth Illinois (Colonel Allen Buckner)
Fifteenth Missouri (Lieutenant Colonel Theodore Meumann)
Sixty-fourth Ohio (Lieutenant Colonel Samuel M. Wolff)
Sixty-fifth Ohio (Major Orlow Smith)

Third Division
Major General Thomas J. Wood

First Brigade
Colonel Charles T. Hotchkiss

Eighty-ninth Illinois (Lieutenant Colonel William D. Williams)
Fifty-first Indiana (Major William N. Denny)
Eighth Kansas (Lieutenant Colonel John Conover)
Fifteenth Ohio (Lieutenant Colonel John McClenahan)
Forty-ninth Ohio (Lieutenant Colonel Joseph R. Bartlett)

Second Brigade
Colonel Henry K. McConnell

Fifty-ninth Illinois (Lieutenant Colonel Clayton Hale)
Forty-first Ohio (Lieutenant Colonel Ephraim S. Holloway)
Seventy-first Ohio (Captain John W. Moody)
Ninety-third Ohio (Lieutenant Colonel Daniel Bowman)
124th Ohio (Lieutenant Colonel James Pickands)

Third Brigade
Brigadier General Samuel Beatty

Seventy-ninth Indiana (Colonel Frederick Knefler)
Eighty-sixth Indiana (Colonel George F. Dick)
Third Michigan (Colonel Moses B. Houghton)
Fourth Michigan (Colonel Jairus W. Hall)
Thirteenth Ohio (Major Joseph T. Snider)
Nineteenth Ohio (Lieutenant Colonel James M. Nash)
Thirteenth Wisconsin (Colonel William P. Lyon)

Artillery Brigade
Major Wilbur F. Goodspeed

Kentucky Light, First Battery (Captain T. S. Thomasson)
First Ohio Light, Battery G (Captain A. Marshall)
Ohio Light, Sixth Battery (Captain Aaron P. Baldwin)
Pennsylvania Light, Battery B (Captain J. Ziegler)

Appendix B

Estimating the Strength of the Cavalry Division of the District of East Tennessee

Due to a paucity of records, the exact strength of Alvan C. Gillem's Cavalry Division of the District of East Tennessee is not known. However, a fair estimate may be calculated by surveying the records that do exist. A starting point is a review of the totals given by several raid participants:

* General Stoneman expected to take a column of six thousand men on the march[1]
* Ohioan Frank Mason, observing that many participating regiments were reduced from effective strength to about half their maximum, placed the size of the division at between six thousand and seven thousand men[2]
* A Pennsylvanian calculated that the division contained about five thousand men, not counting the personnel of the artillery battery[3]
* A trooper who rode with First Brigade headquarters thought that the brigade totaled fifteen hundred or eighteen hundred men and that the division had four or five thousand;[4] this agrees substantially with William J. Palmer's personal guess that his brigade contained about two thousand horsemen[5]
* Finally, U. S. Grant himself figured that Stoneman took about five thousand men on his journey[6]

While none of these estimates purports to be exact, all of them hover between four thousand and six thousand. They also suggest that the First Brigade was the largest of the division. A regiment-by-regiment review arrives at a similar conclusion:

First Brigade (1,589–2,162)

Fifteenth Pennsylvania Cavalry: 506–914[7]
Twelfth Ohio Cavalry: 683[8] or 798[9]
Tenth Michigan Cavalry: 400–450[10]

Second Brigade (1,510)

Eleventh Kentucky Cavalry: 450[11]
Twelfth Kentucky Cavalry: 430[12]
Eleventh Michigan Cavalry: 630[13]

Third Brigade (600)

Eighth Tennessee Cavalry: 200[14]
Ninth Tennessee Cavalry: 0[15]
Thirteenth Tennessee Cavalry: 400[16]

Artillery (fewer than 50)

Battery E, First Tennessee Light Artillery: ?

Taking these estimates in total, then, a reasonable estimate of the size of Stoneman's command is between thirty-seven hundred and forty-three hundred men. Most likely, the division totaled almost exactly four thousand.

It should be added that forty-five hundred men were in Davis Tillson's command.[17]

Notes

The following abbreviations are used in the Notes:

AG	Alvan C. Gillem
CC	Special Collections and Archives, Tutt Library, The Colorado College, Colorado Springs, Colo.
CHS	Steven H. Hart Library, Colorado Historical Society, Denver, Colo.
CSR	Compiled Service Records of Union Soldiers Who Served in Organizations from the State of Tennessee, Record Group 109, National Archives, 1960.
CV	*Confederate Veteran* Magazine
CWLM	The Civil War Library & Museum, Philadelphia, Pa.
DU	Rare Book, Manuscript, and Special Collections Library, Duke University, Durham, N.C.
FHS	The Filson Historical Society, Louisville, Ky.
GR	U.S. Army Generals' Reports of Civil War Service, 1864–87, Record Group 94, M1098, National Archives, Washington, D.C.
GS	George Stoneman
HSP	The Historical Society of Pennsylvania, Philadelphia, Pa.
KY	Military Records and Research Branch, Department of Military Affairs, Frankfort, Ky.
LC	Library of Congress
M	Microcopy
MA	Moravian Archives—Southern Province, Winston-Salem, N.C.
MOLLUS	Military Order of the Loyal Legion of the United States
NA	National Archives, Washington, D.C.
NCDC	National Climactic Data Center, Asheville, N.C.
NCSA	North Carolina State Library and Archives, Raleigh, N.C.
OM	Department of Archives and Special Collections, The University of Mississippi, Oxford, Miss.
OR	U.S. War Department, *The War of the Rebellion: A Compilation of the Official Records of the Union and Confederate Armies.* All references are to Series I unless otherwise noted.
PAJ	*Papers of Andrew Johnson*
R	Reel(s), Roll(s)
RG	Record Group
RR	Civil War Union Volunteer Regiment Records, Record Group 94, Entries 112–15, National Archives, Washington, D.C.
SC	Rare Books and Special Collections, University of South Carolina Libraries
SHC	Southern Historical Collection, Wilson Library, The University of North Carolina at Chapel Hill
SHSP	*Southern Historical Society Papers*
THS	Tennessee Historical Society, Nashville, Tenn.
TSLA	Tennessee State Library and Archives, Nashville, Tenn.
UCB	The Bancroft Library, University of California, Berkeley, Calif.
UM	Bentley Historical Library, University of Michigan, Ann Arbor, Mich.
USAMHI	U.S. Army Military History Institute, Carlisle Barracks, Carlisle, Pa.
UT	The University of Tennessee at Knoxville, Hoskins Library, Special Collections, Knoxville, Tenn.

VHS   Virginia Historical Society, Richmond, Va.
VMI   Virginia Military Institute Archives, Lexington, Va.
WP   William J. Palmer
WV   West Virginia University, West Virginia and Regional History Collection, West
         Virginia Libraries, Morgantown, W. Va.
YU   Beinecke Rare Book and Manuscript Library, Yale University, New Haven, Conn.

PREFACE

[1] J. Robbie Robertson, "The Night They Drove Old Dixie Down," *The Band*. Canaan Music, 1970.

[2] Peter Viney, "The Night They Drove Old Dixie Down (Revisited)," http://theband.hiof. no/articles/dixie_viney.html; "The Band's 'The Night They Drove Dixie Down,'" *Mix: Professional Audio and Music Production*, October 1, 2002.

[3] "The Night They Drove Old Dixie Down," Wikipedia, http://en.wikipedia.org/wiki/The_Night _They_Drove_Old_Dixie_Down.

[4] Brown, *Salisbury Prison*, 13; D.L. David L. Swain to Samuel F. Patterson, in Hickerson, *Echoes of Happy Valley*, May 2, 1866, 110–11; Samuel F. Patterson to David L. Swain, May 15, 1866, Patterson papers, NCSA. There is also a novel, Theresa Meroney's *Tall Gray Gates*, in which George Stoneman and his raiders liberate the inmates of the Salisbury Prison.

[5] Catton, *Never Call Retreat*, 412; Van Noppen, *Stoneman's Last Raid*, ix; Foote, *The Civil War* 3: 848–50.

[6] Grant, *Memoirs*, 571; OR 47 (1), 29; *10th Cavalry*, vol. 40, 15–16; Trowbridge, *Brief History of the 10th Michigan*, 39–40; Mason, *12th Ohio Cavalry*, 100.

[7] *Winston-Salem Journal*, June 8, 2002.

[8] Calvin J. Cowles to unknown, June 22, 1866, Calvin J. Cowles papers, NCSA; Hill, *Guide to North Carolina Highway Markers*, 160; Interview with Dr. William S. Powell, September 11, 1999.

Chapter 1
HAS STONEMAN STARTED YET?
Preparations: Winter 1864–65

[1] Warner, *Generals in Blue*, 426.

[2] OR 49 (2): 28.

[3] George Stoneman autobiographical statement, UCB; *Philadelphia Times*, September 6, 1894; *National Tribune*, September 13, 1894; Fordney, *Stoneman at Chancellorsville*, 7. Busti was later incorporated as the village of Lakewood (Fordney, *Stoneman at Chancellorsville*, 7). Warner (*Generals in Blue*, 481) lists GS's date of birth as August 22.

[4] George Stoneman autobiographical statement, UCB; Fordney, *Stoneman at Chancellorsville*, 8; Robertson, *Stonewall Jackson*, 40; Warner, *Generals in Blue*, 481; *San Marino Tribune*, March 29, 1981. Stoneman claimed that the magazine was the *Southern Literary Messenger*, but that publication published no such article during the time period in question. Seven other young men, including the son of the local Congressman, competed for the Academy's slot (George Stoneman autobiographical statement, UCB).

[5] Fordney, *Stoneman at Chancellorsville*, 9; Warner, *Generals in Blue*, 481; Cullum, *Biographical Register* 1: 280; George Stoneman autobiographical statement, UCB; GS to Miss Lucy Williams, June 3, 1853, Lucy Williams Polk papers, NCSA.

[6] GS to Miss Lucy Williams, June 21, 1853, Lucy Williams Polk papers, NCSA; Fordney, *Stoneman at Chancellorsville*, 9–10; *Philadelphia Times*, September 6, 1894; *In Memoriam: George Stoneman*, MOLLUS pamphlet; Cullum, *Biographical Register* 1: 280–81.

[7] Pennsylvania Commandery—MOLLUS scrapbook No. 1 (Insignia Records, 1–60), Insignia Record No. 30—George Stoneman, CWLM; *In Memoriam: George Stoneman*, MOLLUS pamphlet; Warner, *Generals in Blue*, 574; Cullum, *Biographical Register* 1: 281; Fordney, *Stoneman at Chancellorsville*, 10; Sears, *Union Cavalry* 1: 54; Longacre, *Lincoln's Cavalrymen*, 5.

[8] Welsh, *Medical Histories*, 323; "Hemorrhoids," National Digestive Diseases Information Clearinghouse, http://www.niddk.nih.gov/health/digest/pubs/hems/hemords.htm; "Hemorrhoids (piles)," MedicineNet.com, http://www.medicinenet.com/Script/Main/art.asp?articlekey=383; GS to Miss Lucy Williams, March 28, 1853, Lucy Williams Polk papers, NCSA; Proceedings of a Board to Retire Disabled Officers, case of Col. George Stoneman, 21st Infantry, Letter to the Secretary of War, November 2, 1871, Service Record of George Stoneman; Fordney, *Stoneman at Chancellorsville*, 40; Longacre, *Lincoln's Cavalrymen*, 56. GS traveled extensively in Europe from 1857–59, probably in an effort to heal his malady (George Stoneman autobiographical statement, UCB).

[9] *Philadelphia Times*, September 6, 1894; Fordney, *Stoneman at Chancellorsville*, 40; Evans, *Sherman's Horsemen*, 48; Cullum, *Biographical Register* 1: 281.

[10] *In Memoriam: George Stoneman*, MOLLUS pamphlet; *National Tribune*, September 13, 1894; Fordney, *Stoneman at Chancellorsville*, 10; Longacre, *Lincoln's Cavalrymen*, 12; Roberts, *Encyclopedia of Historic Forts*, 755. Fort Brown was originally named Fort Taylor, but was renamed in honor of an officer who died in the Mexican War (Roberts, *Encyclopedia of Historic Forts*, 755).

[11] Charles F. Adams, Jr. to his mother, May 12, 1863, in Ford, *Cycle of Adams Letters*, 2:8; O'Neill, "Federal Cavalry Operations in the Peninsula Campaign," 86–87; Sears, ed., *Papers of McClellan*, 61; Boatner, *Civil War Dictionary*, 907–8; Fordney, *Stoneman at Chancellorsville*, 10; Starr, *Union Cavalry* 1: 236–37, 266; Longacre, *Lincoln's Cavalrymen*, 56. GS applied for service on McClellan's staff (George Stoneman autobiographical statement, UCB).

[12] Longacre, *Lincoln's Cavalrymen*, 57–58.

[13] Fordney, *Stoneman at Chancellorsville*, 51; *San Marino Tribune*, March 29, 1981; W.W. Averell, "With the Cavalry on the Peninsula," *Battles and Leaders* 2: 429–33; O'Neill, "Federal Cavalry Operations in the Peninsula Campaign," 99 ff., 120, 141; Welsh, *Medical Histories*, 323; Starr, *Union Cavalry* 1: 266, 275–76; Longacre, *Lincoln's Cavalrymen*, 95.

[14] *In Memoriam: George Stoneman*, MOLLUS pamphlet; *Report to Accompany S. 205*, Senate Calendar No. 632; Starr, *Union Cavalry* 1: 319–20; Fordney, *Stoneman at Chancellorsville*, 11.

[15] Greene, "Stoneman's Raid," 68; Starr, *Union Cavalry* 1: 339, 352; Fordney, *Stoneman at Chancellorsville*, 13, 17–19; Cullum, *Biographical Register* 1: 281.

[16] Greene, "Stoneman's Raid," 69–70; Starr, *Union Cavalry* 1: 353–55; OR 25 (2): 244; Longacre, *Lincoln's Cavalrymen*, 141.

[17] Greene, "Stoneman's Raid," 75–89; Fordney, *Stoneman at Chancellorsville*, 20–21, 30–40; Longacre, *Lincoln's Cavalrymen*, 142–43; OR 25 (1): 1060.

[18] Greene, "Stoneman's Raid," 91–96; OR 25 (1): 1062; Fordney, *Stoneman at Chancellorsville*, 41–43.

[19] Greene, "Stoneman's Raid," 96–100; Starr, *Union Cavalry* 1: n.6, 357, 361–62; Journal of Maj. Gen. Samuel P. Heintzelman, May 6 and May 8, 1863, in OR Supplement 25: 467, 469; Fordney, *Stoneman at Chancellorsville*, 43–47, 50–51; Longacre, *Lincoln's Cavalrymen*, 145; Charles F. Adams, Jr. to his mother, May 12, 1863, in Ford, *Cycle of Adams Letters*, 2:8. Historians such as Starr, Greene, and Fordney are less hard on GS, pointing out that the New Yorker did not command a perfect raid, but his effort compares favorably with other Civil War raids. For the "wet shirt" comment, see Joseph Hooker to Samuel P. Bates, December 24, 1878 and n.d., in Bates papers, Pennsylvania State Archives, quoted in Greene, "Stoneman's Raid," 97–98.

[20] Greene, "Stoneman's Raid," 99; OR 25 (3): 11; Welsh, *Medical Histories*, 323; Starr, *Union*

Cavalry 1: 367–68 and n.6; Fordney, *Stoneman at Chancellorsville*, 47, 57.

[21] Flower, *Edwin McMasters Stanton*, 365.

[22] Cullum, *Biographical Register* 1: 281; Fordney, *Stoneman at Chancellorsville*, 58; Wittenberg, "Learning the Hard Lessons of Logistics," *North & South*, January 1999, 76–77; Poulter, "The Cavalry Bureau," *North & South*, January 1999, 70; Longacre, *Lincoln's Cavalrymen*, 221–22.

[23] Fordney, *Stoneman at Chancellorsville*, 58–59; Fordney, "Stoneman's Failed Bid for Glory," *America's Civil War*, May 1998, 26–28; Evans, *Sherman's Horsemen*, xv, 66; Sherman, *Memoirs* 2: 5; *OR* 38 (2): 509; *OR* (4): 507; Bragg, "Union General Lost," 16. Only one division of the cavalry corps took to the field for the Atlanta campaign.

[24] Sherman, *Memoirs* 2: 87–88; Starr, *Union Cavalry* 3: 465; *OR* 38 (1): 75. In his memoirs, Sherman reported that GS commanded 6,500 men, but his report credited GS with 5,000 men.

[25] Starr, *Union Cavalry* 3: 465; Sherman, *Memoirs* 2: 87–88; *OR* 38 (1): 75–76; Evans, *Sherman's Horsemen*, 295–98.

[26] Starr, *Union Cavalry* 3: 466, 468; Sherman, *Memoirs* 2: 98; *OR* 38 (2): 914; Evans, *Sherman's Horsemen*, 293–94, 296–97; Bragg, "Union General Lost," 16–17.

[27] Starr, *Union Cavalry* 3: 469–70; Sherman, *Memoirs* 2: 98; *OR* 38 (1): 75–76; *OR* (2): 914; Evans, *Sherman's Horsemen*, 297, 300, 304, 310–15, 318, 324, 340; Bragg, "Union General Lost," 19–22.

[28] Fordney, "Failed Bid," 32; Evans, *Sherman's Horsemen*, 340; Warner, *Generals in Blue*, 481–82; Welsh, *Medical Histories*, 323; Fordney, *Stoneman at Chancellorsville*, 60; *OR* 38 (2): 914; Bragg, "Union General Lost," 22–23.

[29] "Burst like a shell" quoted in Evans, *Sherman's Horsemen*, n. 21, 591; 474; Sherman, *Memoirs* 2: 98; Starr, *Union Cavalry* 3: 556; Fordney, "Failed Bid," 30, 32; Bragg, "Union General Lost," 23. GS was imprisoned in Macon and Charleston, S.C., before being exchanged for Confederate Brig. Gen. Daniel C. Govan.

[30] Longacre, *Lincoln's Cavalrymen*, 37; *OR* 45 (1): 1074; *OR* (2): 54; Starr, *Union Cavalry* 3: 556.

[31] Warner, *Generals in Blue*, 425; Marvel, "The Battle for Saltville," 11–13, 50; Miller, *Our Service in East Tennessee*, 10; Whisonant, "Union Raiders in the New River Valley," 30.

[32] *OR* 45 (2): 54, 402; Fordney, *Stoneman at Chancellorsville*, 58.

[33] *OR* 45 (2): 54, 80, 402.

[34] Evans, *Sherman's Horsemen*, 50.

[35] Warner, *Generals in Blue*, 54–55; Ramsey, *The Raid*, 14, 18–19; *OR* 45 (1): 807, 809 1073; Starr, *Union Cavalry* 3: 557–58; Scott, *13th Tennessee*, 219.

[36] *OR* 45 (1): 807, 810–11, 813; Ramsey, *The Raid*, 9–10, 19–23, 25–26, 28, 31, 33, 37–38, 39, 41, 44, 50–52, 58, 63, 69–70, 85, 87–89, 92–93, 94–99, 101, 103–4, 126, 128–38; Scott, *13th Tennessee*, 220–24, 228; *11th Cavalry*, 734; *OR* 45 (1): 810–14; Starr, *Union Cavalry* 3: 559; *Michigan in the War* 41: 735–36; Marvel, "Saltville," 54; Report of AG, December 29, 1873, 534, 538–40, GR; *Confederate Military History* 3: 535; Donnelly, "Confederate Lead Mines," 411–12; Starr, *Union Cavalry* 3: 559; Whisonant, "Wythe County Lead Mines," 17.

[37] Ramsey, *The Raid*, 144, 186; *OR* 45 (1): 813–15; *OR* (2): 402; GS to John Breckinridge, January 26, 1865, George Stoneman papers, Chicago Historical Society; Marvel, "Saltville," 54; Graf, *PAJ* 7: xxx; *CV* 10 (July 1902): 305.

[38] *OR* 45 (2): 52, 402.

[39] Warner, *Generals in Blue*, 411; Sherman, *Memoirs* 2: 213, 225, 237–39; Grant, *Memoirs*, 513, 516; Barrett, *Sherman's March*, 25–26.

[40] *OR* 45 (2): 621; Sherman, *Memoirs* 2: 213; Grant, *Memoirs*, 517; Foote, *Civil War*, 737; Grant, *Memoirs*, 514; *OR* 47 (2): 859; *OR* 49 (1): 342, 616–17; Simon, *Papers of U.S. Grant* 13: 360.

[41] *OR* 46 (2) 606; Grant, *Memoirs*, 516; McPherson, *Battle Cry of Freedom*, 825; Foote, *Civil War*, 737–38, 803.

[42] *OR* 49 (1): 616, 663.

[43] Warner, *Generals in Blue*, 500–501; Boatner, *Civil War Dictionary*, 836; Sherman, *Memoirs* 2: 216, 223.

[44] *OR* 49 (2): 534; *OR* (1): 616, 636–37, 663, 680–81, 710, 805, 882; *Tennesseans in the Civil War* 1: 342, 344, 352. On February 9, GS reported 1,993 men under his command.

[45] *OR* 49 (1): 616, 636–37, 693, 680–81, 710, 732, 738.

[46] *OR Supplement* 65: 551; *Tennesseans in the Civil War* 1: 342, 352; Mason, *12th Ohio Cavalry*, 95–96; Reid, *Ohio in the War* 2: 824; *Bucyrus Journal*, September 17, 1886; Banks, "Memoranda," diary entry for March 1, 1865, 291. While in Kentucky, the 12th Ohio was separated and stationed at three locations: Irvine, Richmond, and Crab Orchard. For reference to one of these detachments, see *OR* 49 (1): 766.

[47] Mason, *12th Ohio Cavalry*, 97–98; Reid, *Ohio in the War* 2: 824; Banks, "Memoranda," diary entries for March 1–March 11, 1865, 291–93; *Bucyrus Journal*, September 17, 1886.

[48] *Annual Report of the Adjutant General of Michigan* 1: 98; Robertson, *Michigan in the War*, 737; Entries for February 21–23, March 7, and March 14, 1865, Henry Birdsall diary, SHC; Dyer, *Compendium* 3: 1194–95; *Union Regiments of Kentucky*, 228, 236; *Union Army* 4: 354; *OR* 49 (1): 851. A detachment of the 11th Kentucky Cavalry did not accompany the regiment on the raid (*OR* 49 [2]: 438).

[49] *OR* 49 (1): 326; March 19, 1865, Allen Frankenberry diaries, WV. Frankenberry was originally assigned to the signal corps unit attached to Davis Tillson's infantry, but was transferred to the cavalry on March 22 (March 22, 1865, Allen Frankenberry diaries, WV).

[50] *OR* 49 (1): 732–33, 750–51, 753.

[51] Dyer, *Compendium* 1: 473; *10th Cavalry*, 12; Trowbridge, *Brief History of the 10th Michigan*, 32; *OR Supplement* 65: 637.

[52] WP to "My Dear Mother", February 12, 1865, and WP to Frank Jackson, (March 20, 1865), William J. Palmer Collection, CHS; Dyer, *Compendium* 1: 473; *OR* 49 (1): 840; Betts, "Stoneman's Great Cavalry Raid;" Septimus W. Knight diary, March 6, March 16, 1865, VMI; Frederic Antes diary, March 18, 1865, Civil War Miscellaneous Collection, USAMHI. One witness reported that GS arrived at Wauhatchie on the morning of March 7 with about 3,000 cavalrymen. These were probably the men of the 11th and 12th Kentucky. (Wilson, *Column South*, 267.)

[53] *OR* 49 (2): 12; Special orders No. 60, March 17, 1865, Department of the Cumberland Endorsement and Memoranda Book, Records of the U.S. Army continental commands, RG 393, pt. 2, entry 2780, NA. The command was formally organized on March 17, under Special Orders No. 60. See the Appendix, "Estimating the Strength of the Cavalry Division of the District of East Tennessee," for a detailed analysis of its manpower.

[54] *OR* 49 (1): 863, 874; GS to L. Thomas, April 30, 1865, and GS to unknown, June 19, 1865, both in Letters Sent, District of East Tennessee, Records of the U.S. Army continental commands, RG 393, pt. 2, entry 2740; NA; *OR* 31 (1): 279.

[55] AG to Andrew Johnson, August 16, 1861, in Graf and Haskins, *PAJ* 4: 680; *OR* 49 (2): 12; *OR* 49 (1): 330.

[56] *OR* 49 (1): 679, 680–681, 693–94, 700–701, 732; *11th Cavalry*, 733; Entry for January 8, 1865, Henry Birdsall diary, SHC; Simon, *Papers of U.S. Grant* 13: 416; WP to Frank Jackson, February 12, 1865, William J. Palmer Collection, CHS.

[57] *OR* 49 (1): 697, 700, 728, 732; Grant, *Memoirs*, 516; Simon, *Papers of U.S. Grant* 13: 416. The War Department sent more than 6,000 horses to Canby between October 20, 1864 and March 31, 1865 (*OR* 46 [3]: 718).

[58] *OR* 49 (1): 744.

[59] *OR* 49 (1): 810; Paul Hersh to "Jim", March 2, 1865, Paul Hersh letters, Civil War Miscellaneous Collection, USAMHI; Wilson, *Column South*, 266–67, 269; WP to "My Dear Mother,"

February 22, 1865, William J. Palmer Collection, CHS. Estimates on the number of horses received by the regiment range from 250–400.

[60] *Bucyrus Journal*, September 17, 1886; *Official Roster of Ohio* 11: 587.

[61] March 6, March 14, and March 15, 1865, Henry Birdsall diary, SHC.

[62] OR 49 (2): 438; *Tennesseans in the Civil War* 1: 342, 344, 352; Hewitt, *Supplement*, pt. 2, 65: 558–59, 574–79; Morning Reports, Companies A–F, March 25, 1865, 10th Michigan Cavalry, RR; Regimental Letter, Endorsement, Order, and Guard Report for the 10th Michigan Cavalry, RR; Evans, *Court Martial of Samuel K.N. Patton*, 1; Scott, *13th Tennessee*, 250. A report dated April 3, 1865, lists 540 men present with a detachment of the 10th Michigan Cavalry at Knoxville, Tenn. Company M provides an example why. Of ninety-two men and three officers on the company's rolls, only one officer and forty-nine men went on the raid—because they only had sixty-two horses available (Morning Reports, Companies G–M, 10th Michigan Cavalry, RR).

[63] OR 49 (1): 744, 773; McAulay, *Carbines of the U.S. Cavalry*, 40, 58, 61, 65; Garavaglia and Worman, "Many Were Broken," *North & South*, June 1999, 53–54; Trotter, *Bushwhackers*, 115; Longacre, *Lincoln's Cavalrymen*, 40–41; WP to Frank Jackson, February 12, 1865, William J. Palmer Collection, CHS; Regimental Orders Book for the 11th Kentucky Cavalry, RR. The men of the 11th Kentucky also carried Colt repeating pistols.

[64] Regimental Order and Ordnance Book for the Cos. H and M, 10th Michigan Cavalry, RR; Morning Reports for the 11th Michigan Cavalry, RR; OR 49 (1): 732; Special Orders #33, Regimental Orders Book for Companies A–H, 8th Tennessee Cavalry, and Special Orders #9, Regimental Order Book for the 13th Tennessee Cavalry, RR; Longacre, *Lincoln's Cavalrymen*, 41–42. According to Marvel, "Saltville," 46, both the 11th Michigan and the 12th Ohio used Spencer repeaters during the Saltville raid.

[65] Wilson, *Column South*, 266–67, 269; Paul Hersh to "Jim," March 2, 1865, Paul Hersh letters, Civil War Miscellaneous Collection, USAMHI; Ordnance and Ordnance Stores Receipt, March 16, 1865, William J. Palmer papers, CC. Recipients of the Spencer turned in their Sharps carbines.

[66] OR 49 (1): 717, 725.

[67] OR 47 (2): 859–60; OR 49 (1): 773. The reports Grant saw were generated by George Kirk, who, on February 1, took six hundred Federals on a raid into Haywood County (Trotter, *Bushwhackers*, 237, 240–41).

[68] OR 49 (1): 344, 777–78.

[69] OR 49 (1): 778, 810. In his report of these events, Thomas again blamed "the difficulty of procuring animals for his command and the bad condition of the roads" (OR 49 [1]: 344).

[70] *Brownlow's Knoxville Whig*, March 15, 1865; Precipitation records for South Carolina, Tennessee, and Virginia, 1865, NCDC; OR 49 (1): 848, 856; *Carolina Watchman*, March 3, 1865; February 24, March 5, March 8, March 14, 1865, Allen Frankenberry diaries, WV. Washington's weather station would record more rainfall in 1865 than any year since 1843.

[71] OR 49 (1): 344, 854, 894; OR (2): 28, 30, 43, 103–4; Bradley, *Astounding Close*, 15; Simon, *Papers of U.S. Grant* 14: 196, 198. Phil Sheridan did not march on Lynchburg as originally planned. If he had, Thomas told Stoneman to leave the East Tennessee and Virginia Railroad alone and focus on Danville.

[72] OR 49 (1): 616, 848, 854; Simon, *Papers of U.S. Grant* 14: 198.

[73] OR 49 (1): 873–74, 883; GS to William D. Whipple, March 9, 1865, Letters Sent, District of East Tennessee, Records of U.S. Army continental commands, Entry 2740, RG 393, pt. 2, NA; OR 49 (2): 21.

[74] OR 49 (1): 873; Robert Morrow to William J. Palmer, March 10, 1865, Letters Sent, District of East Tennessee, Records of the U.S. Army continental commands, RG 393, pt. 2, entry 2740, NA; William J. Palmer to "My Dear Colonel," February 8, 1865, William Jackson Palmer papers, YU; Regimental Orders Book for Companies D, F, G, J, and K, 12th Kentucky Cavalry,

RR; Robert Morrow to various commands, March 13, 1865, Letters Sent, District of East Tennessee, Records of the U.S. Army continental commands, RG 393, pt. 2, entry 2740, NA; Diary, March 10, 1865, Charles M. Betts papers, HSP; Ordnance and Ordnance Stores Receipt, March 16, 1865, William J. Palmer papers, CC. Commands were even reminded to secure at least ten lariats for each company to use as picket ropes.

[75] *OR* 49 (1): 883, 916; *OR* 49 (2): 46, 103; WP to Frank Jackson, March 21, 1865, William J. Palmer Collection, CHS; *Brownlow's Knoxville Whig*, March 22, 1865.

[76] *OR* 49 (2): 46.

Chapter 2
A COLUMN OF FIRE
Tennessee: March 14–27, 1865

[1] *OR* 49 (1): 918; *OR* 49 (2): 5.

[2] *OR* 49 (1): 5–6, 918; *OR* 49 (2): 5; March 18–22, 1865, Henry Birdsall diary, SHC.

[3] Mason, *12th Ohio Cavalry*, 98; Banks, "Memoranda," diary entries for March 13, March 14, March 16, 1865, 293–94. One writer reported in error that Palmer's brigade left for Strawberry Plains on the morning of March 20 (Mason, *12th Ohio Cavalry*, 98).

[4] Fordney, "Tailed Bid," 2; Langellier, et. al., *Myles Keogh*, 73; Kirk, *15th Pennsylvania*, 524; Betts, "Stoneman's Great Cavalry Raid."

[5] Diary, March 18, 1865, Charles M. Betts papers, HSP; Wilson, *Column South*, 276; Betts, "Stoneman's Great Cavalry Raid;" Septimus W. Knight diary, March 21, 1865, VMI; Kirk, *15th Pennsylvania*, 492, 520; Morning Reports for Companies A–D and F–L, 15th Pennsylvania Cavalry, RR. At least two companies of the 15th, A and C, did not leave Knoxville until March 22 (Morning Reports for Companies A–D, 15th Pennsylvania Cavalry, RR).

[6] *OR* 49 (2): 21; Trowbridge, *Brief History of the 10th Michigan*, 32–33; *10th Cavalry*, 1; Kirk, *15th Pennsylvania*, 520; Maj. John H. Standish to Brig. Gen. S. Thomas, June 4, 1865, in Regimental Letter, Endorsement, Order, and Guard Report Book, 10th Michigan Cavalry, RR; Morning Reports for Companies A–F, March 21, 1865, 10th Michigan Cavalry, RR. The author of the cited letter is listed only by rank and position, but Standish held the position when the incident in the text occurred (*10th Cavalry*, vol. 40, 12).

[7] *Brownlow's Knoxville Whig*, March 15, 1865; Scott, *13th Tennessee*, 233; *OR* 49 (1): 326, 330; Barchfield's Memoranda, Arnell Collection, UT; Descriptive List, Companies A–D and F–L, 1st Tennessee Light Artillery, RR; March 16, March 18, 1865, Allen Frankenberry diaries, WV. The author of Barchfield's Memoranda is unknown, but internal evidence suggests that he was a member of a Tennessee regiment who participated in Stoneman's raid.

[8] Circular Order, March 15, 1865, Charles M. Betts papers, HSP; Kirk, *15th Pennsylvania*, 520; Longacre, *Lincoln's Cavalrymen*, 45. Since the command carried several different types of small arms, each company's pack mule solved the problem of supplying a variety of arms from a divisional cache.

[9] *Eleventh Cavalry*, 733; Ordnance and Ordnance Stores Receipt, March 16, 1865, William J. Palmer papers, CC; Sample Autobiography, p. 11–12, CC; *Official Roster of Ohio* 11: 615; Mason, "Stoneman's Last Campaign," 22–24.

[10] *OR* 49 (1): 19, 330, 339, 616, 848, 854, 874; *OR* (2): 12–13; Warner, *Generals in Blue*, 506–7; Van Noppen, *Stoneman's Last Raid*, 11; GS to Davis Tillson, March 10, 1865, Letters Sent, District of East Tennessee, Records of the U.S. Army continental commands, RG 393, pt. 2, entry 2740, NA; Miller, *History of the First Ohio Heavy Artillery*, 23, 44; Wilson, *Column South*, 276. Tillson's second brigade remained at Knoxville with its commander, Horatio G. Gibson, who ran district headquarters in Stoneman's absence (*OR* 49 [2]: 54, 438).

[11] Septimus W. Knight diary, March 22, 1865, VMI; Kirk, *15th Pennsylvania*, 492; March 21, 1865, Allen Frankenberry diaries, WV.

[12] Angelo Wiser maps, LC.

[13] *OR* 49 (2): 534; Precipitation records for Tennessee and Virginia in 1865, NCDC; *Brownlow's Knoxville Whig*, March 22 and 29, 1865. Stoneman's District of East Tennessee reported 16,756 men aggregate present for duty during April 1865. Stoneman took less than four of his total six brigades into the field (AG's three-brigade Cavalry Division was missing part of the Tennessee Brigade; Tillson's two-brigade division left one brigade behind).

[14] March 25, 1865, Allen Frankenberry diaries, WV.

[15] Warner, *Generals in Blue*, 175; Cullum, *Biographical Register* 1: 445, 448; Welsh, *Medical Histories*, 131–32.

[16] Warner, *Generals in Blue*, 175; Cullum, *Biographical Register* 1: 443, 445.

[17] James W. Scully to "My Dear Wife," November 22, 1861, James Wall Scully papers, DU; Cullum, *Biographical Register* 1: 443.

[18] *OR* 1: 344; James Chester, "Inside Sumter In '61," *Battles and Leaders* 1: 50; *Encyclopedia of Historic Forts*, 209–10; Cullum, *Biographical Register* 1: 444; Boatner, *Civil War Dictionary*, 436; AG to Andrew Johnson, August 16, 1861, in Graf and Haskins, *PAJ* 4: 679–80.

[19] James W. Scully to "My Dear Wife," November 10, 1861, James Wall Scully papers, DU; Warner, *Generals in Blue*, 175; Cullum, *Biographical Register* 1: 444–45; Graf and Haskins, *PAJ* 4: 681, n. 7; James W. Scully to "My Dear Wife," December 6, 1861; James W. Scully to "My darling wife," February 8, 1862, both in James Wall Scully papers, DU; *OR* 7: 81.

[20] Boatner, *Civil War Dictionary*, 487–89; R.M. Kelly, "Holding Kentucky for the Union," *Battles and Leaders* I: 387–90; James W. Scully to "My Dear Wife," January 17, 1862; James W. Scully to "My Dear Wife," January 20, 1862, both in James Wall Scully papers, DU; *OR* 7: 81. AG was breveted major for his service at Mill Springs (Cullum, *Biographical Register* 1: 444).

[21] Warner, *Generals in Blue*, 175; Cullum, *Biographical Register* 1: 445; *OR* 10: 296.

[22] James W. Scully to his wife, April 13, 1862; James W. Scully to his wife, April 20, 1862, both in James Wall Scully papers, DU; James W. Scully to "My Dear Wife," December 12, 1861, James Wall Scully papers, DU; Report of AG, December 29, 1873, 524, GR; Graf and Haskins, *PAJ* 4: 680, n. 1; AG to Andrew Johnson, April 27, 1862, in Graf and Haskins, *PAJ* 5: 337; W.G. Brownlow, Horace Maynard, and Andrew Johnson to Abraham Lincoln, November 24, 1862, in Graf and Haskins, *PAJ* 6: 71.

[23] Warner, *Generals in Blue*, 175; AG to Andrew Johnson, May 14, 1862, in Graf and Haskins, *PAJ* 5: 390–91, n. 1. The 10th Tennessee had been known as the 1st Middle Tennessee Infantry (General Orders No. 2, June 10, 1865, in Graf, ed., *PAJ* 7: 386); Cullum, *Biographical Register* 1: 444, 446; Andrew Johnson to Don C. Buell, August 8, 1862, in Graf and Haskins, *PAJ* 5: 600; Report of AG, December 29, 1873, 524–25, GR.

[24] Report of AG, December 29, 1873, 525, GR; Warner, *Generals in Blue*, 175–76; Cullum, *Biographical Register* 1: 444, 446.

[25] Report of AG, December 29, 1873, 527, GR; Warner, *Generals in Blue*, 175; Cullum, *Biographical Register* 1: 444, 446; James W. Scully to Andrew Johnson, October 25, 1863, in Graf and Haskins, *PAJ* 6: 436–38; AG to Andrew Johnson, January 7, 1864, in Graf and Haskins, *PAJ* 6: 540–43; AG to Andrew Johnson, March 15, 1864, in Graf and Haskins, *PAJ* 6: 646, n.1. AG's rank was not confirmed by Congress until 1864, and only then at Johnson's urging (Andrew Johnson to Abraham Lincoln, September 12, 1864, in Graf, ed., *PAJ* 7: 157).

[26] Graf and Haskins, *PAJ* 6: xxxvi, 198–99, 199 n.3; Cullum, *Biographical Register* 1: 444, 446; Warner, *Generals in Blue*, 176; Executive Order, August 1, 1864, in Graf, *PAJ* 7: 70; Cullum, *Biographical Register* 1: 444, 446; Report of AG, December 29, 1873, 527–31, 548, GR.

[27] Graf and Haskins, *PAJ* 6: xxxvi, 199 n. 3; Cullum, *Biographical Register* 1: 444, 446; AG to Andrew Johnson, November 15, 1864, in Graf, *PAJ* 7: 290–91; Report of AG, December 29, 1873, 531–33, GR.

[28] William J. Palmer to "My Dear Colonel," February 8, 1865, William Jackson Palmer letters, YU; Warner, *Generals in Blue*, 176; Cullum, *Biographical Register* 1: 444, 446–47; Report of AG, December 29, 1873, 533–34, 540, GR. Wrote Palmer, "I spent last evening with Gen. Gillem—who is full of the East Tennessee and West Virginia Campaign."

[29] James W. Scully to "My Dear Wife," November 28, 1861; James W. Scully to "My Dear Wife," December 3, 1861; James W. Scully to "My Dear Wife," December 22, 1861, all in James Wall Scully papers, DU; James W. Scully to Andrew Johnson, September 9, 1864, in Graf, ed., *PAJ* 7: 145; Haskins, *PAJ* 7: xxxviii. In fact, Schofield attributed the Bull's Gap setback to a lack of cooperation between AG and Brig. Gen. Jacob Ammen. The two men had quarreled when Schofield assigned Ammen to command AG and the Governor's Guard without Johnson's permission (*OR* 39 [1]: 887; *OR* 45 [1]: 884).

[30] Cullum, *Biographical Register* 1: 448–49; Andrew Johnson to Abraham Lincoln, November 8, 1862, in Graf and Haskins, *PAJ* 6: 49; Petition to Abraham Lincoln, December 4, 1862, in Graf and Haskins, *PAJ* 6: 85.

[31] AG to Andrew Johnson, August 16, 1861, in Graf and Haskins, *PAJ* 1: 680. For his staff, AG recruited Cpt. W.J. Patterson, a member of Battery E of the 1st Tennessee Light Artillery, to serve as acting assistant adjutant general; Lt. Col. Israel C. Smith, an efficient soldier, to be his acting assistant inspector general; Lt. O.C. French, to be the division's commissary of subsistence; Lt. D.M. Nelson, to serve as acting aide-de-camp; Surgeon A.L. Carrick, to be medical director; and Maj. S. Hambright, to be provost marshal (*OR* 49 [2]: 13; *OR* 49 [1]: 336; Report of AG, December 29, 1873, in U.S. Army Generals' Reports of Civil War Service, 550, GR).

[32] Wilson, *Column South*, 276; Banks, "Memoranda," diary entry for March 22, 1865, 294; Frederic Antes diary, March 22, 1865, Civil War Miscellaneous Collection, USAMHI; Sample Autobiography, p. 12, CC; Trotter, *Bushwhackers*, 68; Septimus W. Knight diary, March 22, 1865, VMI; Scott, *13th Tennessee*, 233; *OR* 49 (1): 326, 330; Diary, March 22, 1865, Charles M. Betts papers, HSP; Morning Reports for Companies A–F, March 22, 1865, 10th Michigan Cavalry, RR.

[33] McKenzie, "'Oh! Ours is a Deplorable Condition,'" 201–2; Trowbridge, *Desolate South*, 124.

[34] Longstreet, *Manassas to Appomattox*, 520, 538; Trotter, *Bushwhackers*, 43.

[35] March 12, 1865, Henry Birdsall diary, SHC; Charles F. Weller to "Dear Kate", March 13, 1865, and Charles F. Weller to "Dear Annie", March 20, 1865, Charles F. Weller memoirs and letters, *Civil War Times Illustrated* Collection, USAMHI; Banks, "Memoranda," diary entry for March 22, 1865, 294; Trowbridge, "Stoneman Raid," 99; Paul Hersh to "Jim", March 2, 1865, Paul Hersh letters, Civil War Miscellaneous Collection, USAMHI.

[36] Sample Autobiography, 11, CC. The identity of "General Johnson" is not clear, but it was probably Brig. Gen. Richard W. Johnson, a Kentuckian who commanded a cavalry division under James H. Wilson (Warner, *Generals in Blue*, 254).

[37] March 23, 1865, Allen Frankenberry diaries, WV.

[38] Septimus W. Knight diary, March 23, 1865, VMI; March 23, 1865, Allen Frankenberry diaries, WV; Frederic Antes diary, March 23, 1865, Civil War Miscellaneous Collection, USAMHI; Wilson, *Column South*, 277; March 23, 1865, Henry Birdsall diary, SHC; *OR* 49 (1): 326, 338; Angelo Wiser maps, LC; Kirk, *15th Pennsylvania*, 493; Wert, *Longstreet*, 357; Longstreet, *From Manassas to Appomattox*, 520; Morning Reports for Companies A–D and F–L, 15th Pennsylvania Cavalry, RR.

[39] Scott, *13th Tennessee*, 233; *OR* 49 (1): 330; Kirk, *15th Pennsylvania*, 493; Diary, March 23, 1865, Charles M. Betts papers, HSP; Steven Thomas to "My Dear Wife," June 5, 1865, Calvin Thomas papers, UM; Thomas Hutton diary, March 23, 1865, courtesy TSLA. Michigan cavalryman Steven Thomas remembered drawing these rations on March 24, but the preponderance of evidence indicates that he was incorrect by a day (Steven Thomas to "My Dear Wife," June 5, 1865, Calvin Thomas papers, UM).

⁴⁰ Barchfield's Memoranda, Arnell Collection, UT; Frederic Antes diary, March 23, 1865, Civil War Miscellaneous Collection, USAMHI; *OR* 49 (1): 326; Wilson, *Column South*, 277; March 23, 1865, Allen Frankenberry diaries, WV; March 23, 1865, Henry Birdsall diary, SHC. The dates given in Barchfield's account inaccurately place the Tennesseans as arriving in Morristown on March 26.

⁴¹ March 24, 1865, Allen Frankenberry diaries, WV; Septimus W. Knight diary, March 24, 1865, VMI; Diary, March 24, 1865, Charles M. Betts papers, HSP; Morning Reports, Companies A–F, March 25, 1865, 10th Michigan Cavalry, RR; Regimental Letter, Endorsement, Order, and Guard Report for the 10th Michigan Cavalry, RR.

⁴² Wilson, *Column South*, 276–77; *OR* 49 (1): 330, 338; Trowbridge, "Stoneman Raid," 99; Trowbridge, "The Stoneman Raid of 1865," *JUSCA* 4 (June 1891): 189; Moderwell, "Outline of Stoneman's Raid," Civil War (Federal, Miscellaneous) papers, SHC. Miller was to take the "north or Snapp's Ferry Road" at Bull's Gap. Tillson reported reaching Bull's Gap on March 23, but again he appears to have been in error.

⁴³ *OR* 49 (1): 330, 1022; Betts, "Stoneman's Great Cavalry Raid;" Frederic Antes diary, March 24, 1865, Civil War Miscellaneous Collection, USAMHI; Wilson, *Column South*, 277; Diary, March 24, 1865, Charles M. Betts papers, HSP; Angelo Wiser maps, LC; Morning Reports for Companies A–D and F–L, 15th Pennsylvania Cavalry, RR. Estimates of the mileage covered by these two brigades vary.

⁴⁴ March 24, 1865, Allen Frankenberry diaries, WV.

⁴⁵ March 25, 1865, Allen Frankenberry diaries, WV; *OR* 49 (1): 330; Angelo Wiser maps, LC; Frederic Antes diary, March 25, 1865, Civil War Miscellaneous Collection, USAMHI; Septimus W. Knight diary, March 25, 1865, VMI; Trowbridge, *Desolate South*, 124. For one example of the 15th Pennsylvania's previous experience in East Tennessee, see Trotter, *Bushwhackers*, 99–101.

⁴⁶ March 25, 1865, Allen Frankenberry diaries, WV.

⁴⁷ Kirk, *15th Pennsylvania*, 493; Frederic Antes diary, March 25, 1865, Civil War Miscellaneous Collection, USAMHI; Septimus W. Knight diary, March 25, 1865, VMI; Diary, March 25, 1865, Charles M. Betts papers, HSP; Morning Reports for Companies F–L, 15th Pennsylvania Cavalry, RR.

⁴⁸ *OR* 49 (1): 338; Miller, *History of the First Ohio Heavy Artillery*, 44; Miller, *Our Service in East Tennessee*, 13.

⁴⁹ Miller, *History of the First Ohio Heavy Artillery*, 44; Wert, *Longstreet*, 369; Thomas Hutton diary, March 25, 1865, courtesy TSLA; Trowbridge, *Desolate South*, 124; *OR* 49 (1): 337–39.

⁵⁰ Angelo Wiser maps, LC; Diary, March 25, 1865, Charles M. Betts papers, HSP; Banks, "Memoranda," diary entry for March 25, 1865, 295; Morning Reports, Companies A–F, March 25, 1865, 10th Michigan Cavalry, RR; Frederic Antes diary, March 25, 1865, Civil War Miscellaneous Collection, USAMHI; Septimus W. Knight diary, March 25, 1865, VMI; March 25, 1865, Henry Birdsall diary, SHC; March 25, 1865, Allen Frankenberry diaries, WV.

⁵¹ *OR* 49 (1): 330, 338; March 25–26, 1865, Henry Birdsall diary, SHC; Wilson, *Column South*, 276–77; Trowbridge, "The Stoneman Raid of 1865," *JUSCA* 4 (June 1891): 189; Trowbridge, "Stoneman Raid," 99; Steven Thomas to "My Dear Wife," June 5, 1865, Calvin Thomas papers, UM. The cited sources conflict over the number of vehicles that stayed with the column. AG's official report is followed in the text.

⁵² Angelo Wiser maps, LC; *OR* 49 (2): 55; Circular, March 22, 1865, letters sent, District of East Tennessee, Records of the U.S. Army continental commands, RG 393, pt. 2, entry 2740, NA; Circular, March 25, 1865, Book of Regimental Orders, Courts Martial, Rosters, & Muster Rolls for the 15th Pennsylvania Cavalry, RR; *Brownlow's Knoxville Whig*, March 29, 1865 and April 5, 1865.

⁵³ James W. Scully to Andrew Johnson, September 9, 1864, in Graf, ed., *PAJ* 7: 145; Letters of March 11 and March 22, 1865 and Maj. John H. Standish to Brig. Gen. S. Thomas, June 4,

1865, in Regimental Letter, Endorsement, Order, and Guard Report Book, 10th Michigan Cavalry, RR; Letter of Maj. Standish, June 4, 1865, Register of Letters Received and Endorsements Sent, District of East Tennessee, Records of U.S. Army continental commands, RG 393, pt. 2, entry 2774, NA. The Kentucky officer in question was probably Captain Andrew G. Hamilton of the 12th Kentucky Cavalry, although the letters both identified the perpetrator as a Major Hamilton (*Union Regiments of Kentucky*, 237).

[54] March 26, 1865, Allen Frankenberry diaries, WV; March 26, 1865, Henry Birdsall diary, SHC; Wilson, *Column South*, 277; *OR* 49 (1): 330; Morning Reports of Companies F–L, 15th Pennsylvania Cavalry, RR; Frederic Antes diary, March 26, 1865, Civil War Miscellaneous Collection, USAMHI; Septimus W. Knight diary, March 26, 1865, VMI; Kirk, *15th Pennsylvania*, 493; Banks, "Memoranda," diary entry for March 26, 1865, 295; Diary, March 26, 1865, Charles M. Betts papers, HSP; Angelo Wiser maps, LC; Trowbridge, *Desolate South*, 124; March 26, 1865, Allen Frankenberry diaries, WV. The party that had remained at Morristown rejoined the column on March 26.

[55] Wilson, *Column South*, 277; *OR* 49 (1): 330; Morning Reports of Companies A–D and F–L, 15th Pennsylvania Cavalry, RR; March 26, 1865, Henry Birdsall diary, SHC; Frederic Antes diary, March 26, 1865, Civil War Miscellaneous Collection, USAMHI; Septimus W. Knight diary, March 26, 1865, VMI; Kirk, *15th Pennsylvania*, 493; Banks, "Memoranda," diary entry for March 26, 1865, 295; Diary, March 26, 1865, Charles M. Betts papers, HSP; Angelo Wiser maps, LC.

[56] *CV* 27 (May 1919): 182–85.

[57] Steven Thomas to "My Dear Wife," June 5, 1865, Calvin Thomas papers, UM; Morning Reports for Companies A–F, March 26, 1865, 10th Michigan Cavalry, RR.

[58] *To the Members of the 15th Pennsylvania Cavalry*, 23rd Annual Banquet, 8–9.

[59] Steven Thomas to "My Dear Wife," June 5, 1865, Calvin Thomas papers, UM.

[60] *OR* 49 (1): 338; Thomas Hutton diary, March 26–March 30, 1865, courtesy TSLA; Miller, *History of the First Ohio Heavy Artillery*, 44.

[61] *OR* 47 (3): 712, 731; *CV* 10 (July 1902): 305; Warner, *Generals in Gray*, 316–17; Davis, *Headquarters Diary*, 665; Evans, *Confederate Military History* 8: 340–41; R.E. Lee to J.C. Breckinridge, March 21, 1865, R.E. Lee Headquarters papers, VHS. According to Vaughn, Stoneman tried to suggest that Federal forces were evacuating East Tennessee (R.E. Lee to J.C. Breckinridge, March 21, 1865, R.E. Lee Headquarters papers, VHS).

[62] *OR* 47 (3): 712; *CV* 10 (July 1902): 305–6; Warner, *Generals in Gray*, 80. The *Confederate Veteran* article features the report Echols wrote in December 1865 at the request of Robert E. Lee. Echols had replaced Maj. Gen. John C. Breckinridge as department commander in early 1865 when Breckinridge became Confederate secretary of war.

[63] *CV* 10 (July 1902): 305–6; *OR* 49 (1): 1021; Duke, *Morgan's Cavalry*, 617–18; Davis, *Headquarters Diary*, 665.

[64] *CV* 10 (July 1902): 305–6; *OR* 49 (1): 1021; Warner, *Generals in Gray*, 80. Page's artillery batteries were Cpt. Henry C. Douthat's Virginia battery, Cpt. J. Peyton Lynch's Tennessee battery, Cpt. William H. Burrough's Tennessee battery, and King's Saltville Battery or McClung's Tennessee battery under Lt. W.G. Dobson.

[65] *OR* 49 (1): 330; Warner, *Generals in Gray*, 153–54; Trotter, *Bushwhackers*, 112; Scott, *13th Tennessee*, 233; Barchfield's Memoranda, Arnell Collection, UT; *Philadelphia Weekly Times*, January 18, 1879.

[66] Ramsey, *The Raid*, 166; *OR* 49 (1): 330; Scott, *13th Tennessee*, 233, 263–64; Descriptive Book for the 13th Tennessee Cavalry, Companies G–M, RR; *Report of the Adjutant General of Tennessee*, 610; *Tennesseans in the Civil War* 1: 339, 351. After the war, Miller lived in Bristol, Tennessee, perhaps to get away from Carter County, which saw terrible atrocities during the war.

[67] Trowbridge, "The Stoneman Raid of 1865," *JUSCA* 4 (June 1891): 189; Wilson, *Column South*, 277; *OR* 49 (1): 330; Frederic Antes diary, March 27, 1865, Civil War Miscellaneous Col-

lection, USAMHI; Angelo Wiser maps, LC; Betts, "Stoneman's Great Cavalry Raid;" Septimus W. Knight Diary, March 27, 1865, VMI; March 27, 1865, Allen Frankenberry diaries, WV.

[68] Wilson, *Column South*, 277.

[69] Scott, *13th Tennessee*, 234; OR 49 (1): 330; Arthur, *Western North Carolina*, 617; Barchfield's Memoranda, Arnell Collection, UT. Doe River Cove is known today as Hampton, Tennessee.

[70] Kirk, *15th Pennsylvania Cavalry*, 520–21; Angelo Wiser maps, LC; Betts, "Stoneman's Great Cavalry Raid;" OR 49 (1): 330; Frederic Antes diary, March 27, 1865, Civil War Miscellaneous Collection, USAMHI; Septimus W. Knight diary, March 27, 1865, VMI; Diary, March 27, 1865, Charles M. Betts papers, HSP; Kirk, *15th Pennsylvania*, 493, 521; OR 49 (2): 112; March 27, 1865, Henry Birdsall diary, SHC.

[71] Kirk, *15th Pennsylvania*, 493, 521; March 27, 1865, Allen Frankenberry diaries, WV; *National Tribune*, July 9, 1914. According to Company G, 15th Pennsylvania Cavalry's Record of Events, the road was the Old State Road (OR *Supplement* 57: 383)

[72] Angelo Wiser maps, LC; Betts, "Stoneman's Great Cavalry Raid;" OR 49 (1): 330; Frederic Antes diary, March 27, 1865, Civil War Miscellaneous Collection, USAMHI; Wilson, *Recollections and Experiences*, 110; Septimus W. Knight diary, March 27, 1865, VMI; Diary, March 27, 1865, Charles M. Betts papers, HSP.

Chapter 3
WE ARE GETTING ALONG VERY WELL
Boone to Mount Airy: March 28–April 2, 1865

[1] Graf, ed., *Papers of Andrew Johnson* 5: 391, n. 2. Only a few letters survive from Stoneman's North Carolina relationship. See GS to Miss Lucy Williams, June 21, 1853, Lucy Williams Polk papers, NCSA. Lucy Williams later married Maj. William H. Polk, the brother of President James K. Polk.

[2] Arthur, *Watauga County*, 177; Kirk, *15th Pennsylvania*, 494; Frederic Antes diary, March 28, 1865, Civil War Miscellaneous Collection, USAMHI; Scott, *13th Tennessee*, 234; Barchfield's Memoranda, Arnell Collection, UT.

[3] Angelo Wiser Maps, LC; Stevens, *Rebels in Blue*, 5, 29–41, 174; Barrett, *Civil War in North Carolina*, 237–38.

[4] Stevens, *Rebels in Blue*, 68, 116–18; Barrett, *Civil War in North Carolina*, 237–38.

[5] Stevens, *Rebels in Blue*, 170, 173–74; Angelo Wiser maps, LC; OR 49 (1): 330.

[6] *Union Regiments of Kentucky*, 233–36; Dyer, *Compendium* 3: 1194–95.

[7] Orders for March 14, 1864, and November 4, 1864, and Special Orders No. 31, in Order Book for the 12th Kentucky Cavalry, Companies D, F, G, J, and K, RR.

[8] Arthur, *Watauga County*, 177–78; Beall, "Stoneman's Raid," *The North Carolina Review*, November 11, 1910; R.L. Beall's Account of Stoneman's Raid, Cornelia Phillips Spencer papers, SHC; Stevens, *Rebels in Blue*, 175; Angelo Wiser maps, LC; Polson and McFarland, *Sketches*.

[9] James W. Scully to "My Dear Wife," November 28, 1861, James Wall Scully papers, DU; *National Tribune*, October 13, 1898, quoted in Evans, *Sherman's Horsemen*, 327; Langellier, et. al., *Myles Keogh*, 52.

[10] Langellier, et. al., *Myles Keogh*, 49–50, 51, 54–58, 60–63.

[11] Myles Keogh to unknown, December 24, 1865, Letters of Myles Keogh, National Library of Ireland; Langellier, et. al., *Myles Keogh*, 70–72, 76. For the best summary of Keogh's experience in the Civil War, see Brian C. Pohanka, "Unsurpassed in Dash: Keogh in the American Civil War," in Langellier, et. al., *Myles Keogh*, 67–86.

[12] Langellier, et. al., *Myles Keogh*, 72, 78, 81–82; Longacre, *Lincoln's Cavalrymen*, 231; George Stoneman to Edwin M. Stanton, June 19, 1865, 89.218.11.16, Keogh family papers and

photographs, Museum of the American West, Autry National Center; AG to Ulysses S. Grant, December 21, 1865, 89.218.11.1, Keogh family papers and photographs, Museum of the American West, Autry National Center.

[13] Hatcher, *Last Four Weeks*, 33, 53; *New York Herald*, April 1, 1865; Beall, "Stoneman's Raid," *The North Carolina Review*, October 2, 1910; R.L. Beall's account of Stoneman's Raid, Cornelia Phillips Spencer papers, SHC; Spencer, *Last Ninety Days*, 192; Corey, "Following Stoneman," 13. Historians of Stoneman's Raid are indebted to Dr. Robert LaMarr Beall. As a young man Beall studied at Davidson College, UNC, and Jefferson Medical College, and went on to become a respected physician and citizen in Lenoir, N.C. ("Dr. R.L. Beall," *Lenoir News-Topic*, September 12, 1941). In 1866, at the request of Cornelia Phillips Spencer, Beall researched and wrote a paper about the raid that Spencer used in writing *The Last Ninety Days of the War in North Carolina*. Beall's work was also serialized the 1910 *North Carolina Review* magazine.

[14] Trotter, *Bushwhackers*, 36–45, 75, 168; Inscoe and McKinney, *Heart of Confederate Appalachia*, 74, 86, 166–67, 181. Over nine thousand North Carolinians joined Federal forces during the war (Trotter, *Bushwhackers*, 43). Union leaders once toyed with the idea of sending an army through the North Carolina mountains to threaten Lee's rear. Grant personally checked out mountain passes with that thought in mind, but Sherman talked him out of the idea (Trotter, *Bushwhackers*, 44–45).

[15] Stevens, *Rebels in Blue*, 52, 58, 171–72; *Watauga Democrat*, June 14, 1999; Altmayer, *Family History*, 148; Trotter, *Bushwhackers*, 240–41.

[16] Arthur, *Watauga County*, 180, 335; Altmayer, *Family History*, 148; Dugger, *War Trails*, 124; Hardy, *Watauga County and the Civil War*, 4; Hartley, *Roster of the 1st North Carolina Cavalry*, n.p.; Manarin and Jordan, *North Carolina Troops* 9: 485.

[17] Stevens, *Rebels in Blue*, 45, 174; Arthur, *Watauga County*, 335, 177; *Watauga Democrat*, June 14, 1999. According to the *Watauga Democrat* article, Gragg and others may have dashed to the Councill house when they first saw the Federals enter town. The muster grounds were located where the Boone town utility complex stands on King Street today. Keogh led his raiders along King Street.

[18] Altmayer, *Family History*, 148; Dugger, *War Trails*, 124; Van Noppen, *Stoneman's Last Raid*, 17. Some sources suggest that the home guards had gathered to chase bushwhackers, but an 1866 source verifies that no one knew the Federals were coming (Beall, "Stoneman's Raid," *The North Carolina Review*, November 11, 1910; R.L. Beall's account of Stoneman's Raid, Cornelia Phillips Spencer papers, SHC).

[19] Stevens, *Rebels in Blue*, 174; Trowbridge, *Stoneman Raid*, 99; *Union Regiments of Kentucky*, 236; Beall, "Stoneman's Raid," *The North Carolina Review*, November 11, 1910; R.L. Beall's account of Stoneman's Raid, Cornelia Phillips Spencer papers, SHC; Spencer, *Last Ninety Days*, 193.

[20] Arthur, *Watauga County*, 335, 177; Beall, "Stoneman's Raid," *The North Carolina Review*, November 11, 1910; R.L. Beall's account of Stoneman's Raid, Cornelia Phillips Spencer papers, SHC.

[21] *Watauga Democrat*, June 14, 1999; Arthur, *Watauga County*, 177, 335; Beall, "Stoneman's Raid," *The North Carolina Review*, November 11, 1910; R.L. Beall's account of Stoneman's Raid, Cornelia Phillips Spencer papers, SHC. The *Watauga Democrat* article reported Norris as sixty-two, but Arthur gives Norris's birthday as July 12, 1819. Margaret, Norris's wife of twenty-one years, also survived him.

[22] Jones, *Last Raid*, 14.

[23] Arthur, *Watauga County*, 177; *Watauga Democrat*, June 14, 1999; Stevens, *Rebels in Blue*, 175; Beall, "Stoneman's Raid," *The North Carolina Review*, November 11, 1910; R.L. Beall's account of Stoneman's Raid, Cornelia Phillips Spencer papers, SHC.

[24] *Cincinnati Daily Commercial*, May 10, 1865; Van Noppen, *Stoneman's Last Raid*, 18; *Watauga Democrat*, June 14, 1999; Trowbridge, *Stoneman Raid*, 99; *OR* 49 (1): 331; Manarin and

Jordan, *North Carolina Troops* 9: 485; Banks, "Memoranda," diary entry for March 28, 1865, 295. Sources disagree on the exact number of prisoners; most list fifty to sixty-odd prisoners (see, for example, Kirk, *15th Pennsylvania*, 493–94) but one account (Bushong, *Last Great Stoneman Raid*) even claimed that the raiders captured four hundred prisoners. AG's official report is followed in the text.

[25] Dugger, *War Trails*, 124; Beall, "Stoneman's Raid," *The North Carolina Review*, November 11, 1910; R.L. Beall's account of Stoneman's Raid, Cornelia Phillips Spencer papers, SHC; Kirk, *15th Pennsylvania*, 493–94; *Chicago Tribune*, April 3, 1865; Banks, "Memoranda," diary entry for March 28, 1865, 295; *Union Regiments of Kentucky*, 236; Arthur, *Watauga County*, 177, 179, n. 8; *Watauga Democrat*, June 14, 1999; Stevens, *Rebels in Blue*, 175. Councill was buried in the Boone City Cemetery on Howard Street (Heaton, *Registry of Cemeteries*, 6). Ephraim Norris was laid to rest at the Brown Cemetery in Meat Camp, about six miles northeast of Boone ("Cemeteries of Watauga County").

[26] OR 49 (1): 330–31; OR (2): 112; *Chicago Tribune*, April 3, 1865; AG to Ulysses S. Grant, December 21, 1865, 89.218.11.1, Keogh family papers and photographs, Museum of the American West, Autry National Center. Other Federals on the scene also agreed that nine enemy were killed but listed slightly different prisoner totals (March 28, 1865, Henry Birdsall diary, SHC; March 28, 1865, Allen Frankenberry diaries, WV). Newspaper reports printed similar tallies. See *Daily Ohio State Journal*, April 1, 1865, which reported ten enemy killed and 65 wounded and captured, and repeated the *Chicago Tribune's* brag.

[27] Arthur, *Watauga County*, 177, 335; Beall, "Stoneman's Raid," *The North Carolina Review*, November 11, 1910; R.L. Beall's account of Stoneman's Raid, Cornelia Phillips Spencer papers, SHC; Steven Thomas to "My Dear Wife," June 5, 1865, Calvin Thomas papers, UM.

[28] Septimus W. Knight diary, March 28, 1865, VMI; Diary, March 28, 1865, Charles M. Betts papers, HSP; Kirk, *15th Pennsylvania*, 493–94; Frederic Antes diary, March 28, 1865, Civil War Miscellaneous Collection, USAMHI; Betts, "Stoneman's Great Cavalry Raid;" Morning Reports for Companies A–D and F–L, 15th Pennsylvania Cavalry, RR; Scott, *13th Tennessee*, 234.

[29] Wilson, *Column South*, 278.

[30] Frederic Antes diary, March 28, 1865, Civil War Miscellaneous Collection, USAMHI; Dugger, *War Trails*, 124; Stevens, *Rebels in Blue*, 176; OR 49 (1): 323; OR (2): 112, 331.

[31] OR 49 (1): 331. Stoneman's route generally followed present-day U.S. 421; AG's route followed U.S. 321 and 268.

[32] Beall, "Stoneman's Raid," *The North Carolina Review*, November 11, 1910; R.L. Beall's account of Stoneman's Raid, Cornelia Phillips Spencer papers, SHC; Spencer, *Last Ninety Days*, 194–95.

[33] OR 49 (1): 326, 331.

[34] *Eleventh Cavalry*, 1; *Michigan in the War* 41: 729, 737; OR 39 (2): 71; OR 49 (1): 5–6; Dyer, *Compendium* 1: 536; Long and Hunt, *Brevet Brigadier Generals in Blue*, 84.

[35] OR 49 (1): 331; Buxton, *Village Tapestry*, 3; *Lenoir News-Topic*, September 12, 1941; Trotter, *Bushwhackers*, 257. According to Scott, *Annals of Caldwell County*, 221, the mill had been built in 1828, but this date seems unlikely since its founder was living in Raleigh at the time.

[36] J.C. Norwood to Walter W. Lenoir, April 2, 1865, Lenoir papers, SHC; Mrs. George Harper to George Harper, March 25, 1865, Harper papers, SHC.

[37] OR 49 (1): 331; Arthur, *Watauga County*, 180; Arthur, *Western North Carolina*, 617; Alexander, *Here Will I Dwell*, 139; Alexander, *These Eternal Hills*, 81–82. Accounts of Osborne's adventure vary. Scott, *Annals of Caldwell County*, 221–22, claims that Osborne, his wagon loaded with blankets and other goods for the Confederate army, was napping when the Federals arrived. Somehow, he managed to hide in the factory's bell tower until the Federals decided to burn the building. That brought Osborne from his hiding place. Scott's account seems unlikely, however, since the decision to burn the factory was not made until the next day. Scott also reported that the Federals provided Osborne with a guide, which seems equally doubtful.

[38] *Lenoir News-Topic*, September 12, 1941.

[39] Ashe, *Biographical History* 2: 334–43; Powell, *Dictionary* 5: 35–36; *Heritage of Caldwell*, 454; Inscoe and McKinney, *Heart of Confederate Appalachia*, 234; *Western Sentinel*, May 9, 1862.

[40] Powell, *Dictionary* 5: 36–37; Samuel F. Patterson to David L. Swain, May 15, 1866, Patterson papers, NCSA; Beall, "Stoneman's Raid," *The North Carolina Review*, October 2, 1910; R.L. Beall's account of Stoneman's Raid, Cornelia Phillips Spencer papers, SHC; J.C. Norwood to Walter W. Lenoir, April 2, 1865, Lenoir papers, SHC; Spencer, *Last Ninety Days*, 196.

[41] J.C. Norwood to Walter W. Lenoir, April 2, 1865, Lenoir papers, SHC; Alexander, *Here Will I Dwell*, 140; *OR* 49 (1): 331; Mrs. George Harper to George Harper, March 25 & April 2, 1865, Harper papers, SHC; Samuel F. Patterson to David L. Swain, May 15, 1866, Patterson papers, NCSA; J.C. Norwood to Walter W. Lenoir, April 2, 1865, Lenoir papers, SHC; March 29, 1865, Allen Frankenberry diaries, WV; Beall, "Stoneman's Raid," *The North Carolina Review*, October 2, 1910; R.L. Beall's account of Stoneman's Raid, Cornelia Phillips Spencer papers, SHC; Spencer, *Last Ninety Days*, 196. The civilian, Webb Austin, would be released as the column neared Wilkesboro.

[42] Samuel F. Patterson to David L. Swain, May 15, 1866, Patterson papers, NCSA; Ashe, *Biographical History* 2: 334–43; Powell, *Dictionary* 5: 36; *Heritage of Caldwell*, 454. According to legend, Stoneman reprimanded AG for burning the mill, but Stoneman was not present and AG received no official censure (Trotter, *Bushwhackers*, 257).

[43] J.C. Norwood to Walter W. Lenoir, April 2, 1865, Lenoir papers, SHC; Mrs. George Harper to George Harper, March 25, & April 2, 1865, Harper papers, SHC; J. Gwyn to Rufus T. Lenoir, April 30, 1865, Lenoir papers, SHC; J.C. Norwood to Walter W. Lenoir, April 2, 1865, Lenoir papers, SHC; Johnson, *Touring the Carolinas' Civil War Sites*, 137.

[44] GS to Miss Lucy Williams, March 20, 1853, Lucy Williams Polk papers, NCSA.

[45] Wilson, *Column South*, 278; Septimus W. Knight diary, March 28, 1865, VMI; Claim of Joshua Winkler, #20074, Box 233, Entry 732, Watauga County, N.C., RG 217, settled files of the SCC, NA. Winkler guessed that between eight and ten thousand men camped on his plantation.

[46] Dyer, *Compendium* 3: 1275; *10th Cavalry*, vol. 40, 2–12; Kirk, *15th Pennsylvania*, 524; Trowbridge, *Brief History of the 10th Michigan*, 9.

[47] Trowbridge, "Stoneman Raid," 99; Trowbridge, "The Stoneman Raid of 1865," *JUSCA* 4 (June 1891): 189–90.

[48] Jones, *Last Raid*, 17; Trowbridge, "Stoneman Raid," 100; Trowbridge, "The Stoneman Raid of 1865," *JUSCA* 4 (June 1891): 190; Letter of Luther Trowbridge, June 20, 1865, Register of Letters Received and Endorsements Sent, District of East Tennessee, Records of U.S. Army continental commands, RG 393, pt. 2, entry 2774, NA.

[49] Septimus W. Knight diary, March 29, 1865, VMI; Kirk, *15th Pennsylvania*, 494; Diary, March 29, 1865, Charles M. Betts papers, HSP; Betts, "Stoneman's Great Cavalry Raid;" Frederic Antes diary, March 29, 1865, Civil War Miscellaneous Collection, USAMHI; Wilson, *Column South*, 278; Angelo Wiser maps, LC; Claim of Smith P. Green, #15276, Box 233, Entry 732, Watauga County, N.C., RG 217, Settled Files of the SCC, NA.

[50] Kirk, *15th Pennsylvania*, 494; Diary, March 29, 1865, Charles M. Betts papers, HSP; Betts, "Stoneman's Great Cavalry Raid;" Angelo Wiser maps, LC; Wilson, *Column South*, 278.

[51] Dyer, *Compendium* 3: 1479; Reid, *Ohio in the War* 2: 823–24; *Official Roster of Ohio* 11: 583; Mason, *12th Ohio Cavalry*, 7, 16–17, 96, 98; Kirk, *15th Pennsylvania*, 524. For the regiment's arms, see Marvel, "Saltville," 46; *Bucyrus Journal*, September 17, 1886.

[52] Richardson, *Secret Service*, 451; Hartley, *To Restore The Old Flag*, 26–27; Inscoe and McKinney, *Heart of Confederate Appalachia*, 93.

[53] Banks, "Memoranda," diary entry for March 29, 1865, 295; Calvin J. Cowles to the Reverend C.R. Reddick, 29 March 1865; Precipitation report for South Carolina, Tennessee and Virginia in 1865, NCDC; Hartley, *To Restore the Old Flag*, 8; Calvin J. Cowles to unknown, 22 June 1866; Calvin J. Cowles to Arthur Cowles, 6 April 1865, Calvin J. Cowles papers, NCSA.

"The boys" here apparently refers to some locals who joined the Federals. In a letter to the Reverend C.R. Reddick of April 6, 1865, Cowles related that "The greater number of Negro fellows did likewise."

[54] Clark, *Histories of the Several Regiments* 4: 650; Calvin J. Cowles to Arthur Cowles, 6 April 1865, Calvin J. Cowles papers, NCSA; *The Journal-Patriot*, April 9, 1987; Moderwell, "Outline of Stoneman's Raid," Civil War (Federal, Miscellaneous) papers, SHC; Banks, "Memoranda," diary entry for March 29, 1865, 295; *OR* 49 (1): 331. Minie balls, parts of swords, other artifacts have been found on Barricks Hill, but these artifacts are more likely related to wartime encampments instead of skirmishes.

[55] Kirk, *15th Pennsylvania*, 494, 520–21; Diary, March 29, 1865, Charles M. Betts papers, HSP; Betts, "Stoneman's Great Cavalry Raid;" Hancock, *Four Brothers In Gray*, 49–50; Angelo Wiser maps, LC; Diary, March 29, 1865, Charles M. Betts papers, HSP; Betts, "Stoneman's Great Cavalry Raid;" Frederic Antes diary, March 29, 1865, Civil War Miscellaneous Collection, USAMHI; *OR Supplement* 57: 356; Kirk, *15th Pennsylvania*, 494; Wilson, *Column South*, 278; Septimus W. Knight diary, March 29, 1865, VMI; Morning Reports for Companies A–D and F–L, 15th Pennsylvania Cavalry, RR. It should also be pointed out that Buzby's account is garbled; some of the events in his account, "With Gillem's Tennesseans on the Yadkin," occurred on the march over the mountains into North Carolina and not the approach to Wilkesboro.

[56] Trowbridge, "Stoneman Raid," 100; Trowbridge, "The Stoneman Raid of 1865," *JUSCA* 4 (June 1891): 190; Steven Thomas to "My Dear Wife," June 5, 1865, Calvin Thomas papers, UM; Jones, *Last Raid*, 17.

[57] Trowbridge, "Stoneman Raid," 100–101; Trowbridge, "The Stoneman Raid of 1865," *JUSCA* 4 (June 1891): 190; Steven Thomas to "My Dear Wife," June 5, 1865, Calvin Thomas papers, UM; Jones, *Last Raid*, 17.

[58] Trowbridge, "Stoneman Raid," 101; Trowbridge, "The Stoneman Raid of 1865," *JUSCA* 4 (June 1891): 190–91; *OR* 49 (1): 331; Angelo Wiser maps, LC. Hendricks remembered camping at about 2:00 A.M. (Jones, *Last Raid*, 17).

[59] March 29–30, 1865, Allen Frankenberry diaries, WV.

[60] Scott, *13th Tennessee*, 234; Ferguson, *Home on the Yadkin*, 27–28; George Stoneman to John Breckinridge, January 26, 1865, George Stoneman papers, Chicago History Museum.

[61] *OR* 49 (1): 326, 331; Scott, *13th Tennessee*, 234; J.C. Norwood to Walter W. Lenoir, April 2, 1865, Lenoir papers, SHC; Mrs. George Harper to George Harper, March 25, 1865, Harper papers, SHC. Crouch, *Historical Sketches*, 43 relates the story about the loss of the cannon. Crouch, who is sometimes unreliable, reported that the cannon and ammunition were found after the war. If so, it is unknown what became of them.

[62] Trowbridge, "Stoneman Raid," 101–2; Trowbridge, "The Stoneman Raid of 1865," *JUSCA* 4 (June 1891): 191.

[63] Steven Thomas to "My Dear Wife," June 5, 1865, Calvin Thomas papers, UM; Trowbridge, "Stoneman Raid," 101–2; Trowbridge, "The Stoneman Raid of 1865," *JUSCA* 4 (June 1891): 191; Morning Reports, Companies A–F, March 30, 1865, 10th Michigan Cavalry, RR; Frederic Antes diary, March 30, 1865, Civil War Miscellaneous Collection, USAMHI; Kirk, *15th Pennsylvania*, 494; Diary, March 30, 1865, Charles M. Betts papers, HSP; Betts, "Stoneman's Great Cavalry Raid;" Wilson, *Column South*, 278; Septimus W. Knight diary, March 30, 1865, VMI; Morning Reports for Companies A–D and F–L, 15th Pennsylvania Cavalry, RR. Knight called the Reddies the "little Yadkin."

[64] *OR* 49 (1): 331; Kirk, *15th Pennsylvania*, 522. The 12th Ohio apparently camped for the night on or near Barricks Hill, astride Cub Creek (Crouch, *Historical Sketches*, 43).

[65] Banks, "Memoranda," diary entry for March 30, 1865, 295; Betts, "Stoneman's Great Cavalry Raid;" Frederic Antes diary, March 30, 1865, Civil War Miscellaneous Collection, USAMHI; *OR* 49 (1): 331. Reportedly, as many as six men drowned during the crossing, but this is questionable. The *Official Roster of Ohio* 11: 583–617 does not record a death during the Yadkin River

crossing. Only Pennsylvanians reported the drownings. Incidentally, Buzby claimed that a Pennsylvanian was among those who died.

⁶⁶ Kirk, *15th Pennsylvania*, 522–23.

⁶⁷ *OR Supplement* 65: 637; *OR* 49 (1): 326, 331; Scott, *13th Tennessee*, 234; March 30, 1865, Allen Frankenberry diaries, WV.

⁶⁸ Kirk, *15th Pennsylvania*, 523; *The Journal-Patriot*, April 9, 1987.

⁶⁹ *OR* 49 (1): 331; Kirk, *15th Pennsylvania*, 494, 523. Writing many years after the event, a Tennesseean later claimed that the 13th managed to cross the rising river. The author was apparently confused, because the crossing he describes sounds remarkably like that of the 12th Ohio (Scott, *13th Tennessee*, 234).

⁷⁰ Kirk, *15th Pennsylvania*, 523–24. Buzby tends to mix events in his writings and admits that he is relying on memory, so some allowance should be made for exaggeration.

⁷¹ March 30, 1865, Allen Frankenberry diaries, WV; *OR* 49 (1): 331, 336; Wilson, *Column South*, 278; Frederic Antes diary, March 30, 1865, Civil War Miscellaneous Collection, USAMHI; Kirk, *15th Pennsylvania*, 525. No source specifies the whereabouts of Brown's Brigade, but it probably spent the day as the rear brigade after leading the way on March 28.

⁷² Crouch, *Historical Sketches*, 42; Spencer, *Last Ninety Days*, 196; *National Tribune*, July 12, 1900.

⁷³ March 30, 1865, Henry Birdsall diary, SHC; March 30, 1865, Allen Frankenberry diaries, WV.

⁷⁴ Bettie Dobson to "My Dear Sister," April 8, 1865, Dobson Family papers, SHC; "Notes of Stoneman's Raid in Burke County, and the Town of Morganton," Cornelia P. Spencer papers, SHC; Kirk, *15th Pennsylvania*, 523; GS Note and Receipt, March 30, 1865, J. Jay Anderson Collection, James Larkin Pearson Library, Wilkes Community College.

⁷⁵ Winkler Interview; Beall, "Stoneman's Raid," *The North Carolina Review*, November 11, 1910; R.L. Beall's account of Stoneman's Raid, Cornelia Phillips Spencer papers, SHC; Spencer, *Last Ninety Days*, 197; Hartley, *Stuart's Tarheels*, 374; Ogburn, "Preface," xii. The late Mrs. Winkler grew up in Oakland.

⁷⁶ Diary of Calvin J. Cowles, March 29, 1865, quoted in J. Jay Anderson, "The Home Front in the Civil War," *The Journal-Patriot* Bicentennial Edition; Crouch, *Historical Sketches*, 43. The jail, which still stands today, is famous as the prison of Tom Dooley.

⁷⁷ *OR* 49 (1): 326, 331; Kirk, *15th Pennsylvania*, 525; Wilson, *Column South*, 278; Jones, *Last Raid*, 19.

⁷⁸ *OR* 47 (3): 718–19; Roman, *Beauregard* 2: 382–83; Warner, *Generals in Gray*, 22–24; T. Michael Parrish, "Introduction," in Roman, *Beauregard* 1: vi, viii–x, xvi.

⁷⁹ Trudeau, *Out of the Storm*, 209; Warner, *Generals in Gray*, 22–24; T. Michael Parrish, "Introduction," in Roman, *Beauregard* 1: vi, viii–x, xvi; *OR* 47 (3): 731.

⁸⁰ *OR* 47 (3): 712; Warner, *Generals in Gray*, 157, 214.

⁸¹ R.E. Lee to J.C. Breckinridge, March 20, 1865; J.C. Breckinridge to R.E. Lee, March 21, 1865; R.E. Lee to James Longstreet, March 21, 1865, all in R.E. Lee Headquarters papers, VHS; Warner, *Generals in Gray*, 300.

⁸² Jefferson Davis to Robert E. Lee, March 30, 1865, in Rowland, *Jefferson Davis*, 524; *OR* 47 (3): 718–19, 722–23; Warner, *Generals in Gray*, 182; Johnston, *Narrative*, 371; Bradley, *Astounding Close*, 64, 80; Roman, *Beauregard* 2: 382–83.

⁸³ *OR* 47 (3): 718–19, 736–37; Roman, *Beauregard* 2: 382–83, 385.

⁸⁴ *OR* 47 (3): 736; Duke, *Morgan's Cavalry*, 618–19; Roman, *Beauregard* 2: 383; Holsworth, "VMI at the Battle of New Market," 20; Evans, *Confederate Military History* 3: 591–93; Davis, *Headquarters Diary*, 669–70; *CV* 10 (July 1902): 306.

⁸⁵ *CV* 10 (July 1902): 306; Davis, *Headquarters Diary*, 669–70.

⁸⁶ *OR* 47 (3): 703, 718, 727; *OR* 49 (1): 1044; Richard Taylor to Stephen D. Lee, March

11, 1865, Stephen Dill Lee papers, SHC; Bradley, *Astounding Close*, 64; Roman, *Beauregard* 2: 382–83; Johnston, *Narrative*, 394–95; Warner, *Generals in Gray*, 183; Barrett, *Sherman's March*, 165, 201. For Lee's strength, see *OR* 47 (3): 731.

[87] *OR* 47 (3): 718, 722–24, 736; Trotter, *Bushwhackers*, 235–36; Bradley, *Astounding Close*, 62–63; Hallock, *Braxton Bragg* 2: 254–55; Adams, "To Prepare our Sons," 24; Inscoe and McKinney, *Heart of Confederate Appalachia*, 129; Barrett, *Civil War in North Carolina*, 20, 232; Clark, *Histories of the Several Regiments* 4: 649, 651, 654; J.C. Norwood to Walter W. Lenoir, April 2, 1865, Lenoir papers, SHC. All told, about 12,500 men were mobilized into the home guards statewide (Clark, *Histories of the Several Regiments* 4: 649).

[88] *OR* 47 (3): 723; Bradley, *Astounding Close*, 80, 153, 293, 296; Krick, *Lee's Colonels*, 246; *SHSP* 18 (1890): 421; Clark, *Histories of the Several Regiments* 1: 386; Roman, *Beauregard*, 387; *CV* 30 (May 1922): 101–2.

[89] *OR* 47 (3): 723; Bradley, *Astounding Close*, 80, 153, 293, 296; Krick, *Lee's Colonels*, 246; *SHSP* 18 (1890): 421; Clark, *Histories of the Several Regiments* 1: 386; Roman, *Beauregard*, 387.

[90] *OR* 47 (3): 724, 726–27, 728; Roman, *Beauregard* 2: 383.

[91] Bradley, *Astounding Close*, 294; Roman, *Beauregard* 2: 383; *OR* 47 (3): 725, 728–29, 738; Warner, *Generals in Gray*, 86; J.E. Johnston to W.W. Loring, April 30, 1865, "General Winfield Scott Featherston," and "A Statement of Facts, Incidents, & Data," all in Winfield Scott Featherston Collection, OM; "Diary of Nicholas Gibbon," *Mecklenburg, N.C. Genealogical Society Quarterly* 3: 73–74, 128; Warner, *Generals in Blue*, 172.

[92] *OR* 47 (3): 725–27; John M. Otey to G.L. Dudley, March 31, 1865, Letters and Orders Book, P.G.T. Beauregard papers, LC; Lindsley, *Military Annals of Tennessee* 2: 837.

[93] *OR* 47 (2): 1073; *OR* 47 (3): 725; Warner, *Generals in Gray*, 87; "Memoirs of S.W. Ferguson," Heyward and Ferguson family papers, SHC; Evans, *Sherman's Horsemen*, 433–34.

[94] *OR* 47 (3): 722, 725, 729, 754.

[95] *OR* 47 (3): 725, 728; Roman, *Beauregard* 2: 383.

[96] Scott, *13th Tennessee*, 234; Kirk, *15th Pennsylvania*, 525. Morning Reports for Companies A–D, 15th Pennsylvania Cavalry, RR described the weather as "clearing."

[97] *OR* 49 (1): 326–27; March 31, 1865, Allen Frankenberry diaries, WV.

[98] *OR* 49 (1): 331; Scott, *13th Tennessee*, 234; Claim of John Glass, #19221, Box 235, Entry 732, Wilkes County, N.C., RG 217, Settled Files of the SCC, NA; March 31, 1865, Henry Birdsall diary, SHC; Steven Thomas to "My Dear Wife," June 5, 1865, Calvin Thomas papers, UM; *Cincinnati Daily Commercial*, May 10, 1865; Morning Reports for Companies A–D, 15th Pennsylvania Cavalry, RR. AG estimated that the men moved about four miles; Scott, who produced his recollections much later than AG, doubled that estimate.

[99] Calvin J. Cowles to Arthur Cowles, 6 April 1865, Calvin J. Cowles papers, NCSA; *Heritage of Iredell County*, 30; *Charlotte Daily Bulletin*, April 4, 1865; Morning Reports for Companies B, G, and H, 11th Kentucky Cavalry, RR; Beall, "Stoneman's Raid," *The North Carolina Review*, October 2, 1910; R.L. Beall's account of Stoneman's Raid, Cornelia Phillips Spencer papers, SHC; *Greensborough Patriot*, April 6, 1865; Spencer, *Last Ninety Days*, 197; R.L. Beall to Cornelia P. Spencer, September 20, 1866, Cornelia Phillips Spencer papers, SHC; "Stoneman's Raid Brought Civil War to Iredell," June 3, 1954, unprovenienced, Stoneman's Raid file, local history collection, Iredell County Public Library.

[100] "Notes on Stoneman's Raid in Iredell County," Stoneman's Raid file, local history collection, Caldwell County Public Library; "Stoneman's Raid Brought Civil War Home," unprovenienced article, Stoneman's Raid file, local history collection, Iredell Public Library.

[101] John Wadkins to WP, August 22, 1865, William J. Palmer Collection, CHS; Steven Thomas to "My Dear Wife," June 5, 1865, Calvin Thomas papers, UM; Morning Reports, Companies A–F, March 31, 1865, 10th Michigan Cavalry, RR; Banks, "Memoranda," diary entry for March 31, 1865, 295; Kirk, *15th Pennsylvania*, 494; Wilson, *Column South*, 278; Diary, March 31,

1865, Charles M. Betts papers, HSP; Frederic Antes diary, March 31, 1865, Civil War Miscellaneous Collection, USAMHI; Morning Reports for Companies A–D and F–L, 15th Pennsylvania Cavalry, RR.

[102] *The Journal-Patriot*, April 9, 1987; J. Gwyn to Rufus T. Lenoir, April 30, 1865, Lenoir papers, SHC.

[103] March 31, 1865, Allen Frankenberry diaries, WV.

[104] *OR* 49 (2): 204–5; *OR* (1): 337–38.

[105] Frederic Antes diary, April 1, 1865, Civil War Miscellaneous Collection, USAMHI; Betts, "Stoneman's Great Cavalry Raid;" Diary, April 1, 1865, Charles M. Betts papers, HSP; Morning Reports for Companies A–D, 15th Pennsylvania Cavalry, RR; Wilson, *Recollections and Experiences*, 111; Kirk, *15th Pennsylvania*, 494.

[106] Wilson, *Recollections and Experiences*, 111; Kirk, *15th Pennsylvania*, 494; *Elkin 1889–1989*, 5; Morning Reports for Companies A–D, 15th Pennsylvania Cavalry, RR.

[107] *Elkin 1889–1989*, 5–6; *Mount Airy News*, March 11, 1990; Jackson, *Surry County Soldiers in the Civil War*, 423; Canipe, *Early Elkin-Jonesville*, 7, 12, 154.

[108] Wilson, *Recollections and Experiences*, 111; Kirk, *15th Pennsylvania*, 494; *Elkin 1889–1989*, 5; Betts, "Stoneman's Great Cavalry Raid;" Scott, *13th Tennessee*, 234–35; April 2, 1865, Allen Frankenberry diaries, WV.

[109] Descriptive Book for Companies A–E, 10th Michigan Cavalry, RR; *OR* 49 (1): 327.

[110] *Elkin 1889–1989*, 4; Frederic Antes diary, April 1, 1865, Civil War Miscellaneous Collection, USAMHI; Steven Thomas to "My Dear Wife," June 5, 1865, Calvin Thomas papers, UM; Wilson, *Column South*, 279; Septimus W. Knight diary, April 1, 1865, VMI; Morning Reports, Companies A–F, April 1, 1865, 10th Michigan Cavalry, RR.

[111] April 1, 1865, Allen Frankenberry diaries, WV; *OR* 49 (1): 327; *OR Supplement* 65: 556, 567, 637.

[112] Scott, *13th Tennessee*, 234; *OR* 49 (1): 327, 331; *OR Supplement* 65: 556–67, 614, 637; April 1, 1865, Henry Birdsall diary, SHC.

[113] Canipe, *Early Elkin-Jonesville*, 58–59, 61, 89.

[114] *OR Supplement* 65: 556–67, 637; *OR* 49 (1): 327–28; *Mount Airy News*, March 11, 1990; Jackson, *Surry County Soldiers in the Civil War*, 423–24.

[115] Betts, "Stoneman's Great Cavalry Raid;" Diary, April 2, 1865, Charles M. Betts papers, HSP; Mason, "Stoneman's Last Campaign," 24; *OR* 49 (2): 103–4.

[116] *OR* 49 (1): 327–28; Septimus W. Knight diary, April 2, 1865, VMI; *Mount Airy News*, April 1, 1990. The route of march from Elkin followed C.C. Camp Road to Highway 268.

[117] *Winston-Salem Journal*, October 22, 1989; Bettie Dobson to "My Dear Sister," April 8, 1865, Dobson family papers, SHC; Houck, *Story of Rockford*, 52; *Mount Airy News*, April 6, 1983.

[118] *Mount Airy News*, April 1, 1990; *Mount Airy News*, November 11, 1897, reproduced in Jackson, *Surry County Soldiers in the Civil War*, 426–28.

[119] Betts, "Stoneman's Great Cavalry Raid;" *OR* 49 (1): 331; Scott, *13th Tennessee*, 234–35.

[120] *OR* 49 (1): 328; Wilson, *Column South*, 280; April 2, 1865, Henry Birdsall diary, SHC; Frederic Antes diary, April 2, 1865, Civil War Miscellaneous Collection, USAMHI; Wilson, *Recollections and Experiences*, 111; Kirk, *15th Pennsylvania*, 494–95; Angelo Wiser maps, LC; Banks, "Memoranda," diary entry for April 2, 1865, 295; *Mount Airy News*, March 18, 1990 & April 6, 1983.

[121] Scott, *13th Tennessee*, 234–35; *Mount Airy News*, March 18, 1990; April 6, 1983; March 31, 1988; April 1, 1990.

[122] *Mount Airy News*, April 6, 1983; April 1, 1990; May 16, 1986.

[123] Wilson, *Recollections and Experiences*, 111; Kirk, *15th Pennsylvania*, 494–95; Diary, April 2, 1865, Charles M. Betts papers, HSP; Wallace and Wallace, *The Two*, 248. Another tale relates how the raiders decided to draft locals and drew Eng's name but not Chang's, leaving Stoneman

with a dilemma. Rather than take both, he relinquished his claim. No Federal account corroborates this story, so it is probably apocryphal.

[124] Scott, *13th Tennessee*, 234–35; Frederic Antes diary, April 2, 1865, Civil War Miscellaneous Collection, USAMHI; Wilson, *Recollections and Experiences*, 111; Kirk, *15th Pennsylvania*, 494–95; Diary, April 2, 1865, Charles M. Betts papers, HSP; Septimus W. Knight diary, April 2, 1865, VMI; Moderwell, "Outline of Stoneman's Raid," Civil War (Federal, Miscellaneous) papers, SHC; OR 49 (1): 328; Morning Reports, Companies A–F, April 2, 1865, 10th Michigan Cavalry, RR. Colton, in Wilson, *Column South*, 280, estimated that they camped ten miles beyond Mount Airy.

[125] *Mount Airy News*, May 16, 1986; Jackson, *Surry County Soldiers in the Civil War*, 425; April 2, 1865, Allen Frankenberry diaries, WV. Apparently the raiders left behind a pair of binoculars, which is currently in the Greensboro Historical Museum.

[126] OR 49 (1): 331; Wilson, *Column South*, 280. The supply train may have assembled at Oakdale Cemetery in Mount Airy (*Mount Airy News*, April 6, 1983; March 8, 1990).

[127] OR 47 (3): 738, 740; Roman, *Beauregard* 2: 385–86; Hamilton, *Ruffin Papers*, March 31, 1865, 3: 449; P.G.T. Beauregard to R.E. Lee, April 1, 1865, R.E. Lee headquarters papers, VHS; *People's Press*, April 6, 1865.

[128] OR 47 (3): 738, 740, 742–43, 746; Roman, *Beauregard* 2: 385; P.G.T. Beauregard to R.E. Lee, April 1, 1865, R.E. Lee headquarters papers, VHS. For Shelley's and Govan's strengths, see Bradley, *Astounding Close*, 291, 294.

[129] John M. Otey to W.S. Featherston, April 1, 1865, Letters and Orders Book, P.G.T. Beauregard papers, LC; OR 47 (3): 739, 746.

[130] Hendricks, *Imperiled City*, 123, 125–26; John M. Otey to Maj. J.C. Holmes, April 2, 1865, Letters and Orders Book, P.G.T. Beauregard papers, LC; Roman, *Beauregard* 2: 387.

[131] Roman, *Beauregard* 2: 386; OR 47 (3): 746; Hanna, *Flight Into Oblivion*, 11.

[132] Roman, *Beauregard* 2: 387.

Chapter 4
GLORY ENOUGH FOR ONE DAY
Virginia: April 3–9, 1865

[1] Gerhardt, "E.T. Clemmons Bequeathed Money To Build Moravian Church & School," *The Village Gazette*, 1; *People's Press*, April 6, 1865; "Last Year of the War," Civil War and Reconstruction papers, MA. Clemmons was the great-grandson of the founder of Clemmons, N.C. One of Clemmons's stagecoaches is on display at the Clemmons Village Hall today (2010).

[2] OR 49 (1): 331.

[3] Davis, *Headquarters Diary*, 674; Steven Thomas to "My Dear Wife," June 5, 1865, Calvin Thomas papers, UM; April 3, 1865, Henry Birdsall diary, SHC.

[4] Betts, "Stoneman's Great Cavalry Raid;" Wilson, *Recollections and Experiences*, 111; Kirk, *15th Pennsylvania*, 494–95; April 3, 1865, Allen Frankenberry diaries, WV.

[5] Betts, "Stoneman's Great Cavalry Raid;" diary entry for April 2, 1865, Charles F. Weller memoirs and letters, *Civil War Times Illustrated* Collection, USAMHI; Wilson, *Recollections and Experiences*, 111; Kirk, *15th Pennsylvania*, 494–95; OR Supplement 57: 383; Frederic Antes diary, April 3, 1865, Civil War Miscellaneous Collection, USAMHI; OR 49 (1): 331. The site of the wagon-train capture is lost to history. Antes placed the spot at about seven miles from Hillsville. Local legend also suggests a place near Dalton in Stokes County because of some burned wagon tires that were piled there, but the spot was more likely associated with the wagon train the raiders burned near Dalton on April 9. See Chapter 5. (Van Noppen, *Stoneman's Last Raid*, 32; Carter, *Footprints in the Hollows*, 90; J.G. Hollingsworth, "Stoneman's Invasion of Western N.C. Was Destructive," unprovenienced newspaper article, Winston-Salem Public Library clipping file).

⁶ Wilson, *Column South*, 280; *To the Members of the 15th Pennsylvania Cavalry*, 23rd Annual Banquet, 35; Kirk, *15th Pennsylvania*, 533.

⁷ *To the Members of the 15th Pennsylvania Cavalry*, 23rd Annual Banquet, 35; *Cincinnati Daily Commercial*, May 10, 1865; Kirk, *15th Pennsylvania*, 535.

⁸ Wallace, *Guide to Virginia Military Organizations*, 231; OR 49 (1): 331; Betts, "Stoneman's Great Cavalry Raid;" Wilson, *Recollections and Experiences*, 111; Kirk, *15th Pennsylvania*, 494–95; Septimus W. Knight diary, April 3, 1865, VMI; Morning Reports for Companies B, G, and H, 11th Kentucky Cavalry, April 3, 1865, RR.

⁹ Kirk, *15th Pennsylvania*, 534–35; *To the Members of the 15th Pennsylvania Cavalry*, 23rd Annual Banquet, 35.

¹⁰ Kirk, *15th Pennsylvania*, 533.

¹¹ OR Supplement 65: 614; OR 49 (1): 331; *Philadelphia Weekly Times*, January 18, 1879.

¹² Frederic Antes diary, April 3, 1865, Civil War Miscellaneous Collection, USAMHI; Morning Reports, Companies A–F, April 3, 1865, 10th Michigan Cavalry, RR; Jones, *The Last Raid*, 22; Betts, "Stoneman's Great Cavalry Raid;" Wilson, *Recollections and Experiences*, 111; Kirk, *15th Pennsylvania*, 494–95; Morning Reports of Companies A–D, 15th Pennsylvania Cavalry, RR; April 3, 1865, Allen Frankenberry diaries, WV; OR 49 (1): 331; *People's Press*, April 6, 1865; *To the Members of the 15th Pennsylvania Cavalry*, 23rd Annual Banquet, 35. Jacksonville or Floyd Court House is now called Floyd.

¹³ Banks, "Memoranda," diary entry for April 3, 1865, 295; Diary, April 3, 1865, Charles M. Betts papers, HSP; Wilson, *Column South*, 280; OR 49 (1): 328, 331.

¹⁴ OR 49 (2): 331; Hendricks, *Imperiled City*, 48, 92; Calkins, *Appomattox Campaign*, 138.

¹⁵ Hanna, *Flight Into Oblivion*, 15, 17–19; Davis, *Jefferson Davis*, 607; Calkins, *Appomattox Campaign*, 199; Entries for April 2 and April 3, 1865, J.T. Wood diary, SHC; Anna Trenholm diary, SHC.

¹⁶ Davis, *Jefferson Davis*, 609; John M. Otey to W.S. Featherston, April 3, 1865, and John M. Otey to Major Edmonson, April 3, 1865, both in Letters and Orders Book, P.G.T. Beauregard papers, LC; Krick, *Lee's Colonels*, 173; OR 47 (3): 750, 760; "Diary of Nicholas Gibbon," *Mecklenburg, N.C. Genealogical Society Quarterly* 3: 128; Clark, *Histories of the Several Regiments* 1: 386.

¹⁷ Roman, *Beauregard* 2: 388; John M. Otey to W.S. Featherston, April 4, 1865, Letters and Orders Book, P.G.T. Beauregard papers, LC; OR 47 (3): 750.

¹⁸ Roman, *Beauregard* 2: 385–86; OR 47 (3): 746, 751, 753, 756, 760; John M. Otey to Colonel Wheeler, April 4, 1865, Letters and Orders Book, P.G.T. Beauregard papers, LC. Earlier in April, when Stoneman was held up by the Yadkin, Beauregard dispatched Colonel Wheeler to Shallow Ford to observe the enemy (OR 49 [3]: 747).

¹⁹ Banks, "Memoranda," diary entry for April 3, 1865, 295; Septimus W. Knight diary, April 4, 1865, VMI; Morning Reports for Companies A–D, 15th Pennsylvania Cavalry, RR.

²⁰ Jones, *The Last Raid*, 22; Frederic Antes diary, April 4, 1865, Civil War Miscellaneous Collection, USAMHI; Septimus W. Knight diary, April 4, 1865, VMI; Diary, April 4, 1865, Charles M. Betts papers, HSP; Wilson, *Recollections and Experiences*, 111; Kirk, *15th Pennsylvania*, 495; Betts, "Stoneman's Great Cavalry Raid."

²¹ Stigleman, *When the Yankees Came Through Our Town*, 1, courtesy of Gino Williams.

²² Stigleman, *When the Yankees Came Through Our Town*, 1; Interview with Gino Williams, February 15, 2002. Howard is buried in Floyd.

²³ Jones, *The Last Raid*, 22; Frederic Antes diary, April 4, 1865, Civil War Miscellaneous Collection, USAMHI; Septimus W. Knight diary, April 4, 1865, VMI; Diary, April 4, 1865, Charles M. Betts papers, HSP; Wilson, *Recollections and Experiences*, 111; Kirk, *15th Pennsylvania*, 495; Betts, "Stoneman's Great Cavalry Raid."

²⁴ Stigleman, *When the Yankees Came Through Our Town*, 2, courtesy of Gino Williams.

²⁵ Frederic Antes diary, April 4, 1865, Civil War Miscellaneous Collection, USAMHI; Sti-

gleman, *When the Yankees Came Through Our Town*, 2, courtesy of Gino Williams; Mason, *12th Ohio Cavalry*, 99.

[26] Wilson, *Recollections and Experiences*, 111; Kirk, *15th Pennsylvania*, 495; Frederic Antes diary, April 4, 1865, Civil War Miscellaneous Collection, USAMHI.

[27] Stigleman, *When the Yankees Came Through Our Town*, 3, courtesy of Gino Williams.

[28] Ibid., 3–4, courtesy of Gino Williams.

[29] Kirk, *15th Pennsylvania*, 536–37; April 4, 1865, Allen Frankenberry diaries, WV. According to his postwar reminiscences, Frankenberry paid the ladies $1,000 in bonds, but according to Frankenberry's diary, he gave them only $20.

[30] Claim of Elijah W. Hylton, #17710, Box 366, Entry 732, Floyd County, Va., RG 217, Settled Files of the SCC, NA.

[31] *OR* 49 (1): 328; *OR Supplement* 65: 637; Diary, April 4, 1865, Charles M. Betts papers, HSP; Wilson, *Column South*, 280; Septimus W. Knight diary, April 4, 1865, VMI; Banks, "Memoranda," diary entry for April 4, 1865, 295–96.

[32] Diary, April 4, 1865, Charles M. Betts papers, HSP; Wilson, *Column South*, 280; Septimus W. Knight diary, April 4, 1865, VMI; Maj. William Wagner to Lt. Col. Charles M. Betts, May 6, 1865, Charles M. Betts papers, HSP; *OR* 49 (1): 331; *To the Members of the 15th Pennsylvania Cavalry*, 30th Annual Banquet, 8; Morning Reports for Companies A–D, 15th Pennsylvania Cavalry, RR.

[33] Angelo Wiser maps, April 4, 1865, LC.

[34] Diary entry for April 4, 1865, Charles F. Weller memoirs and letters, *Civil War Times Illustrated* Collection, USAMHI; Frederic Antes diary, April 4, 1865, Civil War Miscellaneous Collection, USAMHI; Morning Reports, Companies A–F, April 4, 1865, 10th Michigan Cavalry, RR; Angelo Wiser maps, April 4, 1865, LC; April 4, 1865, Allen Frankenberry diaries, WV.

[35] Banks, "Memoranda," diary entry for April 4, 1865, 295–96; Mason, *12th Ohio Cavalry*, 99–100. A fellow Ohioan, William C. Bushong of Company C, echoed Mason's distance estimate. See Bushong, *Last Great Stoneman Raid*.

[36] Brock, *History of Montgomery County*, 17–18, 34; Crush, *Montgomery County Story*, 105; Wilson, *Recollections and Experiences*, 111–12; Kirk, *15th Pennsylvania*, 495–96.

[37] *Cincinnati Daily Commercial*, May 10, 1865.

[38] Diary, April 4, 1865, Charles M. Betts papers, HSP; Mason, "Stoneman's Last Campaign," 24–25; Bushong, *Last Great Stoneman Raid*; Mason, *12th Ohio Cavalry*, 99.

[39] Trowbridge, *Stoneman Raid*, 102; Trowbridge, "The Stoneman Raid of 1865," *JUSCA* 4 (June 1891): 192; Brock, *History of Montgomery County*, 34; Crush, *Montgomery County Story*, 105; *OR* 49 (1): 328, 331; *OR Supplement* 30: 230; Diary, April 4, 1865, Charles M. Betts papers, HSP; April 4, 1865, Henry Birdsall diary, SHC; Morning Reports for Companies F–L, 15th Pennsylvania Cavalry, April 4, 1865, RR; Whisonant, "Union Raiders in the New River Valley," 30–32, 37; Mason, "Stoneman's Last Campaign," 24–25; Kegley, *Glimpses of Wythe County*, 84. Frank Frankenberry wrote that his force entered the town from the south (April 6, 1865, Allen Frankenberry diaries, WV).

[40] Bushong, *Last Great Stoneman Raid*; Mason, "Stoneman's Last Campaign," 24–25; "Yankee Cavalry Raided Southwest in War's Closing Days," unprovenienced newspaper article in the author's possession; *To the Members of the 15th Pennsylvania Cavalry*, 23rd Annual Banquet, 36; Brock, *History of Montgomery County*, 34; Crush, *Montgomery County Story*, 105; Mason, *12th Ohio Cavalry*, 99–100; Mason, "Stoneman's Last Campaign," 25.

[41] Whisonant, "Union Raiders in the New River Valley," 30–31; *OR* 49 (1): 331; Diary, April 5, 1865, Charles M. Betts papers, HSP; *Cincinnati Daily Commercial*, May 10, 1865; Crush, *Montgomery County Story*, 105.

[42] *Cincinnati Daily Commercial*, May 10, 1865; Kirk, *15th Pennsylvania*, 499–500; Brock, *History of Montgomery County*, 34; Crush, *Montgomery County Story*, 105; *OR Supplement* 22 (2):

4; Morning Reports, Companies F–L, 15th Pennsylvania Cavalry, April 5, 1865, RR.

[43] Moderwell, "Outline of Stoneman's Raid," Civil War (Federal, Miscellaneous) papers, SHC; *OR Supplement* 49: 970.

[44] Whisonant, "Union Raiders in the New River Valley," 32, 34, 39. Central Depot is now called Radford.

[45] Trowbridge, *Stoneman Raid*, 102; Trowbridge, "The Stoneman Raid of 1865," *JUSCA* 4 (June 1891): 192; *OR* 49 (1): 331; Morning Reports for Companies B, G, and H of the 11th Kentucky Cavalry, April 5, 1865, RR; *CV* 10 (July 1902): 307; Davis, *Headquarters Diary*, 680–81. Before the raid, Thomas told Stoneman "not to destroy the bridge over New River west of Christianburg," probably to preserve it for an anticipated Union advance (Simon, *Papers of U.S. Grant* 14: 199).

[46] Frederic Antes diary, April 5, 1865, Civil War Miscellaneous Collection, USAMHI; Diary entry for April 5, 1865, Charles F. Weller memoirs and letters, *Civil War Times Illustrated* Collection, USAMHI.

[47] Banks, "Memoranda," diary entry for April 5, 1865, 296; Bushong, *Last Great Stoneman Raid*; Mason, *12th Ohio Cavalry*, 100; Mason, "Stoneman's Last Campaign," 25. Bushong makes almost the same statement as Mason, and probably borrowed heavily from Mason when writing his account.

[48] Trowbridge, *Stoneman Raid*, 102; Trowbridge, "The Stoneman Raid of 1865," *JUSCA* 4 (June 1891): 192; L.S. Trowbridge to "My Dear Judie," April 12, 1865, L.S. Trowbridge papers, UM; Trowbridge, "Lights and Shadows," 106; Steven Thomas to "My Dear Wife," June 5, 1865, Calvin Thomas papers, UM; *OR Supplement* 30: 230; *10th Cavalry*, vol. 40, 13; Trowbridge, *Brief History of the 10th Michigan*, 34; *OR* 49 (1): 331.

[49] L.S. Trowbridge to "My Dear Judie," April 12, 1865, L.S. Trowbridge papers, UM; Trowbridge, "Lights and Shadows," 106; Trowbridge, *Stoneman Raid*, 102–3, 106–7; Trowbridge, "The Stoneman Raid of 1865," *JUSCA* 4 (June 1891): 192.

[50] *Cincinnati Daily Commercial*, May 10, 1865; Betts, "Stoneman's Great Cavalry Raid;" Steven Thomas to "My Dear Wife," June 5, 1865, Calvin Thomas papers, UM; L.S. Trowbridge to "My Dear Judie," April 12, 1865, L.S. Trowbridge papers, UM; *OR* 49 (1): 328; Diary, April 5, 1865, Charles M. Betts papers, HSP; Diary entry for April 5, 1865, Charles F. Weller memoirs and letters, *Civil War Times Illustrated* Collection, USAMHI; April 5, 1865, Allen Frankenberry diaries, WV; Crush, *Montgomery County Story*, 105. Crush states that the celebration took place on Sunday night, but it probably occurred that Wednesday when the news was received.

[51] L.S. Trowbridge to "My Dear Judie," April 12, 1865, L.S. Trowbridge papers, UM; *OR Supplement* 57: 402; *OR* 49 (1): 331; April 6, 1865, Henry Birdsall diary, SHC; *Cincinnati Daily Commercial*, May 10, 1865. At some point, a rebel squadron of twenty-five men ventured toward Christiansburg but was bloodily repulsed. See Davis, *Headquarters Diary*, 682.

[52] Kirk, *15th Pennsylvania*, 500; April 6, 1865, Allen Frankenberry diaries, WV.

[53] Jones, *The Last Raid*, 24; Trowbridge, "Lights and Shadows," 107–8. Van Noppen, *Stoneman's Last Raid*, 34–35, is garbled in its description of these events; it confuses the achievements of Wagner's detachment with those of the main body. *The Last Raid* is based on this account.

[54] Morning Reports, Companies A–F, April 6, 1865, 10th Michigan Cavalry, RR; Maj. John H. Standish to Brig. Gen. S. Thomas, June 4, 1865, in Regimental Letter, Endorsement, Order, and Guard Report Book, 10th Michigan Cavalry, RR; C.J. Mather to George Stoneman, April 6, 1865, with endorsements, Charles M. Betts papers, HSP.

[55] Betts, "Stoneman's Great Cavalry Raid;" diary entry for April 6, 1865, Charles F. Weller memoirs and letters, *Civil War Times Illustrated* Collection, USAMHI; *OR Supplement* 30: 230, 65: 637; Banks, "Memoranda," diary entry for April 6, 1865, 296; Frederic Antes diary, April 6, 1865, Civil War Miscellaneous Collection, USAMHI; April 6, 1865, Allen Frankenberry diaries, WV. Betts claimed that the circular was issued on April 5, but it probably appeared on April 6 because railroad work continued that day. Federal forces in the area may also have captured Brig.

Gen. Henry B. Davidson, but did not realize the identity of their prisoner. Davidson later escaped. See Davis, *Headquarters Diary*, 682–83.

[56] Roman, *Beauregard* 2: 387; *Charlotte Daily Bulletin*, April 4, 1865; OR 47 (3): 756.

[57] Roman, *Beauregard* 2: 388.Trudeau, *Out of the Storm*, 213; OR 47 (3): 756, 760; John M. Otey to W.S. Featherston, April 4, 1865, Letters and Orders Book, P.G.T. Beauregard papers, LC; John M. Otey to Major Edmensen, April 5, 1865, Letters and Orders Book, P.G.T. Beauregard papers, LC; John M. Otey to G.C. Shew[?], April 5, 1865, Letters and Orders Book, P.G.T. Beauregard papers, LC; "Reminiscences of Confederate days," Fries papers, NCSA. The relieved volunteers had served as scout relays from Shallow Ford to Greensboro. According to one volunteer, this was uncomfortable duty. "I spent the night lying on the ground by my horse, under a little cedar tree by Mr. Crater's front gate. At day light I mounted and rode down the hill to the mill, and it was not long until the Lieutenant came up with his other men, and the report that Stoneman had turned north somewhere in Yadkin County." Afterward, Beauregard thanked Lieutenant Colonel Shew and Colonels Armfield and Corley for their service around Shallow Ford. Shew and Corley were probably local defense commanders. Col. Robert Armfield, a graduate of Trinity College and a lawyer, served with the 38th North Carolina until he was wounded in 1862. (Krick, *Lee's Colonels*, 36). Another colonel, Alfred H. Belo, also commanded at the ford ("Last Year of the War," Civil War and Reconstruction papers, MA).

[58] John M. Otey to W.S. Featherston, April 5, 1865, Letters and Orders Book, P.G.T. Beauregard papers, LC; "A Statement of Facts, Incidents, & Data," Winfield Scott Featherston Collection, OM; Roman, *Beauregard* 2: 388; Lindsley, *Military Annals of Tennessee* 2: 837; OR 47 (3): 756, 760, 761, 768.

[59] Trowbridge, "Stoneman Raid," 102; Trowbridge, "The Stoneman Raid of 1865," *JUSCA* 4 (June 1891): 191; Beall, "Stoneman's Raid," *The North Carolina Review*, October 2, 1910; R.L. Beall's account of Stoneman's Raid, Cornelia Phillips Spencer papers, SHC; *10th Cavalry*, vol. 40, 13; Trowbridge, *Brief History of the 10th Michigan*, 33–34; L.S. Trowbridge to "My Dear Judie," April 12, 1865, L.S. Trowbridge papers, UM.

[60] OR *Supplement* 65: 614; OR 49 (1): 331; *Philadelphia Weekly Times*, January 18, 1879; Scott, *13th Tennessee*, 235; AG to Andrew Johnson, January 7, 1864, in Graf and Haskins, *PAJ* 6: 541. Andrew Thomas Campbell of the 13th Tennessee claimed to have been the man who killed Morgan (Ramsey, *The Raid*, 28, 30).

[61] *Tennesseans in the Civil War* 1: 351–52; Scott, *13th Tennessee*, 112–13, 117, 138, 227, 255, 260; AG to Andrew Johnson, January 7, 1864, in Graf and Haskins, eds., *Papers of Andrew Johnson* 6: 540–41, 542 n. 2, n. 5; Orders No. 25, August 11, 1865, Regimental Order Book, 13th Tennessee Cavalry, RR; OR 45 (1): 813; Dyer, *Tennessee Civil War Veterans Questionnaires*, entry for David Moss; Wallenstein, "Helping to Save the Union," 20. The regiment originally was dubbed the 12th Tennessee Cavalry before Governor Andrew Johnson renamed it.

[62] *Tennesseans in the Civil War* 1: 338–42; AG to Andrew Johnson, January 7, 1864, in Graf and Haskins, eds., *Papers of Andrew Johnson* 6: 540–42 n. 2, 543 n. 9, n. 13; Regimental Orders, Endorsements, and Court Martial Book, 8th Tennessee Cavalry, RR; Descriptive Book, 8th Tennessee Cavalry, RR.

[63] Descriptive Book, 13th Tennessee Cavalry, RR; Scott, *13th Tennessee*, 260–61. Several North Carolina counties, including Wilkes, Caldwell, and Guilford, were represented.

[64] Kirk, *15th Pennsylvania*, 507.

[65] AG to Andrew Johnson, January 7, 1864, in Graf and Haskins, eds., *Papers of Andrew Johnson* 6: 540, 542 n. 3; AG to Andrew Johnson, August 9, 1864, in Graf, ed., *Papers of Andrew Johnson* 7: 87; *Tennesseans in the Civil War* 1: 351; Ramsey, *The Raid*, 10–12; Scott, *13th Tennessee*, 215, 217.

[66] OR 49 (1): 663; Borcherdt, *Story of Austinville*, 43–44; "When Surry Was Invaded," March 21, 1918, unprovenienced newspaper article in the author's collection. Borcherdt places this event at or near dusk, but it probably occurred later in the evening.

[67] Whisonant, "Union Raiders in the New River Valley," 32; Borcherdt, *Story of Austinville*, 44; Kegley, *Wythe County*, 201; Kegley, *Glimpses of Wythe County*, 63; Donnelly, "Confederate Lead Mines," 413; Hoch, *Wythe County During the War*, 38. Porter's Ford is also referred to as Porter's Ferry in some sources.

[68] Barchfield's Memoranda, Arnell Collection, UT; *OR Supplement* 65: 614; *OR* 49 (1): 331; Scott, *13th Tennessee*, 235, 269–70, 278–79; Ramsey, *The Raid*, 169; *Philadelphia Weekly Times*, January 18, 1879; CSR for Barzillah P. Stacy, Microcopy 395, Roll 108; Borcherdt, *Story of Austinville*, 44. Alternate spellings for Stacy's first name include Barzilla, Brazlilliah, and Barzillai. He died on September 20, 1882, and is buried in the Old Gray Cemetery in Knoxville. Borcherdt timed this incident on April 4, but other evidence suggests that it took place during the original crossing of the New. See the text.

[69] Scott, *13th Tennessee*, 235–36; *Philadelphia Weekly Times*, January 18, 1879; Wallace, *Guide to Virginia Military Organizations*, 234, 223; *Cincinnati Daily Commercial*, May 10, 1865; *OR* 49 (1): 323–24. Scott estimated that the detachment marched fifty-five miles, but his estimate is high.

[70] *Cincinnati Daily Commercial*, May 10, 1865; Barchfield's Memoranda, Arnell Collection, UT; *OR* 49 (1): 323–24, 332; Hoch, *Wythe County During the War*, 38; Kegley, *Glimpses of Wythe County*, 84; Orders for April 10, 1865, Wythe County Order Book, Wythe County Court House, Wytheville, Virginia.

[71] Donnelly, "Confederate Lead Mines," 403; *Cincinnati Daily Commercial*, May 10, 1865; *OR* 49 (1): 323–24, 331; *OR Supplement* 65: 614; *Philadelphia Weekly Times*, January 18, 1879; Scott, *13th Tennessee*, 235–36; Davis, *Headquarters Diary*, 679–80; Trowbridge, "The Stoneman Raid of 1865," *JUSCA* 4 (June 1891): 191; Kegley, *Glimpses of Wythe County*, 84; Sullins, *Recollections*, 289–92. Max Meadows depot was the point where lead from the lead mines was loaded onto the railroad.

[72] Donnelly, "Confederate Lead Mines," 403; *Cincinnati Daily Commercial*, May 10, 1865; *OR* 49 (1): 323–24, 331; *OR Supplement* 65: 614; *Philadelphia Weekly Times*, January 18, 1879; Scott, *13th Tennessee*, 235–36; Trowbridge, "The Stoneman Raid of 1865," *JUSCA* 4 (June 1891): 191; Davis, *Headquarters Diary*, 679.

[73] Davis, *Headquarters Diary*, 671–72; *OR* 49 (1): 422; Kegley, *Glimpses of Wythe County*, 62–63; Whisonant, "Wythe County Lead Mines," 17; Donnelly, "Confederate Lead Mines," 413.

[74] *CV* 10 (July 1902): 306; Davis, *Headquarters Diary*, 675–76; Kegley, *Glimpses of Wythe County*, 62–63; Whisonant, "Wythe County Lead Mines," 17; Donnelly, "Confederate Lead Mines," 413; Hoch, *Wythe County During the War*, 38. Most modern sources garble the timing of the movements leading up to the fighting at Wytheville, as well as the skirmish itself.

[75] Davis, *Headquarters Diary*, 677–78.

[76] Scott, *13th Tennessee*, 236; Barchfield's Memoranda, Arnell Collection, UT.

[77] Davis, *Headquarters Diary*, 678; *OR Supplement* 65: 561, 614; *Cincinnati Daily Commercial*, May 10, 1865; Kegley, *Wythe County*, 201; Scott, *13th Tennessee*, 236; Borcherdt, *Story of Austinville*, 44; Kegley, *Glimpses of Wythe County*, 63; Donnelly, "Confederate Lead Mines," 413; Hoch, *Wythe County During the War*, 38; Whisonant, "Wythe County Lead Mines," 13. The ford is located near present-day Ivanhoe, Virginia.

[78] Davis, *Headquarters Diary*, 678–79; *OR* 49 (1): 331, 332; *CV* 10 (July 1902): 306; *CV* 39 (December 1926): 452; Trotter, *Bushwhackers*, 262; Morning Reports for the 13th Tennessee Cavalry, April 6–7, 1865, RR. Giltner's command camped around Wytheville after the fight, and did not further threaten Miller's command (Davis, *Headquarters Diary*, 679). One of Miller's wounded was eighteen-year-old James F. Smith, who received a gunshot wound in the chest (*Report of the Adjutant General of Tennessee*, 623).

[79] Whisonant, "Wythe County Lead Mines," 15; Whisonant, "Union Raiders in the New River Valley," 29–30; Donnelly, "Confederate Lead Mines," 402–4, 409. The mines were located near present-day Austinville, Virginia. Little remains of them today, except for a seventy-foot-tall

shot tower about a quarter mile northeast of the mines, at the site of Jackson's Ferry. Built in 1820, the shot tower is now a historic site.

⁸⁰ Whisonant, "Wythe County Lead Mines," 13, 15–18; Donnelly, "Confederate Lead Mines," 403–4, 409–10, 412–14; Kegley, *Glimpses of Wythe County*, 62–63; Hoch, *Wythe County During the War*, 38; Davis, *Headquarters Diary*, 679; Borcherdt, *Story of Austinville*, 44; Kegley, *Wythe County*, 201; Kegley, *Glimpses of Wythe County*, 63; *OR Supplement* 65: 614. As Donnelly points out, neither AG's report nor the regimental history of the 13th Tennessee reports the destruction of the mines, but both local sources and the Supplement to the Official Records confirm the Tennesseans' activities there.

⁸¹ *OR* 49 (1): 332. Taylorsville is presently called Stuart (Perry, "Civil War Comes to Patrick County"). According to Scott, *13th Tennessee*, 236, Miller received his orders to join the division on April 7 after they passed through Hillsville. AG's report, however, establishes that the order directed Miller to move to Hillsville first and then to Taylorsville, so the orders must have reached Miller in the vicinity of Porter's Ford on April 6.

⁸² Davis, *Headquarters Diary*, 679–80; *CV* 10 (July 1902): 307.

⁸³ *To the Members of the 15th Pennsylvania Cavalry*, 30th Annual Banquet, 7–8; WP to Frank Jackson, February 27, 1865, William J. Palmer Collection, CHS. The watch given to Wagner was presented to him in May 1865 "by the Line Officers of the Regiment" in honor of his promotion.

⁸⁴ *OR* 49 (1): 331; Betts, "Stoneman's Great Cavalry Raid;" *To the Members of the 15th Pennsylvania Cavalry*, 23rd Annual Banquet, 35; Morning Reports of Companies A–D, 15th Pennsylvania Cavalry, RR; Report of Operations of Wagner's Detachment, April 1865, Charles M. Betts papers, HSP; Diary, April 4, 1865, Charles M. Betts papers, HSP; Whisonant, "Union Raiders in the New River Valley," 30–31; Kirk, *15th Pennsylvania*, 529. The Bent Mountain Road generally followed the line of present-day U.S. 221 northward from Floyd. Wagner's command contained six officers and about 240 men.

⁸⁵ Morning Reports for Companies A–D, 15th Pennsylvania Cavalry, RR; Kirk, *15th Pennsylvania*, 496, 529, 530; Wilson, *Recollections and Experiences*, 112; Septimus W. Knight diary, April 4, 1865, VMI; Wilson, *Column South*, 280; Septimus W. Knight diary, April 5, 1865, VMI.

⁸⁶ Kirk, *15th Pennsylvania*, 496, 529; Septimus W. Knight diary, April 5, 1865, VMI; Wilson, *Column South*, 281; Deposition of James Ferguson, August 31, 1900, copy provided to author by Kevin G. Carle. Remnants of the Old Bent Mountain Road still remain in the Back Creek area, near U.S. 221.

⁸⁷ Wilson, *Column South*, 281; Septimus W. Knight diary, April 5, 1865, VMI; Report of Operations of Wagner's Detachment, April 1865, and Maj. William Wagner to Lt. Col. Charles M. Betts, May 6, 1865, both in Charles M. Betts papers, HSP.

⁸⁸ Wilson, *Column South*, 281; Septimus W. Knight diary, April 5, 1865, VMI; Brock, *History of Montgomery County*, 34. See above for details of the 10th Michigan's actions along the Roanoke River.

⁸⁹ Wilson, *Column South*, 281; Maj. William Wagner to Lt. Col. Charles M. Betts, May 6, 1865, and Report of Operations of Wagner's Detachment, April 1865, both in Charles M. Betts papers, HSP; Morning Reports of Companies A–D, 15th Pennsylvania Cavalry, RR; Kirk, *15th Pennsylvania*, 496, 530; Wilson, *Recollections and Experiences*, 112; Septimus W. Knight diary, April 5, 1865, VMI. Big Lick is now called Roanoke.

⁹⁰ Betts, "Stoneman's Great Cavalry Raid;" Morning Reports of Companies A–D, 15th Pennsylvania Cavalry, RR; Septimus W. Knight diary, April 5, 1865, VMI; Kirk, *15th Pennsylvania*, 496, 530; Wilson, *Recollections and Experiences*, 112; Wilson, *Column South*, 281. Wagner's intelligence about Burkeville was false. The Army of Northern Virginia left its Petersburg trenches on the evening of April 2. On April 5, the army left Amelia Court House en route to Jetersville. Coyner Springs is outside of present-day Roanoke, along U.S. 460/221.

⁹¹ Wilson, *Column South*, 281; *Cincinnati Daily Commercial*, May 10, 1865; Maj. William

Wagner to Lt. Col. Charles M. Betts, May 6, 1865, and Report of Operations of Wagner's Detachment, April 1865, both in Charles M. Betts papers, HSP; Septimus W. Knight diary, April 5, 1865, VMI; Wilson, *Recollections and Experiences*, 112; Kirk, *15th Pennsylvania*, 496, 530; Morning Reports of Companies A–D, 15th Pennsylvania Cavalry, RR. A late source notes that the column arrived at Buford at 10:00 P.M. Some troopers spelled the name of the station and their host as "Bufort" or "Beafote."

[92] Morning Reports for Companies A–D, 15th Pennsylvania Cavalry, RR; Report of Operations of Wagner's Detachment, April 1865, Charles M. Betts papers, HSP; *To the Members of the 15th Pennsylvania Cavalry*, 23rd Annual Banquet, 36; Wilson, *Column South*, 281; Wilson, *Recollections and Experiences*, 112–13; Kirk, *15th Pennsylvania*, 496–97, 530; Septimus W. Knight diary, April 6, 1865, VMI. These sources differ on the time the command left for Liberty. Estimates range between 7:00 and 10:00 A.M. Possibly, Wagner sent some men to scout ahead.

[93] Report of Operations of Wagner's Detachment, April 1865, Charles M. Betts papers, HSP; Wilson, *Recollections and Experiences*, 113; Kirk, *15th Pennsylvania*, 497, 530; Septimus W. Knight diary, April 6, 1865, VMI; Wilson, *Column South*, 281. Liberty is now called Bedford and is the site of the National D-Day Memorial. On April 7, one of Phil Sheridan's scouts reported the presence of Stoneman's men in Liberty (Simon, *Papers of U.S. Grant* 14: 366).

[94] Wilson, *Recollections and Experiences*, 113; Kirk, *15th Pennsylvania*, 497, 530–31; Septimus W. Knight diary, April 7, 1865, VMI; Morning Reports for Companies A–D, 15th Pennsylvania Cavalry, RR.

[95] Maj. William Wagner to Lt. Col. Charles M. Betts, May 6, 1865, and Report of Operations of Wagner's Detachment, April 1865, both in Charles M. Betts papers, HSP; Wilson, *Column South*, 281; Septimus W. Knight diary, April 7, 1865, VMI; Wilson, *Recollections and Experiences*, 113; Kirk, *15th Pennsylvania*, 497, 530–31; Morning Reports of Companies A to D, 15th Pennsylvania Cavalry, RR. Colton rejoined the command at the Big Otter bridge around 4:00 P.M. He described the bridge's location as along a "left hand road" that left the pike. Colton also recorded a later time for the camping—1:00 A.M.

[96] Wilson, *Column South*, 281–82; Morning Reports of Companies A–D, 15th Pennsylvania Cavalry, RR; Septimus W. Knight diary, April 6, 1865, VMI; Report of Operations of Wagner's Detachment, April 1865, Charles M. Betts papers, HSP; Wilson, *Column South*, 281–82; Wilson, *Recollections and Experiences*, 113; Kirk, *15th Pennsylvania*, 497, 530–31.

[97] Report of Operations of Wagner's Detachment, April 1865, Charles M. Betts papers, HSP; Wilson, *Column South*, 281–82; Wilson, *Recollections and Experiences*, 113; Kirk, *15th Pennsylvania*, 497, 530–31; *To the Members of the 15th Pennsylvania Cavalry*, 23rd Annual Banquet, 36; OR 49 (1): 324. Only Wilson, *Column South*, records Wagner's council of war, but there is no evidence to discount it. Kirk, *15th Pennsylvania*, 531, and Wilson, *Column South*, 281, report that the bridges were burned on the evening of April 6. The bulk of the evidence, however, suggests that the bridges were destroyed on April 7.

[98] Wilson, *Column South*, 281–82; Morning Reports of Companies A–D, 15th Pennsylvania Cavalry, RR; Kirk, *15th Pennsylvania*, 497, 531; Septimus W. Knight diary, April 7, 1865, VMI; Wilson, *Recollections and Experiences*, 113.

[99] Morris, *Confederate Lynchburg*, 1–6; Blackford, *Campaign and Battle of Lynchburg*, 1.

[100] Morris, *Confederate Lynchburg*, 126–30; Durkin, *John Dooley*, 175; Entry of April 14, 1865, Janet Cleland diary, Jones Memorial Library, Lynchburg; Simon, *Papers of U.S. Grant* 14: 363, 365. For Confederate fears of Thomas's army, see the remarkably accurate articles from *The Lynchburg Virginian* and the *Richmond Enquirer* reprinted in *The New York Herald*, April 2, 1865, and April 3, 1865.

[101] R.E. Colston to R.E. Lee, April 5, 1865; R.E. Lee to R.E. Colston, April 6, 1865, both in R.E. Lee headquarters papers, VHS; Warner, *Generals in Gray*, 58.

[102] Morris, *Confederate Lynchburg*, 126–30; OR 43 (2): 928; Krick, *Lee's Colonels*, 205; "Memoir of the Demise of the Confederacy," George Alexander Martin papers, Jones Memorial Library, Lynchburg.

[103] "Memoir of the Demise of the Confederacy," George Alexander Martin papers, Jones Memorial Library, Lynchburg; R.E. Colston to Major Milligan, April 8, 1865, R.E. Lee headquarters papers, VHS. Martin later claimed that his command alone totaled six hundred men, but given Colston's contemporary claims of only four hundred defenders, Martin's estimate must be inflated.

[104] *OR Supplement* 57: 417; Septimus W. Knight diary, April 7, 1865, VMI; Wilson, *Recollections and Experiences*, 113; Kirk, *15th Pennsylvania*, 497, 531; Morning Reports of Companies A–D, 15th Pennsylvania Cavalry, RR; Wilson, *Column South*, 282; Report of Operations of Wagner's Detachment, April 1865, Charles M. Betts papers, HSP; Descriptive Book for Companies A–F, 15th Pennsylvania Cavalry, RR. Each source varies on the proximity of the command to Lynchburg during the events noted. It is therefore impossible to determine the exact location of these events.

[105] Septimus W. Knight diary, April 7–8, 1865, VMI; Wilson, *Recollections and Experiences*, 113; Kirk, *15th Pennsylvania*, 497, 531; Report of Operations of Wagner's Detachment, April 1865, Charles M. Betts papers, HSP; Wilson, *Column South*, 282.

[106] Septimus W. Knight diary, April 8, 1865, VMI; Report of Operations of Wagner's Detachment, April 1865, Charles M. Betts papers, HSP; Wilson, *Recollections and Experiences*, 113; Kirk, *15th Pennsylvania*, 497, 531; *To the Members of the 15th Pennsylvania Cavalry*, 23rd Annual Banquet, 36; *OR* 49 (1): 324; Wilson, *Column South*, 282; Sample Autobiography, p. 12, CC; Morning Reports for Companies A–D, 15th Pennsylvania Cavalry, RR; R.E. Colston to Major Milligan, April 8, 1865, R.E. Lee headquarters papers, VHS; Evans, *Confederate Military History* 4: 542.

[107] Kirk, *15th Pennsylvania*, 529; Sample Autobiography, p. 12, CC.

[108] Kirk, *15th Pennsylvania*, 499. Actually, Lee's halt at Amelia Court House had nothing to do with news from Lynchburg. When the Army of Northern Virginia arrived there on April 4, they expected to find rations. Finding none, Lee paused for a day to collect food from the countryside (Calkins, *Appomattox Campaign*, 76, 85).

[109] Grant, *Memoirs*, 519.

[110] Marvel, *A Place Called Appomattox*, 230; Calkins, *Appomattox Campaign*, 117, 150; R.E. Colston Letter, April 4, 1865; R.E. Colston to R.E. Lee, April 5, 1865; and R.E. Colston to Major Milligan, April 8, 1865, R.E. Lee headquarters papers, VHS.

[111] *OR Supplement* 57: 344, 417; Septimus W. Knight diary, April 7, 1865, VMI; Morning Reports of Companies A–D, 15th Pennsylvania Cavalry, RR; Septimus W. Knight diary, April 9, 1865, VMI; Wilson, *Column South*, 282; Kirk, *15th Pennsylvania*, 497–98, 531; Wilson, *Recollections and Experiences*, 113; Report of Operations of Wagner's Detachment, April 1865, Charles M. Betts papers, HSP.

[112] Miller, *History of the First Ohio Heavy Artillery*, 45; Thomas Hutton diary, April 3–5, 1865, courtesy TSLA: *OR* 49 (1) 337–38; *OR* (2): 204–5, 337–38; Miller, *Our Service in East Tennessee*, 15–17; Ellis, *Thrilling Adventures*, 396.

[113] *OR* 49 (2): 204–5, 337–38. The 2nd North Carolina was officially led by Col. William Bartlett, but Bahney was in command because Bartlett was serving as a staff officer with another command (Bumgarner, *Kirk's Raiders*, 59).

[114] Barrett, *Civil War in North Carolina*, 233; Trotter, *Bushwhackers*, 29, 113; *OR* 49 (2): 204–5, 337–38; Bumgarner, *Kirk's Raiders*, 59; Arthur, *Watauga County*, 178; *Watauga Democrat*, June 14, 1999; Hardy, *Watauga County and the Civil War*, 6; Beall, "Stoneman's Raid," *The North Carolina Review*, November 11, 1910; Bumgarner, *Kirk's Raiders*, 15.

[115] *OR* 49 (2): 204–5, 337–38; Trotter, *Bushwhackers*, 29; Arthur, *Watauga County*, 178–79; *Watauga Democrat*, June 14, 1999; Hardy, *Watauga County and the Civil War*, 6; Claim of John Horton, #15276, Box 233, Entry 732, Watauga County, N.C., RG 217, Settled Files of the SCC, NA; Descriptive and Consolidated Morning Report Book for the 2nd North Carolina Mounted Infantry, RR; Bumgarner, *Kirk's Raiders*, 24–26; Inscoe and McKinney, *Heart of Confederate Appalachia*, 103–4, 110–11; *Winston-Salem Journal*, October 23, 1994; November 5, 1995; *OR* 49

(2): 204–5, 337–38; Dugger, *War Trails*, 124–25; Buxton, *Village Tapestry*, 3; Arthur, *Western North Carolina*, 617; Van Noppen, *Stoneman's Last Raid*, 21.

[116] Miller, *History of the First Ohio Heavy Artillery*, 10; OR 49 (1): 19–23, 344, 908; OR (2): 338, 394, 534; *Cincinnati Daily Enquirer*, April 12, 1865. For Stanley's raid on Asheville, see Chapter 10.

[117] OR 49 (1): 328, 331; OR Supplement 65: 637; April 7, 1865, Henry Birdsall diary, SHC; *The Wood Family of Patrick Springs*, 14; April 7–8, 1865, Allen Frankenberry diaries, WV; Morning Reports for Companies B, G, and H, 11th Kentucky Cavalry, April 6–April 7, 1865, RR.

[118] OR 49 (1): 331; Morning Reports for Companies B, G, and H, 11th Kentucky Cavalry, April 8, 1865, RR; Perry, "Civil War Comes to Patrick County;" "1865 Raid Shocked Piedmont Towns," Civil War clipping file, Mount Airy Public Library; R. L. Beall to Mrs. Spencer, September 20, 1866, Cornelia Phillips Spencer papers, SHC; *CV* 32 (September 1924): 344.

[119] R. L. Beall to Mrs. Spencer, September 20, 1866, Cornelia Phillips Spencer papers, SHC; Perry, "Civil War Comes to Patrick County;" Claim of James Light, #8901, Box 384, Entry 732, Patrick County, Va., RG 217, Settled Files of the SCC, NA; Claim of Thomas Shelton, #12917, Box 384, Entry 732, Patrick County, Va., RG 217, Settled Files of the SCC, NA; *Winston-Salem Journal*, November 16, 1997; Millhouse, *Recollections of Major A.D. Reynolds*, iii–vi, 17; Reynolds, *Gilded Leaf*, 19, 25–26.

[120] April 7–8, 1865, Allen Frankenberry diaries, WV; April 8, 1865, Henry Birdsall diary, SHC.

[121] Scott, *13th Tennessee*, 236–37; *Philadelphia Weekly Times*, January 18, 1879; OR Supplement 65: 614.

[122] OR 49 (1): 331; Van Noppen, *Stoneman's Last Raid*, 37; Kirk, *15th Pennsylvania*, 500; L.S. Trowbridge to "My Dear Judie," April 12, 1865, L.S. Trowbridge papers, UM; Diary, April 6, 1865, Charles M. Betts papers, HSP.

[123] Angelo Wiser maps, LC; Banks, "Memoranda," diary entry for April 7, 1865, 296; Bushong, *Last Great Stoneman Raid*; Betts, "Stoneman's Great Cavalry Raid;" Kirk, *15th Pennsylvania*, 500; Wilson, *Recollections and Experiences*, 115.

[124] Kirk, *15th Pennsylvania*, 500; Diary, April 6–April 8, 1865, Charles M. Betts papers, HSP; Betts, "Stoneman's Great Cavalry Raid;" Frederic Antes diary, April 7, 1865, Civil War Miscellaneous Collection, USAMHI; Diary entry for April 7, 1865, Charles F. Weller memoirs and letters, *Civil War Times Illustrated* Collection, USAMHI; Angelo Wiser maps, LC; Wilson, *Recollections and Experiences*, 115. Time estimates for the break on the morning of April 7 vary between 9:00 A.M. and noon. Quite possibly, parts of the regiment halted at different times.

[125] Trowbridge, "The Stoneman Raid of 1865," *JUSCA* 4 (June 1891): 192–93; *10th Cavalry*, vol. 40, 13; Trowbridge, *Brief History of the 10th Michigan*, 34; Steven Thomas to "My Dear Wife," June 5, 1865, Calvin Thomas papers, UM.

[126] *10th Cavalry*, vol. 40, 13; Trowbridge, *Brief History of the 10th Michigan*, 34; Morning Reports, Companies A–F, 10th Michigan Cavalry, RR; Trowbridge, "The Stoneman Raid of 1865," *JUSCA* 4 (June 1891): 193; OR Supplement 30: 230; Frederick N. Field to "Dear Brother," September 27, 1865, Frederick N. Field correspondence, UM; Jones, *Last Raid*, 25; *Martinsville and Henry County*, 20; "Stoneman's Raid," in the *Henry County Horse Show*, 56–57, Stoneman's Raid notebook, Bassett Branch Historical Center; *Martinsville Daily Bulletin*, July 31, 1939.

[127] *Martinsville Daily Bulletin*, July 31, 1939; Steve Giegerich, "The Day the Civil War Came to Henry," unprovenienced newspaper article in the author's possession; Hilda G. Marshall, "Stoneman's Raid in Sixty-Five," Stoneman's Raid notebook, Bassett Branch Historical Center. The above sources indicate that this incident occurred the day before the raid, but it must have occurred on April 8, the only time the Federals were near Rough and Ready Mills.

[128] Frederick N. Field to "Dear Brother," September 27, 1865, Frederick N. Field correspondence, UM.

[129] Frederick N. Field to "Dear Brother," September 27, 1865, Frederick N. Field correspondence, UM; Trowbridge, *Brief History of the 10th Michigan*, 7.

[130] Frederick N. Field to "Dear Brother," September 27, 1865, Frederick N. Field correspondence, UM.

[131] "Memorabilia," Henry County, Virginia During the Civil War—miscellaneous notebook, Bassett Branch Historical Center; *10th Cavalry*, vol. 40, 13; Trowbridge, *Brief History of the 10th Michigan*, 34–35; Frederick N. Field to "Dear Brother," September 27, 1865, Frederick N. Field correspondence, UM. Cummins commanded Company L.

[132] *10th Cavalry*, vol. 40, 13; Trowbridge, *Brief History of the 10th Michigan*, 34–35.

[133] Roman, *Beauregard* 2: 385–86; *OR* 47 (3): 751, 753, 756; John M. Otey to Colonel Wheeler, April 4, 1865, Letters and Orders Book, P.G.T. Beauregard papers, LC; *OR Supplement*, pt. 2, Vol. 66, 115–26; Lindsley, *Military Annals*, 883–85, 893, 895–97. Ohioan Joseph Banks estimated the enemy force at five hundred men, but AG credited the force with only 250 (Banks, "Memoranda," diary entry for April 8, 1865, 296; *OR* 49 (1): 332).

[134] "Memorabilia," Henry County, Virginia During the Civil War—miscellaneous notebook, Bassett Branch Historical Center; *Martinsville Daily Bulletin*, July 31, 1939; Steve Giegerich, "The Day the Civil War Came to Henry," unprovenienced newspaper article in the author's possession; "Stoneman's Raid," in the *Henry County Horse Show*, Stoneman's Raid notebook, Bassett Branch Historical Center, 56–57; *10th Cavalry*, vol. 40, 13; *OR* 47 (3): 769; Angelo Wiser maps, LC. According to "Stoneman's Raid," in the *Henry County Horse Show*, Stoneman's Raid notebook, Bassett Branch Historical Center, 56–57, the skirmish took place on the site of the Lester Lumber Company.

[135] Frederick N. Field to "Dear Brother," September 27, 1865, Frederick N. Field correspondence, UM; *OR* 49 (1): 556–57; Descriptive Book for Companies A–E and G–M, 10th Michigan Cavalry, RR.

[136] Trowbridge, "The Stoneman Raid of 1865," *JUSCA* 4 (June 1891): 193; Frederick N. Field to "Dear Brother," September 27, 1865, Frederick N. Field correspondence, UM.

[137] Frederick N. Field to "Dear Brother," September 27, 1865, Frederick N. Field correspondence, UM.

[138] Frederick N. Field to "Dear Brother," September 27, 1865, Frederick N. Field correspondence, UM; Trowbridge, *Brief History of the 10th Michigan*, 8, 35; *10th Cavalry*, vol. 40, 13; *OR* 47 (3): 769; Banks, "Memoranda," diary entry for April 8, 1865, 296. A modern observer identified the depression in which Wheeler's men took refuge as the "deep, steep-sided valley between the C & N W railway tracks and Commonwealth Boulevard, down which Stillhouse Branch flows to empty into Jones' Creek" ("Memorabilia," Henry County, Virginia During the Civil War—miscellaneous notebook, Bassett Branch Historical Center).

[139] Companies A–F, April 8, 1865, 10th Michigan Cavalry, RR; Morning Reports, Companies G–M, April 9, 1865, 10th Michigan Cavalry, RR; Frederick N. Field to "Dear Brother," September 27, 1865, Frederick N. Field correspondence, UM; *10th Cavalry*, vol. 40, 13; Trowbridge, *Brief History of the 10th Michigan*, 35; L.S. Trowbridge to "My Dear Judie," April 12, 1865, L.S. Trowbridge papers, UM; "Stoneman's Raid 3/20/1865–4/23/1865, Notes," Stoneman's Raid notebook, Bassett Branch Historical Center; *OR Supplement* 30: 230; Steven Thomas to "My Dear Wife," June 5, 1865, Calvin Thomas papers, UM; Descriptive Book for Companies A–E and G–M, 10th Michigan Cavalry, RR; *OR* 49 (1): 332; *OR* 47 (3): 769; Stoneman's Raid," in the *Henry County Horse Show*, 56–57, Stoneman's Raid notebook, Bassett Branch Historical Center; *Martinsville Daily Bulletin*, July 31, 1939; Steve Giegerich, "The Day the Civil War Came to Henry," unprovenienced newspaper article in the author's possession; *Martinsville Daily Bulletin*, July 31, 1939; Lindsley, *Military Annals*, 897.

[140] Frederick N. Field to "Dear Brother," September 27, 1865, Frederick N. Field correspondence, UM; Trowbridge, *Brief History of the 10th Michigan*, 8; Trowbridge, "The Stoneman Raid of 1865," *JUSCA* 4 (June 1891): 193; *OR* 47 (3): 769.

[141] *OR* 47 (3): 769, 774–75; *Charlotte Daily Bulletin*, April 11, 1865. Soon afterward, Wheeler's regiment was ordered to rejoin Johnston's army.

[142] "Memorabilia," Henry County, Virginia During the Civil War—miscellaneous notebook,

Bassett Branch Historical Center; *OR* 47 (3): 769; Banks, "Memoranda," diary entry for April 8, 1865, 296; Frederic Antes diary, April 8, 1865, Civil War Miscellaneous Collection, USAMHI; Diary entry for April 8, 1865, Charles F. Weller memoirs and letters, *Civil War Times Illustrated Collection*, USAMHI.

[143] Wiencek, *Hairstons*, 45, 167–68.

[144] *Martinsville Daily Bulletin*, July 31, 1939; Hill, *History of Henry County*, 23; *OR* 49 (1): 328, 331; "Memorabilia," Henry County, Virginia During the Civil War—miscellaneous notebook, Bassett Branch Historical Center. Stoneman is the general named in these accounts, but he was not present at Henry Court House.

[145] *OR* 49 (1): 324, 328, 331; *Philadelphia Weekly Times*, January 18, 1879; *OR Supplement* 65: 614; *OR Supplement* 65: 63.

[146] Moderwell, "Outline of Stoneman's Raid," Civil War (Federal, Miscellaneous) papers, SHC; *OR* 49 (1): 331, 345; *Annual Report of the Adjutant General of Michigan* 1: 95; *Chicago Tribune*, April 19, 1865; *Cincinnati Daily Commercial*, May 10, 1865; *Daily Ohio State Journal*, April 19, 1865. Trowbridge's estimate was 150 miles of railroad (L.S. Trowbridge to "My Dear Judie," April 12, 1865, L.S. Trowbridge papers, UM).

[147] Barchfield's Memoranda, Arnell Collection, UT.

Chapter 5
YONDER THEY COME
Danbury to Salem: April 9–10, 1865

[1] Davis, *Jefferson Davis*, 612; Tetley, *Last Days*, 42; Semmes, *Memoirs of Service Afloat*, 818, 819; Bradley, *Astounding Close*, 234–35.

[2] Evans, *Confederate Military History* 2: 104; 4: 542; 8: 340; 9: 190; *CV* 10 (July 1902): 307; Duke, *History of Morgan's Cavalry*, 621; Duke, *Reminiscences*, 462–63; Durkin, *John Dooley*, 179–80, 184.

[3] Duke, *History of Morgan's Cavalry*, 622; Wilson, *Recollections and Experiences*, 76; *CV* 34 (June 1926): 225; *To the Members of the 15th Pennsylvania Cavalry*, 23rd Annual Banquet, 12; Duke, *History of Morgan's Cavalry*, 622.

[4] Hanna, *Flight into Oblivion*, 22–24; Davis, *Jefferson Davis*, 612–613.

[5] Beall, "Stoneman's Raid," *The North Carolina Review*, October 2, 1910; R.L. Beall's account of Stoneman's Raid, Cornelia Phillips Spencer papers, SHC; Precipitation records for South Carolina and Virginia in 1865, NCDC.

[6] Wiencek, *Hairstons*, 168–69; Interview with Peter Hairston, July 6, 1997. According to Wiencek, *Hairstons*, 227, Stoneman met Goolsby along present-day Highway 311, but it more than likely occurred along either present-day Highway 65 or 8 in Stokes County.

[7] *OR* 49 (1): 324, 328, 332; *Philadelphia Weekly Times*, January 18, 1879; *OR Supplement* 65: 63, 614; Frederic Antes diary, April 9, 1865, Civil War Miscellaneous Collection, USAMHI; Wilson, *Recollections and Experiences*, 115; Kirk, *15th Pennsylvania*, 500; Angelo Wiser maps, LC.

[8] Morning Reports, Companies A–F, April 9, 1865, 10th Michigan Cavalry, RR; Frederick N. Field to "Dear Brother," September 27, 1865, Frederick N. Field correspondence, UM; Morning Reports, Companies G–M, 10th Michigan Cavalry, RR.

[9] Jones, *The Last Raid*, 27; Banks, "Memoranda," diary entry for April 9, 1865, 297.

[10] Barchfield's Memoranda, Arnell Collection, UT; April 9, 1865, Allen Frankenberry diaries, WV; Scott, *13th Tennessee*, 237; April 9, 1865, Henry Birdsall diary, Birdsall papers, SHC.

[11] Johnson, *Touring the Carolinas' Civil War Sites*, 147; Claim of William M. McCanless, #11063, Box 231, Entry 732, Stokes County, N.C., RG 217, Settled Files of the SCC, NA; Woodard, *Heritage of Stokes County*, 86–87; *Winston-Salem Journal*, November 1, 2006. Dr. McCanless purchased the hotel from Moody after the war and assumed the losses, so he submitted

the claim to the Southern Claims Commission.

[12] Woodard, *Heritage of Stokes County*, 314.

[13] *Winston-Salem Journal*, June 8, 2002; Lester, *Seasons in Stokes*, 57; April 9, 1865, Henry Birdsall diary, Birdsall papers, SHC; *OR* 49 (1): 328; Morning Reports for Companies B, G, and H, 11th Kentucky Cavalry, April 9, 1865, RR; Diary, April 9, 1865, Charles M. Betts papers, HSP; Wilson, *Recollections and Experiences*, 115; Kirk, *15th Pennsylvania*, 500; Diary entry for April 9, 1865, Charles F. Weller memoirs and letters, *Civil War Times Illustrated* Collection, USAMHI; *OR* 49 (1): 328, 332; Woodard, *Heritage of Stokes County*, 87; Martin, *Saga of the Sauratowns*, 170.

[14] Woodard, *Heritage of Stokes County*, 156, 225. As of 1981, the broken weapon was still in the family.

[15] Woodard, *Heritage of Stokes County*, 156–57.

[16] Claim of William M. McCanless, #11063, Box 231, Entry 732, Stokes County, N.C., RG 217, Settled Files of the SCC, NA; April 9, 1865, Allen Frankenberry diaries, WV; *OR* 49 (1): 332; *Winston-Salem Journal*, June 8, 2002; Lester, *Seasons in Stokes*, 57.

[17] Johnson, *Touring the Carolinas' Civil War Sites*, 148; Woodard, *Heritage of Stokes County*, 87; Martin, *Saga of the Sauratowns*, 170.

[18] Martin, *Saga of the Sauratowns*, 170.

[19] Morning Reports for Companies B, G, and H, 11th Kentucky Cavalry, April 10, 1865, RR; April 10, 1865, Henry Birdsall diary, Birdsall papers, SHC.

[20] Morning Reports for the 13th Tennessee Cavalry, April 9, 1865, RR; Scott, *13th Tennessee*, 237; *Philadelphia Weekly Times*, January 18, 1879.

[21] Diary, April 10, 1865, Charles M. Betts papers, HSP; Wilson, *Recollections and Experiences*, 115; Kirk, *15th Pennsylvania*, 500, 538; Diary entry for April 10, 1865, Charles F. Weller memoirs and letters, *Civil War Times Illustrated* Collection, USAMHI; *OR* 49 (1): 333.

[22] Morning Reports, Companies G–M, April 10, 1865, 10th Michigan Cavalry, RR; Descriptive Book, Companies A–E, 10th Michigan Cavalry, RR; *Annual Report of the Adjutant General of Michigan* 2: 293; Morning Reports of Companies A–F, 10th Michigan Cavalry, RR.

[23] April 10, 1865, Allen Frankenberry diaries, WV; *OR* 49 (1): 328.

[24] *OR* 49 (1): 328, 332; Trotter, *Bushwhackers*, 264–65; *CV* 29 (May 1921): 185.

[25] Claim of Samuel Stoltz, #15085, Box 23, Entry 732, Forsyth County, N.C., RG 217, Settled Files of the SCC, NA.

[26] *OR* 49 (1): 324, 332–33; Mason, "Stoneman's Last Campaign," 25–26; Trowbridge, *Stoneman Raid*, 105.

[27] Mason, "Stoneman's Last Campaign," 25–26; Trowbridge, *Stoneman Raid*, 105; *OR* 49 (1): 324, 333; Morning Reports for Companies B, G, and H, 11th Kentucky Cavalry, April 10, 1865, RR; April 10, 1865, Henry Birdsall diary, Birdsall papers, SHC; Morning Reports for the 13th Tennessee Cavalry, April 9, 1865, RR; Scott, *13th Tennessee*, 237; *Philadelphia Weekly Times*, January 18, 1879.

[28] Scott, *13th Tennessee*, 237; "Negro Folk Lore of the Piedmont."

[29] *CV* 20 (June 1912): 306.

[30] Crews, *Storm in the Land*, 1–3.

[31] Johnson, *Touring the Carolinas' Civil War Sites*, 149–50; Crews, *Storm in the Land*, 38; Clewell, *History of Wachovia*, 250; Fries, *Forsyth*, 141.

[32] April 10, 1865, Allen Frankenberry diaries, WV; Fries, *Forsyth*, 141; Claim of Samuel Stoltz, #15085, Box 23, Entry 732, Forsyth County, N.C., RG 217, Settled Files of the SCC, NA. Old Town was also known as Bethabara, which is today preserved as a historic site.

[33] Claim of Thomas B. Lash, #3501, Box 23, Entry 732, Forsyth County, N.C., RG 217, Settled Files of the SCC, NA.

[34] Scott, *13th Tennessee*, 237; *Winston-Salem Journal, Clemmons Journal* insert, March 29, 2001; *OR* 49 (1): 333; Casstevens, *Historic Structures and Sites*, 1. Almost a dozen fords were

located between Elkin to the north and Trading Ford to the south, but few accepted wagon traffic as well as the Shallow Ford.

[35] Casstevens, *The Civil War and Yadkin County*, 80; "Last Year of the War," Civil War and Reconstruction papers, MA; "Shallow Ford," Clingman and Puryear family papers, SHC; Wright, *Memoirs of Belo*, 29; *People's Press*, April 14, 1866; *OR* 49 (1): 333; *OR* 47 (3): 790. The account "Last Year of the War" was also reprinted in the *Twin City Sentinel* of October 3, 1925.

[36] "Shallow Ford," Clingman and Puryear family papers, SHC; Reynolds, *Shallow Ford Country*, 175–76; Warner, *Generals in Gray*, 54–55; "Gen. Stoneman's Army in Iredell," Stoneman's Raid file, Local History Collection, Iredell County Public Library.

[37] "Memoir of the Demise of the Confederacy," George Alexander Martin papers, Jones Memorial Library; *Philadelphia Weekly Times*, January 18, 1879; Casstevens, *Heritage of Yadkin County*, 24, 34, 80, 107; Scott, *13th Tennessee*, 237; *OR* 49 (1): 328; April 11, 1865, Allen Frankenberry diaries, WV.

[38] "Gen. Stoneman's Army in Iredell," Stoneman's Raid file, Local History Collection, Iredell County Public Library.

[39] R.L. Beall to Cornelia P. Spencer, September 20, 1866, Cornelia Phillips Spencer papers, SHC.

[40] Casstevens, *Heritage of Yadkin County*, 22; Rutledge, *Illustrated History*, 26.

[41] "Shallow Ford," Clingman and Puryear family papers, SHC.

[42] Claim of Margaret Elizabeth Hauser, #3497, Box 235, Entry 732, Yadkin County, N.C., RG 217, Settled Files of the SCC, NA.

[43] Claim of Sarah Dalton, #3487, Box 235, Entry 732, Yadkin County, N.C., RG 217, Settled Files of the SCC, NA; Reynolds, *Shallow Ford Country*, 184. Although in disrepair, Mrs. Dalton's home still stands (2010), on the Farmington Road near Shallow Ford. It was built in 1855.

[44] Claim of Sarah Dalton, #3487, Box 235, Entry 732, Yadkin County, N.C., RG 217, Settled Files of the SCC, NA; April 11, 1865, Allen Frankenberry diaries, WV; Scott, *13th Tennessee*, 237; *OR* 49 (1): 328.

[45] *Archaeological Survey of the Forsyth County Memorial Park*; Diary, April 10, 1865, Charles M. Betts papers, HSP; Morning Reports of Companies A–F, 10th Michigan Cavalry, RR. The raiders passed just west of the park property (today called Horizons Park) but left no evidence. Germanton Road is today also known as Highway 8.

[46] Wilson, *Recollections and Experiences*, 163; McClure, *Lincoln and Men of War-Times*, 368; "The General's Story," 61.

[47] Peabody, *William Jackson Palmer*, 6; Kirk, *15th Pennsylvania*, 524; WP to Frank Jackson, February 27, 1865, William J. Palmer Collection, CHS.

[48] Fisher, *Builder of the West*, 19, 21; Peabody, *William Jackson Palmer*, v; Clothier, *Letters*, facing p. 34. Palmer's birthplace, a farm named Kinsale, was located near Dover.

[49] Fisher, *Builder of the West*, 17, 21; Peabody, *William Jackson Palmer*, v, 6–7; William J. Palmer to Isaac W. Clothier, April 19, 1859, in Clothier, *Letters*, 14, and William J. Palmer to Isaac W. Clothier, July 24, 1859, in Clothier, *Letters*, 35.

[50] Fisher, *Builder of the West*, 24, 50–51; Anderson, "General William Jackson Palmer," 3; William J. Palmer to Isaac W. Clothier, April 19, 1859, in Clothier, *Letters*, 14; Fisher, *Builder of the West*, 53.

[51] Clothier, *Letters*, 109, 120–28. Palmer, a Mason, was well connected in Philadelphia (William J. Palmer to Isaac W. Clothier, June 25, 1859, in Clothier, *Letters*, 25–26).

[52] Fisher, *Builder of the West*, 70–74.

[53] Clothier, *Letters*, 91–93; Fisher, *Builder of the West*, 74–75.

[54] Dyer, *Compendium* 3:1569; *OR* 16 (2): 177; *OR* 20 (2): 350–51; Fisher, *Builder of the West*, 77–78, 80–81; Wilson, *Recollections and Experiences*, 3, 4; *National Tribune*, July 12, 2000.

[55] Longacre, *Lincoln's Cavalrymen*, 31, 37; "From Carlisle to Murfreesboro," Conrad Lewis Diehl papers, FHS; Wilson, *Recollections and Experiences*, 5; Williams, *Leaves*, 80.

[56] McClure, *Lincoln and Men of War-Times*, 366–68; Wilson, *Recollections and Experiences*, 5–6; Sears, *Landscape Turned Red*, 366; "The General's Story," 61.

[57] Statement, February 12, 1865, William J. Palmer Collection, CHS.

[58] McClure, *Lincoln and Men of War-Times*, 368.

[59] "The General's Story," 61–74; Fisher, *Builder of the West*, 88, 92–94, 103; Statement, February 12, 1865, William J. Palmer Collection, CHS; Wilson, *Recollections and Experiences*, 7.

[60] McClure, *Lincoln and Men of War-Times*, 368–70; Fisher, *Builder of the West*, 88, 92–94, 103.

[61] Fisher, *Builder of the West*, 103–4; "From Carlisle to Murfreesboro," Conrad Lewis Diehl papers, FHS; Williams, *Leaves*, 81, 87.

[62] Fisher, *Builder of the West*, 105–8; WP to Frank Jackson, February 5, 1865, William J. Palmer Collection, CHS; Williams, *Leaves*, 103.

[63] Wilson, *Recollections and Experiences*, 40, 43–45; OR 20 (1): 218, 617; Dyer, *Compendium* 3: 1555.

[64] OR 45 (1): 641–44, 798–800; OR 45 (2): 542; OR 49 (1): 647; Bates, *History of Pennsylvania Volunteers*, 4: 909; Van Noppen, *Stoneman's Last Raid*, 2.

[65] *To the Members of the 15th Pennsylvania Cavalry*, 28th Annual Banquet, 11–12; WP to Frank Jackson, February 12, 1865, and WP to "My Dear Mother," February 22, 1865, William J. Palmer Collection, CHS.

[66] WP to Frank Jackson, February 12, 1865, William J. Palmer Collection, CHS; WP to Frank Jackson, March 20, 1865, William J. Palmer Collection, CHS.

[67] Diary, March 16, 1865, Charles M. Betts papers, HSP; WP to Frank Jackson, February 12, 1865, and February 7, 1865, William J. Palmer Collection, CHS; First Cavalry Brigade, Cavalry Division, District of East Tennessee, General Orders No. 1, March 20, 1865, in Book of Regimental Orders, Court Martials, Rosters, Muster Rolls, etc., RR; Wilson, *Recollections and Experiences*, 3–4; Hinchman, *Biographical Sketch of Charles S. Hinchman*, 26.

[68] Fries, *Forsyth*, 135; Brownlee, *Winston-Salem*, 40; Rights, "Salem in the War," 277–79, 281, 285; Reynolds, *Gilded Leaf*, 18. The town of Salem, eighteenth-century style, is today thoroughly interpreted at the historic site of Old Salem. Thanks to this well-preserved attraction, visitors can gain a real sense of what Salem looked like when the raiders arrived.

[69] Crews, *Storm in the Land*, 1–3, 9–11; Wellman, *Winston-Salem in History* 2: 23; Tursi, *Winston-Salem*, 102; Rights, "Salem in the War," 286; "Last Year of the War," Civil War and Reconstruction papers, MA; Crews, *Storm in the Land*, 36; *People's Press*, April 14, 1866.

[70] *Twin City Sentinel*, June 30, 1969; "Last Year of the War," Civil War and Reconstruction papers, MA; Clewell, *History of Wachovia*, 249–50; Fries, *Forsyth*, 141; Griffin, *Less Time for Meddling*, 267; Owen, *Old Salem*, 72; *People's Press*, April 14, 1866. "Last Year of the War" was also reprinted in the *Twin City Sentinel* of October 3, 1925.

[71] "Last Year of the War," Civil War and Reconstruction papers, MA; Johnson, *Touring the Carolinas' Civil War Sites*, 151; "Reminiscences of Confederate days," Fries papers, NCSA; Griffin, *Less Time for Meddling*, 267; Hall & McMurray, *Tanglewood*, 50. The coffeepot is a symbol of Moravian hospitality, and remains outside Salem today. The home of the little boy in question, remodeled and enlarged into the Manor House, and the site of the fort can still be seen in Tanglewood Park in western Forsyth County.

[72] "Fannie and Louisa," 10, Salem Civil War Recollections, MA; Owen, *Old Salem*, 54; "Reminiscences of Confederate days," Fries papers, NCSA.

[73] Griffin, *Less Time for Meddling*, 267; *People's Press*, April 14, 1866; "Reminiscences of Confederate days," Fries papers, NCSA; "Last Year of the War," Civil War and Reconstruction papers, MA; *People's Press*, April 14, 1866; Frederic Antes diary, April 10, 1865, Civil War Miscellaneous Collection, USAMHI; Angelo Wiser maps, LC; Morning Reports, Companies G–M, 10th Michigan Cavalry, RR; Descriptive Book, Companies G–M, 12th Ohio Cavalry, RR.

[74] Kirk, *15th Pennsylvania*, 538; OR 49 (1): 324, 332–33; Mason, "Stoneman's Last

Campaign," 25–26; Trowbridge, *Stoneman Raid*, 105.

[75] Kirk, *15th Pennsylvania*, 538–39.

[76] Griffin, *Less Time for Meddling*, 267; "Reminiscences of Confederate days," Fries papers, NCSA. According to Fries, the three scouts met the raiders on the Walkertown Road (present-day Highway 311), near Dennis Station (present-day Dennis). Fries may have been in error; it is more likely that they encountered raiders along the Germanton Road (present-day Highway 8). Or these could have been outriders.

[77] Kirk, *15th Pennsylvania*, 539; Brownlee, *Winston-Salem*, 40; Wellman, *Winston-Salem in History* 2: 24; "Last Year of the War," Civil War and Reconstruction papers, MA.

[78] Kirk, *15th Pennsylvania*, 539; *People's Press*, April 14, 1866; "Reminiscences of Confederate days," Fries papers, NCSA; Griffin, *Less Time for Meddling*, 267; "Last Year of the War," Civil War and Reconstruction papers, MA.

[79] "Last Year of the War," Civil War and Reconstruction papers, MA.

[80] Kirk, *15th Pennsylvania*, 539–40; "Last Year of the War," Civil War and Reconstruction papers, MA.

[81] "Fannie and Louisa," 10, Salem Civil War recollections, MA.

[82] The story of the Federals' approach to Salem is compiled from *People's Press*, April 14, 1866; Memorabilia of the Congregation at Salem, 1865, in Crews, *Storm in the Land*, 36; Yearns and Barrett, *North Carolina Civil War Documentary*, 116–17; Tursi, *Winston-Salem*, 103; Wellman, *Winston-Salem in History* 2: 24; Griffin, *Less Time for Meddling*, 267–68, 276; *Twin City Sentinel*, June 30, 1969; Fries, *Forsyth*, 142; Clewell, *History of Wachovia*, 250–51; Owen, *Old Salem*, 74; "Last Year of the War," Civil War and Reconstruction papers, MA. Owen's account claims that the meeting between Palmer and town officials took place on Church Street, but the suggestion that it happened on Liberty Street is more likely. The *Twin City Sentinel* offers the best primary source on this meeting—words directly from Blackburn, who was present.

[83] Crews, *Storm in the Land*, 37; Sample Autobiography, p. 13–14, CC. See also Van Noppen, *Stoneman's Last Raid*, 41 n. 121, which explains that de Schweinitz did meet an officer among the Federal raiders who had once been a classmate. After the war, Sample's Littiz friends would thank him profusely for treating their kinsfolk well.

[84] Fries, *Forsyth*, 141–42; *People's Press*, April 14, 1866; Clark, *Histories of the Several Regiments* 4: 650; Kirk, *15th Pennsylvania*, 539–40; "Fannie and Louisa," 11, Salem Civil War recollections, MA

[85] Memorabilia of the Congregation at Salem, 1865, in Yearns and Barrett, *North Carolina Civil War Documentary*, 116–17; Johnson, *Touring the Carolinas' Civil War Sites*, 151; Betts, "Stoneman's Great Cavalry Raid;" Diary, April 10, 1865, Charles M. Betts papers, HSP; Wilson, *Recollections and Experiences*, 115–16; Kirk, *15th Pennsylvania*, 501; Sample Autobiography, p. 13–14, CC; Clewell, *History of Wachovia*, 251.

[86] Wilson, *Recollections and Experiences*, 115–16; Kirk, *15th Pennsylvania*, 501; Frederic Antes diary, April 10, 1865, Civil War Miscellaneous Collection, USAMHI.

[87] Kirk, *15th Pennsylvania*, 501, 545; Wilson, *Recollections and Experiences*, 115–16; Owen, *Old Salem*, 74; Johnson, *Touring the Carolinas' Civil War Sites*, 151; Wellman, *Winston-Salem in History* 2: 24; Griffin, *Less Time for Meddling*, 269. Owen's text confuses Palmer with Stoneman, who was not present. Sources also disagree on the young lady's location, some placing her on the second floor, others the third.

[88] Rights, "Salem in the War," 287; "Last Year of the War," Civil War and Reconstruction papers, MA. The Blum print shop was across the street from Palmer's headquarters. It still stands today.

[89] "Last Year of the War," Civil War and Reconstruction papers, MA; *Twin City Sentinel*, June 30, 1969; Rights, "Salem in the War," 287; Owen, *Old Salem*, 54; Crews, *Storm in the Land*, 36; *People's Press*, April 14, 1866; Clewell, *History of Wachovia*, 251; *People's Press*, April 14, 1866; Kirk, *15th Pennsylvania*, 545; Tise, *Yadkin Melting Pot*, 128; Memorabilia of the Congregation at Salem, 1865, in Yearns and Barrett, *North Carolina Civil War Documentary*, 116–17; Fries,

Forsyth, 142; Owen, *Old Salem,* 54; "Last Year of the War," Civil War and Reconstruction papers, MA; *Twin City Sentinel,* October 3, 1925 and June 30, 1969. The Boner house still stands today on Main Street in Old Salem, while the camp was probably situated in and around present-day Central Park and Happy Hill Park, at a spot once known as Centerville.

[90] Griffin, *Less Time for Meddling,* 268–69; Crews, *Storm in the Land,* 36–37.

[91] Trelease, *North Carolina Railroad,* 181–82, 191–92.

[92] *To the Members of the 15th Pennsylvania Cavalry,* 15th Annual Banquet, 11–12; Kirk, *15th Pennsylvania,* 541; Trowbridge, *Stoneman Raid,* 105.

Chapter 6
THE PROUDEST DAY IN OUR HISTORY
Salem to Abbott's Creek: April 10–11, 1865

[1] Durkin, *John Dooley,* 188; O'Keefe, *Greensboro,* 15; *Greensborough Patriot,* March 23, 1866; Konkle, *John Motley Morehead,* 408–9; Wright, *Memoirs of Belo,* 30.

[2] *Greensborough Patriot,* April 6, 1865; *OR* 47 (3): 774, 777, 788–89.

[3] *OR* 47 (3): 774, 777, 788–89; Bradley, *Astounding Close,* 137; Roman, *Beauregard* 2: 387, 390; Robinson, *History of Guilford County,* 94; *Greensborough Patriot,* March 23, 1866; Arnett, *Greensboro,* 394; Konkle, *John Motley Morehead,* 409.

[4] *Greensborough Patriot,* March 23, 1866; *SHSP* 41 (September 1916): 60; Robinson, *History of Guilford County,* 94; Arnett, *Greensboro,* 394; Hanna, *Flight Into Oblivion,* 31–3.

[5] Konkle, *John Motley Morehead,* 409; Entry for April 11, 1865, Anna Holmes Trenholm diary, SHC; Clark, *Last Train South,* 55; Roman, *Beauregard* 2: 390–91; Davis, *Short History,* 486; *OR* 47 (3): 788; Davis, *Jefferson Davis,* 613–14; Hanna, *Flight Into Oblivion,* 26. On April 10, Beauregard had wrongly assured Davis that it would be safe to travel. "Road between this place [Greensboro] and Danville safe. Raiders are at or near Salem." Roman, *Beauregard* 2: 389–90. This narrow miss was also reported in Northern newspapers; see *Cincinnati Daily Commercial,* May 3, 1865.

[6] Davis, *Jefferson Davis,* 614; Hanna, *Flight Into Oblivion,* 26–28; Trudeau, *Out of the Storm,* 202–3.

[7] Roman, *Beauregard* 2: 390–91; Trudeau, *Out of the Storm,* 202–3; Davis, *Jefferson Davis,* 614–17; Hanna, *Flight Into Oblivion,* 35–37.

[8] *OR* 47 (3): 788; Roman, *Beauregard* 2: 389–90; "Diary of Nicholas Gibbon," *Mecklenburg, N.C. Genealogical Society Quarterly* 3: 128; Clark, *Histories of the Several Regiments* 1: 386; Howard, *Forgotten Heroes,* 58–59; *OR* 47 (3): 723; Bradley, *Astounding Close,* 80, 153, 293, 296; Krick, *Lee's Colonels,* 246; *SHSP* 18 (1890): 421.

[9] *OR* 47 (3): 774, 777, 788–89, 800.

[10] *OR* 47 (3): 777, 788; Robinson, *History of Guilford County,* 94; *Greensborough Patriot,* March 23, 1866; Arnett, *Greensboro,* 394; Konkle, *John Motley Morehead,* 409; Wright, *Memoirs of Belo,* 30; *OR* 47 (3): 800.

[11] Wright, *Memoirs of Belo,* 30; Entry for April 10, 1865, J.T. Wood diary, SHC; *Greensborough Patriot,* March 23, 1866; *OR* 47 (3): 711–12, 733, 774, 788–91; Warner, *Generals in Gray,* 185; Durkin, *John Dooley,* 179–80, 184.

[12] *To the Members of the 15th Pennsylvania Cavalry,* 15th Annual Banquet, 11–12; Kirk, *15th Pennsylvania,* 501, 541–42, 550; Diary, April 10, 1865, Charles M. Betts papers, HSP.

[13] *OR* 20 (2): 506; *OR* 49 (1): 555; *National Tribune,* July 19, 1900; Kirk, *15th Pennsylvania,* 492; Application of Officer for Correction of Muster, Document File 341655, Records of the Adjutant General Record and Pension Office, RG 94, NA; *America's Medal of Honor Recipients,* 712.

[14] Kirk, *15th Pennsylvania,* 545, 550; Wilson, *Recollections and Experiences,* 116; Diary, April 10, 1865, Charles M. Betts papers, HSP.

[15] Kirk, *15th Pennsylvania*, 550.

[16] Diary, April 10, 1865, Charles M. Betts papers, HSP; *To the Members of the 15th Pennsylvania Cavalry*, 15th Annual Banquet, 12; Kirk, *15th Pennsylvania*, 542–43, 550–51; Betts, "Stoneman's Great Cavalry Raid." Many sources claim that the Federals were within five miles of Greensboro, but it was actually twice that distance.

[17] Kirk, *15th Pennsylvania*, 552; OR 2: 611–12; OR 14: 185–87, 309–10; OR 35 (1): 440–41; OR 47 (2): 1421.

[18] Lt. Col. L.H. Johnson to John C. Breckinridge, April 20, 1865, copy courtesy of Boyd Lamberth; *To the Members of the 15th Pennsylvania Cavalry*, 15th Annual Banquet, 12; Kirk, *15th Pennsylvania*, 542, 550–51; Diary, April 10, 1865, Charles M. Betts papers, HSP; Betts, "Stoneman's Great Cavalry Raid."

[19] Kirk, *15th Pennsylvania*, 502, 546, 551; Betts, "Stoneman's Great Cavalry Raid."

[20] Kirk, *15th Pennsylvania*, 545; Wilson, *Recollections and Experiences*, 116.

[21] Diary, April 10, 1865, Charles M. Betts papers, HSP; *To the Members of the 15th Pennsylvania Cavalry*, 15th Annual Banquet, 12; Kirk, *15th Pennsylvania*, 542–43, 545; OR 49 (1): 555. For Johnson, see Krick, *Lee's Colonels*, 453; Wilson, *Recollections and Experiences*, 116.

[22] Kirk, *15th Pennsylvania*, 502; Betts, "Stoneman's Great Cavalry Raid;" Document File 341655, Records of the Adjutant General Record and Pension Office, RG 94, NA; Wilson, *Recollections and Experiences*, 116; Diary, April 10, 1865, Charles M. Betts papers, HSP; *To the Members of the 15th Pennsylvania Cavalry*, 15th Annual Banquet, 12.

[23] Wilson, *Recollections and Experiences*, 116–17; Kirk, *15th Pennsylvania*, 543, 545–46. According to Boyd Lamberth, this ambush took place near present-day Piedmont Triad International Airport.

[24] *To the Members of the 15th Pennsylvania Cavalry*, 15th Annual Banquet, 12; Kirk, *15th Pennsylvania*, 551–52.

[25] Wilson, *Recollections and Experiences*, 116; Kirk, *15th Pennsylvania*, 545. According to this account, Reiff exchanged words with Johnson's adjutant. Betts's official report is clear, however. It was Johnson who had a personal battle with Reiff.

[26] William J. Palmer to "My Dear Charley," May 20, 1865, William Jackson Palmer papers, Yale; OR 49 (1): 555; *America's Medal of Honor Recipients*, 712; Memorandum of Record and Pension Division, September 30, 1892; Charles M. Betts to the Office Chief, October 14, 1892, and Adjutant General to B. Franklin Betts, April 16, 1911, all in Document File 341655, Records of the Adjutant General Record and Pension Office, RG 94, NA. Betts died in 1905.

[27] *To the Members of the 15th Pennsylvania Cavalry*, 15th Annual Banquet, 12; Diary, April 10, 1865, Charles M. Betts papers, HSP.

[28] Wilson, *Recollections and Experiences*, 117; Kirk, *15th Pennsylvania*, 546.

[29] Trelease, *North Carolina Railroad*, 192; *Annual Report of the North Carolina Railroad, 1865 and 1866*, 17; Wilson, *Recollections and Experiences*, 117; Kirk, *15th Pennsylvania*, 546.

[30] *To the Members of the 15th Pennsylvania Cavalry*, 15th Annual Banquet, 13; Wilson, *Recollections and Experiences*, 117–18; Kirk, *15th Pennsylvania*, 546.

[31] Wilson, *Recollections and Experiences*, 117–18; Kirk, *15th Pennsylvania*, 546–47. According to Mr. Boyd Lamberth, the site of the bridge is near present-day Interstate 40, not far from the Wendover Avenue exit.

[32] Wilson, *Recollections and Experiences*, 118.

[33] Wilson, *Recollections and Experiences*, 118; Kirk, *15th Pennsylvania*, 503, 547.

[34] Konkle, *John Motley Morehead*, 409; *To the Members of the 15th Pennsylvania Cavalry*, 15th Annual Banquet, 13; Diary, April 10, 1865, Charles M. Betts papers, HSP; Kirk, *15th Pennsylvania*, 543. Strickler was the regimental bugler.

[35] *To the Members of the 15th Pennsylvania Cavalry*, 15th Annual Banquet, 13; Diary, April 10, 1865, Charles M. Betts papers, HSP; Kirk, *15th Pennsylvania*, 543.

[36] William J. Palmer to Col. Betts, April 11, 1865, Charles M. Betts papers, HSP; *To the*

Members of the 15th Pennsylvania Cavalry, 15th Annual Banquet, 13; Diary, April 10, 1865, Charles M. Betts papers, HSP; Kirk, *15th Pennsylvania*, 543.

[37] *To the Members of the 15th Pennsylvania Cavalry*, 15th Annual Banquet, 11–12; Kirk, *15th Pennsylvania*, 541–42, 550; Diary, April 10, 1865, Charles M. Betts papers, HSP; "The Burning of Deep River R.R. Bridge, North Carolina, April 10, 1865," Charles M. Betts papers, HSP.

[38] Kirk, *15th Pennsylvania*, 501, 541, 553; Adam Kramer to Lt. Col. Charles M. Betts, April 22, 1865, and "The Burning of Deep River R.R. Bridge, North Carolina, April 10, 1865," both in Charles M. Betts papers, HSP; Wilson, *Recollections and Experiences*, 120. A report apparently written by Kramer, "The Burning of the Deep River R.R. Bridge, North Carolina, April 10, 1865," claims fifty men rode with the detachment, but a note in the margin indicates that this number is uncertain. Later accounts from Kirk's regimental history put eighty-six men in Kramer's detachment.

[39] Hoole, "Admiral on Horseback," 143; Adam Kramer to Lt. Col. Charles M. Betts, April 22, 1865, and "The Burning of Deep River R.R. Bridge, North Carolina, April 10, 1865," both in Charles M. Betts papers, HSP; Kirk, *15th Pennsylvania*, 501, 541, 553; Wilson, *Recollections and Experiences*, 120.

[40] Trelease, *North Carolina Railroad*, 192; Adam Kramer to Lt. Col. Charles M. Betts, April 22, 1865 and "The Burning of Deep River R.R. Bridge, North Carolina, April 10, 1865," both in Charles M. Betts papers, HSP; Kirk, *15th Pennsylvania*, 553; Wilson, *Recollections and Experiences*, 120; *Cincinnati Daily Commercial*, May 10, 1865; *Annual Report of the North Carolina Railroad, 1865 and 1866*, 17; Diary, April 10, 1865, Charles M. Betts papers, HSP.

[41] Adam Kramer to Lt. Col. Charles M. Betts, April 22, 1865, Charles M. Betts papers, HSP; Wilson, *Recollections and Experiences*, 120; Kirk, *15th Pennsylvania*, 501, 541, 553, 555; Diary, April 10, 1865, Charles M. Betts papers, HSP.

[42] Kirk, *15th Pennsylvania*, 553–54.

[43] Kirk, *15th Pennsylvania*, 554–55; Wilson, *Recollections and Experiences*, 120; Adam Kramer to Lt. Col. Charles M. Betts, April 22, 1865, Charles M. Betts papers, HSP. In recognition, Alexander would be praised during dress parade.

[44] Wilson, *Recollections and Experiences*, 120–21; Adam Kramer to Lt. Col. Charles M. Betts, April 22, 1865, and "The Burning of Deep River R.R. Bridge, North Carolina, April 10, 1865," both in Charles M. Betts papers, HSP.

[45] Johnson, *Touring the Carolinas' Civil War Sites*, 152–53; Cadia B. Welborn papers, SHC; *High Point Enterprise*, January 20, 1935; Thomas, *Roads to Jamestown*, 19; Jack L. Perdue, "Fact or Fiction?" *The Commander's Tent*, January 1998; Robinson, *History of Guilford County*, 57; Adam Kramer to Lt. Col. Charles M. Betts, April 22, 1865, Charles M. Betts papers, HSP. The mill was owned by James R. Mendenhall and Duncan McRae.

[46] "An Eyewitness Account," *The Commander's Tent*, July 1995; Cadia B. Welborn papers, SHC; Adam Kramer to Lt. Col. Charles M. Betts, April 22, 1865, and "The Burning of Deep River R.R. Bridge, North Carolina, April 10, 1865," both in Charles M. Betts papers, HSP; Kirk, *15th Pennsylvania*, 501, 541, 555; Diary, April 10, 1865, Charles M. Betts papers, HSP; Wilson, *Recollections and Experiences*, 120.

[47] Wilson, *Recollections and Experiences*, 120–21; Kirk, *15th Pennsylvania*, 501, 541; Adam Kramer to Lt. Col. Charles M. Betts, April 22, 1865, and "The Burning of Deep River R.R. Bridge, North Carolina, April 10, 1865," both in Charles M. Betts papers, HSP; Morning Reports of Companies F–L, 15th Pennsylvania Cavalry, RR; OR 49 (1): 555.

[48] Frederic Antes diary, April 10, 1865, Civil War Miscellaneous Collection, USAMHI; Diary, April 10, 1865, Charles M. Betts papers, HSP; Kirk, *15th Pennsylvania*, 501, 541. For the timing of this, see above. Many sources also claim that Garner's detachment left for its objective from Kernersville, but Betts's diary is clear that it occurred five miles down the road.

[49] Kirk, *15th Pennsylvania*, 501; Frederic Antes diary, April 11, 1865, Civil War Miscellaneous Collection, USAMHI; M. Baldwin Colton to his mother, May 5, 1865, Colton, ed., *Civil*

War Journal and Correspondence of Matthias Baldwin Colton, 394; Abraham B. Garner to Charles W. Betts, April 13, 1865, Charles M. Betts papers, HSP; *National Tribune*, July 19, 1900.

[50] Report quoted in Wilson, *Recollections and Experiences*, 119; Frederic Antes diary, April 11, 1865, Civil War Miscellaneous Collection, USAMHI; M. Baldwin Colton to his mother, May 5, 1865, Colton, ed., *Civil War Journal and Correspondence of Matthias Baldwin Colton*, 394; Abraham B. Garner to Charles W. Betts, April 13, 1865, Charles M. Betts papers, HSP. The site of the bridge was located near Browns Summit, North Carolina. Evidence of the skirmish has been found nearby. My thanks to Boyd Lamberth for his knowledge and research on this event.

[51] Kirk, *15th Pennsylvania*, 502; Abraham B. Garner to Charles W. Betts, April 13, 1865, Charles M. Betts papers, HSP; Diary, April 10, 1865, Charles M. Betts papers, HSP.

[52] Kirk, *15th Pennsylvania*, 502; Abraham B. Garner to Charles W. Betts, April 13, 1865, Charles M. Betts papers, HSP; Frederic Antes diary, April 12, 1865, Civil War Miscellaneous Collection, USAMHI.

[53] Kirk, *15th Pennsylvania*, 502; Abraham B. Garner to Charles W. Betts, April 13, 1865, Charles M. Betts papers, HSP. Glenn's Ferry was located near the present-day Yadkinville Road Bridge. Kirk's regimental history confuses the Yadkin with the South River, and it also identifies the crossing spot as Conrad's Ferry. Conrad's was the name of a nearby crossing where the unit camped that night, but it crossed at Glenn's Ferry.

[54] Kirk, *15th Pennsylvania*, 502; Frederic Antes diary, April 12–13, 1865, Civil War Miscellaneous Collection, USAMHI; Abraham B. Garner to Charles W. Betts, April 13, 1865, Charles M. Betts papers, HSP; OR 49 (1): 555.

[55] *Greensborough Patriot*, March 23, 1866; Robinson, *History of Guilford County*, 101; Kirk, *15th Pennsylvania*, 502; Trelease, *North Carolina Railroad*, 192; Durkin, *John Dooley*, 180; Davis, *Jefferson Davis*, 613–14; Hanna, *Flight Into Oblivion*, 26; Trudeau, *Out of the Storm*, 202.

[56] Diary, April 10, 1865, Charles M. Betts papers, HSP; Trowbridge, *Brief History of the 10th Michigan*, 35; Steven Thomas to "My Dear Wife," June 5, 1865, Calvin Thomas papers, UM.

[57] Claim of Samuel Yokeley, #10959, Box 221, Entry 732, Davidson County, N.C., RG 217, Settled Files of the SCC, NA.

[58] High Point Chamber of Commerce, *The Building and Builders of a City*, 39; CV 37 (March 1930): 95; Cadia B. Welborn papers, SHC.

[59] *Greensboro News & Record*, September 2, 1993; *Annual Report of the North Carolina Railroad, 1865 and 1866*, 11; Johnson, *Touring the Carolinas' Civil War Sites*, 152; CV 37 (March 1930): 95–96; Cadia B. Welborn papers, SHC; Beall, "Stoneman's Raid," *The North Carolina Review*, October 2, 1910; R.L. Beall's account of Stoneman's Raid, Cornelia Phillips Spencer papers, SHC; Spencer, *Last Ninety Days*, 198; Trowbridge, *Stoneman Raid*, 105; Trowbridge, "The Stoneman Raid of 1865," *JUSCA* 4 (June 1891): 194.

[60] Beall, "Stoneman's Raid," *The North Carolina Review*, October 2, 1910; R.L. Beall's account of Stoneman's Raid, Cornelia Phillips Spencer papers, SHC; Spencer, *Last Ninety Days*, 198; CV 37 (March 1930): 95–96; Cadia B. Welborn papers, SHC; Trowbridge, *Stoneman Raid*, 105; Trowbridge, "The Stoneman Raid of 1865," *JUSCA* 4 (June 1891): 194; "Reminiscences of Confederate Days," Fries papers, NCSA; High Point Chamber of Commerce, *The Building and Builders of a City*, 47.

[61] Robert Alexander Jenkins, "From Harper's Ferry to the Surrender," in *Endurin' the War*, Gertrude Jenkins papers, DU.

[62] Jack L. Perdue, "U.S. Cavalry Raids High Point, N.C." *The Commander's Tent*, April 1995; *Greensboro News & Record*, September 2, 1993.

[63] Steven Thomas to "My Dear Wife," June 5, 1865, Calvin Thomas papers, UM; OR Supplement 30: 231; Trowbridge, *Stoneman Raid*, 105; Trowbridge, "The Stoneman Raid of 1865," *JUSCA* 4 (June 1891): 194; OR 49 (1): 556.

[64] Cadia B. Welborn papers, SHC; CV 37 (March 1930): 95–96; *Greensboro News & Record*, September 2, 1993; Steven Thomas to "My Dear Wife," June 5, 1865, Calvin Thomas papers, UM; Collett Leventhorpe to Zebulon Vance, Zebulon Vance Governor's papers, NCSA.

⁶⁵ L.S. Trowbridge to "My Dear Judie," April 12, 1865, L.S. Trowbridge papers, UM; Diary, April 10, 1865, Charles M. Betts papers, HSP; Trowbridge, *Brief History of the 10th Michigan*, 35; Trowbridge, *Stoneman Raid*, 105–6; Trowbridge, "The Stoneman Raid of 1865," *JUSCA* 4 (June 1891): 194; *10th Cavalry*, vol. 40, 14.

⁶⁶ Trowbridge, *Stoneman Raid*, 105–6; Trowbridge, "The Stoneman Raid of 1865," *JUSCA* 4 (June 1891): 194; *10th Cavalry*, vol. 40, 13–14.

⁶⁷ Beall, "Stoneman's Raid," *The North Carolina Review*, October 2, 1910; R.L. Beall's account of Stoneman's Raid, Cornelia Phillips Spencer papers, SHC; Spencer, *Last Ninety Days*, 198; Memoirs of S.W. Ferguson, Heyward and Ferguson family papers, SHC; John M. Otey to W.S. Featherston, April 3, 1865, Letters and Orders Book, P.G.T. Beauregard papers, LC; Krick, *Lee's Colonels*, 422; *OR* 47 (2): 1072; 49 (3): 747; *Carolina Watchman*, April 12, 1865; *OR Supplement* 30: 231.

⁶⁸ *Carolina Watchman*, April 12, 1865; Howard, *Forgotten Heroes*, 1–2, 5; *Heritage of Davidson County*, 5; Donnelly, "Confederate Lead Mines," 404; Clark, *Histories of the Several Regiments* 4: 650, 653; Hoole, "Admiral on Horseback," 143–44.

⁶⁹ Jones, *The Last Raid*, 27–28; L.S. Trowbridge to "My Dear Judie," April 12, 1865, L.S. Trowbridge papers, UM.

⁷⁰ Trowbridge, *Stoneman Raid*, 106; Trowbridge, "The Stoneman Raid of 1865," *JUSCA* 4 (June 1891): 194; L.S. Trowbridge to "My Dear Judie," June 25, 1865, L.S. Trowbridge papers, UM.

⁷¹ Leonard, *Centennial History*, 211–12, 214; *OR Supplement* 30: 231; L.S. Trowbridge to "My Dear Judie," April 12, 1865, L.S. Trowbridge papers, UM; *Annual Report of the North Carolina Railroad, 1865 and 1866*, 17; Beall, "Stoneman's Raid," *The North Carolina Review*, October 2, 1910; R.L. Beall's account of Stoneman's Raid, Cornelia Phillips Spencer papers, SHC; William J. Palmer to Col. Betts, April 11, 1865, Charles M. Betts papers, HSP; *10th Cavalry*, vol. 40, 14. Steven Thomas told his wife (June 5, 1865, Calvin Thomas Papers, UM) that the detachment failed to burn the Abbott's Creek bridge. Trelease, *North Carolina Railroad*, 219–20, writes that Stoneman destroyed two North Carolina Railroad spans (the Deep River at Jamestown and Buffalo Creek at Greensboro), but that the Abbott's Creek bridge had been destroyed in 1864 by an unknown incendiary. However, it seems unlikely that the bridge at Abbott's Creek would not have been repaired by 1865.

⁷² *10th Cavalry*, vol. 40, 14; Trowbridge, *Brief History of the 10th Michigan*, 36–38.

⁷³ William J. Palmer to Col. Betts, April 11, 1865, Charles M. Betts papers, HSP; Trowbridge, *Stoneman Raid*, 106–7; *10th Cavalry*, vol. 40, 14; Trowbridge, "The Stoneman Raid of 1865," *JUSCA* 4 (June 1891): 194–95; *OR Supplement* 30: 231.

⁷⁴ L.S. Trowbridge to "My Dear Judie," April 12, 1865, L.S. Trowbridge papers, UM; Trowbridge, *Stoneman Raid*, 107; Trowbridge, "The Stoneman Raid of 1865," *JUSCA* 4 (June 1891): 195.

⁷⁵ Jones, *The Last Raid*, 27–28, 32; Stevens, *Rebels in Blue*, 177.

⁷⁶ William J. Palmer to Col. Betts, April 11, 1865, Charles M. Betts papers, HSP.

⁷⁷ L.S. Trowbridge to "My Dear Judie," April 12, 1865, L.S. Trowbridge papers, UM; Trowbridge, *Stoneman Raid*, 107–8; *10th Cavalry*, vol. 40, 14; Trowbridge, "The Stoneman Raid of 1865," *JUSCA* 4 (June 1891): 195; *OR Supplement* 30: 231.

⁷⁸ Trowbridge, *Stoneman Raid*, 107–8; Trowbridge, "The Stoneman Raid of 1865," *JUSCA* 4 (June 1891): 195; *OR Supplement* 30: 231; Morning Reports of Companies A–F, 10th Michigan Cavalry, RR; *10th Cavalry*, vol. 40, 14; L.S. Trowbridge to "My Dear Judie," April 12, 1865, L.S. Trowbridge papers, UM. Trowbridge's estimates of enemy casualties grew over the years, from fifty to sixty right after the fight, to seventy-five or even one hundred a quarter century afterward. The lower, contemporary estimates are used in the text. It should also be added that twelve bodies were moved from Lexington to the Salisbury National Cemetery. It is unknown if any of these were casualties from the Abbott's Creek fight (*Statement of the Disposition of Bodies* 3: 8).

⁷⁹ Memoirs of S.W. Ferguson, Heyward and Ferguson family papers, SHC.

[80] *OR Supplement* 30: 231; L.S. Trowbridge to "My Dear Judie," April 12, 1865, L.S. Trowbridge papers, UM; *OR* 49 (1): 556; *10th Cavalry*, vol. 40, 14–15. The Salem to Abbott's Creek march covered about thirty-two miles in roughly sixteen hours.

[81] *To the Members of the 15th Pennsylvania Cavalry*, 15th Annual Banquet, 13; Kirk, *15th Pennsylvania*, 503, 543; Diary, April 10, 1865, Charles M. Betts papers, HSP.

[82] Kirk, *15th Pennsylvania*, 503; Diary, April 10, 1865, Charles M. Betts papers, HSP; Banks, "Memoranda," diary entry for April 11, 1865, 297; "The Burning of Deep River R.R. Bridge, North Carolina, April 10, 1865," Charles M. Betts papers, HSP. According to Betts, the troopers arrived at 2:00; Kramer thought it was 4:00 P.M.

[83] Crews, *Storm in the Land*, 36; "Fannie and Louisa," 11, Salem Civil War Recollections, MA.

[84] Clewell, *History of Wachovia*, 250–51; *People's Press*, April 14, 1866; "Last Year of the War," Civil War and Reconstruction papers, MA; Stone, *Walk Through Old Salem*, 41; "Reminiscences of Confederate days," Fries papers, NCSA; Crews, *Storm in the Land*, 36.

[85] Mason, *12th Ohio Cavalry Roster*, 2, 14; Banks, "Memoranda," diary entry for April 11, 1865, 297; Beall, "Stoneman's Raid," *The North Carolina Review*, November 11, 1910; R.L. Beall's account of Stoneman's Raid, Cornelia Phillips Spencer papers, SHC; Spencer, *Last Ninety Days*, 198; *People's Press*, May 27, 1865.

[86] "Last Year of the War," Civil War and Reconstruction papers, MA; Crews, *Storm in the Land*, 36–37; *People's Press*, May 27, 1865; *People's Press*, April 14, 1866; Wilson, *Recollections and Experiences*, 116; "Last Year of the War," Civil War and Reconstruction papers, MA. John T. Wheeler's cavalry arrived in Salem after Palmer's men left, and continued on toward Salisbury via Friedberg. The tailor shop was probably in the Zevely House, today a popular Winston-Salem restaurant.

[87] "Fannie and Louisa," 11, Salem Civil War recollections, MA; Claim of John Butner, #16000, Box 221, Entry 732, Forsyth County, N.C., RG 217, Settled Files of the SCC, NA. Butner lived on a farm five miles southwest of Salem.

[88] Mason, "Stoneman's Last Campaign," 25; Trowbridge, *Stoneman Raid*, 105; *Journal and Sentinel*, October 4, 1953; Beall, "Stoneman's Raid," *The North Carolina Review*, October 2, 1910; *People's Press*, April 14, 1866; R.L. Beall's account of Stoneman's Raid, Cornelia Phillips Spencer papers, SHC; "Last Year of the War," Civil War and Reconstruction papers, MA; "Appeal for the Return of Articles, Stolen from H.W. Fries Factory, April 14, 1865," Civil War and Reconstruction papers, MA; Tursi, *Winston-Salem*, 104; *People's Press*, May 27, 1865; Crews, *Storm in the Land*, 36–37.

[89] Fries, *Forsyth*, 135; Brownlee, *Winston-Salem*, 40; Clewell, *History of Wachovia*, 254; Wellman, *Winston-Salem in History* 2: 21; "Reminiscences of Confederate days," Fries papers, NCSA; *Journal and Sentinel*, October 4, 1953; D.H. Hill, Jr. to Henry E. Fries, August 5, 1916; J.W. Fries to D.H. Hill, Jr., August 25, 1916, D.H. Hill, Jr. papers, NCSA.

[90] "Appeal for the Return of Articles, Stolen from H.W. Fries Factory, April 14, 1865," Civil War and Reconstruction papers, MA; Tursi, *Winston-Salem*, 104; *People's Press*, April 14, 1866; Shirley, *From Congregation Town to Industrial City*, 136; "Last Year of the War," Civil War and Reconstruction papers, MA; Reminiscences of Confederate days," Fries papers, NCSA; *People's Press*, May 27, 1865; Crews, *Storm in the Land*, 36–37; *Journal and Sentinel*, October 4, 1953. Fries's mill is today the Brookstown Inn, a hotel in Winston-Salem. Elsewhere in town, quartermaster stores of cloth at Waughtown also disappeared.

[91] "Appeal for the Return of Articles, Stolen from H.W. Fries Factory, April 14, 1865," Civil War and Reconstruction papers, MA; Tursi, *Winston-Salem*, 104; Reminiscences of Confederate days," Fries papers, NCSA. Rufus Patterson later confirmed to his father that the factory was not burned, but a Federal officer who passed through Patterson said that both factories at Salem had been burned (Samuel F. Patterson to Rufus L. Patterson, April 19, 1865, Patterson papers, NCSA).

[92] Banks, "Memoranda," diary entry for April 11, 1865, 297; "Last Year of the War," Civil War and Reconstruction papers, MA; *People's Press*, April 14, 1866; Mason, *12th Ohio Cavalry Roster*, 18–19; *Official Roster* 11: 600; Griffin, *Less Time for Meddling*, 270.

[93] Crews, *Storm in the Land*, 37; *People's Press*, April 14, 1866; Clewell, *History of Wachovia*, 251; "Last Year of the War," Civil War and Reconstruction papers, MA; Memorabilia of the Congregation at Salem, 1865, in Yearns and Barrett, *North Carolina Civil War Documentary*; Griffin, *Less Time for Meddling*, 270–71.

[94] Kirk, *15th Pennsylvania*, 547–48; Wilson, *Recollections and Experiences*, 118–19; Diary, April 10, 1865, Charles M. Betts papers, HSP; *OR* 49 (1): 555. Wilson mistakenly identified the town as Salem, Georgia.

[95] Diary, April 10, 1865, Charles M. Betts papers, HSP; Banks, "Memoranda," diary entry for April 11, 1865, 297; Memorabilia of the Congregation at Salem, 1865, in Yearns and Barrett, *North Carolina Civil War Documentary*; Crews, *Storm in the Land*, 37; "Last Year of the War," Civil War and Reconstruction papers, MA; Kirk, *15th Pennsylvania*, 503.

[96] "Last Year of the War," Civil War and Reconstruction papers, MA; Mason, *12th Ohio Cavalry Roster*, 12–13; Griffin, *Less Time for Meddling*, 270–71; *The People's Press*, May 27, 1865.

[97] *Cincinnati Daily Commercial*, May 10, 1865; *Annual Report of the North Carolina Railroad, 1865 and 1866*, 17; Wilson, *Recollections and Experiences*, 121; *OR* 49 (1): 324.

[98] Crews, *Storm in the Land*, 37; *Twin City Sentinel*, October 3, 1925; "Fannie and Louisa," 11, Salem Civil War recollections, MA.

Chapter 7
THE GREATEST CALAMITY THAT EVER BEFELL OUR CITY
Mocksville to Salisbury: April 12–13, 1865

[1] Annie Laurie Etchison, "When the Yankees Came Through," Military–Civil War, Stoneman's Raid file, Davie County Public Library.

[2] Morning Reports for Companies B, G, and H, 11th Kentucky Cavalry, April 11, 1865, RR; Foote, *Civil War*, 737; Grant, *Memoirs*, 514; *OR* 47 (2): 859; *OR* 49 (1): 342, 616–17; Simon, *Papers of U.S. Grant* 13: 360.

[3] Report of AG, December 29, 1873, in U.S. Army Generals' Reports of Civil War Service, M1098, vol. IV, R19, p. 525–26, NA; Kirk, *15th Pennsylvania*, 523; *Daily Carolina Watchman*, March 7, 1865.

[4] Spencer, *Last Ninety Days*, 198–99; Wall, *History of the First Presbyterian Church*, 40; *Davie County Heritage*, 52; Wall, *History of Davie*, 179–80; "The Day Stoneman Came Through," Military-Civil War, Stoneman's Raid file, Davie County Public Library; Beall, "Stoneman's Raid," *The North Carolina Review*, November 11, 1910; R.L. Beall's account of Stoneman's Raid, Cornelia Phillips Spencer papers, SHC; Clark, *Histories of the Several Regiments* 4: 650; April 11, 1865, Allen Frankenberry diaries, WV; *OR* 49 (1): 333.

[5] Spencer, *Last Ninety Days*, 198–99; Beall, "Stoneman's Raid," *The North Carolina Review*, November 11, 1910; R.L. Beall's account of Stoneman's Raid, Cornelia Phillips Spencer papers, SHC; Raynor, *Rebels and Yankees*, 34; Wall, *History of the First Presbyterian Church*, 40; Wall, *History of Davie*, 179–80; "The Day Stoneman Came Through," Military-Civil War, Stoneman's Raid file, Davie County Public Library; *Davie County Heritage*, 52; "The Corner Cupboard," March 4, 1937, in Military-Civil War, Stoneman's Raid file, Davie County Public Library.

[6] Copy of passage from Louise Wiseman Parks, *Captain Wiseman*, Military–Civil war, Stoneman's Raid file, Davie County Public Library; Wall, *History of the First Presbyterian Church*, 40; *Davie County Heritage*, 52; Wall, *History of Davie*, 180; "Miss Alice" to Miss Flossie Martin, in Military-Civil War, Stoneman's Raid file, Davie County Public Library.

[7] Beall, "Stoneman's Raid," *The North Carolina Review*, October 2, 1910; R.L. Beall's account

of Stoneman's Raid, Cornelia Phillips Spencer papers, SHC; Wall, *History of Davie*, 182; *OR* 49 (1): 333; Raynor, *Rebels and Yankees*, 34; Wall, *History of the First Presbyterian Church*, 40; *Davie County Heritage*, 52, 53; Wall, *History of Davie*, 180; *Davie Record*, August 11, 1938, Military-Civil War, Stoneman's Raid file, Davie County Public Library; April 11, 1865, Allen Frankenberry diaries, WV; April 12, 1865, Henry Birdsall diary, SHC.

[8] GS to Miss Lucy Williams, June 21, 1853, Lucy Williams Polk papers, NCSA; April 12, 1865, Allen Frankenberry diaries, WV; Scott, *13th Tennessee*, 237; *OR* 49 (1): 333; "Sun and Moon Data for One Day," April 12, 1865, Salisbury, N.C.

[9] Hairston, *Cooleemee Plantation*, 59, 68–69. The magnificent plantation still stands today. It remains the private property of the Hairston family.

[10] Claim of Joseph A. Hendrix, #11192, Box 221, Entry 732, Forsyth County, N.C., RG 217, Settled Files of the SCC, NA; Raynor, *Rebels and Yankees*, 42; *OR* 49 (1): 328, 333; Scott, *13th Tennessee*, 237; April 12, 1865, Allen Frankenberry diaries, WV.

[11] *OR* 49 (1): 333; Raynor, *Rebels and Yankees*, 42; *National Tribune*, October 31, 1907. The Old Mocksville Road crossed the creek about a half-mile north of the new crossing (Raynor, *Rebels and Yankees*, 42). An alternative spelling for Grant's Creek is Grant Creek.

[12] *OR* 49 (1): 333; Scott, *13th Tennessee*, 237–38; "Sun and Moon Data for One Day," April 12, 1865, Salisbury, N.C.

[13] Brown, *Salisbury Prison*, 1.

[14] *Daily Carolina Watchman*, March 4, 1865; Brown, *Salisbury Prison*, 13–14; Chamberlain, *This Was Home*, 50–51.

[15] Curtis, "Salisbury National Cemetery," 4–5; Andrews, *The South Since the War*, 102–3; Ford, *The Captive*, 207; B.T. Johnson to William G. Gardner, February 17, 1865, Bradley Tyler Johnson papers, DU. Estimates of the size of the prison vary from six to eleven acres.

[16] Brown, *Salisbury Prison*, 69, 159; Ford, *The Captive*, 24–25; Jones, *The Last Raid*, 45; Trelease, *North Carolina Railroad*, 193; Henry Gee to G.W. Booth and G.W. Booth to Zebulon B. Vance, February 3, 1865, Zebulon B. Vance Governor's papers, NCSA; Ford, *The Captive*, 53–54; Chamberlain, *This Was Home*, 119; Clark, *Histories of the Several Regiments* 4: 769–70.

[17] Brown, *Salisbury Prison*, 160; "Stoneman's Raid on Salisbury," A.G. Brenizer papers, NCSA; Kaplan, *Search for Stoneman's Legacy*, 113–14; Van Noppen, *Stoneman's Last Raid*, 50; Ford, *The Captive*, 319, 345–44; Raynor, *Rebels and Yankees*, 33; Bradley, *Astounding Close*, 95; Black, *Railroads of the Confederacy*, 277; Zebulon B. Vance to Cornelia P. Spencer, February 17 [1866], Cornelia Phillips Spencer papers, SHC; Beall, "Stoneman's Raid," *The North Carolina Review*, October 2, 1910; R.L. Beall's account of Stoneman's Raid, Cornelia Phillips Spencer papers, SHC.

[18] Bradley, *Astounding Close*, 13; Trelease, *North Carolina Railroad*, 191, 193.

[19] Beall, "Stoneman's Raid," *The North Carolina Review*, October 2, 1910; R.L. Beall's account of Stoneman's Raid, Cornelia Phillips Spencer papers, SHC; B.T. Johnson to AAG, February 15, 1865, Bradley Tyler Johnson papers, DU; Warner, *Generals in Gray*, 155–56; Hartley, "Don't Bury Me Among the ---- Yankees," 1–5; Beall, "Stoneman's Raid," *The North Carolina Review*, October 2, 1910; Clark, *Histories of the Several Regiments* 4: 375; R.L. Beall's account of Stoneman's Raid, Cornelia Phillips Spencer papers, SHC.

[20] *Memphis Commercial Appeal*, June 17, 1901; Warner, *Generals in Gray*, 97–98; Clark, *Histories of the Several Regiments* 4: 375; Ballard, *Pemberton*, 185–86; Pemberton, *Pemberton: Defender of Vicksburg*, 265–66, 362.

[21] *Carolina Watchman*, April 16, 1866; Beall, "Stoneman's Raid," *The North Carolina Review*, October 2, 1910; Mansion House Register, April 12, 1865; R.L. Beall's account of Stoneman's Raid, Cornelia Phillips Spencer papers, SHC; *Daily Carolina Watchman*, March 8, 1865; Bradley, *North Carolina Confederate Militia and Home Guard Records* 3: 125; *Philadelphia Weekly Times*, December 14, 1878; Clark, *Histories of the Several Regiments* 4: 650–51; Spencer, *Last Ninety Days*, 199; *OR* 46 (2): 1090; *OR*, Series 2, 8:254; *OR*, Series 4, 3: 822–23, 825, 1029; Ford, *The*

Captive, 116, 260, 468; G.W. Booth to Zebulon B. Vance, February 3, 1865, Zebulon B. Vance Governor's papers, NCSA; Brown, *Salisbury Prison*, 83, n. 53.

[22] Beall, "Stoneman's Raid," *The North Carolina Review*, October 2, 1910; R.L. Beall's account of Stoneman's Raid, Cornelia Phillips Spencer papers, SHC; Daniel, *Cannoneers in Gray*, 182–84; *OR* 47 (3): 756; Spencer, *Last Ninety Days*, 199; *CV* 6 (November 1898): 505; *CV* 10 (August 1902): 359; *CV* 11 (September 1903): 394; Lindsley, *Military Annals of Tennessee* 2: 838.

[23] Bradley, *Astounding Close*, 330, n. 6; Daniel, *Cannoneers in Gray*, 182–84; *OR* 47 (3): 756; *OR Supplement*, Part I, 7: 85; Lindsley, *Military Annals of Tennessee* 2: 836–38; Beall, "Stoneman's Raid," *The North Carolina Review*, October 2, 1910; R.L. Beall's account of Stoneman's Raid, Cornelia Phillips Spencer papers, SHC; Spencer, *Last Ninety Days*, 199; *CV* 6 (November 1898): 505; *CV* 10 (August 1902): 359; *CV* 11 (September 1903): 394. According to Lindsley, Bradley Johnson ordered the battalion to follow the engineer's orders. Since Johnson was not present, it was probably either Gardner or Pemberton who referred the gunners to the engineer.

[24] Kirk, *15th Pennsylvania*, 503–4; *Salisbury Post*, May 23, 1999.

[25] Aull and Brandon, *Dr. Josephus Wells Hall*, 80; Beall, "Stoneman's Raid," *The North Carolina Review*, October 2, 1910; R.L. Beall's account of Stoneman's Raid, Cornelia Phillips Spencer papers, SHC; Daniel, *Cannoneers in Gray*, 182–84; *OR* 47 (3): 756; Spencer, *Last Ninety Days*, 199; *CV* 6 (November 1898): 505; *CV* 10 (August 1902): 359; *CV* 11 (September 1903): 394; *Salisbury Post*, May 23, 1999; Lindsley, *Military Annals of Tennessee* 2: 838.

[26] Brown, *Salisbury Prison*, 171; Van Noppen, *Stoneman's Last Raid*, 58; Aull and Brandon, *Dr. Josephus Wells Hall*, 79; Chamberlain, *This Was Home*, 116–18.

[27] Aull and Brandon, *Dr. Josephus Wells Hall*, 79–80; Lindsley, *Military Annals of Tennessee* 2: 841; "Stoneman's Raid on Salisbury," A.G. Brenizer papers, NCSA; Brown, *Salisbury Prison*, 172; Jarnagin Diary, Civil War Collection, Confederate Collection, p. 30, courtesy TSLA; "Stoneman's Raid was 69 Years Ago Today," *Salisbury Post*, April 12, 1934, copy in Brawley file, Edith M. Clark History Room, Rowan Public Library; Lindsley, *Military Annals of Tennessee* 2: 838.

[28] Yeatman, "Awful and Grand Spectacle," 41. The original material on which this source is based can be found in the diary of Mary Polk Yeatman, Yeatman–Polk Collection, courtesy TSLA, April 12, 1865.

[29] Chamberlain, *This Was Home*, 50–51; *Daily Carolina Watchman*, March 22, April 6, April 12, 1865; Raynor, *Rebels and Yankees*, 34.

[30] E.H.M. Summerell to Cornelia Spencer, September 4, 1866, Cornelia Phillips Spencer papers, SHC.

[31] Mason, "Stoneman's Last Campaign," 26–27; Thomas F. Safley, "Our Long Visit East and South and Return Home," Brawley file, Edith M. Clark History Room, Rowan Public Library.

[32] *OR* 49 (1): 333; *10th Cavalry*, vol. 40, 15; *History of the 10th Michigan*, 38; Trowbridge, *Stoneman Raid*, 108; Trowbridge, "The Stoneman Raid of 1865," *JUSCA* 4 (June 1891): 195–96; *Cincinnati Daily Commercial*, May 10, 1865; Scott, *13th Tennessee*, 237–38.

[33] George Stoneman autobiographical statement, UCB; *OR* 49 (1): 333; *Cincinnati Daily Commercial*, May 10, 1865; Scott, *13th Tennessee*, 237–38.

[34] *OR* 49 (1): 333; Scott, *13th Tennessee*, 273–74.

[35] *10th Cavalry*, vol. 40, 15; *History of the 10th Michigan*, 38; Trowbridge, *Stoneman Raid*, 108; Trowbridge, "The Stoneman Raid of 1865," *JUSCA* 4 (June 1891): 195–96; *Cincinnati Daily Commercial*, May 10, 1865. The exact target of Donnelly's and Smith's movements are debatable; according to AG, Donnelly was to assault a point "lower" than Slater, and Smith a point "lower still." AG probably meant that these two groups should cross downstream from Slater.

[36] *OR* 49 (1): 328, 333; *Cincinnati Daily Commercial*, May 10, 1865.

[37] CSR for James M. Reagan, Microcopy 395, Roll 114; *OR* 49 (1): 333, 336; Mason, "Stoneman's Last Campaign," 27; *10th Cavalry*, vol. 40, 15; *History of the 10th Michigan*, 38; Trowbridge, *Stoneman Raid*, 108; Trowbridge, "The Stoneman Raid of 1865," *JUSCA* 4 (June 1891): 195–96; *OR Supplement* 65: 637. According to Wayne Boone, who has closely studied the Salisbury fight,

Reagan used ten-pound Parrott guns.

[38] Scott, *13th Tennessee*, 237–38, 260.

[39] *OR* 49 (1): 333; *National Tribune*, October 31, 1907; *The Union Army* 4: 355; *Union Regiments of Kentucky*, 236.

[40] *CV* 6 (November 1898): 505.

[41] *National Tribune*, October 31, 1907; Brawley, *Rowan Story*, 197.

[42] *OR* 49 (1): 333; Connell, *Son of the Morning Star*, 290–94; *Cincinnati Daily Commercial*, May 10, 1865. Morrow was GS's assistant adjutant general.

[43] "Synopsis of the 11th Kentucky Cavalry," KY.

[44] *OR* 49 (1): 333; Connell, *Son of the Morning Star*, 290–94; *Cincinnati Daily Commercial*, May 10, 1865.

[45] *OR Supplement*, Part I, 7: 85; Lindsley, *Military Annals of Tennessee* 2: 805–38, 841, 843; *CV* 7 (October 1899): 445. Macay's Mill was in disrepair and was no longer in operation during the Civil War. The three-hundred-acre mill pond, McNeely's Pond, was blamed for malarial fever that affected citizens living nearby. The pond was later drained in 1875, but the mill stood well into the twentieth century (*Salisbury Evening Post*, June 3, 1956; *Salisbury Sunday Post*, May 15, 1983).

[46] Lindsley, *Military Annals of Tennessee* 2: 838.

[47] Lindsley, *Military Annals of Tennessee* 2: 827, 842–43.

[48] Lindsley, *Military Annals of Tennessee* 2: 838; *Cincinnati Daily Commercial*, May 10, 1865; Spencer, *Last Ninety Days*, 203; Beall, "Stoneman's Raid," *The North Carolina Review*, November 11, 1910; R.L. Beall's account of Stoneman's Raid, Cornelia Phillips Spencer papers, SHC. Polk was born in Raleigh. His nephew, who rose to the rank of brigadier general, was a native of Salisbury.

[49] Lindsley, *Military Annals of Tennessee* 2: 838–39. This source mistakenly identifies the captured man as Col. Clarke M. Avery of the 33rd North Carolina, but Avery died in June 1864 (Krick, *Lee's Colonels*, 39). See Chapter 8 for more on Alphonso C. Avery and his mission to Salisbury.

[50] Lindsley, *Military Annals of Tennessee* 2: 839. This may have been the same train that bore Jefferson Davis to Greensboro (*Cincinnati Daily Commercial*, May 3, 1865).

[51] Lindsley, *Military Annals of Tennessee* 2: 839.

[52] *Cincinnati Daily Commercial*, May 10, 1865; George Stoneman to Edwin M. Stanton, June 19, 1865, 89.218.11.16, Keogh family papers and photographs, Museum of the American West, Autry National Center; AG to Ulysses S. Grant, December 21, 1865, 89.218.11.1, Keogh family papers and photographs, Museum of the American West, Autry National Center; *OR* 49 (1): 333, 325; Raynor, *Rebels and Yankees*, 44; *The Union Army* 4: 355; *Union Regiments of Kentucky*, 228; GS to unknown, June 19, 1865, Letters Sent, District of East Tennessee, Records of the U.S. Army continental commands, RG 393, pt. 2, entry 2740, NA. For a photo purported to be of both Morrow and Keogh after the battle, see Langellier, et. al., *Myles Keogh*, 85.

[53] Lindsley, *Military Annals of Tennessee* 2: 827, 840, 842–43.

[54] *OR Supplement*, Part I, 7: 85; Lindsley, *Military Annals of Tennessee* 2: 843; 805–7, 839–40; *CV* 7 (October 1899): 445. The claim of firing the Army of Tennessee's last gun is debatable, mainly because of the tenuous assertion that the unit was part of the Army of the Tennessee at the time. However, Marshall's was probably the last Confederate battery to fire in anger east of the Mississippi. An artillery action did occur the next day at Morrisville, North Carolina, but only Union artillery was present (Bradley, *Astounding Close*, 128–29).

[55] Lindsley, *Military Annals of Tennessee* 2: 840, 843.

[56] George Stoneman to Edwin M. Stanton, June 19, 1865, 89.218.11.16, Keogh family papers and photographs, Museum of the American West, Autry National Center; AG to Ulysses S. Grant, December 21, 1865, 89.218.11.1, Keogh family papers and photographs, Museum of the American West, Autry National Center; *OR* 49 (1): 325, 333.

[57] *OR Supplement* 65: 614; *OR* 49 (1): 333, 336; *10th Cavalry*, vol. 40, 15; *History of the 10th Michigan*, 38; Trowbridge, *Stoneman Raid*, 108; Trowbridge, "The Stoneman Raid of 1865," *JUSCA* 4 (June 1891): 195–96; *Cincinnati Daily Commercial*, May 10, 1865. The cited *OR Supplement* report places Donnelly north of town, but he must have struck a point south of town for there is no railroad north of Salisbury. The *Cincinnati Daily Commercial* of May 10, 1865, confirms that AG and GS also sent a party to take the railroad to Charlotte.

[58] *OR* 49 (1): 324, 333–34.

[59] J.K. Miller to Southard Hoffman, June 8, 1865, in CSR for John K. Miller, Microcopy 395, Roll 106; *OR* 49 (1): 336; *10th Cavalry*, vol. 40, 15. *History of the 10th Michigan*, 38; *OR Supplement* 65: 614; Scott, *10th Tennessee*, 237–38.

[60] Brewer, *History of the 46th Alabama*, 39; Beall, "Stoneman's Raid," *The North Carolina Review*, October 2, 1910; R.L. Beall's account of Stoneman's Raid, Cornelia Phillips Spencer papers, SHC; Lindsley, *Military Annals of Tennessee* 2: 839; Kirk, *15th Pennsylvania*, 503–4; G.T. Beauregard to Brig. Gen. William Gardner or Brig. Gen. Bradley T. Johnson, April 14, 1865, MS. Coll. #33, Gen. G.T. Beauregard correspondence, Andrew Joyner, Jr. Collection, Collection 1979.11.261, Greensboro Historical Museum Archives.

[61] *Carolina Watchman*, April 16, 1866; Beall, "Stoneman's Raid," *The North Carolina Review*, October 2, 1910; R.L. Beall's account of Stoneman's Raid, Cornelia Phillips Spencer papers, SHC; Moderwell, "Outline of Stoneman's Raid," Civil War (Federal, Miscellaneous) papers, SHC; Pemberton, *Pemberton: Defender of Vicksburg*, 362, 265–66; Daniel, *Cannoneers in Gray*, 184–85.

[62] *Salisbury Post*, May 23, 1999.

[63] Bushong, *Last Great Stoneman Raid*; *OR* 49 (1): 333; *10th Cavalry*, vol. 40, 15; *History of the 10th Michigan*, 38; Trowbridge, *Stoneman Raid*, 108; Trowbridge, "The Stoneman Raid of 1865," *JUSCA* 4 (June 1891): 195–96; *Cincinnati Daily Commercial*, May 10, 1865; Mason, "Stoneman's Last Campaign," 27; Raynor, *Rebels and Yankees*, 36, 44; *OR* 49 (1): 333; Scott, *13th Tennessee*, 237–38; Beall, "Stoneman's Raid," *The North Carolina Review*, October 2, 1910; R.L. Beall's account of Stoneman's Raid, Cornelia Phillips Spencer papers, SHC. According to the *Philadelphia Inquirer* of April 19, 1865, the Federals entered Salisbury at 10 A.M.

[64] Report of AG, December 29, 1873, 541–42, GR; Sample Autobiography, p. 12, CC.

[65] *Carolina Watchman*, April 16, 1866; Raynor, *Rebels and Yankees*, 33.

[66] Linn, "There Is No Music In My Soul Today," 19–20. The Linn source states that the sounds of gunfire came from the Yadkin River bridge, but that battle did not occur until after Salisbury fell.

[67] Aull and Brandon, *Dr. Josephus Wells Hall*, 80; *CV* 13 (November 1905): 503; "General Stoneman's Raid on Salisbury, North Carolina," Harriet Ellis Bradshaw papers, SHC.

[68] Yeatman, "Awful and Grand Spectacle," 42.

[69] Raynor, *Rebels and Yankees*, 43–44; *Daily Ohio State Journal*, April 19, 1865; E.H.M. Summerell to Cornelia Spencer, September 4, 1866, Cornelia Phillips Spencer papers, SHC; Spencer, *Last Ninety Days*, 200; Brown, *Salisbury Prison*, 173; "General Stoneman's Raid on Salisbury, North Carolina," Harriet Ellis Bradshaw papers, SHC; Lindsley, *Military Annals of Tennessee* 2: 840; "Stoneman's Raid was 69 Years Ago Today," *Salisbury Post*, April 12, 1934, copy in Brawley file, Edith M. Clark History Room, Rowan Public Library. One source (*Cincinnati Daily Commercial*, May 10, 1865) places the entry into town at 8:00 A.M., but the later time seems likelier.

[70] Mansion House Register, April 12, 1865, Rowan Museum.

[71] "General Stoneman's Raid on Salisbury, North Carolina," Harriet Ellis Bradshaw papers, SHC; Petrucelli, *Heritage of Rowan* 1: 7–8.

[72] Beall, "Stoneman's Raid," *The North Carolina Review*, November 11, 1910; R.L. Beall's account of Stoneman's Raid, Cornelia Phillips Spencer papers, SHC; Spencer, *Last Ninety Days*, 201; Aull and Brandon, *Dr. Josephus Wells Hall*, 81; April 12, 1865, Allen Frankenberry diaries, WV; "Stoneman's Raid was 69 Years Ago Today," *Salisbury Post*, April 12, 1934, copy in Brawley file, Edith M. Clark History Room, Rowan Public Library. Another source (Raynor, *Rebels and*

Yankees, 44), states that McNeely's fight occurred on East Innes Street. According to local historian Wayne Boone, the wounded McNeely died that night after being beaten. McNeely was a retired Confederate infantry officer who was then serving as an employee of the arsenal.

[73] "Stoneman's Raid was 69 Years Ago Today," *Salisbury Post*, April 12, 1934, copy in Brawley file, Edith M. Clark History Room, Rowan Public Library. Shaver believed that the Confederate who won the sabre duel was Frank McNeely.

[74] *CV* 13 (November 1905): 503; Beall, "Stoneman's Raid," *The North Carolina Review*, November 11, 1910; R.L. Beall's account of Stoneman's Raid, Cornelia Phillips Spencer papers, SHC. Spencer in *Last Ninety Days*, 201, uses "d----d rebel" instead of "infernal." The officer Stokes shot was thought to be one of Stoneman's staff, but this is not supported by Federal sources.

[75] Spencer, *Last Ninety Days*, 201; Linn, "There Is No Music In My Soul Today," 20; Beall, "Stoneman's Raid," *The North Carolina Review*, November 11, 1910; R.L. Beall's account of Stoneman's Raid, Cornelia Phillips Spencer papers, SHC.

[76] Raynor, *Rebels and Yankees*, 44; Chamberlain, *This Was Home*, 120–21; *Cincinnati Daily Commercial*, May 10, 1865; *Philadelphia Weekly Times*, December 14, 1878.

[77] Linn, "There Is No Music In My Soul Today," 19–20.

[78] Beall, "Stoneman's Raid," *The North Carolina Review*, November 11, 1910; R.L. Beall's account of Stoneman's Raid, Cornelia Phillips Spencer papers, SHC; Linn, "There Is No Music In My Soul Today," 20. On her 100th birthday, Mrs. Ramsey is said to have sat down at her piano and played, "There'll Be a Hot Time in the Old Town Tonight."

[79] Beall, "Stoneman's Raid," *The North Carolina Review*, November 11, 1910; Spencer, *Last Ninety Days*, 195.

[80] Yearns and Barrett, *North Carolina Civil War Documentary*, 119; "General Stoneman's Raid on Salisbury, North Carolina," Harriet Ellis Bradshaw papers, SHC. The prison flag (now the property of the state of North Carolina) was huge, so it is doubtful it figured in the above story.

[81] Petrucelli, *Heritage of Rowan* 1: 7; Chamberlain, *This Was Home*, 118, 120; *Philadelphia Weekly Times*, December 14, 1878; Mason, "Stoneman's Last Campaign," 28–29; Diary of Mary Polk Yeatman, April 12, 1865, Yeatman–Polk Collection, courtesy TSLA; Spencer, *Last Ninety Days*, 194–95, 202–3; E.H.M. Summerell to Cornelia Spencer, September 4, 1866, Cornelia Phillips Spencer papers, SHC; Aull and Brandon, *Dr. Josephus Wells Hall*, 80. Theories abound about why GS did not burn Salisbury. According to Summerell, AG was anxious to lay every house in ashes. "He stated 'repeatedly' that … he would have burned the place could he have had." No other source corroborates this claim. According to one source, GS spared the town because he and a Salisbury resident had been schoolmates, but that was untrue. Other sources state that the Red-Strings (a secret Unionist organization), persuaded GS not to burn the town, or that fellow Masons convinced him. The truth is that GS never intended to destroy civilian property. (Brown, *Salisbury Prison*, 177–78; Brawley, *Rowan Story*, 198).

[82] Trelease, *North Carolina Railroad*, 194; Chamberlain, *This Was Home*, 1–2; Hoole, "Admiral on Horseback," 144; *CV* 30 (May 1922): 101–2; *Carolina Watchman*, February 27, 1890. Old earthworks were still visible in 1890 as they are today.

[83] *Trading Ford*, 3–6.

[84] *Trading Ford*, 5; Raynor, *Rebels and Yankees*, 34; Van Noppen, *Stoneman's Last Raid*, 353.

[85] *OR* 39 (1): 234; *OR* 47 (3): 729, 738–39, 746, 761; Shiman, *Fort York*, 14–15; Spencer, *Last Ninety Days*, 204. Other artillerymen doubtless helped design the earthworks, including John Pemberton. One source suggests that Beauregard's nephew was responsible for the design. (*Carolina Watchman*, February 27, 1890). Beauregard's son was present, not his nephew, but he had little time to assist while his battery was in town.

[86] *Salisbury Post*, September 2, 1951; Shiman, *Fort York*, 6–7, 10, 14–15. The name of the fort in 1865 is in debate. It may have been called Camp Yadkin; Jefferson Davis referred to such a facility in an April 18 message (*OR* 47 [3]: 810), but it is unclear exactly what post Davis is talking

about. The fort has also been called Fort Beauregard and York Hill.

[87] Trelease, *North Carolina Railroad*, 194; "Stoneman's Raid on Salisbury," A.G. Brenizer papers, NCSA; Brawley, *Rowan Story*, 199; Howard, *Forgotten Heroes*, 58–59; *Salisbury Post*, September 2, 1951; E.H.M. Summerell to Cornelia Spencer, September 4, 1866, Cornelia Phillips Spencer papers, SHC; Beall, "Stoneman's Raid," *The North Carolina Review*, October 2, 1910; *Carolina Watchman*, February 27, 1890; R.L. Beall's account of Stoneman's Raid, Cornelia Phillips Spencer papers, SHC; Spencer, *Last Ninety Days*, 203–4.

[88] *Lee's Lieutenants* 3: 512; Warner, *Generals In Gray*, 347–48; *CMH* 10: 320; *Carolina Watchman*, February 27, 1890; "Stoneman's Raid on Salisbury," A.G. Brenizer papers, NCSA; *CV* 30 (May 1922): 101–2.

[89] Brawley, *Rowan Story*, 199; *Carolina Watchman*, February 27, 1890. Although many sources list Clement as a captain, historian Wayne Boone suggests that Clement was a lieutenant with the 54th North Carolina Infantry Regiment.

[90] *Carolina Watchman*, February 27, 1890; Spencer, *Last Ninety Days*, 204; *Salisbury Post*, September 2, 1951; *OR* 49 (1): 334; Barchfield's Memoranda, Arnell Collection, UT; Beall, "Stoneman's Raid," *The North Carolina Review*, October 2, 1910; R.L. Beall's account of Stoneman's Raid, Cornelia Phillips Spencer papers, SHC; Spencer, *Last Ninety Days*, 203–4.

[91] E.H.M. Summerell to Cornelia Spencer, September 4, 1866, Cornelia Phillips Spencer papers, SHC; Brawley, *Rowan Story*, 199; *Salisbury Post*, September 2, 1951; "Stoneman's Raid on Salisbury," A.G. Brenizer papers, NCSA; *Carolina Watchman*, February 27, 1890.

[92] Barchfield's Memoranda, Arnell Collection, UT; Beall, "Stoneman's Raid," *The North Carolina Review*, October 2, 1910; R.L. Beall's account of Stoneman's Raid, Cornelia Phillips Spencer papers, SHC; Spencer, *Last Ninety Days*, 203–4; *Carolina Watchman*, February 27, 1890; Descriptive Book for Companies G–M, 13th Tennessee Cavalry, RR. According to Howard, *Forgotten Heroes*, 58–59, the Federal dead were buried in a small graveyard just down the road.

[93] Shiman, *Fort York*, 14–15; Barchfield's Memoranda, Arnell Collection, UT; E.H.M. Summerell to Cornelia Spencer, September 4, 1866, Cornelia Phillips Spencer papers, SHC; Beall, "Stoneman's Raid," *The North Carolina Review*, October 2, 1910; R.L. Beall's account of Stoneman's Raid, Cornelia Phillips Spencer papers, SHC; Spencer, *Last Ninety Days*, 203–4; Brewer, *History of the 46th Alabama*, 40; Bradley, *Astounding Close*, 297.

[94] E.H.M. Summerell to Cornelia Spencer, September 4, 1866, Cornelia Phillips Spencer papers, SHC; Yearns and Barrett, *North Carolina Civil War Documentary*, 120; *CV* 30 (May 1922): 101–2.

[95] Mason, "Stoneman's Last Campaign," 29; April 12, 1865, Allen Frankenberry diaries, WV; Ford, *The Captive*, 69; Angelo Wiser maps, LC; Betts, "Stoneman's Great Cavalry Raid". One report describing skeletal prisoners found its way into the April 19, 1865, *The Sandusky Register*. According to Wiser, the troopers liberated 400 galvanized Yankees, including a Pennsylvania cavalryman.

[96] April 12, 1865, Allen Frankenberry diaries, WV; Mason, "Stoneman's Last Campaign," 29; Ford, *The Captive*, 50.

[97] *OR* 49 (1): 328, 334; Barchfield's Memoranda, Arnell Collection, UT; April 12, 1865, Allen Frankenberry diaries, WV; *Philadelphia Weekly Times*, December 14, 1878; Ford, *The Captive*, 69. Hambright was a member of the 10th Tennessee Cavalry.

[98] *OR* 49 (1): 325, 334; *Cincinnati Daily Commercial*, May 10, 1865; Mason, "Stoneman's Last Campaign," 28–29; Ford, *The Captive*, 68–69, 478–79; Thomas White to Zebulon B. Vance, April 17, 1865, Zebulon B. Vance Governor's papers, NCSA. Federal tallies of captured supplies are remarkably consistent, and at least one witness stated soon after that the general's figures were probably correct (E.H.M. Summerell to Cornelia Spencer, September 4, 1866, Cornelia Phillips Spencer papers, SHC). The amount of powder, corn, and bacon captured is open to dispute. The lower numbers—the ones AG reported—are used above. The *Philadelphia*

Inquirer of April 19, 1865, provides a list that is similar but provides different amounts of small arms, bacon, and medical supplies.

[99] *OR* 49 (1): 333; *10th Cavalry*, vol. 40, 15; *History of the 10th Michigan*, 38; Trowbridge, *Stoneman Raid*, 108; Trowbridge, "The Stoneman Raid of 1865," *JUSCA* 4 (June 1891): 195–96; *Annual Report of the Adjutant General of Michigan* 1: 98; *11th Cavalry*, vol. 41, 3; Robertson, *Michigan in the War*, 738; *Cincinnati Daily Commercial*, May 10, 1865.

[100] Mason, "Stoneman's Last Campaign," 28–29; Yeatman, "Awful and Grand Spectacle," 42; Diary of Mary Polk Yeatman, April 12, 1865, Yeatman–Polk Collection, courtesy TSLA; "Stoneman's Raid was 69 Years Ago Today," *Salisbury Post*, April 12, 1934, copy in Brawley File, Edith M. Clark History Room, Rowan Public Library; Beall, "Stoneman's Raid," *The North Carolina Review*, October 2, 1910; R.L. Beall's account of Stoneman's Raid, Cornelia Phillips Spencer papers, SHC; Spencer, *Last Ninety Days*, 204–5; Yearns and Barrett, *North Carolina Civil War Documentary*, 119–20; "General Stoneman's Raid on Salisbury, North Carolina," Harriet Ellis Bradshaw papers, SHC.

[101] Chamberlain, *This Was Home*, 120; Spencer, *Last Ninety Days*, 205; Ford, *The Captive*, 68–69, 478–79; "Stoneman's Raid was 69 Years Ago Today," *Salisbury Post*, April 12, 1934, copy in Brawley file, Edith M. Clark History Room, Rowan Public Library; Sample Autobiography, p. 12, CC; Mason, "Stoneman's Last Campaign," 28–29; Diary of Mary Polk Yeatman, April 12, 1865, Yeatman-Polk Collection, courtesy TSLA; *Carolina Watchman*, April 16, 1866; *Philadelphia Weekly Times*, December 14, 1878; Raynor, *Rebels and Yankees*, 38.

[102] *Philadelphia Weekly Times*, December 14, 1878; Spencer, *Last Ninety Days*, 204–5; Yearns and Barrett, *North Carolina Civil War Documentary*, 119–20; "General Stoneman's Raid on Salisbury, North Carolina," Harriet Ellis Bradshaw papers, SHC; Trudeau, *Out of the Storm*, 203; Durkin, *John Dooley*, 192.

[103] April 13, 1865, Henry Birdsall diary, SHC; "Stoneman's Raid was 69 Years Ago Today," *Salisbury Post*, April 12, 1934, copy in Brawley File, Edith M. Clark History Room, Rowan Public Library; *Philadelphia Weekly Times*, December 14, 1878; *Carolina Watchman*, April 16, 1866.

[104] "Sun and Moon Data for One Day," April 12, 1865, Salisbury; Mason, "Stoneman's Last Campaign," 29; Spencer, *Last Ninety Days*, 206; Lindsley, *Military Annals of Tennessee* 2: 841; Moderwell, "Outline of Stoneman's Raid," Civil War (Federal, Miscellaneous) papers, SHC; Ford, *The Captive*, 67; *The Sandusky Register*, April 19, 1865; *Cincinnati Daily Commercial*, May 10, 1865; Beall, "Stoneman's Raid," *The North Carolina Review*, October 2, 1910; R.L. Beall's account of Stoneman's Raid, Cornelia Phillips Spencer papers, SHC; *OR* 49 (1): 325, 334; Sample Autobiography, p. 13, CC; Chamberlain, *This Was Home*, 119; Clark, *Histories of the Several Regiments* 4: 770. Sunset was at 6:53 P.M. Despite Marshall's statement, it would have been difficult for the Ohioans to fire the prison on April 12 since they did not reach Salisbury until 10:00 P.M. Another witness, Nathaniel Sample, stated that the Ohioans destroyed the prison and other structures on April 13 when the raiders left town (Sample Autobiography, 13, CC), but he may have confused the date. One historian claims that some of the raiders were former prisoners, including AG himself, but he was never a prisoner (Spencer, *Last Ninety Days*, 206).

[105] "Sun and Moon Data for One Day," April 12, 1865, Salisbury; Andrews, *The South Since the War*, 105–6, 107. One building—a guardhouse—survived the destruction. Confederate soldiers used it as a command post after GS left. It still stands today on Bank Street. Brewer, *History of the 46th Alabama*, 40.

[106] *Philadelphia Weekly Times*, December 14, 1878; *OR* 49 (1): 325, 334; *Cincinnati Daily Commercial*, May 10, 1865; Mason, "Stoneman's Last Campaign," 28–29; Beall, "Stoneman's Raid," *The North Carolina Review*, October 2, 1910; *Carolina Watchman*, April 16, 1866; R.L. Beall's account of Stoneman's Raid, Cornelia Phillips Spencer papers, SHC; "Stoneman's Raid was 69 Years Ago Today," *Salisbury Post*, April 12, 1934, copy in Brawley file, Edith M. Clark History Room, Rowan Public Library; Diary of Mary Polk Yeatman, April 12, 1865, Yeatman-Polk Collection, courtesy TSLA; *Philadelphia Weekly Times*, December 14, 1878. The tannery was

owned by John Holt and accidentally caught fire from the neighboring buildings (Erwin, *The Village That Disappeared*, 52); Jarnagin Diary, Civil War Collection, Confederate Collection, 30, courtesy TSLA; Ford, *The Captive*, 326. The distillery produced 250,000 gallons of whiskey a year. "Who drinks all this whisky?" asked the *Carolina Watchman* (Brawley, *Rowan County*, 106). The courthouse was not destroyed, even though it was a government building. According to one source, GS had intended to burn it, and had even piled up fuel around the building, but a resident whose father had known GS before the war dissuaded him ("Stoneman's Raid was 69 Years Ago Today," *Salisbury Post*, April 12, 1934, copy in Brawley file, Edith M. Clark History Room, Rowan Public Library).

[107] *Carolina Watchman*, April 16, 1866; *Philadelphia Weekly Times*, December 14, 1878; Spencer, *Last Ninety Days*, 205–6; Betts, "Stoneman's Great Cavalry Raid." One of Spencer's witnesses was R.L. Beall, who wrote, "I could plainly see the conflagration at the distance of fifteen miles, and for several hours the incessant and distinct explosion of shells and fixed ammunition conveyed the impression that a fierce battle with musketry and artillery was raging." Beall, "Stoneman's Raid," *The North Carolina Review*, October 2, 1910; R.L. Beall's account of Stoneman's Raid, Cornelia Phillips Spencer papers, SHC.

[108] Mason, "Stoneman's Last Campaign," 28–29; Diary of Mary Polk Yeatman, April 12, 1865, Yeatman-Polk Collection, courtesy TSLA; *Philadelphia Weekly Times*, December 14, 1878; Yearns and Barrett, *North Carolina Civil War Documentary*, 119–20; "General Stoneman's Raid on Salisbury, North Carolina," Harriet Ellis Bradshaw papers, SHC; April 13, 1865, Allen Frankenberry diaries, WV.

[109] *OR* 49 (1): 324, 334; Mason, "Stoneman's Last Campaign," 28–29; *Governor's Message in Relation to the Western North Carolina Railroad*, 6–7, 8; Trelease, *North Carolina Railroad*, 193; *Annual Report of the North Carolina Railroad, 1865 and 1866*, 11, 17; Trelease, *North Carolina Railroad*, 193; Ford, *The Captive*, 391, 393; Aull and Brandon, *Dr. Josephus Wells Hall*, 80. Federal reports claim the destruction of fifteen miles of track.

[110] *Governor's Message in Relation to the Western North Carolina Railroad*, 34; *Report of the President of the Western North Carolina Railroad*, 17, 41–42, 45. Other estimates of destruction can be found in various sources (for example, the *Philadelphia Weekly Times*, December 14, 1878, and Beall, "Stoneman's Raid," *The North Carolina Review*, October 2, 1910; R.L. Beall's account of Stoneman's Raid, Cornelia Phillips Spencer papers, SHC). None approach the accuracy of the railroad line's official reports, which are presented in the text.

[111] Linn, "There Is No Music In My Soul Today," 19–20; *Davie County Heritage*, 53; Yeatman, "Awful and Grand Spectacle," 42; Brawley, *Rowan County*, 107.

[112] *OR* 49 (1): 334; L.S. Trowbridge to "My Dear Judie," April 12, 1865, L.S. Trowbridge papers, UM; WP to Frank Jackson, February 12, 1865, William J. Palmer Collection, CHS.

[113] Kirk, *15th Pennsylvania*, 498, 531–32; Report of Operations of Wagner's Detachment, April 1865, Charles M. Betts papers, HSP; Wilson, *Column South*, 285–86; Wilson, *Recollections and Experiences*, 113–14; Septimus W. Knight diary, April 10–12, 1865, VMI; Diary, April 13, 1865, Charles M. Betts papers, HSP; Maj. William Wagner to Lt. Col. Charles M. Betts, May 6, 1865, Charles M. Betts papers, HSP; *OR Supplement* 57: 384; *To the Members of the 15th Pennsylvania Cavalry*, 30th Annual Banquet, 8. Wilson recalls rejoining the regiment at 3:00 A.M., and Betts recorded it as 5:00 A.M. Some accounts also suggest incorrectly that the reunion with Wagner took place in Statesville.

[114] Maj. William Wagner to Lt. Col. Charles M. Betts, May 6, 1865, and Report of Operations of Wagner's Detachment, April 1865, both in Charles M. Betts papers, HSP; Diary, April 13, 1865, Charles M. Betts papers, HSP; *OR Supplement* 57: 337, 351, 360, 367, 388; Kirk, *15th Pennsylvania*, 504; *OR* 49 (1): 555.

[115] *Philadelphia Weekly Times*, December 14, 1878; Yeatman, "Awful and Grand Spectacle," 42; *OR* 49 (1): 334; Spencer, *Last Ninety Days*, 204–5; Entry for April 17, 1865, J.T. Wood diary, SHC; Durkin, *John Dooley*, 192; Chamberlain, *This Was Home*, 119. Some subsistence stores did

454

survive. See Thomas White to Zebulon B. Vance, April 17, 1865, Zebulon B. Vance Governor's papers, NCSA.

[116] *Daily Ohio State Journal*, April 19, 1865; *Chicago Tribune*, April 19, 1865; Bushong, *Last Great Stoneman Raid*; Moderwell, "Outline of Stoneman's Raid," Civil War (Federal, Miscellaneous) papers, SHC; Lindsley, *Military Annals of Tennessee* 2: 840; *OR Supplement* 65: 554, 556, 561–62, 566–67, 570, 573, 637; Descriptive Book for Companies G–M, 13th Tennessee Cavalry, RR; Morning Reports for the 13th Tennessee Cavalry, RR; *Report of the Adjutant General of Tennessee*, 609, 632; Robertson, *Michigan in the War*, 738; "Stoneman's Raid was 69 Years Ago Today," *Salisbury Post*, April 12, 1934, copy in Brawley file, Edith M. Clark History Room, Rowan Public Library; *Salisbury Post*, May 23, 1999; *Official Roster* 11: 613, 617; Descriptive Book for Companies G–M, 12th Ohio Cavalry, RR; Mason, *12th Ohio Cavalry Roster*, 34–35, 38–39; Descriptive Book for Companies G–M, 13th Tennessee Cavalry, RR. Jenkins died on April 13. One young Salisbury citizen claims that he saw a Federal trooper die at the foot of the hill where Arlington Street enters Innes Street. The man was buried where he fell.

[117] *Chronological Summary of Engagements and Battles*, CXXXIX; Beall, "Stoneman's Raid," *The North Carolina Review*, October 2, 1910; R.L. Beall's account of Stoneman's Raid, Cornelia Phillips Spencer papers, SHC; *Salisbury Post*, May 23, 1999; Spencer, *Last Ninety Days*, 200; Lindsley, *Military Annals of Tennessee* 2: 840; *OR* 49 (1): 324, 333–34, 345; *Cincinnati Daily Commercial*, May 10, 1865; Mason, "Stoneman's Last Campaign," 27–28; Barchfield's Memoranda, Arnell Collection, UT; *Chicago Tribune*, April 19, 1865; *Annual Report of the Adjutant General of Michigan* 1: 98; *11th Cavalry*, vol. 41, 3; Robertson, *Michigan in the War*, 738; *10th Cavalry*, vol. 40, 15; *History of the 10th Michigan*, 38–39; Bushong, *Last Great Stoneman Raid*; *The Union Army* 4: 355; *Union Regiments of Kentucky*, 236; April 13, 1865, Henry Birdsall diary, SHC; *OR Supplement* 65: 614; Steven Thomas to "My Dear Wife," June 5, 1865, Calvin Thomas papers, UM; Trowbridge, *Stoneman Raid*, 108; Trowbridge, "The Stoneman Raid of 1865," *JUSCA* 4 (June 1891): 195–96; Morning Reports for Companies B, G, and H, 11th Kentucky Cavalry, April 12, 1865, RR; April 12, 1865, Allen Frankenberry diaries, WV. In the margins of his map, Angelo Wiser noted the capture of 1,165 men (Angelo Wiser maps, LC), while the *Philadelphia Inquirer* of April 19, 1865, claimed the capture of 1,164.

[118] *Statement of the Disposition of Bodies* 3: 8; Curtis, "Salisbury National Cemetery," 5; Lindsley, *Military Annals of Tennessee* 2: 840; Robertson, *Michigan in the War*, 738; Beall, "Stoneman's Raid," *The North Carolina Review*, October 2, 1910; R.L. Beall, "Stoneman's Raid," *The North Carolina Review*, October 2, 1910; R.L. Beall's account of Stoneman's Raid, Cornelia Phillips Spencer papers, SHC; Spencer, *Last Ninety Days*, 200; *Salisbury Post*, May 23, 1999. Some of the original burial places included a ravine near the cemetery, the Lutheran graveyard, the English churchyard, the Gold Hill road, the bank of the Yadkin, and Mrs. Sarah Johnston's garden. The body of Hugh Berry was found in the latter spot; Berry had died while in Mrs. Johnston's care.

[119] *OR* 49 (1): 324, 328, 333–34, 345; Angelo Wiser maps, LC; *The Sandusky Register*, April 19, 1865; *Cincinnati Daily Commercial*, May 10, 1865; Mason, "Stoneman's Last Campaign," 27–28; Barchfield's Memoranda, Arnell Collection, UT; *Chicago Tribune*, April 19, 1865; *Annual Report of the Adjutant General of Michigan* 1: 98; *11th Cavalry*, vol. 41, 3; Robertson, *Michigan in the War*, 738; *10th Cavalry*, vol. 40, 15; *History of the 10th Michigan*, 38–39; Bushong, *Last Great Stoneman Raid*; *The Union Army* 4: 355; *Union Regiments of Kentucky*, 236; Steven Thomas to "My Dear Wife," June 5, 1865, Calvin Thomas papers, UM; April 13, 1865, Henry Birdsall diary, SHC; *OR Supplement* 65: 614; Trowbridge, *Stoneman Raid*, 108; Trowbridge, "The Stoneman Raid of 1865," *JUSCA* 4 (June 1891): 195–96; Report of AG, December 29, 1873, 541–42, GR; Morning Reports for Companies B, G, and H, 11th Kentucky Cavalry, April 12, 1865, RR; *National Tribune*, October 31, 1907. The *Philadelphia Inquirer* of April 19, 1865, claims the Federals captured eight stands of colors and nineteen guns.

[120] Roman, *Beauregard* 2: 394–95; Davis, *Jefferson Davis*, 615; Johnston, *Narrative*, 396–99; Trudeau, *Out of the Storm*, 203.

Chapter 8
There Are Bad Men in All Crowds
Salisbury to Lenoir: April 13–17, 1865

[1] For the details behind Stoneman's orders, see Chapter One.

[2] Inscoe and McKinney, *Heart of Confederate Appalachia*, 23; Barrett, *Civil War in North Carolina*, 299–300; *OR* 49 (1): 324. Wilmington was already in Federal hands and Sherman's army had destroyed part of the Wilmington, Charlotte, and Rutherford railroad, so it had little strategic value beyond its ability to shuttle men and supplies locally.

[3] *OR Supplement* 57: 319; Septimus W. Knight diary, April 13, 1865, VMI; Morning Reports for Companies A–D, 15th Pennsylvania Cavalry, RR; Diary, April 13, 1865, Charles M. Betts papers, HSP; Kirk, *15th Pennsylvania*, 504; April 13, 1865, Allen Frankenberry diaries, WV; *OR* 49 (1): 328, 334; April 14, 1865, Henry Birdsall diary, SHC; Scott, *13th Tennessee*, 239; Chamberlain, *This Was Home*, 119; Banks, "Memoranda," diary entry for April 13, 1865, 297; Steven Thomas to "My Dear Wife," June 5, 1865, Calvin Thomas papers, UM; Morning Reports, Companies A–F, 10th Michigan Cavalry, RR. Birdsall's diary account is garbled, dating actions a day later than they actually occurred.

[4] "General Stoneman's Raid on Salisbury, North Carolina," Harriet Ellis Bradshaw papers, SHC; Yearns and Barrett, *North Carolina Civil War Documentary*, 120.

[5] Yeatman, *Awful and Grand Spectacle*, 43; John W. Otey to Zebulon B. Vance, April 12, 1865, Zebulon B. Vance Governor's papers, NCSA; *OR* 47 (3): 789; Bradley, *Astounding Close*, 297; Brewer, *History of the 46th Alabama*, 40; *Philadelphia Weekly Times*, December 14, 1878.

[6] *OR Supplement* 57: 319; Septimus W. Knight diary, April 13, 1865, VMI; Morning Reports for Companies A–D, 15th Pennsylvania Cavalry, RR; Diary, April 13, 1865, Charles M. Betts papers, HSP; Kirk, *15th Pennsylvania*, 504.

[7] Steven Thomas to "My Dear Wife," June 5, 1865, Calvin Thomas papers, UM; Morning Reports for Companies A–F, 10th Michigan Cavalry, RR.

[8] April 13, 1865, Allen Frankenberry diaries, WV; *OR* 49 (1): 328.

[9] Angelo Wiser maps, LC; *Governor's Message in Relation to the Western North Carolina Railroad*, 6–8, 12, 33; *OR* 49 (1): 328; *Report of the President of the Western North Carolina Railroad*, 42.

[10] Banks, "Memoranda," diary entry for April 14, 1865, 298.

[11] *Landmark*, December 1, 1882. This *Landmark* article appeared when Stoneman became governor of California.

[12] Angelo Wiser maps, LC.

[13] Bush, "Pair of Historical North Carolina Letters," 8–9. The quoted letter was dated April 10, 1865.

[14] *Landmark*, April 28, 1907. This article, another of the several Stoneman's Raid stories published intermittently by the *Landmark*, was a response to an April 23, 1907 *Landmark* article. It contains the observations of eyewitness S.W. Stevenson, and appears to be a solid source.

[15] *Landmark*, April 28, 1907.

[16] *Landmark*, April 28, 1907; December 1, 1882.

[17] *Landmark*, April 23, 1907; "Stoneman's Raid Closest Brush with Civil War," Stoneman's Raid File, Local History Collection, Iredell County Public Library. The April 23 *Landmark* article was also written by an eyewitness. It appears to present reliable information as well, despite its late date.

[18] *Ibid.*

[19] *Landmark*, December 1, 1882; Morning Reports for the 11th Michigan Cavalry, RR; April 13, 1865, Henry Birdsall diary, SHC. The officer commanding the advance guard could also have been Israel Smith, mentioned in the previous chapter, but a regimental commander is a more likely candidate than a staff officer.

[20] *Landmark*, April 23, 1907; "Stoneman's Raid Closest Brush with Civil War," Stoneman's Raid file, Local History Collection, Iredell County Public Library; *Landmark*, December 1, 1882.

[21] *Landmark*, April 28, 1907.

[22] *Landmark*, December 1, 1882. The Bogle home was also reported to have been on Main Street (*Landmark*, April 23, 1907).

[23] "Stoneman's Raid Closest Brush with Civil War," Stoneman's Raid File, Local History Collection, Iredell County Public Library; April 13–14, 1865, Allen Frankenberry diaries, WV; April 14, 1865, Henry Birdsall diary, SHC; Kirk, *15th Pennsylvania*, 504; *OR* 49 (1): 328, 334; Scott, *13th Tennessee*, 239; Spencer, *Last Ninety Days*, 213; *OR Supplement* 65: 614.

[24] *Landmark*, April 23, 1907; December 1, 1882; Diary of Annie Olympia Donnell, April 14, 1865, Loula Donnell papers, SHC; "Stoneman's Raid," unprovenienced article, Stoneman's Raid file, Local History Collection, Iredell County Public Library; "Gen. Stoneman's Army in Iredell," Stoneman's Raid File, Local History Collection, Iredell County Public Library; Van Noppen, *Western North Carolina*, 153; Brown, *Salisbury Prison*, 175.

[25] *Governor's Message in Relation to the Western North Carolina Railroad*, 6–8, 33; *Landmark*, December 1, 1882; *Landmark*, April 28, 1907; R.L. Beall's account of Stoneman's Raid, Cornelia Phillips Spencer papers, SHC; Beall, "Stoneman's Raid," *The North Carolina Review*, October 2, 1910; Spencer, *Last Ninety Days*, 213; "Wars—Civil War—Landmark—September 28, 1900," Stoneman's Raid file, Local History Collection, Caldwell County Public Library.

[26] *Landmark*, December 1, 1882; Bush, "Pair of Historical North Carolina Letters," 9. The quoted letter was dated April 27, 1865; MacBryde, *Ellie's Book*, 133; Keever, *Iredell–Piedmont County*, 254.

[27] Diary of Annie Olympia Donnell, April 14, 1865, Loula Donnell papers, SHC. Since none of the division's ranking officers were "foreigners," Ms. Donnell may have confused the Irish-born Myles Keogh with the general.

[28] *Landmark*, April 23, 1907; "Stoneman's Raid Closest Brush with Civil War," Stoneman's Raid file, Local History Collection, Iredell County Public Library.

[29] *Landmark*, April 28, 1907; Spencer, *Last Ninety Days*, 214; R.L. Beall's account of Stoneman's Raid, Cornelia Phillips Spencer papers, SHC; Beall, "Stoneman's Raid," *The North Carolina Review*, November 11, 1910.

[30] R.L. Beall's account of Stoneman's Raid, Cornelia Phillips Spencer papers, SHC; Beall, "Stoneman's Raid," *The North Carolina Review*, October 2, 1910; Spencer, *Last Ninety Days*, 213–14; *Iredell Neighbors*, November 30, 1988; *Iredell Express*, April 13, 1865; *Landmark*, April 23, 1907.

[31] *Landmark*, April 23, 1907; Diary of Annie Olympia Donnell, April 14, 1865, Loula Donnell papers, SHC; *Iredell Neighbors*, November 30, 1988; R.L. Beall's account of Stoneman's Raid, Cornelia Phillips Spencer papers, SHC; Beall, "Stoneman's Raid," *The North Carolina Review*, November 11, 1910; Spencer, *Last Ninety Days*, 213–14; *Landmark*, December 1, 1882.

[32] Watt, *Statesville*, 59; Inscoe and McKinney, *Heart of Confederate Appalachia*, 234; Bradley, *Astounding Close*, 108; Spencer, *Last Ninety Days*, 214–16; "Gen. Stoneman's Army in Iredell," Stoneman's Raid file, Local History Collection, Iredell County Public Library.

[33] Diary of Annie Olympia Donnell, April 14, 1865, Loula Donnell papers, SHC; Van Noppen, *Western North Carolina*, 153.

[34] Trowbridge, "A Continuation of the Narrative of the Stoneman Raid of 1865," L.S. Trowbridge papers, UM; Betts, "Stoneman's Great Cavalry Raid;" Wilson, *Recollections and Experiences*, 121; Kirk, *15th Pennsylvania*, 504; Diary, April 14, 1865, Charles M. Betts papers, HSP; *Landmark*, December 1, 1882. According to the *Landmark*, Stoneman also told Palmer to "stop burning," but the Pennsylvania solider was doing very little of that as it was.

[35] *Landmark*, April 23, 1907; "Stoneman's Raid Closest Brush with Civil War," Stoneman's Raid file, Local History Collection, Iredell County Public Library; *OR* 49 (1): 323–25. The dis-

patch would go by courier from Lenoir and by telegraph from Jonesborough, Tennessee (George Stoneman to Maj. Gen. George Thomas, April 13, 1865, Letters Sent, District of East Tennessee, RG 393, Part 2, Entry 2740, NA).

[36] *OR* 47 (3): 777; Memoirs of S.W. Ferguson, Heyward and Ferguson family papers, SHC; *Landmark*, December 1, 1882; *Landmark*, April 23, 1907; "Stoneman's Raid Closest Brush with Civil War," Stoneman's Raid file, Local History Collection, Iredell County Public Library; Miller and Cross, *Time Is, Time Was*, 5; *Landmark*, April 28, 1907; *Sunday Record & Landmark*, April 14, 1985.

[37] *Landmark*, December 1, 1882; Diary of Annie Olympia Donnell, April 18, 1865, Loula Donnell papers, SHC; *Landmark*, December 1, 1882, April 28, 1907; Miller and Cross, *Time Is, Time Was*, 5; "Stoneman's Raid Closest Brush with Civil War," Stoneman's Raid file, Local History Collection, Iredell County Public Library; Confederate Gravestone Records, NCSA. The wounded Coffee was taken to either the home of Mrs. Simonton or Mayor Surleton, where he died and thus became one of the last Confederates to be killed in the war. In later years, members of the 15th Pennsylvania Cavalry thought incorrectly that they had encountered Duke's men, and claimed the loss of an officer on the Federal side, a former member of the 13th Illinois Cavalry who had killed John Hunt Morgan (Wilson, *Recollections and Experiences*, 76; *To the Members of the 15th Pennsylvania Cavalry*, 23rd Annual Banquet, 12). There is no other evidence to support this contention.

[38] Descriptive Book, 8th Tennessee Cavalry, RR; Diary, April 15, 1865, Charles M. Betts papers, HSP; Frederic Antes diary, April 15, 1865, Civil War Miscellaneous Collection, USAMHI; Morning Reports for Companies A–D, 15th Pennsylvania Cavalry, RR; Kirk, *15th Pennsylvania*, 504–5; Diary Entry for April 14–15, 1865, Charles F. Weller memoirs and letters, *Civil War Times Illustrated* Collection, USAMHI; Wilson, *Column South*, 290; Septimus W. Knight diary, April 14–15, 1865, VMI. Hysinger died at Salisbury after being shot the day before.

[39] *Landmark*, December 1, 1882; Diary of Annie Olympia Donnell, April 14, 1865, Loula Donnell papers, SHC; Entry for May 7, 1865, Fielder diaries, courtesy THS.

[40] Angelo Wiser maps, LC. Wiser called it Little's Ferry.

[41] Report of AG, December 29, 1873, 543, GR; *Annual Report of the Adjutant General of Michigan* 1: 98; Robertson, *Michigan in the War*, 738; *OR* 49 (1): 328; Scott, *13th Tennessee*, 239; April 15, 1865, Henry Birdsall diary, SHC; *Annual Report of the Adjutant General of Michigan* 1: 98; Robertson, *Michigan in the War*, 738; White, *History of Alexander*, 60; Allen, *Heritage of Alexander County* 1: 382.

[42] White, *History of Alexander*, 60; Allen, *Heritage of Alexander County* 1: 382.

[43] Ibid.

[44] April 14–15, 1865, Allen Frankenberry diaries, WV; Claim of John M. Carson, #20185, Box 215, Entry 732, Alexander County, N.C., RG 217, Settled Files of the SCC, NA.

[45] White, *History of Alexander*, 64–65.

[46] Allen, *Heritage of Alexander County* 1: 382.

[47] Allen, *Heritage of Alexander County* 1: 23, 37.

[48] Morning Reports for Companies A–F, 10th Michigan Cavalry, RR; *Annual Report of the Adjutant General of Michigan* 1: 98; Robertson, *Michigan in the War*, 738; *OR Supplement* 65: 615; April 14–15, 1865, Allen Frankenberry diaries, WV; Banks, "Memoranda," diary entry for April 15, 1865, 298; Morning Reports of Companies A–F, 10th Michigan Cavalry, RR; Descriptive Book for Companies A–E, 10th Michigan Cavalry, RR.

[49] Kirk, *15th Pennsylvania*, 504–5; Frederic Antes diary, April 15, 1865, Civil War Miscellaneous Collection, USAMHI; Diary, April 15, 1865, Charles M. Betts papers, HSP; Septimus W. Knight diary, April 14–15, 1865, VMI; Morning Reports for Companies A–D, 15th Pennsylvania Cavalry, RR; Frederic Antes diary, April 15, 1865, Civil War Miscellaneous Collection, USAMHI; Angelo Wiser maps, LC; *OR Supplement* 57: 319; Wilson, *Column South*, 290.

[50] White, *History of Alexander*, 60–61; Allen, *Heritage of Alexander County* 1: 383.

[51] White, *History of Alexander*, 60, 65; Allen, *Heritage of Alexander County* 1: 382–83.

[52] Some sources suggest incorrectly that Easter Sunday was on April 9, but U.S. Naval Observatory Records confirm April 16 as the date (http://aa.usno.navy.mil/data/docs/easter.html).

[53] James W. Albright diary and reminiscences, entry for April 16, 1865, MS. Coll. #16, Civil War Collection 12:1, Greensboro Historical Museum Archives; Brig Gen. Alfred Iverson to P.G.T. Beauregard, April 16, 1865, MS. Coll. #33, Gen. G.T. Beauregard correspondence, Andrew Joyner, Jr. Collection, Collection 1979.11.261, Greensboro Historical Museum Archives; Hoole, "Admiral on Horseback," 131–32, 140–41; Semmes, *Memoirs of Service Afloat*, 819; Bradley, *Astounding Close*, 234–35.

[54] Bradley, *Astounding Close*, 135, 137–43, 154; Davis, *Jefferson Davis*, 614–19; Hanna, *Flight Into Oblivion*, 35–37, 38–41, 44; Entry for April 15, 1865, Anna Holmes Trenholm diary, SHC; Entry for April 15, 1865, J.T. Wood diary, SHC; *Heritage of Davidson County*, 8; Trelease, *North Carolina Railroad*, 194; Konkle, *John Motley Morehead*, 409; *Greensborough Patriot*, March 23, 1866.

[55] Hanna, *Flight Into Oblivion*, 38–41, 44; Diary, John Taylor Wood papers, April 15–17, SHC; Entry for April 16, 1865, Anna Holmes Trenholm diary, SHC; Ford, *Life in the Confederate Army*, 64–66.

[56] *Annual Report of the Adjutant General of Michigan* 1: 98; Robertson, *Michigan in the War*, 738; *OR Supplement* 65: 615.

[57] Scott, *13th Tennessee*, 239; *OR* 49 (1): 328–29; April 15, 1865, Allen Frankenberry diaries, WV. Trotter, *Bushwhackers*, 280, estimated that nine hundred or one thousand prisoners were with the column; Gillem's estimate of prisoners captured at Salisbury is higher. See Chapter Seven.

[58] Downs, "About the Time of the 'Surrender,'" 1–2; Alexander, *Here Will I Dwell*, 139; *OR* 39 (1): 853–54; Clark, *Histories of the Several Regiments* 4: 372–75.

[59] Downs, "About the Time of the 'Surrender,'" 1–2. For more on the raiders' first incursion into Caldwell County, see Chapter 3.

[60] Downs, "About the Time of the 'Surrender,'" 2; Alexander, *Here Will I Dwell*, 140; "Notes of Stoneman's Raid in Burke County, and the Town of Morganton," Cornelia P. Spencer papers, SHC; Bradley T. Johnson telegram, April 8, 1865, Civil War clipping file, Morganton Public Library, Morganton, N.C.; Clark, *Histories of the Several Regiments* 4: 375.

[61] Louisa Norwood to Walter Lenoir, April 24, 1865, Lenoir papers, SHC; *Lenoir News-Topic*, September 12, 1941.

[62] R.L. Beall's account of Stoneman's Raid, Cornelia Phillips Spencer papers, SHC; Beall, "Stoneman's Raid," *The North Carolina Review*, December 4, 1910; Downs, "About the Time of the 'Surrender,'" 3–4.

[63] Downs, "About the Time of the 'Surrender,'" 3; *Lenoir News-Topic*, March 31, 1992.

[64] Downs, "About the Time of the 'Surrender,'" 3.

[65] *Ibid.*, 4.

[66] Downs, "About the Time of the 'Surrender,'" 4–5; *Lenoir News-Topic*, March 31, 1992; Clark, *Histories of the Several Regiments* 4: 375–76.

[67] *Annual Report of the Adjutant General of Michigan* 1: 98; Robertson, *Michigan in the War*, 738; *OR Supplement* 65: 615; Trotter, *Bushwhackers*, 280; *OR Supplement* 65: 637; Downs, "About the Time of the 'Surrender,'" 4–5; *Lenoir News-Topic*, March 31, 1992. According to *OR Supplement* 65: 637, the gunners stopped in "Lattimore," but that is doubtless a misnomer for Lenoir.

[68] Louisa Norwood to Walter Lenoir, April 24, 1865, Lenoir papers, SHC; *Lenoir News-Topic*, September 12, 1941.

[69] *Ibid.*

[70] *Annual Report of the Adjutant General of Michigan* 1: 98; Robertson, *Michigan in the War*, 738; *OR Supplement* 65: 615; Alexander, *Here Will I Dwell*, 142; Alexander, *These Eternal Hills*,

81–82; *Heritage of Caldwell*, 46; Louisa Norwood to Walter Lenoir, April 24, 1865, Lenoir papers, SHC; *Lenoir News-Topic*, September 12, 1941; Bush, "Pair of Historical North Carolina Letters," 9; Van Noppen, *Western North Carolina*, 153.

[71] R.L. Beall's account of Stoneman's Raid, Cornelia Phillips Spencer papers, SHC; Beall, "Stoneman's Raid," *The North Carolina Review*, December 4, 1910; Bush, "Pair of Historical North Carolina Letters," 9.

[72] Diary entry for April 15, Mrs. George W.F. Harper, in Barrett, *Civil War in North Carolina*, 361; R.L. Beall to Cornelia Phillips Spencer, September 20, 1866, Cornelia Phillips Spencer papers, SHC.

[73] Spencer, *Last Ninety Days*, 222–23; R.L. Beall's account of Stoneman's Raid, Cornelia Phillips Spencer papers, SHC; Beall, "Stoneman's Raid," *The North Carolina Review*, December 4, 1910.

[74] "Stoneman's Raid Described in Diary," *The Uplift*, 18–19.

[75] Louisa Norwood to Walter Lenoir, April 24, 1865, Lenoir papers, SHC; *Lenoir News-Topic*, September 12, 1941; R.L. Beall's account of Stoneman's Raid, Cornelia Phillips Spencer papers, SHC; Beall, "Stoneman's Raid," *The North Carolina Review*, December 4, 1910. Rankin died in 1876.

[76] Louisa Norwood to Walter Lenoir, April 24, 1865, Lenoir papers, SHC; *Lenoir News-Topic*, September 12, 1941.

[77] Alexander, *Here Will I Dwell*, 141; Samuel F. Patterson to Rufus L. Patterson, April 19, 1865, Patterson papers, NCSA.

[78] Barrett, *Civil War in North Carolina*, 361; April 16, 1865, Allen Frankenberry diaries, WV.

[79] *OR* 49 (1): 329, 334; Alexander, *Here Will I Dwell*, 142; Downs, "About the Time of the 'Surrender,'" 5; Report of AG, December 29, 1873, in U.S. Army Generals' Reports of Civil War Service, M1098, vol. IV, R19, p. 543, NA; Scott, *13th Tennessee*, 239.

[80] *Lenoir News-Topic*, September 12, 1941; Downs, "About the Time of the 'Surrender,'" 6; Bumgarner, *Kirk's Raiders*, 69; Louisa Norwood to Walter Lenoir, April 24, 1865, Lenoir papers, SHC; *Lenoir News-Topic*, September 12, 1941; Spencer, *Last Ninety Days*, 216–17; Barrett, *Civil War in North Carolina*, 361; R.L. Beall's account of Stoneman's Raid, Cornelia Phillips Spencer papers, SHC; Beall, "Stoneman's Raid," *The North Carolina Review*, December 4, 1910.

[81] Louisa Norwood to Walter Lenoir, April 24, 1865, Lenoir papers, SHC; *Lenoir News-Topic*, September 12, 1941.

[82] R.L. Beall's account of Stoneman's Raid, Cornelia Phillips Spencer papers, SHC; Beall, "Stoneman's Raid," *The North Carolina Review*, December 4, 1910; *CV* 29 (March 1921): 107; Louisa Norwood to Walter Lenoir, April 24, 1865, Lenoir papers, SHC; *Lenoir News-Topic*, September 12, 1941.

[83] Barrett, *Civil War in North Carolina*, 361; Scott, *13th Tennessee*, 152; Spencer, *Last Ninety Days*, 216–18; R.L. Beall's account of Stoneman's Raid, Cornelia Phillips Spencer papers, SHC; Beall, "Stoneman's Raid," *The North Carolina Review*, December 4, 1910; Alexander, *Here Will I Dwell*, 142.

[84] Downs, "About the Time of the 'Surrender,'" 2, 5, 6; Bumgarner, *Kirk's Raiders*, 69.

[85] Downs, "About the Time of the 'Surrender,'" 5–6; Barrett, *Civil War in North Carolina*, 362; Moderwell, "Outline of Stoneman's Raid," Civil War (Federal, Miscellaneous) papers, SHC; Bumgarner, *Kirk's Raiders*, 69. Mason, "Stoneman's Last Campaign," 29, claims that the prisoners and captured artillery went with Gillem, but the evidence is clear that they traveled with Stoneman.

[86] Betts, "Stoneman's Great Cavalry Raid;" Report of AG, December 29, 1873, 542–43, GR.

[87] Downs, "About the Time of the 'Surrender,'" 5–6; Barrett, *Civil War in North Carolina*, 362; Moderwell, "Outline of Stoneman's Raid," Civil War (Federal, Miscellaneous) papers, SHC;

Bumgarner, *Kirk's Raiders*, 69; *OR* 49 (2): 407; Report of AG, December 29, 1873, in U.S. Army Generals' Reports of Civil War Service, M1098, vol. IV, R19, p. 543, NA; Mason, "Stoneman's Last Campaign," 29.

[88] Spencer, *Last Ninety Days*, 217; R.L. Beall's account of Stoneman's Raid, Cornelia Phillips Spencer papers, SHC; Beall, "Stoneman's Raid," *The North Carolina Review*, December 4, 1910; Spencer, *Last Ninety Days*, 219.

[89] R.L. Beall's account of Stoneman's Raid, Cornelia Phillips Spencer papers, SHC; Beall, "Stoneman's Raid," *The North Carolina Review*, December 4, 1910; Spencer, *Last Ninety Days*, 219–22.

[90] Report of AG, December 29, 1873, in U.S. Army Generals' Reports of Civil War Service, M1098, vol. IV, R19, p. 543, NA; *OR Supplement* 65: 637; *OR* 49 (1): 334; R.L. Beall's account of Stoneman's Raid, Cornelia Phillips Spencer papers, SHC; Beall, "Stoneman's Raid," *The North Carolina Review*, December 4, 1910; Downs, "About the Time of the 'Surrender,'" 6; Mason, "Stoneman's Last Campaign," 29; April 17, 1865, Allen Frankenberry diaries, WV.

[91] Scott, *Annals of Caldwell County*, 249–50; R.L. Beall's account of Stoneman's Raid, Cornelia Phillips Spencer papers, SHC; Beall, "Stoneman's Raid," *The North Carolina Review*, December 4, 1910.

[92] Downs, "About the Time of the 'Surrender,'" 4; Louisa Norwood to Walter Lenoir, April 24, 1865, Lenoir papers, SHC; *Lenoir News-Topic*, September 12, 1941.

Chapter 9
WATCH ON THE CATAWBA
Taylorsville to Morganton: April 16–22, 1865

[1] *OR* 49 (1): 334; *OR* 49 (2): 407; Barrett, *Civil War in North Carolina*, 360; R.L. Beall's account of Stoneman's Raid, Cornelia Phillips Spencer papers, SHC; Beall, "Stoneman's Raid," *The North Carolina Review*, October 2, 1910; Trotter, *Bushwhackers*, 277; *Cincinnati Daily Commercial*, May 10, 1865, 279; Betts, "Stoneman's Great Cavalry Raid;" Mason, "Stoneman's Last Campaign," 30.

[2] Angelo Wiser maps, LC; Banks, "Memoranda," diary entry for April 16, 1865, 298. See Chapter 8 for the story of Bingham and Shearer.

[3] Kirk, *15th Pennsylvania*, 504–5; Frederic Antes diary, April 16, 1865, Civil War Miscellaneous Collection, USAMHI; Morning Reports for Companies A–D, 15th Pennsylvania Cavalry, RR; Diary, April 16, 1865, Charles M. Betts papers, HSP; Angelo Wiser maps, LC; Diary entry for April 16, 1865, Charles F. Weller memoirs and letters, *Civil War Times Illustrated* Collection, USAMHI; Septimus W. Knight diary, April 16–17, 1865, VMI; Banks, "Memoranda," diary entry for April 16, 1865, 298.

[4] Diary entry for April 17, 1865, Charles F. Weller memoirs and letters, *Civil War Times Illustrated* Collection, USAMHI; Wilson, *Column South*, 291; Septimus W. Knight diary, April 17, 1865, VMI; Frederic Antes diary, April 17, 1865, Civil War Miscellaneous Collection, USAMHI. Weller called the engineers "mechanics." In his diary, Antes called the Catawba the Watauga by mistake.

[5] Morning Reports for Companies A–F and G–M, 10th Michigan Cavalry, RR; Trowbridge, "A Continuation of the Narrative of the Stoneman Raid of 1865," L.S. Trowbridge papers, UM; *Mountain Scenery*, 21–22; Preslar, *History of Catawba County*, 280–81; Freeze, *The Catawbans*, 200; Huffman and Huffman, *Catawba Journey*, 38; Sherrill, *Annals of Lincoln County*, 182; R.L. Beall's account of Stoneman's Raid, Cornelia Phillips Spencer papers, SHC; Beall, "Stoneman's Raid," *The North Carolina Review*, October 2, 1910.

[6] Morning Reports of Companies A–F and G–M, 10th Michigan Cavalry, RR; Freeze, *The Catawbans*, 200; Trowbridge, "A Continuation of the Narrative of the Stoneman Raid of 1865,"

L.S. Trowbridge papers, UM; *Mountain Scenery*, 21–22.

[7] Septimus W. Knight diary, April 17, 1865, VMI; Diary entry for April 17, 1865, Charles F. Weller memoirs and letters, *Civil War Times Illustrated* Collection, USAMHI. Hickory Station, also called Hickory Tavern by some sources, is present-day Hickory.

[8] Freeze, *The Catawbans*, 200; Preslar, *History of Catawba County*, 281; Frederic Antes diary, April 17, 1865, Civil War Miscellaneous Collection, USAMHI.

[9] Kirk, *15th Pennsylvania*, 505; Frederic Antes diary, April 17, 1865, Civil War Miscellaneous Collection, USAMHI.

[10] Freeze, *The Catawbans*, 200.

[11] Preslar, *History of Catawba County*, 281–82; Freeze, *The Catawbans*, 199–200; "A Catawba Lady Makes a Point," unprovenienced article, copy in the History/Genealogy area of the Catawba County Public Library.

[12] Governor's Message in Relation to the Western North Carolina Railroad, 6–7, 8, 32–33; Report of the President of the Western North Carolina Railroad, 42. Although it is possible that the main body with Gillem caused the damage at Icard's, the most likely unit was Palmer's brigade due to their proximity to Icard and Hickory. The $111,000 in losses is the equivalent to more than $2 million in present-day value (Samuel H. Williamson, "What is the Relative Value?" Economic History Services, June 2005, URL: http://www.eh.net/hmit/compare).

[13] Frederic Antes diary, April 17, 1865, Civil War Miscellaneous Collection, USAMHI; Morning Reports for Companies A–D, 15th Pennsylvania Cavalry, RR; Banks, "Memoranda," diary entry for April 17, 1865, 298; Descriptive Book for Companies G–M, 12th Ohio Cavalry, RR.

[14] CV 10 (July 1902): 307–8; Evans, *Confederate Military History* 2: 104; 8: 340; 9: 190; Duke, *Reminiscences*, 462–63; Duke, *History of Morgan's Cavalry*, 621; John Echols to Robert E. Lee, December 15, 1865, R.E. Lee headquarters papers, VHS.

[15] CV 10 (July 1902): 307; John Echols to Robert E. Lee, December 15, 1865, R.E. Lee headquarters papers, VHS; Duke, *Reminiscences*, 462–65; Duke, *A History of Morgan's Cavalry*, 624, 626.

[16] Diary of Annie Olympia Donnell, April 14, 1865, Loula Donnell papers, SHC; Duke, *Reminiscences*, 462–65; Duke, *History of Morgan's Cavalry*, 624, 626. S.W. Stevenson may have seen Napier's troopers in Statesville. See Chapter 8.

[17] Duke, *History of Morgan's Cavalry*, 624; Duke, *Reminiscences*, 464–65; Moderwell, "Outline of Stoneman's Raid," Civil War (Federal, Miscellaneous) papers, SHC. Duke's path is unknown, but it probably took him west from Statesville to the vicinity of the Catawba and then south along Murray's Mill and Buffalo Shoals Roads. Palmer's cavalrymen followed the direct route along present-day U.S. 321.

[18] Duke, *Reminiscences*, 465; Duke, *History of Morgan's Cavalry*, 624–26. For the distances between Hickory, Newton, and Lincolnton, see Angelo Wiser maps, LC.

[19] Mason, *12th Ohio Cavalry*, 103; Bushong, *Last Great Stoneman Raid*.

[20] Kirk, *15th Pennsylvania*, 505; Frederic Antes diary, April 17, 1865, Civil War Miscellaneous Collection, USAMHI; Hoole, "Admiral on Horseback," 145; Banks, "Memoranda," diary entry for April 17, 1865, 298; Wilson, *Recollections and Experiences*, 121–22. Company A did not reach town, and instead camped just north of Lincolnton at the end of the day (Morning Reports for Companies A–D, 15th Pennsylvania Cavalry, RR).

[21] Sherrill, *Annals of Lincoln County*, 181–82.

[22] Kirk, *15th Pennsylvania*, 505; Wilson, *Recollections and Experiences*, 121. See also Fisher, *Builder of the West*, 120, which incorrectly places this incident in Hickory. The 12th Ohio clearly led the way into town, so the "advance guard" referred to in the paragraph was probably the advance of the 15th Pennsylvania.

[23] Banks, "Memoranda," diary entry for April 17, 1865, 298; Descriptive Book for Companies G–M, 12th Ohio Cavalry, RR; Sherrill, *Annals of Lincoln County*, 182; Wilson, *Recollections and*

Experiences, 122; Kirk, *15th Pennsylvania*, 507. According to Darrell Harkey, Lincoln County's Historical Coordinator, Palmer and Peiffer became good friends, even though two of Peiffer's sons had been killed in the war.

[24] Septimus W. Knight diary, April 21, 1865, VMI; Wilson, *Column South*, 293; Maj. William Wagner to Col. Charles Betts, April 19, 1865, Charles M. Betts papers, HSP; Kirk, *15th Pennsylvania*, 506–7; Morning Reports for Companies A–D, 15th Pennsylvania Cavalry, RR; Brotherton, *Lake Norman*, v, 120; Kirk, *15th Pennsylvania*, 506–7; Bradley, *Astounding Close*, 169–76, 198.

[25] Morning Reports for Companies A–D, 15th Pennsylvania Cavalry, RR; Maj. William Wagner to Col. Charles Betts, April 19, 1865, Charles M. Betts papers, HSP. Kirk, *15th Pennsylvania*, 506–7; Sherman, *Memoirs* 2: 333, 345; *OR* 47 (3): 151, 207. Raleigh newspapers of April 10 and a message from Halleck from the same date confirmed that Stoneman was near Greensboro, so Sherman had an idea of where to find the raiders.

[26] *OR* 47 (3): 245, 249; Report of AG, December 29, 1873, in U.S. Army Generals' Reports of Civil War Service, M1098, vol. IV, R19, p. 543–44, NA; Bradley, *Astounding Close*, 148.

[27] *CV* 10 (July 1902): 307; John Echols to Robert E. Lee, December 15, 1865, R.E. Lee headquarters papers, VHS; Report of AG, December 29, 1873, in U.S. Army Generals' Reports of Civil War Service, M1098, vol. IV, R19, p. 543–44, NA; *OR* 49 (1): 335; Morning Reports for Companies A–D, 15th Pennsylvania Cavalry, RR; Maj. William Wagner to Col. Charles Betts, April 19, 1865, Charles M. Betts papers, HSP; Kirk, *15th Pennsylvania*, 506–7; Diary entry for April 20, 1865, Charles F. Weller memoirs and letters, *Civil War Times Illustrated* Collection, USAMHI. Echols wrote from Salisbury, where he arrived on April 16 after placing Duke's and Vaughn's Brigades to cover Statesville and Charlotte. "Here I received the first full information in regard to the situation of affairs, and remained communicating by telegraph with and receiving orders from Gen. Johnston, then falling back from Raleigh to Greensboro," he wrote.

[28] Wilson, *Column South*, 293; *To the Members of the Society of the 15th Pennsylvania Cavalry*, 18th Annual Banquet, 25; Kirk, *15th Pennsylvania*, 564–65; *OR* 49 (1): 335; Report of AG, December 29, 1873, in U.S. Army Generals' Reports of Civil War Service, M1098, vol. IV, R19, p. 543–44, NA. According to Moderwell, "Outline of Stoneman's Raid," Civil War (Federal, Miscellaneous) papers, SHC, the cease-fire order did not arrive until April 23, but the evidence indicates that it occurred sooner. For the story of the couriers sent to Gillem, see the next chapter. For the acknowledgement, see *SHSP* 12 (1884): 102–3.

[29] Claim of Mary Carpenter, #4174, Box 225, Entry 732, Lincoln County, N.C., RG 217, Settled Files of the SCC, NA; Claim of George Ditherow, #3060, Box 225, Entry 732, Lincoln County, N.C., RG 217, Settled Files of the SCC, NA; Morning Reports for Companies A–D, 15th Pennsylvania Cavalry, RR; Sherrill, *Annals of Lincoln County*, 182; Wilson, *Recollections and Experiences*, 122.

[30] Kirk, *15th Pennsylvania*, 505–7; Barrett, *Civil War in North Carolina*, 361.

[31] Diary entries for April 19–22, 1865, Charles F. Weller memoirs and letters, *Civil War Times Illustrated* Collection, USAMHI; Frederic Antes diary, April 21, 1865, Civil War Miscellaneous Collection, USAMHI; Diary, April 20, 1865, Charles M. Betts papers, HSP; Wilson, *Column South*, 292–93; Morning Reports for Companies A–D, 15th Pennsylvania Cavalry, RR; Septimus W. Knight diary, April 21, 1865, VMI.

[32] *To the Members of the Society of the 15th Pennsylvania Cavalry*, 40th Annual Banquet, 37; Sample Autobiography, p. 14, CC; Wilson, *Recollections and Experiences*, 122; *OR Supplement* 57: 319; Kirk, *15th Pennsylvania*, 505–7, 518; *OR* 49 (1): 329, 335–36; Frederic Antes diary, April 18, 1865, Civil War Miscellaneous Collection, USAMHI; Morning Reports for Companies F–L, 15th Pennsylvania Cavalry, RR; Diary entry for April 18, 1865, Charles F. Weller memoirs and letters, *Civil War Times Illustrated* Collection, USAMHI; Mason, "Stoneman's Last Cam-

paign," 30; Wilson, *Recollections and Experiences*, 86–87.

[33] Kirk, *15th Pennsylvania*, 505–7; Frederic Antes diary, April 18, 1865, Civil War Miscellaneous Collection, USAMHI; Diary entry for April 18, 1865, Charles F. Weller memoirs and letters, *Civil War Times Illustrated* Collection, USAMHI; Mason, "Stoneman's Last Campaign," 30.

[34] Kirk, *15th Pennsylvania*, 505–6; Frederic Antes diary, April 18, 1865, Civil War Miscellaneous Collection, USAMHI; Diary entry for April 18, 1865, Charles F. Weller memoirs and letters, *Civil War Times Illustrated* Collection, USAMHI.

[35] Robertson, *Stonewall Jackson*, 175; "Reminiscence of Dr. Paul B. Barringer," Paul B. Barringer papers, 11–13, NCSA. As Robertson pointed out in his biography of Stonewall (note 119, p. 819), Barringer's writings are somewhat suspect as he was quite young at the time of the events he wrote about in relation to the Jackson family—including the event related in the text.

[36] Morning Reports for Companies A–D, 15th Pennsylvania Cavalry, RR; Frederic Antes diary, April 19, 1865, Civil War Miscellaneous Collection, USAMHI; Diary, April 19, 1865, Charles M. Betts papers, HSP.

[37] Diary, April 18, 1865, Charles M. Betts papers, HSP; Descriptive Lists for Companies G–M, 15th Pennsylvania Cavalry, RR. French was six feet tall, and had a light complexion. He had enlisted in August 1862, and was a member of Company I. The regimental history (Kirk, *15th Pennsylvania*, 506) claimed that French was shot while on picket duty. Betts's contemporary account is followed in the text.

[38] Kirk, *15th Pennsylvania*, 506; Wilson, *Recollections and Experiences*, 122; Diary, April 18, 1865, Charles M. Betts papers, HSP.

[39] Wilson, *Recollections and Experiences*, 122; Diary, April 18, 1865, Charles M. Betts papers, HSP; *To the Members of the 15th Pennsylvania Cavalry*, 30th Annual Banquet, 9; Kirk, *15th Pennsylvania*, 507.

[40] Trowbridge, "A Continuation of the Narrative of the Stoneman Raid of 1865," L.S. Trowbridge papers, UM.

[41] *OR Supplement* 57: 384; Morning Reports of Companies A–F, 10th Michigan Cavalry, RR; *Governor's Message in Relation to the Western North Carolina Railroad*, 12, 33; Steven Thomas to "My Dear Wife," June 5, 1865, Calvin Thomas papers, UM; *10th Cavalry*, vol. 40, 15; *History of the 10th Michigan*, 39; Trowbridge, "A Continuation of the Narrative of the Stoneman Raid of 1865," L.S. Trowbridge papers, UM.

[42] Septimus W. Knight diary, April 17, 1865, VMI; Wilson, *Column South*, 291.

[43] Septimus W. Knight diary, April 17, 1865, VMI; Wilson, *Column South*, 291; Morning Reports for Companies A–D, 15th Pennsylvania Cavalry, RR.

[44] Wilson, *Column South*, 291; Septimus W. Knight diary, April 18, 1865, VMI. Diary, April 19, 1865, Charles M. Betts papers, HSP. See Chapter 8 for more on the Vances and the trunk.

[45] Septimus W. Knight diary, April 19–20, 1865, VMI; Morning Reports for Companies A–D, 15th Pennsylvania Cavalry, RR; Angelo Wiser maps, LC. Morning reports state that the company returned to Lincolnton on April 21.

[46] Diary, April 17, 1865, Charles M. Betts papers, HSP; Maj. William Wagner to Col. Charles Betts, April 19, 1865, Charles M. Betts papers, HSP; *To the Members of the Society of the 15th Pennsylvania Cavalry*, 18th Annual Banquet, 25.

[47] *OR Supplement* 57: 319, 329; Morning Reports for Companies A–D, 15th Pennsylvania Cavalry, RR; Diary, April 17, 1865, Charles M. Betts papers, HSP. The morning report mentions "Plank bridge ford" as the site of the fight's conclusion, but there was no such location. The action probably took place at or near a key crossing southwest of Lincolnton, near present-day Belmont and Mount Holly.

[48] Diary of Annie Olympia Donnell, April 14, 1865, Loula Donnell papers, SHC; Duke,

Reminiscences, 462–65; Duke, *History of Morgan's Cavalry*, 624–26.

⁴⁹ Maj. William Wagner to Col. Charles Betts, April 19, 1865, Charles M. Betts papers, HSP; Angelo Wiser maps, LC.

⁵⁰ Maj. William Wagner to Col. Charles Betts, April 19, 1865, Charles M. Betts papers, HSP; Angelo Wiser maps, LC; Hoole, "Admiral on Horseback," 144. Beatty's Ford was eighteen miles from Lincolnton.

⁵¹ Maj. William Wagner to Col. Charles Betts, April 19, 1865, Charles M. Betts papers, HSP; Kirk, *15th Pennsylvania*, 506.

⁵² Morning Reports for Companies A–D, 15th Pennsylvania Cavalry, RR; Brotherton, *Lake Norman*, v, 120; Maj. William Wagner to Col. Charles Betts, April 19, 1865, Charles M. Betts papers, HSP. Kirk, *15th Pennsylvania*, 506–7. The dispatches included the messages from both Sherman and Thomas; see above. Alternative spellings for Beatty's include Beaties, Beaty's or Beatties. The Federals apparently preferred Beatty's, as confirmed by Angelo Wiser maps, LC.

⁵³ Morning Reports for Companies A–D, 15th Pennsylvania Cavalry, RR; Brotherton, *Lake Norman*, v, 120; Maj. William Wagner to Col. Charles Betts, April 19, 1865, Charles M. Betts papers, HSP. Sherrill's Ford, Beatty's Ford, and Cowan's Ford no longer exist, because the crossings lie under the waters of Lake Norman. The lake was created in the late 1950s and early 1960s with the construction of Duke Power Company dams at Cowan's Ford and elsewhere. The lake occupies 32,000 acres in Lincoln, Gaston, Catawba, Iredell, and Mecklenburg counties.

⁵⁴ A.G. Brenizer papers, NCSA; Warner, *Generals in Gray*, 162–63. Warner states that Johnston was sent in March 1865 to guard the Roanoke River and collect deserters, but Johnston does not mention this in his Brenizer papers account. Perhaps Warner meant the Catawba River. For a list of the Tennessee regiments under Vaughn, see *OR* 49 (1): 1022.

⁵⁵ A.G. Brenizer papers, NCSA.

⁵⁶ *Ibid.*

⁵⁷ *Illinois-Mollus War Papers*, 7: 382–84; *Minutes of the 22nd Annual Reunion, 12th Ohio Volunteer Cavalry*. After the war, Moderwell became the city attorney and mayor of Geneseo, Illinois. After suffering a severe cerebral hemorrhage and dropping into a coma, Moderwell died on November 25, 1906, at the age of sixty-eight. He was buried in Geneseo's Oakwood Cemetery. His wound at Mt. Sterling, Kentucky, in 1864 was thought to have contributed to his death.

⁵⁸ Mason, "Stoneman's Last Campaign," 30–31; Mason, *12th Ohio Cavalry*, 103; Moderwell, "Outline of Stoneman's Raid," Civil War (Federal, Miscellaneous) papers, SHC; Banks, "Memoranda," diary entry for April 18, 1865, 298. For an example of the movement of Confederate troops over the bridge, see *OR* 47 (3): 695. Some sources give Moderwell two hundred men; others, including Moderwell's own recollections, claim 250. Moderwell's recollection is followed in the text. Another account, Bushong, *Last Great Stoneman Raid*, stated incorrectly that the bridge was eighty miles away.

⁵⁹ Moderwell, "Outline of Stoneman's Raid," Civil War (Federal, Miscellaneous) papers, SHC; Smith, *Drama in April 1865*, 34; Mason, *12th Ohio Cavalry*, 103; *Official Roster* 11: 58. Mason places these events two days later than Moderwell and Banks. Banks's timing is presented in the text since it is based on a diary kept at the time.

⁶⁰ Banks, "Memoranda," diary entry for April 18, 1865, 298. The bridge stood near present-day Fort Mill, South Carolina (Smith, *Drama in April 1865*, 34; Blythe and Brockman, *Hornets' Nest*, 405).

⁶¹ Banks, "Memoranda," diary entry for April 18, 1865, 298; Mason, *12th Ohio Cavalry*, 103–4.

⁶² Mason, *12th Ohio Cavalry*, 103–4; Bushong, *Last Great Stoneman Raid*. There is no record of a Maj. E.M. Jones in the Confederate service.

⁶³ Bushong, *Last Great Stoneman Raid*; *Official Roster* 11: 58; Barrett, *Civil War in North Carolina*, 361; *Chronological Summary of Engagements and Battles*, CXL; Banks, "Memoranda," diary entry for April 19, 1865, 298–99; Bushong, *Last Great Stoneman Raid*; Mason, *12th Ohio*

Cavalry, 103–5; Moderwell, "Outline of Stoneman's Raid," Civil War (Federal, Miscellaneous) papers, SHC.

⁶⁴ Moderwell, "Outline of Stoneman's Raid," Civil War (Federal, Miscellaneous) papers, SHC; Banks, "Memoranda," diary entry for April 19, 1865, 298–99; Bushong, *Last Great Stoneman Raid*; Mason, *12th Ohio Cavalry*, 103–5; Trelease, *North Carolina Railroad*, 194.

⁶⁵ Moderwell, "Outline of Stoneman's Raid," Civil War (Federal, Miscellaneous) papers, SHC; Banks, "Memoranda," diary entry for April 19, 1865, 298–99; Bushong, *Last Great Stoneman Raid*; Mason, *12th Ohio Cavalry*, 105. In OR 47 (3): 818–19, 830, President Davis corresponded with Ferguson's command about replacing the bridge, either with a pontoon bridge or by establishing a ferry. Ferguson does not mention this in his memoirs.

⁶⁶ Bushong, *Last Great Stoneman Raid*; Mason, *12th Ohio Cavalry*, 105; Moderwell, "Outline of Stoneman's Raid," Civil War (Federal, Miscellaneous) papers, SHC; Banks, "Memoranda," diary entry for April 20, 1865, 299.

⁶⁷ Mason, "Stoneman's Last Campaign," 30–31; Mason, *12th Ohio Cavalry*, 103; Moderwell, "Outline of Stoneman's Raid," Civil War (Federal, Miscellaneous) papers, SHC; Bushong, *Last Great Stoneman Raid*; Mason, *12th Ohio Cavalry*, 105.

⁶⁸ Mason, "Stoneman's Last Campaign," 30, 31; Smith, *Drama in April 1865*, 33; *Guide to North Carolina Highway Historical Markers*, 120; Barrett, *Civil War in North Carolina*, 361; Mason, *12th Ohio Cavalry*, 106; Reid, *Ohio in the War* 2: 822; *Bucyrus Journal*, September 17, 1886. Dallas remained Gaston's county seat until 1911. Several alternative spellings exist for the ford, including Tuckasiege.

⁶⁹ Banks, "Memoranda," diary entry for April 21, 1865, 299.

⁷⁰ Ibid., 299–300.

⁷¹ Ovens, *If This Be Treason*, 107; Durkin, *John Dooley*, 193–94.

⁷² Bradley, *Astounding Close*, 301; Krick, *Lee's Colonels*, 195; Runyan, *Eight Days*, 14. Hoke was assigned to command the post in July 1864 (OR 40 [3]: 818).

⁷³ Barrett, *Civil War in North Carolina*, 361; Parker, *Recollections of a Naval Officer*, 355–56; Hanna, *Flight Into Oblivion*, 5–6, 31–32.

⁷⁴ Runyan, *Eight Days*, 14; Bumgarner, *Legacy of the Carolina and Northwestern Railway*, 1, 4–5.

⁷⁵ Entry for April 19, 1865, J.T. Wood diary, SHC; "Reminiscence of Dr. Paul B. Barringer," Paul B. Barringer papers, 45–50, NCSA; Arthur, "Checkmate, Mr. President," *The State*, January 1995, 13; Durkin, *John Dooley*, 197; Davis, *Jefferson Davis*, 619; Blythe and Brockman, *Hornets' Nest*, 404; Alexander, "Confederate States Navy Yard," 33. Paul Barringer's father was the North Carolina cavalry general, Rufus Barringer. Paul went on to become a leading physician. On pages 10–11 of his book, Barringer related how the Charlotte-to-Lincolnton mail coach passed through Concord. "We had ample notice because the driver of the mail coach had a long brass horn and regularly sounded it half a mile down the road," he wrote. "This day, while waiting, we heard other sounds from afar. Two or three rifle shots in the distance and the coming of a rider at full speed told us that the war had reached us, for we were expecting Stoneman's raid." A lone Confederate on a mule passed them, and threw a heavy object over a fence and into some shrubs as he passed. A half-dozen raiders rounded the bend behind him, firing as they rode. The man escaped by sliding off his mule and hiding but sending his mule onward. This story is suspect as there is no evidence that any raiders entered Concord. As for Mrs. Davis, she resided in a home at the corner of North Brevard and East Fifth streets.

⁷⁶ Hanna, *Flight Into Oblivion*, 45–47; Davis, *Jefferson Davis*, 619–20; *To the Members of the 15th Pennsylvania Cavalry*, 23rd Annual Banquet, 12; Duke, *Reminiscences*, 465–66; Wilson, *Recollections and Experiences*, 76–77.

⁷⁷ CV 10 (July 1902): 307; John Echols to Robert E. Lee, December 15, 1865, R.E. Lee headquarters papers, VHS; Davis, *Jefferson Davis*, 621–22; Hanna, *Flight Into Oblivion*, 50.

⁷⁸ Spencer, *Last Ninety Days*, 223.

[79] *OR* 49 (2): 407; Report of AG, December 29, 1873, in U.S. Army Generals' Reports of Civil War Service, M1098, vol. IV, R19, p. 543, NA.

[80] *Mountain Scenery*, 21–22; Inscoe and McKinney, *Heart of Confederate Appalachia*, 23; Entry for May 9, 1865, Fielder diaries, Courtesy THS.

[81] Erwin, *The Village That Disappeared*, 51.

[82] "Notes of Stoneman's Raid in Burke County, and the Town of Morganton," Cornelia P. Spencer papers, SHC; Clark, *Histories of the Several Regiments* 4: 376, 650; 5: 635; Krick, *Lee's Colonels*, 366–67; Spencer, *Last Ninety Days*, 223; *The News-Herald*, Feb. 20, 1930; Barrett, *Civil War in North Carolina*, 362; Cozzens, *No Better Place to Die*, 213–14; Warner, *Generals in Gray*, 199–200; Phifer, *Burke*, 327. Colonel Walton was 86 when he gave the account in vol. 5 of Clark's *Histories of the Several Regiments*.

[83] "Notes of Stoneman's Raid in Burke County, and the Town of Morganton," Cornelia P. Spencer papers, SHC; Spencer, *Last Ninety Days*, 223; *The News-Herald*, Feb. 20, 1930; Barrett, *Civil War in North Carolina*, 362; W.L. Twitty to Alphonso C. Avery, April 7, 1896, Alphonso C. Avery papers, SHC; Clark, *Histories of the Several Regiments* 4: 376, 5: 635; Scott, *13th Tennessee*, 239. The artillery piece the Confederates had is unknown. It is described in various sources as a Dahlgren piece, a "brass four inch howitzer," a little cannon, and a gun of large caliber.

[84] "Notes of Stoneman's Raid in Burke County, and the Town of Morganton," Cornelia P. Spencer papers, SHC; W.L. Twitty to Alphonso C. Avery, April 7, 1896, Alphonso C. Avery papers, SHC; Clark, *Histories of the Several Regiments* 4: 376. Sources disagree on the number of defenders, but it is certain that the force never reached one hundred strong.

[85] *OR* 49 (1): 329, 334; Extract from Report of Theodore Mallaby, Jr., W.J. Palmer Collection, Colorado Historical Society; April 17, 1865, Allen Frankenberry diaries, WV; "Notes of Stoneman's Raid in Burke County, and the Town of Morganton," Cornelia P. Spencer papers, SHC; Report of AG, December 29, 1873, in U.S. Army Generals' Reports of Civil War Service, M1098, vol. IV, R19, p. 543–44, NA. Mallaby's report of the fight at Morganton is dated April 18 in the Official Records, but that date is rendered correctly as the 17 in his manuscript report at the Colorado Historical Society.

[86] W.L. Twitty to Alphonso C. Avery, April 7, 1896, Alphonso C. Avery papers, SHC; "Notes of Stoneman's Raid in Burke County, and the Town of Morganton," Cornelia P. Spencer papers, SHC.

[87] April 17, 1865, Henry Birdsall diary, SHC; Clark, *Histories of the Several Regiments* 5: 635; "Notes of Stoneman's Raid in Burke County, and the Town of Morganton," Cornelia P. Spencer papers, SHC; *Heritage of Burke County*, 16; April 17, 1865, Allen Frankenberry diaries, WV. Besides West, the gunners were Lieutenant Peters, John Sherman, David Hennessee, William Kellar, and Daniel Stacy. Another source, Clark, *Histories of the Several Regiments* 5: 635, states that Lt. Mark Erwin commanded the cannon.

[88] "Notes of Stoneman's Raid in Burke County, and the Town of Morganton," Cornelia P. Spencer papers, SHC; *The News-Herald*, Feb. 20, 1930; W.L. Twitty to Alphonso C. Avery, April 7, 1896, Alphonso C. Avery papers, SHC; Spencer, *Last Ninety Days*, 223; Clark, *Histories of the Several Regiments* 5: 635; Barrett, *Civil War in North Carolina*, 362; *Heritage of Burke County*, 16; *OR* 49 (1): 334–35.

[89] "Notes of Stoneman's Raid in Burke County, and the Town of Morganton," Cornelia P. Spencer papers, SHC; Erwin, *The Village That Disappeared*, 52; Samuel F. Patterson to Rufus L. Patterson, April 19, 1865, Patterson papers, NCSA; Barrett, *Civil War in North Carolina*, 362; *OR* 49 (1): 334; *OR Supplement* 65: 550, 554, 556, 561; *The News-Herald*, Feb. 20, 1930; Spencer, *Last Ninety Days*, 223–24; Clark, *Histories of the Several Regiments* 5: 635; *Heritage of Burke County*, 16. Miller's brigade apparently bore the brunt of the fight, but the 11th Michigan was engaged on April 17 (*Annual Report of the Adjutant General of Michigan* 1: 98; Robertson, *Michigan in the War*, 738).

[90] "Notes of Stoneman's Raid in Burke County, and the Town of Morganton," Cornelia P. Spencer papers, SHC.

⁹¹ Davis, "Prominent People in Early Burke County," Civil War clipping file, Morganton Public Library, Morganton, N.C.; "Notes of Stoneman's Raid in Burke County, and the Town of Morganton," Cornelia P. Spencer papers, SHC; *Heritage of Burke County*, 16; Johnson, *Touring the Carolinas' Civil War Sites*, 117–18; *The News-Herald*, Feb. 20, 1930; *OR* 49 (1): 329, 334–35; Extract from Report of Theodore Mallaby, Jr., William J. Palmer Collection, CHS; Clark, *Histories of the Several Regiments* 5: 635.

⁹² *OR* 49 (1): 329; Extract from Report of Theodore Mallaby, Jr., William J. Palmer Collection, CHS; W.L. Twitty to Alphonso C. Avery, April 7, 1896, Alphonso C. Avery papers, SHC. Twitty recalled that the Confederates had two guns present, but the evidence points to the presence of only one artillery piece.

⁹³ *OR* 49 (1): 329; Extract from Report of Theodore Mallaby, Jr., William J. Palmer Collection, CHS; W.L. Twitty to Alphonso C. Avery, April 7, 1896, Alphonso C. Avery papers, SHC; *The News-Herald*, Feb. 20, 1930.

⁹⁴ *OR* 49 (1): 334–35; Barrett, *Civil War in North Carolina*, 362; April 17, 1865, Allen Frankenberry diaries, WV; Report of AG, December 29, 1873, in U.S. Army Generals' Reports of Civil War Service, M1098, vol. IV, R19, p. 543–44, NA; Scott, *13th Tennessee*, 239.

⁹⁵ "Notes of Stoneman's Raid in Burke County, and the Town of Morganton," Cornelia P. Spencer papers, SHC; *The News-Herald*, Feb. 20, 1930; *Heritage of Burke County*, 16; Clark, *Histories of the Several Regiments* 5: 635.

⁹⁶ Louisa Norwood to Walter Lenoir, April 24, 1865, Lenoir papers, SHC; *Lenoir News-Topic*, September 12, 1941.

⁹⁷ Spencer, *Last Ninety Days*, 223; Johnson, *Touring the Carolinas' Civil War Sites*, 117–18; *The News-Herald*, Feb. 20, 1930; "Notes of Stoneman's Raid in Burke County, and the Town of Morganton," Cornelia P. Spencer papers, SHC; Morning Reports for the 13th Tennessee Cavalry, April 15, April 22, 1865, RR; *OR Supplement* 65: 550, 554, 556, 561–62, 637; *OR* 49 (1): 329, 335; Extract from Report of Theodore Mallaby, Jr., William J. Palmer Collection, CHS; W.L. Twitty to Alphonso C. Avery, April 7, 1896, Alphonso C. Avery papers, SHC. The Tennessee cavalryman was shot in the arm.

⁹⁸ Clark, *Histories of the Several Regiments* 5: 635–36; W.L. Twitty to Alphonso C. Avery, April 7, 1896, Alphonso C. Avery papers, SHC.

⁹⁹ April 17, 1865, Henry Birdsall diary, SHC.

¹⁰⁰ "Notes of Stoneman's Raid in Burke County, and the Town of Morganton," Cornelia P. Spencer papers, SHC; Trotter, *Bushwhackers*, 283; Louisa Norwood to Walter Lenoir, April 24, 1865, Lenoir papers, SHC; *Lenoir News-Topic*, September 12, 1941.

¹⁰¹ "Notes of Stoneman's Raid in Burke County, and the Town of Morganton," Cornelia P. Spencer papers, SHC; Davis, "Prominent People in Early Burke County," Civil War clipping file, Morganton Public Library, Morganton, N.C.; *Heritage of Burke County*, 16.

¹⁰² *Heritage of Burke County*, 16; Alexander, *Here Will I Dwell*, 142; April 14 & 17, 1865, Henry Birdsall diary, SHC; Report of AG, December 29, 1873, in U.S. Army Generals' Reports of Civil War Service, M1098, vol. IV, R19, p. 543–44, NA; Barchfield's Memoranda, Arnell Collection, UT.

¹⁰³ April 17, 1865, Allen Frankenberry diaries, WV.

¹⁰⁴ "Notes of Stoneman's Raid in Burke County, and the Town of Morganton," Cornelia P. Spencer papers, SHC.

¹⁰⁵ Ibid.

¹⁰⁶ Louisa Norwood to Walter Lenoir, April 24, 1865, Lenoir papers, SHC; *Lenoir News-Topic*, September 12, 1941; *The News-Herald*, Feb. 20, 1930.

¹⁰⁷ *Governor's Message in Relation to the Western North Carolina Railroad*, 6–7, 32; R.L. Beall's account of Stoneman's Raid, Cornelia Phillips Spencer papers, SHC; Beall, "Stoneman's Raid," *The North Carolina Review*, December 4, 1910; Spencer, *Last Ninety Days*, 223–24; *The Morganton Herald*, April 16, 1891; Phifer, *Burke*, 327; Johnson, *Touring the Carolinas' Civil War Sites*, 118;

Historic Sites Inventory, 36; Erwin, *The Village That Disappeared*, 52–53; "Notes of Stoneman's Raid in Burke County, and the Town of Morganton," Cornelia P. Spencer papers, SHC.

[108] April 18, 1865, Allen Frankenberry diaries, WV.

[109] *OR* 49 (2): 407; *The News-Herald*, Feb. 20, 1930; April 19, 1865, Henry Birdsall diary, SHC; April 19, 1865, Allen Frankenberry diaries, WV; Scott, *13th Tennessee*, 239. According to the 1930 newspaper account, the raiders followed what was then N.C. 10 toward Asheville.

[110] "Notes of Stoneman's Raid in Burke County, and the Town of Morganton," Cornelia P. Spencer papers, SHC; Phifer, *Burke*, 327; Davis, "Prominent People in Early Burke County," Civil War clipping file, Morganton Public Library, Morganton, N.C.; *Heritage of Burke County*, 16.

[111] "Notes of Stoneman's Raid in Burke County, and the Town of Morganton," Cornelia P. Spencer papers, SHC; *The News-Herald*, Feb. 20, 1930.

Chapter 10
God Only Knows What Will Be the End of This
Marion to Mooresboro: April 19–30, 1865

[1] Kirk, *15th Pennsylvania*, 564; Report of AG, December 29, 1873, in U.S. Army Generals' Reports of Civil War Service, M1098, vol. IV, R19, p. 543–44, NA. Reppert has left several accounts of this mission, which conflict regarding the number of men, varying from six to eight.

[2] *To the Members of the Society of the 15th Pennsylvania Cavalry*, 18th Annual Banquet, 25.

[3] *To the Members of the Society of the 15th Pennsylvania Cavalry*, 18th Annual Banquet, 25, 564–65.

[4] Inscoe and McKinney, *Heart of Confederate Appalachia*, 122; Trotter, *Bushwhackers*, 62–63, 95, 106–7, 126–27; Warner, *Generals in Gray*, 213–14; Clark, *Histories of the Several Regiments* 4: 371; *OR* 31 (3): 711; *OR* 33 (3): 741–42, 865; *OR* 39 (1): 235; *OR* 40 (2): 699, 772, 788; Series 4, 3: 822–23; Arthur, *Western North Carolina*, 621; Stevens, *Rebels in Blue*, 131; Robertson, *Stonewall Jackson*, 50, 59; Ready, *Asheville*, 29; Barrett, *Civil War in North Carolina*, 129, 211, 254.

[5] *OR* 42 (3): 1279; Series 4, 3: 520; Ready, *Asheville*, 29; Evans, *Confederate Military History* 5: 280; Trotter, *Bushwhackers*, 235–36; Crow, *Storm in the Mountains*, 112–13; Clark, *Histories of the Several Regiments* 4: 372–73.

[6] Clark, *Histories of the Several Regiments* 4: 372–73; Ready, *Asheville*, 29; Evans, *Confederate Military History* 5: 280; Inscoe and McKinney, *Heart of Confederate Appalachia*, 164; *OR* 47 (3): 730–31; *OR* 49 (1): 1034–35; Trotter, *Bushwhackers*, 235–42.

[7] Crow, *Storm in the Mountains*, 125–26; *OR* 49 (1): 20, 31–34; *OR* (2): 534. For Martin's warnings about the raid, see Chapter 3.

[8] Ready, *Asheville*, 30; *Asheville Citizen-Times*, July 17, 1960, Civil War clipping file, Pack Memorial Library, Asheville, N.C.; Sondley, "The Battle of Asheville," *Asheville Citizen*, October 9, 1924, Civil War clipping file, Pack Memorial Library, Asheville, N.C.; Day, *Story of the One Hundred and First Ohio*, 324; Crow, *Storm in the Mountains*, 125–26; Trotter, *Bushwhackers*, 292–94; *CV* 8 (June 1900): 277–78; Langley, *Yesterday's Asheville*, 9–10, 28; Ready, *Asheville*, 31; *Asheville Citizen Times*, March 31, 1963, Civil War clipping file, Pack Memorial Library; *Enka-Candler Record*, April 7, 1865, Pack Memorial Library, Asheville, N.C.

[9] *OR* 49 (1): 333, 338–39, 381; *OR* 49 (2): 381–8, 438–39; Miller, *Our Service in East Tennessee*, 17–18.

[10] Downs, "About the Time of the 'Surrender,'" 5–6; Barrett, *Civil War in North Carolina*, 362; Moderwell, "Outline of Stoneman's Raid," Civil War (Federal, Miscellaneous) papers, SHC; Bumgarner, *Kirk's Raiders*, 69; *OR* 49 (2): 407; Report of AG, December 29, 1873, in U.S. Army Generals' Reports of Civil War Service, M1098, vol. IV, R19, p. 543, NA; Mason, "Stoneman's Last Campaign," 29; R.L. Beall's account of Stoneman's Raid, Cornelia Phillips Spencer papers, SHC; Beall, "Stoneman's Raid," *The North Carolina Review*, November 11, 1910; Spencer, *Last Ninety Days*, 195.

[11] *Cincinnati Daily Commercial*, May 10, 1865; *OR* 49 (2): 407–8.

[12] *OR* 49 (2): 437; General Order No. 24, April 22, 1865, General Orders Issued by the District of East Tennessee, Records of U.S. Army Continental Commands, RG 393, pt. 2, entry 2749, NA; April 25, 1865, Letters Sent, District of East Tennessee, Records of U.S. Army continental commands, RG 393, pt. 2, entry 2740, NA.

[13] *OR Supplement* 65: 637; Barrett, *Civil War in North Carolina*, 362; *OR* 49 (1): 329; April 19, 1865, Allen Frankenberry diaries, WV; Scott, *13th Tennessee*, 239. Barchfield's Memoranda, Arnell Collection, UT, confirms the itinerary but is incorrect on the date.

[14] *Mountain Scenery*, 21–22; Fossett, *History of McDowell*, 28–29; *Lenoir News-Topic*, September 12, 1941; *In Memoriam*, 3–4, 9, 18, Emma L. Rankin papers, SHC. Emma Rankin died on February 28, 1908.

[15] *In Memoriam*, 18–19, 20, 22–24, Emma L. Rankin papers, SHC.

[16] *In Memoriam*, 24–25, Emma L. Rankin papers, SHC; Fossett, *History of McDowell*, 28–29.

[17] *In Memoriam*, 25, Emma L. Rankin papers, SHC.

[18] *In Memoriam*, 25–26, Emma L. Rankin papers, SHC. A rumor had it that a raider was killed in the skirmish, but Federal records do not mention it.

[19] *In Memoriam*, 26–27, Emma L. Rankin papers, SHC.

[20] R.L. Beall's account of Stoneman's Raid, Cornelia Phillips Spencer papers, SHC; Beall, "Stoneman's Raid," *The North Carolina Review*, December 4, 1910; Trotter, *Bushwhackers*, 284; *In Memoriam*, 32, Emma L. Rankin papers, SHC.

[21] *In Memoriam*, 26–28, Emma L. Rankin papers, SHC; R.L. Beall's account of Stoneman's Raid, Cornelia Phillips Spencer papers, SHC; Beall, "Stoneman's Raid," *The North Carolina Review*, December 4, 1910; Trotter, *Bushwhackers*, 284.

[22] *In Memoriam*, 29, Emma L. Rankin papers, SHC. Emma Rankin recalled years later that April 20 dawned clear, but she was in error as Frankenberry's contemporary account verifies.

[23] *In Memoriam*, 30–31, Emma L. Rankin papers, SHC; *Union Regiments of Kentucky*, 231.

[24] Scott, *13th Tennessee*, 239; *OR* 49 (1): 335; April 20, 1865, Henry Birdsall diary, SHC; April 20, 1865, Allen Frankenberry diaries, WV.

[25] Allen, *Annals of Haywood*, 90; "Relative to Civil War," Civil War clippings file, Pack Memorial Library, Asheville, N.C.; Trotter, *Bushwhackers*, 67–71; Barrett, *Civil War in North Carolina*, 196; Crow, *Storm in the Mountains*, 126–27; "A Mountain Tragedy," George E. Lee papers, SHC; Arthur, *Western North Carolina*, 619.

[26] Clark, *Histories of the Several Regiments* 4: 376; "A Mountain Tragedy," George E. Lee papers, SHC; Interview with George Fortune, Civil War clipping file, Pack Memorial Library, Asheville, N.C. The soldiers belonged to Capt. John Carson's company of Avery's 17th Battalion. Carson was a veteran of the 6th North Carolina who had been disabled at Sharpsburg.

[27] April 20, 1865, Allen Frankenberry diaries, WV; *OR* 49 (1): 335; Report of AG, December 29, 1873, in U.S. Army Generals' Reports of Civil War Service, M1098, vol. IV, R19, p. 543–44, NA; *Annual Report of the Adjutant General of Michigan* 1: 98.

[28] *OR Supplement* 65: 563; Scott, *13th Tennessee*, 494; "A Mountain Tragedy," George E. Lee papers, SHC; Allen, *Annals of Haywood*, 90; "Relative to Civil War;" *Asheville Citizen-Times*, May 22, 2000, "Relate's Story of Prisoner's Death," "More Details of the Lonely Mountain Grave," and Interview with Charles Wesley White, all in clipping file, Pack Memorial Library, Asheville, N.C. The author wishes to thank Mr. Dan Slagle for providing helpful information about the history of the gap and a guided tour of Bill's gravesite. One account says that Bill belonged to a four-man patrol Love sent down the mountain. Laurel bushes and other mountain foliage impeded sight lines. "Before they knew, the foremost men of either party were breast to breast, so close that they could not use their guns," the account claims. The two in front grabbed each other; the Confederate pinned his opponent's arms, grabbed his foe's knife, and then plunged it into the man's breast. The Federal sank to the ground; his comrades ran away, shouting "Come on, Bill," but Bill was dead. This account does not ring true, because the approaching raiders would probably

have been mounted, not on foot, and the grave is marked for a Federal soldier, not a Confederate soldier.

²⁹ Crow, *Storm in the Mountains*, 126–27; April 20, 1865, Henry Birdsall diary, SHC; April 20, 1865, Allen Frankenberry diaries, WV; *OR* 49 (1): 329, 335; Dyer, *Compendium* 3: 1642; Arthur, *Western North Carolina*, 619; Report of AG, December 29, 1873, in U.S. Army Generals' Reports of Civil War Service, M1098, vol. IV, R19, p. 543–44, NA.

³⁰ *In Memoriam*, 33–34, 36–40, Emma L. Rankin papers, SHC; Barchfield's Memoranda, Arnell Collection, UT; R.L. Beall's account of Stoneman's Raid, Cornelia Phillips Spencer papers, SHC; Beall, "Stoneman's Raid," *The North Carolina Review*, December 4, 1910. Emma identified Davis's superior officer as a Colonel Howard, but there were no officers by that name in the 11th Kentucky. Perhaps the officer was Maj. Frederick Slater, then the commander of the regiment, or the commander of Davis's Company F, Robert S. Curd (*Union Regiments of Kentucky*, 231).

³¹ *OR* 49 (1): 329, 335; April 22, 1865, Allen Frankenberry diaries, WV; Report of AG, December 29, 1873, in U.S. Army Generals' Reports of Civil War Service, M1098, vol. IV, R19, 543–44, NA; Crow, *Storm in the Mountains*, 126–27; *Annual Report of the Adjutant General of Michigan* 1: 99; Robertson, *Michigan in the War*, 738; April 21–22, 1865, Henry Birdsall diary, SHC; *Annual Report of the Adjutant General of Michigan* 1: 98. The latter source misdates the Rutherfordton arrival of the 11th Michigan to April 20.

³² April 22, 1865, Allen Frankenberry diaries, WV. Frankenberry was probably referring to Bradley Falls, which today can be seen off Holbert Cove Road near Interstate 26 in Polk County, North Carolina.

³³ Ray, "Asheville in 1865;" *CV* 6 (June 1898): 263.

³⁴ *OR* 49 (1): 335; Patton, *Sketches of Polk*, 45–46; *Guide to North Carolina Highway Historical Markers*, 117; Crow, *Storm in the Mountains*, 127; Arthur, *Western North Carolina*, 619; April 22, 1865, Allen Frankenberry diaries, WV. In 1873, AG mistakenly wrote that he found the gap "entirely undefended" (Report of AG, December 29, 1873, in U.S. Army Generals' Reports of Civil War Service, M1098, vol. IV, R19, 543–44, NA); Scott, *13th Tennessee*, 239–40.

³⁵ Ray, "Asheville in 1865;" *CV* 6 (June 1898): 263; *OR* 49 (1): 329, 335–36; *OR Supplement* 65: 550, 554, 556, 615; Dyer, *Compendium* 3: 1642; April 23, 1865, Allen Frankenberry diaries, WV; April 23, 1865, Henry Birdsall diary, SHC; *OR* 49 (1): 329; Report of AG, December 29, 1873, in U.S. Army Generals' Reports of Civil War Service, M1098, vol. IV, R19, p. 543–44, NA; *Union Army* 4: 354; *Union Regiments of Kentucky*, 228, 236; Crow, *Storm in the Mountains*, 127; "MacBeth Light Artillery," Civil War clipping file, Pack Memorial Library, Asheville, N.C.; *Report of the Adjutant General of Michigan* 1: 98; Jones, *Heritage of Henderson County* 2: 57. Reportedly the battery's horses were in poor condition at the time, no doubt a key reason for capture. The artillery unit had originally been ordered to the district in May 1864 (*OR* 34 [2]: 470).

³⁶ *To the Members of the Society of the 15th Pennsylvania Cavalry*, 18th Annual Banquet, 25, 564–65.

³⁷ April 22–23, 1865, Allen Frankenberry diaries, WV; Report of AG, December 29, 1873, in U.S. Army Generals' Reports of Civil War Service, M1098, vol. IV, R19, p. 543–44, NA; *OR* 49 (1): 335; Kirk, *15th Pennsylvania*, 507; *OR Supplement* 65: 615. According to Frankenberry, news of the armistice first reached the column at Rutherfordton, but the sequence of events in AG's report place it on April 23 at Hendersonville. For the controversy over GS's role in Davis's escape, see Chapter 12.

³⁸ Claim of A.E. Phillips, #16668, Box 223, Entry 732, Henderson County, N.C., RG 217, Settled Files of the SCC, NA; *Michigan in the War* 41: 1; Claim of James Jimison, #7655; Claim of James Drake, #3399, Claim of Walter Williams, #19055; all in Box 223, Entry 732, Henderson County, N.C., RG 217, Settled Files of the SCC, NA.

³⁹ Trotter, *Bushwhackers*, 175; Capers, *Life and Times of Memminger*, 365, 370–72; Boatner, *Civil War Dictionary*, 542; April 23, 1865, Allen Frankenberry diaries, WV; Grizzle, "Hender-

sonville," *Our State* 69 (September 2001): 115–16; *Winston-Salem Journal*, November 1, 1998; FitzSimons, *From the Banks of the Oklawaha* 2: 111–13. According to local legend, the Great Seal of the Confederacy lies buried beneath Glassy Mountain. Memminger died in 1888, and the author-poet Carl Sandburg moved into Memminger's home in 1945. Calling the home Connemara, Sandburg published more than a third of his works during his twenty-two years there. Today the house is a National Park Service site.

[40] *Annual Report of the Adjutant General of Michigan* 1: 99; Robertson, *Michigan in the War*, 738; Descriptive Book for Companies A–K, 11th Michigan Cavalry, RR; Bynum, *Heritage of Rutherford*, xxii; Scott, *13th Tennessee*, 240; FitzSimons, *From the Banks of the Oklawaha* 2: 190; Jones, *Heritage of Henderson County* 2: 57; Hughes, *Hendersonville in Civil War Times*, 26; Patton, *Story of Henderson County*, 129.

[41] Allen, *Annals of Haywood*, 90; "Relative to Civil War," Civil War clippings file, Pack Memorial Library, Asheville, N.C.; Ward, *Heritage of Old Buncombe*, 44; Van Noppen, *Western North Carolina*, 83. A ghost story is also told in Fletcher about a young woman who died after learning of her husband's death in the war. It is said that she rides the roads of Fletcher on a palomino horse. Supposedly twenty-three raiders were killed after following the specter into a Confederate ambush, but no such casualties were incurred ("The Phantom Rider," http://www.prairieghosts.com/episcopal.html).

[42] Morning Reports of Companies A–F, 10th Michigan Cavalry, RR; *OR Supplement* 57: 319, 329, 384; Mason, *12th Ohio Cavalry*, 106; Morning Reports for Companies A–D and F–L, 15th Pennsylvania Cavalry, RR; Frederic Antes diary, April 23, 1865, Civil War Miscellaneous Collection, USAMHI; Diary entry for April 23, 1865, Charles F. Weller memoirs and letters, *Civil War Times Illustrated* Collection, USAMHI; Wilson, *Column South*, 293; Diary, April 20, 1865, Charles M. Betts papers, HSP; Angelo Wiser maps, LC; Septimus W. Knight diary, April 24, 1865, VMI; Kirk, *15th Pennsylvania*, 507; Steven Thomas to "My Dear Wife," June 5, 1865, Calvin Thomas papers, UM.

[43] Kirk, *15th Pennsylvania*, 507–8; Wilson, *Column South*, 294; Wilson, *Recollections and Experiences*, 122.

[44] "Mr. Sondley's Work," *Asheville Citizen*, May 27, 1918, Civil War clipping file, Pack Memorial Library, Asheville, N.C.; Van Noppen, *Stoneman's Last Raid*, 85; *OR* 49 (1): 329, 335–36; Crow, *Storm in the Mountains*, 127–28; Statement of Alvan C. Gillem, June 5, 1865, Register of Letters Received and Endorsements Sent, 1st Cavalry Division, Department of the Cumberland, Records of U.S. Army continental commands, RG 393, Pt. 1, Entry 2774, NA; Tessier, *State of Buncombe*, 36; *Asheville Citizen-Times*, July 17, 1960, Civil War clipping file, Pack Memorial Library, Asheville, N.C. For the weather that day, see April 24, 1865, Allen Frankenberry diaries, WV.

[45] Statement of Alvan C. Gillem, June 5, 1865, Register of Letters Received and Endorsements Sent, 1st Cavalry Division, Department of the Cumberland, Records of U.S. Army continental commands, RG 393, Pt. 1, Entry 2774, NA; "The Edney Letter," June 19, 1865; "Mr. Sondley's Work," *Asheville Citizen*, May 27, 1918, Civil War clipping file, Pack Memorial Library, Asheville, N.C.; *OR* 47 (3) 244–45; *OR* 49 (1): 329, 335–36; Crow, *Storm in the Mountains*, 127–28; Bradley, *This Astounding Close*, 172. Charles Weller delivered a dispatch to AG that evening, arriving "tired and hungry" (Diary entry for April 24, 1865, Charles F. Weller memoirs and letters, *Civil War Times Illustrated* Collection, USAMHI). The contents of the dispatch are unknown, but presumably it was from Palmer.

[46] Inscoe, *Mountain Masters*, 265–66; Inscoe and McKinney, *Heart of Confederate Appalachia*, 5–6, 9, 19, 23–24, 74–75, 211; Benjamin Sloan, "Reminiscent: Making Implements of War for the Confederates," Civil War clipping file, Pack Memorial Library, Asheville, N.C.; *Enka-Candler Record*, April 7, 1865, Pack Memorial Library, Asheville, N.C.; Ray, "Asheville in 1865;" *CV* 6 (June 1898): 263; Langley, *Yesterday's Asheville*, 28; Trotter, *Bushwhackers*, 175, 291; Ready,

Asheville, 27, 28; Ella Reed Matthews, "Our Town in the War Between the States," Civil War clipping file, Pack Memorial Library, Asheville, N.C.; McKinney, "Premature Industrialization," 233.

[47] Robertson, *Small Boy's Recollections*, 97; *OR* 49 (1): 336; "The Edney Letter," June 19, 1865; Scott, *13th Tennessee*, 240–41; April 25, 1865, Allen Frankenberry diaries, WV; "Mr. Sondley's Work," *Asheville Citizen*, May 27, 1918, Civil War clipping file, Pack Memorial Library, Asheville, N.C.; April 25, 1865, Henry Birdsall diary, SHC; *OR* 47 (3) 244–45; *OR* 49 (1): 329, 335–36; Crow, *Storm in the Mountains*, 127–28; *OR Supplement* 65: 615; Bradley, *This Astounding Close*, 172; Ray, "Asheville in 1865;" *CV* 6 (June 1898): 263.

[48] Bradley, *This Astounding Close*, 206–9.

[49] Bradley, *This Astounding Close*, 209–11; *OR* 47 (3): 334, 457–58; Sherman, *Memoirs* 2: 358.

[50] GS to AG, April 24, 1865, Part 2, Entry 2740, Letters Sent, District of East Tennessee, RG 393, NA; *OR* 49 (2): 457–58; Report of AG, December 29, 1873, in U.S. Army Generals' Reports of Civil War Service, M1098, vol. IV, R19, p. 543, NA.

[51] Scott, *13th Tennessee*, 240–41; *OR* 49 (2): 475; *OR Supplement* 65: 615; April 25, 1865, Allen Frankenberry diaries, WV; April 25–26, 1865, Henry Birdsall diary, SHC. In his postwar general's report, AG stated that he received these orders on April 25, but the sequence of events suggests that April 26 is the correct date (Report of AG, December 29, 1873, in U.S. Army Generals' Reports of Civil War Service, M1098, vol. IV, R19, p. 543, NA); *10th Cavalry*, vol. 40, 15; *History of the 10th Michigan*, 39; Steven Thomas to "My Dear Wife," June 5, 1865, Calvin Thomas papers, UM.

[52] *OR Supplement* 65: 573, 637; *OR* 49 (2): 475, 508. The artillery arrived in Greeneville on April 30 but AG arrived that same afternoon of April 26.

[53] *OR* 49 (1): 329; April 26, 1865, Allen Frankenberry diaries, WV; Crow, *Storm in the Mountains*, 128; "The Edney Letter," June 19, 1865; April 25, 1865, Henry Birdsall diary, SHC; Ward, *Heritage of Old Buncombe*, 7; Marcus Lafayette Reed, Jr., "Swannanoa Valley Civil War Men," Copy courtesy of Dan Slagle; James G. Martin to Cornelia Phillips Spencer, June 27, 1866, Cornelia Phillips Spencer papers, SHC.

[54] *OR* 49 (1): 329; April 26, 1865, Allen Frankenberry diaries, WV; Crow, *Storm in the Mountains*, 128; "The Edney Letter," June 19, 1865; Ward, *Heritage of Old Buncombe*, 7; Marcus Lafayette Reed, Jr., "Swannanoa Valley Civil War Men," copy courtesy of Mr. Dan Slagle; James G. Martin to Cornelia Phillips Spencer, June 27, 1866, Cornelia Phillips Spencer papers, SHC; Scott, *13th Tennessee*, 241; *Annual Report of the Adjutant General of Michigan* 1: 99; Robertson, *Michigan in the War*, 738; *OR Supplement* 65: 550, 554, 563; April 27, 1865, Henry Birdsall diary, SHC; *Annual Report of the Adjutant General of Michigan* 1: 98.

[55] "Plundering in Asheville is Described by Rockwell," *Asheville Citizen-Times*, January 28, 1962, in Civil War clipping file, Pack Memorial Library, Asheville, N.C.; Ray, "Asheville in 1865;" *CV* 6 (June 1898): 263; James G. Martin to Cornelia Phillips Spencer, June 27, 1866, Cornelia Phillips Spencer papers, SHC; *Asheville Citizen Times*, March 31, 1963, Civil War clipping file, Pack Memorial Library, Asheville, N.C.; "The Edney Letter," June 19, 1865.

[56] James G. Martin to Cornelia Phillips Spencer, June 27, 1866, Cornelia Phillips Spencer papers, SHC.

[57] "Col. Ray Tells Story of Wild Night of Fear," Civil War clipping file, Pack Memorial Library, Asheville, N.C.; "Mr. Sondley's Work," *Asheville Citizen*, May 27, 1918, Civil War clipping file, Pack Memorial Library, Asheville, N.C.

[58] *OR* 49 (1): 329; *Annual Report of the Adjutant General of Michigan* 1: 99; Robertson, *Michigan in the War*, 738; Scott, *13th Tennessee*, 241; *Annual Report of the Adjutant General of Michigan* 1: 98; *OR Supplement* 65: 550, 554, 563; Ray, "Asheville in 1865;" *CV* 6 (June 1898): 263; James G. Martin to Cornelia Phillips Spencer, June 27, 1866, Cornelia Phillips Spencer papers, SHC; *Asheville Citizen Times*, March 31, 1963, Civil War clipping file, Pack Memorial Library, Asheville, N.C.; "Plundering in Asheville is Described by Rockwell," *Asheville Citizen-*

Times, January 28, 1962, in Civil War clipping file, Pack Memorial Library, Asheville, N.C.; "Col. Ray Tells Story of Wild Night of Fear," Civil War clipping file, Pack Memorial Library, Asheville, N.C.; Scott, *13th Tennessee,* 241.

[59] "The Edney Letter," June 19, 1865.

[60] Robertson, *Small Boy's Recollections,* 18, 83, 98, 100, 105.

[61] "The Edney Letter," June 19, 1865; Robertson, *Small Boy's Recollections,* 108–9; Unknown to "My Dear Brother," August 14, 1865, Lenoir papers, SHC; Marcus Lafayette Reed, Jr., "Swannanoa Valley Civil War Men," copy courtesy of Mr. Dan Slagle.

[62] Marcus Lafayette Reed, Jr., "Swannanoa Valley Civil War Men," copy courtesy of Mr. Dan Slagle; April 26–27, 1865, Allen Frankenberry diaries, WV.

[63] Robertson, *Small Boy's Recollections,* 102–3.

[64] James G. Martin to Cornelia Phillips Spencer, June 27, 1866, Cornelia Phillips Spencer papers, SHC; James G. Martin to AG, May 23 & 26, 1865 and C.W. Polk to AG, May 31, 1865, all in Register of Letters and Endorsements Sent, District of East Tennessee, Records of U.S. Army continental commands, RG 393, pt. 2, entry 2774, NA.

[65] Bvt. Brig. Gen. William J. Palmer to Brig. Gen. J.G. Martin, April 28, 1865, Cornelia Phillips Spencer papers, SHC; Van Noppen, *Stoneman's Last Raid,* 90; Crow, *Storm in the Mountains,* 128.

[66] Descriptive Book for Companies G–M, 13th Tennessee Cavalry, RR; Morning Reports for Companies A–F, 10th Michigan Cavalry, RR; Descriptive Book for Companies A–E, 10th Michigan Cavalry, RR.

[67] Davis, *Jefferson Davis,* 625–26; Hanna, *Flight Into Oblivion,* 52–53; Memoirs of S.W. Ferguson, Heyward and Ferguson family papers, SHC; Duke, *Reminiscences,* 462–68; Duke, *History of Morgan's Cavalry,* 624–26.

[68] Mason, *12th Ohio Cavalry,* 106; CV 39 (December 1926): 452; Entry for April 25, 1865, J.T. Wood diary, SHC; Hanna, *Flight Into Oblivion,* 58.

[69] Duke, *History of Morgan's Cavalry,* 626; Hanna, *Flight Into Oblivion,* 59–60; Davis, *Jefferson Davis,* 627–28. Yorkville is known today as York, and Unionville is present-day Union.

[70] OR 49 (1): 545–47. Indeed, on April 27 Sherman attempted to issue GS yet another order, this time directing GS's cavalry to return to East Tennessee. See OR 47 (3): 323.

[71] OR 49 (1): 545–47; OR 49 (2): 489–90, 508.

[72] OR 49 (2): 508; Crow, *Storm in the Mountains,* 128; April 28, 1865, Allen Frankenberry diaries, WV; Scott, *13th Tennessee,* 241; April 28–29, 1865, Henry Birdsall diary, SHC. Frank Mason of the 12th Ohio, who was not present, indicates that Miller's brigade stayed behind to send prisoners and cannon to Knoxville, and that the men respected private property (Mason, *12th Ohio Cavalry,* 106). The evidence suggests otherwise on both counts.

[73] OR Supplement 65: 550, 554, 556, 561, 615; OR 49 (1): 329; OR 49 (2): 555; April 30, 1865, Allen Frankenberry diaries, WV; Scott, *13th Tennessee,* 241; April 30, 1865, Henry Birdsall diary, SHC; *11th Cavalry,* vol. 41, 3; OR Supplement 65: 550, 554, 563; *Annual Report of the Adjutant General of Michigan* 1: 98–99; Robertson, *Michigan in the War,* 738. The last two named sources incorrectly state that these events occurred on May 27. Meanwhile, in OR 49 (2): 555, Brown called Saluda Gap Jones's Gap.

[74] OR 49 (1): 336; (2): 475.

[75] Banks, "Memoranda," diary entry for April 26, 1865, 300.

[76] *Mountain Scenery,* 27–28; Morning Reports of Companies A–F and G–M, 10th Michigan Cavalry, RR; Frederic Antes diary, April 26, 1865, Civil War Miscellaneous Collection, USAMHI; Kirk, *15th Pennsylvania,* 508; Morning Reports for Companies A–D, 15th Pennsylvania Cavalry, RR; Wilson, *Column South,* 294.

[77] Septimus W. Knight diary, April 27, 1865, VMI; Morning Reports for Companies A–D, 15th Pennsylvania Cavalry, RR; Bushong, *Last Great Stoneman Raid;* Morning Reports of Companies A–F, 10th Michigan Cavalry, RR; Morning Reports for Companies A–D, 15th Pennsylvania

Cavalry, RR; Banks, "Memoranda," diary entry for April 27, 1865, 300. Presumably the separate road taken by the 12th Ohio probably did not lead through Hickory Nut Gap, as no extant Ohio source even mentions the gap. Possible routes include Deep Gap, Low Gap, and Howard's Gap, all of which are south of Hickory Nut Gap and offer a more direct path to Hendersonville.

[78] Griffin, *Western North Carolina Sketches*, 41–42, 52–54; *Mountain Scenery*, 30; Jones, *Heritage of Henderson County* 2: 56. Some of the defenders of Swannanoa Gap disbanded at Hickory Nut Gap after learning of the surrender of Confederate forces (Interview with George Fortune, Civil War clipping file, Pack Memorial Library, Asheville, N.C.). Lake Lure was the backdrop for the 1987 film *Dirty Dancing*.

[79] Clark, *Histories of the Several Regiments* 4: 650; Wilson, *Column South*, 294; Diary, April 27, 1865, Charles M. Betts papers, HSP; Kirk, *15th Pennsylvania*, 508; Angelo Wiser maps, LC.

[80] Septimus W. Knight diary, April 27, 1865, VMI; Morning Reports for Companies A–D, 15th Pennsylvania Cavalry, RR; Bushong, *Last Great Stoneman Raid*; Morning Reports of Companies A–F, 10th Michigan Cavalry, RR; Wilson, *Column South*, 294; Kirk, *15th Pennsylvania*, 508; Wilson, *Recollections and Experiences*, 122–23; Banks, "Memoranda," diary entry for April 27, 1865, 300; OR 49 (2): 508.

[81] *Charlotte Daily Observer*, May 10, 1901; Griffin, *Western North Carolina Sketches*, 52, 54; Clarke, *History of Sherrill's Tavern*; Blackmun, *Western North Carolina*, 2; Jones, *Heritage of Henderson County* 2: 57; Angelo Wiser maps, LC. That same day, while on detached duty, Charles Weller of the 15th Pennsylvania captured a Confederate captain and three enlisted men (Diary entry for April 27, 1865, Charles F. Weller memoirs and letters, *Civil War Times Illustrated* Collection, USAMHI).

[82] Wilson, *Column South*, 294; Banks, "Memoranda," diary entry for April 27, 1865, 300; Frederic Antes diary, April 27, 1865, Civil War Miscellaneous Collection, USAMHI.

[83] Kirk, *15th Pennsylvania*, 508–9; Wilson, *Column South*, 294; *Charlotte Daily Observer*, May 10, 1901; Griffin, *Western North Carolina Sketches*, 52; Diary, April 26, 1865, Charles M. Betts papers, HSP; Morning Reports for Companies A–D, 15th Pennsylvania Cavalry, RR; Septimus W. Knight diary, April 27, 1865, VMI; Mason, "Stoneman's Last Campaign," 31; Mason, *12th Ohio Cavalry*, 107; *OR Supplement* 65: 615; Sample Autobiography, p. 14, CC; Wilson, *Recollections and Experiences*, 123; GS to AG, April 24, 1865, Part 2, Entry 2740, Letters Sent, District of East Tennessee, RG 393, NA; OR 49 (2): 457–58; Report of AG, December 29, 1873, in U.S. Army Generals' Reports of Civil War Service, M1098, vol. IV, R19, p. 543, NA. The sources are contradictory, so the exact time when Palmer received the orders of April 24 and April 27 is in some doubt. The sequence presented in the text follows the most likely scenario, for it is based on the surviving contemporary sources.

[84] *Charlotte Daily Observer*, May 10, 1901; Griffin, *Western North Carolina Sketches*, 52; Angelo Wiser maps, LC; Wilson, *Column South*, 301; OR 49 (2): 508. Palmer's night at Esmeralda may have occurred on April 28.

[85] OR 49 (2): 508.

[86] Diary entry for April 28, 1865, Charles F. Weller memoirs and letters, *Civil War Times Illustrated* Collection, USAMHI; Septimus W. Knight diary, April 28, 1865, VMI; *OR Supplement* 57: 319, 329; Morning Reports of Companies A–F, 10th Michigan Cavalry, RR; Frederic Antes diary, April 28, 1865, Civil War Miscellaneous Collection, USAMHI; Morning Reports for Companies A–D, 15th Pennsylvania Cavalry, RR; Wilson, *Recollections and Experiences*, 123; Kirk, *15th Pennsylvania*, 508–9; Capt. Henry McAllister to Lt. Col. Charles M. Betts, April 28, 1865, Charles M. Betts papers, HSP. The Morning Reports for Companies A–D, 15th Pennsylvania Cavalry, RR, place the march back to Rutherfordton on April 29. Either the reports are in error, or a rear guard followed a day behind the main body of the brigade.

[87] Banks, "Memoranda," diary entry for April 28, 1865, 300–301; Mason, "Stoneman's Last Campaign," 31–32; Mason, *12th Ohio Cavalry*, 106–7; Moderwell, "Outline of Stoneman's Raid," Civil War (Federal, Miscellaneous) papers, SHC; Bushong, *Last Great Stoneman Raid*; OR Supple-

ment 49: 969. Several accounts, including Mason's, other 12th Ohio accounts, and the *National Tribune* of July 19, 1900, garble the sequence of events of these confusing days.

[88] Banks, "Memoranda," diary entry for April 28, 1865, 300–301; Mason, *12th Ohio Cavalry*, 107.

[89] Banks, "Memoranda," diary entry for April 29, 1865, 301; Mason, *12th Ohio Cavalry*, 107; Bushong, *Last Great Stoneman Raid*; Mason, *12th Ohio Cavalry*, 107; Davis, *Jefferson Davis*, 627–28; Moderwell, "Outline of Stoneman's Raid," Civil War (Federal, Miscellaneous) papers, SHC; *OR Supplement* 49: 969; *OR* 49 (1): 547–48. Both Mason and Bushong mistakenly stated that the Ohioans camped on April 29 on the Pacolet River instead of the Broad. Also, Mason and Bushong judged incorrectly that they missed Davis by forty-eight hours.

[90] Morning Reports for Companies A–D and F–L, 15th Pennsylvania Cavalry, RR; Septimus W. Knight diary, April 29, 1865, VMI; Morning Reports of Companies A–F, 10th Michigan Cavalry, RR; *OR Supplement* 57: 384.

[91] Capt. Henry McAllister to Lt. Col. Charles M. Betts, April 29, 1865, Charles M. Betts papers, HSP; Diary, April 29, 1865, Charles M. Betts papers, HSP; *OR* 49 (1): 329, 547–48; Frederic Antes diary, April 29, 1865, Civil War Miscellaneous Collection, USAMHI; Diary entry for April 29, 1865, Charles F. Weller memoirs and letters, *Civil War Times Illustrated* Collection, USAMHI; Wilson, *Column South*, 301; Morning Reports for Companies A–D and F–L, 15th Pennsylvania Cavalry, RR; Septimus W. Knight diary, April 29, 1865, VMI; Morning Reports of Companies A–F, 10th Michigan Cavalry, RR; *OR Supplement* 57: 384. According to a report he wrote from Athens a week later, Palmer said that he was in the vicinity of the Cowpens battlefield when he received the order to intercept Davis. His memory was in error, as he had yet to enter South Carolina on April 29, although his 12th Ohio Cavalry was near the old battlefield at the time.

[92] Wilson, *Recollections and Experiences*, 123; Kirk, 15th *Pennsylvania*, 509.

Chapter 11
WE WOULD HAVE LIKED TO SPARE THEM
The End of Stoneman's Raid: May 1–November 25, 1865

[1] Hanna, *Flight Into Oblivion*, 84, 95; Foote, *The Civil War* 3: 850, 1008; Keenan, *Wilson's Cavalry Corps*, 212–13; Starr, *Union Cavalry in the Civil War* 1: 21, 27; 3: 563–65.

[2] Mason, *12th Ohio Cavalry*, 110–14; Mason, "Stoneman's Last Campaign," 40–41.

[3] Wilson, *Column South*, 320; Frederic Antes diary, May 18–21, 1865, Civil War Miscellaneous Collection, USAMHI; Betts, "Stoneman's Great Cavalry Raid;" Morning Reports for Companies F–L, 15th Pennsylvania Cavalry, RR; Kirk, *15th Pennsylvania*, 518; Wilson, *Recollections and Experiences*, 135; Wilson, *Column South*, 321; Morning Reports for Companies A–D, 15th Pennsylvania Cavalry, RR; Septimus W. Knight diary, May 20, 1865, VMI; Morning Reports for Companies A–F, 10th Michigan Cavalry, RR; Descriptive Book for Companies G–M, 12th Ohio Cavalry, RR; Banks, "Memoranda," diary entry for May 19–20, 1865, 306; Bushong, *Last Great Stoneman Raid*; Mason, *12th Ohio Cavalry*, 113–14. Morrison was reported killed at Greenville, S.C., but the regiment was obviously not there at the time.

[4] *OR* 47 (3): 334–35; *OR* 49 (2): 981; Bradley, *Astounding Close*, 228.

[5] *OR* 49 (2): 852, 875.

[6] *OR* 49 (2): 1105.

[7] Wilson, *Column South*, 324; Sample Autobiography, p. 14, CC.

[8] *OR* 49 (1): 547; Wilson, *Column South*, 322.

[9] Bushong, *Last Great Stoneman Raid*; L.S. Trowbridge to "My Dear Judie," April 12, 1865, L.S. Trowbridge papers, UM; *10th Cavalry*, vol. 40, 15; Trowbridge, *Brief History of the 10th Michigan*, 39; *Brownlow's Knoxville Whig*, May 31, 1865.

[10] Diary of Annie Olympia Donnell, April 28, 1865, Loula Donnell papers, SHC; *Philadelphia Weekly Times*, December 14, 1878; W.W. Lenoir to "Dear Joe," August 4, 1865, Lenoir papers, SHC; Bush, "Pair of Historical North Carolina Letters," 9.

[11] Weigley, *American Way of War*, 133, 137–38, 143–45.

[12] Van Noppen, *Stoneman's Last Raid*, 111–12; Hatcher, *Last Four Weeks*, 243.

[13] Spencer, *Last Ninety Days*, 207–8; R.L. Beall, "Stoneman's Raid," *The North Carolina Review*, October 2, 1910; R.L. Beall's account of Stoneman's Raid, Cornelia Phillips Spencer papers, SHC; Diary entry for May 25, 1865, Charles F. Weller memoirs and letters, *Civil War Times Illustrated* Collection, USAMHI.

[14] Grant, *Memoirs*, 571; Foote, *The Civil War* 3: 848–50; Calvin J. Cowles to W.J. Palmer, 1 October 1870, Calvin J. Cowles papers, NCSA.

[15] Grant, *Memoirs*, 571.

[16] Van Noppen, *Stoneman's Last Raid*, 111–12.

[17] Trowbridge, *Stoneman Raid*, 109; Trowbridge, "The Stoneman Raid of 1865," *JUSCA* 4 (June 1891): 196; Trowbridge, "A Continuation of the Narrative of the Stoneman Raid of 1865," L.S. Trowbridge papers, UM; Cullum, *Biographical Register* 1: 447; *Cincinnati Daily Commercial*, May 10, 1865; *OR* 49 (1): 336; Badeau, *Military History of U.S. Grant* 3: 637; WP to "My Dear Charley," May 20, 1865, William J. Palmer papers, Yale; *Philadelphia Inquirer*, April 19, 1865.

[18] Trowbridge, *Stoneman Raid*, 109; Trowbridge, "The Stoneman Raid of 1865," *JUSCA* 4 (June 1891): 196; Trowbridge, "A Continuation of the Narrative of the Stoneman Raid of 1865," L.S. Trowbridge papers, UM; Cullum, *Biographical Register* 1: 447; *Cincinnati Daily Commercial*, May 10, 1865; *OR* 49 (1): 336; Badeau, *Military History of U.S. Grant* 3: 637.

[19] *OR Supplement* 57: 319, 329, 337, 351, 360, 368, 384; 22: 4; Scott, *13th Tennessee*, 249–50; Taylor, *Philadelphia in the Civil War*, 178; Fisher, *Builder of the West*, 124, 125; Roll of Co. A, 15th Pa. Cav., Septimus W. Knight diary, VMI; Mason, "Stoneman's Last Campaign," 43; Kirk, *15th Pennsylvania*, 519; *Michigan in the War* 41: 725; Wilson, *Column South*, 322.

[20] Diary entry for May 25, 1865, Charles F. Weller memoirs and letters, *Civil War Times Illustrated* Collection, USAMHI.

[21] Cullum, *Biographical Register* 1: 447; Trowbridge, *Stoneman Raid*, 109; Trowbridge, "The Stoneman Raid of 1865," *JUSCA* 4 (June 1891): 196; Trowbridge, "A Continuation of the Narrative of the Stoneman Raid of 1865," L.S. Trowbridge papers, UM; Betts, "Stoneman's Great Cavalry Raid;" *Cincinnati Daily Commercial*, May 10, 1865.

[22] *National Tribune*, July 9, 1914.

[23] Weigley, *American Way of War*, 140; *10th Cavalry*, vol. 40, 15; Trowbridge, *Brief History of the 10th Michigan*, 39; Trowbridge, *Stoneman Raid*, 109; Trowbridge, "The Stoneman Raid of 1865," *JUSCA* 4 (June 1891): 196; Trowbridge, "A Continuation of the Narrative of the Stoneman Raid of 1865," L.S. Trowbridge papers, UM.

[24] Trowbridge, *Stoneman Raid*, 109; Trowbridge, "The Stoneman Raid of 1865," *JUSCA* 4 (June 1891): 196; Trowbridge, "A Continuation of the Narrative of the Stoneman Raid of 1865," L.S. Trowbridge papers, UM; *OR* 49 (1): 336.

[25] Calvin J. Cowles to W.J. Palmer, 1 October 1870, Calvin J. Cowles papers, NCSA.

[26] Foote, *Civil War*, 737; Grant, *Memoirs*, 514; *OR* 47 (2): 859; *OR* 49 (1): 342, 616–17; Simon, *Papers of U.S. Grant* 13: 360.

[27] Report of AG, December 29, 1873, in U.S. Army Generals' Reports of Civil War Service, M1098, vol. IV, R19, p. 543–44, NA; Kirk, *15th Pennsylvania*, 516–17; Wittenberg and Petruzzi, *Plenty of Blame to Go Around*, 276.

[28] *Cincinnati Daily Commercial*, May 10, 1865; Kirk, *15th Pennsylvania*, 528; "Stoneman's Raid on Salisbury," A.G. Brenizer papers, NCSA; "When Surry Was Invaded," March 21, 1918, unprovenienced newspaper article in the author's collection; Van Noppen, *Stoneman's Last Raid*, 111; Spencer, *Last Ninety Days*, 207–8; R.L. Beall, "Stoneman's Raid," *The North Carolina Review*, October 2, 1910; R.L. Beall's account of Stoneman's Raid, Cornelia Phillips Spencer papers, SHC.

[29] *Cincinnati Daily Commercial*, May 10, 1865.

[30] *OR* 49 (1): 326; AG to Andrew Johnson, April 27, 1862, and AG to Andrew Johnson, May 14, 1862, both in Graf, ed. *Papers of Andrew Johnson* 5: 337, 391. Gillem's father was named Samuel. Gillem's brothers, Luke and John, had been born in or around 1834 and 1836 respectively.

[31] *Cincinnati Daily Commercial*, May 10, 1865; *OR* 49 (1): 336.

[32] WP to G.M. Bascom, May 24, 1865, William J. Palmer papers, CC.

[33] WP to G.M. Bascom, May 24, 1865, William J. Palmer papers, CC; *OR* 49 (1): 336.

[34] Ibid.

[35] *OR* 49 (1): 336.

[36] Van Noppen, *Stoneman's Last Raid*, 110; Weigley, *American Way of War*, 149; Sherman, *Memoirs of William T. Sherman* 2: 126; Charles F. Adams, Jr. to his mother, May 12, 1863, in Ford, *Cycle of Adams Letters*, 2:5.

[37] "When Surry Was Invaded," March 21, 1918, unprovenienced newspaper article in the author's collection; Van Noppen, *Stoneman's Last Raid*, 111; Spencer, *Last Ninety Days*, 207–8; R.L. Beall, "Stoneman's Raid," *The North Carolina Review*, October 2, 1910; R.L. Beall's account of Stoneman's Raid, Cornelia Phillips Spencer papers, SHC.

[38] *OR* 49 (2): 407–8; Calvin J. Cowles to W.J. Palmer, 1 October 1870, Calvin J. Cowles papers, NCSA.

[39] Report of AG, December 29, 1873, in U.S. Army Generals' Reports of Civil War Service, M1098, vol. IV, R19, p. 543–44, NA; *National Tribune*, July 19, 1900; R.B.B. Houston to Gov. Worth, May 15, 1866, Governor's Papers, NCSA. The cavalry veteran added, "When they [the flap-jacks] were cooked on one side they were turned by shaking the skillet and tossing them in the air. This requires considerable skill; and the successful flap-jack baker was an individual of much importance. On our forced march we had but few opportunities to forage or cook, and consequently went hungry for days and nights in succession."

[40] *National Tribune*, July 19, 1900; "When Surry Was Invaded," March 21, 1918, unprovenienced newspaper article in the author's collection; Kirk, *15th Pennsylvania*, 516–17; C. Plyler to J. Worth, January 1, 1866, Governor's papers, NCSA.

[41] Betts, "Stoneman's Great Cavalry Raid;" Taylor, *Philadelphia in the Civil War*, 178; Fisher, *Builder of the West*, 124–25.

[42] Van Noppen, *Stoneman's Last Raid*, 46, 111; J.A. Billups to WP, May 10, 1865, William J. Palmer papers, CC; *To the Members of the Society of the 15th Pennsylvania Cavalry*, 23rd Annual Banquet, 8–10.

[43] R.L. Beall's account of Stoneman's Raid, Cornelia Phillips Spencer papers, SHC; Beall, "Stoneman's Raid," *The North Carolina Review*, December 4, 1910; Spencer, *Last Ninety Days*, 219–22.

[44] Governor's papers for Jonathon Worth, 1865–68, NCSA.

[45] Blackmun, *Western North Carolina*, 356; Hill, *History of Henry County*, 25; "General Stoneman's Raid on Salisbury, North Carolina," Harriet Ellis Bradshaw papers, SHC; Yearns and Barrett, *North Carolina Civil War Documentary*, 120.

[46] Noe and Wilson, *Civil War in Appalachia*, xxvi; Blackmun, *Western North Carolina*, 357, 376; Howard, *Forgotten Heroes*, 62; "Reminiscences by O.J. Lehman, 1857–1904," p. 4, Civil War and Reconstruction papers, MA; R.B.B. Houston to Gov. Worth, May 15, 1866, Governor's papers, NCSA.

[47] Blackmun, *Western North Carolina*, 357; Inscoe and McKinney, *Heart of Confederate Appalachia*, 262, 267, 269, 275; Howard, *Forgotten Heroes*; Unknown to "My Dear Brother," August 14, 1865, Lenoir papers, SHC. The population of western North Carolina doubled in the thirty years after the war.

[48] Griffin and Standard, "The Cotton Textile Industry in Antebellum North Carolina," 159, 160, 161–65; Keever, *Iredell—Piedmont County*, 264. North Carolina mills affected by the raid included the Patterson Cotton Factory in Caldwell County, the Mocksville Cotton Factory, the Salem Manufacturing Company, the Hunting Creek Factory, the Lexington Cotton Factory, the

F&H Fries Cotton and Woolen Mills, the Mount Airy Cotton Mill, the Salisbury Manufacturing Company, the Buck Creek Shoals Factory, the Elkin Manufacturing Company, the Yadkin Cotton Factory in Wilkes, Eagle Cotton Mills, S.F. Patterson and Company Cotton Mill, Tomlinson's Cotton Factory, and the Wachovia Steam and Cotton Mill.

[49] McKenzie, "'Oh! Ours Is a Deplorable Condition,'" 199; Inscoe and McKinney, *Heart of Confederate Appalachia*, 186.

[50] Blackmun, *Western North Carolina*, 377; Inscoe and McKinney, *Heart of Confederate Appalachia*, 283; Howard, *Forgotten Heroes*, 62; Kegley, *Glimpses of Wythe County*, 85; *Cincinnati Daily Commercial*, May 10, 1865.

[51] *Governor's Message in Relation to the Western North Carolina Railroad*, 6–7, 12–13, 36; Abrams, *Western North Carolina Railroad*, 18–21; Inscoe and McKinney, *Heart of Confederate Appalachia*, 280–81; McKinney, "Premature Industrialization," 238. According to the governor's report, the details of the Western North Carolina Railroad's losses due to Stoneman's raid are as follows: Joint Passenger Depot and Shed in Salisbury, $12,000; Depot, $6,000; Shops, $20,000; Round House damaged, $5,000; Water Tank, $1,500; Fence and Scales, $1,500; material, $5,000; tools, $8,000; water tank at the six mile post, $1,500; Second Creek Bridge, $3,000; Third Creek Station, $3,500; Third Creek Bridge, $3,000; depot and tank at Statesville, $4,500; depot at Icard's, $2,500; Depot at the Head of the Road, $500; saw mill, $600; 10 box cars, $3,800; 3 flats, $900; 2 passenger coaches, $4,000; 1 second class car, $1,200; 2 seriously damaged locomotives, $7,000; 1 locomotive slightly damaged, $500; dump cars, $2,000; damage to truck and iron, $2,000. Total: $111,000.

[52] Inscoe and McKinney, *Heart of Confederate Appalachia*, 186; Blackmun, *Western North Carolina*, 376; *SHSP* 1: 188–89; Mansion House Register, April 12, 1865; *Philadelphia Weekly Times*, December 14, 1878.

[53] Inscoe and McKinney, *Heart of Confederate Appalachia*, 110–11, 115, 127–28.

[54] *Landmark*, December 1, 1882.

[55] Louisa Norwood to Walter Lenoir, April 24, 1865, Lenoir papers, SHC; *Lenoir News-Topic*, September 12, 1941; "Reminiscences by O.J. Lehman, 1857–1904," p. 4, Civil War and Reconstruction papers, MA; Samuel F. Patterson to Rufus L. Patterson, April 19, 1865, Patterson papers, NCSA; "Shallow Ford," Clingman and Puryear family papers, SHC.

[56] Kirk, *15th Pennsylvania*, 562.

[57] Blackmun, *Western North Carolina*, 359; Inscoe and McKinney, *Heart of Confederate Appalachia*, 125–26; *Martinsville Daily Bulletin*, July 31, 1939.

[58] Descriptive Book for Companies A–E, 10th Michigan Cavalry, RR; Gwaltney, "Capture of Fort Hamby," 2; Harper, *Reminiscences of Caldwell County in the Great War*, 46; "History of Fort Hamby," A.C. Avery papers, SHC; Harvey Augustus Eller to Adolphus Hill Eller, Sept. 21, 1931, in Hubell, "The James Eller Family and the Bushwhackers of Wilkes County." A Lockwood is also mentioned in local histories of the gang, confirming the official record.

[59] Gwaltney, "Capture of Fort Hamby," 2–3; Harper, *Reminiscences of Caldwell County in the Great War*, 45–46; Crouch, *Historical Sketches of Wilkes*, 39; "History of Fort Hamby," A.C. Avery papers, SHC; Harvey Augustus Eller to Adolphus Hill Eller, Sept. 21, 1931, in Hubell, "The James Eller Family and the Bushwhackers of Wilkes County."

[60] Gwaltney, "Capture of Fort Hamby," 2–4, 12; Harper, *Reminiscences of Caldwell County in the Great War*, 45–47; Crouch, *Historical Sketches of Wilkes*, 39–41; "History of Fort Hamby," A.C. Avery papers, SHC; Arthur, *Watauga County*, 183; Keever, *Iredell—Piedmont County*, 236–37; Allen, *Heritage of Alexander County* 1: 37–38; Clark, *Histories of the Several Regiments* 4: 376–77; *Lenoir News-Topic*, March 31, 1992.

[61] Gwaltney, "Capture of Fort Hamby," 4–10; Harper, *Reminiscences of Caldwell County in the Great War*, 47–48; "History of Fort Hamby," A.C. Avery papers, SHC; Crouch, *Historical Sketches of Wilkes*, 40, 41; Keever, *Iredell—Piedmont County*, 236–37; Allen, *Heritage of Alexander County* 1: 37–38; Hubell, "The James Eller Family and the Bushwhackers of Wilkes County;" Harvey

Augustus Eller to Adolphus Hill Eller, Sept. 21, 1931, in Hubell, "The James Eller Family and the Bushwhackers of Wilkes County;" Clark, *Histories of the Several Regiments* 4: 376–77.

[62] Harvey Augustus Eller to Adolphus Hill Eller, Sept. 21, 1931, in Hubell, "The James Eller Family and the Bushwhackers of Wilkes County;" Gwaltney, "Capture of Fort Hamby," 10–13; "History of Fort Hamby," A.C. Avery papers, SHC; Crouch, *Historical Sketches of Wilkes*, 42; Harper, *Reminiscences of Caldwell County in the Great War*, 49; *The Journal-Patriot*, April 19, 1990. Today the site has been altered by the waters of the W. Kerr Scott Reservoir, but archaeology has been performed there.

[63] *SHSP* 21: 343–46.

[64] Inscoe and McKinney, *Heart of Confederate Appalachia*, 275–76.

[65] "Reminiscences by O.J. Lehman, 1857–1904," p. 4, Civil War and Reconstruction papers, MA.

Appendix A
ORDER OF BATTLE

[1] *OR* 49 (1) 325–26; *OR* 49 (2): 12–13, 534, 539. The organization of Confederate forces is not presented here as a hodgepodge of home guard and regular units from various commands were engaged.

[2] The organization presented in the Official Records listed Standish as the commander of the 10th Michigan, but clearly Trowbridge was present during the raid, as the narrative discusses. Trowbridge must have been absent when the document was prepared.

[3] Due to a shortage of horses, portions of the 8th Tennessee Cavalry, including Company C, did not participate in the raid. Although extant records are unclear, it is also likely that Company D stayed behind as well (Hewitt, *Supplement*, pt. 2, 65: 558–59; *Tennesseans in the Civil War* 1: 342).

[4] Patton was arrested prior to the raid and did not participate. Lieutenant Colonel Andrew J. Brown would normally have commanded the regiment in Patton's absence (AG to Andrew Johnson, January 7, 1864, in Graf and Haskins, eds., *Papers of Andrew Johnson* 6: 540–42 n. 2, 543 n. 9, n. 13; Regimental Orders, Endorsements, and Court Martial Book, 8th Tennessee Cavalry, RR; Descriptive Book, 8th Tennessee Cavalry, RR), but for some reason Maj. John M. Sawyers commanded the 8th instead during the campaign (*Tennesseans in the Civil War* 1: 342).

[5] Although listed as a participant in *OR* 49 (2): 12, the 9th Tennessee Cavalry actually did not go on the raid. The unit was stationed at various Tennessee camps during the early Spring of 1865 (Morning Reports for Companies A–M, 9th Tennessee Cavalry, Record Group 94, Entries 112–15, Records of the Adjutant General's Office, Regimental Records, NA; *Tennesseans in the Civil War* 1: 344; Hewitt, *Supplement*, pt. 2, 65: 574–79).

[6] Although not originally listed as part of the division in Special Orders No. 60, this battery did participate in the raid (OR 49 [1] 325–26; OR 49 [2]: 12–13; Hewitt, *Supplement*, pt. 2, 65: 637).

[7] Seven companies.

[8] Eight companies.

[9] Also known as Thomas's Battery.

[10] From second brigade, 4th Division, 23rd Corps.

[11] Special Orders No. 60, dated March 17, 1865, lists Tillson's Second Brigade with seven more light artillery batteries: 21st Ohio, 22nd Ohio, 11th Michigan (Battery L, 1st Michigan), Henshaw's Illinois Battery, Colvin's Illinois Battery, Battery B, 1st Tennessee, and Battery M, 1st Michigan (OR 49 [2]: 13).

[12] Nine companies strong.

[13] Three companies strong.

[14] In addition to Stanley's Fourth Army Corps, George Thomas's department included the Districts of Middle Tennessee, West Tennessee, and the Etowah, as well as miscellaneous infantry and artillery. Only the First Division of the Fourth Corps is recounted here since Thomas's other forces did not play a role in the raid. See *OR* 49 (2): 534.

Appendix B
Estimating the Strength of the Cavalry Division of the District of East Tennessee

[1] *OR* 49 (2): 35.

[2] Mason, "Stoneman's Last Campaign," 22–24; Mason, *12th Ohio Cavalry*, 98.

[3] Kirk, *15th Pennsylvania*, 493.

[4] Kirk, *15th Pennsylvania*, 520.

[5] WP to Frank Jackson, March 20, 1865, William J. Palmer Collection, CHS.

[6] Simon, *Papers of U.S. Grant* 14: 196.

[7] This range of 506–914 is taken from five different strength estimates of 506, 650, 789, and 914. These come from the following sources. Five hundred and six equals the number of men reported in Wilson, *Recollections and Experiences*, 122, as composing the various detachments of the 15th during the raid; 650 equals the number of Spencer carbines the 15th procured in February 1865 (Paul Hersh to "Jim", March 2, 1865, Paul Hersh letters, Civil War Miscellaneous Collection, USAMHI) and all Sharps turned in; 789 equals the 627 men the regiment mustered out in June 1865, plus 162 men who were not mustered out but remained on duty, as recorded in Kirk, *15th Pennsylvania*, 519; and 914 equals the number of men mentioned by Charles M. Betts in "Stoneman's Great Cavalry Raid in 1865," *The National Tribune*, December 9, 1926. Most likely, the correct total falls between 650 and 789, as this data is derived from the best contemporary sources.

[8] *OR* 49 (1): 763; as of February 24, 1865.

[9] Mason, *12th Ohio Cavalry*, 96. It should be added that the 12th Ohio Cavalry boasted over 1,400 members in 1863. Soliday, J.A., *Sixth Annual Reunion*, 7.

[10] Trowbridge claimed to be outnumbered at Henry Court House by a force of four or five hundred enemy (see Chapter 4). He also claimed that two of his three battalions numbered less than three hundred men (see Chapter 5). Assuming the third battalion was equal in force to the other two, he probably had no more than 450 men on hand at most. The weakness of the regiment is attributed to the fact that 540 men of the regiment, including Companies K and L, were on detached duty at Knoxville (April 3, 1865 report, Regimental Letter, Endorsement, Order, and Guard Report for the 10th Michigan Cavalry, RR; Morning Reports, Companies G–M, 10th Michigan Cavalry, RR).

[11] A detachment of the 11th Kentucky Cavalry (under Major Lawson) of unknown size remained with Davis Tillson's Fourth Division, District of East Tennessee (*OR* 49 [2]: 438). Four hundred is the author's estimate, assuming that the 11th was the smallest of the three regiments but still strong enough to operate independently, as it did on occasion during the raid.

[12] *OR* 49 (1): 763; as of February 24, 1865.

[13] Ibid.

[14] Miller had only five hundred men on hand when he raided Wytheville (see Chapter 5). While this apparently did not account for the entire contingent of Tennesseans in the division, it was doubtless close. It is also known that the 8th was short at least two companies on the raid (C and D), so it was the smaller of the two Tennessee regiments in the division. This estimate reflects that.

[15] Did not participate in the raid.

[16] Despite the seventy-five-man detachment that was subtracted before the raid began (*OR* 49 [2]: 438), the 13th was still Gillem's largest Tennessee regiment, so this estimate is larger. However, it should be noted that Gillem requested 1,500 horses for his command prior to the raid (*OR* 49 [1]: 744). This may have been because the entire Tennessee brigade was larger, but Gillem's request also doubtless accounted for more than one horse per man.

[17] OR 49 (1): 339, 549.

Bibliography

Manuscripts

Bassett Branch Historical Center, Bassett, Va.
   Henry County, Virginia, During the Civil War—miscellaneous notebook
   Stoneman's Raid notebook
Chicago History Museum, Chicago, Ill.
   George Stoneman papers
Civil War Library and Museum, Philadelphia, Pa.
   Pennsylvania Commandery—MOLLUS scrapbooks
Colorado College, Tutt Library, Special Collections and Archives, Colorado Springs, Colo.
   Nathaniel Sample autobiographical sketch
   William J. Palmer papers
Colorado Historical Society, Stephen H. Hart Library, Denver, Colo.
   William J. Palmer Collection, manuscript #477
Davie County Public Library, Mocksville, N.C.
   Military–Civil War, Stoneman's Raid file
Duke University, William R. Perkins Library, Manuscripts Department, Durham, N.C.
   Bradley Tyler Johnson papers
   Gertrude Jenkins papers
   James Wall Scully papers
Filson Historical Society, Louisville, Ky.
   Conrad Lewis Diehl Papers
Greensboro Historical Museum Archives, Greensboro, N.C.
   General P. G. T. Beauregard correspondence, Andrew Joyner, Jr., Collection
   James W. Albright diary and reminiscences, Civil War Collection
Historical Society of Pennsylvania, Philadelphia, Pa.
   Charles M. Betts papers, collection #1889
Iredell County Public Library, Statesville, N.C.
   Stoneman's Raid file, Local History Collection
Jones Memorial Library, Lynchburg, Va.
   George Alexander Martin papers
   Janet Cleland diary
Library of Congress, Washington, D.C.
   Angelo Wiser maps
   P. G. T. Beauregard papers
Military Records and Research Branch, Department of Military Affairs, Frankfort, Ky.
   T. Graham, "A Synopsis of the Organization, Travels, and Expeditions of the 11th Kentucky Cavalry, U.S. Vol. Cav.," September 9, 1866
Mississippi Department of Archives and History, Jackson, Miss.
   John M. Stone papers, Z/0026.000
Moravian Archives, Winston-Salem, N.C.
   Civil War and Reconstruction papers
   Henry E. Fries Collection
   Salem Civil War recollections

Mount Airy Public Library, Mount Airy, N.C.
  Civil War clipping file
Museum of the American West, Autry National Center, Los Angeles, Calif.
  Keogh family papers and photographs
National Archives, Washington, D.C.
  Civil War Union volunteer regiment records, RG 94, entries 112–15
  Compiled service records of Union soldiers who served in organizations from the state of
    Tennessee, record group 109, 1960
  Records of attending officers of the Department of the Treasury, settled case files
    for claims approved by the Southern Claims Commission, RG 217
  Records of the Adjutant General Record and Pension Office, RG 94
  Records of United States Army continental commands, RG 393
  United States Army generals' reports of Civil War service, 1864–87, RG 94, M1098
National Climatic Data Center, Asheville, NC
  Precipitation records for South Carolina, Tennessee, and Virginia, 1865
National Library of Ireland, Dublin, Ireland
  Letters of Myles Keogh, 1861–69
North Carolina State Library and Archives, Raleigh, N.C.
  A. G. Brenizer papers
  Calvin J. Cowles papers
  Confederate gravestone records, North Carolina Division, United Daughters of the
    Confederacy, 1956–67, 13 vols.
  D. H. Hill, Jr., papers
  Fries papers
  Governor's papers—Jonathon Worth
  Lucy Williams Polk papers
  Military Collection, Civil War Collection
  Patterson papers
  Paul B. Barringer papers
  Zebulon B. Vance governor's papers
Pack Memorial Library, Asheville, N.C.
  Civil War clipping file
Rowan Museum, Inc., Salisbury, N.C.
  Mansion House register
Rowan Public Library, Edith M. Clark History Room, Salisbury, N.C.
  Brawley file
  Ramsey Confederate cannon file
Tennessee Historical Society, Nashville, Tenn.
  Alfred T. Fielder diaries
  James Douglas Anderson papers
Tennessee State Library and Archives, Nashville, Tenn.
  Jarnagin diary, Civil War Collection, Confederate Collection
  Thomas Hutton diary
  Yeatman-Polk Collection
United States Army Military History Institute, Carlisle Barracks, Carlisle, Pa.
  Charles F. Weller memoirs and letters, *Civil War Times Illustrated* Collection
  Frederic Antes diary, Civil War Miscellaneous Collection

Paul Hersh letters, Civil War Miscellaneous Collection
Theodore Ramsey papers, Civil War Miscellaneous Collection
University of California, Bancroft Library, Berkeley, Calif.
George Stoneman autobiographical statement
University of Michigan, Bentley Historical Library, Ann Arbor, Mich.
Calvin Thomas papers
Frederick N. Field correspondence
L. S. Trowbridge papers
University of Mississippi, Oxford, Miss.
Winfield Scott Featherston Collection
University of North Carolina at Chapel Hill, Southern Historical Collection,
Wilson Library, Chapel Hill, N.C.
Alphonso C. Avery papers, #3456
Anna Holmes Trenholm diary, #1402-z
Cadia Barbee Welborn papers, #2755
Civil War (Federal, miscellaneous) papers, #150
Clingman and Puryear family papers, #2661
Cornelia Phillips Spencer papers, #683
Dobson family papers, #4654-z
Emma Lydia Rankin papers, #621-z
G. W. F. Harper papers, #313
George E. Lee papers, #02629-z
Harriet Ellis Bradshaw papers, General Stoneman's raid on Salisbury, #1444-z
Henry A. Birdsall diary, #4667-z
Heyward and Ferguson family papers, #2754-z
John Taylor Wood diary, #2381
Joseph Smith Fowler papers, #2239
Lenoir family papers, #426
Loula Hendon Donnell papers, #4206
Stephen Dill Lee papers, #2440
University of South Carolina Libraries, Rare Books and Special Collections, Columbia, S.C.
Alvan C. Gillem papers, Lord Civil War Collection
University of Tennessee, Special Collections Library, Knoxville, Tenn.
Samuel Mayes Arnell Collection
Virginia Historical Society, Richmond, Va.
Robert E. Lee headquarters papers
Virginia Military Institute, Lexington, Va.
Septimus W. Knight diary, ms. #0317
Virginia Tech, Special Collections Department, University Libraries, Blacksburg, Va.
Piedmont Railroad Company papers
Western North Carolina Railroad papers
Watauga County Public Library, Boone, N.C.
Listing of cemeteries of Watauga County
West Virginia University, West Virginia and Regional History Collection, Morgantown, W.V.
Allen D. Frankenberry diaries
Wilkes Community College, James Larkin Pearson Library, Wilkesboro, N.C.
J. Jay Anderson Collection

Williams, Gino, Floyd, Va.
   Waitman Stigleman, *When the Yankees Came Through Our Town*
Wythe County Courthouse, Wytheville, Va.
   Order book, 1860–65
Wytheville Community College Library, Wytheville, Va.
   Mary B. Kegley Collection
Yale University, Beinecke Rare Book and Manuscript Library, New Haven, Conn.
   William Jackson Palmer papers

NEWSPAPERS

Brownlow's Knoxville Whig
Bucyrus (Ohio) *Journal*
Carolina Watchman (Salisbury, N.C.)
Charlotte Daily Bulletin
Charlotte Daily Observer
Chicago Tribune
Cincinnati Daily Commercial
Greensboro News & Record
High Point (N.C.) *Enterprise*
Iredell (County, N.C.) *Express*
Journal and Sentinel (Winston-Salem N.C.)
Journal-Patriot (North Wilkesboro, N.C.)
Landmark (Statesville, N.C.)
Lenoir (N.C.) *News-Topic*
Martinsville (Va.) *Daily Bulletin*
Memphis Commercial Appeal
Mount Airy (N.C.) *News*
Nashville Tennessean
National Tribune (Washington, D.C.)
North Carolina Review (Raleigh, N.C.)
Ohio State Journal
Patriot, The (Greensboro, N.C.)
People's Press (Salem, N.C.)
Philadelphia Times
Record & Landmark (Statesville, N.C.)
Salisbury (N.C.) *Post*
Sandusky (Ohio) *Register*
Twin City Sentinel (Winston-Salem, N.C.)
Watauga (N.C.) *Democrat*
Winston-Salem Journal

INTERVIEWS

Hairston, Peter. Interview by the author. Advance, N.C., July 6, 1997.
Powell, Dr. William S. Interview by the author. September 11, 1999.
Williams, Gino. Interview by the author. Floyd, Va., Feb. 15, 2002.
Winkler, Annie F. Interview by the author. North Wilkesboro, N.C., July 20, 1989.

BOOKS, ARTICLES, AND PAMPHLETS

Abrams, William H., Jr. "The Western North Carolina Railroad, 1855–1894." Master's thesis, Western Carolina University, 1976.

Alexander, Nancy. *Here Will I Dwell: The Story of Caldwell County*. Salisbury, N.C.: Rowan Printing Co., 1956.

———. *These Eternal Hills: A Collection of Columns Which Have Appeared in the* Lenoir News-Topic. Reprint, Caldwell County Historical Society.

Alexander, Violet G. "The Confederate States Navy Yard at Charlotte, N.C., 1862–1865." *North Carolina Booklet* 3 (1926): 28–37.

Allen, Sara C., ed. *Heritage of Alexander County, North Carolina*. Vol. 1. Winston-Salem, N.C.: Alexander County Genealogical Society and Hunter Publishing Co., 1986.

Allen, W. C. *The Annals of Haywood County, N.C.* Privately published, 1935.

Altmayer, Bud. *A Family History of Watauga County*. Boone, N.C.: Minor's Printing Co., 1994.

America's Medal of Honor Recipients: Complete Official Citations. Golden Valley, Minn.: Highland Publishing, 1980.

Anderson, George L. "General William Jackson Palmer: Man of Vision." *Colorado College Studies* 4 (Spring 1960): 1–23.

Andrews, Sidney. *The South Since the War: As Shown by Fourteen Weeks of Travel and Observation in Georgia and the Carolinas*. Boston: Ticknor and Fields, 1866.

Annual Report of the Adjutant General of the State of Michigan, for the Years 1865–6. Vol. 1. Lansing, Mich.: John A. Kerr and Co., 1866.

Annual Report of the Adjutant General of Pennsylvania, Transmitted to the Governor in Pursuance of Law, for the Year 1866. Harrisburg, Pa.: Singerly and Myers, State Printers, 1867.

Annual Report of the North Carolina Railroad Company, 1865 and 1866. Executive document 24, sections 1866–67. Raleigh, N.C.: William E. Bell, Printer to the State, 1867.

Archaeological Survey of the Forsyth County Memorial Park. Earth Systems Division of SSI, 1978.

Arnett, Ethel Stephens. *Greensboro, North Carolina: The County Seat of Guilford*. Chapel Hill: University of North Carolina Press, 1955.

Arthur, Billy. "Checkmate, Mr. President." *The State* (Jan. 1995).

Arthur, John Preston. *A History of Watauga County, North Carolina, With Sketches of Prominent Families*. Richmond, Va.: Everett Waddey Co., 1915.

———. *Western North Carolina: A History, 1730–1913*. Reprint, Spartanburg, S.C.: Reprint Co., 1973.

Ashe, Samuel A., Stephen B. Weeks, and Charles L. Van Noppen. *Biographical History of North Carolina: From Colonial Times to Present*. 8 vols. Greensboro, N.C.: Charles L. Van Noppen, Publisher, 1905.

Ashmore, Otis. "The Story of the Confederate Treasure." *Georgia Historical Quarterly* 2 (Sept. 1918): 119–38.

Aull, Sara, and Mary Brandon. *Dr. Josephus Wells Hall: A Man of Energy and Enterprise, Salisbury, North Carolina.* Salisbury, N.C.: Historic Salisbury Foundation, 1994.

Averell, W. W. "With the Cavalry on the Peninsula." In vol. 2 of *Battles and Leaders of the Civil War*, edited by Robert U. Johnson and Clarence C. Buel, 429–33. New York: Century, 1887–88.

Badeau, Adam. *Military History of U. S. Grant, from April 1861 to April 1865.* 3 vols. New York: D. Appleton and Co., 1881.

Ballard, Michael B. *Pemberton: A Biography.* Jackson and London: University Press of Mississippi, 1991.

Banks, Joseph. "Memoranda of a Raid Through the Southern States in 1865." *Georgia Historical Quarterly* 26 (Sept.–Dec. 1942): 291–307.

Barrett, John G. *The Civil War in North Carolina.* Chapel Hill: University of North Carolina Press, 1963.

———. *Sherman's March Through the Carolinas.* Chapel Hill: University of North Carolina Press, 1956.

Bates, Samuel P. *History of Pennsylvania Volunteers, 1861–1865.* Vol. 4. Harrisburg, Pa.: B. Singerly, State Printers, 1870.

Beall, R. L. "Stoneman's Raid Was Riot of Ruin." *North Carolina Review* (Oct. 2, Nov. 11, and Dec. 4, 1910).

Betts, Charles M. "Stoneman's Great Cavalry Raid in 1865." *National Tribune* (Dec. 9, 1926).

Black, Robert C., III. *The Railroads of the Confederacy.* Chapel Hill: University of North Carolina Press, 1952.

Blackford, Charles M. *Campaign and Battle of Lynchburg, Virginia.* Lynchburg, Va.: Warwick House Publishers, 1994.

Blackmun, Ora. *Western North Carolina: Its Mountains and Its People to 1880.* Boone, N.C.: Appalachian Consortium Press, 1977.

Blythe, LeGette, and Charles Raven Brockman. *Hornets' Nest: The Story of Charlotte and Mecklenburg County.* Charlotte, N.C.: Public Library of Mecklenburg County, 1961.

Boatner, Mark M., III. *The Civil War Dictionary.* Rev. ed. New York: David McKay Co., 1988.

Borcherdt, W. D. "The Story of Austinville." Photocopy available at Wytheville Community College Library, Wytheville, Va.

Born in Slavery: Slave Narratives from the Federal Writers Project, 1936–1938. North Carolina narratives 11: 1; South Carolina narratives 14: 2. http://lcweb2.loc.gov/ammem/snhtml/snhome.html.

Bradley, Mark L. *This Astounding Close: The Road to Bennett Place.* Chapel Hill and London: University of North Carolina Press, 2000.

Bradley, Stephen E., Jr. *North Carolina Confederate Militia and Home Guard Records.* 3 vols.

Bragg, William Harris. "The Union General Lost in Georgia." *Civil War Times Illustrated* 24 (June 1985): 16–23.

Brawley, James S. *Rowan County: A Brief History.* Raleigh: North Carolina Department of Cultural Resources, Division of Archives and History, 1974.

———. *The Rowan Story, 1753–1953: A Narrative History of Rowan County, North Carolina.* Salisbury, N.C.: Rowan Printing Co., 1953.

Brewer, George E. *History of the Forty-Sixth Alabama Regiment Volunteer Infantry, 1862–1865.*

Reprint, Montgomery, Ala.: Confederate Publishing Co., 1985.

Brock, Robert Alonzo. *History of Montgomery County, Copied from Hardesty's Historical and Geographical Encyclopedia, Special Virginia Edition.* H. H. Hardesty and Co., 1884.

Brotherton, Marvin K. *Lake Norman: Piedmont History.* Davidson, N.C.: Warren Publishing, 1993.

Brown, Louis A. *The Salisbury Prison: A Case Study of Confederate Military Prisons, 1861–1865.* Rev. ed. Wilmington, N.C.: Broadfoot Publishing Co., 1992.

Brownlee, Fambrough L. *Winston-Salem: A Pictorial History.* Norfolk, Va.: Donning Co., Publishers, 1977.

Bumgarner, Matthew. *Kirk's Raiders: A Notorious Band of Scoundrels and Thieves.* Hickory, N.C.: Piedmont Press, 2000.

———. *The Legacy of the Carolina and Northwestern Railway.* Johnson City, Tenn.: Overmountain Press, 1996.

Bush, Conrad L. "A Pair of Historical North Carolina Letters." *North Carolina Postal History Society Newsletter* (Summer 1988), 8–9.

Bushong, William. "The Last Great Stoneman Raid." Address delivered at regimental reunion at Bellefontaine, Ohio, 1910.

Buxton, Barry M. *A Village Tapestry: The History of Blowing Rock.* Boone, N.C.: Appalachian Consortium Press, 1989.

Bynum, William B., ed. *The Heritage of Rutherford County, North Carolina.* Vol. 1. Winston-Salem, N.C.: Genealogical Society of Old Tryon County, 1984.

Calkins, Chris M. *The Appomattox Campaign: March 29–April 9, 1865.* Conshohocken, Pa: Combined Books, 1997.

Campbell, James B. "East Tennessee During the Federal Occupation, 1863–1865." *East Tennessee Historical Society Publications* 19 (1947): 64–80.

Canipe, Ruby Bray, comp. *Early Elkin-Jonesville History and Genealogy.* Jonesville, N.C.: Tarheel Graphics, 1981.

Capers, Henry D. *The Life and Times of C. G. Memminger.* Richmond, Va.: Everet Wadday Co., Publishers, 1893.

Carter, William F., Jr., and Carrie Y. Carter. *Footprints in the "Hollows," or Surry County and Her People.* Elkin, N.C.: Northwestern Regional Library. Available at Forsyth County Public Library.

Casstevens, Frances H. *The Civil War and Yadkin County, North Carolina.* Jefferson, N.C.: McFarland and Co., Publishers, 1997.

———. "Historic Structures and Sites: Huntsville Community, Yadkin County, North Carolina." Not published, 1992. Available at Forsyth County Public Library.

Casstevens, Frances H., ed. *The Heritage of Yadkin County.* 1981. Reprint, Winston-Salem, N.C.: Hunter Publishing Co., 1991.

Catton, Bruce. *Never Call Retreat.* New York: Washington Square Press, 1965.

Chamberlain, Hope Summerell. *This Was Home.* Chapel Hill: University of North Carolina Press, 1938.

Chesnut, Mary Boykin. *A Diary From Dixie.* Edited by Ben Ames Williams. Reprint, Cambridge, Mass., and London: Harvard University Press, 1976.

Chester, James. "Inside Sumter in '61." In vol. 1 of *Battles and Leaders of the Civil War*, edited by Robert U. Johnson and Clarence C. Buel, 50–73. New York: Century, 1887–88.

Chronological Summary of Engagements and Battles in the Medical and Surgical History of the War of the Rebellion (1861–1865). 8 vols. Reprint, Wilmington, N.C.: Broadfoot Publishing, 1991.

Clark, Walter, ed. *Histories of the Several Regiments and Battalions from North Carolina in the Great War, 1861-65*. 5 vols. Goldsboro, N.C.: Nash Brothers, 1901.

Clarke, Mrs. James McClure. "A History of Sherrill's Tavern: Presented before a Meeting of the Western North Carolina Historical Association, October 28, 1978." http://toto.lib.unca.edu/findingaids/mss/sherrills_inn/clarke_history.htm.

Clewell, John Henry. *History of Wachovia in North Carolina*. New York: Doubleday, Page and Co., 1902.

Clothier, Isaac W., comp. *Letters, 1853–1868, Gen'l Wm. J. Palmer*. Philadelphia: 1906.

Colton, Henry E. *Mountain Scenery: The Scenery of the Mountains of Western North Carolina and Northwestern South Carolina*. Raleigh, N.C.: W. L. Pomeroy, 1859.

Colton, Jessie Sellers, ed. *The Civil War Journal and Correspondence of Matthias Baldwin Colton*. Philadelphia: Macrae-Smith Co., 1931.

Colton, Suzanne Wilson, comp. *Column South with the Fifteenth Pennsylvania Cavalry: From Antietam to the Capture of Jefferson Davis*. Flagstaff, Ariz.: J. F. Colton and Co., 1960.

"Complete Sun and Moon Data for One Day: U.S. Cities and Towns." *Astronomical Applications Department, Naval Oceanography Portal, U.S. Naval Observatory*. http://www.usno.navy.mil/USNO/astronomical-applications/data-services/rs-one-day-us.

Confederate Veteran magazine. 40 vols. (1893–1934).

Connell, Evan S. *Son of the Morning Star: Custer and the Little Big Horn*. San Francisco: North Point Press, 1984.

Cook, Gerald Wilson. "The Last Tarheel Militia, 1861–1865." Not published.

Corey, John. "Following Stoneman's Footsteps." *The State* 25 (March 8, 1958): 13, 16.

Cozzens, Peter. *No Better Place to Die: The Battle of Stones River*. Urbana and Chicago: University of Illinois Press, 1991.

Crews, C. Daniel. *A Storm in the Land: Southern Moravians and the Civil War*. Winston-Salem, N.C.: Moravian Archives, 1997.

Crouch, John. *Historical Sketches of Wilkes County*. Wilkesboro, N.C.: Wilkes Genealogical Society, 1902.

Crow, Vernon H. *Storm in the Mountains: Thomas' Confederate Legion of Cherokee Indians and Mountaineers*. Cherokee, N.C.: Press of the Museum of the American Indian, 1982.

Crush, Charles W., ed. *The Montgomery County Story: 1776–1957*. Christiansburg, Va.: Montgomery County Festival Committee, 1957.

Cullum, George W. *Biographical Register of the Officers and Graduates of the U.S. Military Academy at West Point, New York, From Its Establishment in 1802 to 1890*. 3 vols. Boston: Houghton Mifflin, 1891.

Curtis, Sue. "The Salisbury National Cemetery: A Legacy of the Salisbury Confederate Prison." *Ramrod: Newsletter of the North Carolina Civil War Round Table* (July 1998): 3–5.

Daniel, Larry J. *Cannoneers in Gray: The Field Artillery of the Army of Tennessee, 1861–1865*. Tuscaloosa: University of Alabama Press, 1984.

Darrow, Caroline Baldwin. "Recollections of the Twiggs Surrender." In vol. 1 of *Battles and Leaders of the Civil War*, edited by Robert U. Johnson and Clarence C. Buel, 33–39. New York: Century, 1887–88.

Davie County Heritage, North Carolina, 1997. Walsworth Publishing Co., Davie County Heritage, and Don Mills, Inc., 1997.

Davis, Jefferson. *A Short History of the Confederate States of America.* New York: Belford Co., Publishers, 1890.

Davis, William C. *Jefferson Davis: The Man and His Hour.* Baton Rouge: Louisiana State University Press, 1991.

Davis, William C., and Meredith L. Swentor, eds. *Bluegrass Confederate: The Headquarters Diary of Edward O. Guerrant.* Baton Rouge: Louisiana State University Press, 1999.

Day, L. W. *Story of the One Hundred and First Ohio Infantry.* Cleveland, Ohio: W. M. Bayne Printing Co., 1894.

Day, W. A. *A True History of Company I, 49th Regiment North Carolina Troops.* Reprint, Baltimore, Md.: Butternut and Blue, 1997.

"Diary of Nicholas Gibbon, 28th Regt. North Carolina Volunteers." *Mecklenburg, N.C., Genealogical Society Quarterly* 2: 124–33, 151–56; 3: 11–17, 69–74, 128–32.

Dodson, W. C., ed. *Campaigns of Wheeler and His Cavalry, 1862–1865, from Material Furnished by Gen. Joseph Wheeler, to Which Is Added His Concise and Graphic Account of the Santiago Campaign of 1898.* Atlanta, Ga.: Hudgins Publishing Co., 1899. Reprint, Memphis, Tenn., and Camden, S.C.: E. F. Williams and J. J. Fox, 1997.

Donnelly, Ralph W. "The Confederate Lead Mines of Wythe County, Va." *Civil War History* 5 (Dec. 1959): 402–14.

Downs, R. L. "About the Time of the 'Surrender.'" Published in the *Lenoir Topic* in a series of five articles from December 17, 1890, to January 14, 1891.

"Dr. R. L. Beall." *Lenoir News-Topic,* September 12, 1941.

Duke, Basil W. *A History of Morgan's Cavalry.* Reprint, West Jefferson, Ohio: Genesis Publishing Co., 1997.

———. *Reminiscences of General Basil W. Duke.* Reprint, West Jefferson, Ohio: Genesis Publishing Co., 1997.

Dugger, Shepherd M. *The War Trails of the Blue Ridge.* Reprint, Banner Elk, N.C.: Puddingstone Press, 1974.

Duncan, Wade, coordinator. *The Heritage of Stokes County, North Carolina.* Vol. 2. Charlotte, N.C.: Stokes County Historical Society, Inc., in cooperation with Delmar Printing and Publishing Co., 1990.

Dunn, J. P., Jr. *Massacres of the Mountains: A History of the Indian Wars of the Far West.* Reprint, Stackpole Books, 1992.

Durkin, Joseph T., ed. *John Dooley, Confederate Soldier: His War Journal.* Washington, D.C.: Georgetown University Press, 1945.

Dyer, Frederick H. *A Compendium of the War of the Rebellion.* 3 parts. Des Moines, Iowa: Dyer Publishing Co., 1908.

Dyer, Gustavus W., and John Trotwood Moore. *The Tennessee Civil War Veterans Questionnaires.* 5 vols. Easley, S.C.: Southern Historical Press, 1985.

"Edney Letter, The." *A Lot of Bunkum* (Nov. 1997): 85–86.

Eleventh Cavalry. Vol. 41, *Record of Service of Michigan Volunteers in the Civil War, 1861–1865.* Kalamazoo, Mich.: Ihling Bros. and Everard, Printers, 1905.

Elkin, 1889–1989: A Centennial History. Charlotte, N.C.: Elkin Historical Collection.

Eller, Ernest McNeill. *Salem: Star and Dawn.* Jarboc Printing Co., 1962.

Ellis, Daniel. *Thrilling Adventures of Daniel Ellis: The Great Union Guide of East Tennessee for a Period of Nearly Four Years During the Great Southern Rebellion.* New York: Harper and Brothers, Publishers, 1867.

Erwin, Susan Graham. *The Village That Disappeared.* Charlotte, N.C.: Laney-Smith, Inc., 1996.

Evans, Clement A., ed. *Confederate Military History Extended Edition: A Library of Confederate States History in Seventeen Volumes, Written by Distinguished Men of the South.* 17 vols. Atlanta, Ga.: Confederate Publishing, 1899.

Evans, David. *Sherman's Horsemen: Union Cavalry Operations in the Atlanta Campaign.* Bloomington and Indianapolis: Indiana University Press, 1996.

Evans, Richard L. *Court Martial of Samuel K. N. Patton, 8th Regiment, Tennessee Cavalry Volunteers.* Houston, Tex.: privately published, 1999.

"Eyewitness Account, An." *Commander's Tent* (July 1995).

Ferguson, Thomas W. *Home on the Yadkin.* Winston-Salem, N.C.: Clay Printing Co., 1957.

Fisher, John S. *A Builder of the West: The Life of General William Jackson Palmer.* Caldwell, Idaho: Caxton Printers, Ltd., 1939.

FitzSimons, Frank L. *From the Banks of the Oklawaha: Facts and Legends of the North Carolina Mountains.* Vol. 2. Garden Glow Publishing Co., 1977.

Flower, Frank A. *Edwin McMasters Stanton: The Autocrat of Rebellion, Emancipation, and Reconstruction.* Reprint, New York: AMS Press, 1973.

Fonvielle, Chris E., Jr. *The Wilmington Campaign: Last Rays of Departing Hope.* Campbell, Calif.: Savas Publishing Co., 1997.

Foote, Shelby. *The Civil War: A Narrative.* Vol. 3, *Red River to Appomattox.* New York: Vintage Books, 1974.

Ford, Annette Gee, comp. and ed. *The Captive: Major John H. Gee, Commandant of the Confederate Prison at Salisbury, North Carolina, 1864–1865, A Biographical Sketch with Complete Court-Martial Transcript.* Salt Lake City, Utah: Annette Gee Ford, 2000.

Ford, Arthur P. *Life in the Confederate Army, Being the Personal Experiences of a Private Soldier in the Confederate Army, and Some Experiences and Sketches of Southern Life.* New York and Washington, D.C.: Neale Publishing Co., 1905.

Ford, Worthington Chauncey. *A Cycle of Adams Letters: 1861–1865.* 2 vols. Boston and New York: Houghton Mifflin Co., Riverside Press, 1920.

Fordney, Ben F. *George Stoneman: A Biography of the Union General.* Jefferson, N.C., and London: McFarland and Co., Inc., Publishers, 2008.

———. *Stoneman at Chancellorsville: The Coming of Age of Union Cavalry.* Shippensburg, Pa.: White Mane Publishing Co., 1998.

———. "Stoneman's Failed Bid for Glory." *America's Civil War* 11 (May 1998): 26–32.

Fossett, Mildred B. *History of McDowell County.* Marion, N.C.: McDowell County American Revolution Bicentennial Commission, Heritage Commission, 1976.

Freeze, Gary R. *The Catawbans: Crafters of a North Carolina County, 1747–1900.* Newton, N.C.: Catawba County Historical Association, 1995.

Fries, Adelaide, Stuart T. Wright, and J. Edwin Hendricks. *Forsyth: The History of a County on the March.* Chapel Hill: University of North Carolina Press, 1976.

Fulbright, Lucille M., ed. *The Heritage of Catawba County, North Carolina.* Vol. 1. Winston-Salem, N.C.: Catawba County Genealogical Society, 1986.

Garavaglia, Louis A., and Charles G. Worman. "Many Were Broken By Very Slight Shocks As in Mounting and Dismounting." *North & South* 2 (June 1999): 40–47, 50–55.

"General's Story, The." *Harper's New Monthly Magazine* 35 (June 1867): 60–74.

Gerhardt, Lois. "E. T. Clemmons Bequeathed Money to Build Moravian Church & School," *Village Gazette* 2 (Spring 2001): 1, 4.

Goodwin, E. L. *A Small Boy's Recollections of the War: To My Children.* Wytheville, Va.: E. L. Godwin, 1906.

"Governor's Message in Relation to the Western North Carolina Railroad." Document 10, *Legislative Documents, 1865–1866*. Raleigh, N.C.: William E. Bell, Printer to the State, 1866.

Graf, Leroy P., ed. *The Papers of Andrew Johnson*. Vol. 7, *1864–1865*. Knoxville: University of Tennessee Press, 1986.

Graf, Leroy P., and Ralph W. Haskins, eds. *The Papers of Andrew Johnson*. Vol. 4, *1860–1861*. Knoxville: University of Tennessee Press, 1976.

———. *The Papers of Andrew Johnson*. Vol. 5, *1861–1862*. Knoxville: University of Tennessee Press, 1979.

———. *The Papers of Andrew Johnson*. Vol. 6, *1862–1864*. Knoxville: University of Tennessee Press, 1983.

Grant, Ulysses S. *Personal Memoirs of U. S. Grant*. Edited by E. B. Long. Reprint, New York: Da Capo Press, 1982.

Greene, A. Wilson. "Stoneman's Raid." In *Chancellorsville: The Battle and its Aftermath*, edited by Gary W. Gallagher. Chapel Hill and London: University of North Carolina Press, 1996.

Greenwood, Janette Thomas. *Bittersweet Legacy: The Black and White "Better Classes" in Charlotte, 1850–1910*. Chapel Hill and London: University of North Carolina Press, 1994.

Griffin, Clarence W. *Western North Carolina Sketches*. Forest City, N.C.: Forest City Courier, 1941.

Griffin, Frances. *Less Time for Meddling: A History of Salem Academy and College, 1772–1866*. Winston-Salem, N.C.: John F. Blair, Publisher, 1979.

Griffin, Richard W., and Diffee W. Standard. "The Cotton Textile Industry in Ante-bellum North Carolina. Part Two: An Era of Boom and Consolidation, 1830–1860." *North Carolina Historical Review* 34 (Apr. 1957): 131–64.

Grizzle, Ralph. "Hendersonville." *Our State: Down Home in North Carolina* 69 (Sept. 2001): 114–20.

Gwaltney, W. R. "Capture of Fort Hamby: A Thrilling Story of the War." *Mountain Scout Library* 4 (June 1903). A copy is in the North Carolina Collection at the University of North Carolina.

Hairston, Peter W. *The Cooleemee Plantation and Its People*. Winston-Salem and Lexington, N.C.: History Division, Hunter Publishing Co., and Davidson County Community College, 1986.

Hall, William James, and Helen Johnson Ferguson. *Tanglewood: Historic Gem of Forsyth County, North Carolina*. Winston-Salem, N.C.: Helen J. McMurray, 1979.

Hallock, Judith Lee. *Braxton Bragg and Confederate Defeat*. 2 vols. Tuscaloosa and London: University of Alabama Press, 1991.

Hamilton, J. G. de Roulhac, ed. *The Papers of Thomas Ruffin*. 3 vols. Raleigh, N.C.: Edwards and Broughton Printing Co., State Printers, 1920.

Hancock, Mary Alice. *Four Brothers in Gray*. Copy in author's collection.

Hanna, A. J. *Flight Into Oblivion*. Reprint, Baton Rouge: Louisiana State University Press, 1999.

Hardy, Michael C. "Watauga County and the Civil War." Paper presented at the Watauga County History Symposium, October 7, 1999.

Harper, G. W. F., comp. *Reminiscences of Caldwell County, North Carolina, in the Great War of 1861–1865*. Lenoir, N.C.: G. W. F. Harper, 1913.

Hartley, Chris J. "'Don't Bury Me Among the _____ Yankees': An Introduction to the Maryland Line in the Confederate States Army." Unpublished article in the author's possession.

———. *Roster of the 1st North Carolina Cavalry Regiment, Army of Northern Virginia*. Copy in author's collection.

———. *Stuart's Tarheels: James B. Gordon and His North Carolina Cavalry*. Baltimore, Md.: Butternut and Blue, 1996.

———. *To Restore the Old Flag: Proceedings of a Symposium on the Civil War and Wilkes County*. Wilkesboro, N.C.: Old Wilkes, Inc., 1990.

Hatcher, Edmund N. *The Last Four Weeks of the War*. Columbus, Ohio: Co-operative Publishing Co., 1892.

Heaton, John William, comp. *A Registry of Cemeteries Located in the Town of Boone, North Carolina*. Available at Watauga County Public Library.

Hendricks, Howard O. *Imperiled City: The Movements of the Union and Confederate Armies Toward Greensboro in the Closing Days of the Civil War in North Carolina*. Master's thesis, University of North Carolina at Greensboro, 1987.

Heritage of Burke County, North Carolina. Winston-Salem, N.C.: Burke County Historical Society in Cooperation with Hunter Publishing Co., 1981.

Heritage of Caldwell County, North Carolina. Vol. 1. Winston-Salem, N.C.: Caldwell County Heritage Book Committee in Cooperation with Hunter Publishing Co., 1983.

Heritage of Davidson County, 1982. Winston-Salem, N.C.: Genealogical Society of Davidson County in Cooperation with Hunter Publishing Co., 1982.

Heritage of Iredell County, 1980. Statesville, N.C.: Genealogical Society of Iredell County in Cooperation with Hunter Publishing Co., 1980.

Hesseltine, William B. *Dr. J. G. M. Ramsay: Autobiography and Letters*. Nashville: Tennessee Historical Commission, 1954.

Hickerson, Thomas F. *Echoes of Happy Valley: Letters and Diaries, Family Life in the South, Civil War History*. Chapel Hill, N.C.: Thomas F. Hickerson, 1962.

High Point Chamber of Commerce, comp. *The Building and Builders of a City: High Point, North Carolina*. High Point, N.C.: Hall Printing Co., 1947.

Hill, Judith Parks America. *A History of Henry County, Virginia, with Biographical Sketches of its Most Prominent Citizens and a Genealogical History of Half a Hundred of its Oldest Families*. Baltimore, Md.: Regional Publishing Co., 1976.

Hill, Michael, ed. *Guide to North Carolina Highway Historical Markers*. Raleigh, N.C.: Division of Archives and History, Department of Cultural Resources, 1990.

Hinchman, Lydia S. *Biographical Sketch of Charles S. Hinchman, from Records and Recollections*. Privately published, 1930.

Hoch, Beverly Repass, ed. *Wythe County, Virginia, During the War Between the States*. Wytheville, Va.: Town of Wytheville and Wytheville County Historical Society, 1996.

Holsworth, Jerry. "VMI at the Battle of New Market, and Sigel's Defeat in the Shenandoah Valley." *Blue and Gray* 16 (Spring 1999): 20.

Hoole, W. Stanley, ed. "Admiral on Horseback: The Diary of Brigadier General Raphael Semmes, February–May 1865." *Alabama Review* 28 (Apr. 1975): 129–50.

Houck, Lucy Hamlin. "The Story of Rockford." Not published, 1972. Available at Forsyth County Public Library.

Howard, Joshua B. *Forgotten Heroes: Davidson County, N.C., and the War Between the States*. Thomasville, N.C.: Graphic Design Printing, 1997.

Hubell, Paul E. "The James Eller Family and the Bushwhackers of Wilkes County, North Carolina, 1864–1865." *Eller Chronicles* 6. Feb. 1992. http://freepages.family.rootsweb.com/~adelr/feb92/feb92p9.htm.

Huffman, Linda B., and Barry G. Huffman. *Catawba Journey*. Newton, N.C.: Catawba County

Historical Association, 1982.

Hughes, N. Collin. *Hendersonville in Civil War Times.* Hendersonville, N.C.: Blue Ridge Specialty Printers, 1936.

Hunt, Roger D., and Jack R. Brown. *Brevet Brigadier Generals in Blue.* Gaithersburg, Md.: Olde Soldier Books, Inc., 1990.

In Memoriam: George Stoneman. Military Order of the Loyal Legion of the United States, Headquarters Commandery of the State of California, circular 21. San Francisco, Calif.: 1894.

Inscoe, John C. *Mountain Masters: Slavery and the Sectional Crisis in Western North Carolina.* Knoxville: University of Tennessee Press, 1989.

Inscoe, John C., and Gordon B. McKinney. *The Heart of Confederate Appalachia: Western North Carolina in the Civil War.* Chapel Hill and London: University of North Carolina Press, 2000.

Jackson, Hester Bartlett, ed. *Surry County Soldiers in the Civil War.* Charlotte, N.C.: Surry County Historical Society, 1992.

Johnson, Clint. *Touring the Carolinas' Civil War Sites.* Winston-Salem, N.C.: John F. Blair, Publisher, 1996.

Johnson, Robert U., and Clarence C. Buel, eds. *Battles and Leaders of the Civil War.* 4 vols. New York: Century, 1887–88.

Johnston, Joseph E. *Narrative of Military Operations During the Civil War.* Reprint, New York: Da Capo Press, 1990.

Jones, George Alexander, ed. *The Heritage of Henderson County.* Vol. 2. Winston-Salem, N.C.: Hunter Publishing Co. in cooperation with the Henderson County Genealogical and Historical Society, 1988.

Jones, Robert E. *The Last Raid.* Copy in author's collection.

Kaplan, Steven E. "The Search for General Stoneman's Legacy." *Treasure Quest Magazine* 5 (Spring 1994): 113–15.

Kapp, Louise Bowles. *Bethania: The First Industrial Town of Wachovia.* Bethania, N.C.: Bethania Historical Association, 1995.

Keenan, Jerry. *Wilson's Cavalry Corps.* Jefferson, N.C., and London: McFarland and Co., Inc., Publishers, 1998.

Keever, Homer M. *Iredell: Piedmont County.* Statesville, N.C.: Iredell County Bicentennial Commission, 1976.

Kegley, Mary B., comp. *Glimpses of Wythe County.* Orange, Va.: Central Virginia Newspapers, Inc., 1986.

———. *Wythe County, Virginia: A Bicentennial History.* Wytheville, Va.: Wythe County Board of Supervisors, 1989.

Kirk, Charles H., ed. *History of the Fifteenth Pennsylvania Cavalry, Which Was Recruited and Known as the Anderson Cavalry in the Rebellion of 1861–1865.* Philadelphia: Historical Committee of the Society of the Fifteenth Pennsylvania Cavalry, 1906.

Konkle, Burton Alva. *John Motley Morehead and the Development of North Carolina, 1796–1886.* Reprint, Spartanburg, S.C.: Reprint Co., 1971.

Krick, Robert K. *Lee's Colonels: A Biographical Register of the Field Officers of the Army of Northern Virginia.* Dayton, Ohio: Morningside Press, 1992.

Langellier, John P., Kurt Hamilton Cox, and Brian C. Pohanka. *Myles Keogh: The Life and Legend of an "Irish Dragoon" in the Seventh Cavalry.* El Segundo, Calif.: Upton and Sons, 1991.

Langley, Joan, and Wright Langley. *Yesterday's Asheville.* Miami, Fla.: E. A. Seemann Publishers, Inc., 1975.

Leonard, Jacob Calvin. *Centennial History of Davidson County, N.C.* Raleigh, N.C.: Edwards and Broughton Co., 1927.

Lester, Darrel. *Seasons in Stokes: A Proud Look Back.* Madison, N.C.: Twin Rivers Printing Co., 1984.

Lindsley, John Berrien, ed. *The Military Annals of Tennessee: Confederate.* Nashville, Tenn.: J. M. Lindsley and Co., Publishers, 1886.

Linn, Joe White. "There Is No Music in My Soul Today." *UDC Magazine* (Oct. 1994): 19–20.

Longacre, Edward G. *Lincoln's Cavalrymen: A History of the Mounted Forces of the Army of the Potomac.* Mechanicsburg, Pa.: Stackpole Books, 2000.

Longstreet, James. *From Manassas to Appomattox: Memoirs of the Civil War in America.* Reprint, Secaucus, N.J.: Blue and Grey Press, 1985.

Lovin, Clifford R., ed. *Our Mountain Heritage: Essays on the Natural and Cultural History of Western North Carolina.* Cullowhee, N.C.: North Carolina Humanities Commission and Mountain Heritage Center, 1979.

MacBryde, Ann C., transcriber. *Ellie's Book: The Journal Kept by Ellie M. Andrews From January 1862 Through May 1865.* Davidson, N.C.: Briarpatch Press, 1984.

Manarin, Louis, and Weymouth T. Jordan, Jr. comps. *North Carolina Troops, 1861–1865: A Roster.* Multivolume series. Raleigh, N.C.: Division of Archives and History, 1968–2000 ff.

Martin, J. Franklin. "Saga of the Sauratowns: A History of Stokes County, North Carolina." Not published. Available at Forsyth County Public Library.

Martinsville and Henry County: Historic Views. Martinsville, Va.: Henry County Woman's Club, 1976.

Marvel, William. "The Battle for Saltville: Massacre or Myth?" *Blue and Gray* 8 (Aug. 1991): 10–19, 46–54.

———. *A Place Called Appomattox.* Chapel Hill and London: University of North Carolina Press, 2000.

Mason, Frank H. "General Stoneman's Last Campaign and the Pursuit of Jefferson Davis." In *Ohio-MOLLUS War Papers,* vol. 3, 21–43.

———. *The Twelfth Ohio Cavalry: A Record of Its Organization and Services in the War of the Rebellion, Together with a Complete Roster of the Regiment.* Cleveland, Ohio: Nevins' Steam Printing House, 1871.

McAulay, John D. *Carbines of the U.S. Cavalry, 1861–1905.* Lincoln, R.I.: Andrew Mowbray Publishers, 1996.

McClure, A. K. *Abraham Lincoln and Men of War-Times: Some Personal Recollections of War and Politics During the Lincoln Administration.* Philadelphia: Times Publishing Company, 1892.

McKenzie, Robert Tracy. " 'Oh! Ours Is a Deplorable Condition': The Economic Impact of the Civil War in Upper East Tennessee." In *The Civil War in Appalachia: Collected Essays,* edited by Kenneth W. Noe and Shannon W. Wilson. Knoxville: University of Tennessee Press, 1997.

McKinney, Gordon B. "Premature Industrialization in Appalachia: The Asheville Armory, 1862–1863." In *The Civil War in Appalachia: Collected Essays,* edited by Kenneth W. Noe and Shannon H. Wilson. Knoxville: University of Tennessee Press, 1997.

McPherson, Holt. *High Pointers of High Point.* High Point, N.C.: Hall Printing Co., 1976.

McPherson, James M. *Battle Cry of Freedom: The Civil War Era.* New York: Oxford University Press, 1988.

Miller, Hillborn C. *History of the First Ohio Heavy Artillery.* Ohio Historical Society.

———. "Our Service in East Tennessee, 1864–5: First Ohio Heavy Artillery History." Paper read at reunion at Gallipolis, Ohio, September 21, 1899.

Miller, Mildred J., and Pam M. Cross. *Time Is, Time Was: Gravestone Art, Burial Customs and History, Iredell County, North Carolina*. Statesville, N.C.: Genealogical Society of Iredell County, 1990.

Millhouse, Barbara Babcock, ed. *Recollections of Major A. D. Reynolds, 1847–1925*. Winston-Salem, N.C.: Reynolda House, Inc., 1978.

Minutes of the 22nd Annual Reunion, 12th Ohio Volunteer Cavalry, September 5, 1907, Columbus, Ohio.

Morris, George Graham. *Confederate Lynchburg, 1861–1865*. Master's thesis, Virginia Tech, 1977.

Murray, Keith A. *The Modocs and Their War*. Norman: University of Oklahoma Press, 1959.

Noe, Kenneth W., and Shannon H. Wilson, eds. *The Civil War in Appalachia: Collected Essays*. Knoxville: University of Tennessee Press, 1997.

Official Roster of the Soldiers of the State of Ohio in the War of the Rebellion, 1861–1866. Vol. 11. Akron, Ohio: Werner Pig and Litho Co., 1891.

Ogburn, Jane C. Preface in *North Wilkesboro: The First Hundred Years, 1890-1990*, by J. Jay Anderson. North Wilkesboro, N.C.: North Wilkesboro Centennial Committee, 1990.

O'Keefe, Patrick. *Greensboro: A Pictorial History*. Norfolk, Va.: Donning Co., Publishers, 1977.

O'Neill, Robert. "'What Men We Have Got are Good Soldiers and Brave Ones Too': Federal Cavalry Operations in the Peninsula Campaign." In *The Peninsula Campaign of 1862: Yorktown to the Seven Days*, vol. 3, edited by William J. Miller. Campbell, Calif.: Savas Publishing Co., 1997.

Ovens, David. *If This Be Treason: A Look at His Town and Times*. Charlotte, N.C.: Heritage House, 1957.

Owen, Mary B. *Old Salem, North Carolina*. Garden Club of North Carolina, 1941.

Parker, William H. *Recollections of a Naval Officer*. New York: Charles Scribner's Sons, 1883.

Patton, Sadie S. *Sketches of Polk County History*. Asheville, N.C.: Miller Printing Co., 1950.

———. *The Story of Henderson County*. Asheville, N.C.: Miller Printing Co., 1947.

Peabody, George. *William Jackson Palmer, Pathfinder and Builder: A Compilation of Addresses at Presentations of Bronze Bas Reliefs and Equestrian Statue Commemorating His Life and Work*. Boston: Thomas Todd Co., Printers, 1931.

Pemberton, John C. *Pemberton: Defender of Vicksburg*. Chapel Hill: University of North Carolina Press, 1942.

Perdue, Jack L. "Fact or Fiction?" *Commander's Tent* (January 1998).

———. "U.S. Cavalry Raids, High Point, N.C." *Commander's Tent* (April 1995).

Perry, Thomas J. "The Civil War Comes to Patrick County." Paper prepared for presentation at the Reynolds Homestead, Critz, Va., 1995.

Petrucelli, Katherine S., ed. *The Heritage of Rowan County, North Carolina*. Vol. 1. Charlotte, N.C.: Genealogical Society of Rowan County, 1991.

Phifer, Edward William, Jr. *Burke: The History of a North Carolina County, 1777–1920*. Morganton, N.C.: privately published, 1977.

Polson, Peggy, and Betty McFarland. *Sketches of Early Watauga*. Boone, N.C.: Boone Branch, American Association of University Women, 1973.

Porter, Horace. *Campaigning with Grant*. New York: Century Co., 1897. Reprint, Time-Life Books, Inc., 1981.

Poulter, Keith. "The Cavalry Bureau." *North & South* 2 (Jan. 1999): 70–71.

Powell, William S. *Dictionary of North Carolina Biography*. 6 vols. Chapel Hill and London: University of North Carolina Press, 1994.

Preslar, Charles J., ed. *A History of Catawba County*. Salisbury, N.C.: Rowan Printing Co., 1954.

Ramsey, Thomas R., Jr. *The Raid: East Tennessee, Western North Carolina, Southwest Virginia*. Kingsport, Tenn.: Kingsport Press, Inc., 1973.

Ray, James M. "Asheville in 1865." *The Lyceum* (September 1890). Copy in Civil War clipping file, Pack Memorial Library, Asheville, N.C.

Raynor, George. *Rebels and Yankees in Rowan County*. Vol. 4, *Piedmont Passages*. Salisbury, N.C.: *Salisbury Post*, 1991.

Ready, Milton. *Asheville: Land of the Sky*. Northridge, Calif.: Windsor Publications, Inc., 1986.

Regan, John H. "The Flight and Capture of Jefferson Davis." In *The Annals of the War: Written by Leading Participants North and South, Originally Published in the* Philadelphia Weekly Times. Reprint, Morningside Press, 1988.

Reid, Whitelaw. *Ohio in the War: Her Statesmen, Her Generals, and Soldiers*. 2 vols. Cincinnati, Ohio: Moore, Wilstach and Baldwin, 1868.

Report of the Adjutant General of the State of Tennessee of the Military Forces of the State from 1861 to 1866. Nashville, Tenn.: S. C. Mercer, Printer to the State, 1866.

Report of the President of the Western North Carolina Railroad Company. Executive document 23, series 1866–67. Raleigh, N.C.: William E. Bell, Printer to the State, 1867.

Reynolds, G. Galloway. *Shallow Ford Country*. Lewisville, N.C.: 1992. Copy in Forsyth County Public Library.

Reynolds, Patrick, and Tom Shachtman. *The Gilded Leaf: Triumph, Tragedy, and Tobacco*. Boston, Toronto, and London: Little, Brown and Co., 1989.

Richardson, Albert D. *The Secret Service, The Field, The Dungeon, and The Escape*. Hartford, Conn.: American Publishing Co., 1865.

Rights, Douglas LeTell. "Salem in the War Between the States." *North Carolina Historical Review* 27 (July 1950): 277–88.

Roberts, Robert B. *Encyclopedia of Historic Forts: The Military, Pioneer, and Trading Posts of the United States*. New York: Macmillan, 1988.

Robertson, George F. *A Small Boy's Recollection of the Civil War*. Reprint, Clover, S.C.: George F. Robertson, 1932.

Robertson, James I., Jr. *Stonewall Jackson: The Man, the Soldier, the Legend*. New York: Macmillan, 1997.

Robertson, John, comp. *Michigan in the War*. Lansing, Mich.: W. S. George and Co., State Printers and Binders, 1882.

Robertson, Robbie. "The Night They Drove Old Dixie Down." Canaan Music, 1970.

Robinson, Blackwell P. *The History of Guilford County, North Carolina, U.S.A*. Vol. 1, *Guilford County's First 150 Years*. Greensboro, N.C.: Guilford County Bicentennial Commission and the Guilford County American Revolution Bicentennial Commission, 1971.

Roman, Alfred. *The Military Operations of General Beauregard in the War Between the States, 1861 to 1865*. 2 vols. Reprint, New York: Da Capo Press, 1994.

Ross, Stephen A. "To 'Prepare our Sons for All the Duties that May Lie before Them': The Hillsborough Military Academy and Military Education in Antebellum North Carolina." *North Carolina Historical Review* 79 (Jan. 2002): 1–27.

Rowland, Dunbar, ed. *Jefferson Davis, Constitutionalist: His Letters, Papers, and Speeches*. Jackson.: Mississippi Department of Archives and History, 1923.

Runyan, Morris C. *Eight Days with the Confederates and the Capture of their Archives, Flags, etc., by Company G, Ninth New Jersey Volunteers*. Princeton, N.J.: William C. C. Zapf, Printer, 1896.

Rutledge, William E., Jr. *An Illustrated History of Yadkin County, 1850–1980*. Yadkinville, N.C.: privately published, 1981.

Scott, Samuel W., and Samuel P. Angel. *History of the Thirteenth Regiment Tennessee Volunteer Cavalry, U.S.A*. Reprint, Overmountain Press, 1987.

Scott, W. W. *Annals of Caldwell County*. Reprint, Lenoir, N.C.: Caldwell County Genealogical Society, 1996.

Sears, Stephen W., ed. *The Civil War Papers of George B. McClellan*. New York: Ticknor and Fields, 1989.

———. *Landscape Turned Red: The Battle of Antietam*. New York: Popular Library, 1983.

Semmes, Raphael. *Memoirs of Service Afloat During the War Between the States*. Reprint, Baton Rouge and London: Louisiana State University Press, 1996.

Sherman, William T. *Memoirs of William T. Sherman*. 2 vols. Reprint, New York: Da Capo Press, 1984.

Sherrill, William L. *The Annals of Lincoln County*. Charlotte, N.C.: Observer Printing House, 1937.

Shiman, Philip. *Fort York: A Late War Confederate Fort on the Yadkin River*. Copy in author's collection.

Shirley, Michael. *From Congregation Town to Industrial City: Culture and Social Change in a Southern Community*. New York and London: New York University Press, 1994.

Simon, John Y., ed. *The Papers of Ulysses S. Grant*. 20 vols. Carbondale: Southern Illinois University Press, 1967–99.

Smith, Ed. "Drama in April 1865." In *Charlotte Remembers*. Charlotte, N.C.: Community Publishing Co., 1972.

Soliday, J. A. *Sixth Annual Reunion of the 12th Ohio Volunteer Cavalry and Joint Meeting with the 11th Michigan Cavalry, Held at Detroit, Michigan, on Wednesday and Thursday, August 5th and 6th, 1891*. Fort Wayne, Ind.: Daily Press Job Room, 1891.

Southern Historical Society Papers. 52 vols. Richmond, Va.: 1876–1959.

Spencer, Cornelia Phillips. *The Last Ninety Days of the War in North Carolina*. Reprint, Wilmington, N.C.: Broadfoot Publishing Co., 1993.

Stabler, James, comp. "Thy Affectionate Son . . ." *A Collection of Letters of Three Brothers, John Palmer, William T. Palmer, and Edward L. Palmer, from the 1860s*. 1993. Copy in U.S. Army Military History Institute.

Starr, Stephen Z. *The Union Cavalry in the Civil War*. 3 vols. Baton Rouge and London: Louisiana State University Press, 1985.

Statement of the Disposition of Some of the Bodies of Deceased Union Soldiers and Prisoners of War Whose Remains Have Been Removed to National Cemeteries in the Southern and Western States. 4 vols. Washington, D.C.: GPO, 1868.

Stevens, Peter F. *Rebels in Blue: The Story of Keith and Melinda Blalock*. Dallas, Tex.: Taylor Publishing Co., 2000.

Stone, Walter. *A Walk Through Old Salem*. Winston-Salem, N.C.: John F. Blair, Publisher, 2000.

"Stoneman's Raid Described in Diary." *The Uplift* 35 (Aug. 30, 1947): 18–19.

Sullins, David D. *Recollections of An Old Man: Seventy Years in Dixie, 1827–1897*. Bristol, Tenn.: King Printing Co., 1910.

Supplement to the Official Records of the Union and Confederate Armies. 94 vols. in 3 parts. Wilmington, N.C.: Broadfoot Publishing Co., 1997.

Tennesseans in the Civil War: A Military History of Confederate and Union Units with Available Rosters of Personnel. 2 parts. Nashville, Tenn.: Civil War Centennial Commission, 1964.

Tenth Cavalry. Vol. 40, Record of Service of Michigan Volunteers in the Civil War, 1861–1865. Kalamazoo, Mich.: Ihling Bros. and Everard, Printers, 1905.

Tessier, Mitzi Schaden. *The State of Buncombe.* Virginia Beach, Va.: Donning Co., Publishers, 1992.

Tetley, Gerald. "Last Days of the Confederacy." *The Commonwealth* 28 (Oct. 1961): 32–33, 42.

Thomas, C. Yvonne Bell. *Roads to Jamestown: A View and Review of the Old Town.* Fredericksburg, Va.: Bookcrafters, 1997.

Thomas, Theresa. *Tall Gray Gates.* New York: Daniel Ryerson, Inc., 1942.

Tise, Larry E. *The Yadkin Melting Pot: Methodism and the Moravians in the Yadkin Valley, 1750–1850, and Mount Tabor Church, 1845–1966.* Clay Printing Co., 1967.

To the Members of the Society of the 15th Pennsylvania Volunteer Cavalry: A Short Account of the 15th Annual Banquet, Held at Philadelphia, Pa., December 7, 1887. Philadelphia: Edward Patteson, Steam Power Printers, 1888.

To the Members of the Society of the 15th Pennsylvania Volunteer Cavalry: A Short Account of the 18th Annual Banquet, Held at Philadelphia, Pa., November 12, 1890. Philadelphia: Edward Patteson, Steam Power Printers, 1891.

To the Members of the Society of the 15th Pennsylvania Volunteer Cavalry: A Short Account of the 22nd Annual Banquet, Held at Pittsburgh, Pa., September 12, 1894. Philadelphia: Patteson Printing House, 1895.

To the Members of the Society of the 15th Pennsylvania Volunteer Cavalry: A Short Account of the 23rd Annual Banquet, Held at Philadelphia, Pa., November 26, 1895. Philadelphia: Patteson Printing House, 1896.

To the Members of the Society of the 15th Pennsylvania Volunteer Cavalry: A Short Account of the 28th Annual Banquet, Held at Philadelphia, Pa., December 6, 1900. Philadelphia: Patteson Printing House, 1900.

To the Members of the Society of the 15th Pennsylvania Volunteer Cavalry: A Short Account of the 30th Annual Banquet.

To the Members of the Society of the 15th Pennsylvania Volunteer Cavalry: A Short Account of the 31st Annual Banquet, Held at Philadelphia, Pa., November 10, 1903.

To the Members of the Society of the 15th Pennsylvania Volunteer Cavalry: A Short Account of the 40th Annual Banquet, Held at Philadelphia, Pa., November 19, 1912. Philadelphia: Press of Review Publishing and Printing Co., 1912.

To the Members of the Society of the 15th Pennsylvania Volunteer Cavalry: A Short Account of the 51st Annual Banquet, Held at Philadelphia, Pa., October 17, 1923. Philadelphia: Press of Review Publishing and Printing Co., 1923.

Trading Ford on the Yadkin River: 10,000 Years of Piedmont North Carolina History. Salisbury, N.C.: Friends of the Trading Ford. Available at Forsyth County Public Library.

Trelease, Allen W. *The North Carolina Railroad, 1849–1871, and the Modernization of North Carolina.* Chapel Hill and London: University of North Carolina Press, 1991.

Trotter, William R. *Bushwhackers: The Civil War in North Carolina, The Mountains.* Winston-Salem, N.C.: John F. Blair, Publisher, 1988.

Trowbridge, John W. *The Desolate South, 1865–1866: A Picture of the Battlefields of the Devastated Confederacy.* New York: Duell, Sloan, and Pearce, 1956.

Trowbridge, Luther S. *A Brief History of the Tenth Michigan Cavalry.* Detroit: Friesema Bros. Printing Co., 1906.

———. "Lights and Shadows of the Civil War." In *Michigan-MOLLUS War Papers*, vol. 2, 101–9. Detroit: Ostler Printing Co., 1888.

———. "The Stoneman Raid of 1865." *Journal of the U.S. Cavalry Association* 4 (June 1891): 188–96.

———. "The Stoneman Raid of 1865: A Paper Prepared and Read Before Michigan Commandery of the Military Order of the Loyal Legion of the United States, January 8, 1888." In *Michigan-MOLLUS War Papers*, vol. 1, 95–109. Detroit: Ostler Printing Co., 1888.

Trudeau, Noah Andre. *Out of the Storm: The End of the Civil War, April–June 1865.* Baton Rouge: Louisiana State University Press, 1994.

Tursi, Frank V. *Winston-Salem: A History.* Winston-Salem, N.C.: John F. Blair, Publisher, 1994.

Union Army: A History of Military Affairs in the Loyal States, 1861–1865. Vol. 4. Reprint, Wilmington, N.C.: Broadfoot Publishing Co., 1998.

Union Regiments of Kentucky, The. Louisville, Ky.: *Courier-Journal* Job Printing Co., 1897.

United States Congress. *Report to Accompany S. 205.* Senate calendar #632, report 576, 54th Congress, 1st sess., March 26, 1896.

United States War Department. *The War of the Rebellion: A Compilation of the Official Records of the Union and Confederate Armies.* 128 vols. Washington, D.C.: GPO, 1880–1901.

Van Noppen, Ina W. *Stoneman's Last Raid.* Raleigh, N.C.: North Carolina State University Print Shop, 1961.

Van Noppen, Ina W., and John J. Van Noppen. *Western North Carolina since the Civil War.* Boone, N.C.: Appalachian Consortium Press, 1973.

Viney, Peter. "The Night They Drove Old Dixie Down (Revisited)." http://theband.hiof.no/articles/dixie_viney.html.

Wall, James W. *History of Davie County in the Forks of the Yadkin.* Spartanburg, S.C.: Reprint Co., Publishers, 1997.

———. *A History of the First Presbyterian Church of Mocksville, N.C.* Salisbury, N.C.: Rowan Printing Co., 1963.

Wallace, Irving, and Amy Wallace. *The Two.* New York: Simon and Schuster, 1978.

Wallace, Lee A., Jr., comp. *A Guide to Virginia Military Organizations: 1861–1865.* Richmond: Virginia Civil War Commission, 1964.

Wallenstein, Peter. "'Helping to Save the Union': The Social Origins, Wartime Experiences, and Military Impact of White Union Troops from East Tennessee." In *The Civil War in Appalachia: Collected Essays,* edited by Kenneth W. Noe and Shannon H. Wilson. Knoxville: University of Tennessee Press, 1997.

Ward, Davis Cline, ed. *The Heritage of Old Buncombe County.* Vol. 1. Winston-Salem, N.C.: Hunter Publishing Co. in cooperation with the Old Buncombe County Genealogical Society, 1981.

Warner, Ezra J. *Generals in Blue: Lives of the Union Commanders.* Baton Rouge: Louisiana State University Press, 1964.

Watt, W. N. *Statesville: My Home Town, 1789–1920.* W. N. Watt, 1996.

Weigley, Russell F. *The American Way of War: A History of United States Military Strategy and Policy.* Bloomington: Indiana University Press, 1973.

Wellman, Manly Wade. *Winston-Salem in History.* Vol. 2, *The War Record.* Winston-Salem, N.C.: Historic Winston, 1976.

Wellman, Paul I. *The Indian Wars of the West.* New York: Modern Literary Editions Publishing Co., 1963.

Welsh, Jack D. *Medical Histories of Union Generals.* Kent, Ohio, and London: Kent State University Press, 1996.

Wert, Jeffry D. *General James Longstreet: The Confederacy's Most Controversial Soldier—A Biography*. New York: Simon and Schuster, 1993.

Western Piedmont Council of Governors. *Historic Sites Inventory, Region E*. 1975.

Whisonant, Robert C. "Geology and the Civil War in Southwestern Virginia: The Wythe County Lead Mines." *Virginia Minerals* 42 (May 1996): 13–19.

———. "Geology and the Civil War in Southwestern Virginia: Union Raiders in the New River Valley, May 1864." *Virginia Minerals* 43 (Nov. 1997): 29–40.

White, William E. *A History of Alexander County, North Carolina*. Taylorsville, N.C.: *Taylorsville Times*, 1926.

Wiencek, Henry. *The Hairstons: An American Family in Black and White*. New York: St. Martin's Press, 1999.

Williams, John A. B. *Leaves From a Trooper's Diary*. Philadelphia: John A. B. Williams, 1869.

Wilson, Selden L. *Recollections and Experiences During the Civil War, 1861–1865, in the 15th Pennsylvania Volunteer Cavalry, Better Known as the Anderson Cavalry*. Washington, Pa.: 1913.

Wilson, Suzanne Colton, comp. *Column South with the Fifteenth Pennsylvania Cavalry, From Antietam to the Capture of Jefferson Davis*. Edited by J. Ferrell Colton and Antoinette G. Smith. Flagstaff, Ariz.: J. F. Colton and Co., 1960.

"Wilson's Raid Through Alabama and Georgia." In vol. 4 of *Battles and Leaders of the Civil War*, edited by Robert U. Johnson and Clarence C. Buel, 759–61. New York: Century, 1887–88.

Wittenberg, Eric J. "Biography of George Stoneman, Jr." http://www.bufordsboys.com/StonemanBiography.htm.

———. "Learning the Hard Lessons of Logistics: Arming and Maintaining the Federal Cavalry." *North & South* 2 (Jan. 1999): 62–69, 72–78.

Wittenberg, Eric J., and J. David Petruzzi. *Plenty of Blame to Go Around: Jeb Stuart's Controversial Ride to Gettysburg*. New York and Calif.: Savas Beatie LLC, 2006.

Wood, Jim. *The Wood Family of Patrick Springs, Virginia, and Their Kinsmen*. Beckley, W.V.: Jim Wood, 2001.

Woodard, John R. *The Heritage of Stokes County, North Carolina*. Winston-Salem, N.C.: Stokes County Historical Society in Cooperation with Hunter Publishing, 1981.

Wright, Stuart, ed. *Memoirs of Alfred Horatio Belo*. Reprint, Gaithersburg, Md.: Olde Soldier Books, Inc.

Yearns, W. Buck, and John G. Barrett, eds. *North Carolina Civil War Documentary*. Chapel Hill: University of North Carolina Press, 1980.

Yeatman, Ted, ed. "What An Awful and Grand Spectacle It Is!" *Civil War Times Illustrated* 22 (Jan. 1984): 41–43.

Index